To:

_____

*N*ot one of all the good promises
the Lord your God gave you
has failed. Every promise has
been fulfilled.

Joshua 23:14

From:

_____

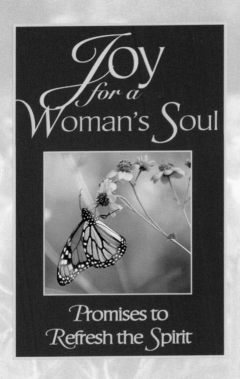

Joy for a Woman's Soul

Promises to Refresh the Spirit

Zondervan *Gifts*

We have a gift for inspiration™

Table of Contents

Part I: Discovering Joy

The Joy of Being Me   8
Make a Joyful Pit Stop   11
The Joy All Around Us   14
The Joy of God's Everlasting Love   17
The Joy of God's Creation   20
Our Unique Treasures   23
God Is in Control   26
The Joy of God's Gifts   29
The Joy of Good Friends   32
Secure in God's Love   35
A Joyful Child of God   38
Joyful Companions   41
God Always Remembers   44
The Joy of God's Touch   47

Part II: A Joyful Up-look

The Joy of Change   52
Finding Hope in Jesus   55
No Regrets   58
Joy Sappers   61
Soaring Through Struggles   64
The Joy of Persevering   67
The Joy of a Godly Perspective   70
The Joy of Possibilities   73
The Joy of Trusting God's Plan   76
Standing With Others in Prayer   79
The Joy of God's Great Faithfulness   82
Catastrophe or Happy Ending?   85
The Blessing of Courage   88
Trusting Through the Tears   91
The Joy Buster of Fear   94

Part III: Give Joy a Boost

The Boost of a Joyful Outlook 100
A Second Look Yields Forgiveness 103
Walking With a Gratitude Attitude 106
The Joy of Aging 109
The Joy Buster of Worry 112
A Respite From Our Tasks 115
Stop, Look, & Sniff 118
A Green Thumb of Beauty 121
The Joy of Enjoying Life 124
The Joy of Following God's Direction 127
Remembering and Being Remembered 130
The Joy of Thankfulness 133
The Seven Deadly Joy Busters 136
The Joy of Godly Relationships 139
The Joy of Receiving Advice 142
Think About Your Heart Attitude 145

Part IV: Share the Joy

The Joy of a Reassuring Word 150
The Joy of Sharing Your Witness 153
The Deep Calling of Friendship 156
The Joy of a Good Attitude 159
The Joy of a Loving Letter 162
Celebrate Joy! 165
The Joy of Family 168
The Days of Your Life 171
Renew Your Hope with Prayer 174
Focus on Christ & Find Joy 177
The Joy of Helping Others Help You 180
Blessed Sidekicks 183
The Joy Buster of Pride 186
The Joy of Fellowship 189
The Joy of Being Different 192
Put on a Smiley Face 195
The Joy of Caring for Family Members 198
A Positive Perspective 201
Wrapped in Jesus' Joy 204

Discovering
Joy

The *Joy* of *Being* *Me*

*A*s I travel across the country to various speaking engagements, I meet concealed hurt, disguised hurt, disjointed hurt. Pain is a normal part of life.

That's why I think: *Why not take as much joy as possible along the way so when hurt comes, we assimilate it better?*

Every day now I take joy—by refusing to accept the lie that I have to feel miserable about the baggage, the stuff, and the sickness that trails me no matter how I try to hide or outwit it. I choose to do zany, kooky, and funny things to make myself and others laugh.

And I fling joy—beyond my next-door neighbor's fence, clear across town, and into the universe. Then it curves right back to me. Sometimes with a whack on the head when I need it. Sometimes with a thwack into my heart. Sometimes landing with a crack at my feet. But it always comes back. No doubt about it.

BARBARA JOHNSON

DISCOVERING JOY

*W*ho am I? Me. I'm myself. No other. No duplicate. No clone. God created me, and I'm who He wants me to be. Nothing more. Nothing less. Nothing else. That's true for you, as well.

The writer of Job says each of us has been uniquely shaped by God's hand. He has formed us exactly. The great I AM made us and shaped us. A blessed thought! I don't have to be anybody but me. And, as I walk with Christ, he's in the process of making me more like himself. God created us into who we are and "nothing is to be rejected" (1 Timothy 4:4).

Being who you are is sometimes difficult because you don't like who you are. Accept yourself as God's wonderful creation. Then you are free to be you without fear.

Who are you? God's unique creation. There's nobody just like you. Never has been, never will be. Only you can be you. Be whom God made you.

LUCI SWINDOLL

Promises About Me

God saw all that he had made, and it was very good.

Genesis 1:31

You created my inmost being; you knit me together in my mother's womb. I praise you because I am fearfully and wonderfully made; your works are wonderful, I know that full well. My frame was not hidden from you when I was made in the secret place. When I was woven together in the depths of the earth, your eyes saw my unformed body. All the days ordained for me were written in your book before one of them came to be.

Psalm 139:13–16

Your hands made me and formed me; give me understanding.

Psalm 119:73

Make a Joyful Pit Stop

If you're speeding down the freeway, the police might pull you over. But no one ever makes you take pit stops. You have to choose them. It's the same with life. Emergencies force us to stop, but pit stops of joy are events we plan for and savor.

It's good to let go and to bring a little relief into the noise when life is clamoring at you. It won't change any of the circumstances you find yourself in, but when you can laugh at the antics of others, perhaps because you can see yourself in them, that helps to lighten the load.

Does something come to mind for you? It might be a video of family and friends that makes you laugh when watching it. Or maybe it's an old tearjerker movie with a happy ending.

Whatever makes you feel warm and cozy and helps you celebrate the moment, keep an episode or two at hand and stock up on snacks. There's nothing like a vat of praline pecan ice cream when the bills are due, the laundry is piled to the ceiling, and the cat just coughed up a fur ball on the dog!

 SHEILA WALSH

*H*uman beings thrive on laughter. Since most of us can't afford vacations in Hawaii, we have to learn to make our own fun! The best way to do that is to keep your state of mind green and golden: find, recycle, or produce joy wherever and however you can. A good humorist is a work of heart! The Hasidic Jews believe that the best way to worship God is by being happy. They even incorporate dance and celebration into their spiritual walk.

Humor is the chocolate chips in the ice cream of life. Remember the old-time "Good Humor man" who drove his ice cream truck down every street in the neighborhood, chiming a jingle on those hot summer days? All the kids came running as soon as they heard the sound. But good humor doesn't drive down many streets anymore. You have to go out and get it yourself.

Fortunately, it's not that hard to find.

BARBARA JOHNSON

Promises About Joy

*H*e will yet fill your mouth with laughter and your lips with shouts of joy.

Job 8:21

*W*eeping may remain for a night, but rejoicing comes in the morning.

Psalm 30:5

*G*od has brought me laughter, and everyone who hears about this will laugh with me.

Genesis 21:6

*O*ur mouths were filled with laughter, our tongues with songs of joy. Then it was said among the nations, "The LORD has done great things for them."

Psalm 126:2

The Joy All Around Us

Luci, two other dear friends, and I flew to Chile and headed off for what proved to be an off-the-charts, fantastic trip to the Magallenic penguin rookery. I wasn't prepared for the utter delight I felt as our bus made its way down to the coastal rookery, carefully threading its way through hundreds of little penguins who didn't care whose parking lot they were on or how big our bus was.

As we exited the bus, one particularly friendly penguin turned to a woman and began an energetic effort to loosen her shoelaces. When the shoelaces would not yield, the penguin pummeled the woman's leg with a succession of flipper slaps that sent us all into hysterics. The woman was not hurt, but she was sporting some memorable bruises the next day.

To my knowledge, penguins don't serve any useful purpose in life other than to give people like me immense pleasure. From the grandeur of the snow-capped glacier peaks to the awkward land inefficiency of penguins, what fun it is simply to "sing for joy" about God's creation.

MARILYN MEBERG

DISCOVERING JOY

*R*ecently I stopped for breakfast at the local pancake house. I intended to steal a moment to be alone before the day began and its many demands crowded my time.

"Just an egg and a homemade biscuit," I told the waitress, "And a coffee, please." I handed back the menu and turned to the book I'd brought to jump-start my mind.

I had barely finished the second page before she returned with my breakfast. She poured the coffee and asked if there'd be anything else. "No, I'm fine, thank you," I answered.

She smiled. "Enjoy!" she said, then hurried back to deliver someone else's order.

Her final word hung in the air above my corner booth like a blessing. It was a choice she had offered me. I could go through this day oblivious to the miracles all around me or I could tune in and "enjoy!"

I've heard a lot of sermons in my day, but the best sermon I'd heard in a long time was preached in one word by a busy waitress as she poured a cup of coffee. God has given us this day. I don't want to miss it.

Enjoy!

GLORIA GAITHER

Promises About the *Joy* Around *Us*

He performs wonders that cannot be
fathomed, miracles that cannot be counted.
He bestows rain on the earth; he sends
water upon the countryside. The lowly he
sets on high, and those who mourn are
lifted to safety.

Job 5:9–11

Great are the works of the LORD; they are
pondered by all who delight in them.

Psalm 111:2

Tell the righteous it will be well with
them, for they will enjoy the fruit of their
deeds.

Isaiah 3:10

My chosen ones will long enjoy the
works of their hands.

Isaiah 65:22

The Joy of God's Everlasting Love

God's love is a gift that can make you forget yourself at times. The Scottish writer George MacDonald said, "It is the heart that is not yet sure of its God that is afraid to laugh in his presence."

So often with old people and children all sense of what would be appropriate is swallowed up in what feels right. That's refreshing. We waste too many years between childhood and our older years measuring our behavior on a scale we think we see in someone else's eyes.

God loves us as we are right now! That's one of the things I'm most grateful for. I love the freedom to be myself in God. I pray that a year from now, five years from now, I will be a godlier woman, but I know God won't love me any more than he does right this minute.

Let me tell you, you can run in out of the cold, sit by the fire, put up your feet, and just be yourself. You are loved, you are loved, you are loved!

 SHEILA WALSH

$\mathcal{D}$o you enjoy hearing tender words from your spouse, children, family, and friends? Of course you do. However, to know that we are loved by an omnipotent, omnipresent, omniscient Lord is the grandest feeling of acceptance anyone can have. When other people fail to express their love to us, we can always depend on Jesus.

Imagine Jesus himself saying to you:

"Child of mine, I love you with an everlasting love. I love you with unconditional love. I love you because I want to! I love you when others think you are unlovable. I love you when you have sinned and come short of my glory. I love you in the good times and in the bad."

THELMA WELLS

Promises About God's Everlasting Love

The LORD appeared to us in the past, saying: "I have loved you with an everlasting love; I have drawn you with loving-kindness."

Jeremiah 31:3

We love because he first loved us.

1 John 4:19

From everlasting to everlasting the LORD's love is with those who fear him, and his righteousness with their children's children.

Psalm 103:17

Give thanks to the LORD, for he is good; his love endures forever.

Psalm 118:1

The *Joy* of *God's Creation*

*O*ne of the things I find fascinating about God's creation is the way he seems to temper the negative environmental elements with corresponding positive ones. For instance, without the nearly ceaseless rains of the Northwest, no incomparable green scenery would greet the eye from all directions. And the snow that snuggles atop Mt. Hood, Mt. Rainier, and Mt. St. Helens would not exist if, at lower elevations, there were no rain.

By the same token, if God had not created water for the desert environment, it would indeed be an ashtray. But because of water, we have luxuriously green golf courses, languidly swaying palm trees, and even streams in the desert.

God's creative style ensures that something wonderful will offset something less than wonderful. In everything God seems so balanced.

MARILYN MEBERG

DISCOVERING JOY

*W*hy the gardening mania? Why the books, calendars, accessories, decorations, tools, music, picture frames, furniture, clothes? Why are we so enchanted with white picket fences made into tables and chairs and headboards for the bed? Why the silk grapevines, sweet peas, and ficus trees for the bathroom, kitchen, and hall? Because we crave the sweet serenity of greens and golds and deep brown earth. Because fellowship with God began in a garden, and we long for that time and place. Because leaves quivering in the wind, blossoms nodding, grass ruffled by a breeze, remind us of our real home and the peaceful destiny awaiting us. Because when I cheer up with my geraniums, smile at my pansies, laugh with my petunias, they teach me about God's big greenhouse bursting with joy.

Take the seedlings on loan from heaven and share the growth. Get your gloves muddy, your face tanned, and your knees crinkled here on earth. Nurture faith and love. Keep believing in the harvest. God will make something beautiful out of your effort and energy.

BARBARA JOHNSON

Promises About God's Creation

How many are your works, O Lord! In wisdom you made them all; the earth is full of your creatures.

Psalm 104:24

These are but the outer fringe of his works; how faint the whisper we hear of him! Who then can understand the thunder of his power?

Job 26:14

You alone are the Lord. You made the heavens, even the highest heavens, and all their starry host, the earth and all that is on it, the seas and all that is in them. You give life to everything, and the multitudes of heaven worship you.

Nehemiah 9:6

Our Unique Treasures

*M*en have such a different angle of viewing things than women. We girls call to others to come see a playful puppy, a snugly kitten, or a cooing baby. Meanwhile the guys dangle a grass snake like a charm bracelet, point out the newest road kill, and burp loud enough to register 6.3 on the Richter scale.

That's not to say all guys—just a fair portion—go for the yucky stuff of life. But I find the he-men in my vicinity would rather investigate a spider's nest than check out the new lace curtains. Even though we did start out in the same garden, we don't seem to be smelling the same rose bush.

We need to respect our differences and to value another's contribution. Our differences enable us to enlarge each other's angle of viewing life. Treasure each other's uniqueness and remember to see from another angle.

PATSY CLAIRMONT

*M*other loves to philosophize. "We humans are real pack rats," she once said. "We hold on to the past for dear life." She leaned forward in her chair: "We're not limited just to fine china and snapshots or old leather-bound books. All our lives, we are making collections that are far more significant . . . fears, phobias, and suspicions . . . hopes, dreams, and illusions . . . attributes, persuasions, and prejudices."

As a result of our conversation, I am learning to discard the redundancies of my life. I would be willing to give up nearly every collection I have, except one—my family and friends. They are truly a part of my life that gives me warmth, color, and texture, courage, comfort, and strength, joy, tears, and very often, laughter in large doses!

If I were asked what I cherish most, my answer would surely be my faith in God, but without so much as a comma between, I would have to add my exquisite treasure of friends and family. The simple, basic pleasures of our daily lives, are the significant, valuable treasures.

 PEGGY BENSON

Promises About Our Unique Treasures

The body is a unit, though it is made up of many parts; and though all its parts are many, they form one body. So it is with Christ.

1 Corinthians 12:12

There is one body and one Spirit— just as you were called to one hope when you were called—one Lord, one faith, one baptism; one God and Father of all, who is over all and through all and in all. But to each one of us grace has been given as Christ apportioned it.

Ephesians 4:4–7

Just as each of us has one body with many members, and these members do not all have the same function, so in Christ we who are many form one body, and each member belongs to all the others. We have different gifts, according to the grace given us.

Romans 12:4–6

God Is in Control

I see God's fingerprints in his handi-work: a sunrise, a shooting star, a lilac bush, and a newborn's smile. I observe a measure of his strength in a hurricane, an earthquake, a thunderbolt. I see his creativity in a kanga-roo, the Grand Canyon, and a blue-eyed, red-headed baby. I detect his humor in a porpoise, a cactus, and a two-year-old's twinkling eyes. I am aware of his mysterious-ness when I consider the Trinity, the solar system, and his desire to be in communion with us. "What is man that you are mindful of him?" (Psalm 8:4)

But how do we find God? Sometimes we search him out, and sometimes he "finds" us. Every time we think of God it is because he first had us on his mind. The Lord is always the initiator. He has been from the beginning (Genesis 1:1), and he will be to the end (Revelation 1:7). So know that once you have invited him to enter your life, you are on his mind and he is in your heart.

PATSY CLAIRMONT

DISCOVERING JOY

*W*hen I say "The LORD is my shepherd," I remember that he has charge over my life. As my shepherd, he watches over me to see that I stay in the fold. He loves me unconditionally in spite of going my own willful way sometimes. He protects me from danger. He provides everything for me. He chastises me when I do wrong. He comforts me when I am distressed. He bandages my wounds when I get hurt. He calms my fears when I am afraid. He takes care of my relationships when they become shaky. He bathes me in his Spirit when I seek his face. He communicates with me in ways I can understand.

God promises to provide all our *needs* according to his riches in glory in Christ Jesus. I know he will do that. And he delights in often giving us what we want, too.

You can depend on him to watch over you, to protect you, to provide for you, to comfort you, to chastise you when you need it, to bandage your wounds, to calm your fears, to care for your relationships, to communicate with you, and to love you unconditionally.

THELMA WELLS

Promises About God's Care & Control

He who did not spare his own Son, but gave him up for us all—how will he not also, along with him, graciously give us all things?

Romans 8:32

My God will meet all your needs according to his glorious riches in Christ Jesus.

Philippians 4:19

Keep your lives free from the love of money and be content with what you have, because God has said, "Never will I leave you; never will I forsake you." So we say with confidence, "The Lord is my helper; I will not be afraid."

Hebrews 13:5–6

The LORD is my light and my salvation— whom shall I fear? The LORD is the stronghold of my life—of whom shall I be afraid?

Psalm 27:1

The *Joy* of *God's Gifts*

*O*ur God is a gift giver. His generosity is obvious in how lavishly he bestows on us rainbows, waterfalls, canyons, and white caps.

One day when I was visiting in the desert a marshmallow cloud formation drizzled over the mountaintop like so much whipped cream. I brought my bike to a standstill and just beheld this delicious scene for thirty-five minutes. Another evening the sunset turned the skyline into a saucer of peaches and cream—absolutely dreamy. The Lord serves up his scrumptious beauty in liberal portions and then invites us to partake.

I have often joined Marilyn Meberg at nightfall for the spectacular performance as the sun sets. The mountains go through a series of thrilling changes. From pinks to lavenders to deep purples, the setting sun and emerging evening appear to cover the hillside for sleep. Marilyn and I never tire of the Lord's thrilling displays. We "ooh!" and "ah!" in all the right places, and we can feel our blood pressure balancing out as smiles and giggles of pleasure help us to express our gratitude.

PATSY CLAIRMONT

*O*ur support group has met monthly in a church across from Disneyland. During the summer months the 9:30 PM fireworks over Disneyland always interrupt our meetings. I'd usually get irritated and annoyed until one evening a couple from Iowa joined us. As soon as the fireworks started, they sat up, eyes twinkling. "Oh, the fireworks!" they exclaimed. There was wonder in their faces. They were excited and suddenly animated. "Can we stop for a few minutes to watch them?" they asked.

Think of everything you normally take for granted. Make a list of the most ordinary, tedious things that happen every day over and over in your life. Now imagine a homeless man or woman coming to live with you for a day. What do you think they would say about the linens and soft blankets? The furnace that blows heat through the floor?

"Oh, the fireworks!" The marvelous kingdom of our God is right across the street regardless of where we live. We may as well get enthused and infect everyone we meet with his amazing love and power. Let the fireworks begin!

BARBARA JOHNSON

Promises About God's Gifts

Every good and perfect gift is from above, coming down from the Father of the heavenly lights, who does not change like shifting shadows.

James 1:17

Who gave man his mouth? Who makes him deaf or mute? Who gives him sight or makes him blind? Is it not I, the Lord? Now go; I will help you speak and will teach you what to say.

Exodus 4:11-12

If you, then, though you are evil, know how to give good gifts to your children, how much more will your Father in heaven give good gifts to those who ask him!

Matthew 7:11

The Joy of Good Friends

*S*ometimes, when I can't sleep, I lie in bed, and instead of counting sheep, I count all the fun people God has put in my life.

On one such occasion, I'd gone to bed at 10:30 PM. When I woke up, I was sure it must be morning and was shocked to see that the clock on my bedside table said it was only 12:30 AM. I slipped out of bed, went downstairs, made some hot tea, and switched on the TV. But when the clock said it was 3:30 AM, I went back upstairs determined to fall asleep.

That's when I remembered some of the stories Luci, Patsy, and Marilyn tell when they speak at the conferences, and I started to laugh. I don't know if you've ever felt like laughing while the person next to you is fast asleep, but it makes you laugh even more. I stuck my head under the covers to try to muffle my snorts.

Who can make you giggle and snort under the covers just thinking about them and their antics? The next time you can't sleep, thank God for all those who make your life richer!

SHEILA WALSH

DISCOVERING JOY

*L*ike people, plants are born with personality. The difference, I think, is that in his plan for people, God added humor!

Some plants feed upon a seed beneath the earth. Others push the seed case forth—some with methodical care, others with reckless abandonment.

I am often gently nourished by a friend whose quiet company provides wisdom and comfort for my spirit.

I am sometimes coquettishly coaxed from my comfortable environment and persistently urged through the crusty surface soil by friends.

But, on occasion, I have been catapulted from my warm bed to worlds beyond my experience by the likes of my professional colleagues or family members.

We nurture and are nourished by our friends in different ways. In his plan for friends, I think God often paints way outside the lines. The color may not rival that of the flower garden, but the comedy is superb!

JOY MACKENZIE

Promises About Good Friends

A friend loves at all times, and a brother is born for adversity.

Proverbs 17:17

I no longer call you servants, because a servant does not know his master's business. Instead, I have called you friends, for everything that I learned from my Father I have made known to you.

John 15:15

Perfume and incense bring joy to the heart, and the pleasantness of one's friend springs from his earnest counsel.

Proverbs 27:9

Two are better than one, because they have a good return for their work: If one falls down, his friend can help him up.

Ecclesiastes 4:9–10

Secure in God's Love

*H*ow does one find God? He is in our prayers guiding our words, he is in our songs as we worship him, and he is filling our mouths when we comfort a friend or speak wisdom to someone who needs hope. Sometimes we can search so hard for the miraculous we miss the obvious reality of his ever-present nearness. Count your blessings. He is in them, too.

We can't command the Lord into our awareness. He is King; we are his beloved subjects. When our hearts are tenderly responsive ("Whatever, Lord") and it suits his greater plan, then the Lord will lift the thin veil that separates us. And we will be stunned to realize that he has been closer than our own breath all along.

By the way, it has been my experience that I keep refinding him, which has helped to define me. You, too, may lose track of your faith. Remember, it is never too late to step back on the path.

PATSY CLAIRMONT

*M*y baby boy has no sense of what's appropriate on the noise-making front. On the first Sunday we took him to church, we opted to sit in the back row, knowing that at the first squawk we could be up and out fast. As the sermon started, everything seemed fine. Christian was cuddled up in my arms, deep in sleep, or so I thought. Suddenly, Christian burst into a baby version of "Moon River" at a decibel level that could have burst a dog's eardrums. I jumped up so quickly I nearly dropped him. I hurried out whispering "Shh!" vainly in his ear. That only seemed to encourage him, and he moved into verse two, grinning from ear to ear.

By the time we were outside, I was laughing so hard I could barely walk or breathe. There is something so charming about that kind of innocence. When children are secure, they feel free to be who they really are. That's how you and I can live too. God is the only one who knows everything about us. He knows it all, and he loves you. What a gift in a world where there is so much uncertainty!

SHEILA WALSH

Promises About God's Love

God so loved the world that he gave his one and only Son, that whoever believes in him shall not perish but have eternal life.

John 3:16

God demonstrates his own love for us in this: While we were still sinners, Christ died for us.

Romans 5:8

I love those who love me, and those who seek me find me.

Proverbs 8:17

So we know and rely on the love God has for us. God is love. Whoever lives in love lives in God, and God in him.

1 John 4:16

A Joyful Child of God

Early Christmas morning! Waking up in a cold bedroom, frost on the window panes, snow draping the trees outside my window. Wrapping up in warm dressing gowns and slippers. Creeping down the stairs barely able to contain the excitement. Opening the living room door . . . a wonderland, a transformation overnight from the ordinary to every unspoken wish laid out in gold and red and green packages. Tangerines wrapped in silver paper. The aroma of turkey filling every room.

I wonder why our vision becomes impaired with the turning of calendar pages. We have forgotten what joy looks like. We were made for joy, but we have forgotten what it smells like. We've forgotten how it sounds.

Before you go to bed tonight, do one thing that will bring back a little joy from childhood. Have some cookies and milk or throw a duckie in your bath. Buy a children's book and curl up by the fire and read. Welcome to . . . joy!

SHEILA WALSH

DISCOVERING JOY

I love playful people! People who aren't too sophisticated or too proper to engage in zany antics draw me like a two-year-old to mud.

Sometimes I think we responsible adults assume that being playful might be interpreted as being childish, maybe even silly. Admittedly, nothing is more tragic than an adult who fails to gain the maturity and wisdom necessary to live a productive life. But equally tragic are adults who forget how to vent their play instincts.

The mature person is able to recognize the distinction between the two worlds and choose which world is appropriate for the moment.

Jesus said it's impossible to enter the Kingdom unless we become as little children (Mark 10: 15). He seemed to place a high premium on that childlike quality. He reminds us of how preferable it is at times to be childlike.

MARILYN MEBERG

Promises About Being a Child of God

To all who received him, to those who believed in his name, he gave the right to become children of God—children born not of natural descent, nor of human decision or a husband's will, but born of God.

John 1:12–13

Do everything without complaining or arguing, so that you may become blameless and pure, children of God without fault in a crooked and depraved generation, in which you shine like stars in the universe.

Philippians 2:14–15

How great is the love the Father has lavished on us, that we should be called children of God! And that is what we are!

1 John 3:1

Joyful Companions

Given first dibs on travel companions, I would pick Thelma, Luci, Marilyn, Sheila, and Barbara right off the bat.

Thelma often is tucked in a corner behind the scenes, Bible spread open, preparing herself for ministry.

Luci can guide us into stimulating conversations as well with her witty, thought-provoking questions.

Marilyn keeps us all chortling and challenged with her comedic sense and her insightful offerings.

Sheila's brilliant mind, lightning humor, and sterling devotion brighten my path.

Barbara's a seasoned journeyer who has taught me how to travel on with smiles in my miles.

Who are your traveling chums? Do they promote smiles in your miles? Do they add joy to your journey? When we choose companions may we be wise and select those who are wholesome, humorous, helpful, and honorable.

PATSY CLAIRMONT

*O*ne of my favorite early spring flowers is the Johnny Jump-up. It is a first cousin to the pansy. They have sweet smiling faces, each with its own personality. Each morning, the sweet smiling faces of the small flowers look up at me as they settle their roots into the earth.

I smile back as I see in them the faces of my "jump-up" friends—people who have come into my life over the years at just the exact time I needed to see a friendly, smiling face. They are people who believe in me and let me know it in many ways. They are quick to send a note of encouragement, make a phone call, or surprise me with a birthday gift. What a tremendous rescue team!

During the days of spring, as I walk into my garden and think and pray about my life— where I've been and where I might be next—I smile to myself and remember, and I thank God for all of my Johnny Jump-ups!

PEGGY BENSON

Promises About Joyful Companions

*S*hout for joy to the LORD, all the earth. Worship the LORD with gladness; come before him with joyful songs. Know that the LORD is God. It is he who made us, and we are his; we are his people, the sheep of his pasture.

Psalm 100:1–3

*I*f two lie down together, they will keep warm. But how can one keep warm alone? Though one may be overpowered, two can defend themselves. A cord of three strands is not quickly broken.

Ecclesiastes 4:11–12

*R*uth replied, "Don't urge me to leave you or to turn back from you. Where you go I will go, and where you stay I will stay. Your people will be my people and your God my God. Where you die I will die, and there I will be buried."

Ruth 1:16–17

God Always Remembers

*C*hristi at New Life Clinics asked me to be the surprise guest for the employees at their annual Christmas dinner. I agreed. But I didn't write it down.

The day of the event, I kept feeling this annoying tug that said, "You're supposed to do something today." But I couldn't think of what it was.

On Christmas Day someone asked me how the surprise appearance at New Life had worked out. Oh, no! My heart was sick. I forced myself to face up to what I had done.

Wouldn't it be horrible if Jesus were so busy he couldn't remember what we talked to him about?

Thank God we don't have to endure that kind of treatment from our Lord! Hallelujah, we are never forgotten! God can be depended on. We disappoint loved ones. We inconvenience people we care about. But how wonderful, how beautiful, how comforting to know we have a God who is always near to console and cheer, just when we need him most.

THELMA WELLS

Les and I were in an antique shop the other day when we spotted a photo album on a table. Interested, we peeked inside only to find a family peering back at us.

We both felt sad seeing someone's snapshots cast aside for strangers to peruse. We wondered who would throw away his or her history (a few family members maybe, but the whole clan)? How does one toss out a picture without guilt? A person's likeness is so personal it seems like a violation to discard them. After all, what if these individuals have rejection issues? And who would purpose to buy more relatives?

Ever feel like your identity is lost in a world full of people? We have a God whose heart is expansive enough to hold us all and yet who's so intently focused on each of us that he knows our rising up and our sitting down. Our faces are no surprise to the Lord, and our identities are engraved in the palms of his hands.

PATSY CLAIRMONT

Promises About Remembering

Can a mother forget the baby at her breast and have no compassion on the child she has borne? Though she may forget, I will not forget you!

Isaiah 49:15

God is not unjust; he will not forget your work and the love you have shown him as you have helped his people and continue to help them.

Hebrews 6:10

Only be careful, and watch yourselves closely so that you do not forget the things your eyes have seen or let them slip from your heart as long as you live. Teach them to your children and their children after them.

Deuteronomy 4:9

Get wisdom, get understanding; do not forget my words or swerve from them.

Proverbs 4:5

The *Joy* of *God's* *Touch*

I was a guest singer at a Billy Graham crusade. Billy's message was simple and uncompromising. No bells or whistles "wowed" the crowd, just a simple call was made to "Come home." I wondered what the response would be. I wondered if the message sounded too good to be true. I wondered if it sounded too simple.

But then it began. People began to stream to the front to receive Christ. I had to bury my face in my hands, overwhelmed with pure joy at being a spectator to such a homecoming.

It would be such a shame to sit in church every Sunday and listen to what's being said about God but never grasp that this is a personal invitation—a welcome mat just for you.

"If we confess our sins, he is faithful and just and will forgive us our sins and purify us from all unrighteousness" (1 John 1:9). Isn't that great? Isn't that simple? All you have to do is pray:

"Father, thank you that you love me. Thank you that Jesus died for me. I want to come home. Thank you for waiting for me. Amen."

SHEILA WALSH

*W*e want and need to know who we are. Of course, for the believer, there need not be a puzzle. Specific attention, thought, and planning about me took place before God actually formed me in the womb. That implies I am much more than a cozy encounter between my parents nine months before I was born. No matter the circumstances surrounding my conception, I am a planned event.

Not only am I a planned event, I was "set apart." I have a specific task to do for God. We all have a specific task to do for God, and it was planned in his head before we were ever formed in the womb. That is an incredible truth!

Not only is my identity and calling known, but also Isaiah 43:1 says, "I have called you by name; you are Mine!" (NAS). He considers me unique and set apart, and he calls me his own.

May we sink into that cushion of joyful peace and never forget "whose we be."

MARILYN MEBERG

Promises About God's Touch

This is what the Lord says . . . "Fear not, for I have redeemed you; I have summoned you by name; you are mine."

Isaiah 43:1

I will do the very thing you have asked, because I am pleased with you and I know you by name.

Exodus 33:17

I, the Lord, have called you in righteousness; I will take hold of your hand.

Isaiah 42:6

I will refine them like silver and test them like gold. They will call on my name and I will answer them; I will say, "They are my people," and they will say, "The Lord is our God."

Zechariah 13:9

A Joyful Up-look

The *Joy* of *Change*

*L*ike it or not, constant change is part of modern life. What in the world *doesn't* change?

1. God's love.
2. Friendship with his Son.
3. The power of the Holy Spirit.

When you think you've had just about all the change you can stand, reach out and take one step further into God's wide arms. Though his love, friendship, and power never change, he made you with a big, elastic spiritual cord that stretches with every tug and pull. He knows exactly how much give it's got. If he's calling you to stretch, he knows you've got what it takes. Reach!

God knows change can make your life richer. Live for today but hold your hands open to tomorrow. Anticipate the future and its changes with joy. There is a seed of God's love in every event, every circumstance, every unpleasant situation in which you may find yourself. Don't get stuck in a rut or hung up on an outdated blessing. You serve a God of change!

BARBARA JOHNSON

A Joyful Up-look

*C*hange! You can count on it! Life boasts very few things that are absolutely dependable, but change is one of them, and it is the one we seem to fear most.

The moon and the ocean both provide exquisite models of the rhythm of life—consistent in their waxing and waning, advance and retreat, ebb and flow. But in our brief earthly journey, most of us just haven't quite been able to get the hang of it. We dread the ebbing, fearing the flow will never return. We demand a constancy that is impossible.

If the joy is in the flow—the moments of great advance, the rush—then the maturing and growing is in the retreat, the pulling back, the ebb, during which there is a grand preparation and anticipation of the next exciting surge forward. The mighty ocean wave retreats to empower its next forward motion.

In God's infinite understanding of the human condition, he reaches out to assuage the dread and fear of change: "Trust me," he says. "I will never leave you. Come to me . . . and I will give you rest. In my presence is fullness of joy."

JOY MACKENZIE

Promises About Change

You have made known to me the path of life; you will fill me with joy in your presence, with eternal pleasures at your right hand.

Psalm 16:11

There is a time for everything, and a season for every activity under heaven: a time to be born and a time to die, a time to plant and a time to uproot, a time to kill and a time to heal, a time to tear down and a time to build, a time to weep and a time to laugh, a time to mourn and a time to dance, a time to scatter stones and a time to gather them, a time to embrace and a time to refrain, a time to search and a time to give up, a time to keep and a time to throw away, a time to tear and a time to mend, a time to be silent and a time to speak, a time to love and a time to hate, a time for war and a time for peace.

Ecclesiastes 3:1–8

Finding Hope in Jesus

I attended a gala occasion recently to which I wore a dressy pants outfit with stylish heels. My hair was fluffed, and my ears were adorned with a new pair of dazzling earrings. I felt spiffy . . . until I arrived at the event. I was the only woman with slacks on, and I felt awkward. After a considerable time I spotted another gal in slacks, and I wondered if she would want to sit with me and be best friends. Soon several others arrived in similar attire, and I no longer felt the need to bond.

Aren't we funny? We work hard to be originals and then fear our originality has made us different. I enjoy being center stage unless it's under a critical spotlight. Like the time I spoke only to learn afterward that my slip was hanging in a southerly direction waving to the onlookers. Following the sessions, several hundred women alerted me so I could hike it up. Believe me, I wanted to take a hike . . . an exceedingly long one to another land. Despite today's fads I prefer to keep my underwear undercover. Know what I mean?

PATSY CLAIRMONT

A JOYFUL UP-LOOK

The ocean is a favorite place of mine. I love to listen to sounds that only the waves can make. I walk miles along the shoreline leaving my footprints in the sand, which are then invaded by an endless ebb and flow of the tide. These moments bring an unspeakable calm. I can see with a clear mind and heart all the ways God has held my life and walked me through the violent storms to bring me to a restful place. Even the bad memories—those painful reminders of hurt and disappointment—somehow get covered with sweet forgiveness and a yearning for all to be right and true under the warm blanket of the Lord's mercy.

It is when my mind is stayed on Jesus, when my eyes look toward eternal things, when my ears listen way beyond the voices of the day, that I hear the ocean sing. The Lord miraculously puts everything into his perspective when my mind and heart are set on all that he is, on all that he's done, on all that he's promised. I become more thankful, I become more hopeful, and most importantly, I am humbled.

KATHY TROCCOLI

Promises About
Hope in Jesus

Surely God is my salvation; I will trust and not be afraid. The LORD, the LORD, is my strength and my song; he has become my salvation.

Isaiah 12:2

I am not ashamed, because I know whom I have believed, and am convinced that he is able to guard what I have entrusted to him for that day.

2 Timothy 1:12

Do not let your hearts be troubled. Trust in God; trust also in me.

John 14:1

May the God of hope fill you with all joy and peace as you trust in him, so that you may overflow with hope by the power of the Holy Spirit.

Romans 15:13

No Regrets

Did you know that an opal is a stone with a broken heart? Made of dust, sand, and silica, it is full of minute fissures that allow air to be trapped inside. The trapped air refracts the light, resulting in the lovely hues that inspire the opal's nickname, the Lamp of Fire. When kept in a cold, dark place, the opal loses its luster. But when held in a warm hand or when the light shines on it, the luster is restored. So it is with us. A broken heart becomes a lamp of fire when we allow God to breathe on it and warm us with his life.

If things are tough, remember that every flower that ever bloomed had to go through a whole lot of dirt to get there. The Almighty Father will use life's reverses to move you forward. So do not keep grieving about a bitter experience. The present is slipping by while you are regretting the past and worrying about the future. Regret will not prevent tomorrow's sorrows; it will only rob today of its strength. So keep on believing. With Jesus you have not a hopeless end but an endless hope!

Barbara Johnson

A Joyful Up-look

*E*ver wish you could start over? Probably all of us have longed for another chance in some area of our lives. We wouldn't necessarily have done things differently, just more or perhaps less.

The truth is we can't go backward, only forward into uncharted territory. To sit in our sorrow would lead to misery. Although regret that leads to change is a dear friend, regret that leads to shame is a treacherous enemy.

There is no guarantee that if we had done a part of our lives differently things would end any differently. We have to trust the God of the universe who directs the outcome of all things that he will do that which ultimately needs to be done.

Many things are now out of our control but never his. So next time you and I need something to lean on, let's make it the Lord.

◼ PATSY CLAIRMONT

*P*romises About *R*egrets

*G*odly sorrow brings repentance that leads to salvation and leaves no regret, but worldly sorrow brings death.

2 Corinthians 7:10

*R*epent! Turn away from all your offenses; then sin will not be your downfall. Rid yourselves of all the offenses you have committed, and get a new heart and a new spirit.

Ezekiel 18:30–31

*W*hen God saw what they did and how they turned from their evil ways, he had compassion and did not bring upon them the destruction he had threatened.

Jonah 3:10

*R*epent, then, and turn to God, so that your sins may be wiped out, that times of refreshing may come from the Lord.

Acts 3:19

Joy Sappers

Some say truth is stranger than fiction; others say it isn't stranger, just more rare. (One thing is sure: if you tell the truth, there's less to remember!)

No matter what, don't ever let yesterday use up too much of today. If it sneaks up on you, turn the tables on it. Like interest rates, make trouble work *for* you, not *against* you. You don't always need a comedian to make you laugh. Once you get started, you can pull a few one-liners out of the bag yourself. When someone says, "Life is hard," say, "I prefer it to the alternative, don't you?" When somebody else complains about getting old, answer, "Right now, I'm just sitting here being thankful that wrinkles don't hurt!"

Life is too short to spend it being angry, bored, or dull. That was never God's intention. Maybe boredom and dullness aren't on any list of sins in the Bible, but they will sap your joy if you tolerate them.

BARBARA JOHNSON

A JOYFUL UP-LOOK

"*D*id you mail that insurance form, sweetie?" I asked Barry one afternoon.

He seemed to lose a little color. "I forgot," he said.

"Why would you forget something as important as that?" I snapped.

"I'm sorry, honey. I just forgot," he said.

I found myself standing on the edge of a cliff and knew I had to choose whether I would dive off or back off. I asked Barry to excuse me for a moment, and I made a conscious, determined choice to get on my knees and to let my anger go. As I released my fury, I was filled with joy.

Choosing to let go of my tempestuous responses may not seem big to you, but it's making a huge difference in our lives. I want to be the fragrance of Christ in the midst of the storms of life, not part of the storm front.

If you struggle with old behaviors that are as familiar to you as the spider veins on your legs, I encourage you to invite Christ into the moment and to let those old patterns go. You can choose. You can be a drip of rain or a ray of sunshine.

SHEILA WALSH

Promises About Joy Sappers

Take note of this: Everyone should be quick to listen, slow to speak and slow to become angry.

James 1:19

Your attitude should be the same as that of Christ Jesus: Who, being in very nature God, did not consider equality with God something to be grasped, but made himself nothing, taking the very nature of a servant.

Philippians 2:5–7

Take my yoke upon you and learn from me, for I am gentle and humble in heart, and you will find rest for your souls.

Matthew 11:29

Whoever claims to live in him must walk as Jesus did.

1 John 2:6

Soaring Through Struggles

I was flying from Minneapolis to California, or so I thought, when the pilot announced we were returning to our port of departure. "Whatever for?" we all wondered, groaning and complaining. The pilot explained that the aircraft couldn't get enough altitude to clear the Rocky Mountains near Denver. Despite our mutterings, we turned around and headed back.

Once on the ground, it wasn't long before the airplane mechanics found the problem. One of them had left a vacuum hose in the door, preventing the seal from being tight enough to allow the cabin to be pressurized and thus enable the plane to clear the Rockies. A simple error by a careless mechanic drained the airplane's power to soar.

What's your personal vacuum hose that keeps you from soaring? Pray for illumination. Let go of worry. Follow the disciplines outlined in the Bible. Communicate with the Pilot as well as the ground crew. Do whatever is necessary to remove the hoses that drain your energy or force you backward. Don't give up and take the bus. It's better to fly. Remember that underneath are the "everlasting arms".

BARBARA JOHNSON

A Joyful Up-look

*D*efying odds, breaking barriers, not being held back. I know people like that. They're a source of encouragement to me. They hang tough when others give up, forge ahead when others lag behind, choose to be cheerful when others sink in defeat.

Yet even more powerful are the words of Jesus, who challenged his followers to move mountains, walk on water, and prepare a picnic for five thousand. He assured us we would do no less than the impossible.

I don't know the circumstances of your life. Maybe you're experiencing a financial crisis, a relational struggle, or a genuine feeling of inadequacy. Whatever your biggest problems, be sure you aren't surrendering to the odds. You may look at yourself and say, "I can't. I can't rise above this, get beyond it, or overcome," and so you give up. Let me say with all the love in the world, my friend, don't quit. You're just starting this ride. You have the whole sky above your head. God wants to free you from bondage, and he knows just how to do it.

■ LUCI SWINDOLL

Promises About Soaring Through Struggles

Even to your old age and gray hairs I am he, I am he who will sustain you. I have made you and I will carry you; I will sustain you and I will rescue you.

Isaiah 46:4

The eternal God is your refuge, and underneath are the everlasting arms.

Deuteronomy 33:27

He knows the way that I take; when he has tested me, I will come forth as gold.

Job 23:10

For a little while you may have had to suffer grief in all kinds of trials. These have come so that your faith—of greater worth than gold, which perishes even though refined by fire—may be proved genuine and may result in praise, glory and honor when Jesus Christ is revealed.

1 Peter 1:6–7

66

The Joy of Persevering

A calmer faith. That's the quiet place within us where we don't get whiplash every time life tosses us a curve. Where we don't revolt when his plan and ours conflict. Where we relax (versus stew, sweat, and swear) in the midst of an answerless season. Where we accept (and expect) deserts in our spiritual journey as surely as we do joy. Where we are not intimidated or persuaded by other people's agendas but moved only by him. Where we weep in repentance, sleep in peace, live in fullness, and sing of victory.

PATSY CLAIRMONT

*M*y daughter Vikki, with her free spirit, discovered that once you start to climb a mountain, it's so steep and rough your only option is to keep your sights on finishing and your mind on the rocks and boulders up ahead. You have to keep looking forward and not back, and you have to pray every step of the way that you will make it.

The road to glory is difficult with its rocks and boulders, its strain and struggle. Things aren't always as easy as we would like. Surprises and pitfalls wait for us along the road of life. We're going to sweat and sway, we're going to wonder why things are the way they are.

But every road has an end; every mountain has its peak. If we can just hold on and keep climbing, knowing that God is aware of how we're straining, he will bring us up and over the mountains. It's consoling to know God is in control of every part of our journey to glory, even over the steep mountains.

THELMA WELLS

Promises About Persevering

To him who overcomes, I will give
the right to eat from the tree of life,
which is in the paradise of God.

Revelation 2:7

Let us not become weary in doing
good, for at the proper time we will
reap a harvest if we do not give up.

Galatians 6:9

To those who by persistence in
doing good seek glory, honor and
immortality, [God] will give eternal life.

Romans 2:7

Stand firm. Let nothing move you.
Always give yourselves fully to the
work of the Lord, because you know
that your labor in the Lord is not in
vain.

1 Corinthians 15:58

The Joy of a Godly Perspective

Charles Darrow didn't set out to become a millionaire when he developed "Monopoly," the game that was later marketed around the world by Parker Brothers, but that's what happened. The little gift he developed from scraps of cardboard and tiny pieces of wood was simply a way to keep his wife's spirits up during her Depression-era pregnancy. Darrow created a gift of joy, shared it with the world, and the gift came right back to him a thousandfold.

Are times tough in your little apartment—or lavish mansion? Are you weary from standing in lines that lead to nowhere? If it seems as if your world is collapsing around you or you feel yourself slipping down into the depths of depression, don't despair.

Remember that the right temperature in a home is maintained by warm hearts, not by icy glares, lukewarm enthusiasm—or hotheads! Your attitude can set the tone for your whole family. So use whatever scraps you can find—even if, in the beginning, it's just a scrap of a smile, then watch the gifts come back to you.

BARBARA JOHNSON

Life is a process. To God process isn't a means to an end; it is the goal. Whatever sends us running to him, makes us embrace him, causes us to depend on him, is the best good in our lives.

We have been at times so full of gratitude and awe that we haven't been able to do anything else but sing "Let's just praise the Lord." At other times we haven't been able to see how God could possibly be there in the dark circumstances of life, yet we have learned that he was always—in all things—up to something good in our lives. That "good" is always eternal good.

Some of life's circumstances seem sense-less, and others, too painful to bear. But when we base our confidence on a perspective broader than this world's view, we can trust that what our sovereign God is working to accomplish is not the servant of this world's circumstances; rather, this world's circum-stances are always being made the servant of his purposes.

Let's just praise the Lord!

GLORIA GAITHER

Promises for a Godly Perspective

"*For* I know the plans I have for you," declares the LORD, "plans to prosper you and not to harm you, plans to give you hope and a future."

Jeremiah 29:11

"*For* my thoughts are not your thoughts, neither are your ways my ways," declares the LORD. "As the heavens are higher than the earth, so are my ways higher than your ways and my thoughts than your thoughts."

Isaiah 55:8–9

Oh, the depth of the riches of the wisdom and knowledge of God! How unsearchable his judgments, and his paths beyond tracing out! "Who has known the mind of the Lord? Or who has been his counselor?" "Who has ever given to God, that God should repay him?" For from him and through him and to him are all things. To him be the glory forever! Amen.

Romans 11:33–36

The *Joy* of *Possibilities*

Though the fig tree should not blossom, and there be no fruit on the vines, though the yield of the olive should fail, and the fields produce no food, though the flock should be cut off from the fold, and there be no cattle in the stalls, yet I will exult in the Lord, I will rejoice in the God of my salvation. The Lord God is my strength, and he has made my feet like hinds' feet, and makes me walk on my high places.

Habbukuk 3:17-19 NASB

The Lord is my strength and my shield; my heart trusts in him, and I am helped. My heart leaps for joy and I will give thanks to him in song.

Psalm 28:7

But I will sing of your strength, in the morning I will sing of your love; for you are my fortress, my refuge in times of trouble.

Psalm 59:16

A Joyful Up-look

*T*here are moments in the harsh bleakness of winter that would be unbearable if there were not, tucked deep within its bosom, the promise of spring. But spring always comes. Dark moments in the life and heart of a mother or wife are mitigated only in the light of God's sovereignty. We must learn to draw upon the resources of a Sovereign God—One who unreservedly offers us not solutions, not answers, not happy-ever-after endings, but his glad welcome—the assurance of his presence with us.

The desert has its edge, and in God's timing the darkness will give way to light. Ephesians 3:12 is our warranty: "We may approach God with freedom and confidence." Assured of his glad welcome, we can take our places in a world full of people like ourselves—people who don't know where to turn, who never in a million years expected to find themselves in their present circumstances—people for whom there are no answers but Jesus Christ. And we can do it joyfully!

◼ Joy MacKenzie

Promises About Possibilities

Everyone born of God overcomes the world. This is the victory that has overcome the world, even our faith.

1 John 5:4

I have told you these things, so that in me you may have peace. In this world you will have trouble. But take heart! I have overcome the world.

John 16:33

With God all things are possible.

Matthew 19:26

Sovereign LORD, you have made the heavens and the earth by your great power and outstretched arm. Nothing is too hard for you.

Jeremiah 32:17

The Joy of Trusting God's Plan

Look at the life you hold in your own two hands. Is it tattered and shabby? Think about it. Might it bring opportunities for growth and gladness? What is going to be important one hundred years from now that doesn't seem important now? What seems important now that will not be important a century from now?

In moments that appear unredeemable, watch and wait. Recognize the precious things. Refuse to trash anything! Ask God to help you see things from his perspective. Take one step after another. Before long, in spite of yourself, you may notice surprising signs of hope in your own backyard.

Trial and triumph are what God uses to scribble all over the pages of our lives. They are signs that he is using us, loving us, shaping us to his image, enjoying our companionship, delivering us from evil, and writing eternity into our hearts. Be happy through everything because today is the only thing you can be sure of. Right here, right now, cherish the moment you hold in your hands.

BARBARA JOHNSON

In God's infinite plan for my life, he allowed me to be born out of wedlock to a crippled girl whose parents were so embarrassed by the situation they forced her to leave their home and find her own way. My great grandmother convinced my mother to let me live at Granny's house. Granny and my great grandfather, Daddy Harrell, became very attached to me. Daddy Harrell and I became best friends. He was blind, but as soon as I was old enough to learn my way around the neighborhood, I became his eyes. I held his hand and led him down the street to the doctor's office, to visit his friends, or to church.

Just as Daddy Harrell trusted me to lead him from place to place without fear of falling or being run over by a car, he taught me to trust God by turning over to him my fears and anxieties. God knew my great grandparents' nurturing would be the catalyst that would propel me to learn the truths about who God is and how he works in our everyday lives. I know my heavenly Father because I have seen him in the people I love.

THELMA WELLS

Promises About Trusting God's Plan

It is not for you to know the times or dates the Father has set by his own authority.

Acts 1:7

Those who know your name will trust in you, for you, LORD, have never forsaken those who seek you.

Psalm 9:10

Blessed is the man who trusts in the LORD, whose confidence is in him. He will be like a tree planted by the water that sends out its roots by the stream. It does not fear when heat comes; its leaves are always green. It has no worries in a year of drought and never fails to bear fruit.

Jeremiah 17:7–8

Fear the LORD, you his saints, for those who fear him lack nothing.

Psalm 34:9

Standing With Others in Prayer

*A*nytime we stop to be present with others in their trouble, we carry the opportunity to bring boomerang joy. You don't have to be famous or important. You don't have to be acclaimed or much sought after. Just be you. Stay true to yourself and those values that keep you grounded in kindness.

Keep looking for the boomerang surprise in your life. Listen for the whirring sound that means it may be getting close. Always stay connected to people and seek out things that bring you joy. Dream with abandon. Pray confidently. But be careful what you pray for—because everything and anything is possible through the power of prayer!

BARBARA JOHNSON

*A*s a mother, I find solace in praying for my children during the good times and the bad. To help my children and myself to get focused on how to deal with problems, I ask my children if they have listened to praise music before they called to tell me about their woes. If they haven't, I ask them to call back after they have—unless, of course, it's an emergency.

I believe one of the best ways to get in a praying mood is to listen to music that ushers you into a spirit of adoration. That, in turn, takes your mind off the problem and helps you to focus on the Problem-Solver.

While I wait for them to call back, I follow my own instructions. I sing, listen to gospel music, and pray. Usually, when they phone me again, both of us are in harmony with each other and the Lord.

We are admonished to pray without ceasing because prayers assert God's power in our lives. Even our unuttered thoughts can be prayers, which enables us to pray without ceasing. When we fail to pray, we aren't cheating God; we're cheating ourselves.

THELMA WELLS

Promises About Standing With Others in Prayer

Call to me and I will answer you and tell you great and unsearchable things you do not know.

Jeremiah 33:3

The LORD is near to all who call on him, to all who call on him in truth.

Psalm 145:18

And I will do whatever you ask in my name, so that the Son may bring glory to the Father. You may ask me for anything in my name, and I will do it.

John 14:13–14

Carry each other's burdens, and in this way you will fulfill the law of Christ.

Galatians 6:2

The *Joy* of *God's* *Great* *Faithfulness*

*C*hristians sometimes have more trouble handling trouble than the world does, because we think we should be perfect. As things veer out of control, you may find yourself asking, "Who stopped payment on my reality check?"

Too often our faith is shallow. We cling to the padded cross instead of the "old rugged" cross of the hymn. What should set us apart is our trust, our ability to let God loose in our circumstances rather than forever trying to control them ourselves.

Admit it and save yourself years of worry. There are no superfamilies. There are no perfect people. You are right where "X" marks the spot on the map of life. Whatever dilemma you're facing, ask yourself what difference it will make one hundred years from today. The difference is in letting go and letting God. He'll never let you down. He'll help you face tomorrow with open hands, open heart, open mind, and tons of confidence.

BARBARA JOHNSON

A Joyful Up-look

$\mathcal{O}$ne night, Bill and I were listening to an African-American pastor on the radio encouraging his congregation. With a heartfelt genuine compassion for his people, he kept repeating Psalm 30:5. "Weeping endures for the night!" he would say, "But joy comes in the morning! Let me hear you, now. Weeping endures for the night . . ." The people would sing that phrase back to him.

"But *joy* comes in the morning!" With one great voice they returned the affirmation. "Joy comes in the morning!"

As we listened, the problems in our own lives seemed to settle into perspective in the immense power of God and his great faithfulness.

No matter how tragic the circumstances seem, no matter how long the spiritual drought, no matter how long and dark the days, the dawn will come. We will know that our God has been there all along. We will hear him say, through it all, "Hold on, my child, joy comes in the morning!"

GLORIA GAITHER

Promises of God's Great Faithfulness

Because of the LORD's great love we are not consumed, for his compassions never fail. They are new every morning; great is your faithfulness.

Lamentations 3:22–23

The Lord is faithful, and he will strengthen and protect you from the evil one.

2 Thessalonians 3:3

He who began a good work in you will carry it on to completion until the day of Christ Jesus.

Philippians 1:6

Your love, O LORD, reaches to the heavens, your faithfulness to the skies.

Psalm 36:5

Catastrophe or Happy Ending?

*W*e need to recognize the vast difference between *mere inconvenience* and a *major catastrophe*. Nobody ever said life is easy, trouble free, or without problems. Everyone knows that. The secret to handling problems is how we view them. It's an attitude thing. Running out of coffee is inconvenient. A rained out picnic is inconvenient. But a smashed jaw, broken cheekbone, crushed nose, and missing eye? We're talking catastrophe!

Maybe I'm just a cockeyed optimist, but I think life is to be experienced joyfully rather than endured grudgingly. We know it brings complexities and trouble. Scripture affirms that. But why do we take minor irritations so seriously? Why do we act as though it's the end of the world? Think of the pain and conflict we would spare ourselves, the stress we would forego, if we just realized mere inconveniences can be survived.

LUCI SWINDOLL

I believe the world is shaped by the hand of a loving God. The Bible shows that we are an Easter people living in a Good Friday world, not Good Friday people living in an Easter world. That means we are destined for joy no matter how difficult our daily life. Something in us responds to the happiness other people experience, because we glimpse life as God intends it to be! It is an image imprinted in the spirit of Easter morning—pure, powerful, and potent, like the resurrection.

So go out there and help create all the happy endings you can. Don't be afraid of tears—your own or those of neighbors, family, friends, or strangers. You will have your share of Good Fridays, but Easter will come. Remember, moist eyes are good. Trembling lips are acceptable. Quivering voices won't hurt anybody. Though tears may disorient some people or send others running for cover, they are signals there is something deeper to be understood.

Go ahead and let the tears flow. But know too, that the blue of heaven is far bigger than gray clouds beneath.

Barbara Johnson

Promises for Catastrophes and Happy Endings

Do not fear, for I am with you; do not be dismayed, for I am your God. I will strengthen you and help you; I will uphold you with my righteous right hand.

Isaiah 41:10

No temptation has seized you except what is common to man. And God is faithful; he will not let you be tempted beyond what you can bear. But when you are tempted, he will also provide a way out so that you can stand up under it.

1 Corinthians 10:13

Let us acknowledge the LORD; let us press on to acknowledge him. As surely as the sun rises, he will appear; he will come to us like the winter rains, like the spring rains that water the earth.

Hosea 6:3

The *Blessing* of *Courage*

*W*henever I find myself feeling weary and overwhelmed by the commitments I've made to my family, friends, publishers, and the Women of Faith tour, I remember Jesus' words: "From everyone who has been given much, much will be demanded; and from the one who has been entrusted with much, much more will be asked" (Luke 12:48).

Many blessings have been given to me. I know God didn't bless me with these gifts so I could sit back in the recliner and keep them all to myself.

Sometimes life becomes so complicated we feel as if we've gone as far as we can down this stressful highway. We imagine ourselves smashed up against a brick wall, unable to answer one more call, hear one more complaint, and take one more breath. When that's the image that fills your mind, change the brick wall to God. Imagine yourself pressed tightly against his heart, wrapped in his everlasting arms, soothed by his life-giving breath. Picture yourself encircled in God's love, soaked in his strength. Then step out onto the highway once more.

BARBARA JOHNSON

*C*ourage and fear. Those two attributes are strange bedmates. It would seem impossible to experience both of them at the same time; yet I believe that's the challenge of the Christian life. Fear tells us that life is unpredictable, anything can happen, but courage replies quietly, "Yes, but God is in control."

If we will stop for a moment during our cluttered lives to reflect, we will realize this life is not a rehearsal. This is it. How will we choose to live?

I want to live a passionate life. I want to live a life that recognizes the fears but moves out with courage. I want to show the world the eternal mystery of what God can do through a miserable sinner sold out to him. Why would I settle for anything less? Life is tough, but God is faithful.

Sheila Walsh

Promises for Courage

Have I not commanded you? Be strong and courageous. Do not be terrified; do not be discouraged, for the LORD your God will be with you wherever you go.

Joshua 1:9

Fear not, for I have redeemed you; I have summoned you by name; you are mine.

Isaiah 43:1

He gives strength to the weary and increases the power of the weak. Even youths grow tired and weary, and young men stumble and fall; but those who hope in the LORD will renew their strength. They will soar on wings like eagles; they will run and not grow weary, they will walk and not be faint.

Isaiah 40:29–31

God did not give us a spirit of timidity, but a spirit of power, of love and of self-discipline.

2 Timothy 1:7

Trusting Through the Tears

God washes us and cleans us up. His love rinses away the residue we pick up trying to protect ourselves from life's scratchy circumstances. When he is finished with us, we are shining, transparent and lustrous.

Certainly the rain falls on the just and the unjust (chiefly on the just, because the unjust steal their umbrellas). But a few splashes of pain don't get me down for long. In the cesspools of life, I remember the colorful splashes of joy. I take my rainbow with me and share it with others!

We cannot protect ourselves from trouble, but we can dance through the puddles of life with a rainbow smile, twirling the only umbrella we need—the umbrella of God's love. His covering of grace is sufficient for any problem we may have.

BARBARA JOHNSON

*N*o matter who you are, you are made in God's image. Your life has eternal significance through Christ. Even in the most stable relationships at times we can't be there for each other. But Christ will always be there. Christ is with you today as he was yesterday and will be tomorrow, and when you lay your head down for the last time, your life will be just beginning.

Where do you find yourself today? Perhaps you are worried about a child who has wandered away from God, and fear grips your heart for him or her. Perhaps you look at a pile of bills and a fragile balance in your checkbook, and fear squeezes tight.

How can you trust? I encourage you to take a leap into the arms of the One who is able to fill your heart with love and throw your fears to the wind. Christ did not come to remove all our troubles but to walk with us through every one of them. So, take a leap. Take a flying leap!

Sheila Walsh

Promises
About Trusting
Through Tears

You will keep in perfect peace him whose mind is steadfast, because he trusts in you. Trust in the LORD forever, for the LORD, the LORD, is the Rock eternal.

Isaiah 26:3–4

Trust in the LORD with all your heart and lean not on your own under-standing; in all your ways acknowl-edge him, and he will make your paths straight.

Proverbs 3:5–6

Those who trust in the LORD are like Mount Zion, which cannot be shaken but endures forever.

Psalm 125:1

The *Joy Buster* of *Fear*

I have envisioned certain fears that I kept trying to keep ahead of, only to find that when I stopped and faced them, there really was nothing to fear after all. What I needed to do was quit trying to avoid them and face them instead.

After my husband died, I didn't think I could handle money matters like taxes, interest rates, and investments. I had no choice but to turn and face that fear. I would still rather deal with investments like broccoli, cauliflower, and grapefruit, but I have learned it won't leave me dead on the beach to read a tax form.

Facing fears with a prayer on my lips and faith in my heart allows me not only to trust God more but also to experience victory that comes from no one but him. Actually, that is a rather exhilarating way to stay fit.

MARILYN MEBERG

A Joyful Up-look

*S*ometimes, despite our best intentions, we find ourselves wandering in a wilderness of anxiety, lost and unable to find our way out. I know. For years I felt that way. Nothing seemed to work; I felt stripped and anxious, unable to determine what my mission in life should be.

I didn't know how to set my sights on God and let him lead me where to go.

It's true that goals help us to be disciplined and to aim our energies toward accomplishing what we've set out to do. So goals in and of themselves aren't bad. But for me, setting goals and not leaning on God had led me into a perplexing and fretful place. I learned that first I needed to humbly go before God and give him my concerns. Then he would provide me with direction.

You may be in the same wilderness I was, anxiously wandering around, feeling aimless and without a map, fearful disaster is headed toward you. Relinquish your anxieties to God. For he cares for you. Directions will come in God's good time.

THELMA WELLS

Promises About Overcoming Fear

Jesus immediately said to them: "Take courage! It is I. Don't be afraid."

Matthew 14:27

Peace I leave with you; my peace I give you. I do not give to you as the world gives. Do not let your hearts be troubled and do not be afraid.

John 14:27

"Do not fear what they fear; do not be frightened." But in your hearts set apart Christ as Lord.

1 Peter 3:14–15

Do not fear, for I am with you; do not be dismayed, for I am your God. I will strengthen you and help you; I will uphold you with my righteous right hand.

Isaiah 41:10

He who dwells in the shelter of the Most
   High will rest in the shadow of the
   Almighty.
I will say of the LORD, "He is my refuge and
   my fortress, my God, in whom I trust."

If you make the Most High your dwelling—
   even the LORD, who is my refuge—
then no harm will befall you, no disaster
   will come near your tent.
For he will command his angels
   concerning you to guard you in all
   your ways;
they will lift you up in their hands, so that
   you will not strike your foot against a
   stone.
You will tread upon the lion and the cobra;
   you will trample the great lion and the
   serpent.

"Because he loves me," says the LORD,
   "I will rescue him; I will protect him,
   for he acknowledges my name.
He will call upon me, and I will answer
   him; I will be with him in trouble,
   I will deliver him and honor him.
With long life will I satisfy him and show
   him my salvation."

Psalm 91: 1,2; 9-16

Give *Joy* A Boost

The Boost of a Joyful Outlook

I've decided to get into a good humor and stay that way. That's why I want to treat people with kindness and a smile wherever I meet them, regardless of how they treat me. The smile, the kindness, comes back.

Let your joy out. One way I do that is to give people something to laugh about. How? I collect jokes and write down everything that I hear that makes me brighten up. I make amusement a ministry because chuckles are better than a therapist. They are aloe vera for the sunburns of life. When the dumps take their toll, laughter provides the exact change to get you through.

Whatever your troubles, try looking at them by the light of a different star. Go ahead; don't be afraid. Find a wacky angle, a new twist. Offer trouble a little serious thought, then turn it upside down and look at it through God-colored glasses. Chew on trouble's possibilities for making you smarter, better, stronger, kinder. Then take the curved weapon I call joy and toss trouble by its funny side out into the world.

BARBARA JOHNSON

I wasn't all that thrilled about flying. If the good Lord had meant for us to be up in the air, he would have required us to live in hangers instead of homes.

Yet one day I realized navigating the airways was to be a constant part of my life, and I was going to lose my joy a lot if I didn't make some altitude adjustments. I needed another perspective. So I'll put on a gratitude attitude before boarding because:

1. It provides a way to travel that allows me to dart about the country and do things I could never do otherwise.

2. I might be able to offer a word of kindness to an anxious traveler or a stressed flight attendant.

3. As unskilled at cooking as I am, I can still offer up a better meal than the airlines!

Maybe you find yourself taxiing around your home or office with a jet-sized 'tude. Try sitting still and ask the Lord for a fresh perspective for an old routine. Then prepare for take-off and enjoy the amazing view.

PATSY CLAIRMONT

Promises for a Joyful Outlook

Everyone born of God overcomes the world.

> 1 John 5:4

The one who is in you is greater than the one who is in the world.

> 1 John 4:4

In all their distress he too was distressed, and the angel of his presence saved them. In his love and mercy he redeemed them; he lifted them up and carried them all the days of old.

> Isaiah 63:9

Whoever touches you touches the apple of [God's] eye.

> Zechariah 2:8

A Second Look Yields Forgiveness

*H*ave you heard of International Forgiveness Week? Sure enough, I found it on the calendar, smack-dab in the middle of winter. In winter you feel dull and drab and closed in, as though spring will never come. You are restless, cold, and irritable, the way you feel when you hold a grudge.

Forgiveness enables you to bury your grudge in the icy earth and put the past behind you. You flush resentment away by being the first to forgive. Forgiveness fashions your future. It is a brave and brash thing to do. The gutsiest decision you can make. As you forgive others, winter will soon make way for springtime as fresh joy pushes up through the soil of your heart.

Forgiveness is a stunning principle, your ticket out of hate and fear and chaos. I know what regret feels like; I've earned my credentials. But I also know what forgiveness feels like, because God has so graciously forgiven me. Forgiveness frees you of the past so you can make good choices today. Look to Jesus as your example.

BARBARA JOHNSON

GIVE JOY A BOOST

I walked into a Dallas bank to meet with an executive vice president about customer service training. I went up to the secretary's desk, smiled, and announced my name and my reason for being there. The secretary stopped working, looked me up and down, gave me no response, stood up, and walked off leaving me standing there. She had decided I wasn't worth a nod let alone a smile or a handshake.

When I taught the customer service class, she was a top participant. She was pleasant, positive, polite, and poised. But none of that held any meaning for me. Her lasting impression remained my first impression of her.

But I wasn't following Christ's admonition to give people room to make a second impression. I needed to give her a second chance.

Maybe you have written a person off as someone you want nothing to do with. That person just might deserve a second chance.

God knows us inside out and outside in. He understands what motivates us and accepts us even in our worst moments. I want to be able to do the same for others.

THELMA WELLS

Promises About Forgiveness

In him we have redemption through his blood, the forgiveness of sins, in accordance with the riches of God's grace.

Ephesians 1:7

For he has rescued us from the dominion of darkness and brought us into the kingdom of the Son he loves, in whom we have redemption, the forgiveness of sins.

Colossians 1:13–14

The Lord our God is merciful and forgiving, even though we have rebelled against him.

Daniel 9:9

Be kind and compassionate to one another, forgiving each other, just as in Christ God forgave you.

Ephesians 4:32

Walking With a Gratitude Attitude

*G*od is at work in all of life if we will only see his hand and listen and learn. God is talking to us all the time. We imagine that if good things happen, then God loves us, and if life seems difficult, then he doesn't. This isn't true. Join hands with God in your life. Throw open the doors and let the sun come pouring in. God is at work! God is at work! God is at work! God's grace shows up to plug our leaky lives. That's the gospel. That's the good news.

Do you *really* want to find the joy? Then reach out. Pure joy learns to take one day—one hour at a time. Throw yourself at God's mercy. Ask him to show you his love. Give him some room to move in. The gift is yours. Ask God here and now to allow you a glimpse of his love.

Let God love you, and even before you "feel" the warmth, start walking a thank-you journey.

SHEILA WALSH

Harvest time in Indiana. The wide plows turn the traces of cornstalks and dry soybean plants under, leaving the fresh black earth like a velvet carpet laid in neat squares. The squirrels skitter around the yard stuffing acorns and walnuts in their jaws, racing off to bury their treasure.

This is the season to finish things, to tie up loose ends, to save and store, to harvest and be sure there is enough of everything that matters to last us through the hard times.

And how does one finish a season of the heart? How can we harvest and store the bounty of the spirit and save the fruits we cannot see? Gratitude is the instrument of harvest. It ties the golden sheaves in bundles; it plucks the swollen kernels in great bales.

Thank God for harvest time, a time for finishing what's been started, a time to be aware, to take account, and to realize the life we've been given.

God has promised that if we harvest well with the tools of thanksgiving, there will be seeds for planting in the spring.

GLORIA GAITHER

Promises for a Gratitude Attitude

Speak to one another with psalms, hymns and spiritual songs. Sing and make music in your heart to the Lord, always giving thanks to God the Father for everything, in the name of our Lord Jesus Christ.

Ephesians 5:19–20

Know that the LORD is God. It is he who made us, and we are his; we are his people, the sheep of his pasture. Enter his gates with thanksgiving and his courts with praise; give thanks to him and praise his name.

Psalm 100:3–4

Whatever you do, whether in word or deed, do it all in the name of the Lord Jesus, giving thanks to God the Father through him.

Colossians 3:17

The Joy of Aging

Television journalist Dan Rather once asked a 106-year-old man to disclose his secret of long life. The old man rocked back and forth in his chair before answering. Finally he replied, "Keep breathing."

Sure, growing older is stressful, but using your funny bone to subdue that kind of stress works wonders! When you hear *snap, crackle, pop,* and it isn't your cereal don't panic. Laughter defuses insults, soothes aching muscles, and counteracts the humiliation of what is happening to your body and mind.

Gerontologist Ann E. Gerike says we can develop a new way of thinking about our physical limitations as we age. After a lifetime of straining to be "the perfect perky ideal," finally your breasts can relax. And that extra weight around the middle (hence the term "middle age"?)—it's just cuddlier body lines! So as birthdays come, don't think of yourself as growing old; you've just reached that vibrant metallic age: silver in your hair, gold in your teeth, and lead in your bottom!

BARBARA JOHNSON

GIVE JOY A BOOST

I feel encased within a timepiece that can at times rob me of my peace. Left unto ourselves, some of us would race and others of us would rust. Either way we would speed past or sleep through the joy. We need to make peace with the timepiece so we don't spend our time beating our heads against the clock.

Here are some tips. I'll try them if you will.

1. Don't cram everyday so full you can't enjoy the journey.

2. Don't under-plan and miss the thrill of a fruitful day.

3. Don't underestimate a nap, a rocking chair, and a good book.

4. Don't become a sloth.

5. Do offer your gratitude for the moments assigned to you.

6. Do celebrate even the passing of days.

PATSY CLAIRMONT

Promises About Aging

Your beauty should not come from outward adornment, such as braided hair and the wearing of gold jewelry and fine clothes. Instead, it should be that of your inner self, the unfading beauty of a gentle and quiet spirit, which is of great worth in God's sight.

1 Peter 3:3–4

Even to your old age and gray hairs I am he, I am he who will sustain you. I have made you and I will carry you; I will sustain you and I will rescue you.

Isaiah 46:4

Gray hair is a crown of splendor; it is attained by a righteous life.

Proverbs 16:31

Age should speak; advanced years should teach wisdom.

Job 32:7

The *Joy Buster* of *Worry*

✿

"*D*ear Lord, like a child with her mom, when I say now, I mean right now! Thank you for not always dropping everything in the universe and rushing to my rescue. Instead, you have allowed me to feel my neediness and experience my limitations so I will understand that it is you who will (eventually) save me. I don't want to refuse your perfect plan; I want to find refuge in you. Then I will have the stamina to make it to the end. Amen."

🌼 PATSY CLAIRMONT

I have a bit of a "germ-thing"; and I don't like cafeterias. So I was eating my entire meal [at a cafeteria] with an oversized spoon I had found in an obscure container slightly behind the soft ice-cream machine.

"How long have you had this germ thing?" Luci asked.

"Since the sixth grade," I replied. "Our science teacher had us all touch some specially treated sponge, and overnight it grew bacteria cultures that we watched develop into various colorful and horrifying configurations. I've never been the same since."

Luci slowly put down her fork and studied it for a second. Then, with renewed enthusiasm, she announced, "If those germs haven't gotten me by this time in my life, I don't think they ever will!"

Her healthy response reminded me that for me to fear the unseen and worry about its potential to do harm throttles my joy. Of course one should observe hygienic health practices, but if carried to an extreme, they can lead to wrestling with a too-large spoon in a cafeteria with plenty of right-sized forks.

MARILYN MEBERG

Promises About Freedom From Worry

Cast your cares on the LORD and he will sustain you; he will never let the righteous fall.

Psalm 55:22

Look at the birds of the air; they do not sow or reap or store away in barns, and yet your heavenly Father feeds them. Are you not much more valuable than they? Who of you by worrying can add a single hour to his life? And why do you worry about clothes? See how the lilies of the field grow. They do not labor or spin. Yet I tell you that not even Solomon in all his splendor was dressed like one of these. If that is how God clothes the grass of the field, which is here today and tomorrow is thrown into the fire, will he not much more clothe you, O you of little faith? So do not worry, saying, "What shall we eat?" or "What shall we drink?" or "What shall we wear?" . . . But seek first his kingdom and his righteousness, and all these things will be given to you as well. Therefore do not worry about tomorrow, for tomorrow will worry about itself.

Matthew 6:26–34

A Respite From Our Tasks

*M*mmm . . . So good to get away from the everyday of life. Perfect solitude. Time to reflect, read, write, and pray.

God has manifested himself in breathtaking sunsets and a dancing porpoise show. "Together now, up and out of the water. Smile and dive," say the porpoise. "Under the boat and out. Higher this time. They love us!"

Today we saw a rainbow—a complete rainbow. We considered sailing off to find the pot of gold. But whatever would we do with a pot of gold? And who would believe our story?

Tonight we made up silly songs and poetry, even a joint venturing one about the captain of our ship. We were silly beyond words.

And to think we almost didn't come. "Too busy," we said. Busy doing what? It slips my mind just now.

🌿 SUE BUCHANAN

GIVE JOY A BOOST

*A*s a child raised in rural communities with few libraries, I was thrilled when the bookmobile rolled into my area every other week. With my books strapped to the back carrier of my bike, I would eagerly pedal a little more than a mile to where the bookmobile was parked. Happily fortified with new reading selections, I'd pedal back home, clamor up the makeshift ladder to my tree house, and settle in.

When was the last time you settled in for a mindlessly pleasant read? Why don't you do that more often? What's driving you continually to be productive?

Perhaps some of you, like me, are missing out on recreational activity that has no purpose other than to give a needed respite from our task-oriented lives. Wouldn't it be fun occasionally to produce nothing, accomplish nothing, and contribute to nothing? Maybe that means reading a book that doesn't require a pen; maybe it's a cup of something at a coffee house, or maybe it's a meander through the mall or a stroll (not a jog) through the park. The possibilities for nothing are endless.

MARILYN MEBERG

Promises About a Respite From Our Tasks

Come to me, all you who are weary and burdened, and I will give you rest. Take my yoke upon you and learn from me, for I am gentle and humble in heart, and you will find rest for your souls.

Matthew 11:28–29

Be at rest once more, O my soul, for the Lord has been good to you.

Psalm 116:7

There remains, then, a Sabbath-rest for the people of God; for anyone who enters God's rest also rests from his own work, just as God did from his. Let us, therefore, make every effort to enter that rest.

Hebrews 4:9–11

Stop, Look & Sniff

Two young children were playing a bed-time game they called "God is . . ." They took turns finishing the sentence with positive descriptions of God. Six-year-old Missy finally ventured, "God smells good all the time."

"That's dumb," her older brother said.

But Missy insisted. "Sometimes he smells like orange blossoms and sometimes like apples. Tonight he smells like strawberries."

Maybe Missy was really just enjoying the smell of the strawberry bubble bath that was hardly dry on her skin. But maybe Missy can lead us to a new appreciation of a spiritual metaphor. In 2 Corinthians 2:15, Paul says that we believers are "the aroma of Christ."

God wants to use you to spread the aroma of Christ. Are you able to joy in that metaphor? Can you inhale a little deeper and longer to enjoy the fragrance yourself?

Stop the rat race. Enjoy the rich aromas in your life—the ones God gives in nature and the ones God gives through the witness of human kindness. Stop and enjoy the sights, tastes, and smells of God's good gifts.

SHEILA WALSH

GIVE JOY A BOOST

*I*t is often in the small things—the ordinary moments turned extraordinary—that I recognize his presence and can sense his kindness and tenderness.

My friend Allyson's baby, Logan, seems to have an inner joy that comes straight from heaven. One day as Allyson and I were running errands she left me in the car with him. Every time I turned to look at him he would giggle with such zeal that I wondered whether he could catch his breath. Any sadness I felt that day was washed away as I listened to Logan laugh.

Once, hurrying through a busy airport to get to my gate on time for a connecting flight, I came upon a lady in a wheelchair. Amidst the chaos of the hundreds of people rushing around us, my eyes met hers. The sweetest smile appeared on her face. I smiled back, but I knew she would never fully realize how that small gesture had filled my soul.

I believe that God is in our everyday. Many moments occur in our lives which reveal his face, his touch, his voice. Look for him today. He will be found.

 KATHY TROCCOLI

Promises About Stopping and Looking

This is the day the LORD has made; let us rejoice and be glad in it.

Psalm 118:24

Taste and see that the LORD is good; blessed is the man who takes refuge in him.

Psalm 34:8

A cheerful look brings joy to the heart, and good news gives health to the bones.

Proverbs 15:30

Light is sweet, and it pleases the eyes to see the sun.

Ecclesiastes 11:7

For we are to God the aroma of Christ among those who are being saved and those who are perishing.

2 Corinthians 2:15

A Green Thumb
of Beauty

Gardening fever is upon us. It seems as
though everyone is a gardener, even if they
live in a big-city apartment. Even if they have
eleven green thumbs. Even if they wouldn't
pull weeds for a million dollars. Even if they
don't know the difference between a spade
and a rake. Even if they hate vegetables and
bugs, are allergic to bees, or have spring aller-
gies. Suddenly everyone is a gardening
maniac.

Well, there are certain things anybody can
plant—sweet P's in a straight row, for
instance: prayer, patience, peace, passion.
But it's not enough for a gardener to love
flowers. A gardener also must hate weeds. As
good plants grow, you pinch off bitter ones
like panic, paranoia, and passivity. And by the
way, while gardening, do squash pride. And
please, lettuce love one another at all times.

Begin now to cultivate your half-acre of
love. All it takes is a few seeds no larger than
grains of sand. The blossom of a good deed
fades with time but that lasting perfume is
the joy you receive from doing it.

BARBARA JOHNSON

I was driving down a familiar road in Nashville one fall day when I almost drove off the road, the beauty was so intense. It looked as if God had sent in a team of the world's finest artists overnight, and I was privy to the opening day of his spectacle.

The show was a sight to behold. Every tree had changed to shades of deepest gold and robin red, to sun-kissed yellow and pumpkin orange. Leaves danced in the air and brushed against my windshield.

Notice the colors in your world! Look around your own home. How can you add a touch of beauty? Every one of us can do one small thing to add beauty to our workplace or kitchen or bedroom. File the papers cluttering the desk. Re-cover a pillow. Rearrange the furniture. Light a candle on the table.

Maybe it's time for a new hairstyle or makeover. The makeup counters at the mall will give you a complimentary makeover with no obligation to buy. A friend tells me there's nothing like a professional shoeshine for lifting up a bad day. Open your eyes. Brighten your world.

 SHEILA WALSH

Promises About Beauty

He has made everything beautiful in its time.

Ecclesiastes 3:11

Charm is deceptive, and beauty is fleeting; but a woman who fears the LORD is to be praised.

Proverbs 31:30

Your beauty should not come from outward adornment, such as braided hair and the wearing of gold jewelry and fine clothes. Instead, it should be that of your inner self, the unfading beauty of a gentle and quiet spirit, which is of great worth in God's sight. For this is the way the holy women of the past who put their hope in God used to make themselves beautiful.

1 Peter 3:3–5

The *Joy* of *Enjoying Life*

*G*od can use you even when you're living between estrogen and death. Age on, girls, the best is yet to be! Remember that each day is like a suitcase—every person gets the same size, but some people figure out how to pack more into theirs.

Life is short. Each year passes more quickly than the previous one. It's easy to deny yourself many of life's simple pleasures because you want to be practical. Forget about practical and decide instead to become a joy collector. Always be on the lookout for gifts without ribbons. God is strewing them across your path right now. His gifts come tagged with a note: "Life can be wonderful. Do your best not to miss it!" Enjoy what is before it isn't anymore.

God will scatter surprise blessings across your path in the next few years. Don't be like the woman who described herself as passive and bored, a "mush melon living in a middle-aged frame." Instead be zany and giddy. Dare to slip on a pair of bunny slippers once in a while! Surprise yourself! Enjoy the little things because one day you'll look back and realize they were the big things!

BARBARA JOHNSON

GIVE JOY A BOOST

*S*ince I travel most weekends, Monday is the day I unpack. That's always a mess, with stuff everywhere and suitcases lying about.

Then there's the laundry ... piles of clothes that need washing. And those piles multiply! I have this theory that, after the Lord comes and time is no more, somewhere, in a corner of the world, dirty laundry will still be waiting.

On Monday I must make stops at the grocery store, the cleaners, the bank, the post office, the service station, the hairdresser. Mondays annoy me.

But in another way, I love Mondays. I love unloading all my stuff out of the suitcase and organizing it back where it belongs. I love pulling fresh laundry from the dryer and folding it while it's still warm.

On Monday nights, I feel genuine joy, having such a sense of accomplishment. So what's the difference? Why do I sometimes get bogged down with chores, hating the day? Then, at other times, I get fired up with enthusiasm, loving the day? Perspective! Perspective is everything. The busiest days can become our most joyful.

LUCI SWINDOLL

Promises for Enjoying Life

All the days ordained for me were written in your book before one of them came to be.

Psalm 139:16

It is God who arms me with strength and makes my way perfect. He makes my feet like the feet of a deer; he enables me to stand on the heights.

Psalm 18:32–33

Go, eat your food with gladness, and drink your wine with a joyful heart, for it is now that God favors what you do.

Ecclesiastes 9:7

That everyone may eat and drink, and find satisfaction in all his toil—this is the gift of God.

Ecclesiastes 3:13

The Joy of Following God's Direction

My experience with the prompting of the Holy Spirit has been that when he directs you, there is an indescribable peace in your body, mind, and spirit that you feel but can't explain to anyone who hasn't experienced it. God's Spirit would never direct us to do anything contrary to Scripture, so we have a guidebook that can help us too.

You've probably said in certain situations, "I knew in my heart that such and such was . . ." Those are probably times God's Spirit was prompting you.

I need to be responsive to the Holy Spirit. I have found him to be the greatest organizer, time manager, administrator, and scheduler.

What will you do when you think you're being prompted by the Holy Spirit to take a certain action? I'd suggest you ask for clarity. Wait for the answer. I can't tell you how you will know when the answer comes, but I can tell you that you will experience peace in your mind, body, and soul that you can't describe. Listen to your heart.

 THELMA WELLS

*V*ision is when you see it and others don't. Faith is when you do it and others won't. With vision and faith things can be done.

One of the greatest by-products of believing in something, and then going for it is joy. I've often said, "My favorite thing in life is doing something new while having a good time." That's the essence of joy.

Let's get practical. Perhaps you have an idea of something you would like to do, but you're scared. You've never done anything like it before. Maybe the idea just won't go away. But it's outside your comfort zone, and you don't feel adequate for the task. Start to pray, "Lord, if this desire is from you, will you bring it to pass? Help me know where to start."

And then start. This is the faith part. Work hard. Do what makes sense to you. Ask the Lord whom to talk to who might help you. Talk with them.

What has he given you the desire to do? You can do it.

LUCI SWINDOLL

Promises About
God's Direction

In your unfailing love you will lead the people you have redeemed. In your strength you will guide them to your holy dwelling.

Exodus 15:13

Teach me to do your will, for you are my God; may your good Spirit lead me on level ground.

Psalm 143:10

If you are pleased with me, teach me your ways so I may know you and continue to find favor with you.

Exodus 33:13

Good and upright is the LORD; therefore he instructs sinners in his ways. He guides the humble in what is right and teaches them his way.

Psalm 25:8–9

Remembering and Being Remembered

*A*t the call center in Denver International Airport, each of the thirty-six operators may answer as many as 260 calls per day. Then they relay messages to some of the ninety-thousand passengers and others that pass through the concourses within any twenty-four-hour period.

Sometimes the messages are frantic, such as one from a daughter who helped her father carry his luggage to the check-in counter for his trip to Bangkok and then returned to the parking lot to discover a major problem. That's when the call center might relay a message begging, "Don't get on that plane! You have Sarah's only set of car keys in your pocket."

When I read about these relayed messages, I chuckled, but then I thought of how fortunate we are that when we need to get an urgent message to our Father in heaven, we don't have to route our plea through a busy call center. Isaiah 58:9 promises, "Then you will call, and the LORD will answer."

❧ BARBARA JOHNSON

*R*emembering is important to God. He encourages us to make memories. In Joshua 3–4, we read the account of the Israelites moving the ark of the covenant across the flooded Jordan River. After the water parted to allow the ark and the Israelites to cross, God commanded the leaders of the twelve tribes to take one stone each from the river and to place it where the priests had stood with the ark when they arrived safely on the other shore. "These stones are to be a memorial to the people of Israel forever" (Joshua 4:7). They are still there today.

We're encouraged to remember days of old, the wonders of God, the Sabbath, God's deeds and our struggles, our Creator, our youth, and that life is short.

If you've not yet begun to create memories, start now. Load up your camera with film, fill that pen with ink, and capture the miracles and wonders that come your way.

Surround yourself with whatever it takes to be reminded. God is faithful. Don't ever forget that.

LUCI SWINDOLL

Promises About Remembering

The eyes of the LORD are on the righteous and his ears are attentive to their cry.

Psalm 34:15

Before they call I will answer; while they are still speaking I will hear.

Isaiah 65:24

You will call upon me and come and pray to me, and I will listen to you. You will seek me and find me when you seek me with all your heart.

Jeremiah 29:12–13

Only be careful, and watch yourselves closely so that you do not forget the things your eyes have seen or let them slip from your heart as long as you live.

Deuteronomy 4:9

The *Joy* of *Thankfulness*

I don't know about you, but I don't want to live my life in the *past* lane. I want to find a zillion things to be thankful for today. One little girl was overjoyed one Thanksgiving Day because broccoli *wasn't* on the table! When God does make broccoli part of the menu, I've learned it's only because he has a greater good in mind.

What are you thankful for right this moment? Start today by being grateful for the tiniest things: water to drink, a moment to rest, the color of a flower or sunset or bird. A piece of bread. A song on the radio. Keep looking for sights, smells, sounds, that make you feel pleasure. Write them down.

Let's decide to be thankful and encourage one another to cultivate grateful hearts. God is thankful for *you*. He gave his Son to reclaim your life. He invites you into the joy of salvation. That's an awful lot to be thankful for right there. And something else to be thankful for? The fact that you are here to be thankful!

BARBARA JOHNSON

Let's be thankful! Thankful for plenty—plenty and more—of things to eat and wear; of shelter and warmth; of beauty. Plenty of things that money can't buy, such as tenderness and inspiration and revelation and insight.

Thankful for health—health that we take so for granted that we schedule our lives, assuming always that everything will be normal.

Thankful for family—family with individual personalities, gifts, needs, and dreams, each such a gift—all feeding into what we are and what we will become.

Thankful for friends—for stimulating, vivacious, provoking, comforting, disturbing, encouraging, agitating, blessing, loving, warming, forgiving friends.

And thankful for the courage to go on trusting people, risking love, daring to believe in what could be, all because of the confirming experience of daily trusting God and finding him utterly trustworthy.

GLORIA GAITHER

Promises About Being Thankful

Just as you received Christ Jesus as Lord, continue to live in him, rooted and built up in him, strengthened in the faith as you were taught, and overflowing with thankfulness.

Colossians 2:6–7

Sing and make music in your heart to the Lord, always giving thanks to God the Father for everything.

Ephesians 5:19–20

Whatever you do, whether in word or deed, do it all in the name of the Lord Jesus, giving thanks to God the Father through him.

Colossians 3:17

Through Jesus, therefore, let us continually offer to God a sacrifice of praise.

Hebrews 13:15

The Seven Deadly Joy Busters

As believers in God, there are places where we should definitely not, under any circumstances, even *think* of parking.

Do not park by life's defeats. Where has life gotten you down? Don't park there! Move on.

Do not park at anger. Storing up hostility will only boomerang on you in the long run.

Do not park at escape. There is no good time for quitting. Don't give up, get going!

Do not park at discouragement. Optimism actually promotes physical as well as emotional healing.

Do not park at worry. Think on what is right and true and lovely (Philippians 4:8). Who knows what possibilities are just around the corner?

Do not park at guilt. Move on by receiving Jesus as your Savior, accepting God's forgiveness and freely forgiving others. Put the past behind you. Begin again. Learn all you can from your mistakes, and with God's help make a U-turn at each one.

Barbara Johnson

GIVE JOY A BOOST

A saboteur of joy is the many ways we are disappointed with ourselves. We live with regrets that drag us down to the depths, sometimes to the depths of despair.

Many of us who have been Christians for years do not perceive ourselves as sinners of the first degree. We get up every morning intending to serve and please God, and yet, with the apostle Paul, we do what we don't want to do. We miss the mark and then live in regret.

I think of the apostle Paul—a Christian— admitting his own weakness: "What a wretched man I am! Who will rescue me from this body of death?" That question is followed by an exclamation: "Thanks be to God—through Jesus Christ our Lord!" (Romans 7:24–25). Jesus is the only one who could rescue me from myself.

God knows about the secret abortion, the private fantasy life, the hatred you hold in your heart. It is only when we confess these things to God that he can fill the broken, empty places with his joy.

SHEILA WALSH

Promises About Overcoming Deadly Joy Busters

There is now no condemnation for those who are in Christ Jesus.

Romans 8:1

I say to myself, "The LORD is my portion; therefore I will wait for him." The LORD is good to those whose hope is in him, to the one who seeks him; it is good to wait quietly for the salvation of the LORD.

Lamentations 3:24–26

Do not worry about your life, what you will eat or drink; or about your body, what you will wear. Is not life more important than food, and the body more important than clothes?

Matthew 6:25

Guard the good deposit that was entrusted to you—guard it with the help of the Holy Spirit.

2 Timothy 1:14

The *Joy* of *Godly Relationships*

I used to find it hard to make deep friendships with other women. I felt such a need for approval and acceptance; yet I was afraid to let the real me be seen in case I wasn't enough. The higher I erected a façade of fear around myself, the more I needed approval but the less I was available to receive it. Hiding behind that wall, I didn't realize how much effort it would take for someone to scale those heights to find the real, scared, and unsure me.

Finally, I figured out I was inadequate to create or maintain relationships. Fortunately, at the same time, I realized Christ is enough for all of us. His mercy helps us to see others mercifully, and his loving acceptance of us enables us to accept ourselves and others. With that as a beginning point, we can relax, be ourselves, and come out from behind the protective walls we've erected. Then we can connect with others who have discovered the joy of just being themselves—flawed and silly but of worth because of Jesus.

SHEILA WALSH

*L*oving and being loved—being connected, valued, befriended, cherished by
another—is a compelling need that perme-
ates the life of every human being on God's
earth. Yet neither love nor friendship can be
manipulated or prescribed. You can't choose
an attractive candidate and merely follow
your top-ten list of things to do to make love
happen. So how then are such relationships
to come about? Is there anything we can do
to develop a bond of companionship that is
intimate, fulfilling, and even joyful?

Jesus Christ created a model of love, as he
did of friendship: along with the reassuring "I
have loved you even as the Father has loved
me . . . I have told you this so that your joy
may be full," we hear from his heart the wel-
coming words, "I have called you friend."
Mind-boggling!

We need not set out in search for a friend,
rather, we must simply set out to be the friend
Christ modeled—anticipating the needs of
others, wearing ourselves out at giving. Jesus
died doing it. The rewards are infinite and
joyous!

JOY MACKENZIE

Promises About Godly Relationships

If we walk in the light, as he is in the light, we have fellowship with one another, and the blood of Jesus, his Son, purifies us from all sin.

1 John 1:7

Greater love has no one than this, that he lay down his life for his friends. You are my friends if you do what I command.

John 15:13–14

I have called you friends, for everything that I learned from my Father I have made known to you.

John 15:15

After Job had prayed for his friends, the LORD made him prosperous again and gave him twice as much as he had before.

Job 42:10

The Joy of Receiving Advice

*G*od warns us of danger. We listen and are careful. But then we slough off. Even when we see warning signs, we think we're smart enough and have our act together. We don't listen or pay attention. That's when we fall and fail.

Whether you're climbing mountains or think you have a firm grip on everything that's important to you, you would be wise to look to the Lord. Remain humble and aware that your footing could slip at any time—or you could feel those things that are so precious to you slip out of your life without warning. We're on the way to glory land, but we ain't there yet!

 THELMA WELLS

GIVE JOY A BOOST

I had been invited for a horseback ride. My husband, Les, didn't think me wise to accept the invitation. Les wasn't worried about the trail paths so much as he was my tailbone being splattered on the roadway.

My husband's cautions rang in my ears as I headed out. The only challenge I had was my stirrups. They were a little too long for my short legs, and I felt like a toe dancer as I stretched to keep my feet in the stirrups.

About six minutes into the ride, my leg muscles began to scream, "Are you out of your mind?" Finally, with my legs stretched far beyond their designed reach and with a kink in my back the size of New Hampshire, I pleaded my cause with the staff. They compassionately headed for the stable. As I deboarded, my legs wobbled as I toddled my way to a bench. For three days afterwards my back felt like the horse had ridden me.

Do you find it difficult to take good advice? To live within your limitations? To admit when you're wrong? Just remember, if you get a backache from carrying your horse, don't be surprised.

PATSY CLAIRMONT

Promises About Receiving Advice

The way of a fool seems right to him, but a wise man listens to advice.

Proverbs 12:15

Let the wise listen and add to their learning, and let the discerning get guidance.

Proverbs 1:5

If you accept my words and store up my commands within you, turning your ear to wisdom and applying your heart to understanding, and if you call out for insight and cry aloud for understanding, and if you look for it as for silver and search for it as for hidden treasure, then you will understand the fear of the LORD and find the knowledge of God. For the LORD gives wisdom, and from his mouth come knowledge and understanding.

Proverbs 2:1—6

Think About Your Heart Attitude

Women have always been able to make do with what life hands them, to create an ordered universe in the midst of chaos and stress. Women have always been able to make something from nothing, stretching the stew, making the worn-out clothes or opportunities into something new, smiling and caressing in spite of their own inclinations to give in to tears and fatigue, mothering the world. Yet, while their hands were performing the task at hand, their minds were racing on. Assimilating. Analyzing. Philosophizing.

So much of men's thinking is applied directly to their work. The result of their thinking is output, income, product. But much of what women think about does not create tangible product. Instead, they ponder the meaning and quality of life. Such pondering may not result in consumable products, but it can produce great souls who ask *why* instead of merely *what* and *how*. Women, after all, are about the industry of the heart.

GLORIA GAITHER

I'm all for nostalgia, but it's hard to be nostalgic when you can't remember anything. At least memory loss helps me dispense with regret and guilt. I'm moving on, anticipating where I'm heading, open to today's answers to today's problems.

Some people pause to reminisce and then get stuck there. Nowadays I may be slowing down, but I am definitely not settling back. I keep trying, just as my first-grade teacher taught me to do. And if at first I *do* succeed, I'll try not to look astonished.

How will the Lord use your life this year? This month? This day? Is there one thing you can do to make life better for someone else? Can you warm the home of an elderly friend? Chill out so a teenager can open up to your love? Knock on the door of a lonely single mom? Invite a seven-year-old for lemonade? The possibilities are endless. God expects us to use our brains and figure out what we can do to make a difference. Find out where he's working and join his crew.

 BARBARA JOHNSON

Promises About Your Heart Attitude

May the God of hope fill you with all joy and peace as you trust in him, so that you may overflow with hope by the power of the Holy Spirit.

Romans 15:13

Whoever finds his life will lose it, and whoever loses his life for my sake will find it.

Matthew 10:39

Since, then, you have been raised with Christ, set your hearts on things above, where Christ is seated at the right hand of God.

Colossians 3:1

Those who hope in the LORD will renew their strength. They will soar on wings like eagles; they will run and not grow weary, they will walk and not be faint.

Isaiah 40:31

Share the
Joy

The Joy of a Reassuring Word

Sometimes the very desire for action leads to the neglect of action. We're so busy searching for the perfect opportunity, the most effective method, the favorable moment that we not only disqualify ourselves for the mission and miss the joy, but an urgent need is left unanswered.

I have often experienced the pull of an inner voice, urging me to call a friend who is in need. Invariably, I address that urge by checking my watch to see if the time is appropriate, or by mentally reprioritizing my schedule to accommodate a more convenient arrangement.

Born of genuine concern for my friend, my determination to provide the most propitious response thwarts the entire effort. The perfect moment never arrives; there is never a convenient time.

When my friend most needed simply to hear a reassuring voice, I wasn't available. I was busy rearranging God's schedule. Are you, too?

JOY MACKENZIE

*O*ne woman went to her doctor to get the results of a checkup. The doctor said, "I have good news and bad news. Which do you want first?"

She answered, "The good news!"

The doctor said, "You have twenty-four hours to live."

"Good grief," exclaimed the woman. "That's the *good* news? Then what's the *bad* news?"

"The bad news," replied the doctor, "is that I was supposed to tell you yesterday."

Don't let your life speed out of control. Live intentionally. Slice the time from your schedule. Do something today that will last beyond your lifetime.

Commit yourself to being a hope bringer no matter what. Hope looks for the good in people, opens doors for people, discovers what can be done to help, lights a candle, does not yield to cynicism. Hope sets people free. Be grateful today for the hope you've been given and then find creative ways to pass it on to someone else.

BARBARA JOHNSON

Promises for Sharing Reassuring Words

How beautiful on the mountains are the feet of those who bring good news.

Isaiah 52:7

A word aptly spoken is like apples of gold in settings of silver.

Proverbs 25:11

Like cold water to a weary soul is good news from a distant land.

Proverbs 25:25

The Spirit of the Sovereign LORD is on me, because the LORD has anointed me to preach good news to the poor. He has sent me to bind up the brokenhearted, to proclaim freedom for the captives and release from darkness for the prisoners.

Isaiah 61:1

The *Joy* of *Sharing Your Witness*

*G*od draws people to himself. Each of us is just his mouthpiece on earth. Whether we say just the right thing or can't think of anything that seems right, all we can do is open our mouths and trust God to use us. That doesn't mean we shouldn't be prepared to offer a reasoned explanation for our faith, but it does take the pressure off of us. We are the instruments, but God is the one who must make the music through us.

Have you tried to explain a spiritual principle to someone lately and sounded only sour notes? Have you been stymied about how to make clear that thing which seems so obvious to you? Remembering your role and God's role can help to comfort you if you've blown it. It may even give you the push you need to increase your knowledge so you can "sound off" more eloquently next time.

THELMA WELLS

SHARE THE JOY

If we want to spread hope and joy, if we want people to know our Lord and Savior Jesus Christ, let's stop faking who we are. The only thing that's separating them from us is that we are forgiven. Our problems are no less tragic. Our lives no less complicated. Our burdens no less heavy. For all of us life is mostly a struggle to keep our weight down and our spirits up. The difference is that Christians have Someone who will go the distance with them.

In your desire to share the gospel, you may be the only Jesus someone else will ever meet. Be real and involved with people. They may be closer to the kingdom of heaven than you think. A good rule of thumb is to keep your heart a little softer than your head!

It's in the darkest places, after all, that the grace of God shines most brightly. That is where people begin to see him. By our scars we are recognized as belonging to him.

Ask the Holy Spirit to help you be genuine in all your relationships. And allow God to answer the world's questions through your life.

BARBARA JOHNSON

Promises About Sharing Your Witness

*T*hen Jesus came to them and said, "All authority in heaven and on earth has been given to me. Therefore go and make disciples of all nations, baptizing them in the name of the Father and of the Son and of the Holy Spirit, and teaching them to obey everything I have commanded you. And surely I am with you always, to the very end of the age."

Matthew 28:18–20

*Y*ou will receive power when the Holy Spirit comes on you; and you will be my witnesses in Jerusalem, and in all Judea and Samaria, and to the ends of the earth."

Acts 1:8

*A*ll the ends of the earth will see the salvation of our God.

Isaiah 52:10

The Deep Calling of Friendship

*O*ne of the deepest callings of friendship is to weep with those who weep. As I write, in autumn, I watch the leaves falling off my favorite tree outside my window. And so there are seasons in all of our lives when the wind blows cold and we feel fragile and exposed. These are the times when we wrap each other up in a blanket of love and friendship and stay right there until the buds begin to show again.

Real friendship grows when we are prepared to be there equally in the bad moments and the good. When we can walk through a field with a few thorns in the grass and make it to the other side, our friendships will be stronger and our joy will be real. We were formed for relationship but we are filled in Christ. Our deepest needs for intimacy will be met only in the "friend who sticks closer than a brother" (Proverbs 18:24). The One who has surely carried our sorrows. The One who has known us since before we were born.

 SHEILA WALSH

I have only a few close friends. We're not talking casual acquaintances here. We're talking people who know me inside out—people I could trade panty hose with, people I can trust with my darkest secret, my most delicate china, and my wildest dream. People for whom I don't have to put on makeup or straighten the house.

Only low-maintenance friends qualify for the short list! I can cut short a telephone conversation without explanation; I can NOT invite them to a dinner party, and they know I must have a good reason. They never demand more than I can give and are willing to let me sacrifice for them when they are in need. The give-and-take is joyful and genuine. (I know lots of folks who are exceptionally generous givers but so self-sufficient that they would die before they let a friend return a favor. A good friend is also a gracious receiver!)

Who are your close friends? Have you told them lately how much you appreciate them?

JOY MACKENZIE

157

Promises About Friendship

Rejoice with those who rejoice; mourn with those who mourn.

Romans 12:15

Her neighbors and relatives heard that the Lord had shown her great mercy, and they shared her joy.

Luke 1:58

Suppose a woman has ten silver coins and loses one. Does she not light a lamp, sweep the house and search carefully until she finds it? And when she finds it, she calls her friends and neighbors together and says, "Rejoice with me; I have found my lost coin."

Luke 15:8–9

Be glad and rejoice with me.

Philippians 2:18

The *Joy* of a *Good Attitude*

*M*y bus driver's name on this particular spring tour was "Shooter." He was kind-hearted, upbeat, and very unassuming.

One day on the road, in dire need of toiletries, I was waiting in the lobby for a cab to take me to the nearest drug store. Shooter also happened to be there.

Out of the blue, he said to me, "Kathy, you get up in the morning with a good attitude. I like that."

Nowhere near every morning, I thought. But I was thankful for his observation.

"This is how I look at it," he said. "The sun comes up every morning, and I'm grateful for another day to be alive. And you know what? If the sun never came up, we could all use a flashlight."

Shooter's words touched me deeply that day. I am a believer in Jesus and his promises. If the sun doesn't shine I do indeed have a flashlight: his Word is a lamp unto my feet guiding my every step. The sweet glow of his presence shines into my darkness.

KATHY TROCCOLI

*W*e live out the kingdom of God within us when we treasure each other and when we find ways to turn unfortunate things around. Laughter is one of those ways. Laughter stirs the blood, expands the chest, electrifies the nerves, and clears the cobwebs from the brain. If you laugh a lot, when you are older all your wrinkles will be in the right places!

If you live to be one hundred, your heart will have beaten 3,681,619,200 times, pumping 27,323,260 gallons of blood weighing over one hundred tons. (If you end up tired, you've earned it!) Think about making every heartbeat a happy one.

BARBARA JOHNSON

Promises About a Good Attitude

*W*ell done, good and faithful servant! You have been faithful with a few things; I will put you in charge of many things. Come and share your master's happiness!

Matthew 25:21

A happy heart makes the face cheerful, but heartache crushes the spirit.

Proverbs 15:13

*J*ust as the sufferings of Christ flow over into our lives, so also through Christ our comfort overflows.

2 Corinthians 1:5

*R*ejoice that you participate in the sufferings of Christ, so that you may be overjoyed when his glory is revealed.

1 Peter 4:13

The *Joy* of a *Loving Letter*

*B*ill and I travel to speaking engagements as many as thirty-nine weekends a year, and sometimes we find ourselves standing in the carport on Sunday afternoons almost too exhausted to unload the luggage.

But as soon as I walk in the door, one of the first things that catches my eye is the huge stack of mail a neighbor has collected for us and left on the kitchen table.

Standing there reading the mail, my batteries are quickly recharged with joy, and pretty soon I'm scurrying around our home with a smile on my face and a song in my heart.

After the complicated work of writing another book or an exhausting trip for an extended speaking engagement, I sometimes feel as if I've given all that I can. But the joyful letters give me the strength. Who do you know who could use an uplifting word today?

BARBARA JOHNSON

$\mathscr{I}$ remember the day I picked up a card that showed Winnie the Pooh and Piglet on the front walking hand in hand. Their conversation went like this:

"Pooh?" Piglet said.

"Yes, Piglet."

"Oh, nothing," Piglet said. "I just wanted to be sure of you."

I stared at it awhile, smiled, and then read it a few more times. I've asked this question of close friends at many different times in my life, in many different ways. I need the safety, the reassurance, the knowing they are right there and that I am loved.

Writing our feelings down and sending them to our loved ones is always worth the time and energy. It's amazing what often transpires. Cold walls melt, hard days take an easier turn, and bitterness gives way to forgiveness.

The saying that life is far too short and unpredictable is absolutely true. I try not to let a day go by without saying what needs to be said—or even what needs to be said again.

KATHY TROCCOLI

163

Promises About Loving Letters

How beautiful on the mountains are the feet of those who bring good news, who proclaim peace, who bring good tidings, who proclaim salvation, who say to Zion, "Your God reigns!"

Isaiah 52:7

A word aptly spoken is like apples of gold in settings of silver.

Proverbs 25:11

The Sovereign LORD has given me an instructed tongue, to know the word that sustains the weary.

Isaiah 50:4

How good is a timely word!

Proverbs 15:23

Celebrate Joy!

*E*very good life is a balance of duty and bliss. We will be called upon to do things we would rather not. We have to weigh decisions by mind and spirit and by the Word of God. So make each year count. Instead of clutching it fast, give it away. "Cast your bread upon the waters" (Ecclesiastes 11:1) and it comes back pretzels!

Do you have a gift for making people laugh? Writing a short story? Baking a great loaf of bread? Do you listen well? Throw a mean softball? Can you organize anything with flair? Are you good at making money? Selling just about anything? Running a race? Put yourself in the center ring. Offer your energy to life and do it heartily, unto the Lord.

Don't forget to celebrate anything you can think of. Do things that make you aware of how great it is to be alive. Every day is worth a party, not just the cookie-cutter moments. Special occasions are everywhere. Don't always be practical and expedient. God gave us license to be outrageously happy, friendly, and rejoicing.

BARBARA JOHNSON

*W*e Christians might look a bit more redeemed if we learned more about partying well—finding ways to celebrate the victories and milestones in each other's lives and also celebrating the traditional (and maybe some untraditional) seasonal holidays and holy days.

Families can celebrate their own events: anniversaries, Mother's Day, Father's Day. Celebrate! I know, putting on a party, even an informal gathering, takes effort, from organizing to cleanup. But I think our society, even our church, is hungry for meaningful interaction. Forget the virtual internet party. Have a real one that includes smiles, laughter, and popcorn. Let people gather around the grill. Skewer their own shish kebabs. Make their own pizzas. Decorate their own Christmas cookies.

Why not share the goodness of God in your life with others? Gather to celebrate because we are made for community. Sign on, sign up for the party. Celebrate the moment. Set up a milestone. Treasure the memory. Share the joy.

SHEILA WALSH

Promises About Celebrations

Let all who take refuge in you be glad; let them ever sing for joy. Spread your protection over them, that those who love your name may rejoice in you. For surely, O LORD, you bless the righteous; you surround them with your favor as with a shield.

Psalm 5:11–12

One generation will commend your works to another; they will tell of your mighty acts. They will speak of the glorious splendor of your majesty, and I will meditate on your wonderful works. They will tell of the power of your awesome works, and I will proclaim your great deeds. They will celebrate your abundant goodness and joyfully sing of your righteousness.

Psalm 145:4–7

The Joy of Family

Recently my cousin Ann, whom I had not heard from since we were children, contacted me. What a surprise, and how tickled I was to learn she wanted to reconnect after all these years. (We were raised in different states, and our life journeys never had occasion to intersect.) Ann said she woke up one day and realized she had lost contact with her father's (my uncle's) family. Now in her sixties, she decided to call all of her first cousins and to reestablish relationships. I couldn't have been more pleased, and so we agreed to meet up at one of my conferences in the South. Our reunion was fun and allowed us to reestablish our family connection. Isn't that what connection is really all about—being like family?

PATSY CLAIRMONT

Since Thanksgiving was only a few days away, I hurried off to buy a frozen turkey. I quickly grabbed a sixteen-pound Jenny O.

The directions on Jenny's frozen back instructed me to place her in my refrigerator where she would thaw. With innocent anticipation, I pulled Jenny out of the refrigerator Thanksgiving morning. She wasn't as stiff as the day we had met, but she certainly wasn't soft and pliable.

Jenny crawled into my oven around eleven o'clock and came out around five in the evening. She was flavorful and moist until I cut more than an inch deep. Then we hit pink meat, which threw me into fits about salmonella potential.

In spite of this mild turkey crisis, my family, some dear friends, and I had a wonderful time together. Sometimes I forget and allow myself to focus on the externals of a celebration, which, of course, throttles my internal experience of joy. Even if we had been reduced to ordering out for pizza and having Jenny join us in eating the meal, we would have had a great time simply because we were together.

MARILYN MEBERG

169

Promises About Family

You are no longer foreigners and aliens, but fellow citizens with God's people and members of God's household.

Ephesians 2:19

Keep your father's commands and do not forsake your mother's teaching. Bind them upon your heart forever; fasten them around your neck. When you walk, they will guide you; when you sleep, they will watch over you; when you awake, they will speak to you.

Proverbs 6:20–22

As for me and my household, we will serve the LORD.

Joshua 24:15

Live in harmony with one another; be sympathetic, love as brothers, be compassionate and humble.

1 Peter 3:8

The Days of Your Life

There are days when I start feeling blue. On those days I've learned to avoid certain things. I won't weigh myself, listen to sad music, get a haircut, open a box of chocolates, or shop for a bathing suit. Instead, on such days I make it a goal to perk up and be happy. The best way is to become a joy germ carrier. Infecting people with joy so they break out in symptoms of laughter— that's the very best way to beat the blues.

I've made it a habit to wring out of every single day all the fun and love I can find. If you don't know where to start next time you're feeling low, take it simply: Fill in the hours with crazy excursions into comedy. You'll learn what makes people laugh and how to communicate through chuckles. The point is simply to get started. The point is never to give up. The point is to be friendly and to focus on the person next to you. People who like people are people that people like!

BARBARA JOHNSON

I like having special days, days set aside to commemorate an event: birthdays, anniversaries, graduations. My journals are full of remembrances like "forty years ago today my parents were married." Or "if my father had lived, he'd be ninety today." Or, "Remember, Luci, three years ago you bought this house."

Days are important. I anticipate them. I'm looking forward to the day my friends come for Thanksgiving, to the next time I'll see my brother in Florida. And I can never quite wait for Christmas.

The word "days" appears more than five hundred times in Scripture, and the Mosaic Law prescribed feast days when the congregation was to celebrate by dancing, singing, resting from labor, and giving praise to God. These were occasions of joy and gladness.

I encourage you to create special days for yourself and your family. Twenty-four hours when you do something entirely different from other days . . . or maybe do nothing.

This is the day the Lord has made. Rejoice. Celebrate all your days.

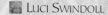 LUCI SWINDOLL

Promises About Your Days

This is the day the LORD has made; let us rejoice and be glad in it.

Psalm 118:24

This day is sacred to our Lord. Do not grieve, for the joy of the LORD is your strength.

Nehemiah 8:10

If you call the Sabbath a delight and the LORD's holy day honorable, and if you honor it by not going your own way and not doing as you please or speaking idle words, then you will find your joy in the LORD.

Isaiah 58:13−14

I tell you, now is the time of God's favor, now is the day of salvation.

2 Corinthians 6:2

Renew Your Hope
With Prayer

One of the most colorful people in my family is Uncle Lawrence Morris, Jr., my mother's only brother. His nickname is Uncle Brother. Although he had accepted Christ as a young man, Uncle Brother had lived like the devil. But I prayed for him to return to the Lord. I didn't want Uncle Brother to die without realizing he could enjoy a better life than the one he had chosen.

Thanks be to God, for the past several years, Uncle Brother has made some major changes. He reads his Bible. He bridles his tongue. He has changed his friends. He is concerned about others.

God was always present. And he was waiting for my uncle to reopen his heart.

Are you dealing with someone whom you feel will never change? Nobody is so far from God that he can't get back to the Lord. Our responsibility is to keep knocking at God's door about that person, to keep believing God will answer our prayers. Thank God for what he will do. Patiently but expectantly wait on the Lord. Renew your hope!

THELMA WELLS

*T*he promise to pray for someone going through hard times rolls easily off our tongues. But do we really mean it? Our sisters, brothers, and children in the faith need our committed involvement in their lives.

Prayer is not a last resort but a first-rate privilege. We don't know how to pray as we ought, but we ought to pray anyway. We never know why some things happen as they do. But we stand upon the rocky shores of life and keep on praying, because prayer changes the one who prays as much as it changes those for whom we pray.

Some people think their prayers have fallen on deaf ears. But they have not. It takes faith to know that. Faith is the ability to let your light shine even after your fuse is blown. Faith is seeing light with the eyes of your heart, when the eyes of your body see only darkness ahead.

God is changing things through our willingness to pray and keep at it. While sorrow looks back and worry looks around, faith looks up. As we pray, we may face finite disappointment, but we must never lose infinite hope.

BARBARA JOHNSON

Promises About
Renewing Your Hope

Be strong and take heart, all you who hope in the LORD.

Psalm 31:24

The LORD longs to be gracious to you; he rises to show you compassion. For the LORD is a God of justice. Blessed are all who wait for him!

Isaiah 30:18

The LORD is good to those whose hope is in him, to the one who seeks him; it is good to wait quietly for the salvation of the LORD.

Lamentations 3:25–26

Put your hope in the LORD, for with the LORD is unfailing love and with him is full redemption.

Psalm 130:7

Focus on Christ & Find Joy

There's really no easy formula for appropriating joy. Joy happens in us as God restores us, teaching us to abide in him as he works in and through us.

Joy is not something that you can buy. You can't get it from a book or a conference. You can't absorb it as if by osmosis by hanging out with people who seem to have it. You can spend your life trying to eliminate all pain and stress from your world in the vain hope that joy will take its place, but it won't. You can beg for it, pray for it, bargain for it to no avail. Joy comes only when you live in relationship with the source of joy.

Remember the promise of John 15:4? "Remain in me, and I will remain in you. No branch can bear fruit by itself; it must remain in the vine. Neither can you bear fruit unless you remain in me." You can't go out and work on joy. We are called to rest in the One who *is* joy. Without him there is no fruit, no joy.

SHEILA WALSH

In this instant world, we often want microwave solutions to crock-pot problems. I'm not ashamed to admit that I lack solutions to overwhelming troubles. Some things belong to the Lord; he alone knows these secrets. On this earth we seek advice from experts, wisdom from counselors, solace from comforters, encouragement from mentors. But when you get right down to it, the bottom line is that we must trust the Lord through it all.

Jesus is there when nobody else is. When one of God's kids hits rock bottom, he or she discovers that Jesus is the only foundation. For you are not just a number in a network in cyberspace. There is Someone who knows your face, your name, your need. That person doesn't punch in a formula on a PC to arrive at a solution to your trouble. He never offers platitudes and never patronizes. Instead he offers love and a place to land. He gives the quiet assurance that he is all you need at any point in life.

Take a chance. Embrace the vision God gives you. Celebrate life.

BARBARA JOHNSON

Promises About Focusing on Christ

Christ Jesus, who died—more than that, who was raised to life—is at the right hand of God and is also interceding for us.

Romans 8:34

He who began a good work in you will carry it on to completion until the day of Christ Jesus.

Philippians 1:6

Since, then, you have been raised with Christ, set your hearts on things above, where Christ is seated at the right hand of God.

Colossians 3:1

Consider him who endured such opposition from sinful men, so that you will not grow weary and lose heart.

Hebrews 12:3

The Joy of Helping Others Help You

*O*ne of the most rewarding ways to relate to others is to give them ownership over what's going on. At home the entire family should share in keeping things up around the house. At work people want to be a part of things and to have responsibility with accountability. And others in your life are waiting for you to take some items off your calendar so they can put them on theirs.

It takes awhile to complete the delegation process. Training, explaining, and overseeing are all part of it. However, when everyone has his or her tasks and can do them with little supervision, you begin to reap the results.

I hypothesize that you have some people to whom you can delegate housework, office work, and church work. Wouldn't it be great not to have the frightening words, "Fire! Another fire!" reverberating in your mind? You have to decide you're tired of fighting these blazes yourself. Trust people enough to give them important tasks. Delegate.

THELMA WELLS

*R*ecently I moved. I moved only seven blocks, but I still had to pick up everything and find a place to set it down in my new abode—that or have an enormous (thirty-four years' worth of stuff) yard sale. Thankfully, I had dear friends come to my rescue and help me pack.

After arriving in our new home, I was overwhelmed at the prospect of settling in. I had thought I would pull it together rapidly. Instead, I roamed from room to room trying to remember my name. Carol came to give support (and to verify my identity) every morning for four days. She assisted me until early evening, when she would then make our dinner, serve us, and clean up. You can only guess what a gift that was to me emotionally. I never expected that kind of beyond-the-call-of-duty effort, but I'm certain our new home ownership would have found me sinking before I could even unload the cargo, if it were not for Carol's life preserver of kindness.

PATSY CLAIRMONT

Promises About Helping Others Help Us

Moses' father-in-law said: "The work is too heavy for you; you cannot handle it alone. Listen now to me and I will give you some advice, and may God be with you. You must be the people's representative before God and bring their disputes to him. Teach them the decrees and laws, and show them the way to live and the duties they are to perform. But select capable men from all the people—men who fear God, trustworthy men who hate dishonest gain—and appoint them as officials over thousands, hundreds, fifties and tens. Have them serve as judges for the people at all times, but have them bring every difficult case to you; the simple cases they can decide themselves. That will make your load lighter, because they will share it with you. If you do this and God so commands, you will be able to stand the strain, and all these people will go home satisfied."

Exodus 18:17–23

Blessed Sidekicks

We need each other. Scripture says two are better than one. We're instructed to love, pray for, care about, accept, forgive, serve, encourage and build up one another.

I love that about my partners in the Women of Faith conferences. We "be-bop" all over the country watching out for each other. We serve one another joyfully, from the heart. When one of us is down, we rally to her. When one celebrates, we rejoice together. We're a team. We never anticipated this kind of bonding, but bonded we are.

People need each other—no matter how much we insist we don't. Nobody is an island, an entity unto herself, or a Lone Ranger. We're in this thing called *community*, and part of the joy of community is sharing the weight. The weight of burdens, losses, loneliness, and fear.

Look around you, my friend. Who's there for you? And who are you there for? Take a careful look. Even those who insist they can make it on their own may be waiting for you to reach out and help. Be there and available. Even the Lone Ranger had a sidekick.

LUCI SWINDOLL

The key to friendship between women—and somehow for us girls, it's not the easiest thing to achieve—is being able to accept each other unconditionally. If we can do that, the rewards are never ending! And the pay dirt is definitely a bonanza! It's a proven fact we will stay young longer, are less likely to be depressed, and will save a fortune in counseling fees!

The secret of friendship is that we *bless each other,* and within the blessing is a kaleidoscope of meaning—to make happy, to praise, to thank, to protect, to sanctify, to favor, to celebrate, to give benediction. It not only applies to best friends, but it applies to every cherished human relationship—husband and wife, parent and child, sister and brother, neighbor with neighbor, church member with church member. It's cross-cultural, cross-racial, cross-generational, and cross-backyardfence-ational—a made-up word, but that too is allowed with friends!

SUE BUCHANAN

Promises About Blessed Sidekicks

Carry each other's burdens, and in this way you will fulfill the law of Christ.

Galatians 6:2

You yourselves have been taught by God to love each other.

1 Thessalonians 4:9

Be devoted to one another in brotherly love. Honor one another above yourselves.

Romans 12:10

If you really keep the royal law found in Scripture, "Love your neighbor as yourself," you are doing right.

James 2:8

Love one another deeply, from the heart.

1 Peter 1:22

The Joy Buster of Pride

How quickly we judge another's outward appearance. We see clothes that don't match, and we judge. We look at another's car, manners, music, posture, or facial characteristics ... judging all the while.

I'll tell you, if human perspective had been the criterion for God's judgment, the Swindolls would have been zapped long ago. Each of us, my brothers and I, live the majority of our lives in well-worn clothes that don't match. More often than not, I go to the store in my oldest sweats. I don't want to change clothes just to pick up a carton of milk, grab a hamburger, or have the car washed.

In Antoine de Saint-Exupery's book, *The Little Prince,* he states, "It is only with the heart that one can see rightly; what is essential is invisible to the eye."

"What is essential is invisible" captures what we read in Scripture. We have no right to pass judgment on another. When I don't put any judgmental demands on others, I'm happiest because I know I'm doing what is right. When nobody puts demands on me, it frees me to be who I am.

LUCI SWINDOLL

*U*ppity is a downer. We are warned about being high-minded, that is, thinking more highly of ourselves than we should. Like the time I thought I was lookin' good only to discover my pantyhose were underfoot—or more accurately, they were streaming behind my foot as I sashayed through the middle of town.

Remember in Genesis when Joseph paraded his new coat for his brothers' viewing? They, in turn, stripped him of his colors and sold him into slavery. Yep, showing off tends to trip us up. Thinking more highly of ourselves than we ought means a downfall is probably up ahead.

I guess God knew for Joseph to grow up, he would have to live down his need to be the center of attention. Here, though, is the amazing truth: Joseph grew to handle his down times as well as he did his up times. He became an example to many as his social position looked an awful lot like a busy elevator.

Which leads me to ask, Who is the central focus of our lives? The Lord? Or our need to be center stage? Are we willing, whether we ascend or descend, to be a shining example?

 PATSY CLAIRMONT

187

Promises About Overcoming Pride

Patience is better than pride.

Ecclesiastes 7:8

Pride only breeds quarrels, but wisdom is found in those who take advice.

Proverbs 13:10

When pride comes, then comes disgrace, but with humility comes wisdom.

Proverbs 11:2

Pride goes before destruction, a haughty spirit before a fall.

Proverbs 16:18

Everyone who exalts himself will be humbled, and he who humbles himself will be exalted.

Luke 18:14

The *Joy* of *Fellowship*

I'm convinced that wherever I am, Christian fellowship is mandatory for my heart and soul. Nothing can take its place.

One day outside a church in Buenos Aires the spirited sounds of singing and clapping met us on the sidewalk, enveloped us, and literally propelled us forward. We were surrounded by radiantly smiling Latin faces singing praises to God with utter abandon. Not only was I moved by the powerful presence of the Holy Spirit in that place, but I also realized how rejuvenated I felt to be enveloped by believers. It felt wonderful to be bathed in the oneness of these dear Christians, who hugged and kissed us with such unaffected genuineness. That sweet Sunday will live forever in my memory, as I reflect on fellowship that was unhindered by language or cultural barriers.

How about you? Are you pining for the fellowship that surpasses all others? Spend time with fellow believers rejoicing over what you have in Jesus. Sing some songs. Laugh together. Pray for one another. Hug each other. Celebrate the blessed tie that binds you to one another in Christian love.

MARILYN MEBERG

A cold day. It swirls snow, kicking up a storm. It takes something extra to stick to the job, keep your kids happy in the house, get to church, and be a good neighbor in those frosty winter months.

We experience frigid temperatures in our faith too. There are cold days when hope dies: love walks out the door, a friend moves out of town, the job ends, the bank fails. God seems distant. Prayer fades in your throat before you barely utter a word. The Bible stares back with a blank page. You might call it spiritual frostbite. It is painful. Poisonous. Dangerous.

The church is God's spiritual stove. In its containment we pile on fuel, stir the embers, strike a match. We need each other's warmth to survive the winters of our lives. Don't be fooled by the facade of strength that some put on to protect themselves. Put a little May and June into someone's life. Don't hide behind propriety. Look both ways—who needs a hand, a word, or one of your ears for a few moments? Lending yours might mean making someone's day. Reach out and warm a heart!

BARBARA JOHNSON

Promises About Fellowship

Honor one another above yourselves. Never be lacking in zeal, but
keep your spiritual fervor, serving the
Lord . . . Share with God's people who
are in need. Practice hospitality . . .
Live in harmony with one another.
Do not be proud, but be willing to
associate with people of low position.
Do not be conceited. Do not repay
anyone evil for evil. Be careful to do
what is right in the eyes of everybody.
If it is possible, as far as it depends
on you, live at peace with everyone.

Romans 12:10–18

Where two or three come together
in my name, there am I with them.

Matthew 18:20

The Joy of Being Different

We rang the doorbell, and I laughed as I looked through the door's glass pane and saw four shaggy dogs running over each other to be first to the door.

As we sat in our friends' study, eventually the dogs all found their places, flopping down exhausted from extending such an effusive welcome.

"Do you make a habit of rescuing dogs from the pound?" I asked.

"Yes, I do," Karalyn answered. "Everyone wants a perfect animal, a new one that looks great with no faults or limitations, but I've found the animals who have been all but tossed away have so much love to give."

Christ said that we shouldn't entertain those who can repay us but rather those who have nothing to give. In every church across America there are those who come lonely and leave lonely every Sunday. Old people's homes are full of forgotten lives. What a blessing it would be to them and to us if we really saw them and included them in our lives.

SHEILA WALSH

*D*o I have the courage to be me? I hope to be a woman who is real and compassionate and who might draw people to nestle within God's embrace.

Any one of us can do that. We may never win any great awards or be named best dressed, most beautiful, most popular, or most revered. But each of us has an arm with which to hold another person. Each of us can pull another shoulder under ours. Each of us can invite someone in need to nestle next to our heart.

We can give a pat on the back, a simple compliment, a kiss on the cheek, a thumbs-up sign. We can smile at a stranger, say hello when it's least expected, send a card of congratulations, take flowers to a sick neighbor, make a casserole for a new mother.

Let's take the things that set us apart, that make us different, that cause us to disagree, and make them an occasion to compliment each other and be thankful for each other. Let us be big enough to be smaller than our neighbor, spouse, friends, and strangers. Every day.

 BARBARA JOHNSON

Promises About Being Different

The Lord *has declared this day that you are his people, his treasured possession as he promised, and that you are to keep all his commands.*

Deuteronomy 26:18

I will give you a new heart and put a new spirit in you; I will remove from you your heart of stone and give you a heart of flesh. And I will put my Spirit in you and move you to follow my decrees and be careful to keep my laws.

Ezekiel 36:26−27

Know that the Lord *has set apart the godly for himself.*

Psalm 4:3

We are God's workmanship, created in Christ Jesus to do good works, which God prepared in advance for us to do.

Ephesians 2:10

Put on a Smiley Face

I believe in having fun, because I know that she who laughs, lasts. Whatever you do, whether it's jumping from airplanes, visiting the sick, surfing the Net, taking care of widows, or goofing off, do it well and never lose your ability to scatter joy. Tuck some in the pocket of the stranger next to you at the grocery store. Sprinkle it on the head of an elderly lady crossing the street in front of you. Leave funny messages in your teenagers' cars or on their e-mail. Wake your spouse up with the scent of roses or honeysuckle. And never ever forget to smile.

Smiles are like two-for-one coupons. Each time you let them spread across your lips, they light up the face and heart of someone else. Sooner or later a smile will come back around to you just when you need it most. And it is something anyone—everyone—can do well. Talk about a win-win situation; move over, Stephen Covey!

BARBARA JOHNSON

*P*icture this: You are asked to travel for most of the weekends of an entire year around the country with five women you've never met. You'll be speaking together, eating together, and praying together. You'll be under pressure together, and you'll share in the joys and tribulations of traveling together. That's an awful lot of togetherness with a bunch of strangers, if you ask me.

If I had known what it was going to be like to travel with these five Women of Faith, I would have . . . why, I would have signed up a lot sooner. I had no idea how exciting and vibrant they were nor what an influence they would have on my life. Through all the pain, sorrow, disappointment, aggravation, and agitation of life, these wonderful women are still funny, adventurous, and silly.

Just as they have influenced and encouraged me, you, too, can be a blessing to the people you meet today. Life has it's serious moments. But being just a bit kooky may be the secret to seeing yourself and others through good times and bad. Go ahead, make someone's day—make her smile.

THELMA WELLS

Promises About Smiles

A happy heart makes the face cheerful.

Proverbs 15:13

A cheerful heart is good medicine, but a crushed spirit dries up the bones.

Proverbs 17:22

*T*he cheerful heart has a continual feast.

Proverbs 15:15

*R*ejoice in the Lord always. I will say it again: Rejoice!

Philippians 4:4

*S*ing joyfully to the Lord, you right-eous; it is fitting for the upright to praise him.

Psalm 33:1

The *Joy* of *Caring* for *Family Members*

*T*rue love demands honesty, taking risks with one another and enduring some difficult moments because we want a real relationship.

A friend of mine recently told me he now only talks to his mother by e-mail because it makes her more bearable. I asked him if he had ever discussed with her the difficulty they had communicating. He looked at me as if I had suggested he stick his hand in a blender. "You've got to be kidding," he said. "Talk to my mother? That's like trying to bargain with a scorpion!"

Often family members behave in set patterns simply because that's what we expect each other to do. It's a dance that has developed over the years between us. We need to take a fresh look. Put on a new record. Say "thank you." Send flowers. Write a note. Take a good look. Move a little closer.

SHEILA WALSH

*C*aring is a gift you give the other person. And Christian women are good at caring. The pain that sometimes results is a value-added premium to let you know that you are alive and well, that you still have a tender heart. Sympathy is nothing other than *your* pain in my heart.

We cannot always head off disaster. Sometimes we discover that the light at the end of the tunnel really is the headlight of an oncoming train. Even so, I've found that the best thing to hold on to in this life is each other. When even that fails, we can be assured that God is holding on to us.

I try to take the cold water thrown upon me, heat it with enthusiasm, and use the steam to push ahead. On the long journey, I seek to love and to live in the strength of the Lord. At the end of each day, before turning down the covers, I turn all my problems over to the Holy Spirit. I'm grateful he stays up late to handle them. Then I lay down, secure in the knowledge that broken things become blessed things if I let Christ do the mending!

BARBARA JOHNSON

Promises About Caring for Family Members

If anyone does not provide for his relatives, and especially for his immediate family, he has denied the faith and is worse than an unbeliever.

1 Timothy 5:8

Let us do good to all people, especially to those who belong to the family of believers.

Galatians 6:10

Children should not have to save up for their parents, but parents for their children.

2 Corinthians 12:14

Which of you fathers, if your son asks for a fish, will give him a snake instead? Or if he asks for an egg, will give him a scorpion? If you then, though you are evil, know how to give good gifts to your children, how much more will your Father in heaven give the Holy Spirit to those who ask him!

Luke 11:11–13

A *Positive* *Perspective*

Stress is everywhere. People stress out because they know today is the tomorrow they worried about yesterday! Dieters know what stress is. Someone said, "I've been on a diet for two weeks, and all I've lost is fourteen days." That's self-imposed stress.

What happens when you think you are winning the rat race and along come faster rats? How do you deal with the stress? The best advice for stress is this: Stress may be a given factor, but your attitude can change the way it affects you.

Stress is nothing but psychological pollution. Flush stuff like that out of your system with a positive outlook. Keep mentally limber; accept what you can't change, and don't dwell on your own or others' shortcomings. Be an imp for a day or an hour, make a neighbor laugh, play a practical joke, delight yourself with a wacky surprise.

Don't waste today's time cluttering up tomorrow's opportunities with yesterday's troubles! God has promised to turn your "hours of stressing into showers of blessing."

BARBARA JOHNSON

I love grocery shopping. I love having all those choices and anticipating the preparation of wonderful meals. I grab up fresh bouquets of flowers and never quite seem to get the smile off my face. Every now and then, I add a jar of pickles, can of hair spray, or package of liverwurst to another shopper's unattended cart, just to entertain myself and give that person whiplash at the checkout counter.

Even the post office can be rewarding. Last week, I bought ten stamps and gave two each to the five people behind me. I told them I hated waiting in line and was sure they did too. So, I was giving them a little present. My own little random act of kindness.

We all have things in life we have to do, but we can choose how we want to do them. It's up to each of us. I can tell you this, though. There's only one way to have joy ... by doing everything "as unto the Lord."

By the way, if you're the one who arrived at home with an extra jar of pickles, enjoy them. You helped bring a smile to someone today. Perspective is everything.

 LUCI SWINDOLL

Promises About a Positive Perspective

*W*hatever you do, work at it with all your heart, as working for the Lord, not for men.

Colossians 3:23

*S*erve wholeheartedly, as if you were serving the Lord, not men, because you know that the Lord will reward everyone for whatever good he does, whether he is slave or free.

Ephesians 6:7–8

*T*he Almighty says: "See if I will not throw open the floodgates of heaven and pour out so much blessing that you will not have room enough for it."

Malachi 3:10

Wrapped in Jesus' Joy

*J*oy. It's a powerful force. It looks in the face of life with all its tears and tragedy, all its ups and downs, and it wraps a blanket of eternal comfort around our shoulders. It doesn't leave the scene. Joy in the midst of pain, on the faces of our friends, in the quiet moments of our days. This gift the world seeks after and sells its soul to buy—found in the arms of the One who *is* joy. It has no substance without his presence.

The Book of Common Prayer includes a beautiful prayer for evening that requests God's help in various circumstances: "Tend the sick, Lord Christ, give rest to the weary, bless the dying, soothe the suffering, pity the afflicted, shield the joyous; and all for your love's sake. Amen."

Did you hear it? It was in there. It's my prayer for you. I tuck it into this page with all the love of heaven: "shield the joyous." I pray: "Wrap them up, dear Lord. Keep them safe and kind and hopeful. Speak to them in the quiet and in the noise and in all the moments of their days . . . for your sake. Amen."

SHEILA WALSH

Promises About Jesus' Joy

Jesus said: "Take my yoke upon you and learn from me, for I am gentle and humble in heart, and you will find rest for your souls. For my yoke is easy and my burden is light."

Matthew 11:29–30

Jesus said: "I have told you these things, so that in me you may have peace. In this world you will have trouble. But take heart! I have overcome the world."

John 16:33

May our Lord Jesus Christ himself and God our Father, who loved us and by his grace gave us eternal encouragement and good hope, encourage your hearts and strengthen you in every good deed and word.

2 Thessalonians 2:16–17

PRAISE FOR ELIZABETH GEORGE
AND HER NOVELS

"A MASTER OF THE ENGLISH MYSTERY."
—*The New York Times*

"MS. GEORGE PROVIDES ENOUGH TWISTS AND SHOCKS...
TO STARTLE AND SATISFY EVEN THE MOST JADED READER."
—*The Wall Street Journal*

"ANOTHER WINNER FROM THE CURRENT MASTER OF THE
CLASSIC ENGLISH MYSTERY."
—*The Atlantic Monthly*

"GEORGE DELIVERS, ONCE AGAIN, A MYSTERY IMBUED WITH
PSYCHOLOGICAL SUSPENSE
AND IN-DEPTH CHARACTERIZATION."
—*Booklist*

PRAISE FOR
BELIEVING THE LIE

"Ms. George, as ever, writes a long and complicated book, with a multiplicity of subplots and a richness of physical detail. In *Believing the Lie*, as often as not, the terrain and the weather are objective correlatives to the characters' stormy patches. Meanwhile, the story strands are untied and retied in satisfying and often moving ways."
—*The Wall Street Journal*

"Elizabeth George is a superstar of the crime-fiction world, British Inspector Division. Deservedly so: Her tales always provide nuanced character studies and insights into social issues along with their intricate mysteries."
—*The Seattle Times*

"Devilishly complicated."   —*Entertainment Weekly*

"A dense, twisty plot with characters who reveal the sad spectrum of human dereliction."   —*People*

"George's . . . ability to continually enhance the portraits of Lynley, Havers, and other recurring characters while generating fully fleshed new ones for each novel is nothing less than superlative, and her atmospheric prose, complete with lovely and detailed descriptions of her setting, combines to add literary gravitas to her work . . . a worthy addition to her portfolio and one that simultaneously disturbs and satisfies."   —*Richmond Times-Dispatch*

"Impossible to put down . . . for the Elizabeth George fan—or any fan of the well-written, intelligent, character-driven novel—I'd say, dig in."   —*AnnArbor.com*

"Although the story is a bit slow to build, when it reaches its climax, look out. This one has at least four different, but related, story lines, all reaching a fever pitch at the same time . . . *Believing the Lie* is more than six hundred pages of bliss for mystery lovers, capped off with a surprise ending."   —*The Gazette* (Montreal)

continued . . .

"George's mastery of impeccable pacing and plot development mercilessly launches you into the latest episode (in this case #17) in D.I. Lynley's life. . . . Although Elizabeth George is an American author who lives and writes in Washington State, she breathes pure Anglican fire and dialogue, not to mention geographic authenticity into her award-winning novels." —Bookreporter.com

"George's many fans, however, will be thrilled with this new episode in the lives of her lovable cast of characters."
—*Library Journal*

"So fascinating that even at a thundering 606 pages, I wished for at least ten more." —*Mystery Scene*

"George's strengths—character development, plot twists, and shocking tragedy—continue to shine. . . . Look for a serious cliff-hanger at the end, which will leave George's fans panting for the next Lynley episode."
—Shelf Awareness

"A page-turning plot." —*World*

"Unsettling and will keep readers on edge."
—SheKnows Book Lounge

PRAISE FOR
ELIZABETH GEORGE

"[Lynley is] one of the great character portraits in contemporary crime fiction." —*The Boston Globe*

"Ms. George can do it all, with style to spare."
—*The Wall Street Journal* on *Careless in Red*

"As always, Georges's subplots provide . . . engrossing moments and memorable characters."
—*Chicago Tribune* on *A Traitor to Memory*

"Crime writing at its best."
—*The Courier-Mail* (Queensland, Australia) on *This Body of Death*

ALSO BY

ELIZABETH GEORGE

A Great Deliverance
Payment in Blood
Well-Schooled in Murder
A Suitable Vengeance
For the Sake of Elena
Missing Joseph
Playing for the Ashes
In the Presence of the Enemy
Deception on His Mind
In Pursuit of the Proper Sinner
A Traitor to Memory
I, Richard
A Place of Hiding
With No One as Witness
What Came Before He Shot Her
Careless in Red
This Body of Death

NONFICTION
*Write Away: One Novelist's Approach
to Fiction and the Writing Life*

ANTHOLOGY
*A Moment on the Edge:
100 Years of Crime Stories by Women*
Two of the Deadliest

ELIZABETH GEORGE

Believing the Lie

A Lynley Novel

A SIGNET SELECT BOOK

SIGNET SELECT
Published by the Penguin Group
Penguin Group (USA) LLC, 375 Hudson Street,
New York, New York 10014

USA | Canada | UK | Ireland | Australia | New Zealand | India | South Africa | China
penguin.com
A Penguin Random House Company

Published by Signet Select, an imprint of New American Library, a division of
Penguin Group (USA) LLC. Previously published in Dutton and New American Library editions.

First Signet Select Printing, March 2014

ISBN 978-0-451-46549-8

Printed in the United States of America
10 9 8 7 6 5 4 3 2 1

In loving memory of

Anthony Mott

brilliant raconteur

adored companion

always Antonio to me

This life's five windows of the soul
Distorts the Heavens from pole to pole,
And leads you to believe a lie
When you see with, not thro', the eye . . .

WILLIAM BLAKE

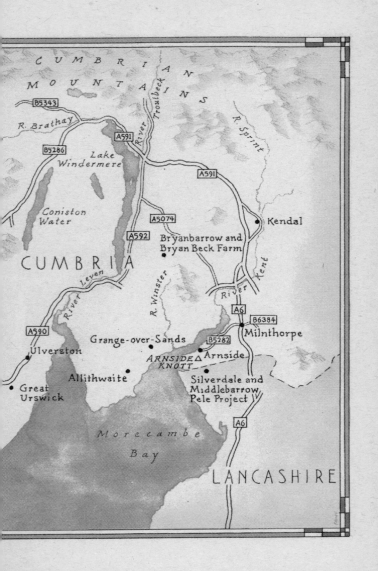

10 OCTOBER

Zed Benjamin had never been called into the office of the editor before, and he found the experience simultaneously disconcerting and thrilling. The disconcerting half of it resulted in massive sweating of the armpits. The thrilling half of it produced a heartbeat he could actually feel, for some reason, in the pads of his thumbs. But since from the first he'd believed it essential to see Rodney Aronson as just another bloke at *The Source*, he attributed both the sweating of armpits and the pulsing of thumbs to the fact that he'd switched from his one summer suit to his one winter suit rather too early in the season. He made a mental note to change back to the summer suit in the morning and he only hoped his mother hadn't taken it out to be cleaned once she saw he'd made the switch. That would be, Zed thought, exactly like her. His mum was helpful and earnest. She was too much of both.

He sought a distraction, easy enough to find in Rodney Aronson's office. While the editor of the newspaper continued to read Zed's story, Zed began to read the headlines on the old issues of the tabloid that were framed and hung along the walls. He found them distasteful and idiotic, their stories a form of pandering to the worst inclinations in the human psyche. *Rent Boy Breaks Silence* was a piece on a kerb-crawling encounter between a sixteen-year-old boy and a member of Parliament in the vicinity of King's Cross Station, an unseemly romantic interlude unfortunately interrupted by the advent of vice officers from the local nick. *MP in Sex Triangle with Teenager* preceded the rent boy breaking his silence and *MP Wife in Suicide Drama* followed hard on its heels. *The Source* had been on top of all these stories, first on the scene, first with the scoop, first with the money to pay informants for salacious details to juice up a report that in any legitimate paper would either be written with discretion or buried deep inside or both. This was particularly the case for such hot topics as *Prince in Bedroom Brouhaha, Kiss-and-Tell Equerry Shocks Palace*, and *Another Royal Divorce?*, all of which, Zed knew very well from gossip in the canteen, had topped *The Source*'s previous circulation figures by over one hundred thousand copies each. This was the sort of reportage for which the tabloid was known. Everyone in the newsroom understood that if you didn't want to get your hands dirty sifting through other people's nasty bits of laundry, then you didn't want to work as an investigative reporter at *The Source*.

Which was, admittedly, the case for Zedekiah Benjamin. He definitely didn't want to work as an investigative reporter at *The Source*. He saw himself as a columnist-for-the–*Financial Times* kind of bloke, someone with a career providing enough respectability and name recognition to support his real passion, which was writing fine poetry. But jobs as respectable columnists were as scarce as knickers under kilts, and one had to do *something* to put food on the table since writing excellent verse wasn't about to do it. Thus Zed knew it behooved him to act at all times like a man who found the pursuit of the social gaffes of celebrities and the peccadilloes of members of the royal family journalistically and professionally fulfilling. Still, he liked to believe that even a paper like *The Source* could benefit from a slight elevation from its usual position in the gutter, from where, it had to be said, no one was gazing at the stars.

The piece that Rodney Aronson was reading demonstrated this. In Zed's mind, a tabloid story did not have to swim in lubricious facts in order to capture the reader's interest. Stories could be uplifting and redemptive like this one and still sell newspapers. True, stories like this one weren't likely to make the front page, but the Sunday magazine would do, although a two-page spread at the centre of the daily edition wouldn't have gone down bad either, just as long as photographs accompanied it and the story made a jump to the following page. Zed had spent ages on this piece and it deserved a gallon of newsprint, he thought. It had exactly what readers of *The Source* liked, but with refinement. Sins of the fathers and their sons were featured, ruined relationships were explored, alcohol and drug usage was involved, and redemption was achieved. Here was a feature about a wastrel, caught in the deadly embrace of methamphetamine addiction, who at the eleventh hour of his life—more or less—managed to turn himself around and live anew, birthing himself through an unexpected devotion to society's lowest of the low. Here was a story with villains and heroes, with worthy adversaries and enduring love. Here were exotic locations, family values, parental love. And above all—

"It's a snore." Rodney Aronson tossed Zed's story to one side of his desk and fingered his beard. He dislodged a flake of chocolate therein and popped it into his mouth. He'd finished a Cadbury Hazelnut while he was reading and his restless eyes took in his desktop as if seeking another indulgence, which he didn't need, considering a girth barely hidden by the overlarge safari jacket he favoured for workday attire.

"What?" Zed thought he'd somehow misheard and he rooted round in his mind for anything that rhymed with *snore* as a means of reassuring himself that his editor hadn't just condemned his piece to the bottom corner of page 20 or worse.

"Snore," Rodney said. "Snore as in sleep as in put me to sleep. You promised me a hot investigative piece if I sent you up there. You guaranteed me a hot investigative piece, as I recall. If I went to the expense of putting you up in a hotel for God knows how many days—"

"Five," Zed said. "Because it was a complicated piece and there were people who needed to be interviewed so that the objectivity one wants to maintain—"

"All right. Five. And I'm going to want a word about your choice of hotel, by the way, because I've seen the bill and I'm wondering if the bloody room came with dancing girls. When someone is sent the hell up to Cumbria for five days at the expense of the paper, promising that a whiz-bang story will be the outcome . . ." Rodney picked up the piece and used it to gesture with. "What the hell exactly have you investigated here? And what in God's name's this title all about? *The Ninth Life*. What is this, something from one of your highbrow *lit*-ra-cher classes? Maybe creative writing, eh? Fancy yourself a novelist, do you?"

Zed knew the editor hadn't been to university. That was part of the canteen gossip as well. Sotto voce had come the advice soon after Zed's joining the staff of *The Source*: For God's sake and for your own good, don't cross Rod with anything that reminds him you have a first or a second or a *whatever* in something even vaguely associated with higher education, mate. Can*not* cope and thinks you're taking the piss, so keep it shut when it comes to that kind of thing.

Thus Zed trod carefully with his reply to Rodney's question about the title of his piece. "I was thinking of cats, actually."

"You were thinking of cats."

"Uh . . . having nine lives?"

"Got it in a basket. But we're not writing about cats, are we."

"No. Of course not. But . . ." Zed wasn't sure what the editor wanted, so he altered direction and plunged on with his explanation. "What I meant was that the bloke's been eight times in rehab, see, in three different countries and nothing worked for him, and I mean *nothing*. Oh, maybe he's been clean for six or eight months or once for a year but after a bit it's back to the meth and he's wasted again. He ends up in Utah, where he meets a very special woman, and suddenly he's a new man and he never looks back."

"Presto, change-o, that's about it? Saved by the power of love, eh?" Rodney's voice sounded affable. Zed took heart from this.

"That's exactly it, Rodney. That's what's so incredible. He's completely cured. He comes home, not to the fatted calf but—"

"The fatted what?"

Zed backpedaled swiftly. Biblical allusion. Obviously a very bad way to go. "Stupid remark, that. So he comes home and he starts a programme to help the unhelpable." Was that a word? Zed wondered. "And not who you'd expect him to help: young blokes and girls with their lives ahead of them. But rejects. Old blokes living rough, society's detritus—"

Rodney glanced his way.

Zed hurried on with, "Social rubbish getting its next meal from the inside of wheelie bins while they spit out their rotting teeth. He saves them. He thinks they're *worth* saving. And they respond. They're cured as well. A lifetime of booze and drugs and living rough and they're cured of it." Zed took a breath. He waited for Rodney's reply.

It came evenly enough but the tone was suggestive of a lack of enthusiasm for Zed's defence of his reportage. "They're rebuilding a bloody tower, Zed. Nobody's cured of anything and when the tower's finished the lot of them will go back to the street."

"I don't think so."

"Why?"

"Because it's a pele tower. And that's what gives the story its power. It's a metaphor." Zed knew the very idea of metaphor put him onto dangerous ground with the editor, so he madly rushed on. "Consider the use of the towers and you'll see how it works. They were built for protection against border reivers—those nasty blokes who invaded from Scotland, eh?—and, for our purposes, the border reivers represent drugs, okay? Meth. Coke. Hash. Smack. Blow. Whatever. The pele tower itself represents redemption and recovery, and each floor of the tower, which in the past contained something different, and by this I mean the ground floor was for animals and the first floor was for cooking and household activities and the second floor was for living and sleeping and then the roof was for fighting off the reivers by showering them with arrows and oh I don't know hot oil or something and when you look at all this and take it to mean what it *ought* to mean and *could* mean in the life of a person who's been on the street for what . . . ten or fifteen years? . . . then—"

Rodney's head dropped onto his desk. He waved Zed off.

Zed wasn't sure what to make of this. It looked like dismissal but he wasn't about to slink off with his tail between . . . God, another metaphor, he thought. He crashed on, saying, "It's what makes this story a cut above. It's what makes this story a Sunday piece. I see it in the magazine, four full pages with photos: the tower, the blokes rebuilding it, the befores and the afters, that sort of thing."

"It's a snore," Rodney said again. "Which, by the way, is another metaphor. And so is sex, which this story has none of."

"Sex," Zed repeated. "Well, the wife *is* glamorous, I suppose, but she didn't want the story to be about her or about their relationship. She said he's the one who—"

Rodney raised his head. "I don't mean sex as in sex, stupid. I mean sex as in *sex*." He snapped his fingers. "The sizzle, the tension, the make-the-reader-want-something, the restlessness, the urge, the rising excitement, the make-her-wet-and-make-him-hard only they don't know why they even feel that way. Am I being clear? Your story doesn't have it."

"But it's not meant to have it. It's meant to be uplifting, to give people hope."

"We're not in the bloody uplifting business and we sure as hell aren't in the business of hope. We're in the business of selling papers. And believe me, this pile of bushwa won't do it. We engage in a certain *type* of investigative reporting here. You told me you knew that when I interviewed you. Isn't that why you went to Cumbria? So *be* an investigative reporter. Investi-bloody-gate."

"I did."

"Bollocks. This is a lovefest. Someone up there seduced your pants off—"

"Absolutely no way."

"—and you soft-pedaled."

"Did not happen."

"So this"—again Rodney gestured with the story—"represents the hard stuff, eh? This is how you go for the story's big vein?"

"Well, I can see that . . . Not exactly, I suppose. But I mean, once one got to know the bloke—"

"One lost one's nerve. One investigated zippo."

This seemed a rather unfair conclusion, Zed thought. "So what you're saying is that an exposé of drug abuse, of a wasted life, of tormented parents who've tried everything to save their kid only to have him save himself . . . this bloke who was about to choke on the silver spoon, Rodney . . . that's not investigative? That's not sexy? The way you want it to be sexy?"

"The son of some Hooray Henry wastes himself on drugs." Rodney yawned dramatically. "This is something new? You want me to tick off the names of ten other useless bags of dog droppings doing the same thing? It won't take long."

Zed felt the fight drain out of him. All the time wasted, all the effort spent, all the interviews conducted, all—he had to admit it—the subtle plans to alter the direction of *The Source* and make it into a paper at least marginally worthwhile and thereby put his name in lights since, let's face it, the *Financial Times* wasn't hiring at the moment. All for nothing. It wasn't right. Zed considered his options and finally said, "Okay. I take your point. But what if I give it another go? What if I go up there and do some more digging?"

"About what, for God's sake?"

That was surely the question. Zed thought about all the individuals he'd spoken to: the reformed addict, his wife, his mother, his sisters, his father, the poor sots he was saving. Was there someone somewhere doing something he'd missed? Well, there had to be, for the simple reason that there always was. "I'm not sure," Zed settled on saying. "But if I nose around . . . Everyone's got secrets. Everyone lies about something. And consider how much we've already spent on the story. It won't be such a waste if I give it another try."

Rodney pushed his chair back from his desk and seemed to roll Zed's offer round in his head. He jabbed a finger onto a button on his phone and barked to his secretary, "Wallace. You there?" and when she responded, "Get me another

Cadbury. Hazelnut again." And then to Zed, "Your time, your dime. And that's the only way I'm going for it."

Zed blinked. That put things in an entirely different light. He was on the bottom rung of the ladder at *The Source* and so were his wages. He tried to do the maths on a train ticket, a hired car, a hotel—perhaps a down-at-heel B & B or some old lady letting out rooms on a backstreet in . . . where? Not by one of the lakes. That would cost too much, even at this time of year, so it would have to be . . . And would he be paid for the time he spent in Cumbria? He doubted it. He said, "C'n I have a think on it? I mean, you won't spike the story straightaway, right? I have to look at my funds, if you know what I mean."

"Look all you want." Rodney smiled, a strange and unnatural stretching of his lips that spoke of how seldom he used them in this manner. "Like I said, your time, your dime."

"Thanks, Rodney." Zed wasn't quite sure what he was thanking the other man for, so he nodded, got to his feet, and headed for the door. As he reached for the knob, Rodney added in a friendly tone, "If you decide to make the trip, I suggest you lose the beanie."

Zed hesitated but before he could speak, Rodney continued. "It's not a religion thing, kid. I could give a bloody crap about your religion or anyone else's. This is a recommendation coming from a bloke who's been in the business since you were in nappies. You can do it or not, but the way I see it, you don't want anything to distract people or give them a reason to think you're anything but their confessor, best friend, shoulder to cry on, psychowhosis, or whatever. So when you show up in anything takes their attention away from the story they want to tell—or better yet and for our purposes *don't* want to tell—you've got a problem. And I mean any of it: turbans, rosary beads swinging from your neck, beanies, full-length beards dyed in henna, daggers at the waist. Are you with me? My point is that an investigative reporter blends in and with the beanie . . . Look, there's nothing you can do about the height and the hair—unless you colour the hair, and I'm not asking you to do that—but the beanie takes it over the top."

As if in reflex Zed touched his yarmulke. "I wear it because—"

"Don't care why you wear it. Don't care *if* you wear it. It's a word from the wise, is all. Your choice."

Zed knew the editor was saying this last bit to avoid a lawsuit. Indeed, he knew the editor had phrased everything he'd said about the yarmulke for the very same reason. *The Source* was not exactly a bastion of political correctness, but that was not the point. Rodney Aronson knew which side of his professional bread bore the butter.

"Just take it on board," Rodney told him as the office door opened and his secretary entered, bearing a family-size chocolate bar.

"Will do," Zed said. "Absolutely."

ST. JOHN'S WOOD
LONDON

Time was of the essence, so he left at once. He planned to take the Tube and switch to the bus at Baker Street. A taxi all the way to St. John's Wood would have been better—with the added benefit of giving him legroom—but he could ill afford it. So he hoofed it down to Blackfriars Station, waited interminably for a Circle Line train, and when it arrived crammed to the gills, he was forced to ride next to the carriage doors where the only way to fit inside was to hunch his shoulders and rest his chin on his chest in the manner of a penitent.

With a crick in his neck, he stopped at a cashpoint before catching the bus for the final leg of his journey. His purpose was to check his bank account in the vain hope that he'd somehow miscalculated the last time he'd balanced his chequebook. He had no savings other than what was contained in that single account. He saw the amount and felt his spirits sink. A trip to Cumbria would clean him out, and he had to think, was it worth it? It was, after all, only a story. Give it up and he'd merely be assigned another. But there were stories and there were stories, and this one . . . He knew it was something special.

Undecided still, he arrived home ninety minutes earlier than usual, and because of this he rang the bell at the building's entrance to announce himself so his mother didn't panic when she heard a key in the lock at a time of day when no one was due at the flat. He said, "It's me, Mum," and she said, "Zede*ki*ah! Wonder*ful!*" which rather puzzled him until he got inside and saw the source of his mother's delight.

Susanna Benjamin was in the midst of finishing up a modest afternoon tea, but she wasn't alone. A young woman sat in the most comfortable chair in the lounge—the chair Zed's mother always reserved for guests—and she blushed prettily and dropped her head for a moment as Zed's mother made the introductions. She was called Yaffa Shaw, and according to Susanna Benjamin, she had membership in the same book discussion group as Zed's mother, who proclaimed this a marvelous coincidence for some reason. Zed waited for more and soon was given it in the form of "I was telling Yaffa only just now that my Zedekiah *always* has his nose in a book. And not only one but four or five at once. Tell Yaffa what you're reading now, Zed. Yaffa is reading the new Graham Swift. Well, we're *all* reading the new Graham Swift. For the book group, Zed. Sit, sit, darling. Have a cup of tea. Oh my goodness, it's cold. I'll get some fresh, shall I?"

Before Zed could manage an answer to this, his mother was gone. He heard her in the kitchen banging about. She turned on the radio for good measure. He knew it would take her a deliberate quarter of an hour to produce the tea because he and his mother had been through this before. The last time it had been the girl working on the till at Tesco. The time before that, and a far better bet, the oldest niece of their rabbi, in London to attend a summer course offered by an American university whose name Zed could not remember. After Yaffa, who was watching him doubtless in hope of conversation, there would be another. This would not cease till he'd married one of them and then the prodding for grandchildren would begin. Not for the first time Zed cursed his older sister, her professional life, and her decision not only not to reproduce but also not to marry.

She had the career in science that had been intended for him. Not that he'd wanted a career in science but if she'd only cooperated and given their mother a son-in-law and grandchildren, he wouldn't be coming home time and again to yet another potential mate lured onto the premises through one pretext or another.

He said to Yaffa, "You and Mum . . . the same book discussion group, is it?"

She blushed more deeply. "Not exactly," she admitted. "I work in the bookshop. I make recommendations to the group. Your mum and I . . . we were talking . . . I mean, the way people do, you know."

Oh, how he knew. And above all the things he knew was the fact that he knew exactly how Susanna Benjamin operated. He could picture the conversation: the sly questions and the trusting replies. He wondered how old the poor girl was and whether his mother had managed to work her fertility into the equation.

He said, "I wager you didn't expect to find she even had a son."

"She didn't say. Only now things're a bit difficult because—"

"Zed, darling," his mother sang out from the kitchen. "Darjeeling's fine? Tea cake as well? What about a scone, dear? Yaffa, you'll have more tea, yes? You young people will want to chat, I know."

That was exactly what Zed didn't want. What he wanted was time to think and to weigh the pros and cons of going into debt to take himself up to Cumbria for the time needed to sex up his story. And when in Cumbria, if he actually went there, he was going to have to determine exactly what constituted the sex: the zing, the snap, the whatever it was supposed to be to excite the readers of *The Source,* who, it was highly probable, had the collective intelligence of gravestones. How to excite a gravestone? Give it a corpse. Zed chuckled inwardly at the extended metaphor. He was only glad he hadn't used it in conversation with Rodney Aronson.

"Here we are, my dears!" Susanna Benjamin rejoined them, bearing a tray of fresh tea, scones, butter, and jam.

"My Zedekiah's a big boy, isn't he, Yaffa? I don't know where he got his height. What is it, exactly, dear heart?" This last to Zed. He was six feet eight inches tall and his mother knew that as well as she knew where the height came from, which was his paternal grandfather, who'd been only three inches shorter. When he didn't reply, she went blithely on with, "And what feet he has. Look at those feet, Yaffa. And hands the size of rugby balls. And you know what they say . . ." She winked. "Milk and sugar, Zedekiah? You want both, yes?" And to Yaffa, "Two years on the kibbutz, he was, this son of mine. Then two years in the army."

"Mum," Zed said.

"Oh, don't be so bashful." She poured more tea into Yaffa's cup. "The *Israeli* army, Yaffa. What do you think of that? He likes to hide everything. Such a humble boy. He's always been that way. Yaffa's like that, too, Zedekiah. Every bit of information must be dragged out of the girl. Born in Tel Aviv, father a surgeon, two brothers working in cancer research, mother a clothing designer, my boy. Clothing designer! Isn't that wonderful? Of course, I couldn't afford a single thing she designs because her clothes are sold in . . . What did you call them, Yaffa dear?"

"Boutiques," Yaffa said, although she'd gone so red in the face that Zed feared a stroke or seizure was in the offing.

"Knightsbridge, Zed," his mother intoned. "Just think of it. She designs all the way in Israel, and the clothing comes *here*."

Zed sought a way to interrupt the flow, so he said to Yaffa, "What brought you to London?"

"Studies!" Susanna Benjamin replied. "She's going to university here. Science, Zedekiah. Biology."

"Chemistry," Yaffa said.

"Chemistry, biology, geology . . . it's all the same because think of the brain in this sweet head of hers, Zed. And isn't she pretty? Have you ever seen a prettier little thing than our Yaffa sitting here?"

"Not recently," Zed said with a meaningful look at his mother. He added, "It's been at least six weeks," in the hope that the sheer embarrassment of having her intentions brought out into the open would force her to wind down.

That was not to be. Susanna added, "He likes to make fun of his mother, Yaffa. He's a tease, my Zedekiah. You'll get used to that."

Used to that? Zed cast a look at Yaffa, who was shifting uneasily in her chair. This told him there was more to be revealed and his mother revealed it forthwith.

"Yaffa's taking your sister's old bedroom," Susanna said to her son. "She's come to look at it and she's said it's just what she needs now she's having to move from her other lodgings. Won't it be lovely to have another young face in the flat? She'll be joining us tomorrow. And you must tell me what you like for breakfast, Yaffa. Starting the day out with a proper meal is going to help you with your studies. It did for Zedekiah, didn't it, Zed? First-class degree in literature, my son. Did I tell you he writes poetry, Yaffa? Something tells me he's likely to write a poem about you."

Zed stood abruptly. He'd forgotten he had his teacup in hand, and the Darjeeling sloshed out. Thankfully, most of it went onto his shoes, saving his mother's carpet. But he would have liked to dump it onto her neatly coifed grey head.

His final decision was as instantaneous as it was necessary. He said, "I'm off to Cumbria, Mum."

She blinked. "Cumbria? But didn't you just—"

"More to the story and I've got to go after it. Very time-sensitive as things turn out."

"But when are you leaving?"

"Soon as I pack my bag."

Which, he decided, ought to take him five minutes or less.

EN ROUTE TO
CUMBRIA

The fact that he wanted and needed to leave posthaste before his mother built the chuppah right in the lounge forced Zed to catch a train that would get him to Cumbria by a most circuitous route. That couldn't be helped. Once he packed his bag and tucked his laptop into its case, he was gone, effectuating a very clean getaway. The bus; the Tube; Euston Station; slapping down a credit card to pay for his ticket, four sandwiches, a copy of *The Economist*, *The Times*, and the *Guardian*; wondering how long it was going to take him to find something—anything—to sex up his story; wondering even more how long it was going to take him to break his mother of bringing women in off the street like his procurer . . . By the time he was able to board the train, he was ready for the distraction of work. He opened up his laptop and as the train left the station, he began to search through his notes, which he'd meticulously recorded during every interview, which he'd meticulously typed into the laptop every night. He also had with him a set of hand-written notes. He would check those as well. For there had to be something, and he *would* find it.

He reviewed the subject of his story first: Nicholas Fair-clough, thirty-two years old, the formerly dissolute son of Bernard Fairclough, first Baron of Ireleth in the county of Cumbria. Born into wealth and privilege—there was that silver spoon—he'd squandered throughout his youth the good fortune that he'd been handed by Fate. He was a man graced with the face of an angel but in possession of the inclinations of Lot's next-door neighbour. A series of reha-bilitation programmes had seen him as an unwilling par-ticipant from his fourteenth year onwards. They read like a travelogue as progressively more exotic—and remote—locations were chosen by his parents in an attempt to entice him into healthy living. When he wasn't taking the cure somewhere, he was using his father's money to travel in a life-owes-me-a-living style that led him time and again directly back into addiction. Everyone threw in the towel on the bloke, after wiping their washed hands upon it. Father, mother, sisters, even a cousin cum brother had—

Now *that* was something he hadn't thought about, Zed realised. The cousin-cum-brother angle. It had seemed a nonstory, and Nicholas himself had certainly emphasized that during interviews, but there was a chance that Zed might have missed something he could now use . . . He flipped through his notebook first and found the name: Ian

Cresswell, employed by Fairclough Industries in a position
of some quite serious responsibility, first cousin to Nicholas,
eight years older, born in Kenya but come to England in
late childhood to be a resident in the Fairclough home . . .
Now that was something, wasn't it, something that could be
moulded somehow?

Zed looked up thoughtfully. He glanced at the window.
It was pitch-dark outside, so all he saw was his own reflection: a redheaded giant with worry lines becoming incised
on his forehead because his mother was attempting to
marry him off to the first willing woman she was able to
find and his boss was ready to deposit his well-written prose
into the rubbish and he himself just wanted to write something marginally worthwhile. And so, what did he have in
these notes? he asked himself. What? *What?*

Zed fished out one of his four sandwiches and began to
devour it as he checked his paperwork. He was looking for
a clue, for the way he could spin his story, or at least for a
hint that further digging in one area or another might produce the sizzle that Rodney Aronson said was required.
The cousins-as-brothers angle *was* possible. Reading, however, Zed found that his thoughts were dominated by Old
Testament tales, which took him into the land of biblical
allusion and metaphor, where he could ill afford to wander.
But if the truth were told, it *was* difficult to read what he'd
uncovered in his interviews with all the principal characters
without thinking of Cain and Abel, my brother's keeper,
burnt offerings of the fruits of one's labour, and being pleasing or not-so-pleasing to whoever was standing in place of
God in the story, which would probably be Lord Fairclough,
Baron of Ireleth. And if one *truly* wanted to be biblical
about things, the Peer could be Isaac, faced with Esau and
Jacob and their battling birthrights to contend with,
although how anyone on earth could have mistaken the skin
of a dead lamb—or whatever it had been—for hairy arms
had always been way, *way* beyond Zed's willingness to
believe. The whole idea of birthrights, however, drove Zed
deeper into his notes to see if he had any information about
who actually stood to inherit what, should something
untoward happen to Lord Fairclough, in addition to who

stood to run Fairclough Industries should the baron meet an untimely end.

Now *that* would be a story, wouldn't it? Bernard Fairclough mysteriously . . . what? Dies or disappears, let's say. He falls down the stairs, becomes incapacitated, has a stroke, or whatever. A little digging turns over the fact that days before his untimely end or whatever it was, he's met with his solicitor and . . . what? A new will is drawn up, his intentions as to the family business are made crystal clear, lifetime settlements are made, language is inserted into his will, his trust, his papers, as to—what would it be?—an indication of an inheritance, a declaration of someone's disinheritance, a revelation of . . . what? The son is not his actual son. The nephew is not his actual nephew. There's a second family in the Hebrides, there's a mad and deformed elder sibling long hidden in the attic, the cellar, the boathouse. There's something explosive. Something *kapow*. Something sexy.

Of course, the problem was that, if Zed wanted to admit the *entire* truth of the matter, the only remotely sexy thing about his story of Nicholas Fairclough's ninth life was the man's wife, and she was sexy in spades. He hadn't wanted to make too much of that fact in his meeting with Rodney Aronson because he'd been fairly certain of Rodney's reaction, which would have come from the photograph-her-tits school of thought. Zed had kept fairly mum on the topic of the wife because she'd wished to remain in the background, but now he wondered if there was something about her that he might explore. He went to that set of notes and saw that words like *caramba* and *yikes* had indicated his initial reaction upon laying his eyes on her. He'd even nonsensically written *South American Siren* by way of describing her, every inch of her a w-o-m-a-n demanding notice from an m-a-n. If Eve had looked remotely like Alatea Fairclough, Zedekiah would have concluded at the end of their only interview, it was no wonder Adam took the apple. The only question was why he hadn't eaten the whole damn crop and the tree as well. So . . . Was *she* the story? The sex? The sizzle? She was stunning in all the right ways, but how did one turn stunning into story? "She's the reason I'm alive today," says the husband, but so what? Run a picture of her and any bloke whose parts are in working order is going to know why Nicholas Fairclough took the cure. Besides, she had nothing to say beyond "What Nick's done, he's done himself. I'm his wife but I'm not important in his real story."

Had that been a hint? Zed wondered. His *real* story. Was there more to uncover? He thought he'd dug, but perhaps he'd been too smitten with the subject of his piece. And perhaps he'd been too smitten with his subject because he wanted to believe such things were possible: redemption, salvation, turning one's life around, finding true love . . .

Perhaps that was the line to follow: true love. Had Nicholas Fairclough really found it? And if he had, did someone envy it? One of his sisters, perhaps, because one of them was unmarried and the other divorced? And how did they feel anyway, now that the prodigal had returned?

Further rustling through his notes. Further reading. Another sandwich. A wander through the train to see if there was a buffet car—what a ludicrous thought in these days of marginal profits—because he was dying for a coffee. Then it was back to his seat, where he finally gave up the ghost altogether and then popped back up with the idea of ghosts because the family home was what had got him started in the first place on this piece, and what if the family home was haunted and the haunting had led to the drug addiction, which had led to the search for a cure, which had led to . . . He was back to the bloody wife again, the South American siren, and the only reason he was back to her was *caramba* and *yikes*, and he'd be better off crawling back home and forgetting this whole damn thing except home meant his mother and Yaffa Shaw and whoever was going to follow Yaffa Shaw in a never-ending procession of women he was meant to marry and get children on.

No. There was a story here somewhere, the kind of story that his editor wanted. If he had to dig further to find something juicy, he'd get out his shovel and aim for China. Anything else was unacceptable. Failure was not an option.

18 OCTOBER

BRYANBARROW
CUMBRIA

Ian Cresswell was setting the table for two when his partner arrived home. He himself had taken off early from work, a romantic evening in mind. He'd bought lamb, which was in the oven with a fragrant blanket of seasoned bread crumbs browning over the shoulder of it, and he'd prepared fresh vegetables and a salad. In the fire house, he'd uncorked wine, polished glasses, and moved before the fireplace two chairs and the old oak game table from one corner of the room. It wasn't quite cold enough for a coal fire although the ancient manor house was always rather chilly, so he lit a bank of candles and fixed them to the cast iron grate; then he lit two more and placed them on the table. As he did so, he heard the kitchen door open, followed by the sound of Kav's keys being tossed into the chipped chamber pot on the window seat. A moment later Kav's footsteps crossed the kitchen flagstones, and the squeak of the old range's door caused Ian to smile. It was Kav's night to cook, not his, and Kav had just discovered the first surprise.

"Ian?" More footsteps across the slate flagstones and then into and across the hallan. Ian had left the door to the fire house open, and he said, "In here," and waited.

Kav paused at the doorway. His gaze went from Ian to

the table with its candles to the fireplace with *its* candles to Ian again. His gaze went then from Ian's face to Ian's clothes and it lingered exactly where Ian wanted it to linger. But after a moment of the kind of tension that, at one time, would have sent the two of them directly to the bedroom, Kav said, "I had to work with the blokes today. We were shorthanded. I'm filthy. I'll have a wash and get changed," and backed out of the room without another word. This was enough to tell Ian that his lover knew what the scene before him presaged. This was also enough to tell Ian what direction their coming conversation was, as usual, going to take. An unspoken message of this kind from Kaveh would at one time have been enough to stymie him, but Ian decided that wouldn't be the case tonight. Three years of concealment and one year in the open had taught him the value of living as he was meant to live.

It was thirty minutes before Kaveh rejoined him, and despite the fact that the meat was ten minutes out of the oven and the vegetables were well on their way to becoming a culinary disappointment, Ian was determined not to feel affronted by the time it had taken the other man to return. He poured the wine—forty quid for the bottle, not that it mattered, considering the occasion—and he nodded to the two glasses. He picked his own up, said, "It's a good Bordeaux," and waited for Kav to join him for a toast. For clearly, Ian thought, Kaveh saw that a toast was Ian's intention, else why would he be standing there with his glass lifted and an expectant smile on his face?

For a second time, Kav's gaze took in the table. He said, "Two places? Did she ring you or something?"

"I rang her." Ian lowered his glass.

"And what?"

"I asked for another night."

"And she actually cooperated?"

"For once. Aren't you having some wine, Kav? I got it in Windermere. That wine shop we were in last—"

"I had words with bloody old George." Kav inclined his head in the direction of the road. "He caught me on the way in. He's complaining about the heating again. He said he's entitled to central heating. *Entitled* he said."

"He's got plenty of coal. Why's he not using it if the cottage is too cold?"

"He says he doesn't want a coal fire. He wants central heating. He says if he doesn't have it, he's looking for another situation."

"When he lived here, he didn't have central heating, for God's sake."

"He had the house itself. I think he saw that as compensation."

"Well, he's going to have to learn to cope, and if he can't do that, he'll have to find another farm to rent. Anyway, I don't want to spend this evening talking about George Cowley's grievances against us. The farm was for sale. We bought it. He didn't. Full stop."

"*You* bought it."

"A technicality soon to be taken care of, I hope, when there'll be no I. No yours and mine. No me, no you. Only we." Ian took up the second glass and carried it to Kav. Kav hesitated for a moment. Then he accepted it. "Jesus God, I want you," Ian said. And then with a smile, "Want to feel how much?"

"Hmmm. No. Let's let it build."

"Bastard."

"I thought that's how you like it, Ian."

"First time you've smiled since you walked in the door. Tough day?"

"Not really," Kav said. "Just a lot of work and not enough help. You?"

"No." They both drank then, eyes on each other. Kav smiled again. Ian moved towards him. Kav moved away. He tried to make it look as if his attention had been caught by the gleam of cutlery or the low bowl of flowers on the table, but Ian wasn't deceived. What he thought in reaction was what any man would think when he's twelve years older than his lover and he's given up everything to be with him.

At twenty-eight there would be any number of reasons Kaveh could give in explanation of why he wasn't ready to settle down. Ian wasn't prepared to hear them, however, because he knew there was only one that served as the truth. This truth was a form of hypocrisy, and the presence of hypocrisy was central to every argument they'd had in the last year.

"Know what today is?" Ian asked, raising his glass again.

Kav nodded but he looked chagrined. "Day we met. I'd forgotten. Too much going on up at Ireleth Hall, I think. But then—" He indicated the table. Ian knew he meant not only the setup but also the trouble he'd gone to with the dinner. "When I saw this, it came to me. And I feel like a bloody wretch, Ian. I've nothing for you."

"Ah. No matter," Ian told him. "What I want is right here and it's yours to give."

"You've already got it, haven't you?"

"You know what I mean."

Kaveh walked to the window and flicked the heavy closed curtains open a crack as if to check where the daylight had gone to, but Ian knew that he was trying to work out what it was he wanted to say and the thought that he might want to say what Ian didn't want to hear caused his head to begin its telltale throbbing and a flash of bright stars to course across his vision. He blinked hard as Kaveh spoke.

"Signing a book in a registry office doesn't make us any more official than we already are."

"That's bollocks," Ian said. "It makes us more than official. It makes us legal. It gives us standing in the community and, what's more important, it tells the world—"

"We don't need standing. We already have it as individuals."

"—and what's more important," Ian repeated, "it tells the world—"

"Well, that's just it, isn't it?" Kaveh said sharply. "The world, Ian. Think about it. The world. And everyone in it."

Carefully, Ian set his wineglass on the table. He knew he should get the meat and carve it, get the veg and serve them, sit, eat, and let the rest go. Go upstairs afterwards and have each other properly. But on this night of all nights, he couldn't bring himself to do anything more but say what he'd already said to his partner more than a dozen times and what he'd sworn he wouldn't say tonight: "You asked me to come out and I did. For you. Not for myself, because it didn't matter to me and even if it had, there were too many people involved and what I did—for you—was as good as stabbing them through their throats. And that was fine by me because it was what you wanted, and I finally realised—"

"I *know* all this."

"Three years is long enough to hide, you said. You said, 'Tonight you decide.' In *front* of them you said it, Kav, and in front of them I decided. Then I walked out. With you. Have you *any* idea—"

"Of course I do. D'you think I'm a stone? I *have* a bloody idea, Ian. But we're not talking about just living together, are we? We're talking about marriage. *And* we're talking about my *parents*."

"People adjust," Ian said. "That's what you told me."

"People. Yes. Other people. They adjust. But not them. We've been through this before. In my culture—*their* culture—"

"You're part of this culture now. All of you."

"That's not how it works. One doesn't just flee to a foreign country, take some magic pill one night, and wake up the next morning with an entirely different system of values. It doesn't happen that way. And as the only son—the only child, for God's sake—I have . . . Oh Christ, Ian, you *know* all this. Why can't you be happy with what we have? With how things are?"

"Because how things are is a lie. You're not my lodger. I'm not your landlord. D'you actually think they'll believe that forever?"

"They believe what I tell them," he said. "I live here. They live there. This works and it will continue to work. Anything else, and they won't understand. They don't need to know."

"So that they can do what? Keep presenting you with suitable Iranian teenagers to marry? Fresh off the boat or the plane or whatever and eager to give your parents grandbabies?"

"That's not going to happen."

"It's happening already. How many have they arranged for you to meet so far? A dozen? More? And at what point do you just cave in and marry because you can't take the pressure from them any longer and you start to feel your duty too much and *then* what do you expect to have? One life here and another in Manchester, her down there— whoever she is—waiting for the babies and me up here and . . . goddamn it, *look* at me." Ian wanted to kick the table over, sending the crockery flying and the cutlery spinning across the floor. Something was building within him, and he knew an explosion was on its way. He headed for the door, for the hallan that would take him to the kitchen and from there outside.

Kaveh's voice was sharper when he said, "Where're you going?"

"Out. The lake. Wherever. I don't know. I just need to get out."

"Come on, Ian. Don't be this way. What we have—"

"What we have is nothing."

"That isn't true. Come back and I'll show you."

But Ian knew where *showing you* would lead, which was where *showing you* always led, which was to a place having nothing to do with the change he sought. He left the house without looking back.

EN ROUTE TO BRYANBARROW
CUMBRIA

Tim Cresswell slouched in the backseat of the Volvo. He tried to close his ears to the sound of his little sister begging their mother once again to let them live with her. "Please please extra pretty please, Mummy" was the way she put it. She was, Tim knew, trying to charm their mother into thinking she was actually missing something without her children in constant attendance. Not that anything Gracie might say or the way she might say it would do any good. Niamh Cresswell had no intention of allowing them to live with her in Grange-over-Sands. She had fish to fry that had nothing to do with any responsibility she might feel towards her offspring. Tim wanted to tell Gracie this, but what was the point? She was ten years old and too young to understand the workings of pride, loathing, and revenge.

"I *hate* Daddy's house," Gracie was adding in hopeful good measure. "There're spiders *every*where. It's dark and creaky and full of draughts and it's got all these corners where there're cobwebs and things. I want to live with you, Mummy. Timmy does 's well." She squirmed round in her seat. "*You* want to live with Mummy 's well, don't you, Timmy?"

Don't call me Timmy, you stupid twit, was what Tim actually wanted to say to his sister, but he couldn't ever get mad at Gracie when she looked at him with that expression of trusting love on her face. When he saw it, though, he wanted to tell her to harden up. The world was a shit hole, and he couldn't understand why she hadn't yet worked that out.

Tim saw that his mother was watching him in the rear-view mirror, waiting to hear how he would answer his sister. He curled his lip and turned to the window, thinking that he could almost not blame his father for dropping the bomb that had destroyed their lives. His mother was a real piece of work, she was.

The bloody cow was acting true to character, even now, all pretence about why they were heading back to Bryan Beck farm. What she didn't know was that he'd picked up the phone in the kitchen the exact same moment she'd taken up the phone in her bedroom, so he'd heard it all: his father's voice asking would she mind keeping the kids another night and his mother's voice agreeing to do so. Pleasantly agreeing, for once, which should have told his father something was up, because it certainly told Tim as much. So he was unsurprised when his mother came out of the bedroom less than ten minutes later dressed to the nines and breezily told him to pack up because his father had phoned and he and Gracie had to go back to the farm earlier that evening than usual.

"Something nice he has planned for you," she said. "He didn't say what. So get yourselves together. Be quick about it."

She went on to search for her car keys, which Tim realised she'd pinched. Not for his own sake, but for Gracie's. She damn well deserved another night with their mother if that's what she wanted.

She was saying, "See, there's not even enough hot water for a proper bath, Mummy. And the water *trick*les out and it's brown and disgusting. Not like your house where I c'n have bubbles. I do so like bubbles. Mummy, why can't we live with *you*?"

"You know very well," Niamh Cresswell finally said.

"No, I don't," countered Gracie. "Most kids live with their *mums* when their parents get divorced. They live with their mums and they *visit* their dads. And you got bedrooms for us anyways."

"Gracie, if you want so much to have all the details about the situation, you can ask your father why it's different for you two."

Oh right, Tim thought. Like Dad was actually going to give Gracie the facts on why they lived on some creeped-out farm in some creeped-out house on the edge of a creeped-out village where there was nothing to do on a Saturday night or a Sunday afternoon but smell the cow shit, listen to the sheep, or—and this would be if one was *truly* lucky—chase the village ducks from their stupid duck house and their holding pen into the stream across the lane. Bryanbarrow was the end of nowhere, but it was just perfect for their father's new life. And about that life . . . Gracie didn't understand. She wasn't meant to. She was meant to think that they took in lodgers, only there was only *one*, Gracie, and after you go to bed where do you think he really sleeps and in what bed exactly and what do you think they do there when the door is closed?

Tim tore at the back of his hand. He dug in his nails till he broke the skin and felt tiny crescents of blood bubbles form. His face was a blank, he knew, because he'd perfected that expression of absolutely nothing going on in his head. That and the hands and the damage he could do to them and his overall appearance kept him where he wanted to be, which was far away from other people and far away from everything else. His efforts had succeeded, even, in getting him out of the local comprehensive. Now he attended a special school near Ulverston, which was miles and miles and miles from his father's house—all the better to cause a mind-boggling inconvenience to him every day, naturally—

and miles upon miles from his mother's house and that was
the way he wanted it because there, near Ulverston, no one
knew the truth of what had happened in his life and he
needed it that way.

Tim watched the passing scenery, silent. The drive from
Grange-over-Sands to his father's farm spun them north in
the fading daylight, up through the Lyth Valley. There the
landscape was patchwork: paddocks and pastures that were
the green of shamrocks and emeralds and that, like a wave,
rolled into the distance to swell up to the fells. On these, great
outcroppings of slate and limestone burst forth, with grey
scree fanning out beneath them. Between the pastures and
the fells stood groups of woodland, alders that were yellow
with the autumn and oaks and maples that were gold and
red. And here and there erupted buildings that marked the
farms: great hulking stone barns and slate-fronted houses
with chimneys from which wood smoke curled.

Some miles along, the landscape altered as the wide Lyth
Valley began to close in. With that closure came the advent
of woods, and the leaves from their trees banked the road,
which began to wind between drystone walls. It had started
to rain now, but when *didn't* it rain in this part of the world?
This part of the world was *known* for its rain, and the result
was moss thickly growing on the stones of the walls, ferns
shoving themselves out of crevices, and lichens underfoot
and on the bark of the trees.

"It's raining," Gracie said unnecessarily. "I hate that old
house when it rains, Mummy. Don't you, Timmy? It's horrible there, all dark and damp and creepy and *horrible*."

No one replied. Gracie dropped her head. Their mother
made the turn into the lane that would take them up to
Bryanbarrow, quite as if Gracie had not spoken at all.

The road here was narrow, and it proceeded upwards in
a series of hairpin bends that carved a route through woodland of birch and chestnut trees. They passed Lower Beck
farm and a disused field that was thick with bracken; they
coursed along Bryan Beck itself, crossed it twice, climbed
a bit more, and finally swung into the approach to the village, which lay below them, nothing much more than the
juncture of four lanes giving onto a green. That it had a

public house, a primary school, a village hall, a Methodist chapel, and a C of E church made it a gathering place of sorts. But only on evenings and Sunday mornings, and even then those gathered in the village either drank or prayed.

Gracie began to cry as they crept over the stone bridge. She said, "Mummy, I *hate* it here. Mummy. Please."

But her mother said nothing, and Tim knew she wouldn't. There were certainly feelings to consider in this matter of where Tim and Gracie Cresswell would live, but the feelings were not those of Tim and Gracie Cresswell. That was the way it was and the way it would be, at least till Niamh gave up the ghost or finally just gave up, whichever came first. And Tim wondered about this last, he did. It seemed that hate could kill a person, although when he thought about it, hate hadn't yet killed him so perhaps it wouldn't kill his mother either.

Unlike so many farms in Cumbria, which maintained a distance from villages and hamlets, Bryan Beck farm sat just at the edge of the village, and it comprised an ancient Elizabethan manor house, an equally ancient barn, and an even more ancient cottage. Beyond these the farm's pastures opened up, and in these grazed sheep, although they were not the property of Tim's father but rather belonged to a farmer who rented the land from him. They lent the farm "an authentic look," Tim's father liked to say, and were in keeping with "the tradition of the Lakes," whatever that was supposed to mean. Ian Cresswell was no bloody farmer and as far as Tim was personally concerned, the stupid sheep were a great deal safer with his father keeping his distance from them.

By the time Niamh had pulled the Volvo into the drive, Gracie was in full blub mode. She seemed to think if she sobbed loud enough, their mother would turn the car around and take them back to Grange-over-Sands instead of what she had planned, which was to give them the boot just to mind-fuck their father and then dash off to Milnthorpe to body-fuck her poor twit of a boyfriend in the kitchen of his stupid Chinese takeaway.

"Mummy! Mummy!" Gracie was crying. "His car's not even *here*. I'm scared to go inside if his car's not here 'cause he's not home and—"

"Grace, stop it this instant," Niamh snapped. "You're acting like a two-year-old. He's gone to the shops, that's all. There're lights on in the house and the other car's here. I expect you can work out what that means."

She wouldn't say the name, naturally. She might have added, "Your father's *lodger* is at home," with that nasty emphasis that communicated volumes. But that would be to acknowledge Kaveh Mehran's existence, which she had no intention of doing. She did say, "Timothy," meaningfully, and inclined her head towards the house. This meant he was to drag Gracie from the car and march her through the garden gate to the door because Niamh didn't intend to do it.

He shoved his door open. He tossed his rucksack over the low stone wall and then jerked open his sister's door. He said, "Out," and grabbed her arm.

She shrieked, "No!" and "I won't!" and began to kick.

Niamh unfastened Gracie's safety belt and said, "Stop making a scene. The whole village will think I'm killing you."

"I don't care! I don't care!" Gracie sobbed. "I want to go with you, Mummy!"

"Oh, for the love of God." Then Niamh was out of the car as well, but not to help Tim manage his sister. Instead, she grabbed up Gracie's rucksack, opened it, and threw it over the wall. It landed—this was a mercy at least—on Gracie's trampoline, where its contents spilled out into the rain. Among those contents was Gracie's favourite doll, not one of those hideously misshapen fantasy women with feet in the wear-high-heels position and nippleless tits at attention but a baby doll so scarily realistic that to toss it out to land on its head in the middle of a trampoline should have been considered child abuse.

At this Gracie screamed. Tim shot his mother a look. Niamh said, "What did you expect me to do?" And then to Gracie, "If you don't want it ruined, I suggest you fetch it."

Gracie was out of the car in a flash. She was into the garden and up onto the trampoline and cradling her doll, still weeping, only now her tears mixed with the falling rain. Tim said to his mother, "Nice one, that."

She said, "Talk to your father about it."

That was, of course, her answer to everything. Talk to your father, as if he, who he was, and what he'd done comprised the excuse for every rotten thing Niamh Cresswell did.

Tim slammed the door and turned away. He went into the garden while behind him he heard the Volvo take off, bearing his mother to wherever because he didn't much care. She could fuck whatever loser she wanted to fuck, as far as he was concerned.

In front of him, Gracie sat howling on her trampoline. Had it not been raining, she would have jumped upon it, wearing herself out, because that's what she did and she did it every day, just as what he did was what he did and he did it every day as well.

He scooped up his rucksack and watched her for a moment. Pain in the arse, she was, but she didn't deserve what she'd been handed. He went over to the trampoline and reached for her rucksack. "Gracie," he said, "let's go inside."

"I'm not," she said. "I'm not, I'm not." She clutched her doll to her bosom, which caused a little tear in Tim's own chest.

He couldn't remember the doll's name. He said, "Look, I'll check for spiders, Gracie, and I'll get rid of cobwebs. You can put . . . whatsername . . . in her cot—"

"Bella. She's called Bella," Gracie sniffed.

"All right. Bella-she's-called-Bella. You can put Bella-she's-called-Bella in her cot and I'll . . . I'll brush your hair. Okay? The way you like it. I'll do it up the way you like it."

Gracie looked at him. She rubbed her arm over her eyes. Her hair, which was a source of unending pride for her, was getting wet and soon enough it would be frizzy and unbrushable. She fingered a long and luxurious lock of it. She said, "French braids?" so hopefully that he couldn't deny her.

He sighed. "All right. French braids. But you got to come now, or I won't."

"'Kay." She scooted to the edge of the trampoline and handed him Bella-she's-called-Bella. He stowed the doll headfirst into Gracie's rucksack and carried this along with his to the house. Gracie followed, scuffling her feet in the gravel on the garden path.

Everything changed when they got inside, though. They went in through the kitchen at the east side of the house, where a roast of some kind stood on the top of the primitive range in the fireplace, its juices congealing in the pan beneath it. A pot next to this pan held sprouts gone cold. A salad was wilting on the draining board. Tim and Gracie hadn't had their dinner, but by the look of things here, neither had their father.

"Ian?"

Tim felt his insides harden at the sound of Kaveh Mehran's voice. Cautious, it was. A little tense?

Tim said roughly, "No. It's us."

A pause. Then, "Timothy? Gracie?" as if it might actually be someone else mimicking his voice, Tim thought. There was noise from the fire house, something being dragged across the flagstones and onto the carpet, a bleak "What a mess," and Tim experienced a wonderful moment in which he understood they'd probably had a fight—his dad and Kaveh going after each other's jugular with blood everywhere and wouldn't *that* be a treat. He headed towards the fire house. Gracie followed.

To Tim's disappointment, all was well within. No overturned furniture, no blood, no guts. The noise had come from Kaveh dragging the heavy old games table from in front of the fireplace back to where it belonged. He looked down-in-the-mouth, though, and that was enough for Gracie to forget that she herself was a walking emotional smash-up. She hurried over to the bloke straightaway.

"Oh, Kaveh," she cried. "Is something wrong?" Whereupon the bugger dropped onto the sofa, shook his head, and put his face in his hands.

Gracie sat on the sofa next to Kaveh and put her arm round his shoulders. "Won't you tell me?" she asked him. "Please tell me, Kaveh."

But Kaveh said nothing.

Obviously, Tim thought, he and their dad had had an argument of some sort and their dad had taken off in a temper. Good, he decided. He hoped they both were suffering. If his dad drove off the side of a cliff, that would be excellently fine by him.

"Has something happened to your mummy?" Gracie was asking Kaveh. She even smoothed the bloke's greasy hair. "Has something happened to your dad? C'n I get you a cup of tea, Kaveh? Does your head hurt? D'you have a tummy ache?"

Well, Tim thought, Gracie was taken care of. Her own cares forgotten, she'd bustle round playing nurse. He dropped her rucksack inside the fire house door and himself crossed to the room's other door, where a small square hall offered an uneven staircase to the first floor of the house.

His laptop occupied a rickety desk beneath the window in his bedroom, and the window itself looked out on the front garden and the village green beyond it. It was nearly dark now and the rain was coming down in sheets. The wind had picked up, piling the leaves from the maples beneath benches on the green and tossing them helter-skelter into the street. Lights were on in the terrace of houses across the green, and in the ramshackle cottage where George Cowley lived with his son, Tim could see movement behind a thin curtain. He watched for a moment—a man and his son and it looked to him like they were conversing but what did he know, really, of what was going on—and then he turned to his computer.

He logged on. The connection was slow. It was like waiting for water to freeze. Below him, he could hear the murmur of Gracie's voice and in a moment the sound of the stereo being turned on. She was thinking that music would make Kaveh feel better. Tim couldn't think why, as music did sod-all for him.

Finally. He got onto his e-mail and checked for messages. There was one especially that he sought. He'd been waiting anxiously to see how things were going to develop, and there was no way he could have assessed this from his mother's laptop. Absolutely no way.

Toy4You had finally made the proposition that Tim had been angling for. He read it over and thought for a while. It was little enough to ask for what Tim expected to get in return, so he typed the message he'd been waiting to type these many weeks of playing Toy4You along.

```
Yeah, but if I do it, I need something in
return.
```

He hit send and couldn't help smiling. He knew exactly what he wanted in exchange for the favour that was being asked of him.

LAKE WINDERMERE
CUMBRIA

Ian Cresswell had cooled off long before he reached the lake, as reaching the lake necessitated a twenty-minute drive. But the cooling off only applied to Ian's need to explode. The feelings beneath that need had not changed, and betrayal was first among them.

Our situations are different didn't appease Ian any longer. It had been fine at first. He'd been so besotted with Kav that the fact that the younger man might not himself do what he'd successfully demanded of Ian had barely registered in Ian's mind. It had been enough to walk out of the house in the company of Kaveh Mehran. It had been enough to leave behind his wife and his children in order—he declared to himself, to Kaveh, and to *them*, for God's sake—to finally and openly be who he was. No more slithering off to Lancaster, no more nameless groping and nameless fucking and feeling the momentary relief of taking part in an act that was, for once, not such a miserable *chore*. He'd done that for years in the belief that protecting others from what he'd admitted to himself when it was too late to do anything about it was more important than owning himself as he knew now he was meant to be owned. Kaveh had taught him that. Kaveh had said, "It's them or it's me," and had knocked on the door and walked into the house and said, "Do you tell them or do I tell them, Ian?" and instead of saying *Who the hell are you and what're you doing here?* Ian had heard himself make the declaration and out he'd walked, leaving Niamh to explain to the kids if she cared to explain, and he wondered now what the hell he'd been thinking, what sort of madness had overcome him, whether he had actually been suffering from a mental disease of one kind or another.

He wondered this not because he didn't love Kaveh Mehran and still wanted him in a manner that felt like a form of insane obsession. He wondered it because he hadn't stopped to consider what that moment had done to them all. And he wondered it because he hadn't stopped to consider what it might mean if Kaveh didn't do the same for Ian as Ian had done for him.

To Ian, Kaveh's making the declaration seemed simple enough and far less damaging than what Ian had done. Oh, he understood that Kav's parents were foreigners, but they were foreigners in culture and religion only. They'd lived in Manchester for more than a decade so they were hardly adrift in an ethnic sea of which they had no understanding. It had been more than a year now that they'd lived together—he and Kaveh—and it was time for Kaveh to speak the truth about what he and Ian Cresswell were to each other. The fact that Kaveh could not embrace that simple fact and share it with his parents . . . The unfairness of it all made Ian rail.

That need to rail was what he wanted to get out of his system. For he well knew that railing would accomplish exactly nothing.

The gates stood open at Ireleth Hall when he arrived, which generally meant that someone was visiting. Ian didn't want to see that someone or anyone else, however, so instead of heading towards the medieval house that loomed above the lake, he took a side route that led directly down to the water and to the stone boathouse built on its shore.

Here he kept his scull. It was sleek, low in the water, tricky to climb into from the stone dock that ran round three sides of the boathouse's dim interior, and just as tricky to climb out of. This trickiness was intensified at the moment by the lack of illumination in the boathouse itself. Generally the light provided by the waterside doorway was sufficient, but the day had been overcast in the first place and now it was getting dark. That, however, couldn't be allowed to matter because Ian needed to be out on the lake, digging the hatchet blades into the water, increasing his speed and burning his muscles, till the sweat pouring from him allowed him to experience nothing but effort alone.

He untied the scull's dock line and held the shell close to the dock's edge. There were three stone steps into the water not far from the lakeside entry to the boathouse, but he'd found that using them was risky. Over time the lake water had encouraged algae to grow upon them, and no one had cleaned the steps in years. Ian could have done it easily enough, but only when he used the scull did he actually think about the matter of seeing to the steps, and when he used the scull it was generally because he *needed* to use it and he needed to use it as soon as possible.

This evening was no different. With the dock line in one hand and the other on the gunwale of the shell to hold it steady, he lowered himself gingerly into the scull, balancing his weight precariously so that he didn't flip the craft and fling himself into the water. He sat. He coiled the line and placed it into the bow. He fixed his feet into the stretchers and he pushed off from the dock. He was facing outwards so it was a simple matter to ease the scull towards the archway and onto the lake.

The rain, which had begun during his drive to Ireleth Hall, was falling more determinedly now and had he not wanted to work the tension out of his body, Ian knew he would not have continued at that point. But rain was a small matter and it wasn't raining as hard as it could. Besides, he didn't intend to be out that long. Just for the time it took him to send himself flying over the water north in the direction of Windermere. When he'd worked up enough sweat, he'd return to the boathouse.

He fixed the long oars into their rectangular locks. He adjusted the position of the looms. He gave an experimental movement of his legs to ensure that the seat ran smoothly on its slides and then he was ready to set out. Less than ten seconds saw him some distance from the boathouse and heading to the centre of the lake.

From there, he could see the shape of Ireleth Hall with its tower, its gables, and its many chimneys telling the tale of the centuries that had gone into its making. Lights shone from the drawing room's bay windows and from the first-floor bedroom of the owners of the place. On the south side of the building the massive geometrical shapes of the topiary garden—gloomy against the evening sky—rose above the stone walls that enclosed them, and some one hundred yards away from this and partly hidden from Ireleth Hall itself, more lights poured from every floor of another tower, twin to the structure that was the earliest part of Ireleth Hall but in this case a folly built to resemble the stern and square pele towers of Cumbria and used to house one of the most useless females that Ian Cresswell had ever encountered.

He turned from the sight of the hall, the tower, and the topiary garden, country home of his uncle, a man whom he loved but did not understand. "I accept you so you must accept me," Bernard Fairclough had said to him, "because we all live lives of accommodation."

Ian wondered about this, however, just as he wondered about debts to be paid and to whom such payment needed to go. It was one other thing on his mind this evening. It was one other thing that kept him out on the water.

The lake was not a lonely place. Because of its size—the largest body of water in Cumbria—a few small towns and villages sprang up intermittently on its shores, and in scattered areas within the rest of the undeveloped landscape the occasional slate-fronted house stood, either a country home long ago converted into a high-priced hotel or a private domicile that usually spoke of a well-heeled individual with the funds to live in more than one place because as autumn gave way to winter, the lakes became unwelcoming to those who weren't prepared for heavy wind and snow.

Thus, Ian felt no sense of isolation out on the water. True, he was the only one rowing at the moment, but there was comfort along the shore where boats used by members of a local club and boats, kayaks, canoes, and sculls belonging to inhabitants of the lakeside houses had not yet been removed from the water for the coming winter.

He couldn't have said how long he rowed. It couldn't have been long, he thought, as it didn't seem as if he'd gained much distance. He'd not yet come upon the Beech Hill Hotel, from which he'd be able to see clearly the hulk of Belle Isle lying low in the water. That usually marked the halfway point of his workout, but he realised he must have been more exhausted than he thought from his discussion with Kaveh because he found his muscles were growing weary, telling him it was time for turning back.

He sat for a moment, still, unmoving. He could hear traffic noises from the A592, which ran along the east shore of the lake. But aside from the rain hitting the water and against his windcheater, that was it. Birds were abed, and everyone of sense was indoors.

Ian breathed deeply. A shiver shuddered through him, someone walking on his grave, he thought wryly. Either that or the weather, which was far more likely. Even in the rain, he caught the scent of wood smoke from a chimney nearby and in his mind he pictured a warming blaze, himself in front of it with his legs stretched out, and next to him Kaveh. In a similar chair, holding in his hand a similar glass of wine, taking part in a desultory end-of-day conversation of the kind millions of couples had in millions of homes all over the planet.

That, he told himself, was what he wanted. That and the peace that came with it. It didn't seem so much to ask: just a life moving forward as other lives did.

Some minutes passed in this way: with limited sounds, Ian at rest, the scull moving gently with the rhythm of the water. Had it not been raining, he might even have dozed. But as it was, he was becoming progressively wetter and it was time to head back to the boathouse.

He reckoned he'd been on the water for more than an hour, and it was in complete darkness that he made his final approach to the shore. By this time, trees were mere shapes on the land: angular conifers as solid as standing stones, wispier birches line-drawn against the sky and among them maples with palmate leaves trembling as the rain beat upon them. A path among them led down to the boathouse, a fanciful structure when seen from the water, for even now despite the weather and the hour, the shape of it formed a mass of crenellation, slate, and limestone and its weatherside doorway rose in a Gothic arch more suitable to a church than to a shelter for boats.

The light had burned out above this doorway, Ian saw. It should have come on with the fall of darkness, illuminating the exterior of the boathouse even if it did little enough to shed light on the building's insides. But where a yellow glow would have—at least in better weather—attracted moths, there was nothing at all. Along with the algae on the jetty steps, it was something else to be seen to.

He aimed for the arched opening and glided within. The boathouse was nowhere near the main house, nor was it near the tower folly, so there was nothing—no hint of distant light—to break the gloom, and the darkness was absolute. There were three other craft stored there. A well-used fishing rowing boat, a speedboat, and a canoe of uncertain vintage and even more uncertain seaworthiness were tied up haphazardly along the front and the right side of the dock. It was necessary to work one's way among them to get back to the far end where the scull had been tied, and Ian was able to do this by feel, although he caught his hand between the rowingboat and the scull and he swore as the fiberglass of one smashed his knuckles into the wood of the other.

The same thing happened against the stone dock, and he felt the blood this time. He said, "God*damn*," and pressed his knuckles against his side for a moment. The damn things hurt like the dickens and told him that whatever else he did, he needed to do it with care.

There was a torch in his car, and he had enough sense of humour remaining to congratulate himself for having left it there where it would do him absolutely no bloody good. More carefully this time, he reached out for the dock, found it, and then sought the cleat to tie up the scull. At least, he thought, he could make a cleat hitch in light or in dark, in rain or in shine. He did so and released his feet from the stretchers. Then he shifted his weight and reached for the dock to heave himself up and out of the shell.

As these things do, it happened when the balance of his weight was on a single stone of the dock and his body was momentarily arched out of the scull and over the water. The stone that should have taken his weight—and now apparently too long in place on the dock to do so—became dislodged.

He fell forward, and the scull—tied only at its bow—shot backwards. Down he went into the frigid water.

On his way, however, his head slammed into the slate from which the dock had long ago been fashioned. He was unconscious when he hit the water, and within a few minutes he was also dead.

25 OCTOBER

Their arrangement was the same as it had been from the first. She would communicate in some way, and he would go to her. Sometimes it was a quarter smile, just an upturn of her lips gone so quickly that anyone unaware of what it meant would not even have noticed. Sometimes it was the word *tonight* murmured as they passed in a corridor. At other times she said something openly if, perhaps, they met on the stairway or in the officers' mess or if, perhaps, they saw each other in the underground car park arriving by chance at the same moment in the morning. But in any case, he waited until she gave the word. He didn't like it this way, but there was no other. She would not under any circumstances come to him, and even had she been willing to do so, she was his superior officer so he was hers to command. It did not work the other way round.

He'd tried it only once, early on in their arrangement. He'd thought it might mean something if she spent the night with him in Belgravia, as if their relationship had turned some sort of corner, although he wasn't exactly certain that he wanted it to do so. She'd said firmly in that way she had of making things so pellucid there were no further avenues of discussion available to him, That will never happen,

Thomas. And the fact she called him Thomas rather than the more intimate Tommy by which his every friend and colleague referred to him said more than the other, larger truth that he knew she would not say: The house in Eaton Terrace was still redolent of his murdered wife, and eight months after her death on the front steps of the building, he hadn't been able to bring himself to do a single thing about that. He was insightful enough to realise that there was little likelihood of any woman's sleeping in his bed while Helen's clothes still hung in the wardrobe, while Helen's scent bottles still stood on the dressing table where Helen's hairbrush still held strands of Helen's hair. Until Helen's presence was eradicated from the house, he could not realistically hope to share it with anyone else, even for a night. So he was caught, and when Isabelle said that word—*Tonight?*—he went to her, drawn by a force that was at once a physical need and a form of oblivion, however brief.

He did as much on this evening. In the afternoon they'd had a meeting with the head of IPCC on the matter of a complaint registered that past summer by a solicitor on the behalf of her client: a paranoid schizophrenic who had run into traffic in a London street while being pursued by the police. The resulting internal injuries and fractured skull demanded monetary compensation, and the solicitor meant to have it. The police complaints commission was investigating the matter and this constituted meeting upon meeting with everyone involved explaining his or her take on the story, with CCTV footage viewed, with eyewitnesses interviewed, and with the London tabloids breathlessly eager to snatch up the story and run with it as soon as the IPCC made a determination as to guilt, innocence, malfeasance, accident, circumstances beyond anyone's control, or whatever else they chose to conclude. The meeting had been tense. He was as tightly strung as Isabelle at its conclusion.

She'd said to him as they walked through the corridors to return to their offices in Victoria Block, I'd like to have you tonight, Thomas, if you've the energy. Dinner and a shag. Very good steaks, very nice wine, very clean sheets. Not Egyptian cotton as I expect yours are, but fresh all the same.

And then the smile and something in her eyes that he'd not yet been able to interpret, these three months after they'd first coupled in the soulless bedroom of her basement flat. Damn if he didn't want her, he thought. It had to do with an act the nature of which allowed him to believe he'd mastered her when the truth was she had quickly mastered him.

The arrangement was simple enough. She would go to the shops, and he could either go straight to the flat and let himself in with his key or go to his own home first on one pretext or another, killing time till making the drive to that dismal street at the halfway point between Wandsworth prison and a cemetery. He chose the latter. It allowed him the semblance of being his own man.

To further this illusion, he took his time with his preparations: reading his mail, having a shower and a shave, returning a phone call from his mother on the matter of rainwater heads along the west side of the house in Cornwall. Should they be replaced or repaired, did he think? Winter's coming, darling, and with the rains getting heavier . . . It was a pretext call on her part. She wanted to know how he was, but she didn't like to ask directly. She knew very well that the rainwater heads had to be repaired. They could not possibly be replaced. It was a listed building, after all. It would probably be falling down round their ears before they'd receive permission to alter it. They chatted on of family matters. How was his brother doing? he asked, which was family code for Is he still coping without turning back to cocaine, heroin, or whatever other substance he might use to remove himself from reality? The answer was Perfectly well, darling. This was family code for I'm monitoring him, as always, and you've no cause to worry about it. How was his sister? meant had Judith yet given up the idea of permanent widowhood, to which the answer Terribly busy as always was code for She has no intention of risking another dreadful marriage, believe me. So went the conversation till all topics were exhausted and his mother said, I do so hope we'll see you for Christmas, Tommy, and he assured her that she would.

After that, with no other reason to hold him in Belgravia, he worked his way over to the river and south from there to

Wandsworth Bridge. He reached the house in which Isabelle lived just after half past seven. Parking was murder in the area, but he got lucky when a van pulled away from the kerb some thirty yards down the street.

At Isabelle's door, he fished out his key. He had it in the lock and was letting himself in when she opened the door from within and quickly stepped outside onto the flagstones of the area at the base of the stairs from the pavement above them. She shut the door behind her.

She said, "We can't tonight. Something's come up. I would have rung your mobile but I couldn't. I'm sorry."

He was nonplussed. Stupidly, he looked over her shoulder at the panels of the closed door. He said, "Who's here?" because that much was obvious enough. Another man, he reckoned, and in that he was right, although it was not a man he expected.

"Bob," she said.

Her former husband. How could this, he wondered, possibly be a problem? "And?" he enquired pleasantly.

"Thomas, it's awkward. Sandra's with him. The boys as well."

Bob's wife. The twin sons that were Isabelle's own, children of her five-year marriage. They were eight years old and he'd had yet to meet them. As far as he knew, they'd not even been in to London to see her.

He said, "This is good, Isabelle. He's brought them to you, then?"

"You don't understand," she said. "I wasn't expecting—"

"I know that, obviously. So I'll meet them, we'll have dinner, and I'll leave."

"He doesn't know about you."

"Who?"

"Bob. I've not told him. This was all a surprise. He and Sandra have come into town for some sort of dinner. A big affair. They're dressed to the nines. They've brought the boys and they thought we could have a visit—the boys and I—while they're at this event."

"They didn't phone you first? What if you hadn't even been at home? What would he have done with them then? Have them wait in the car while he went to dinner?"

She looked irritated. "You know, that's hardly important, Thomas. The fact is, I am at home and they're here in London. I've not seen the boys in weeks, this is the first time he's actually allowing me to be alone with them, and I have no intention of—"

"What?" He looked at her more evenly now. She was pinched round the mouth. He knew what this meant. She was wanting a drink and the last thing she'd now be able to do was to have one. "What is it you suppose I'd do, Isabelle? Corrupt them with my dissolute ways?"

"Don't be difficult. This has nothing to do with you."

"Tell them I'm your colleague, then."

"A colleague with the key to my door?"

"For the love of God, if he knows I have the key to your door—"

"He doesn't. And he won't. I told him I thought I heard someone knock and I've come to check if anyone's at the door."

"Are you aware you're contradicting yourself?" Again, he looked beyond her shoulder to the door. He said, "Isabelle, is there someone else in there? Not Bob at all? Not his wife? Not the boys?"

She drew herself taller. She was six feet tall, nearly his height, and he knew what it meant when she made the most of that fact. "What are you suggesting?" she demanded. "That I've another lover? God in heaven. I can*not* believe you're doing this. You know what this means to me. These are my children. You'll meet them and Bob and Sandra and God only knows who else when I'm ready and not before. Now I've got to get back inside before he comes to see what's happening, and you've got to go. We'll talk about this tomorrow."

"And if I walk in anyway? You leave me out here, I use the key, I come inside? What then?" Even as he spoke the words, he couldn't believe it of himself. His dignity seemed to have gone the way of his brains, his patience, and his self-control.

She knew it. He could see *that* in her eyes no matter what else she was able to hide from him so well. She said, "Let's forget you said that," and she went inside, leaving him to cope with what looked every moment more like a tantrum thrown by a five-year-old.

God, what had he been thinking? he wondered. Thomas Lynley, detective inspector of New Scotland Yard, titled member of the landed gentry, graduate of Oxford University with a first-class degree in being a fool.

28 OCTOBER

He managed to avoid her quite successfully for two days although he was able to tell himself that he wasn't attempting to avoid her at all because he spent those days hanging about the Royal Courts of Justice. There his testimony had been called for in the ongoing trial of a serial killer with whom he'd come into very close and nearly fatal contact the previous February. After those two days, however, his presence being no longer required in the vicinity of Courtroom Number One, he politely refused three requests from journalists for interviews, which he knew would end up touching upon the one subject he could not face touching upon—the death of his wife—and he returned to New Scotland Yard. There Isabelle unsurprisingly asked him if he'd been avoiding her since he'd phoned in his necessary absences not to her but to the departmental secretary. He said of course not and what possible reason had he to avoid her and he'd been at court as had been his longtime partner DS Barbara Havers. Surely Isabelle didn't think DS Havers was also trying to avoid her?

He shouldn't have said this last because it gave too much away, and what it gave away was the truth of the matter, which was, naturally, that he hadn't particularly wished to have a conversation with Isabelle till he'd sorted out in his own head the reasons for his reaction at the door to her flat. Isabelle said that, frankly, avoiding her was precisely what she'd expect DS Havers to be doing as she made a regular habit of that. To which he'd replied, Be that as it may, I'm not trying to do so.

She said, "You're angry and you've a right to be, Tommy. I behaved badly. He turned up with the children and I was completely unnerved. But see it from my position, please. It's not beyond Bob to phone one of the higher-ups here and drop the word: 'Are you aware that Acting Detective Superintendent Ardery is having it off with a subordinate officer? Just thought you might want to know.' And he'd do that, Tommy. He *would* do that. And you know what would happen if he did."

He thought she was being overly paranoid, but he didn't say as much. To do so would lead them into an argument, if not here in her office to which she'd summoned him then somewhere else. He said, "You could be right," and when she said, "So . . . ?" he knew that it was another way of saying *Tonight, then?* so that they could see to what they'd had to postpone. Steaks, wine, a shag that would be very energetic and very, very good. Which, he realised, was the hell of it for him. Isabelle in bed was inventive and exciting, and in bed was the only place she allowed him even a moment of control over her.

He was considering her proposition when Dorothea Harriman, the lithesome and well-turned-out departmental secretary, popped into the doorway, which he'd left open. She said, "Detective Inspector Lynley?" and when he turned, "I've just had a call. I'm afraid you're wanted."

"By whom, Dee?" He assumed he was meant to return to the Old Bailey for some reason.

"Himself."

"Ah." Not the Old Bailey, then. Himself would be the assistant commissioner, Sir David Hillier. When Hillier beckoned, one set off to do his bidding. "Now?" he asked.

"That would be the case. And he's not here. You're to go straight to his club."

"At this hour? What's he doing at his club?"

Harriman shrugged. "Not a clue. But you're meant to be

there as soon as possible. Traffic permitting, he'd like you there in fifteen minutes. His secretary made that clear."

"That seals it, then, doesn't it?" He turned back to Isabelle and said, "If you'll excuse me, guv?" When she gave a curt nod, he went on his way, everything still unresolved between them.

Sir David Hillier's club was near Portland Place, and it was a ludicrous idea that Lynley would be able to get there from New Scotland Yard within fifteen minutes. But the mention of time suggested urgency, so he took a cab and told the driver to rat-run and, for God's sake, to do everything possible to avoid Piccadilly Circus, a regular source of congestion. That got him to Twins—Hillier's club—in twenty-two minutes, something of a record considering the time of day.

Twins had been fashioned from three of the few remaining town houses in the area not razed by someone's idea of redevelopment in the nineteenth century. It was marked only by a discreet bronze plaque to the right of the doorbell and by an azure flag with the eponymous founders of the club memorialised upon it. They'd been conjoined, or so at least it seemed by their depiction on the flag. As far as Lynley knew, no one had delved deeply enough into the history of the place to learn whether this was an apocryphal account of the club's genesis.

He was admitted not by a doorman but rather by an elderly woman in black with a crisp white pinafore apron pinned to her chest. She looked like someone from another century and, as things developed, she moved like that as well. He stated his business in an entry hung with Victorian paintings of uncertain quality that loomed above a marble draughtsboard floor. The woman nodded and negotiated something like a three-point turn before leading him to a door to the right of an impressive staircase broken by a mezzanine. There a sculpture of Venus on the half shell stood, backed by a window that arched to display the upper part of a garden, evidenced by the remains of a tree strangled by ivy.

The woman knocked, opened, and admitted him into a darkly panelled dining room, closing the door behind him.

The room was empty of diners at this hour but occupied by two men at one of the linen-covered tables. They had a porcelain coffee service between them. There were three cups.

One of the men was the assistant commissioner, and the other was a bespectacled bloke who was, perhaps, too well-dressed for the time of day and the present environment, although, for that matter, so was Hillier. They seemed of an age but unlike Hillier, the other man had a receding hairline that he emphasised rather than hid, by combing his remaining locks straight back, where they lay flat against his skull in defiance of fashion and looks. His hair was uniform in colour—mousy brown would have best described it—and thus seemed to be dyed. Also in defiance of fashion, his spectacles were thick rimmed with enormous black frames, and these in combination with an astoundingly overlarge upper lip unmatched to his lower made him look like someone begging to be caricatured. This, in fact, suggested to Lynley that he knew of the man, although he couldn't have stated his name.

Hillier did that. "Lord Fairclough," he said. "Bernard, this is DI Lynley."

Fairclough stood. He was far shorter than both Lynley and Hillier, perhaps five feet five inches, and he carried something of a gut on him. His handshake was firm, and during the ensuing meeting, nothing he said or did indicated that he was anything but strong willed and confident.

"David's told me about you," Fairclough said. "I hope we can work well together." His accent placed him from the north and its nature surprised Lynley, for it spoke of an education decidedly not undergone in a hallowed public school. He glanced at Hillier. It was completely like the AC to rub elbows with someone in possession of a title. It was completely *unlike* the AC, on the other hand, to do this elbow-rubbing with someone whose title had come not via the blood but rather, like his, via the Honours List.

"Lord Fairclough and I were knighted on the same day," Hillier said, as if he felt an explanation for their association was required. He added, "Fairclough Industries," as a means of clarification, as if the name of Fairclough's source of wealth—if he had any—would be apparent at once.

"Ah," Lynley said.

Fairclough smiled. "The Fairloo," he said as means of clarification.

That did it, of course, as it would do. Bernard Fairclough had come to prominence first because of a most unusual lavatory invented and then widely produced by Fairclough Industries. He'd sealed his place in the firmament of those receiving titles from a grateful nation, however, by establishing a charitable foundation whose focus was raising funds to research a cure for pancreatic cancer. However, Fairclough had never been able to escape his association with the lavatory, and much amusement had been generated by tabloids referring to his knighthood and subsequent elevation to the peerage with such declarations as "It was a royal flush."

Hillier gestured at the table. Lynley was meant to join them. Without asking, Hillier poured him a cup of coffee and, as Lynley sat and Fairclough resumed his own place at the table, slid the cup in his direction along with the milk and sugar.

"Bernard's asked a favour of us," Hillier said. "It's an entirely confidential matter."

Which explained their meeting at Twins, Lynley thought. Which also explained their meeting at Twins at a time of day when the only members in the building were probably either dozing over newspapers in the library or playing squash in a basement gym. Lynley nodded but said nothing. He glanced at Fairclough, who removed a white handkerchief from his pocket and patted it against his forehead. This bore a moderate sheen of sweat. It was not overly warm in the room.

He said, "My nephew—Ian Cresswell, my late sister's son—drowned ten days ago. South end of Lake Windermere sometime after seven in the evening. His body wasn't found till the next afternoon. My wife was the one who found him."

"I'm sorry to hear it." It was, of course, an automatic response to being given such information. Hearing it, Fairclough's face remained a blank.

"Valerie likes to fish," he told Lynley, a remark that

sounded apropos of nothing till he went on with, "She takes a small rowing boat out a few times each week. Odd hobby for a woman but there it is. She's fished for years. We keep the boat along with several other craft in a boathouse on the property, and that's where Ian's body was. Facedown in the water, open gash on his head, although at that point there was no blood."

"What seems to have happened?"

"Lost his footing getting out of a single scull. It's how he took his exercise, that, the scull. He went down, hit his head on the dock—it's stone—and fell into the water."

"Couldn't swim or unconscious?"

"The latter. A terrible accident, according to the inquest."

"You think otherwise?"

Fairclough turned in his seat. He seemed to look at a painting over a fireplace at the far side of the room. This was a circus scene painted in the style of Hogarth: part of the rake's progress, with assorted human oddities from the circus in place of the rake. It was another vote for the conjoined twins. They'd have been circus material, certainly. Fairclough studied the scene depicted before he finally said, "He fell because two large stones came loose on the dock. They dislodged."

"I see."

Hillier said, "Bernard thinks there's a chance the stones had some help, Tommy. The boathouse has stood for more than one hundred years and it was built to stand a hundred more. So was the dock."

"Yet if the coroner has ruled an accident—"

"I don't actually disbelieve him," Fairclough said quickly. "But . . . " He looked at Hillier as if asking the AC to finish.

Hillier complied. "Bernard wants to be certain it was an accident, as anyone might. There are family concerns."

"What sort of family concerns?"

The other men were silent. Lynley looked from one to the other. He said, "I can hardly make certain of anything if I'm in the dark, Lord Fairclough."

"It's Bernard," Fairclough said, although Hillier's look

in his direction suggested that such familiarity was going to breed the usual. "It's Bernie, actually, among the family. But Bernard will do." Fairclough reached for his coffee cup. Hillier had topped it up, but it seemed that Fairclough wanted the cup more for something to do with his hands than for drinking. He turned it, examined it, and finally said, "I want to be certain that my son, Nicholas, wasn't involved in Ian's death."

Lynley let a moment hang while he absorbed this information and what it could imply about the father, the son, and the deceased nephew. He said, "Have you reason to believe Nicholas might be involved?"

"No."

"Then?"

Again that glance towards Hillier, which prompted the AC to say, "Nicholas has had a . . . We'd have to call it a troubled youth. He seems to have got over it, but as he's seemed to get over it before, Bernard's fear is that the boy—"

"A man now," Fairclough cut in. "He's thirty-two. He's married as well. When I look at him, things seem to have changed. *He* seems to have changed, but it was drugs, all sorts but particularly methamphetamine, and it went on for years, you see, since he was round thirteen. He's lucky even to be alive at this point, and he swears he knows it. But that's what he always said, isn't it, time after time."

Lynley heard all this with a dawning of understanding as to how he fitted into what was going on. He'd never spoken of his brother to Hillier, but Hillier had snouts in every part of the Met and how unlikely was it that among the information he gathered was that which told the AC of Peter Lynley's battles with addiction?

Bernard continued. "Then he met a woman from Argentina. She's a real beauty, and he fell in love, but she laid down the law. She'd have nothing to do with him till he got the monkey off his back permanently. So he did so. Apparently."

To Lynley this seemed all the more reason that Nicholas Fairclough was uninvolved, but he waited for more and it came in fits and starts. It seemed that the dead man had grown up in the Fairclough home, playing the role of an older brother whose perfection had created footsteps too large for the younger Nicholas ever to hope he'd be able to walk in. Ian Cresswell had successfully completed schooling at St. Bees in Cumbria, and from there achieved further success at university. This put him in position to serve as the chief of finances for Fairclough Industries as well as the man in charge of Bernard Fairclough's personal financial affairs. These affairs, it seemed, were considerable.

"No decision's been made as to who'll take over the daily running of the firm when I'm no longer around," Fairclough said. "But obviously, Ian was very high on the list of contenders."

"Did Nicholas know this?"

"Everyone knew it."

"Does he stand to gain, then, from Ian's death?"

"As I've said, no decision had—or has—been made."

So if everyone knew where Ian stood, everyone— whoever *everyone* was—had a motive for murder, Lynley thought, if murder it was. Yet if the coroner had deemed it an accident, Fairclough should have been relieved, which he clearly was not. Lynley wondered idly if, despite his words, Fairclough in fact *wanted* his son to be the cause of his own cousin's death. It was perverse, but in his time at the Met, Lynley had seen his share of perversity.

"Exactly who is everyone?" Lynley enquired. "I take it there are others besides Nicholas with a vested interest in Fairclough Industries?"

There were, as it turned out: There were two older sisters and a former son-in-law, but it was Nicholas about whom Fairclough had concerns. Lynley could leave the rest of them alone. Not a single one of them was a killer. They lacked the bottle for it. Nicholas, it seemed, did not. And besides, with his history . . . One wished to be sure he had no involvement in this matter. One merely wished to be sure.

"I'd like you to take this on," Hillier told Lynley. "You'll have to go up to the Lakes and all of it has to be done with complete discretion."

A police investigation managed with complete discretion, Lynley thought. He wondered how he was meant to accomplish that.

Hillier elucidated. "No one will know you've gone there. And the local police won't know you're doing this. We don't want to give the impression that the IPCC's about to get involved. No feathers ruffled but no stone unturned. You know how to manage that."

The fact was that he didn't. And there was something else that made him uneasy. He said, "Superintendent Ardery is going to want to—"

"I'll handle Superintendent Ardery. I'll handle everyone."

"So I'm to work on this completely alone?"

"No one at the Yard can be involved," Hillier said.

This seemed to be code for the fact that Lynley was meant to do nothing at all if Nicholas Fairclough turned out to be a killer. He was to leave him to the hands of his father, to the hands of God, or to the hands of the Furies. All of this amounted to an investigation Lynley wanted no part of. But he knew he wasn't being requested to make a trip up to Cumbria. He was being told to do so.

FLEET STREET
THE CITY OF LONDON

Rodney Aronson had clawed his way to his present position as editor of *The Source* through means both fair and foul, and one of those means was the cultivation of an impressive collection of snouts. He was where he wanted to be in his life, which was sitting in an impressive if somewhat chaotic office where he could wield absolute power, but this did not prevent him from feeling grievances. He hated arrogance. He hated hypocrisy. He hated stupidity. But most of all, he hated incompetence.

Following a story was not rocket science. Neither was chivvying it along. Following merely required three things: research, shoe leather, and doggedness. Chivvying required a willingness to see one's fellow humans squirm and, if necessary, be squashed. If this latter requirement itself required a bit of slithering on the part of the reporter, what of it? The end product was the story and if the story was big enough with an appropriate amount of sensation attached to it, big sales were the result. Big sales translated into increased advertising, which translated into increased revenue, which translated into orgasmic delight from *The Source*'s chairman, the cadaverous Peter Ogilvie. At all costs, Ogilvie needed to be kept well oiled with good news in the form of profits. As to whose head or reputation rolled in pursuit of these, it mattered not.

Granted, the story of Nicholas Fairclough's putative redemption from the clutches of drugs had been a snore of monumental proportions. They could have used it in operating theatres in place of anaesthetic, such a soporific had it been. Now, however, things were looking up. Now, it seemed, Rodney might not have to defend the expenditure of Zed Benjamin's initial trip to Cumbria to develop the story, no matter the incredible cost the reporter had incurred.

But that thought brought forward the whole issue of journalistic stupidity. Rodney could not see how idiot Benjamin could have failed yet a *second* time to nose his way into a story when the damn smell of it was right in front of him. Another five days tramping round Cumbria had resulted in nothing but an extension of the tedious panegyric he'd already created about Nicholas Fairclough, his doped-up past, his reformed present, and his doubtless sanctified future. Other than that, there was nada to interest the typical *Source* reader. There was zero, nought, and double nought with nuts.

Receiving the news from a head-hanging Benjamin that there was nothing more he could possibly add to what he'd written, Rodney knew he should kick the bloke out on his ear. He couldn't explain to himself why he hadn't done so, and he thought at first he might be getting soft. But then one of his snouts phoned in, passed along a delectable tip, and Rodney reckoned he might not have to sack Benjamin after all.

What the snout had to say constituted an instructive

moment, and since Rodney Aronson loved instructive moments nearly as much as he loved anything containing cacao, he sent for the red-haired giant and enjoyed a Kit Kat that he washed down with an espresso from his personal machine, this latter a gift from Butterball Betsy, a wife who knew many ways to please. That most of them were gustatory didn't bother him.

Rodney had finished the Kit Kat and was making himself a second espresso when Zed Benjamin lumbered into the room. Damn if he still wasn't wearing the beanie, Rodney thought with a sigh. He had little doubt that the dumbo had yarmulked his way round Cumbria a second time, successfully putting everyone off yet again. Rodney shook his head in resignation. The folly he had to endure as editor of *The Source* sometimes truly offset its delights. He decided not to mention the headgear again. He'd done so once, and if Benjamin wouldn't take his advice, there was nothing for it but to let him sink under the weight of his own nonsensical inclinations. He'd learn or he wouldn't, and Rodney knew which alternative was more likely. End of story.

"Shut the door," he said to the reporter. "Take a seat. Give me a second here." He admired the creamy nature of his concoction and turned off the machine. He carried his drink to the desk and sat. "Death is sex," he said. "I reckoned you'd work that out for yourself, but it seems you can't. Got to tell you, Zedekiah, this line of work might not be for you."

Zed looked at him. He looked at the wall. He looked at the floor. He finally said, "Death is sex," so slowly that Rodney wondered if the man's brains had gone the way of his footwear because for some reason he was wearing not respectable shoes but instead very odd-looking sandals with tire treads for soles, along with striped socks that appeared to be handmade from remnants of yarn.

"I told you the story needed sex. You went up there a second time and tried to find it. That you failed to find it I can understand, more or less. But what I can't understand is how you failed to see the moment of potential rescue when it came. You should've been in here like a flash yelling *eureka* or *cowabunga* or *praise Jesus, I'm saved*. Well, probably not that last, all things considered, but the point is you got handed a way into the story—and this would be a way to save it and to justify the expense the paper went to in sending you up there in the first place—and you missed it. Completely. The fact that I had to discover it myself concerns me, Zed. It really does."

"She still wouldn't talk to me, Rodney. I mean, she talked but she didn't *talk*. She says she's not what's important. She's his wife, they met, they fell in love, they married, they came back to England, and there's an end to her part of the tale. From what I can tell, he's entirely devoted to him. But everything he's done, he's done himself. She *did* tell me that it would benefit him—*encourage* was the word she used—if the story featured his recovery alone and not her part in it. She said something like, 'You need to understand how important it is for Nicholas to be acknowledged as having achieved this on his own.' She meant his recovery. I did get that the reason for her wanting the recognition to go to him has to do with his relationship with his dad, and I shaded the story that way, but there didn't seem to be anything more—"

"I know you're not completely stupid," Rodney cut in, "but I'm beginning to think you're deaf. 'Death is sex,' is what I said. You did hear that, didn't you?"

"Well, yeah. I did. And she's sexy, the wife. You'd have to be blind not to—"

"Forget the wife. She's not dead, is she?"

"Dead? Well, no. I mean, I reckoned you were using a metaphor, Rodney."

Rodney gulped down the rest of his espresso. This gave him time not to strangle the young man, which was what he badly wanted to do. He finally said, "Believe me, when I use a fucking metaphor, you're going to know it. Are you aware— remotely or otherwise—that the cousin of your hero is dead? Recently dead as a matter of fact? That he died in a boathouse where he fell into the water and drowned? That the boathouse I'm speaking of is on the property of your hero's father?"

"Drowned while I was there? No way," Zed declared. "You may think I'm blind, Rod—"

"You'll get no argument from me."

"—but I would have hardly missed that fact. When did he die and which cousin are we talking about?"

"Is there more than one?"

Zed shifted in his chair. "Well, not that I know of. Ian Cresswell drowned?"

"Yes indeedy doodah," Rodney said.

"Murdered?"

"Accident according to the inquest. But that's hardly the point because the death's nicely suspicious and suspicion is our bread and butter. Metaphor, by the way, in case you're thinking otherwise. Our purpose is to fan the fire—another metaphor, I think I'm on a roll here—and see what comes crawling out of the woodwork."

"Mixed," Zed muttered.

"What?"

"Never mind. Is that what you want me to do, then? I take it I'm to suggest there's reason to believe foul play is involved, with Nicholas Fairclough the player. I can see how it fits: The former drug addict falls off the wagon of recovery and does in his cousin for some obscure reason and as of this writing, gentle readers, he apparently has walked away scot-free." Zed slapped his hands against his thighs as if he was about to rise and do Rodney's bidding directly. But instead of getting up to leave, he said, "They grew up as brothers, Rodney. The original story does indicate that. And they didn't hate each other. But of course I could make it sound like Cain going after Abel if that suits you."

"Do not," Rodney said, "take that tone with me."

"What tone?"

"You bloody well know what tone. I should kick your arse from here to down under, but I'm going to do you a favour instead. I'm going to say three little words that I hope to God will make your pointed ears prick up. Are you listening, Zed? I don't want you to miss them. Here they come, now: New Scotland Yard."

That, Rodney saw to his satisfaction, appeared to stop Zed Benjamin in his self-righteous tracks. The reporter frowned. He thought. He finally said, "What about New Scotland Yard?"

"They're in."

"Are you saying they're investigating the drowning?"

"I'm saying something better than that. They're sending a bloke up there wearing brothel-creepers, if you receive my meaning. And he's not a bloke from the IPCC."

"So it's not an internal investigation? What is it, then?"

"A special assignment. Completely hush-hush, mum's the word, and on the big QT. He's apparently been given the job of making a list and checking it twice. And reporting back when he's finished."

"Why?"

"That's the story, Zed. That's the sex behind the death." Rodney wanted to add that it was also what Zed himself would have learned had he put in the effort that Rodney himself would have put in had he been in the same position with his story shit-canned by his editor and, potentially, with his job on the line.

"So I'm not to make something up to add sex to the story," Zed said, as if he needed clarification. "What you're saying is that it's already there."

"At *The Source*," Rodney intoned religiously, "we don't need to make things up. We just need to find them in the first place."

"And can I ask . . . How'd you know this? About the Met, I mean. How'd you find out if it's all hush-hush?"

It was one of those moments when paternal superiority was called for, and Rodney loved those kinds of moments. He rose from behind his desk, went round to the front of it, and lifted a bulky thigh to rest it on the corner. It wasn't the most comfortable position—considering the chafing of his skin against his trousers—but Rodney liked to think it communicated a degree of journalistic savoir faire that would underscore the importance of what he had to say next. "Zedekiah, I've been in this business since I was a kid. I've sat where you're sitting and this is what I learned: We're nothing without the snouts we cultivate, and I've cultivated them from Edinburgh to London and all points in between. Particularly in London, my friend. I've got snouts in places that other people don't even recognise as being places. I scratch their backs with great regularity. They scratch mine whenever they can."

Benjamin looked suitably impressed. Indeed, he looked humbled. He was in the presence of his journalistic better and it seemed that he finally knew it.

Rodney went on, enjoying his moment. "Nicholas Fairclough's dad has a tie to the Met. He's the one asking for an investigation. Can I reckon you know what that means, Zed?"

"He thinks it wasn't an accident that Ian Cresswell drowned. And if it wasn't an accident, we've got a story. Fact is, we've got a story either way because we've got the Met up there nosing round and that suggests something might have gone on and all we ever need for a story is a suggestion."

"Amen to that," Rodney said. "Get back to Cumbria, my good man. On the double."

CHALK FARM
LONDON

Detective Sergeant Barbara Havers arrived home in an uneasy mood that she didn't want to name. Having found a parking space not too far from Eton Villas, she should have been grateful, but she couldn't summon up the appropriate feeling of joy attendant on not having to hike to her front door. As usual, the Mini coughed a few times after Barbara cut the ignition, but she barely took note. Through the windscreen a splattering of rain began to fall, but she hardly clocked that either. Instead, her thoughts remained where they'd been largely fixed—save for one brief distraction—during her long drive home from the Met. Those thoughts battled in her head with a voice that judged them childish, but that didn't matter and it certainly wasn't enough to quash them, although she would, at this point, have been grateful had that only been the case.

No one had noticed, Barbara thought. Not a single, sod-

ding individual. Well, all right, Detective Superintendent
Ardery had noticed, but she hardly counted as she'd given
the initial order—although she'd claimed it was only a
suggestion—and from Barbara's nearly four months of
experience with Isabelle Ardery, she knew the superintendent noticed everything. Ardery seemed to make noticing
a habit. She seemed, in fact, to have raised it to a fine art.
So whenever she took note of something, it mattered not,
unless her taking note was connected intimately to one's
performance at work. If it was connected to anything else,
one could say that Isabelle Ardery was merely engaging in
her irritating habit of sitting in judgement upon the superficial, with the number one superficial within the superintendent's gaze being Barbara Havers's personal appearance.
As to the rest of the team, when Barbara had arrived back
at the Yard from her final appointment with the dentist,
they'd gone about their business without a word, a raised
eyebrow, or anything else.

Barbara had told herself she didn't care, and there was
truth in this since she really didn't care about the notice of
most of her colleagues. But the notice of one of them she
cared about deeply, and it was this caring that sat uneasily
upon her, asking to be acknowledged or at least dealt with
by the downing of something of a pastry orientation. French
would be nice, but it was too late in the day to score a chocolate croissant, although not too late in the day to snag an
entire torte, which of course would have been Austrian, but
at this hour who was quibbling about such minor details as
country of origin? Yet Barbara knew that that direction
would lead her straight into the evils of an extended carb
wallow from which she might not emerge for weeks, so
instead of pausing at a bakery en route to her home, she'd
decided to engage in retail therapy in Camden High Street.
There she'd made the purchase of a scarf and a blouse,
whereupon she'd celebrated the fact that she'd just behaved
in a manner entirely different from her usual mode of reacting to disappointment, stress, frustration, or anxiety, but
this celebration lasted only till she parked the Mini. At that
point, her final encounter with Thomas Lynley forced its
way into her consciousness.

After their time at the Old Bailey that day, they'd parted: Lynley heading back to the Yard and Barbara heading to the dentist. They'd not seen each other again until the end of the day when they met in the ascending lift. Barbara was taking it from the underground car park and when it stopped at the lobby, Lynley got on. She could see that he was preoccupied. He'd been preoccupied outside Courtroom Number One earlier in the day, but she'd reckoned that had to do with having to testify to his near encounter with the Grim Reaper in the back of a Ford Transit kitted out as a mobile murder scene some months earlier. This preoccupation seemed different, though, and when he vanished into Superintendent Ardery's office after the lift doors opened, Barbara reckoned she knew the reason why.

Lynley thought she didn't know what was going on between Ardery and him. Barbara could understand the reason for this conclusion. No one else at the Met had a clue that he and the superintendent were dancing inside each other's knickers two or sometimes three nights a week, but no one else at the Met knew Lynley as well as Barbara did. And while she couldn't imagine anyone actually *wanting* to shag the superintendent—bloody hell, it had to be like going to bed with a cobra—she'd spent the last three months of their affair telling herself that, if nothing else, Lynley deserved it. He'd lost his wife to a street murder at the hands of a twelve-year-old, he'd spent five months afterwards wandering the coast of Cornwall in a sodding daze, he'd returned to London barely functioning ... If he wanted the questionable diversion of plugging Isabelle Ardery's drainpipes for a time, so be it. They could both be in big trouble if anyone found out about it, but no one was going to find out about it because they were discreet and Barbara wasn't going to say a word. Besides, Lynley wasn't going to hook himself up *permanently* to someone like Isabelle Ardery. The man had something like three hundred years of family history to contend with, and if nothing else, he knew his duty and it had very little to do with an interlude in which he bonked a woman on whom the title Countess of Asherton would hang like a hundredweight. His type was meant to reproduce obligingly and send the family name hurtling into the future. He knew this and he'd act accordingly.

Still, it did not sit easily with Barbara that Lynley and the superintendent were lovers. That relationship comprised the malodorous elephant present in every encounter Barbara had with him. She hated this. Not him, not the affair itself, but the fact that he wouldn't talk to her about it. Not that she expected him to. Not that she really wanted him to. Not that she would actually be able to think of something reasonable to say should he turn to her and make a comment alluding to it. But they were partners—she and Lynley—or at least they had been and partners were meant to . . . *What*? she asked herself. But that was a question she preferred not to answer.

She shoved open her car door. The rain wasn't bad enough to use a brollie, so she pulled up her jacket's collar, grabbed the bag that held her new purchases, and hurried towards home.

As was her habit, she glanced at the basement flat of the Edwardian house behind which her tiny bungalow sat. The day was falling towards dusk, and lights were on. She saw her neighbour move past the French windows.

All right, she thought, she was ready to admit it. The truth was, she needed someone to notice. She'd endured hours in the dentist's chair and her reward had been Isabelle Ardery's nod and her words, "See to the hair next, Sergeant," and that had been it. So instead of heading down the side of the house to the back garden where her bungalow sat beneath a towering false acacia, Barbara headed over to the flagstones that marked the outside area of the basement flat, and there she knocked on the door. The notice of a nine-year-old was better than nothing, she decided.

Hadiyyah answered, although Barbara heard the girl's mother say, "Darling, I *do* wish you wouldn't do that. It could be anyone."

"Just me," Barbara called out.

"Barbara, Barbara!" Hadiyyah cried. "Mummy, it's Barbara! Shall we show her what we've done?"

"Of course, silly girl. Do ask her to come in."

Barbara stepped inside to the scent of fresh paint, and

it took less than a moment to see what mother and daughter had accomplished. The lounge of the flat had been repainted. Angelina Upman was putting her mark upon it. She'd arranged decorative cushions on the sofa as well, and there were fresh flowers in two different vases: one low artistic arrangement on the coffee table, another on the mantel above the electric fire.

"Isn't it lovely?" Hadiyyah gazed up at her mother with such adoration that Barbara felt her throat close. "Mummy knows how to make things special and it's simple, really. Isn't it, Mummy?"

Angelina bent and kissed the top of her daughter's head. She lifted the little girl's chin and said to her, "You, my darling, are my biggest admirer, for which I thank you. But a more disinterested eye is required." She shot a smile at Barbara. "What do you think, Barbara? Have Hadiyyah and I made a success of our redecorating?"

"It's meant to be a surprise," Hadiyyah added. "Barbara, think of it. Dad doesn't even *know*."

They'd chosen to cover the heretofore dingy cream walls with the pale green of early spring. It was a colour well suited to Angelina, and she had to have known that. Sensible decision, Barbara thought. Against it, she looked even more attractive than she already was: light haired, blue eyed, delicate, a sprite.

"I like it," she said to Hadiyyah. "Did you help pick out the colour?"

"Well . . ." Hadiyyah shifted on her feet. She was standing next to her mother and she looked up at Angelina and sucked a tiny part of her upper lip.

"She did," Angelina lied blithely. "She had the final say. Her future in interior design is laid out in front of her, I daresay, although it's not likely her father will agree. It'll be science for you, Hadiyyah pet."

"Pooh," Hadiyyah said. "*I* want to be"—with a glance at her mother—"a *jazz* dancer, that's what."

This was news to Barbara, but not surprising. She'd learned that life as a professional dancer had been what Angelina had ostensibly been attempting for the fourteen months during which she'd disappeared from her daughter's life. That she hadn't disappeared alone was something Hadiyyah had not been told.

Angelina laughed. "A jazz dancer, is it? We'll keep that a secret, you and I." And to Barbara, "Will you have a cup of tea with us, Barbara? Hadiyyah, put the kettle on. We need to put our feet up after our day's labours."

"No, no, can't stay," Barbara said. "Just stopped by to . . ."

Barbara realised that they hadn't noticed either. Hours upon hours in the blasted dental chair and no one . . . and that meant . . . She pulled herself together. God, what was *wrong* with her? she wondered.

She remembered the bag in her hand, the scarf and blouse within it. "Bought something in the high street. I reckoned Hadiyyah's approval is all I need to wear it tomorrow."

"Yes, yes!" Hadiyyah cried. "Let's see, Barbara. Mummy, Barbara has been making herself over. She's been buying new clothes and everything. She wanted to go to Marks and Spencer at first, but I wouldn't let her. Well, we bought a skirt there, didn't we, Barbara, but that was *all* because I told her only *grannies* ever go to Marks and Spencer—"

"Not exactly true, darling," Angelina said.

"Well, *you* always said—"

"I say many silly things you're to take no notice of. Barbara, show us. Put it on, in fact."

"Oh yes, will you put it on?" Hadiyyah said. "You *must* put it on. You c'n use my room—"

"Which is chaos unleashed," Angelina said. "Use Hari's and mine, Barbara. Meanwhile, we'll make the tea."

Thus Barbara found herself in the last place she actually would have chosen to be: in the bedroom of Angelina Upman and Hadiyyah's father, Taymullah Azhar. She closed the door behind her with a tiny expulsion of breath. All right, she told herself, she could do this. All she had to do was take the blouse from the bag, unfold it, whip off the pullover she had on . . . She didn't have to look at anything but what was directly in front of her.

Which, naturally, she found impossible to do, and she didn't want to begin to think why. What she saw was what she expected to see: the signs of a man and woman who were partners to each other and specifically partners in the one way necessary to create a child. Not that they were attempting to create another, since Angelina's birth control pills were on the bedside table next to a clock radio. But contained within the fact of them was also the fact of what they meant.

So bloody what? Barbara asked herself. What the dickens had she expected and what business was it of hers anyway? Taymullah Azhar and Angelina Upman were doing the deed. Better said, they had *resumed* doing the deed at some point after Angelina's sudden reappearance in Azhar's life. The fact that she'd left him for another man was now apparently forgiven and forgotten, and there was an end to it. Everyone got to live happily whatever. Barbara told herself it behooved her to do likewise.

She buttoned the blouse and tried to smooth out its wrinkles. She took out the scarf she'd bought to go with it, and she wound this inexpertly round her neck. She moved to a mirror on the back of the door and gazed at herself. She wanted to retch. She should have gone for the torte, she decided. It would have cost less and been infinitely more satisfying.

"Are you changed, Barbara?" Hadiyyah asked from behind the closed door. "Mummy wants to know do you need any help."

"No. Got it," Barbara called. "I'm coming out. You ready? Have your sunglasses on? Be prepared to be dazzled."

Silence greeted her. Then Hadiyyah and her mother spoke at once: "A striking choice, Barbara," came from Angelina, while, "Oh no! You forgot about the jawline and the neckline!" came from Hadiyyah, this latter in something of a wail, to which she added, "They're s'posed to mirror each other, Barbara, and you for*got*."

Another fashion disaster, Barbara thought. There really *was* a reason she'd spent the last fifteen years of her life wearing slogan-fronted tee shirts and drawstring trousers.

Angelina hastened to say, "Hadiyyah, that's not true."

"But she's meant to choose rounded and she's chosen—"

"Darling, she's only failed to use the scarf as it's meant to be used. One can still create the effect by rounding the scarf. One doesn't want to be limited by believing that only a single kind of neckline . . . Here, Barbara, let me show you."

"But, Mummy, the colour—"

"—is perfect and I'm pleased you see that," Angelina said firmly. She removed the scarf from around Barbara's neck and with a few deft and maddening moves, she rearranged it. This put her closer to Barbara than she'd been before, and Barbara caught the scent of her: She was fragrant like a tropical flower. She also had the most flawless skin Barbara had ever seen. "There," Angelina said. "Look in the mirror now, Barbara. Tell me what you think. It's very easy to do. I'll show you."

Barbara went back into the bedroom within sight of those pills, which, this time, she refused to look at. She wanted to dislike Angelina—a woman who'd left her daughter and her daughter's father to have a lengthy fling for which she'd actually been *forgiven*?—but she found that she couldn't. This went some distance, she supposed, in explaining how and why Azhar had apparently forgiven her.

She saw her reflection and she had to admit it: The bloody woman knew how to tie a scarf. And now it was tied, properly, Barbara could see that it wasn't actually the appropriate concomitant garment to the blouse. Damn it all, she thought. *When* would she learn?

She was about to emerge and ask Angelina if she and Hadiyyah would accompany her on her next adventure in Camden High Street since she hadn't a great deal of money to waste on making the wrong sartorial decisions. But she heard the flat door open and the sounds of Taymullah Azhar arriving home. The last place she wanted to be found was in the bedroom he shared with the mother of his child, so she hastily untied the scarf, removed the blouse, shoved them back into the bag, and donned the pullover she'd worn to work that day.

When she rejoined them, Azhar was admiring the new paint on the walls, with Hadiyyah clinging onto his hand and Angelina linked to his arm. He turned, and his surprised face told Barbara that neither Hadiyyah nor her mother had mentioned her presence.

He said, "Barbara! Hullo. And what do you think of their handiwork?"

"I'm hiring them to do my digs next," Barbara said, "although I'm demanding purple and orange for my colours. Think that'll do me right, Hadiyyah?"

"No no no!" Hadiyyah cried.

Her parents laughed. Barbara smiled. Aren't we all a happy family? she thought. Time to exit stage right. She said, "Leave you to your dinner," and to Angelina specifically, "Thanks for the help with the scarf. I could see the difference. If I can get you to dress me every morning, I'll be set for life."

"Anytime," Angelina said. "Truly."

And the damn thing was, she meant it, Barbara thought. Maddening woman. If she'd merely cooperate and be a sodding cow, things would be so much easier.

She nodded a good night to them all and let herself out. She was surprised when Azhar followed her, but she understood when he lit a cigarette, something he would not do indoors now that nonsmoking Angelina had returned.

He said, "Congratulations, Barbara."

She stopped, turned, and said, "For what?"

"Your teeth. I see they've been repaired, and they look very good. I expect people have been telling you that all day, so let me count myself among them."

"Oh. Right. Ta. The guv—she's ordered the entire thing. Well, not *ordered* exactly, 'cause she can't do that in a personal matter like appearance. So let's say she suggested it strenuously. She wants the hair fixed next. I don't know where we go from there but I've a feeling it'll involve liposuction and serious cosmetic surgery. When she's finished with me, I expect I'll be beating men off with a broom."

"You're making light of it and you shouldn't," Azhar told her. "No doubt Angelina and Hadiyyah have already told you—"

"They haven't actually," Barbara cut in. "But thank you for the compliment, Azhar."

So there was irony in a soap dish, she thought: a compliment from the very last man on earth who should have noticed her teeth and the very last man from whom she should have wanted notice in the first place. Well, it didn't mean anything either way, she told herself.

On that set of lies, she walked on to her bungalow, bidding Taymullah Azhar good night.

30 OCTOBER

Forewarned being forearmed, Lynley had spent the next two days following his meeting with Hillier and Bernard Fairclough doing what research he was able to do on the man, his family, and his situation. He didn't wish to walk into this covert investigation blind and as things turned out, there was a fair amount of information available on Fairclough, who had not been born Bernard Fairclough at all but rather Bernie Dexter of Barrow-in-Furness. His initial appearance on earth took place at home, in a two-up and two-down terrace house in Blake Street. This turned out to be a short distance from the railway tracks upon the figurative wrong side of which the Dexter domicile lay.

How he'd morphed from Bernie Dexter into Bernard Fairclough, first Baron of Ireleth, was the kind of tale with which Sunday newspaper magazines justify their existences. As Bernie Dexter at fifteen years of age, he'd finished with what schooling he was ever to have and had gone to work for Fairclough Industries in a lowly position defined by the mindless job of packing chrome bathroom fixtures into shipping containers for eight hours each day. Although it was a job guaranteed to bleed soul, hope, and ambition from an ordinary worker, Bernie Dexter of Blake Street had been no ordinary worker. *Cheeky from the first* was how his wife described him in a post-knighthood interview, and she ought to have known for she had been born Valerie Fairclough, the great-granddaughter of the firm's founder. She'd met the fifteen-year-old when she herself was eighteen and he was performing in the company's Christmas panto. She was there for duty's sake; he was there for fun's sake. They encountered each other in a receiving line: the Fairclough owners doing a yearly bit of noblesse oblige and their employees—among whom was Bernie—moving along the line with an appropriate amount of forelock tugging, downcast eyes, and *aye, sir, thank you, sir* in best Dickensian manner as Christmas bonuses were handed out. This applied to all except Bernie Dexter, who told Valerie Fairclough straightaway and with a wink that he intended to marry her. "A real beauty, you are," he said, "so I reckon I'll set you up for life." He declared this last with utter confidence, as if Valerie Fairclough were somehow not set up for life already.

He'd gone on to keep his word, however, for he had no qualms at all about approaching Valerie's father, telling him, "I could make this firm into something better, you know, you give me half a chance." And so he had done. Not all at once, of course, but over time, and during that time he also managed to impress Valerie with the persistence of his devotion to her. He also managed to impregnate the young woman when she was twenty-five, which resulted in an elopement. In short order, then, he took her family name as his own, improved the efficiency of Fairclough Industries, modernised its products, one of which was—of all things—an entire line of state-of-the-art lavatories, from which he amassed an impressive fortune.

His son, Nicholas, had always been the fly in the ointment of Bernie's otherwise ideal life. Lynley found volumes of information on the bloke. For when Nicholas Fairclough went periodically bad, he did it in a very public manner. Public drunkenness, brawls, break-ins, football hooliganism, drunk driving, car theft, arson, indecent exposure while under the influence . . . The man had a past that read like that of the prodigal son on steroids. He'd played out his dissolution before God and everyone and in particular before the eyes of the local press in Cumbria, and the stories generated from his behaviour caught the eyes of the national tabloids always on the prowl for sensation to feature on their cover pages, especially when the sensation is generated by the scion of someone notable.

Early death was the usual outcome of a life led in the manner Nicholas Fairclough had led his, but in his case love supervened in the person of a young Argentine woman with the impressive name of Alatea Vasquez y del Torres. Fresh out of yet another rehab programme—this one in America, in the state of Utah—Nicholas had taken himself to a former mining town called Park City for what he apparently believed was a well-deserved spate of R & R, financed as usual by his desperate father. The old mining town served this purpose well, for it was nestled in the Wasatch Mountains and into its embrace every year from late November till April came avid skiers from round the world, along with scores of young men and women hired to service their needs.

Alatea Vasquez y del Torres had been among this latter group, and she and Nicholas Fairclough—according to the more breathless reports Lynley was able to scavenge—locked eyes over the till in one of the ski resort's many eateries. The rest, as is generally said, was history. What ensued was a whirlwind courtship, a courthouse marriage effected in Salt Lake City, a final descent into a drug-fuelled pyre of dissolution on Nicholas's part—odd way to celebrate matrimony, but there you have it, Lynley thought—from which the phoenix that was apparently the man's amazing physical constitution arose. The arising of this phoenix, however, had little to do with Fairclough's determination to get the better of the beast on his back and everything to do with Alatea Vasquez y del Torres's decision to walk out on him barely two months into their marriage.

"I'd do anything for her," Fairclough had later declared. "I'd die for her. To take the cure for her was child's play."

She'd returned to him, he'd stuck with sobriety, and everyone was happy. So it seemed from all the accounts that Lynley was able to glean in his twenty-four hours of research into the family. Thus if Nicholas Fairclough had been involved some way in his cousin's death, at this point in his life it seemed wildly out of character, for it was hardly reasonable to assume that his wife would remain loyally at the side of a murderer.

Lynley went on to read about the rest of the family from whatever sources he could find. But information on them was vague, considering how dull they were in comparison to the son of Lord Fairclough. One sister divorced, one sister a spinster, one cousin—this would be the dead man— the master of the Fairclough money, that cousin's wife a homemaker and their two children respectable . . . The Fairclough family were a disparate group but on the surface they all seemed clean.

At the end of his second day of exploration, Lynley stood at the window of his library in Eaton Terrace and looked out at the street, the gas fire burning brightly behind him in the late afternoon. He didn't much like the situation he was in, but he wasn't sure what he could do about it. In his line of work, the objective was to gather evidence in proof of someone's guilt, not to gather evidence in proof of their innocence. If the coroner had declared the death accidental, there seemed little point delving further into the matter. For coroners knew what they were about, and they had evidence and testimony to bolster their findings. That the coroner had deemed the death of Ian Cresswell an accident—unfortunate and untimely as all accidents were, but still an accident—seemed a conclusion that ought to have satisfied everyone, no matter the grief attendant on the sudden loss of a man from the bosom of his family.

It was interesting, though, that Bernard Fairclough wasn't satisfied, Lynley thought. Despite the inquest and its results, Fairclough's doubts in the matter suggested that he might well know more than he'd mentioned at their meeting at Twins. And this suggested there was more to the death of Ian Cresswell than met the superficial eye.

Lynley wondered if someone had dropped a word to Fairclough about the local investigation into the drowning. He also wondered if Fairclough had himself had a word with someone inside of it.

Lynley turned from the window and gazed at his desk; spread out on it were notes, printouts from his computer, the laptop itself. There was, he reckoned, more than one avenue to unearth additional information regarding Ian Cresswell's death—if, indeed, there was additional information—and he was on his way to the phone to make a call in the service of gathering more details when it rang. He thought about allowing the answer machine to take it—that reaction to the phone had become habitual over recent months—but he decided to pick up, and when he did, it was to hear Isabelle say, "What on earth are you doing, Tommy? Why haven't you been at work?"

He'd thought Hillier would handle this detail. Obviously, he'd been wrong.

He said, "It's a small matter Hillier asked me to deal with. I thought he'd tell you."

"Hillier? What sort of matter?" Isabelle sounded surprised, as well she might. He and Hillier didn't rub congenial elbows very often, and if push came to shove, Lynley was surely the last person at the Met to whom Hillier would turn.

"It's confidential," he told her. "I'm not at liberty—"

"What's going on?"

He didn't reply at once. He was trying to think of a way to tell her what he was doing without actually telling her what he was doing, but she apparently took his silence for avoidance because she said tartly, "Ah. I see. Is this to do with what happened?"

"With what? What happened?"

"Please. Don't. You know what I'm saying. With Bob. That night. The fact that we've not been together since—"

"Lord, no. It's nothing to do with that," he cut in, although the truth of the matter, if he had to admit it, was that he wasn't exactly sure.

"Then why've you been avoiding me?"

"I'm not aware that I *have* been avoiding you."

There was a silence that greeted this. He found himself wondering where she was. The time of day suggested she might still be at the Yard, perhaps in her office, and he could see her there at her desk with her head lowered to speak into the phone and her smooth hair—rather the colour of amber—tucked behind one ear to show a conservative but fashionable earring. One shoe off, perhaps, and there she was leaning down to rub her calf as she thought what she would say to him next.

What she said surprised him. "Tommy, I told Bob yesterday. Not who exactly because, as I explained, I do know very well he'd use it against me at some time when he believes I'm out of order. But *that*. I told him that."

"That what?"

"That I'm involved with someone. That you'd come to the door when he and Sandra were there, that I'd sent you off because I thought the boys weren't ready to meet . . . after all, they'd come into London for the first time to see me and they needed to adjust to my being in London and to the flat itself and everything that goes along with it. To have a man there as well . . . I told him I felt it was too soon and I'd asked you to leave. But I wanted him to know that you do exist."

"Ah. Isabelle." Lynley knew what it had cost her: telling her former husband about him when the man held such power over her life and now telling *him* that she'd done so when she was a proud woman and God how he knew that about her.

"I'm missing you, Tommy. I don't want us to be at odds."

"We're not at odds."

"Are we not?"

"We are not."

Another pause. Perhaps she was at home after all, he thought, sitting on the edge of the bed in that claustrophobic bedroom of hers with its single window virtually sealed against anyone's attempt to open it fully and its bed too small to accommodate both of them comfortably for an entire night. Which could or could not have been the point of it, he realised. And what would that mean to him if she admitted to that?

"Things are complicated," he said. "They always are, aren't they?"

"After a certain age, yes. There's so much bloody baggage." And then after an indrawn breath, "I want you tonight, Tommy. Will you come to me?" And most remarkably, "Have you the time?"

He wanted to say that it wasn't at all a matter of time. It was a matter of how he felt and who he wanted to be. But this, too, was complicated. So he said, "I can't say exactly."

"Because of the Hillier thing. I was hoping you'd notice I hadn't insisted on knowing what's going on. And I won't. You've my promise on it. Even afterwards, I won't, and you know what that means because I do know how you are afterwards. Sometimes I think I could get anything out of you afterwards, you know."

"And why don't you?"

"Well, it doesn't seem quite fair, does it? Besides, I like to think I'm not that sort of woman. I don't scheme. Well, not much at least."

"Are you scheming now?"

"Only to have you and it can't be a scheme if I'm admitting to it, can it?"

He smiled at that. He felt a softening towards her and he recognised this as the desire he continued to feel for her, despite the fact that the timing of their relationship was wretched and they were ill matched anyway and always would be. He wanted her. Still.

"It might be late when I arrive," he said.

"That hardly matters. Will you come to me, Tommy?"

"I will," he told her.

CHELSEA
LONDON

He had arrangements to make first, however. While he could have made them over the phone, he decided that making them in person would allow him to gauge whether what he was asking was an inconvenience to the people he needed. For they would never tell him so.

The fact that this was not to be a formal police investigation hobbled him considerably. It also called for a creative approach to appease the demands for secrecy. He could have insisted that Hillier allow him the services of another officer, but the only officers he cared to work with were unlikely candidates for a surreptitious crawl round Cumbria. At six feet four inches tall and with skin the colour of very strong tea, DS Winston Nkata would hardly fade into the autumn scenery of the Lake District. And as for DS Barbara Havers—who under other circumstances would have been Lynley's first choice, despite her score of maddening personal habits—the idea of Barbara chain-smoking her belligerent way round Cumbria under the pretext that she was, perhaps, a walker out for a bracing week on the fells . . . It was too ludicrous to contemplate. She was a brilliant cop, but discretion was not her strong suit. Had Helen been alive, she would have been perfect for the job. She would have loved it, as well. *Tommy darling, we'll be incognito! Lord, how delicious. I've spent my life absolutely long-ing to do a Tuppence.* But Helen was not alive, was *not* alive. The very thought of her sent him on his way as rapidly as he could manage.

He drove to Chelsea, choosing the route that took him down the King's Road. It was the most direct way to get to Cheyne Row but not the quickest as the narrow road led him through the area's trendy shopping district with its fashion boutiques, shoe shops, antiques markets, pubs, and restaurants. There were crowds on the pavements as always, and seeing them—especially seeing their youth—made him melancholy and filled him with what felt like regret. He couldn't have said what he regretted, though. He didn't much want to try to find out.

He parked in Lawrence Street, near Lordship Place. He walked back the way he'd come but rather than going on to Cheyne Row, he went in through the garden gate of the tall brick house that stood on the corner.

The garden was showing its autumn colours and readying itself for the winter. The lawn was strewn with leaves needing gathering while the herbaceous borders offered plants whose flowers were long gone now and whose stalks leaned perilously, as if weighted towards the ground by an unseen hand. The wicker furniture wore canvas shrouds. Moss grew between the bricks. Lynley followed a path of these, which led to the house. There, steps descended to the basement kitchen. A light was on there against the coming evening. He could see a shape moving behind the window, itself steamed from the heat inside.

He knocked sharply twice and when the usual barking of the dog commenced, he opened the door and said, "It's me, Joseph. I've come in the back way."

"Tommy?" It was a woman's voice, however, not the voice Lynley had been expecting but rather the man's daughter. "Are you playing at Victorian tradesman?"

She came round the corner from the kitchen in the wake of the dog, a long-haired dachshund with the unlikely name of Peach. Peach barked, jumped, and did her usual by way of greeting him. She was as undisciplined as always, living proof of what Deborah St. James often declared: that she required a dog she could pick up as she was utterly hopeless at training anything.

"Hullo, you," Deborah said to Lynley. "What a very nice surprise." She scooted the dog to one side and hugged him. She brushed a kiss against his cheek. "You're staying for dinner," she announced. "For many reasons but most of all because I'm cooking it."

"Good Lord. Where's your father?"

"Southampton. Anniversary. He didn't want me to go this year. I expect it's because it's the twentieth."

"Ah." He knew Deborah wouldn't say more, not because it pained her to speak of her mother's death, which, after all, had occurred when Deborah was seven years old, but because of him and the fact of what death might remind him of.

"Anyway," she said, "he'll be back tomorrow. But meanwhile that leaves poor Simon in my culinary clutches. Are you wanting him, by the way? He's only upstairs."

"I'm wanting you both. What're you cooking, then?"

"Shepherd's pie. The mash is instant. More than that I wasn't willing to attempt and besides, potatoes are potatoes, aren't they? I'm doing broccoli for the veg, Mediterranean style. Swimming in olive oil and garlic. And a side salad as well, also swimming in olive oil and garlic. You'll stay? You must. If it's terrible, you can lie and tell me everything tastes like ambrosia. I'll know you're lying, of course. I always know when you lie, by the way. But it won't matter because if you say everything's wonderful, Simon'll be forced to do likewise. Oh yes, and there's pudding as well."

"That'll be the deciding factor."

"Ah. You see? I know you're lying, but I'll play along. It's actually a French tart."

"Leaping out of a cake or something?"

She laughed. "Very amusing, Lord Asherton. Are you staying or not? It's apple and pear, by the way."

"How can I refuse?" Lynley glanced towards the stairs that led up to the rest of the house. "Is he . . . ?"

"In the study. Go up. I'll join you once I check to see how things look in the oven."

He left her. Upstairs, he walked down the corridor. He heard the sound of Simon St. James's voice coming from his study at the front of the house. This took the place of a normal sitting room, and it was crammed floor to ceiling with books on three walls with a fourth dedicated to Deborah's photographs. When Lynley entered the room, his friend was seated at his desk, and the fact that he was driving his hand into his hair with his head bent to the task as he spoke on the phone told Lynley that difficulty was afoot in the other man's life.

St. James was saying, "I thought so as well, David. I still think so. As far as I'm concerned, it's the answer we're looking for . . . Yes, yes. I completely understand . . . I'll speak to her again . . . How much time exactly? . . . When would she want to see us? . . . Yes, I see." He glanced up then, saw Lynley, and nodded a hello. He said, "All right, then. Best to Mother and your family," before ringing off. His final remark told Lynley that he'd been speaking to his eldest brother, David.

St. James rose awkwardly, shoving away from his desk to get purchase on its edge so that he could rise more easily, despite the disability of a leg that hadn't functioned without a brace for years. He greeted Lynley and moved to the drinks trolley beneath the window. "Whisky's the answer," he said to Lynley. "Taller than usual and straight. What about you?"

"Pour away," Lynley said to him. "Trouble?"

"My brother David's come across a girl in Southampton who wants to put up her baby for adoption, a private arrangement made through a solicitor."

"That's excellent news, Simon," Lynley said. "You must be delighted after all this time."

"Under normal circumstances. It's like a gift we weren't expecting." He uncapped a bottle of Lagavulin and poured a good three fingers for each of them. Lynley raised an eyebrow as St. James handed one over to him. "We deserve it," St. James said. "At least I do, and I expect you do as well." He gestured towards the leather armchairs in front of the fireplace. They were worn and cracked, suitable for sinking into and getting properly sloshed.

"What are the circumstances, then?" Lynley asked.

St. James glanced at the doorway, suggesting the conversation was meant to take place without Deborah's knowledge. "The mother wants an open adoption. Not only herself involved in the baby's life but the father as well. She's sixteen. He's fifteen."

"Ah. I see."

"Deborah's reaction was that she doesn't want to share her child."

"Not entirely unreasonable, is it?"

St. James continued. "And decidedly, she doesn't want to share her child with two teenagers. She says it would be like adopting three children instead of one and besides that, there are both extended families to consider and how they'd fit in as well." He took a gulp of the whisky.

"Actually," Lynley said, "I rather see her point."

"As do I. The situation's far from ideal. On the other hand, it seems . . . Well, she's had the rest of the tests, Tommy. It's definite. It's highly unlikely she'd ever be able to carry a child to term."

Lynley knew this. He'd known for more than a year, and it seemed that Deborah had finally told her husband the truth she'd carried alone—aside from his own knowledge of it—for the past twelve months.

Lynley said nothing. Both of them meditated on their glasses of Lagavulin. From the corridor, the clicking of dog nails against wood indicated that Peach was coming to them and if Peach was coming, she was no doubt accompanied by her mistress. Lynley said quietly, "Deborah's asked me to stay to dinner, but I can make an excuse if it's awkward for you tonight."

St. James replied with, "God no. I'd prefer it. You know me. Anything to avoid a difficult conversation with the woman I love."

"I've brought us some predinner goodies," Deborah said as she entered the room. "Cheese straws. Peach has already had one, so I can tell you they're delicious, at least to a dog. Don't get up, Simon. I'll fetch my own sherry." She put a plate of the cheese straws on an ottoman between the two chairs, shooed the dachshund away from them, and went to the drinks trolley. She said to her husband, "Tommy's told me he wants to see both of us. I reckon it's either business or an announcement or both and if it has to do with the Healey Elliott, I vote that we buy it off him straightaway, Simon."

"Clear your mind of that proposition," Lynley said. "I'll be buried in that car."

"Damn." St. James smiled.

"I did try," his wife told him. She came to perch on the arm of his chair and said to Lynley, "What, then, Tommy?"

He thought about how to approach the matter. He settled on saying, "I'm wondering how you two might feel about an autumn's jaunt up to the Lakes."

CHELSEA
LONDON

She always brushed the day's tangles out of her hair before she came to bed. Sometimes he did it for her, and sometimes he watched. Her hair was long and thick and curly and red, ungovernable at most times, which was why he loved it. Tonight he watched from the bed, where he rested against the pillows. She stood across from him at the chest of drawers. There was a mirror above this and she could see him watching her in its reflection.

"Are you sure you can take the time away from work, Simon?"

"It's only a few days. Question is, can you and how do you feel about doing it?"

"Dissembling not being my stock in trade, you mean?" She put down her brush and crossed to the bed. She wore a thin cotton nightgown, but she shed this, as usual, before joining him. He liked that she preferred to sleep naked. He liked turning to find her, warm and soft, while he was dreaming. "It's the sort of thing Helen would have loved," she noted. "I wonder Tommy's not thought of that."

"Perhaps he has."

"Hmm. Yes. Well, I'm ready to help him, for whatever good I can do. I'll want to track down that sidebar about Nicholas Fairclough that Tommy mentioned. I c'n use that as my jumping-off point, I daresay. 'Having read about you and your project in that magazine article on your parents' topiary garden . . .' Et cetera, et cetera. And at least there's a reason that already exists for someone to want a documentary film made. If there weren't, I'd be completely out of my depth. What about you?"

"The inquest material won't present a problem. Nor will the forensic data. As to the rest, I'm not sure. It's an odd situation any way you look at it." And speaking of odd situations, he thought, there was another that remained to be dealt with. He said, "David phoned. I was talking to him when Tommy arrived."

He could actually *feel* the change in her. Her breathing altered, one slow intake followed by one very long pause. He said, "The girl would like to meet us, Deborah. Her parents and the boy would be there as well. She prefers it that way, and the solicitor indicated—"

"I can't," Deborah said. "I've thought about it, Simon. I've looked at it every possible way. Truly, I have. You must believe me. But no matter how I try to twist it, I do think that the bad outweighs the good."

"It's irregular, but other people manage it."

"They may do, but I'm not other people. We'd be asked to share a baby with its birth mother, its birth father, its natural grandparents, and God knows who else, and I *know* this is trendy and modern, but I don't want it. I can't make myself want it."

"They might well lose interest in the child," St. James pointed out. "They're very young."

Deborah looked at him. She'd been sitting up in bed—not at rest against the pillow—and she swung round and said incredulously, "Lose *interest*? This is a child, not a puppy. They're not going to lose interest. Would you?"

"No, but I'm not a fifteen-year-old boy. And anyway, there would be arrangements. They'd be drawn up by the solicitor."

"No," she said. "Please don't ask me again. I just *can't*."

He let a moment pass. She'd turned away. Her hair tumbled down her back nearly to her waist, and he touched a lock of it, saw how it curled naturally round his fingers. He said, "Will you just think about it a bit longer before you decide? As I said, she'd like to meet us. We could do that much if nothing else. You might well like her, her family, the boy. You know, the fact that she wants to keep contact with the child . . . That's not a bad thing, Deborah."

"How is it good?" she asked, still turned from him.

"It indicates a sense of responsibility. She doesn't just want to walk away and get on with her life as if nothing ever happened to change it. In a way she wants to provide for the child, be there to answer questions should questions come up."

"We could answer questions. You know that very well. And why on earth—if she wants to be involved in the child's life—would she choose a couple from London to be the parents anyway, instead of a couple from Southampton? That doesn't make sense. She's from Southampton, isn't she?"

"She is."

"So you see . . ."

He reckoned she couldn't bear another disappointment and he didn't blame her. But if they didn't continue to push forward, if they didn't follow whatever avenue opened up before them, an opportunity could easily be missed and if they wanted a child, if they *truly* wanted a child . . .

That was, of course, the real question. Asking it, however, constituted a minefield, and he'd been married to Deborah long enough to know that some fields were too dangerous to venture into. Still, he said, "Have you another solution, then? Another possibility?"

She didn't reply at once. He had the sense, though, that she did have something else in mind, something she was reluctant to mention. He repeated the question. She quickly responded with, "Surrogacy."

He said, "Good God, Deborah, that route's fraught with—"

"Not a donor mother, Simon, but a host mother. Our embryo, our baby, and someone willing to carry it. It wouldn't be hers. She'd have no attachment. Or at least she'd have no right to an attachment."

His spirits plummeted. He wondered how something that for other people was so damnably natural could have, for them, turned into such a mire of appointments, doctors, specialists, procedures, solicitors, questions, answers, and more questions. And this, now? Months and months would pass while a surrogate was sought and interviewed and checked out in every possible way while Deborah took drugs that would do God only knew what to her system in order to harvest (God, what a word) eggs while he disappeared into a lavatory stall with container in hand to make the required, passionless, and loveless deposit and all of this to result—perhaps, if they were lucky, if nothing went wrong—in a child that was biologically their own. It seemed wildly complicated, inhumanly mechanised, and only partially guaranteed of success.

He blew out a breath. He said, "Deborah," and he knew that she recognised in his tone a form of hesitation that she would not want to hear. That it had to do with his desire to protect her would not occur to Deborah. And that was just as well, he thought. For she hated him to protect her from life, even as she felt life's blows more than he thought either necessary or good.

She said in a low voice, "I know what you're thinking. And this puts us at an impasse, doesn't it?"

"We just see things differently. We're coming at it from different directions. One of us sees an opportunity where the other sees an insurmountable difficulty."

She thought about this. She said slowly, "How odd. It seems there's nothing to be done, then."

She lay next to him, then, but her back was to him. He switched out the light and put his hand on her hip. She didn't respond.

WANDSWORTH
LONDON

It was nearly midnight when Lynley arrived. Regardless of his promise to her, he knew he should have gone home instead and slept however he was meant to sleep on this particular night, which would be fitfully, no doubt. But instead he made his way to Isabelle's, and he let himself in with his key.

She met him at the door. He'd expected she would have long gone to bed, and it did seem she'd been there at first. But a light was on next to the sofa in the sitting area of her flat, and he saw a magazine spread out there, evidently discarded when she'd heard his key in the lock. She'd left her dressing gown on the sofa as well, and as she wore nothing beneath, she came to him nude and when he closed the door behind him, she stepped into his arms and lifted her mouth to his.

She tasted of lemons. For a moment he allowed himself to wonder if the taste of her indicated that she was trying to hide the fact that she'd been drinking again. But then he didn't care as his hands travelled the distance from her hips to her waist to her breasts.

She began to undress him. She murmured, "This is very bad, you know."

He whispered, "What is?"

"That I've thought of little else all day." His jacket fell to the floor and she worked the buttons of his shirt. He bent to her neck, her breasts.

"That," he said, "*is* very bad in your line of work."

"In yours as well."

"Ah, but I've more discipline."

"Have you indeed?"

"I have."

"And if I touch you here, like this?" She did so. He smiled. "What happens to your discipline then?"

"The same thing, I daresay, that happens to yours if I kiss you here, if I decide on more, if I use my tongue . . . rather like this."

She drew in a sharp breath. She chuckled. "You're an evil man, Inspector. But I'm fully able to match evil for evil. Rather, as you say, like this." She lowered his trousers. She made him as naked as she was herself. She used her nakedness to force action from him.

She was, he found, as slick and as ready as he was. He said, "The bedroom?"

She said, "Not tonight, Tommy."

"Here, then?"

"Oh yes. Right here."

2 NOVEMBER

Because of the hour of the day, Zed Benjamin had been able to score a good table at the Willow and Well, and he'd been sitting there for fifty minutes, waiting for something to happen on the other side of a window whose lead mullions were in need of replacement. The cold seeped past them like a visitation of the angel of death, but the benefit of this discomfort was the fact that no one would question the knitted ski cap that Zed was thus able to keep planted on his head. The cap was his bow to making himself less memorable since it fully covered his flame-coloured hair. There was nothing he could do about his extreme height save slouching whenever he remembered to do so.

He was managing just that at his table in the pub. He'd been going from hunching over his pint of lager to slumping in his chair with his legs stretched out till his arse was as numb as the heart of a pimp, but in all the time he'd maintained one posture or another, nothing suggesting that illumination was in the offing had occurred in what he could see of the village of Bryanbarrow just outside of the window.

This was his third day in Cumbria, his third day of searching for the sex that would keep his story on Nicholas

Fairclough from being binned by Rodney Aronson, but so far he'd come up with nothing except fifteen lines of a new poem, which, God knew, he wasn't about to mention to Aronson when the odious editor of *The Source* made his daily phone call to ask meaningfully how things were going and to remind Zed that whatever costs he was incurring would be his own. As if he didn't know that already, Zed thought. As if he were not staying in the most modest room in the most modest bed-and-breakfast he could find in the entire region: an attic bedroom in one of the multitudinous Victorian terraces that lined virtually every street in Windermere, this one on Broad Street within walking distance of the public library. He had to duck to get through the door of the room and practically do the limbo if he wanted to walk to the single window. The loo was on the floor below and the heat was by means of whatever came up from the rest of the house. But all of this made the price extremely right, so he'd snapped it up upon a single glance once he learned how little it was going to cost him. In recompense, it seemed, for the myriad inconveniences of the room, the landlady provided sumptuous breakfasts involving everything from porridge to prunes, so Zed hadn't had to eat lunch since he'd arrived, which was just as well since he used the time he would have otherwise spent in a café trying to suss out who—besides himself—was prowling round the death of Ian Cresswell. But if Scotland Yard was indeed here in Cumbria in the person of a detective on the scent of the unfortunate drowning of Nicholas Fairclough's cousin, Zed had not been able to locate that person, and until he saw him, he wasn't going to be able to mould *The Ninth Life* into the *Nine Lives and a Death* that Rodney Aronson apparently wanted.

Naturally, Aronson knew who the Scotland Yard detective was. Zed would have put a week's meagre wages on that. He would have put a further week's wages on Aronson's having a master plan to give Zed the sack upon his failure to unearth said detective, which would equate to his failure to sex up his story. That was what this was all about because Rodney couldn't cope with the combination of Zed's education and his aspirations.

Not that he was getting far with his aspirations and not that he *would* get far with them. Oh, one might survive artistically in this day and age by producing poetry, but poetry did not put a roof over one's head.

That thought—a roof over his head—put Zed in mind of the roof in London under which he lived. It put him further in mind of the people beneath that roof. Lodged among those people were those people's intentions, his mother's foremost among them.

At least he didn't have to worry about those intentions just now, Zed thought, for one morning soon after the first night of Yaffa Shaw's presence in the family flat—which had been effected with a rapidity astounding even for his mother—the young woman waylaid Zed outside of the bathroom they were going to be forced to share, and sponge bag in hand she'd murmured, "No worries, Zed. All right?" His mind on his job, he thought at first she was speaking of what lay in front of him: yet another trip to Cumbria. But it came to him that Yaffa was actually talking about her presence in the family flat and about his mother's determination to throw them together as much as she could until she wore down their resistance and they succumbed to an engagement, marriage, and babies.

Zed said, "Eh?" and fiddled with the belt of his dressing gown. It was too short for him, as were the trousers of his pyjamas, and he never could find slippers to fit so he was wearing what he usually wore on his feet in the morning, which was a pair of mismatched socks. He felt all at once like what Jack found at the top of the beanstalk, especially in comparison to Yaffa, who was neat and trim and all of a piece with everything on her a coordinated affair in an appealing colour that seemed to enhance both her skin and her eyes.

Yaffa looked over her shoulder in the general direction of the kitchen, from where breakfast sounds were emanating. She said quietly, "Listen, Zed. I have a boyfriend in Tel Aviv, in medical school, so you're not to worry." She'd pushed back a bit of her hair—dark, curly, and hanging down below her shoulders quite prettily, whereas earlier she'd worn it pulled back from her face—and she gave him a look that he'd had to call impish. She said, "I didn't tell her that. You see, this"—with an inclination of her head towards the door of the bedroom she'd been given—"saves me heaps of money. I can cut back my hours at work and take another course. And if I can do that each term, I can finish uni earlier, and if I can do *that*, I'm one step closer to getting back home to Micah."

"Ah," he said.

"When she introduced us—you and me—I could see what your mum had in mind, so I didn't say anything about him. I needed the room—I *need* the room—and I'm willing to play along if you are."

"How?" He realised he seemed only capable of one-word responses to this young woman, and he wasn't at all sure what this meant.

She said, "We develop a pretence."

"Pretence?"

"We're attracted, you and I. We play the role, we 'fall in love'"—she sketched inverted commas in the air—"and then conveniently I break your heart. Or you break mine. It doesn't matter except considering your mum, I'd better break yours. We'd probably have to go on one or two dates and maintain some kind of enraptured contact on our mobiles while you're gone. You could make kissing noises occasionally and look soulfully at me over the breakfast table. It would buy me time to save the money I need to take the extra course each term and it would buy you time to get your mother off your back for a bit about getting married. We'd have to play at a little affection now and then but you're off the hook having to sleep with me as we wouldn't want to show such disrespect to your mum. I think it would work. What about you?"

He nodded. "I see." He was pleased he'd advanced to two words instead of one.

"So?" she said. "Are you willing?"

"Yes." And then in a graduation to four words: "When do we start?"

"At breakfast."

So when Yaffa asked him over the breakfast table to tell her about the story he was working on in Cumbria, he played along. To his surprise, he found that she asked very good questions and her pretence of interest in his affairs caused his mother to beam at him meaningfully. He'd left London with his mother's ecstatic hug and her "You see, you *see,* my boy?" burning in his brain, along with a note from Yaffa in his pocket: "Wait thirty-six hours, phone the flat, ask your mum if you can speak to me. I'll give you my mobile number while she's listening. Good hunting in Cumbria, my friend." He'd phoned at the thirty-six-hour mark exactly, and he'd ended up again surprised to find that he actually enjoyed the brief conversation he had with Yaffa Shaw. This was due, he reckoned, to the fact that everything was out in the open between them. No pressure, he thought. And he always operated best when there was minimal pressure.

He only wished that were the case with regard to this damn story. He couldn't think of what to do to unearth the Scotland Yard detective aside from planting himself in Bryanbarrow and waiting to see who turned up at Ian Cresswell's farm on the scent of the man's untimely death. The Willow and Well afforded him an unobstructed view of this place. For Bryan Beck farm sat across the small triangular green that served as the centre of the village, its ancient manor house visible behind a low stone wall and a tenant cottage making a crumbling statement at right angles to it.

As he watched, into the second hour of nursing his pint and maintaining his vigil, there was finally a sign of life at the farm. It didn't emanate from the manor house, though, but rather from the tenant cottage. From this emerged a man and a teenage boy. They left the property side by side and walked onto the green, where the man placed a step stool that he positioned in the centre of the lawn among the fallen leaves blown from the oak trees that bordered it. He plopped himself on this stool and gestured to the boy, who was carrying what looked like an old bedsheet, along with a shoe box tucked under his arm. The bedsheet he draped round the older man's shoulders, and from the box he took scissors, a comb, and a hand mirror. The older man removed the tweed cap he wore and jerked his head at the boy: the sign to begin. The boy set about cutting his hair.

This, Zed knew, had to be George Cowley and his teenage son, Daniel. They could be no one else. He knew that the dead man Ian Cresswell had a son, but as Cresswell *was* dead, he didn't reckon the son was hanging about the farm and he reckoned even less that that son would be cutting the hair of the tenant farmer. Why they were doing this in the middle of the village green was an interesting question, but cutting it there made cleaning-up simple, Zed supposed, although it wasn't likely to endear George Cowley to the other residents of Bryanbarrow, some of whom lived in the terrace of cottages that comprised one side of the green.

Zed downed the rest of his pint, which at this point had long gone both warm and flat. He lumbered out of the pub and he approached the haircutting on the green. It was chilly outside, with a breeze, and the combined scent of wood smoke and cow dung hung on the air. Sheep were sounding off from beyond Bryan Beck farm and as if in response ducks were quacking with undue volume from Bryan Beck itself, which gushed along the west side of the village out of Zed's view.

"Afternoon." Zed nodded at the man and the boy. "You're Mr. Cowley, I understand." He understood because he'd spoken to the publican at some length during his first hour's deployment within the Willow and Well. As far as the publican knew, Zed was one of the myriad walkers who came to the Lakes either to discover what Wordsworth had spent his creative energies extolling or to see what the profits from *Peter Rabbit* had managed to save from mankind's tendency to build hideous structures upon it. He'd been more than willing to increase Zed's knowledge of the "real Lakes" with a good period of gossip about its denizens, many of whom were "gen-u-ine Cumbrian characters," one of whom was, ultimately and conveniently, George Cowley. "A real piece o' work, is George," the publican had said. "One of those blokes never lets go of a grievance. Love to feud, they do, that sort of bloke. I feel dead sorry for that boy of his 'cause the only thing George has any fondness for is feuding and his bloody dog." His bloody dog was a border collie who'd come as far as the hedge when George Cowley and his son crossed over to the green. A word from George and the dog had dropped to its belly obediently. There it remained, a watchful eye on the proceedings, throughout Zed's conversation with its master.

Cowley eyed Zed with no small degree of suspicion. His son held his scissors poised, but he'd stopped cutting his father's hair. George said over his shoulder to him, "Get on with it, Dan," and looked away from Zed. So much for friendly conversation, Zed thought.

"Lovely farm you've got," Zed said. "Unusual to have it actually part of the village."

"Not mine," George remarked sourly.

"You run it, though, don't you? Doesn't that make it as good as yours?"

George cast him a look indicative of scorn. "Not hardly. And what's it to you anyway?"

Zed glanced at the man's son. Daniel's face flushed. Zed said, "Nothing, actually. It merely looks an interesting place. The big house and all that. I've a curiosity about old buildings. It's an old manor house, isn't it? The bigger building?"

Cowley scowled. "Could be. Dan, are you cutting or not? I'm not 'bout to sit here all day in the cold. We've things to see to."

Daniel said quietly to Zed, "Elizabethan, it is. We used to live there."

"Dan!"

"Sorry." He resumed his cutting. It looked like something he'd been doing for years, as he used both the comb and the scissors efficiently.

Cowley said to Zed, "So who bloody wants to know and why?"

"Eh?"

"The house. The farm. Why're you asking about 'em? What's your interest? You've some sort o' business in the village?"

"Oh." Zed thought of the approach that would glean him the most information with the least revelation on his part. "Just interested in the history of the places I visit. In the Willow and Well, the barman was saying that's the oldest building in the village, that manor house."

"Wrong, he is. Cottage's older by a hundert years."

"Is it really? I expect a place like that could be haunted or something."

"That why you're here? You looking for ghosts? Or"—sharply—"for something else?"

God, the man was suspicious, Zed thought. He wondered idly if the bloke had pieces of silver shoved up the chimney or something very like, with Zed there to case the joint, as the saying went. He said affably to Cowley, "Sorry. No. I'm only here visiting. I don't mean to unnerve you."

"Not unnerved. I c'n take care of m'self and Dan, I can."

"Right. Of course. I expect you can." Zed went for a jolly tone. "I don't expect you get many people asking questions about the farm, eh? Or actually many people here at all, especially this time of year. Asking questions or doing anything else." He winced inwardly. He was going to have to do something about developing a subtlety of approach.

Cowley said, "'F you like history, I c'n give you history," but he crossed his arms beneath the sheet that was keeping the hair from his clothing, and his posture suggested nothing was forthcoming, in spite of his words.

Daniel said, "Dad," in a tone that took a position between advising and warning.

"Didn't say nothing, did I," Cowley said.

"It's only that—"

"Just cut the bloody hair and have done." Cowley looked away, this time to the manor house behind the wall. It was all of stone, neatly whitewashed right to the top of its chimneys, and its roof looked as if it had been recently replaced. "That," he said, "was meant to be mine. Got bought out from under my nose, it did, with no one the wiser till the job was done. And look what happened: what *needed* to happen. That's how it is. 'N am I surprised? Not bloody likely. You pay the wages in the end, you do."

Zed looked at the man in utter confusion. He reckoned "what happened" was the death of Ian Cresswell, who, he knew, had lived in the manor house. But, "Wages?" he asked, while what he was thinking was, What the hell is the man going on about?

"Of sin," Daniel said in a low voice. "The wages of sin."

"That's right, that is," George Cowley said. "He paid the wages of sin right and proper. Well, there he is and here we are and when affairs get settled and the farm goes up for sale again, we'll be there this time and make no mistake. Bryan Beck farm is meant to be ours, 'n we've not been scrimping from day one in our lives to have it go to someone else a second time."

From this it seemed to Zed that Ian Cresswell's sin had been purchasing Bryan Beck farm before George Cowley had been able to do so. Which meant—and this was useful, wasn't it?—that Cowley had a motive to murder Cresswell. And *that* meant it was only a matter of time before New Scotland Yard came calling, which also meant that all he himself had to do was wait for their arrival. Confirm they're here, use their presence to sex up his story, and get the hell back to London, where he could resume his life. Yes. Things were looking up.

He said, "You're talking about Mr. Cresswell's purchase of the farm, I take it."

Cowley looked at him as if he were mad. "Purchase of the farm?"

"You said 'the wages of sin.' I reckoned purchasing the farm was his sin."

"Bah! That was bloody wrong, that was. That put us where it did, me and Dan. But no one pays wages 'cause of property." He loaded the final two words with derision, and he seemed to feel Zed was dim enough to require further elucidation. "Indecent, it was, him and that Arab lodger of his. And what're those kids of his still doing there? That's the question *I* ask, but no one's answering, are they. Well, that's indecent on top of indecent. And I tell you this: More wages are coming, an' they're bound to be big. You can count on that."

SWARTHMOOR
CUMBRIA

Tim Cresswell hated Margaret Fox School, but he put up with it because it spared him from having to go to a comprehensive where he might be expected to make friends, which was pretty much the last thing he wanted. He'd had friends once, but he'd learned that having them meant having to look at the smirks on their faces when they twigged what was going on in his life. Having friends meant having to overhear their murmurs of speculation as he passed them in one corridor or another on his way to lessons. The fact was, he didn't care if he ever had a friend again, since those he'd once possessed had ceased *being* friends just about the time his dad had walked out on the family to arse-fuck a limp-wristed Iranian. Word had gone round about *that* soon enough, for Tim's mum didn't possess the sense to keep her outrage to herself, especially if she was certain about being the aggrieved party in a situation. And she was definitely that, wasn't she. Turned out his dad had been fucking other men for years, exposing her to disease, disaster, disgust, disrespect, all the other disses there were, because one thing Niamh was especially good at was listing those disses to whoever wanted to hear them. She made sure Tim knew them from the word go, and in response he broke a few things, he burned a few things, he hurt a few people, he dismembered a kitten—never mind that the poor thing was already dead—and he ended up in Margaret Fox School just outside of Ulverston. Here Tim intended to stay, but to manage that he had to do just enough to be cooperative and not enough to be given the boot back into the system where the normies were educated.

Most kids boarded at Margaret Fox School because they were too disturbed to live with their families. But there were day pupils as well, and Niamh Cresswell had seen to it that Tim was placed among them. All the better to force his father or Kaveh Mehran to cart him from Bryanbarrow all the way to Ulverston and back each day, a drive that took forever, ate up their time together, and punished them for

putting a real bazooble of a crater in Niamh's pride. Tim
went along with it all because it got him far away from
everyone who knew the story of what had happened to his
parents' marriage, which was just about everyone in
Grange-over-Sands.

But one of the things he hated about Margaret Fox School
was the rule about the stupid Societies, always spelled with
a capital, just like that. In addition to regular lessons, one
was required to belong to three Societies: one each of aca-
demic, creative, and physical. The philosophy was that the
Societies supposedly eased the whacked-out pupils of Margaret Fox School into a semblance of normal behaviour, sort
of tricking them into acting as if they could function beyond
the high walls that enclosed the grounds of the institution.
Tim despised the Societies because they forced him into contact with the other pupils, but he'd managed to find three that
kept that contact to a bare minimum. He'd signed on for the
Ramblers, the Sketchers, and the Philatelists, since each of
these were activities he could do alone even if other people
were present. They didn't require communication of any
kind, other than listening to the staff member in charge of
each Society drone on about the subject of supposed interest.

Which was exactly what was going on just now at the
regular meeting of the Ramblers. Quincy Arnold was doing
his usual blah blah blah at the end of their afternoon walk.
This had been a nothing stagger on the public footpath from
Mansriggs over to Mansriggs Hall and from there up to Town
Bank Road, where the school van picked them up, but the
way QA was banging on about it, you'd think they'd just
scaled the Matterhorn. The big deal had been the view of
Ben Cragg—wahoo to another bloody tooth of limestone,
Tim thought—but the ultimate goal was evidently what all
this afternoon wandering was leading up to: what QA called
the Big Adventure on Scout Scar. Said adventure would not
happen till spring, and in the meantime all the rambling they
were doing was to prepare them for the enchantment to
come. Blah blah blah whatever. QA could blather like no one
else, and he could be positively orgasmic about limestone
escarpments and—pound on, my heart—glacial erratics. Yew
trees blasted by the winds, dangerous screes where sure foot-

ing was crucial, larks and buzzards and cuckoos on the wing, daffodils tucked into hazel coppices. It sounded about as interesting to Tim as learning Chinese writing from a blind man, but he knew the value of looking at QA when the bloke was doing his blah blahs, although he kept his expression hovering between indifference and loathing, always on guard against being deemed cured.

He had to have a piss, though. He knew he should have done a side-of-the-road job before they'd embarked on the ride back to the school at the end of the walk. But he hated pulling his prick out in public because one never knew how it would be taken among this lot with whom he had to walk. So he squeezed back the urges and now he suffered through QA's summary of their afternoon's timeless adventure, and when they were at last released onto the school grounds with the gates shut behind them, he made a dash for the nearest loo and let it flow. He made sure some of it went on the floor and some onto his trouser leg. When he was finished, he examined himself in the mirror and picked at a spot on his forehead. He achieved a bit of blood—always nice—and left to fetch his mobile phone.

They weren't allowed, of course. But the day pupils could have them as long as they got checked in every morning and ticked off on a list that was kept in the headmaster's office. To rescue them every afternoon, one had to trek to the headmaster, receive a permission slip, and then trek back to the tuck shop where in a locked bank of pigeonholes behind the till the mobiles were deposited for safekeeping.

On this day, Tim was the last to retrieve his. He checked for messages as soon as the mobile was in his hand. There was nothing, and he felt his fingers start to tingle. He wanted to throw the mobile at someone, but instead he walked to the tuck shop door and from there to the central path that would take him to the drop-off area where he would wait with the other day pupils to score their lifts for the trip home from school. They could only ride with approved drivers, of course. Tim had three but with his dad dead he was down to two, which meant one, really, because there was no way in hell that Niamh was going to drive to fetch him, so that left Kaveh. And so far Kaveh had done the job because he had no choice and he'd not yet worked how to get out of it.

Tim didn't care. It was nothing to him who came to fetch him. What was important now was the deal he'd struck with Toy4You and the fact that he'd had no response to his latest message, sent this morning on his way into school. He got into contact once again:

Where r u

A moment and then: Here

y didnt u anser

when

u no what i mean we agreed

no way

u promised me

no can do

y y y

not on mobl

u promised u said

lets talk

Tim looked up from the screen. He didn't want to talk. He wanted action. He'd kept his part of the bargain and it was only fair that Toy4You do exactly the same. It always came down to this in the end, he thought bitterly. People played each other like a deck of cards and he was bloody sick and tired of it all. But what choice did he have? He could start all over, but he didn't want that. It had taken long enough to find Toy4You.

He punched in his answer. Where

u no

2day

2night

ok

He flipped the phone closed and shoved it into his pocket. A fat girl whose name he didn't know was watching him from a bench. His eyes met hers and she lifted her school skirt. She spread her legs. She had on no knickers. He wanted to spew all over the path but instead he went for a distant bench and sat down to wait for his ride back to Bryanbarrow. He considered the ways he could torment Kaveh on the long trip home, and he congratulated himself for the piss on his trousers. That would get up old Kaveh's nose in more ways than one, he thought with an inward chuckle.

ARNSIDE
CUMBRIA

Alatea Fairclough was mesmerised by Morecambe Bay. She'd never seen anything like it. The ebb tide emptied its vast expanse, leaving behind one hundred twenty square miles of varying kinds of sands. But these were sands so dangerous that only the unwary, the lifelong fishermen of the area, or the Queen's Guide went out on them. If anyone else wandered into the empty bay—and people did all the time—they ran the risk of ending their days on earth by stumbling onto an area of quicksand that was, to the casual observer, indistinguishable from solid ground. Or far out in the bay they stood too long on rises of sand that seemed safe, like islands, only to find that the flood tide cut them off and then covered them in its return. And when, instead of a mere flood tide, a tidal bore brought the water swirling back into the bay at the speed of a galloping horse, things happened with a dizzying quickness as a vast surge of water covered everything in its path. And that was the thing about the tidal bore that Alatea found so hypnotic. It seemed to come from nowhere, and the speed of the torrent suggested a power driven by a force beyond any man's control. The thought of this generally filled her with peace, however: that there *was* a force beyond man's control and that she could turn to that force for solace when she was most in need.

She loved the fact that this house—a gift from her husband's father to celebrate the occasion of her marriage to his only son—sat just above the Kent Channel, which was itself part of greater Morecambe Bay. From the edge of the property where a stone wall marked a public footpath along the channel and ultimately up to the wild, open hilltop of Arnside Knot, she could stand with a voluminous shawl wrapped round her and watch the renewing return of the salt water. She could pretend she knew something about how to read the eddies that it created.

She was there now, on this November afternoon. The sunlight was dimming as it would do earlier and earlier until late December, and the temperature was fast falling as well. A cloud bank over the rise of Humphrey Head Point across the channel to the west suggested a coming night of rain, but she wasn't bothered by this. Unlike so many people in this adopted country of hers, she always welcomed rain with its promise of both growth and renewal. Still, she found herself uneasy. Her husband was the cause.

She hadn't heard from him. She'd phoned his mobile during the afternoon, once she'd learned from ringing Fairclough Industries that Nicholas hadn't gone into work that day. She'd made that phone call round eleven, when he still should have been there prior to leaving for the Middlebarrow Pele Project, where he now spent half of his workdays. She'd first assumed that he'd gone to the project earlier than usual and she'd then rung his mobile. But all she heard was that disembodied voice telling her that she had to leave a message. This she had done, three times now. The fact that Nicholas had not replied filled her with concern.

His cousin's sudden death loomed large. Alatea didn't want to think about it. Not only did death in general shake her, but this death in particular and the circumstances of this death filled her with a dread that took every ounce of her skill at subterfuge to hide. Ian's drowning had hit the family hard. Particularly had it devastated Nicholas's father. So staggered had Bernard been at first that Alatea had wondered at the nature of his exact relationship with Ian. But it was only when Bernard had begun to distance himself from Nicholas that Alatea had sensed an undercurrent beneath the older man's grief.

Nicholas was not involved in Ian's drowning. Alatea knew this for a hundred and one reasons but most of all she knew it because she knew her husband. He seemed weak to people because of his past, but he was no such thing. He was the rock and substance of her life, and he would become the same to many others if he only had the chance. This was what the Middlebarrow Pele Project was giving to him.

But he hadn't been at the project today any more than he had been at Fairclough Industries. Had he been, he would have had his mobile switched on. He knew it was important to her to have contact with him periodically and he was always willing to allow her the access. He'd said at first, "Do you not trust me, Allie? I mean, if I'm going to use again, I'm going to use again. You can't stop me with a phone call, you know," but that hadn't been the reason she wanted close contact with him, and through partial truths she'd ultimately been able to persuade him that her need had nothing to do with the need he himself had finally managed to conquer.

Whenever he was gone from her, she worried that something might happen to him, entirely unrelated to his addictions. A car crash, a stone falling from the old pele tower, a freak accident . . . exactly like what had happened to Ian. Except she *wouldn't* think about Ian, she told herself. There were too many other things to consider.

She turned from the sight of the floodwaters swirling into the Kent Channel. Up the slope of the lawn in front of her, Arnside House spread out. She allowed herself a momentary feeling of pleasure as she looked upon the building. The house gave her a focus for her energies, and she wondered if Bernard had known that when he presented it to them upon their return to England.

"It was used for convalescing soldiers after the war," he'd said as he'd walked her through it, "and then it spent some thirty years as a girls' school. After that there were two sets of owners who did a few things to restore it to what it once was. But then I'm afraid it stood vacant for a time. Still, there's something about it that's very special, my dear. I think it deserves a family running about inside it. And more, it deserves someone like you to put your touch upon it." He'd kept his hand on the small of her back as he'd walked her through the place. He had a way of looking at her that was a little disturbing. His gaze would go from Nicholas to her and back to Nicholas as if he couldn't understand what they had between them: either where it had come from in the first place or how it was going to endure.

But that didn't matter to Alatea. What mattered was

Bernard's acceptance of her, and she had that. She could tell he thought she possessed a form of magical power that was protecting Nicholas, a kind of sorcery perhaps. She could also tell from Bernard's assessing looks, taking her in from top to toes, that he reckoned exactly what the sorcery was.

She went up the slope of lawn towards the house. A set of stone steps led up to a terrace, and she used these, careful of the damp moss that grew upon them. Across the lawn she made for a doorway tucked into the side of the building. There she let herself into the drawing room, whose pale yellow walls suggested sunlight even on the most dismal of days.

This was the first room she and Nicholas had restored. It overlooked the terrace, the lawn, and the channel. From its bay windows one could even see across the water to Grange-over-Sands forming a fan of lights up the hillside at night. In the evenings she and Nicholas sat here, a fire glowing in the fireplace as the shadows stretched across the floor.

It was early for the fire, but she lit it anyway, for comfort as well as for warmth. Then she checked the phone for a message from her husband and when there was no light blinking to tell her he'd phoned, she decided to ring him another time. She pressed the numbers slowly, the way one does when hoping a previously engaged line will now be unengaged. Before she finished, though, she finally heard him, his footsteps approaching along the uncarpeted corridor.

She hadn't heard either his car or his entering the house. But she knew it was Nicholas just as she knew from the lightness of his step what mood he was in. She slipped her mobile into her pocket. Nicholas called her name and she said, "In here, darling," and in a moment he was with her again.

He paused at the doorway. He looked cherubic in the diffused light, like an overlarge putto from a Renaissance painting, round of face with bright curls spilling over his forehead. He said, "You're an impossibly gorgeous woman. Am I in the right house?" and he crossed the room to her.

She was wearing flat-soled shoes for once, so they were of a height: both of them nearly six feet tall. This made it easier for him to kiss her, and he did so, enthusiastically. His hands went down her back to cup her bum and he pulled her close to him. He finally said with an engaging laugh, "I'm loaded, Allie, like you wouldn't believe," and for a terrible moment she thought he'd got himself high. But then he removed the pins and the slides that kept her hair in order and he loosened it to fall round her face and her shoulders. After that he began to unbutton her blouse and talk about "swimmers and there're millions of them, and they're perfect in form and let me tell you they're ready to be perfect in function as well. Where are we in your cycle just now?" and his mouth went to her neck as his hands deftly unfastened her bra.

Her body responded even as her mind assessed. She sank to the carpet before the fire, pulled Nicholas down with her, and undressed him. He was not a man who coupled in silence. Rather, it was "Christ, the *feel* of you," and "my God, Allie," and "oh yes, just like that" and because of this, she knew every level of his rising excitement.

It matched her own. Even if her thoughts began in another place as they always did, in another time, with one or another man, they ended up centred on this man, here. Of its own accord her body met his and they created for each other a release born of pleasure that made everything else fade into insignificance.

This was enough for her. No. It was more than enough. Enough was the love and protection Nicholas afforded her. That in addition she should have found a man whose body met hers in such a way as to drive off memory and fear . . . This was something she had never expected that day behind the cafeteria till on a mountain in Utah when she looked up, accepted the money for his bowl of chili, and heard him say in wonder, "Jesus God, is it difficult for you?"

She'd said, "What?"

"Being so beautiful. Is it rather like a curse?" And then he'd grinned, scooped up his tray, and said, "Bloody hell. Never mind. What a line, eh? Sorry. I didn't intend it to sound like that," and off he went. But he was back the next day and the day after that. On the fourth time through her queue, he asked her if she'd have coffee with him that afternoon, told her he didn't drink alcohol of any kind, told her he was recovering from methamphetamine addiction, told her he was English, told her he meant to go home to England, told her he meant to prove to his father and his mother that he was finally through with the devils that had ridden him for so many years, told her . . . There was a queue behind him, but he didn't notice. She did, however, and to get him to move along she'd said, "I will meet you, yes. There is a place in the town, across from the town lift. Its name . . ." And she couldn't remember the name. She stared at him in some confusion. He stared at her in much the same way. He'd said, "Believe me, I'll find it," and so he had.

Now they lay on the carpet before the fire, side by side. He said, "You should tilt your hips, Allie. They're brilliant swimmers but it'll be easier if they're going downhill." He rose on one elbow and observed her. "I went to Lancaster," he said frankly. "Did you try to phone me? I switched off the mobile because I knew I wouldn't be able to lie to you."

"Nicky . . ." She heard the disappointment in her voice. She wished she could have hidden it, but at least the sound of it was better than acknowledging the sudden fear that stabbed her.

"No, listen, darling. I needed to check, just to make sure. I did such a job on my body for so many years, it was logical for me to want to know . . . I mean, wouldn't you want to? In my position? With nothing happening yet?"

She turned as well, her arm stretched out over her head and her head resting upon it. She looked not at him but rather over his shoulder. The rain had begun. She could see its pattern on the bay windows. She said, "I am not a machine for babies, Nicky, how do you call it? This thing that grows them?"

"Incubator," he said. "I know you're not. And I don't think of you that way. But it's only natural . . . I mean, it's been two years now . . . We've both been anxious about it . . . You know." He reached out and touched her hair. She didn't have the kind of hair a man could run his fingers through. It was kinky and disordered, the gift of one of her progenitors, and God only knew which one because they represented a mixture of races and ethnicities too varied for logic to explain how they had all ended up reproducing with each other.

She said, "That *is* it, Nicky. The anxious part, you know. My magazine says that anxiety alone can make this difficult for a woman."

"I understand. I *do*, darling. But it could be something else, and it's time we found out, don't you think? That's why I went and it's also why you can—"

"No." She shook his hand off her hair and sat up.

"Don't sit! That'll—"

She cast him a look. "In my country," she said, "women are not made to feel this way: that they exist for one purpose only."

"I don't think that."

"These things take time. We know this where I come from. And a baby is something to cherish. A baby is not . . ." She hesitated. She looked away from him. She knew the truth of the matter, far beyond what her body was and was not doing. That truth needed to be spoken between them, so she finally said, "A baby is not a way to win your father's approval, Nicky."

Another man would have responded in outrage or denial, but this was not Nicholas's way. Part of her love for him derived from his absolute honesty, so strange in a man who'd given years of his life to the worship of drugs. He said, "You're right, of course. I do want it for that reason. I owe him that much for what I put him through. He's desperate for a grandchild and I can do that for him since my sisters didn't. *We* can do that for him."

"So you see—"

"But that's not the only reason, Allie. I want this with you. *Because* of you and because there's an *us*."

"And if I have these tests. If what comes out of it is that I am not able . . . ?" She dropped into silence and in that silence she could feel—she would swear it—his muscles become quite tense. She didn't know what this meant, and that fact pounded the blood down her arms and into her fingers so that she had to move. She got to her feet.

He did as well. He said, "Is that what you actually think?"

"How can I think otherwise when this"—a gesture towards the carpet, the fire, where they had lain, what they had done—"becomes only about a baby? Your little swimmers, as you call them, and how they are shaped and how they can move and how I should position myself afterwards to make certain they do what you want them to do. How am I meant to feel, faced with this and with your insistence that I visit some doctor and spread my legs and have instruments thrust into me and whatever else?"

Her voice had risen. She bent, picked up her discarded clothing, began to dress. "All this day," she said, "I miss you so much. I worry when I phone you and you do not answer. I long for you because it's *you*, while—"

"It's the same for me. You know that."

"I know nothing."

She left him. The kitchen was at the other end of the house, down the long panelled corridor, through the main hall and the dining room. She went there and began their dinner. It was far too early for this, but she wanted something to do with her hands. She was mindlessly chopping onions when Nicholas joined her again. He, too, was dressed, but he'd buttoned his shirt incorrectly and it hung drunkenly from his shoulders in a way that made her soften towards him. He was, she knew, a lost boy without her, just as she would be lost without him.

"I'm sorry," he said. "The last way on earth I want you to feel is like a baby machine. Or whatever."

"I am trying," she said. "The vitamins. All the pills. My temperature. My diet. Whatever will make it easier, possible . . ." She stopped because she'd begun to weep. She used her arm to brush the tears from her face.

"Allie . . ." He came to her, turned her to him.

They stood together, in each other's arms. One minute, two. At last he said, "Just to hold you like this, I feel a kind of awe. D'you know how lucky a man I am? *I* know it, Allie."

She nodded and he released her. He cupped her face in his hands and studied it in that way of his that always made her feel that the thousand truths she had hidden from him were there, openly displayed, and he was reading them all. But he made no mention of anything but, "Forgive me?"

"Of course. And I will do as you ask. Just not quite yet. Please, Nicky. Let us wait a few more months."

He nodded. Then he grinned and said, "Meantime, we'll give those swimmers some exercise, all right? Firm up their sense of direction?"

She smiled in turn. "We can do that."

"Good. Now tell me why you're chopping a mountain of onions, because my eyes are stinging like the devil. What're you making?"

She observed the pile she'd created. "I have no idea."

He chuckled. "Madwoman." He walked over to the day's post, which was in a neat pile near the kitchen phone. He said, "Did you speak with that bloke about restoring the stained glass?"

She had, she told him. He thought he could match the glass in the other windows in the main hall, but it would take some doing. He could either take the original out for a while or he could bring glass to them, but in either case, it would be expensive. Did Nicky want . . . ?

Their conversation found its way back to normalcy: compromise reached and tension gone. They went on to other matters that concerned them till Nicholas found the phone message that Alatea had forgotten she'd written, so intent had she been on getting past babies, doctors in Lancaster, and what Nicholas wanted and expected of her.

"What's this, then?" he said, holding up the paper she'd torn from a notebook earlier in the day.

"Ah. You've had a call. A television film is being made and a woman phoned. She would like to speak with you about it. She is a . . . I think she called it a scout of research, something like that."

He frowned. "What kind of film?"

"Alternative treatments for drug addiction. This is a documentary, she said. Interviews with addicts and doctors and social workers. The involvement of a film crew and someone with them—a celebrity? a presenter? I do not know—to ask the questions. I told her it is not likely you would be interested, but—"

"Why?"

"What?"

"Why'd you tell her that?"

She went for one of her cookbooks. Nicholas had created for her a recessed shelf for them above the cooker hob, and she grabbed one at random, wondering what she could possibly do with three onions chopped into tiny bits. She said, "This sort of thing . . . this is what feeds the ego, Nicky. We have talked about that, you and I. It cannot be good, because of where it leads. Because of all the things you must guard against."

"Right. Right. But it's not about me, Allie." He looked again at the paper he held. "Where's she from? Where're the filmmakers from?"

"I did not ask. I did not think . . ." She looked at the cover of the cookbook she was holding. She gathered her thoughts, considered her approach. She said, "Nicky, you must take care with this sort of thing. You always said that your part is quiet. Behind the scenes. This is best."

"Raising money to keep the project going is best," he countered. "This could be what we need to make that happen."

"And when it does not?"

"Why d'you say that?"

"The other thing . . . that newspaperman who was here so many times . . . what came of that? Nothing. And all the hours you spent with him, the talking, the walking round, the working at the pele tower with him, and what then? More nothing. He promises a story and what comes of his promise? Nothing. I do not wish to see the disappointment in your face," she told him. Because of where it might lead was what he would add in his own head. But that could not be helped.

His expression changed, but not to hardness. Rather, he seemed to glow at her and the source of the glow was his love. He said, "Darling Allie, you're not to worry. I do know what's at risk for me every day." He picked up the phone but didn't punch in the number. "This isn't about ego. This is about saving lives, like mine was saved."

"You always have claimed I saved your life."

"No," he replied. "You made it worth living. I'd like to see what this is about"—he gestured with the phone—"but I won't do it without your agreement."

She saw no other way. He was asking very little. After all that he had given to her, there seemed no course available but to say, "All right, then, Nicky. If you will have a care."

"Brilliant," he replied. He looked at the paper and punched in the number. As he did so, he said to Alatea, "What's the surname, Allie? I can't read your writing."

She came to look over his shoulder at what she'd written. "St. James," she said.

GREAT URSWICK
CUMBRIA

When the gates of Margaret Fox School opened, Manette Fairclough McGhie sighed in relief. She'd thought there was a very good chance that Niamh Cresswell wouldn't have phoned the school to inform them that her son would be fetched on this day by someone not on the previously approved list. It would have been exactly like Niamh to have done so. Niamh knew that Manette had been close to Ian, which in Niamh's eyes made Manette a postdivorce enemy. But it seemed that Ian's former wife had decided that the convenience of having an additional someone willing to fetch her son outweighed her need to avenge all putative sins committed against her. She'd said, "I'll let Gracie know. She'll be upset if Tim doesn't show up at his regular time," and this made Manette feel that she ought to be taking Gracie as well as Tim, but it was Tim she wanted to see today, Tim whose face at his father's funeral still haunted Manette's nights. This would be her tenth attempt to get through to her cousin Ian's son. She'd tried at the reception immediately following the funeral. She'd tried with phone calls. She'd tried by e-mail. And now she was going for the direct approach. Tim could hardly avoid her if she had him in the car.

She'd left work early, stopping by Freddie's office to tell him she'd see him at home. "I'm fetching Tim," she said. "Thought he might like to spend the evening with us. Dinner and a DVD. You know. Perhaps stay the night?" Freddie's reply had somewhat surprised her. Instead of an absent-minded, "Oh, right, Manette," her erstwhile partner in life had turned the red of a very bad sunburn and said, "Oh yes. As to that . . . ," and after a bit of uncharacteristic stumbling round, had gone on with, "I've a date, actually, Manette."

She'd said, "Oh," and tried to hide her surprise.

He'd hurried on with, "I rather thought it was time. I probably should have told you before now, but I didn't quite know how to put it."

Manette didn't like the way she felt about this, but she forced a smile and said, "Oh. Lovely, Freddie. Anyone I know?"

"No, no. Of course not. Just someone . . ."

"How'd you meet?"

He moved back from his desk. On the monitor behind him, she could see a graph and she wondered what he was working on. Profits and losses, probably. He was also due to analyse wages and benefits. And there was the not small matter of formally going through the books following Ian's death. When on earth had Freddie even found the time to meet someone? she wondered. He said, "Actually, I'd rather not talk about it. It feels a bit uncomfortable."

"Oh. Right." Manette nodded. He was watching her earnestly to gauge her reaction so she was careful to give him a cheerful one. "P'rhaps you c'n bring her by, then. I'll want to see if I approve. You don't want to make a second mistake."

"You weren't a mistake," he told her.

"Ah. Thanks for saying that." She fished in her bag and brought out her car keys. She said brightly, "Still my best friend, then?"

"Still and always," he replied.

What he didn't say was what she knew: that they couldn't go on forever as they were, divorced but housemates, everything the same in their lives save where they slept and with whom they made love. What remained was the deep friendship that had always existed between them, which was, at the end, the root of the problem. She'd often thought since the day they'd agreed to divorce that things might have been different had they been able to have children together, that their relationship wouldn't have deteriorated to the point of their dinnertime conversation being all about the benefits of a self-cleaning and self-deodorising lavatory and how to market it. One couldn't go on like that indefinitely without waking up one morning and wondering where the magic had gone. A friendly divorce seemed the best solution.

Well, she'd known Freddie would find someone else eventually. She intended to do the same herself. She just hadn't thought it would happen so quickly. Now she wondered if the truth was that she just hadn't thought it would happen at all.

She eased her car through the gates of Margaret Fox School. She'd not been here before, but Niamh had told her where Tim would be waiting. There was a supervised holding area near the administration building, Tim's mother had said. Manette's name would be on a list matching to Tim's name. She was to take her identification with her. A passport was best if she had one. There would be no quibbling over that.

She found Tim easily enough since the lane into the school led directly to the administration building, with the classrooms and dormitories forming a quadrangle behind it. Her cousin's son was hunched on a bench with a rucksack at his feet. He was doing what, in Manette's experience, most teenagers did with their free time these days. He was texting someone.

She pulled up to the kerb, but he didn't look up, so intent was he upon what he was doing. This gave her the chance to observe him and she did so, reflecting not for the first time upon the extremes to which Tim went in order to hide his resemblance to his father. Like Ian, he'd been late to puberty, and he still hadn't gone through a growth spurt. So he was small for his age, and out of his school uniform, he would look even smaller. For then he donned clothes so baggy that they draped upon him, and even the baseball caps he favoured were too large. They covered his hair, which he'd not cut in ages and which he allowed to hang in his eyes. He would want, of course, to hide those eyes most of all. For like his father's, they were large and brown and limpid and they served perfectly well as those metaphorical windows to the soul.

Manette could see he was scowling. Something wasn't right with whoever was texting in reply to Tim. As she watched, he lifted his hand and tore at his fingers. He bit down so hard that she winced at the sight. She got out of the car quickly and called his name. He looked up. For a moment his face showed surprise—Manette wanted to call it delighted surprise, but she didn't dare go that far—but then his features settled into the scowl again. He didn't move from the bench.

She said, "Hey, Buster, come on. I'm your lift today. I need help with something and you're my man."

He said sullenly, "I got somewhere to go," and went back to texting, or perhaps pretending to.

She replied, "Well, I don't know how else you're going to get there 'cause I'm the only one with wheels that you're going to see."

"Where's bloody Kaveh, then?"

"What's Kaveh got to do with it?"

Tim looked up from his mobile. Manette saw him huff. It was a derisive exhalation of breath intended to convey his judgement of her. It said *stupid cow* without saying *stupid cow*. Fourteen-year-old boys were nothing if not transparent.

"Come on, Tim," she said. "Let's go. The school's not about to let anyone else fetch you today now your mum's rung them."

He would know the drill. Further recalcitrance was pointless. He muttered, shoved himself to his feet, and slouched over to the car, dragging his rucksack behind him. He threw himself into the passenger seat with enough force to rock the car on its wheels. She said, "Steady on," and then, "Seat belt, please," and she waited for him to cooperate.

She felt for Tim. He'd taken too many punches. He'd been the worst possible age for his father to have walked out on the family for any reason. To have had his father walk out on the family for another man had thrown his entire world off its axis. What was he meant to do and how was he meant to understand his own dawning sexuality in such a situation? It was no wonder to Manette that Tim's behaviour had altered on the edge of a knife, propelling him from his comprehensive into the cloistered safety of a school for the disturbed. He *was* disturbed. In his position who wouldn't be?

She made a careful turn into the road outside the school gates, and she said to Tim, "CDs in the glove box. Why don't you find us something?"

"Won't have anything I like." He turned a shoulder to her and stared out of the window.

"Bet I do. Have a look, Buster."

"I got to meet someone," he told her. "I said."

"Who?"

"Someone."

"Your mum know about this?"

That derisive huff of breath again. He muttered something and when she asked him to repeat it, he said, "Nothing. Forget it," and he watched the scenery.

There was little enough of it and certainly nothing to fascinate in this part of the county. For outside of Ulverston and heading south to Great Urswick the land was open and rolling, farmland separated from the road by hedges and limestone walls, pastures in which the ubiquitous sheep grazed, and the occasional woodland of alders and paper birches.

It wasn't a long drive. Manette's home in Great Urswick was closer to Margaret Fox School than the homes of any of Tim's other relatives. It was, she thought not for the first time, the most logical place for Tim to reside during the school terms, and she'd mentioned this to both Ian and Niamh shortly after they'd enrolled the boy there. But Niamh wouldn't hear of it. There was Gracie to consider. It would devastate her to be without her brother in the after-school hours. Manette had reckoned that there was more to the matter than Gracie's devastation, but she had not pressed it. She would, she'd decided, see the boy when she could.

Great Urswick wasn't much of a village, one of those collections of cottages that had grown round the intersection of several country lanes, a distance inland from Bardsea and Morecambe Bay. It possessed a pub, a post office, a restaurant, two churches, and a primary school, but it had the added feature of sitting on the edge of a somewhat large pond. The posh district—as Manette and Freddie liked to call it—consisted of the houses built along the banks of this pond. They were situated near to the road but their large back gardens comprised lawns giving onto the pond itself. Reeds formed occasional barriers between the gardens and the water, and where there were no reeds, miniature jetties allowed residents access to rowing boats or places to sit and watch the ducks and the two resident swans who lived there throughout the year.

Manette and Freddie's house was one of these. Manette pulled up to it—leaving the garage for Freddie's use—and she said to Tim, "Come and look. Here's where I need your help. Back here."

"Why isn't Freddie helping you?" Tim asked abruptly. He didn't move to unhook his seat belt.

"Freddie?" She laughed. "Impossible. He'd have to read instructions and there's no way he's about to do that. The way I reckon it, I read and you build. And afterwards we cook burgers and chips."

"Build? What? I can't build nothing."

"Oh yes you can. Wait and see," she said. "It's round the back. Come on." She set off towards the corner of the house, without waiting to see if he would follow.

The project was a tent. Of course she could have put it up herself, with or without help from anyone. But this was not the point. The point was doing something to engage Tim and to get him talking or at least to get him relaxing enough that he might allow her a modest inroad into his suffering.

She unpacked the tent and laid it out on the lawn. It was a large affair, more suitable for a family of four than for what she had in mind, but as it wasn't the season for tent buying, she'd had to make do with what was on offer. She was sorting through various stakes and cords when she heard Tim finally come round the side of the house. She said, "Good. There you are. Need a snack before we begin?"

He shook his head. He looked from the sprawl of canvas to her to the water. He said, "What're you setting this up here for, then?"

"Oh, this is just practice for you and me," she told him. "When we know what we're doing, we'll take it up Scout Scar."

"What for?"

"For camping out, silly. What else would we use it for? Your mum told me you're walking on the fells now and as I'm walking on the fells as well, we c'n do it together, soon's you're ready."

"You don't walk on the fells."

"A lot you know. I take all kinds of exercise. Besides, Freddie doesn't like me running along the roads any longer. He thinks I'll be hit by a car. Come on, then. What're you waiting for? Sure you don't want a snack? Custard cream? Jaffa cake? Banana? Marmite toast?"

"I said no!" He sounded fierce. "Look. I already told you. I got to meet someone."

"Where?"

"It's important. I said I'd be there."

"Where?"

"Windermere."

"*Windermere?* Who on earth are you meeting in Windermere? Does your mum know you're meeting someone in Windermere?" She'd been crouched among the items intended for setting up the tent, but now she stood. She said, "See here, Tim. What's going on? Are you up to something?"

"What's that s'posed to mean?"

"You know very well. Drugs, drink, some sort of naughty nonsense that—"

"No. Look, I got to be there. I *got* to."

She could hear his desperation, but she couldn't tell what it had to do with or why he was feeling it. Any idea she had in the matter was not a good one. But there was something in his eyes when they flashed in her direction, a form of suffering looking out at her and begging for her help. She said, "I can't take you there without speaking to your mum," and she headed in the direction of the house, saying, "I'm going to phone her and make sure—"

"You can't!"

"Why not? Tim, what's going on?"

"She won't care. She doesn't know. It won't matter. If you ring her . . . oh fuck, fuck, *fuck*." And he stalked across the tent and down to the little wooden jetty that stretched into the pond. There was a rowing boat tied there, but he didn't get into it. Instead he dropped heavily down onto the jetty and his head fell into his hands.

Manette could tell he was crying. Her heart went out to him. She crossed the lawn and went out to join him on the dock. She sat down next to him but didn't touch him. She said, "Buster, this is a bad time for you. This is the worst. But it's going to pass. I promise you. It *is* going to pass because—"

"You don't know anything!" He swung round and shoved her. She fell onto her side. "You don't know shit!" He kicked her, and she felt the force of the blow in the region of her kidneys. She tried to say his name but could not get it past her lips before he kicked her again.

3 NOVEMBER

LAKE WINDERMERE
CUMBRIA

Lynley arrived at Ireleth Hall in the afternoon. Given the choice among flying, driving, or taking the train, he'd opted for driving, despite the length of the trip. He left London long before dawn, stopped twice along the way, and spent the time in the Healey Elliott deep in thought.

He hadn't been with Isabelle on the previous night. She'd asked and he'd wanted, but he reckoned it would be better for them both if he stayed away. Despite her words to the contrary, he knew she intended to get to the bottom of where he was going and why, and he equally intended not to tell her. The conflict between them that this would have doubtless caused was something he wanted to avoid. Isabelle had cut back radically on her drinking in the months they'd been together, and he didn't want anything—like an argument with him—to set her on the path to the bottle again. She needed to stay sober and he liked her sober, and if avoiding a conflict encouraged her to maintain sobriety, then he was happy to avoid anything resembling a conflict with her.

Darling, I had no idea you'd become such a coward with women, Helen would have said about this. But it wasn't cowardice as far as he was concerned. It was the course of wisdom and he was determined to follow it. Still, he thought about this and about Isabelle and himself most of the way to Cumbria. Compatibility was on his mind.

When he reached Ireleth Hall, the great iron gates stood open as if in anticipation of his arrival. He drove beneath the shelter of ancient oaks, winding in the direction of Lake Windermere, and finding himself ultimately pulling up to an impressive many-gabled affair of stone dappled with grey lichen, its central feature a boxy pele tower of enormous proportions that announced the age of at least part of the building. Thirteenth century, Lynley thought. It predated his own home in Cornwall by more than four hundred years.

From the pele tower various extensions had been put onto the building over the centuries. Wisely, however, they were all of a piece so the result was a harmonious blend of architectural periods, with rolling lawns spreading out on either side of it, these copiously dotted with some of the most impressive oaks Lynley had ever seen. Among the oaks stood equally impressive plane trees, and beneath them fallow deer grazed placidly.

He got out of the car and breathed deeply of air fresh from a recent rainfall. From where he stood, the lake wasn't visible, but he reckoned that from inside the west-facing house, the views of the water and the opposite shore would be impressive.

"Here you are, then."

Lynley turned at the sound of Bernard Fairclough's voice. The man was heading his way from a walled garden to the north of the house. He joined Lynley by the Healey Elliott. He admired the old car, ran his hand along its sleek wing, and asked the usual polite questions about the vehicle, its age, its performance, and about Lynley's drive from London. The niceties dispensed with, he ushered him into the house through a door that led directly into a great hall panelled in oak and hung with burnished breastplates of armour. A fire burned in a fireplace here, with two sofas facing each other in front of it. Other than the crackling from flames consuming wood and the ticking from a longcase clock, the place seemed entirely silent.

Fairclough spoke in the low tones of a man at a church

service or one concerned about being overheard, although as far as Lynley could tell they were alone. "I've had to tell Valerie why you're here," he said. "We don't keep secrets in general—more than forty years together and it's impossible anyway—so she's in the picture. She'll cooperate. She's not entirely happy with me for pushing this matter, but she understands . . . as well as a mother can understand when there are concerns about her children." Fairclough pushed his thick-framed spectacles up the bridge of his nose as he considered his words. "She's the only one, though. So for everyone else, you're a fellow member of Twins who's come for a visit. Some of them know about your wife as well. It's made . . . Well, it's made everything more believable. You've no trouble with that, I hope?"

He sounded nervous. Lynley had to wonder what he was nervous about: that Lynley was here, that he was a cop, or that he might uncover something unsavoury as he stumbled round the property. He supposed any of these were possible, but the nerves did make him curious about Fairclough. "Helen's death was in the newspapers," he replied. "I can hardly protest if it's common knowledge."

"Good. Good." Fairclough rubbed his hands together in a let's-get-down-to-work gesture. He shot Lynley a smile. "I'll show you your room and give you a tour. I thought a quiet dinner this evening, just the four of us, and then tomorrow perhaps you can . . . Whatever it is you do, you know."

"The four of us?"

"Our daughter Mignon will be joining us. She lives here on the property. Not in the house as she's of an age when a woman prefers to have her own home. She's not far, though, and as she's unmarried and you're a widower, it did seem possible . . ." Fairclough, Lynley noted, had the grace to look uncomfortable at this. "Something of another excuse for you to be here. I haven't said anything to Mignon directly, but if you keep it in mind that she's unmarried . . . I've a feeling she might be more forthright with you if you . . . perhaps showed her a bit of interest."

"You suspect she has something to hide?" Lynley asked.

"She's a cipher," Fairclough replied. "I've never been

able to have a breakthrough to her. I hope you'll manage it. Come. It's just this way."

The stairs formed part of the pele tower's base and they rose among a collection of landscape watercolours into a corridor panelled in oak much like the great hall but without the great hall's windows to lighten the gloom. Doors opened off this corridor, and Fairclough led Lynley to one at the far north end, where a lead-paned window offered a dim shaft of light in which dust motes floated upward as if released from captivity in the Persian carpets.

The room they entered was a large one, its best feature a set of bay windows with a deep embrasure where a seat had been fashioned. Fairclough walked Lynley over to this spot. "Windermere," he said unnecessarily.

As Lynley had assumed, this west side of the house overlooked the lake. Three terraces made a way down to it: two of lawn and a third of gravel upon which weathered tables, chairs, and chaise longues stood. Beyond this last one, the lake spread out, disappearing round a finger of land that pointed northeast and was called, Fairclough said, Rawlinson Nab. Closer to hand, the tiny island of Grass Holme seemed to float in the water surmounted by a copse of ash trees, and Grubbins Point appeared like a knuckle protruding outward into the water.

Lynley said to Fairclough, "You must quite enjoy living here. Most of the year, at least, as I expect you're fairly overrun in the summer." Tourists, he meant. Cumbria in general and the Lakes in particular would be thronged from June to the end of September. Rain or shine—and God knew most of the time it was rain—they'd be walking, climbing, and camping everywhere there was space to do so.

"Frankly, I wish I had more time to do just that, to live here," Fairclough said. "Between the factory in Barrow, the foundation, my solicitors in London, and the Ministry of Defence, I'm actually fortunate to get here once a month."

"Ministry of Defence?"

Fairclough grimaced. "My life is governed by a complete lack of romance. I've a composting toilet they're interested in. We've been in discussion for months."

"And the solicitors? Is there a problem I should know about? Something related to the family? To Ian Cresswell?"

"No, no," Fairclough said. "Patent lawyers, these are, as well as solicitors for the foundation. All of it keeps me on the run. I rely on Valerie to deal with this place. It's her family home so she's happy to do so."

"Sounds as if you don't see much of each other."

Fairclough smiled. "Secret of a long and happy marriage. Bit unusual, but it's worked all these years. Ah. There's Valerie now."

Lynley moved his gaze from Fairclough to the three terraces, assuming the man's wife had come into view from elsewhere on the property. But he indicated the lake and upon it a rowing boat. A figure had just put oars into water and was bending to the task of rowing towards the shore. It was impossible at this distance to tell if the oarsman was male or female, but Fairclough said, "She'll be heading towards the boathouse. Let me take you to her. You'll be able to see where Ian . . . Well, you know."

Outside, Lynley took note of the fact that the boathouse wasn't visible from the main house. To gain it, Fairclough led him to the south wing of Ireleth Hall, where through shrubbery formed by the autumn red foliage of a mass of spiraea more than six feet tall, an arbour gave way to a path. This wound through a garden thick with the twin of holly, mahonia, which appeared to have grown in the spot for one hundred years. The path curved downwards through a little plantation of poplars and ultimately opened onto a fanlike landing. The boathouse was here: a fanciful structure faced in the stacked slate of the district with a steeply pitched roof and a land-side single door. There were no windows.

The door stood open and Fairclough entered first. Inside, they stood on a narrow stone dock that ran round three sides of the building, the lake water lapping against it. A motorboat and a scull were tied to this dock, as well as an ancient canoe. According to Fairclough, the scull had belonged to Ian Cresswell. Valerie Fairclough had not gained the boathouse yet, but they could see her from its water-side door, and it was obvious she would be with them within minutes.

"Ian capsized the scull when he fell," Fairclough said. "Just over there. You can see where the stones are missing. There were two of them—side by side—and he apparently grasped one and lost his balance when it came loose. He fell and the other stone went as well."

"Where are they now?" Lynley went to the spot and squatted for a better look. The light was bad inside the boathouse. He would need to come back with a torch.

"What?"

"The stones that came loose. Where are they? I'll want a look at them."

"They're still in the water as far as I know."

Lynley looked up. "No one brought them up for examination?" That was unusual. An unexpected death raised all sorts of questions and one of them was the one that asked how a stone on a dock—no matter the dock's age—had loosened. Wear and tear might have done it, of course. So might a chisel, however.

"The coroner ruled it an accident, as I've told you. It looked straightforward to the policeman who came to the scene. He phoned an inspector who came, had a look, and reached the same conclusion."

"Were you here when this happened?"

"In London."

"Was your wife alone when she found the body?"

"She was." And with a glance towards the lake, "Here she is now."

Lynley rose. The rowing boat was approaching quickly, the oarsman applying muscular strokes. When she was close enough for the boat to glide the rest of the way into the boathouse on its own power, Valerie Fairclough removed the oars from the oarlocks, rested them in the bottom of the boat, and floated inside.

She was wearing rainclothes: yellow slicker and waxed trousers, gloves, and boots. She had nothing on her head, however, and her grey hair was managing to look perfectly kempt despite the fact she'd been out on the water.

"Any luck?" Fairclough asked.

She looked over her shoulder but did not appear startled. She said, "There you are, then. Rotten luck entirely, I'm afraid. I was out for three hours and all I managed were two miserable little things who looked at me so pathetically, I was forced to toss them back into the water. You must be Thomas Lynley"—this to Lynley. "Welcome to Cumbria."

"It's Tommy." He extended his hand to her. She threw him the dock line instead of grasping it.

"Cleat hitch," she said. "Or do I speak Greek?"

"Not to me."

"Good man." She handed her fishing gear to her husband: a tackle box, a rod, and a pail of squirming bait that Lynley recognised as maggots. Clearly, she wasn't a squeamish woman.

She clambered out of the rowing boat as Lynley tied it up. She was extremely agile, impressive for her age since Lynley knew she was sixty-seven years old. When she was on the dock, she shook his hand. "Welcome again," she said. "Has Bernie given you the tour?" She tugged off her rain slicker and removed the trousers. She hung these from pegs on the boathouse wall as her husband stowed her fishing kit beneath a wooden workbench. When he turned to her, she offered her cheek for a kiss. She said, "Darling," as ostensible greeting and added, "How long've you been back?" to which he said, "Noon," to which she said, "You should have sent up a flare." She added, "Mignon?" and he said, "Not yet. She's well?" to which she replied, "Slow process, but better." It was, Lynley knew, that shorthand of all couples who've been together so many years.

Valerie said to him with a nod at the scull, "You were having a look at where our Ian drowned, weren't you. Bernie and I aren't of the same mind on this subject, but I expect he's told you that."

"He's mentioned that you found the body. It must have been a shock."

"I hadn't even known he'd gone out rowing. I hadn't known he was on the property at all as he hadn't parked his car near the house. He'd been in the water nearly twenty-four hours when I got to him, so you can imagine what he looked like at that point. Still, I'm glad I found him and not Mignon. Or Kaveh. I can only imagine what would have happened then."

"Kaveh?" Lynley asked.

"Ian's partner. He's doing some work for me here on the property. I'm putting in a children's area and he's done the design. He's overseeing the work as well."

"He's here every day?"

"Perhaps three times a week? He doesn't check in with me, and I don't keep track." She regarded Lynley as if evaluating what was going on in his mind. She said, "As the Americans say on their television programmes, do you like him for the murder?"

Lynley smiled briefly. "It may well turn out that the coroner was right."

"I have every confidence that it will." She looked from Lynley to her husband. Fairclough, Lynley saw, was gazing intently through the water-side opening in the boathouse, out onto the lake. She said, "It was a terrible thing to have happened. We were very fond of Ian, Bernie and I. We should have kept a closer eye on the dock. It's quite old— more than a hundred years—and it's never been out of use. Stones become loose. See here. There's another."

She used her toe against a stone next to the spot from which the other two had fallen. It was, as she said, unsteady as well. But of course, Lynley thought, that might have been owing to the fact that someone had deliberately loosened it.

"When accidents happen, we want to blame someone," Valerie said. "And this was a wretched thing to have happened because it leaves those poor children with one mad parent and no tempering influence whatsoever. If there's fault here, however, it's mine, I'm afraid."

"Valerie," her husband said.

"I'm in charge of Ireleth Hall and the property, Bernie. I fell down on the job. Your nephew died as a result."

"I don't blame you," her husband replied.

"Perhaps you should consider doing so."

They exchanged a look from which Bernard broke away first. That look said more than their words had done. There were, Lynley reckoned, deep waters here. They went far beyond those found in the lake.

4 NOVEMBER

When they'd laid their plans for taking a few days to help Tommy in Cumbria, Deborah St. James had entertained visions of herself and Simon being domiciled in a hotel draped in a stunning display of Virginia creeper in its autumnal glory, overlooking one of the lakes. She would even have settled for a situation viewing a mere waterfall as the county appeared to have a plethora of them. But where she ended up was an old inn called the Crow and Eagle exactly at the point one would expect an inn to be sitting: at an intersection of two roads down which lorries seemed to rumble at all hours of the night. This intersection was in the middle of the market town of Milnthorpe, so far south of the Lakes as not to be considered part of the Lakes at all, and the only water it boasted was the River Bela—nowhere in view—which appeared to be one of the countless tributaries that debouched into Morecambe Bay.

Simon had seen her expression at the first glimpse of the place. He'd said, "Ah," and, "Well, we're not here on holiday, are we, my love, but we'll take a day or two when we've finished. A grand hotel with a view of Windermere, roaring fires, scones, tea, and whatever else." He'd leered at her playfully.

She'd eyed him and said, "I'm planning to hold you to that, Simon."

"I'd have it no other way."

On the evening of their arrival, she'd received on her mobile the call that she'd been awaiting. She answered as she'd been answering every call for the last twenty-four hours, just for the practice. She'd said, "Deborah St. James Photography," and she'd nodded to Simon when the caller identified himself as Nicholas Fairclough. It hadn't taken long to make the arrangements: He was willing to meet with her and discuss the project that she had phoned about. He'd said, "But this documentary . . . it's not about me, is it? At least not about my private life." She'd assured him that it was only about the project he had developed for recovering addicts. It would be a preliminary interview, she told him. She would give a report to a filmmaker from Query Productions, who would ultimately make the decision regarding the project's inclusion in his documentary. "This is purely on spec," she told him. She liked this jargon. Anything to make her seem like the genuine article to this man. "I've no idea if you'd actually be in the film at the end of the day, you understand." This seemed to relieve him. He sounded quite buoyant when he said, "Right, then. When shall we meet?"

She was readying herself for that meeting now. Simon was on his mobile with the coroner, spinning his own tale about a lecture he would be giving to a class at University College, London. He was, she was finding, far more glib than she. This surprised her, for while he had always been the most confident of men and his credentials were impressive enough to *make* him confident, his confidence had always seemed to be connected to his relationship with the truth. That he could dissemble so well gave her pause. One didn't like to know one's husband was quite so adept at lying when he had to.

Her own mobile rang as she was gathering her things. She looked at the number and recognised it. No need to be Deborah St. James Photography at the moment. The caller was Simon's brother, David.

She knew at once why David was ringing her. She was more or less ready for the call.

"Just thought I'd answer any questions you might have," was how David brought up the subject. His voice had that encouraging ring to it, jollying her along. "The girl's quite keen to meet you, Deborah. She's had a look at your Web site: the photos and all that. Simon said you were worrying a bit about the London placement since she lives here in Southampton. I daresay she wouldn't have considered it, but she knows Simon's my brother, and her father's worked at the company here for a good twenty years. Part of the accounting department," he added hastily. That was synonymous with *she's from a good family*, as if he felt that the girl's having a dockworker as a father would constitute the possession of tainted blood.

They wanted her to decide. Deborah understood this. David and Simon both saw the situation as the perfect solution to a problem having gone on for years. They were both the sort of man who takes each difficulty in life as it comes up and deals with it as soon as possible and just as efficiently. Neither of them was like her, projecting into the future and seeing how complicated and potentially heartbreaking was the scenario they were proposing.

She said, "David, I just don't know. I don't think it would work. I can't see how—"

"Are you saying no?"

That was another one of the problems. Saying no meant no. Asking for more time meant not taking a position. Why on earth, Deborah wondered, could she not take a definite position on this matter? *Last chance* and *only chance* seemed like the reasons, but she was still frozen in place, unwilling to speak.

She said she'd ring him back. At the moment, she had to set off for Arnside. A heavy sigh at his end told her he wasn't happy with this, but he rang off. Simon said nothing, although he'd obviously heard her side of the call as he'd finished with his own. They parted at the sides of their respective hire cars, wishing each other luck.

Deborah's drive was the lesser one. Nicholas Fairclough lived just on the far outskirts of the village of Arnside, and Arnside was southwest of Milnthorpe, a short distance along the side of a muddy flat of sand that gave onto the

Kent Channel. There were fishermen here, positioned along
the road and down the bank, although Deborah couldn't
tell exactly where they were fishing. From the car, it didn't
look as if there was any water in the mud flat at all. She
could see, however, where the shifting tide from Morecambe Bay had scoured out depressions in the sand, creat-
ing banks and drops that suggested danger.

Arnside House was the name of Nicholas Fairclough's
property. It sat at the end of the Promenade, an impressive
display of Victorian mansions that had no doubt at one time
served as the summer homes of industrialists from Manchester, Liverpool, and Lancaster. Most of these were
stately-looking conversions now: flats possessing unim-
peded views of the channel, of the railway viaduct that
stretched across the water towards Grange-over-Sands, and
of Grange-over-Sands itself, just visible today through a
mild autumn mist.

Unlike the mansions that preceded it, Arnside House
was an unadorned structure, utterly plain and whitewashed
over a roughcast exterior that was itself a finishing surface
over what was undoubtedly stone or brick. Its windows featured unpainted sandstone surrounds, and its many gables
displayed rounded chimneys whitewashed like the rest of
the building. Only the rainwater heads were other than
plain, and these were highly stylised in a design Deborah
recognised as Arts and Crafts. Shades of Charles Rennie
Mackintosh, she thought. Once inside the structure, however, she discovered a whimsical blend of everything from
the medieval to the modern.

Nicholas Fairclough answered the door. He admitted her
into an oak-panelled entrance hall whose marble floor was
detailed in a pattern of diamonds, circles, and squares. He
took her coat from her and led her down an uncarpeted
corridor and past a large room having the look of a medieval banqueting hall, complete with minstrels' gallery above
a fireplace inglenook. This hall was something of a wreck
as far as Deborah could tell, and as if in explanation of this,
Nicholas Fairclough said, "We're restoring the old pile bit
by bit. That's going to be last, I'm afraid, as we need to find
someone who can cope with the most astounding wallpaper.

Peacocks and Petunias, I call it. *Peacocks* is accurate but I can't swear to the other. Here, we can talk in the drawing room."

This was sunshine yellow with a white plaster frieze of hawthorn berries, birds, leaves, roses, and acorns. In any other room, this elaborate decoration would have been the main feature, but the drawing room's fireplace served as a remarkable focal point of bright turquoise tiles and a hearth that duplicated the diamonds, circles, and squares of the entrance. A fire was burning here and although the fireplace—like the one in the great hall—formed part of an inglenook with bench seats, bookshelves, and stained glass windows, Nicholas motioned Deborah to one of two low-slung chairs in one of the bay windows from which they had a view of the water. A table stood between the chairs, a coffee service and three cups on it, along with a fan of magazines.

"I wanted to speak to you for a moment before I fetch my wife," Nicholas said. "I must tell you that I'm completely on board with talking to you and with having the project featured in this film if it comes to it. But Allie's going to take some convincing. I thought I'd give you a heads-up."

"I see. Can you give me some idea . . . ?"

"She's rather private," he said. "She's from Argentina and she's self-conscious about her English. Frankly, I think she speaks it perfectly well, but there you have it. Plus . . ." He tipped his fingers beneath his chin and looked thoughtful for a moment before saying, "She's protective of me, as well. There's that."

Deborah smiled. "This film isn't an exposé or anything, Mr. Fairclough. Although, to be honest it could turn into that if you're enslaving recovering addicts for your own purposes. I suppose I should ask if you need protecting for some reason?"

She'd meant it lightheartedly, but she couldn't help noting how seriously he took the question. He appeared to be tossing round a few possibilities, and she found this detail rather telling. He finally said, "Here's what I think it is. She worries that I'll be disappointed in some way. And she worries where disappointment will lead me. She wouldn't *say* that, but one has a way of knowing these things about one's wife. After a bit of time together. If you know what I mean."

"How long have you been married?"

"Two years last March."

"You're quite close, then."

"We are indeed, I'm pleased to say. Let me fetch her to meet you. You don't look all that frightening, do you."

He sprang up from his chair and left her in the drawing room. Deborah looked around. Whoever had decorated it had an artistic flair that she could well appreciate. The furniture reflected the period from which the house had come, but it managed to remain secondary to the features of the room. Aside from the fireplace, the most notable of these were columns: slender poles surmounted with capitals that were bowls carved with birds and fruits and leaves. They stood at the sides of the bay windows, they formed the ends of the inglenook's benches, they held up a shelf that ran round the room just beneath the frieze. The restoration of this room alone must have cost a fortune, Deborah reckoned. She wondered where a reformed drug addict had managed to come up with such a sum.

Her gaze went to the bay window. From there it fell upon the table and the coffee service that sat upon it, waiting for someone's use. The fan of magazines next to this caught her attention, and she idly fingered through them. Architecture, interior design, gardening. And then she came to one that caused her hand to stop abruptly. *Conception,* this one was called.

Deborah had seen it often enough during the endless appointments she'd had with specialists before receiving the disheartening diagnosis that had sunk her dreams, but she'd never looked through it. It had seemed too much like tempting fate. She picked it up now, however. There might well be, she thought, a form of sisterhood between Nicholas Fairclough's wife and herself, and this could be useful.

Quickly, she flipped through it. It consisted of the types of articles one might expect in a magazine of such a name. Appropriate diets during pregnancy, antenatal vitamins and supplements, postpartum depression and related problems, midwives, breast-feeding. All of it was here. But in the back was something curious. A number of pages had been torn out.

Footsteps came along the corridor, and Deborah replaced the magazine on the table. She got to her feet and turned as she heard Nicholas Fairclough say, "Alatea Vasquez y del Torres Fairclough," and added with an appealing, boyish laugh, "Forgive me. I rather love saying that name. Allie, this is Deborah St. James."

The woman was, Deborah thought, quite exotic: olive skinned and dark eyed, with cheekbones defining an angular face. She had an abundance of coffee-coloured hair so wiry that it sprang from her head in a billowing mass, and enormous gold earrings shone through it when she moved. She was an odd match for Nicholas Fairclough, former drug addict and family black sheep.

Alatea crossed the room to her, a hand extended. She had large hands, but they were long fingered and slim like the rest of her. "Nicky tells me you seem harmless enough," she said with a smile. Her English was heavily accented. "He has told you I have a concern about this."

"About my being harmless?" Deborah asked. "Or about the project?"

"Let's sit and have a chat." Nicholas was the one to speak, as if worried that his wife wouldn't understand Deborah's mild joke. "I've made coffee, Allie."

Alatea poured. She wore gold bangles on her wrists—first cousins to her earrings—and they slid down her arm as she reached for the coffeepot. Her gaze seemed to fall on the magazines as she did this, and for a moment she hesitated. She cast a glance at Deborah. Deborah smiled in what she hoped was an encouraging fashion.

Alatea said, "I was surprised about this film of yours, Ms. St. James."

"It's Deborah. Please."

"As you wish, of course. It is small up here, what Nicholas is doing. I did wonder how you learned about him."

Deborah was ready for this. Tommy had done his homework on the Faircloughs. He'd found a logical point of entry for her. "It wasn't me, actually," she said. "I just go where I'm pointed and do the preliminary research for the filmmakers at Query Productions. I'm not sure exactly how they decided upon you"—with a nod at Nicholas—"but I think it had to do with an article about your parents' house."

Nicholas said to his wife, "It was that sidebar again, darling." And to Deborah, "There was a piece written about Ireleth Hall, my parents' place. It's an historic old pile on Lake Windermere with a topiary garden round two hundred years old that my mother's brought back. She mentioned this place—our home—to the reporter and as it's a bit of an architectural conversation piece, he trotted over to have a look. Not sure why. Perhaps it was a historical-restorations-are-in-the-blood-of-the-Faircloughs kind of thing. This place was given to us by my father and I reckoned taking it on was better than looking a gift horse. I think Allie and I would have preferred something new with all the mod cons in working order, though. Isn't that the case, darling?"

"It's a beautiful home," Alatea said in reply. "I feel fortunate to live here."

"That's because you always insist upon seeing the glass half-full," Nicholas told her, "which makes me a very lucky man, I suppose."

"One of the film producers," Deborah said to Alatea, "brought up the Middlebarrow Pele Project at an early meeting we had in London, when we were looking at all the possibilities. Frankly, no one knew what a pele tower was, but there were several people who knew about your husband. Who he is, I mean. As well as other things." She didn't elaborate upon those things. It was obvious to them all what they were.

"So this film," Alatea said, "I do not have to be involved? It is, you see, a matter of my English—"

Which sounded, Deborah thought, not only excellent but charming.

"—and the fact that Nicky has done all of this on his own."

"I wouldn't have done it without you in my life," Nicholas put in.

"But that is another matter entirely." She turned as she spoke and her hair lifted, that billowing effect caused by its wiry nature. "The pele project . . . this is about you and what you have done and what you are achieving on your own. I am only your support, Nicky."

"As if that's not important," he said, rolling his eyes at Deborah as if to add, "You see what I have to put up with?"

"Nonetheless, I have no real part and I want no part."

"You've no worries on that score," Deborah assured her. Anything to get their agreement, she thought. "And really, I do want to stress that nothing may come of this anyway. I don't make the decisions. I only do the research. I create a report, take pictures to accompany it, and everything goes to London. The people at the production company decide what will be in the film."

"See?" Nicholas said to his wife. "No worries."

Alatea nodded but she didn't look convinced. Still she gave her blessing with the words, "Perhaps you should then take Deborah to see the project, Nicky. That seems like a good place to begin."

ARNSIDE
CUMBRIA

When her husband had left with the red-haired woman, Alatea sat for a moment looking at the fan of magazines on the table in the bay window's alcove. They had been gone through. While this shouldn't have been odd, considering the woman had been waiting for Nicholas to fetch his wife for an introduction and it *was* natural for one to flip idly through magazines while waiting, there was nonetheless very little that did not set Alatea's nerves on edge these days. She told herself that it meant absolutely nothing that *Conception* was now on the top of the stack. While it was a little embarrassing that a stranger might conclude that Alatea was obsessed with the subject of the magazine, it hardly meant anything would come of her conclusion. This woman from London was not here to talk to her or to wander through the labyrinth of her personal history. She was here because of what Nicholas was doing. And it was likely that she wouldn't have been here at all had Nicholas been just some ordinary individual trying to develop yet another way to help addicts turn their lives around. The fact that he wasn't just some ordinary bloke, the fact that the misdeeds of his misspent youth had garnered him so much publicity because of his father . . . That was what made the story a good one: the son of Lord Fairclough, self-redeemed from a life of dissolution.

Alatea hadn't known about the Baron Fairclough of Ireleth part of Nicholas's past when she'd first met him, or she would have run from his presence. Instead, she'd known only that his father was a manufacturer of everything imaginable that one might find in a bathroom, a fact that Nicholas had made light of. What he hadn't mentioned was his father's title, his father's service to the cause of pancreatic cancer, and his father's subsequent position of prominence. So she'd been prepared to meet a man prematurely aged by his son's having thrown away twenty years of his life. She'd not been prepared to meet the vital presence that was Bernard Fairclough. Nor had she been altogether prepared for that way Nicholas's father looked at her through his heavy-framed spectacles. "Call me Bernard," he'd said, and his eyes had gone from her own to her bosom and back again. "Welcome to the family, my dear."

She was used to men's eyes on her bosom. That had not been the problem. It was natural. Men were men. But men didn't usually then gaze upon her with speculation on their faces. *What is someone like you doing with my son?* was the unspoken question Bernard Fairclough had asked her.

She had seen that look each time Nicholas had introduced her to a member of his family. To them all, she and her husband were unsuited and although she wanted to make her physical appearance the reason for her unsuitability as the wife of Nicholas Fairclough, she reckoned it was more than that. They thought of her as a gold digger. She was not from their country; they knew nothing about her; her courtship had been disturbingly brief. To them this meant she was after something, undoubtedly the family fortune. Especially did Nicholas's cousin Ian think this, because he was the man in charge of Bernard Fairclough's money.

What Nicholas's family didn't think was that she could possibly be in love with him. She'd so far expended a great deal of effort to assure them of her devotion. She'd given them not a single reason to doubt her love for Nicholas, and ultimately, she'd come to believe she'd soothed the concerns of them all.

There was no reason their concerns should not be soothed, for she *did* love her husband. She *was* devoted to him. God in heaven, she was hardly the first woman on earth who had fallen in love with a man less attractive than herself. It happened all the time. So for every person to gaze upon her so speculatively . . . This had to stop, but she wasn't sure how to halt it.

Alatea knew that she had to resolve her anxieties about this and other matters in some way. She had to stop starting at shadows. It was not a sin to enjoy the life she had. She hadn't sought it. It had come to her. That had to mean it was the path that she was intended to follow.

Still, there was the magazine mixed among the others on the table and now on the top of them. Still, there was the way the woman from London had looked at her. How did they really know who this woman was, why she was here, and what she intended? They didn't. They had to wait to find out. Or so it seemed.

Alatea picked up the coffee service on its tray. She carried it into the kitchen. She saw next to the telephone the scrap of paper upon which she'd first written the message from Deborah St. James. She hadn't taken note of the name of the company Deborah St. James represented when she'd taken the message, but the woman herself had mentioned it, thank God, so Alatea had a place to start.

She went to the second floor of the house. Along a corridor where servants once had slept, she had designated a tiny bedroom as their design centre while she and Nicholas worked upon the house. But she also used the room as her lair and it was here that she kept her laptop.

It took forever to access the Internet from this location,

but she managed to do so. She stared at the screen for a moment before she began to type.

It had been easy to bunk off school. Since no one with any brains would actually *want* to cart him all the way to Ulverston and beyond and since Kaveh *did* have brains, it had been a simple matter. Lie in bed, clutch the stomach, say Cousin Manette had served him something that must have been bad on the previous evening, claim he had already been sick twice during the night, and act appreciative when Gracie reacted as he'd known she'd react. She'd flown to Kaveh's bedroom and he'd heard her crying out, "Timmy's been sick! Timmy's not well!" and he did feel a very small twinge of guilt because he knew from Gracie's voice that she was afraid. Poor dumb kid. It didn't take a genius to know she was worried that someone else from her family might suddenly kick the bucket.

She needed to get a grip, did Gracie. People died all the time. One couldn't prevent that by hovering round them and doing their breathing, eating, sleeping, and shitting for them. Besides, as far as Tim was concerned, Gracie had bigger worries now than the potential death of someone else in her life. She had the worry of what the hell was going to become of her now their dad was dead and their mother wasn't making the slightest move to claim them.

Well, at least they weren't the only ones with that worry, he thought. For it was only a matter of time before Kaveh got both the word and the boot, and then it would be out on the street for him. Find a new place to live and a new dick to fuck you. Go back to whatever hole you'd been living in when Dad first found you, Kaveh, my man.

Tim could hardly wait for that moment. And he wasn't the only one, as things turned out.

That morning old George Cowley had waylaid Kaveh on his way to the car with Gracie in tow. Cowley looked like shit from what Tim could see from his bedroom window, but Cowley *always* looked like shit so it didn't mean much to see him with his braces forgotten and his fly so undone that part of his shirt was hanging out of it like a tattersall flag. He must've seen Kaveh and Gracie from the window of his hovel and come running to have it out with the bloke.

Tim couldn't hear what they were saying but he reckoned he knew the topic well enough. For Cowley hitched up his sagging trousers and adopted a posture that suggested a confrontation was in the offing. If that was the case, there was only one reason for confronting Kaveh about anything: Cowley wanted to know when Kaveh was planning to vacate the premises. He wanted to know when Bryan Beck farm was going on to the block.

Outside, Gracie had her rucksack at her feet and was waiting for Kaveh to unlock the car door for her. She was ping-ponging her gaze between Kaveh and Cowley, and Tim could see from her expression that she was scared. Gracie scared created a twinge in Tim, suggesting he ought to go outside and see if there was something he could do to come between Cowley and Kaveh or at least to get Gracie away from them. But doing that would bring himself to the closer attention of Kaveh, who might then tell him to get himself ready to be carted down to Margaret Fox School, and that was the last thing he wanted since he had things to do today.

Tim turned from the window and crossed the room to his bed. He threw himself down on it. He was waiting for the sound of Kaveh's car, which would indicate that Tim was finally alone for the day. When he heard its muted roar—Kaveh was always too heavy on the accelerator, as if he thought the engine needed to be thoroughly flooded before putting the car into gear—Tim reached for his mobile. He began to punch in the number.

So yesterday had been a waste. He'd flipped out with Cousin Manette, and that was bad. What was good in the bad was that he'd not gone so far as to hurt her seriously. He'd come to his senses right at the moment he was about to fall upon her and choke the bloody life out of her and enjoy doing it just to get her to stop being so fucking *concerned* about him. His vision had gone black and he couldn't even see the stupid cow on the ground in front of him. He'd dropped to his knees then and had beaten his fists on the wooden jetty instead of on her and damn it all if she hadn't rolled over and pulled him to her and tried to soothe him. Tim didn't know where his father's cousin had developed her skill in the turn-the-other-cheek department. Her ability to forgive and forget was a strong indication that she had more than one screw loose in a place where screws didn't belong at all.

At any rate, getting into Windermere had been out of the question. Tim had done his part and sobbed awhile. Then he finally calmed down. There they remained on the jetty dock for a good thirty minutes with Cousin Manette holding him and murmuring about things being fine and all right and you and me will go camping up Scout Scar just you wait and see and then who knows what will happen maybe your dad will come back to life like anyone really wanted him to and maybe your mum will develop a different personality which was just as unlikely. Whatever, Tim thought. Who bloody cared anyway. The important thing was not to have to spend the night in Great Urswick, and he'd managed that.

where r u he thumbed into the mobile. 2day ok he added.

There was no reply.

couldnt was his second message. No ride 2 W. There was no need to add the information about Manette, her tent, and all the rest. The fact was he'd not had a way to get to Windermere once Manette had carted him to Great Urswick and it would have taken him hours to thumb it.

There was still no reply. Tim waited. His gut started to feel like there *was* actually bad food inside of it as he'd claimed, and he swallowed a lump of desperation. No, he told himself immediately, he wasn't desperate. He wasn't anything.

He rolled off the bed, tossing the mobile on the bedside table. He went to his laptop and accessed his e-mail. No message.

It was, he decided, time to push matters along. No way in hell was anyone walking away from a bargain Tim had struck. He'd kept his half of it and it was time the other half was kept as well.

LAKE WINDERMERE
CUMBRIA

Lynley had rooted a small pocket torch from the glove box of the Healey Elliott, and he was walking down to the boathouse for a closer look at the dock when his mobile rang. It was Isabelle, he saw. Her first words to him were, "Tommy, I need you in London."

Logically he thought something had come up, which was what he asked her.

She said, "I'm not talking about professional need. There are certain actions I don't want another member of the team to engage in for me."

He smiled at that. "Well, that's good to hear. I didn't much fancy sharing you with DI Stewart."

"Don't push your luck. When will you be back?"

He looked out at the lake. He'd come through the plantation of poplars and he stood on the path with the morning sun falling on his shoulders. It was looking like a very fine day. For a moment he gave casual thought to what it would be like to be sharing the day with Isabelle. He said, "I don't know, actually. I've only just got started."

"What about a brief encounter? I'm missing you, and I don't like to miss you. When I miss you, you start preying on my mind. I can't have that and do my job properly."

"A brief encounter would solve that for you?"

"It would. I have no defence to offer: I enjoy you in bed."

"At least you're forthright."

"And I always will be. So have you the time? I can come to you this afternoon—" She paused and he pictured her checking her diary for a time. When she went on, he knew he'd been right. "Round half past three," she added. "Can you free yourself then?"

"I'm not near London, I'm afraid."

"Really? Where are you?"

"Isabelle . . ." He wondered if she'd been trying to trick him. Dangling the prospect of sex to divert him first and then sweeping in for an inadvertent admission on his part regarding his location. "You know I can't say."

"I know you've been instructed by Hillier to keep your mouth shut. I wouldn't expect that to apply to me. Would it have applied—" She stopped herself. She said, "Never mind," and that told him what she'd been on the edge of asking: *Would it have applied to your wife?* But she wouldn't say that. They never mentioned Helen because to mention Helen ran the risk of taking their relationship in a direction that led from the purely sexual to an area she'd indicated from the first she had no intention of going. "At any rate, this is ridiculous," she said. "What does Hillier think I'm going to do with the information?"

"I don't expect it's personal," he said. "I mean, the fact that he doesn't want you to know. He doesn't want anyone to know. To be honest, I never thought to ask him why."

"That doesn't seem like you. Did you want to leave London for some reason?" And then quickly, "Never mind. This is the sort of conversation that can get us in trouble. I'll speak to you later, Tommy."

She rang off. He was left with the mobile in his hand. He put it back in his pocket and continued to the boathouse. Best to keep his mind in the here and now, he thought. Isabelle was right about conversations that could muddy the waters of what was going on between them.

The boathouse, he found, was kept unlocked. The time of day made its interior darker than it had been on Lynley's previous visit, so he was glad he'd brought the torch and he switched it on. It was quite cool within: the result of the water, the stones, and the time of year. The air bore the tang of damp wood and algae. He worked his way round to the spot where Ian Cresswell's scull was tied.

There, he knelt. He used the torch's light against the edges of the stones that formed three sides of the gap remaining when the other two had gone into the water. There was little enough to see. Mortar was a rough surface anyway, and years of wear and usage had caused cracks, gouges, and splintered edges in more spots than just this one place. But what he was looking for was an indication of some tool used to ease the process of disintegration along: a chisel, perhaps, a screwdriver, a wedge. Anything would have done the job. Anything would also have left a mark.

He could see nothing. He realised that a closer examination under full light was going to be necessary, rather hard to pull off if the pretence he was merely a visitor was to be maintained. He also realised that his previous conclusion about the missing stones was now confirmed: They had to get them up and out of the water. The prospect wasn't a pleasant one. The water wasn't deep, but it would be frigid.

He switched off the torch and left the boathouse. He paused and looked out at the lake. No one was on it, and its surface was a perfect plane that reflected the glowing autumnal trees on its shoreline and above them the cloudless sky. He turned from this view and looked in the direction of the house. It was not visible from where he stood although anyone on the path through the plantation of poplars could easily see it. There was, however, another spot from which the boathouse could probably be seen: The top floor and roof of a square tower rose above a rise of land just south of the poplars. This was the folly where Mignon Fairclough lived. She'd not turned up to dinner on the previous night. Perhaps she wouldn't mind a morning call upon her now.

The folly was a duplication of the defensive pele towers in the district. It was the sort of structure people had once added to their properties to give them a bit of faux history, although, in the case of Ireleth Hall, faux history had hardly been necessary. Nonetheless, at some point in time the folly had been constructed and now it stood four floors tall, with a crenellated roof that suggested access was available at that level as well. And from the roof the view would be all encompassing, Lynley reckoned. One would be able to see Ireleth Hall, the drive up to it, its grounds, and the lake, as well as the boathouse.

When he knocked on the door, he heard a woman call out from inside, "What? *What?*" in some exasperation. He reckoned he was disturbing Mignon in the midst of whatever it was that she did—he hadn't yet learned her occupation—and he called out, "Miss Fairclough? Sorry. Am I disturbing you?"

Her answer sounded surprised. "Oh! I thought it was Mother again," and in a few moments the door swung open to reveal one of Bernard Fairclough's twin daughters. She was supporting herself on a zimmer frame, a woman who'd taken her diminutive height from her father and not her mother. She was swathed in various robes and gowns that gave her a bit of an artistic flair at the same time as effectively shrouding her body. She was also, Lynley noted, fully made up as if planning to go out sometime during the day. She'd done her hair as well, but she'd chosen a rather child-like style. It was held off her face like Alice in Wonderland with a band of blue ribbon, although unlike Alice's its colour was dull brown and not blond.

She said, "You're the Londoner, I take it. What're you doing prowling round this morning? I saw you down at the boathouse again."

"Did you?" Lynley wondered how she'd managed that. Three flights of stairs with a zimmer frame. He also wondered why she'd managed it. "I was getting some air," he said. "I saw the tower from the boathouse and came to introduce myself. I expected to meet you at dinner last night."

"Not up to it, I'm afraid," she said. "Still recovering from a bit of surgery." She looked him over and made no effort to hide her inspection. He thought she was about to say, You'll do, or ask him to open his mouth for a look at his teeth but instead she said, "You may as well come in."

"Am I disturbing you?"

"I was online but it can wait." She stepped back from the door.

Once inside, he could see the entire ground floor at a glance. It comprised a sitting room, a kitchen, and an area for Mignon's computer. It also seemed to be acting as a storage facility for boxes upon boxes stacked in virtually every open area upon the floor. They were sealed and at first he thought she might be in the process of moving house till a glance told him they were all packages addressed to her, with packing slips encased in plastic upon them.

The computer, he saw, was on. The screen of its monitor was lit and the format told him she'd been in the midst of reading and responding to e-mails. She saw the direction of his glance and said, "Virtual living. I find it vastly preferable to the real thing."

"A modern-day version of pen pals?"

"Lord no. I'm having quite a torrid affair with a gentleman in the Seychelles. At least that's where he says he's from. He also says he's married and a teacher in a dead-end job. Poor bloke went there for a sense of adventure and ended up finding the only adventure available was on the Internet." She smiled briefly and insincerely. "Of course, he could be lying about everything since as far as he knows *I'm* a fashion designer terribly busy with getting ready for my next catwalk show. Last time I was a missionary physician doing noble work in Rwanda and before that . . . let me see . . . Oh yes. I was an abused housewife seeking someone to understand my plight. As I said, it's virtual living. Anything is possible. It's open season on the truth."

"Can't that sort of thing backfire?"

"That's half the fun. But I'm careful and once they start talking about getting together in one port or another, I end it with a bang." She moved towards the kitchen, going on to say, "I should offer you coffee or something. I've only the instant kind, I'm afraid. Would you like a cup? Or tea? I've only bags. I could do you a cup of either."

"Coffee is fine. But I hate to trouble you."

"Do you indeed? How well-bred of you to say so." She was out of his line of vision in the kitchen banging about, so he took the opportunity to look round the place. Aside from the plethora of boxes, there was unwashed crockery on most available surfaces. The plates and bowls looked to have been there for some time because when he lifted one, it left a perfect ring beneath it that was untroubled by the dust that formed a fine down elsewhere.

He moved closer to the computer. She hadn't been lying, he saw at a glance. *God how I know what you mean,* she had written. *There are times when life gets in the way of what's really important. In my case, we used to do it every night. And now I'm lucky for once a month. But you should talk to her about it. Really. Of course, I say that and don't myself talk to James. How I wish. But never mind. What I wish can't happen. If only, though.*

"We've advanced to the point of revealing our miserable marriages," Mignon said behind him. "Really, it's incredible. The process is always exactly the same. You'd think someone along the line would have a bit of imagination when they're setting about seduction, but they never do. I've got the kettle on. Coffee'll be just a minute. I'll need you to carry your own cup."

Lynley joined her in the kitchen. It was tiny but kitted out with everything one would need. He saw she would have to do some washing up soon, however. There were very few plates left and she was using the last available mug for his coffee. She was having nothing herself. He said, "Wouldn't you prefer a real relationship?"

She eyed him. "Like my parents', perhaps?"

He lifted an eyebrow. "They seem quite devoted."

"Oh yes. They are. Perfectly devoted, entirely compatible, and everything else that goes along with it. Just look at them. Billing and cooing. Did they do that bit for you?"

"I'm not sure I'd recognise a bill or a coo."

"Well, if they didn't engage in a few rounds of it yesterday, they'll show you today, I'm sure. Watch for an exchange of looks suggesting deep waters. They're good at that."

"All form and no substance?"

"I didn't say that. *Devoted* was what I said. They're devoted and compatible, with all the trimmings. I think it's to do with the fact that my father's rarely here. It's quite perfect for them both. Well, for him at least. As for Mother, she doesn't complain and why should she? As long as she can fish, go to lunch with friends, manage my life, and spend vast amounts of her money on the gardens, I expect her existence is fine. And it *is* her money. Not Dad's, by the way, but he's never minded that as long as he has free use of it. Not what I would want in a marriage but as I don't want a marriage at all, who am I to judge theirs?"

The water came to a boil and the kettle clicked off. Mignon

set about the exercise of making him a cup of coffee, although she didn't bother to do it deftly. She spooned in a heap of the instant powder, leaving a trail of it between jar and mug, and when she stirred it, the liquid slopped over the edge of the mug and onto the worktop. She used the same spoon to dig into a sugar bowl, did a bit more slopping, added milk, and slopped some more. She handed over the mug without wiping off the excess coffee and said in what Lynley judged the understatement of the year, "Sorry. I'm not at all domestic."

"Nor am I," he responded. "Thank you."

She hobbled back to the sitting room, tossing over her shoulder, "What sort of car is that, by the way?"

"Car?"

"That amazing thing you're driving. I saw it when you arrived yesterday. Quite stylish but it must absolutely swill petrol like a camel at the oasis."

"Healey Elliott," he told her.

"Never heard of it." She found a chair unburdened by magazines and boxes. She deposited herself into it with a thud and said to him, "Find a spot. Move anything. It hardly matters." And as he was searching for a place to sit, "So what were you doing at the boathouse? I saw you there yesterday with my father. What's the attraction?"

He made a note about being more careful in his movements. It was appearing that aside from occupying herself with the Internet, Mignon spent her time in observation of what was going on round the property. He said, "I'd thought about taking that scull out on the lake but my natural bent towards sloth got the better of me."

"Just as well." She jerked her head in the general direction of the boathouse. "Last person who used it drowned. I reckoned you were tiptoeing down there to have a look at the scene of the crime." She chuckled grimly.

"Crime?" He took a sip of the coffee. It was ghastly.

"My cousin Ian. Surely you've been informed. No?" She told him much of what he already knew, as blithely as she'd told him everything else. He wondered about her general frankness of conversation. In his experience, such commitment to ostensible veracity hid, in reality, a wealth of information.

Ian Cresswell had definitely been murdered, as far as Mignon was concerned. Her reasoning was that, as far as she knew, people rarely died just because someone else *wished* them to. To his raised eyebrow upon hearing this, she went on. Her brother, Nicholas, had had to stumble along in Cousin Ian's sainted footsteps for most of his life. From the moment dear Ian had arrived from Kenya to take up residence with the Fairclough family upon the death of his mother, it had been Ian this and Ian that and why can't you be more like Ian? First-class pupil at St. Bees, he was, first-class athlete, first-class nephew to his uncle Bernard, shining star, blue-eyed boy, never put so much as a toenail wrong.

"I reckoned when he dumped his family and took up with Kaveh, that would open Dad's eyes to our darling Ian. I'm sure Nicky felt the same. But even deserting his family didn't do it. And now Kaveh's working for my mother and who orchestrated that if not Ian, hmm? No, nothing poor Nicky's done in his life has been enough to shine a light on him that was brighter than the light shone on Ian. And nothing Ian did dimmed his own light in my father's eyes. It does make one wonder."

"About?"

"All sorts of delicious things." Her face wore an I'll-say-no-more expression: saintly and pleased simultaneously.

"So Nicholas killed him?" Lynley enquired. "I assume he stood to gain somehow."

"As to the killing part, personally, I wouldn't be the least surprised. As to the gaining . . . Lord knows." She also seemed to be saying she wouldn't much blame Nicholas for anything that might have happened to Ian Cresswell, and this, along with her remarks about the man himself, was something that bore looking into. As did, Lynley thought, the terms of Cresswell's will.

He said, "It does seem a risky way to go about killing him, though, wouldn't you say?"

"Why?"

"I understand your mother uses the boathouse nearly every day."

Mignon straightened in her chair, receiving this news. She said, "And you're implying . . . ?"

"That your mother might have been a target for murder, assuming in the first place that someone was targeted for murder at all."

"*No* one would be the least interested in seeing my mother die," Mignon declared. She felt the need, apparently, to tick off on her fingers every person devoted to her mother, and topping the list was her father again, and all those claims of his devotion to Valerie.

Lynley thought of *Hamlet* and ladies protesting too much. He also thought of rich people and what they did with their money and how money bought everything from unwilling silence to reluctant cooperation. But all of this begged the question of what Bernard Fairclough had then intended by coming to London and requesting someone to look into the death of his nephew.

Too clever by half came to mind. Lynley just wasn't certain where the expression ought to be applied.

GRANGE-OVER-SANDS
CUMBRIA

Manette Fairclough McGhie had long believed there was no one on earth more manipulative than her own sister, but now she had other ideas. Mignon had used a simple accident at Launchy Gill to control their parents for more than thirty years: slip on the boulders too near the waterfall, knock your head, sustain a skull fracture, and my God, you'd think the world had ended. But really, Mignon was nothing at all in comparison to Niamh Cresswell. Mignon used people's guilt, fear, and anxiety to get what she wanted. But Niamh used her own children. And this, Manette decided, was going to stop.

So she took the day off from work. She had a good reason, being bruised and sore from Tim's attack on her on the previous afternoon. But even had he not kicked her kidneys and her spine so savagely, she would have come up with something. Fourteen-year-old boys did not behave as Tim was behaving without good reason. She'd known, of course, that something more serious than confusion over his father's life choices was behind Tim's attack on her as well as his placement in Margaret Fox School. She just hadn't known the reason was his own miserable excuse for a mother.

Niamh's home was just outside of Grange-over-Sands, some distance from Great Urswick. It was part of a neat and newish housing estate that curled down a hillside overlooking an estuary in Morecambe Bay. The houses here reflected someone's taste for things Mediterranean: They were uniformly a blinding white, uniformly trimmed in dark blue, with uniformly simple front gardens heavily given to gravel and shrubbery. They were of various sizes and, true to form, Niamh possessed the largest of them with the best view of the estuary and the wintering birds who domiciled there. This was the home to which Niamh had decamped upon Ian's desertion of his family. Manette knew from talking to Ian after the divorce that Niamh had been adamant about moving house. Well, who could blame her, really? Manette had thought at the time. The memories within the former home would have been painful, and the woman had two children to care for in the aftermath of the nuclear explosion that had occurred in the centre of her family. She'd have wanted something nice, at least, to help cushion the blow of such a transition in Tim and Gracie's lives.

That conclusion of Manette's, however, existed before she had learned that Tim and Gracie weren't living with their mother at all but rather with their father and his lover. She'd adjusted her thinking to What the hell is going on?, ultimately letting the question go when Ian had told her it was what he wanted as well: having his children with him. Upon Ian's death, Manette had thought that Niamh would naturally have taken the children home with her. That she had evidently not done so brought up What the hell is going on? once again. This time, she intended to have the question answered.

Niamh's estate car was in front of the house, and she came at once to the door when Manette knocked. Her expression was expectant, but this expression altered when she saw that her caller was Manette. Had Niamh not been wearing enough scent to knock over a pony as well as a hot-pink cocktail dress showing a copious amount of cleavage, that altered expression alone would have told Manette someone else was due to arrive quite soon.

Niamh said, "Manette," as a means of greeting. She did not step back from the doorway in unspoken welcome.

No matter, Manette thought. She stepped forward, giving Niamh no choice but to go chest-to-chest with her or to move out of the way. Niamh chose the latter option, although she did not close the door behind them as she followed Manette into the body of the house.

Manette made for the sitting room with its broad windows overlooking the estuary. She gave a passing glance to the mass of Arnside Knot far across the bay and passing thought to the fact that with a powerful enough telescope one would have been able to see not only where the trees of the knot opened up to the crown of bare land and a few wind-scarred conifers at its summit but also lower down the hill and into her brother Nicholas's sitting room.

She turned and faced Niamh. The other woman was watching her but, oddly, her glance shifted several times from Manette to the doorway leading into the kitchen. It was as if someone was hiding in there, which hardly made sense considering Niamh's previous look of expectation. So Manette said, "I could do with a coffee. Mind if I . . ." and strode in that direction.

Niamh said, "Manette, what do you want? I would have appreciated a phone call to tell me—"

But Manette was in the kitchen at that point, putting on the kettle as if she lived here. On the worktop she saw the reason for Niamh's shifty eyes. A bright red tin bucket stood upon it, filled with a variety of items. A black sticker with white letters formed a flag on the bucket and *Bucket of Love* was printed across this. That this intriguing object had just arrived by post was indicated by an open box on the worktop as well. It took no advanced degree in human sexuality to understand that the bucket's contents constituted a variety of suggestive toys meant to be used by a couple looking for spice to add to their sex life. *Very* interesting, Manette thought.

Niamh pushed past her, snatched up the Bucket of Love, and replaced it in the box. She said, "Fine. Now what do you want? And *I'll* make the coffee if it's quite all right with you." She fetched a cafetiere, which she slammed onto the worktop. She did the same with a small bag of coffee and a mug with *I've been to Blackpool!* fading round its middle.

"I've come about the children," Manette said. There was no point in preliminaries that she could see. "Why aren't they back with you yet, Niamh?"

"I don't see that it's any of your business. Did Timothy tell you something yesterday?"

"Tim attacked me yesterday. I think you and I can agree that's normal behaviour for a fourteen-year-old boy."

"Ah. So that's what this is about. Well, you wanted to fetch him from school. It didn't work out? How awful for you." Niamh said this last in a tone that indicated Tim's attack upon Manette had been nothing of the sort. She spooned coffee into the cafetiere and fetched milk from the fridge. She said, "But you can't be that surprised, Manette. He's in Margaret Fox School for a reason."

"And we both know what that reason is," Manette replied. "What the hell is going on?"

"What's going on, as you put it, is the fact that Timothy's behaviour hasn't been *normal*, as you also put it, for quite some time. I expect you can work out why."

God, Manette thought, it was going to be the same song and dance as it always was with Niamh: Tim's birthday and the surprise guest showing up. Wonderful moment to learn one's father has a lover of the same sex or of any sex. Manette wanted to strangle Niamh. How much more mileage was the bloody woman intending to get from what Ian and Kaveh had done? Manette said, "It wasn't Tim's fault, Niamh." To which she added, "And do not attempt to derail this conversation in your usual fashion, all right? That may have worked with Ian, but I assure you it's not going to work with me."

"Frankly, I don't wish to talk about Ian. You've no worry on that score."

What a laugh, Manette thought. *This* would be an exciting change in her cousin's wife since Ian and his outrage against her had been the sole subject of Niamh's conversation for the last year. Well, she was going to take Niamh at her word. She was here to talk about Tim, anyway. She said, "Excellent. I've no wish to talk about Ian either."

"Really?" Niamh examined her fingernails, which were perfectly groomed like the rest of her. "Now that's a change. I thought Ian was one of your favourite topics."

"*What* are you talking about?"

"Please. You may have been trying to hide it all these years, but it was never a secret to me that you wanted him."

"*Ian?*"

"If he left me, you assumed it would be for you. Really, Manette, by all accounts, you should be as enraged as I am that he chose Kaveh as his next life's partner."

God, God, *God*, Manette thought. Niamh had actually managed to slither away from the subject of Tim as smoothly as if she'd been oiled. She said, "Oh stop it. I can see what you're doing. It's not going to work. I'm not leaving till we talk about Tim. Now you can have that conversation with me or we can play cat and mouse for the rest of the day. But *something*"—with a meaningful glance at the box containing the Bucket of Love—"tells me you'd like me to make myself scarce. And that's not going to happen simply because you manage to raise my ire."

Niamh said nothing to this. She was saved by the bell of coffee making. The electric kettle clicked off and she busied herself with filling the cafetiere and stirring the grounds.

Manette said, "Tim's a day pupil at Margaret Fox School. He's not a boarder. He's meant to come home at night to his parents. But he's still going home to Kaveh Mehran, not to you. What's that supposed to be doing for his mental state?"

"What's *what* doing to his mental state, Manette?" Niamh turned from the coffee. "The fact that he's going home to Ian's precious Kaveh or going home at all instead of staying there in lockdown like a criminal?"

"Home is here, not in Bryanbarrow. You know that very well. If you could have seen the state he was in yesterday . . . God in heaven, what's wrong with you? This is your son. Why haven't you moved him home? Why haven't you moved Gracie home? Are you punishing them for some reason? Is this some sort of game you're playing with their lives?"

"What do *you* know about their lives? What have you ever known? You've only been involved with them—when you've been involved at all—because of Ian. Dear beloved sainted Ian who can do no wrong to any bloody Fairclough. Even your father took his side when he left me. Your *father*. Ian with a halo on his head walks out of that door hand-in-hand—or should I say hand-on-arse—with some . . . some . . . some *Arab* barely out of nappies and your father does nothing. None of you do. And now he's working for your mother as if he did absolutely nothing at *all* to destroy my life. And you accuse me of playing games? You question what *I'm* doing when the lot of you did nothing at all to make Ian come home where he belonged, where his duty was, where his children were, where I . . . I . . ." She grabbed a kitchen towel because the tears that had come to her eyes were threatening to spill over. She caught them before they damaged her eyeliner or made a streak through her makeup. This done, she threw the kitchen towel in the rubbish and drove the palm of her hand down upon the cafetiere, separating the coffee from its grounds and putting a full stop to her own remarks.

Manette watched her. For the first time things were becoming clear. She said, "You're not bringing them home, are you? You're intending Kaveh to keep them. Why?"

"Drink your bloody coffee and leave," Niamh replied.

"Not till we get things perfectly clear. Not till I understand every nuance of what you have in mind. Ian's dead, so that's ticked off your list. Now it's Kaveh. Kaveh's not too likely to die, though, unless you kill him—" Manette's words halted of their own accord. She and Niamh were left staring at each other.

Niamh turned away first. "Leave," she said. "Just go. Leave."

"What about Tim? What about Gracie? What happens to them?"

"Nothing."

"Which means you leave them with Kaveh. Until someone forces your hand legally or otherwise, you leave them in Bryanbarrow. Permanently. So Kaveh gets the full experience of what he destroyed. Those two children—who are, by the way, perfectly innocent in this entire matter—"

"Don't be so certain of that."

"What? Are you claiming now that *Tim* . . . My God. You get worse and worse."

There was, Manette knew, no further point in their conversation. Coffee be damned, she began to head towards the front door and she was nearly there when footsteps came up the two exterior steps and someone called out, "Nee? Pet? Where's my girl?"

A man stood at the door, a pot of chrysanthemums in his hands and on his face a look of such eagerness that Manette knew she was looking at the sender of the Bucket of Love. He was there to play with its contents, she reckoned. A slight sheen of anticipation glistened on his pudgy face.

He said, "Oh!" and looked over his shoulder as if thinking he'd come to the wrong house.

Then over Manette's shoulder, Niamh said, "Come in, Charlie. Manette is just leaving."

Charlie. He looked vaguely familiar. Manette couldn't place him, however, till he nodded at her nervously and passed her in the doorway. His proximity brought his scent quite close, and the scent was cooking oils and something else. At first Manette thought of fish and chips, but then she realised he was the owner of one of the three Chinese takeaways in the market square in Milnthorpe. She'd been in there more than once on her way home from Arnside and Nicholas's house, scoring a meal for Freddie. She'd never seen this man out of his kitchen uniform spattered with grease and copious amounts of soy sauce. But here he was, eager to do a job that didn't at all involve slopping chop suey into takeaway cartons.

As he entered the house, he said, "You look good enough to eat," to Niamh.

She giggled. "Hope so. Have you brought your appetite?"

Both of them laughed. The door closed on them, allowing them to get down to business.

Manette felt white heat wash over her. Something, she decided, would have to be done about her cousin Ian's wife. She was wise enough to understand, however, that it might well be a leave-her-to-God situation completely beyond her powers to effect. But what she could effect was a change in Tim and Gracie's lives. And that was something she could see to herself.

WINDERMERE
CUMBRIA

Getting possession of the forensic reports had not been a difficult matter, and this ease of acquisition had been largely due to St. James's reputation as an expert witness. There was, of course, no actual need for his expertise in this matter because the ruling had already been made by the coroner, but a phone call and a spurious tale about a university presentation on basic forensics had been enough to put all the relevant documents into his hands. These confirmed what Lynley had told him about the death of Ian Cresswell, with a few additional salient details. The man had suffered a severe blow to the head—in the near region of the left temple—which had been enough to render him unconscious and fracture his skull. The apparent source of the blow was the stone dock and although his body had been in the water for approximately nineteen hours when it had been found, it had—at least according to the forensic report—still been possible to make a comparison between the wound on his head and the shape of the stone that he had ostensibly hit on the dock before tumbling into the water.

St. James frowned. He wondered how this was possible. Nineteen hours in the water would do much to alter the inflicted wound, making information about it useless unless some sort of reconstruction had been managed. He looked for this, but he didn't see one. He made a note and continued reading.

Death had been by drowning as an examination of the lungs had confirmed. Bruising on the right leg suggested that Cresswell's foot may have become caught in the scull's stretcher as he lost his balance, capsizing the craft and holding the victim beneath the water for a time until—perhaps due to the gentle action of the lake over the hours—his foot had ultimately become dislodged and his body had floated freely next to the dock.

Toxicology showed nothing unusual. Blood alcohol indicated that he'd been drinking but he was not drunk. Everything else in the report indicated that he was a fine specimen of a man in the range of forty to forty-five years, in perfect health and superb physical condition.

Since it had been an unwitnessed drowning, a coroner's ruling had been required. This had necessitated an inquest, preceded by an investigation by the coroner's officers. They had testified at the inquest, as had Valerie Fairclough, the forensic pathologist, the first policeman on the scene, and the subsequent officer called in to confirm the first policeman's conclusion that no SOCO were needed as no crime had occurred. The end product of all this was the ruling of death by accidental drowning.

As far as St. James could see, there was nothing untoward in any of this. However, if mistakes had been made, they'd been made at the initial stage of the process and that was with the first policeman on the scene. A conversation with this police constable was in order. This demanded a trip to Windermere, from where the officer had originally come.

The man's name was PC William Schlicht, and from the look of him when he came into Reception at the Windermere station to meet St. James, he was fresh out of the nearest training facility. This would explain why he'd called in another officer to confirm what he'd concluded. It had likely been the first death scene PC Schlicht had encountered and he wouldn't have wanted to start his career off with a gross error. Aside from that, the death had occurred on the estate of a well-known and semipublic figure. The newspapers in the area would have found this of interest, and the PC would know that eyes were upon him.

Schlicht was a slight man. But he was also wiry and athletic in appearance, and his uniform looked as if he starched and ironed it every morning, as well as polished its buttons. He seemed to be in his early twenties, and his expression was one of a man extremely eager to please. Not the best attitude in a policeman, St. James thought. It put one in the position of being easily manipulated by outside forces.

"A course you're teaching?" PC Schlicht said after their exchange of greetings. He'd taken St. James beyond Reception, into the station itself, and he led him to a coffee room/lunch room where a refrigerator bore a sign reading *Put your *#%*# name on your lunch bag!* and an old coffeemaker circa 1980 was sending forth an odour reminiscent of coal mines in the nineteenth century. Schlicht had been in the midst of eating what looked like leftover chicken pie from a plastic container. A smaller pot of raspberry fool sat next to this, awaiting consumption as his dessert.

St. James made the appropriate noises of agreement upon the mention of the putative course. He lectured frequently at University College London. Should PC Schlicht wish to do some checking up on him, everything he was claiming about his visit to Cumbria was verifiable. St. James told the PC to go on with his lunch, please, as he merely wished to confirm a few details.

"I reckon someone like you would look for a fancier case to present in a lecture, if you know what I mean." Schlicht lifted a leg over the seat of his chair to sit. He scooped up his cutlery and tucked back into his meal. "The Cresswell situation was a straightforward business from the start."

"You must have had one or two doubts, though," St. James said, "since you called in another officer."

"Oh, that." Schlicht waved his fork in acknowledgement. He then confirmed what St. James had suspected: It had been his first death scene, he didn't want a blot on his copy book, and the family was quite well-known in the area. He added, "Not to mention rich as the dickens, if you know what I mean," and he grinned as if the wealth of the Faircloughs demanded that a certain conclusion was in order from the local police. St. James said nothing, merely looking questioning. Schlicht said, "The rich have their ways, you know? Not like you and me, they are. You take my wife: She finds a body in our boathouse—not that we have a boathouse in the first place, mind you—and let me tell you, she'd be screaming down the walls and running in circles and no phone call to nine-nine-nine *she* made would even be understandable, if you get my meaning. That one"—by whom St. James concluded he was referring to Valerie Fairclough— "is cool as cream. 'There appears to be a dead man floating in my boathouse' is how she puts it, 'cording to the dispatch bloke who phoned up the station, and she goes right on to give the address without being asked, which is a bit odd 'cause you'd think under the circumstances she'd need to be asked or reminded or something. And when I get there, she's not waiting on the drive or pacing in the garden or tapping her toe on the front steps or anything you'd expect in such a situation, is she? No. She's inside the house and she comes out dressed like she's going to some posh afternoon tea or something and I wonder, I do, what she went down to the boathouse for in the first place dressed like that. She tells me straightaway and without my asking that she was down there to go out on the lake and do a bit of fishing. Dressed like that, mind you. She says she does it all the time: two, three, perhaps four times a week. All hours, it doesn't matter to her. She likes to be out on the water, she says. She says she didn't expect to find a body floating there and she knows who it is: her husband's nephew. She takes me down there to have a look. We're walking on our way when the ambulance shows up and she waits for them to join us."

"She knew then, for a certainty, that the man in the water was dead."

Schlicht paused, fork midflight to his lips. "She did, that. 'Course, he was floating facedown and he'd been in the water a good long while. Those clothes of hers, though. They do say something, don't they?"

Still, Schlicht said, it was cut-and-dried as far as he could tell when they got to the boathouse, despite any oddity in Valerie Fairclough's attire and behaviour. The scull was capsized, the body was floating next to it, and the condition of the dock with its missing stones told the tale of what had happened. Nonetheless, he put in a call for a DI to have a look just to be on the safe side of things, and the DI in question—a woman called Dankanics—came along, had a look, and agreed with how all evidence seemed to Schlicht. The rest had been more or less routine: filling out paperwork, making reports, showing up at the inquest, et cetera.

"Did DI Dankanics go over the scene with you?"

"Right. She had a look. We all did."

"All?"

"Ambulance crew. Mrs. Fairclough. The daughter."

"Daughter? Where was she?" This was odd. The scene should have been secured. That it had not been was highly irregular, and St. James wondered if this irregularity was the result of Schlicht's inexperience, DI Dankanics's possible indifference, or something else.

"Don't know exactly where she was when she saw the commotion," Schlicht replied, "but what brought her down to the boathouse was the noise. The ambulance had its siren going all the way to the house—those blokes like their siren like I like my dog, let me tell you—and she heard it and came along with her zimmer."

"Disabled, is she?"

"Looks that way. So that was that. The body got carted off for autopsy, DI Dankanics and I took statements, and . . ." He frowned.

"Yes?"

"Sorry. I'd forgotten the boyfriend."

"Boyfriend?"

"Turns out the dead bloke was a poofter. His partner was working on the property. Not at that exact moment, mind you, but he came driving in as the ambulance was driving out. 'Course he wanted to know what was going on—who wouldn't, human nature, eh?—and Mrs. Fairclough told him. Took him to one side and had a word and down he goes."

"He fainted?"

"Face-flat onto the gravel. We didn't know who he was at first and the fainting bit seemed off-kilter for some bloke just driving up to the house and hearing there's been a drowning. So we asked who he was and she told us—this is Valerie—that this bloke did landscapes and the like and the other bloke, the dead one in the boathouse, was his partner. Partner as in *partner*, if you take my meaning. Anyway, he came round soon enough and he starts blubbing. He says it's *his* fault the other bloke drowned, which we take up with some interest—this is me and Dankanics—but it turns out they'd had words on the previous evening about tying the knot. The dead bloke had wanted a civil ceremony with everything front and centre and all aboveboard while the living bloke liked things as they were. And Christ, if that bloke wasn't howling his head off. Makes you wonder, if you know what I mean."

St. James didn't, exactly, although like Alice he was finding the information curiouser and curiouser. He said, "As to the boathouse itself . . ."

"Hmm?"

"Was everything in order? Aside from the missing stones on the dock, of course."

"Far as Mrs. Fairclough could tell."

"What about the boats themselves?"

"They were all inside."

"As usual?"

Schlicht knotted his eyebrows. He'd finished with his chicken pie and was prising the lid from the raspberry fool. "Not sure I receive your meaning."

"Were the boats always kept in the order they were in when you saw the body? Or was that order arbitrary?"

Schlicht's lips rounded into a whistle, but he made no sound. He also gave no reply for a moment, but St. James could tell that in spite of his informal manner of address, he was not a fool. "That's something," he said, "that we didn't ask. Bloody hell, Mr. St. James. I hope it doesn't mean what I think it means."

For an arbitrary order suggested a likely accident. Anything else suggested murder.

MIDDLEBARROW FARM
CUMBRIA

The Middlebarrow Pele Project was situated to the east of the hill that comprised Arnside Wood, which gave entrance to a protected area called Arnside Knot. Deborah St. James and Nicholas Fairclough skirted this hill on the way to the project, curving through the upper part of Arnside village and then down again, following signs that directed them towards a place called Silverdale. As they drove, Nicholas Fairclough chatted in what seemed to Deborah to be a habitually friendly manner. He appeared open and forthright, the least likely individual to have planned the murder of his own cousin, had it actually been a murder. He made no mention of Ian Cresswell's death, of course. The drowning of the man—as unfortunate as it was—bore no relationship to the ostensible reasons for Deborah's visit to this place. She wasn't sure she was meant to keep it this way, however. It seemed to her that one way or another she had to bring Cresswell into the picture.

This wasn't her forte. Chatting up people in general was difficult for her, although she'd improved over the years since she'd learned the value of having her photographic subjects relax while she snapped their pictures. But that kind of chatting up was, at least, honest in its own way. This brand of chatting up—when she was pretending to be someone she utterly was not—left her in a quandary.

Luckily, Nicholas didn't appear to notice. He was too intent upon reassuring her of his wife's support of the work he was doing.

"She'll be standoffish till you get to know her," he told Deborah as they zipped along the narrow road. "It's her nature. You're not to take it personally. Allie doesn't trust people much as a rule. It's to do with her family." He cast her a smile. He had an oddly youthful face—like a boy's when he hasn't come into his manhood yet—and Deborah reckoned he'd remain young looking right to the grave. Some people were lucky that way. "Her dad's the mayor of the town she was born in. In Argentina. He's been mayor for years, so she grew up in the spotlight there and she had to learn to monitor everything she did. So she always thinks someone's watching her, to catch her out doing . . . I don't know what. Anyway, it makes her skittish at first. Everyone has to earn her trust."

"She's quite attractive, isn't she," Deborah said. "I expect that could be a problem for someone in the limelight, even in a small town. All eyes on her, if you know what I mean. Where in Argentina is she from?"

"Santa Maria di something. I always forget. It's about ten words long. It's in the foothills of wherever. Sorry. All the Spanish names flummox me. I'm completely hopeless with languages. I can barely speak English. Anyway, she doesn't like the place. She says it felt like an outpost on the moon. I expect it's not that big, eh? She ran off from home when she was something like fifteen years old. She made it up with her family after a bit, but she never went back."

"Her family must miss her."

"That," he said, "I wouldn't know. Although I expect they would do, wouldn't they?"

"You've not met them, then? They didn't attend your wedding?"

"Actually, there wasn't much of a wedding. Just Allie and me and city hall in Salt Lake City. Someone to do the ceremony and two women we carted in off the street to be witnesses. Afterwards, Allie wrote to tell her parents we'd done the deed, but they didn't write back. They're cheesed off about it, I expect. But they'll come round. People always do. Especially"—he grinned—"when there's a grandchild on the way."

That explained the magazine she'd seen. *Conception* with its countless stories on antenatal this and postnatal that. "You're expecting? Congrat—"

"Not yet. But any day now." He tapped his fingers a bit on the steering wheel. "I'm very lucky," he said. Then he pointed out an autumnal woodland to the east of the road on which they were driving, a rich panoply of umber and gold deciduous trees contrasting against the green of conifers. "Middlebarrow Wood," he told her. "You can see the pele tower from here." He pulled into a lay-by to give her a view.

The tower, Deborah saw, was on a rise of land that looked rather like the prehistoric barrows one found all round the countryside in England. Behind this rise, the woods began, although the tower itself was out in the open. This would have given it a superior position should any border reivers have come calling, a regular occurrence during the centuries when the border between England and Scotland continually shifted. The intent of the reivers was always the same. They were marauders who had taken advantage of the lawlessness of that period of time, perfecting the art of stealing cattle and oxen, invading homes, and stripping their victims of everything they owned. Their objective was always plunder and getting back to their own homes without being killed in the process. If they themselves had to kill to accomplish this, they did so. But that hadn't been their first priority.

The pele towers had been an answer to the question of protection from the reivers. The best of them were indestructible, with stone walls far too thick to be harmed and windows just wide enough for an archer to fire from, and separate floors for animals, their owners, their household activities, and their defence. But the towers had fallen out of use as time went on, after the border was finally firmly established, along with laws and the advent of lawmen willing to make those laws more than someone's passing fancy. Once the towers fell out of use, their materials were employed for other buildings. Or the towers themselves were subsumed into larger structures, becoming part of a great house, a vicarage, or a school.

Middlebarrow Tower was of the first type. It stood tall, with most of its windows intact. A short distance from it and across a field, a group of old farm buildings gave testimony to what some of the tower's original stones had been used for. Between the tower and these farm buildings, a camp had been set up. It was equipped with small tents, honey pots, and several makeshift sheds with a larger tent to accommodate the twelve-step programme, Nicholas Fairclough said. This was also the dining tent. Meals and twelve-stepping went hand in hand.

Nicholas pulled back into the road, which descended to a lane leading off towards the tower. The tower, he said, was on the private land of Middlebarrow farm. He'd got the farmer to consent to the project—not to mention to consent to the presence of the recovering addicts who were currently living and working there—once he saw the benefits of a restored tower that could be used as anything from a holiday rental to a tourist attraction.

"He's settled on turning the place into a camping site,"

Nicholas told her. "It'll bring him some extra money during the season, and he's happy enough to put up with us if that's the end product. That was Allie's idea, by the way, approaching the farmer with the possibilities for the tower if he'd let us renovate it. She was involved with the pele project in its initial stages."

"But not now?"

"She likes to be in the background. Plus . . . well, I daresay when the addicts began to arrive, she was a bit more comfortable being at home than hanging about here." They pulled onto the site where work was in progress, and Nicholas added, "No need to be wary, though. These blokes are far too used up—and far too ready for a change in their lives—to be harmful to anyone."

But they were not, Deborah found, far too used up to work. A team leader had been assigned to the project, and when Nicholas introduced him as Dave K—"It's traditional not to use surnames," he told her—it was clear that work leading to hunger leading to meals leading to twelve-stepping and then to sleep was the order of the day. Dave K had a roll of plans with him, and he unscrolled them on the bonnet of Nicholas Fairclough's car. With a nod at Deborah meant, she assumed, to convey acknowledgement of the introduction, he lit a cigarette and used it as a pointer as he spoke to Nicholas about the project.

Deborah wandered from the car. The tower, she saw, was huge, a bulky mass of a building that looked like the makings of a Norman castle, complete with crenellation. Upon a casual glance, it didn't appear in need of a great deal of restoration, but when Deborah walked round the other side of the structure, she saw what had become of it during the centuries it had lain available for anyone to maraud upon it.

The project was going to be enormous. Deborah couldn't think how they were going to manage the scope of work needing to be done. There were no floors to the building, one of the four external walls was missing, and another wall was partially collapsed. Removing debris alone was going to take ages and then there was the not small matter of obtaining materials to replace those that had long ago been carted off to become part of other buildings in the district.

She gazed upon it with a photographer's eye. In the same fashion, she examined the men who were working there, most of whom seemed to be the age of pensioners. She didn't have any of her cameras with her aside from a small digital one to keep her position as a filmmaker's research scout on the up-and-up. She took this from her bag and applied herself to recording what was round her.

"It's really the act of creation that heals. The process not product, I mean. Of course, at first they focus on the product. That's human nature. But in the end they'll come to see that the real product is self-belief, self-esteem, self-knowledge. Whatever you want to call it."

Deborah turned. Nicholas Fairclough had come up beside her. She said, "To be honest, your workers don't look strong enough to do much, Mr. Fairclough. Why are there no younger men to help them?"

"Because these are the blokes who need saving the most. Here and now. If someone doesn't reach out to them, they're going to die on the streets in the next couple of years. My thinking is that no one deserves to die like that. There're programmes all over the country—all over the world—for young people, and believe me I know, because I spent time in a lot of them. But for blokes like this? Shelters for the night, sandwiches, hot soup, Bibles, blankets, whatever. But not belief. They're not so far gone that they can't read pity at fifty yards. Feel that way towards them and they'll take your money, use it to get high, and spit on your charity. 'Scuse me for a moment, okay? Have a look round if you like. I need to talk to one of them."

Deborah watched as he picked his way through the rubble. He yelled, "Hey, Joe! What d'we hear from that stonemason?"

Deborah wandered in the direction of the large tent, identified by a sign in front of it reading *Eat and Meet*. Inside, a bearded man in a knitted cap and heavy coat—too heavy for the weather, but he seemed to have no body fat at all to insulate his bones—was setting up for a meal. He had positioned large pots over spirit warmers, and a fragrance came from them, redolent of red meat and potatoes.

He saw Deborah, and his eyes lit on the camera in her hands.

Deborah said pleasantly, "Hello. Not to worry. I'm just having a look round."

"Th' always are," he muttered.

"Lots of visitors?"

"Always someone comin' hereabouts. Himself needs the funds."

"Oh. I see. Well, I'm not a potential donor, I'm afraid."

"Nor was the last. Doesn't matter to me. I get food and the meetings and 'f someone wants to ask me do I think this'll work, I say it will."

Deborah approached him. "But you don't believe in this process?"

"Didn't say that. And doesn't matter what I believe. Like I say, I get food and the meetings and that's enough for me. Don't mind the meetings as much as I reckoned I would, so that's not half-bad. Dry place to sleep as well."

"During the meetings?" Deborah asked him.

He looked up sharply. He saw her smile and he chuckled. "Anyway, like I said, they're not half-bad. Bit much with the God bit, bit more with the acceptance bit, but I can cope. Maybe it'll sink in. Willing to try it. Ten years sleeping rough . . . it's enough."

Deborah joined him then at the serving table. He had a large box on a chair next to it, and from this he began taking out cutlery, tin plates, plastic drinking glasses, cups, and a mound of paper napkins. He began to arrange these on the table, and Deborah helped him.

"Teacher," he said quietly.

She said, "What?"

"That's what I was. Secondary comprehensive in Lancaster. Chemistry. I bet you didn't reckon that, did you?"

"No. I didn't." Her words were equally quiet.

He gestured towards the outdoors. "All shapes and sizes," he said. "We got a surgeon, a physicist, two bankers, and an estate agent out there. And those're just the ones willing to say what they left behind. The others . . . ? They're not ready yet. Takes time to admit how far you've fallen.

You don't have to make those table napkins so neat. We're not the Ritz."

"Oh. Sorry. Force of habit."

"Like Himself," he said. "Can't hide your roots."

Deborah didn't bother to tell him that her own roots came from the soil of what in another century would have been called "being in service." Her father had long been employed by the St. James family, and he'd spent the last seventeen years of his life caring for Simon while pretending not to be caring for Simon. It was a very delicate balancing act that had him referring to his own son-in-law as Mr. St. James. Deborah made a murmur of quasi-agreement and said, "You sound fond of him."

"Himself? Decent bloke. Bit too trusting, but good to the core."

"You think he's being taken advantage of? I mean, with these gentlemen here."

"Not hardly. Most of them know they've got something good going and 'less they're too far gone with the drink or with drugs, they're going to hang on here as long as they can."

"Then who?"

"Taking advantage?" He eyed her directly, a very meaningful look. Deborah saw that he had a cataract forming in his left eye and she wondered how old he was. With ten years of life on the street as part of his C.V., it would be nearly impossible to determine his age from his appearance.

"People come round with promises and he believes 'em. He's naïve that way."

"It's to do with money? Donations?"

"Sometimes. Other times, they want something off him." Again, that meaningful look.

Deborah realised that he was placing her in the category of people wanting something from Nicholas Fairclough. It wasn't an unreasonable conclusion, considering who she was supposed to be. Still, she said, "Such as?"

"Well, he's got a good story to tell, doesn't he? He thinks if he tells it, it'll bring in money to help this place. Only it doesn't always work that way, does it. Most of the time it comes to nothing. We had a newspaper bloke here four times promising a story and Himself saw bags of money coming in to help us out when the story got printed. Bloody nothing came of it and we're back where we started, scrabbling for funds. That's what I mean. A bit naïve."

Deborah said, "Four times?"

"Eh?"

"A reporter was here four times and no story came out of it? That's unusual, quite an investment of time with no payoff for anyone. It must have been a true disappointment. What sort of reporter invests all that time in preparing a story without writing it?"

"That's what I want to know. *Said* he was from *The Source* in London, but no one was checking his credentials so he could've been anyone. What *I* think is he was here to find dirt on Himself, hoping to make him look bad. Greasing his own career—this bloke—if you know what I mean. But Himself, he doesn't see it that way. 'The time wasn't right' is how he puts it."

"But you don't agree."

"Way I see it, he needs to be careful. He never is and that's going to be a problem for him. Not now, then later. A problem."

WINDERMERE
CUMBRIA

Yaffa Shaw had been the one to suggest to Zed that more might be in order than his merely hanging about the Willow and Well in Bryanbarrow village waiting for a miraculous revelation to drop into his lap, like the appearance of a Scotland Yard detective complete with magnifying glass in hand and meerschaum pipe clenched between his lips, all the better to identify him. They'd had their regular conversation after Zed had written up his notes regarding everything the old farmer George Cowley had alluded to on the green. He'd made note also of the fact that the man's teenage son had seemed more than uncomfortable with his father's rant. Could be, he decided, that another chat was in order but this time with Daniel Cowley and not his father.

Yaffa, playing the part of his concerned potential life partner since his mum was in the room—when *wasn't* she in the room when it came to his love life? Zed wondered wryly—pointed out that Ian Cresswell's death and George Cowley's intentions might be in conflict with each other instead of what Zed had concluded, which was that they were directly related.

At first, Zed bristled at this. He was, after all, the investigative reporter. She, on the other hand, was merely a student at university attempting to accelerate her course so as to get back to Micah, the medical school boyfriend in Tel Aviv. He said, "I wouldn't be so sure about that, Yaf," without realising at first that the nickname had risen unbidden to his lips. "Sorry. Yaffa," he said, correcting himself.

She said, "I like the other. It makes me smile." And then obviously to his mother in explanation to what had to have been Susanna Benjamin's breathless question about why Yaffa Shaw was smiling while in conversation with her beloved Zed, "Oh, Zed called me Yaf. I thought it was rather sweet." And then to Zed, "Your mum says *sweet* is your middle name. She says that behind that giant exterior of yours, you're a cream puff."

"God." Zed groaned. "Can you get her to leave the room? Or should I just ring off and we can consider the duty done for today?"

"Zed! Stop it!" She laughed. She had, he'd discovered, a most pleasant laugh. She said to his mother, "This man is making kissing noises. Does he always do that when he's speaking on the phone to a woman? . . . He doesn't? Hmmm. I wonder what he'll say next."

"Tell her I'm asking you to take off your knickers or something," Zed said.

"Zedekiah Benjamin! Your mum is standing right here." And then, "He's being very naughty." And then a moment later to Zed and in an altered tone, "She's gone. Really, though, Zed, she's very sweet, your mum. She's started bringing me hot milk and biscuits at night. While I'm studying."

"She knows what she wants. She's been working at it for years. So. Everything going all right, then?"

"Fine. Micah did phone, and I brought him into the picture. Now he's pretending to be brother Ari, phoning from Israel to see how his baby sister is doing with her studies."

"Right. Well. Good." And really, that should have been it since their only obligation to each other was a twice-daily phone call taking place somewhere in his mother's vicinity.

Yaffa, however, took them back to what she'd been saying earlier in their conversation. "What if things aren't how they look?"

"Like us, you mean?"

"Well, I'm not talking about us, but it's a case in point, isn't it? What I mean is what if there's an inherent irony here that in and of itself could sex up your story about Nicholas Fairclough?"

"The Scotland Yard bloke—"

"Beyond the Scotland Yard bloke. Because listen to what you've told me about it all: one man is dead, another man wants the farm that the dead man occupied. Still another man lives on the farm with the dead man's children. Now what does that suggest to you?"

The truth was that it suggested nothing, but Zed was suddenly aware that Yaffa was ahead of him on the curve of the story. He hemmed and hawed and cleared his throat.

She said, mercifully, "There's more here than meets the eye, Zed. Did the dead man leave a will?"

"A will?" What the hell had a will to do with anything? Where was the sex in that?

"Yes. A will. There's potential conflict there, d'you see? George Cowley assumes the farm is going to be his for the taking now because now it will go on the block. But what if that's not the case? What if that farm is paid for free and clear and Ian Cresswell left it to someone? Or what if he put a name besides his own on the deed? What irony, hmm? George Cowley is thwarted once again. It's even more ironic if, perhaps, this man George Cowley had something to do with Ian Cresswell's death, isn't it?"

Zed saw she was right. He also saw she was clever and on his side as well. So after they rang off, he set about delving into the matter of Ian Cresswell and a will. It didn't take long for him to find out that there was indeed a will because wisely Cresswell had registered it online and the information was there for all to see: A copy of this document was at his solicitor's office in Windermere. Another copy—since the bloke was dead—would be available through the probate registry but scoring a look at that would eat up valuable time, not to mention a trip all the way to York, so he knew he had to get either a peek or the information itself in another way.

It would have been nothing short of pure delight for the will to be viewable online, but the lack of privacy in the UK—which was becoming pandemic considering global terrorism, permeable national borders, and the easy access to explosives courtesy of the world's arms manufacturers—had not extended to the requirement that one's last will and testament had to be offered up for public consumption. Still, Zed knew that there was a way to get to it and he also knew which single person on the planet was likely to be able to put his fingers on the document that he needed.

"A will," Rodney Aronson said when he caught up with the editor in his London office. "You're telling me you want to look at the dead man's will. I'm in the middle of a meeting here, Zed. We've a paper to produce. You do know that, don't you?"

Zed reckoned that his editor was also in the middle of consuming a chocolate bar, for over the phone he could hear the wrapper being crinkled even as Rodney Aronson spoke.

He said, "The situation is more complicated than it looks, Rod. There's a bloke up here wanting to put his mitts on that farm owned by Ian Cresswell. *Expecting* it to go on the block, he is. It seems to me that he's got one hell of a motive to do the chop on our guy—"

"Our *guy*, as you say, is Nick Fairclough. The story you're writing is about him, no? That's the story we're looking for the sex in and the sex is the cops. But it's only sex in the Fairclough story if they're *investigating* Fairclough. Zed, my man, do I have to do your job for you, or can you possibly jump on board the moving train?"

"I get it. I know. I'm fully on board. But as no cops have shown a face yet—"

"That's what you're doing up there? Waiting for cops to

show their faces? Jesus Christ, Zed. What sort of reporter are you? Let me spell it out, all right? If this bloke Credwell—"

"Cresswell. Ian Cresswell. And he's got a farm up here and his kids are living on it with some bloke, far as I can tell. So if the farm was left to this bloke or even to the kids and—"

"I don't bloody care who the farm was left to, who it belongs to, or whether it dances the tango when no one's looking. And I don't bloody care if this Cresswell was murdered. What I care about is what the cops are doing up there. If they're not prowling round Nicholas Fairclough, then your story is dead and you're on your way back to London. D'you understand that or do I have to go at it another way?"

"I understand. But—"

"Good. Now get back onto Fairclough and stop bothering me. Or come back to London, have done with the whole thing, and get a job writing greeting cards. The kind that rhyme."

That last was a particularly low blow. Nonetheless, Zed said, "Right."

But it wasn't right. Nor was it good journalism. Not that *The Source* actually practised good journalism, but given a story that was virtually dropping into their laps, one might think it actually possible.

Fine, Zed thought. He would get back to Nicholas Fairclough and Scotland Yard. But first he was determined to find out about that farm and about the terms of that bloody will because he had a gut feeling that that information was crucial to more than one person in Cumbria.

MILNTHORPE
CUMBRIA

Lynley met with St. James and Deborah in the public bar of their hotel. Over glasses of a rather indifferent port, they went over the information they'd gathered. St. James was of the same mind, Lynley discovered, as he himself was.

They had to bring up the missing stones from the dock and St. James had to look at them. He wouldn't mind having a look at the boathouse itself as well, he told Lynley, but he didn't know how an arrangement for this could be made without tipping their hand.

"I daresay it'll be tipped eventually," Lynley said. "I'm not sure how long I can carry off the pretence of idle curiosity for the benefit of anyone who happens to be watching. Fairclough's wife knows, by the way. He did tell her."

"That makes things a bit easier."

"Relatively, yes. And I agree with you, Simon. We need you inside that boathouse for more reasons than one."

"Meaning?" Deborah asked the question. She had her digital camera on the table next to her glass of port, and she'd brought a small notebook out of her shoulder bag as well. She was, Lynley saw, taking seriously her part in this little investigation of theirs. He smiled at her, grateful for the first time in months to be in the presence of longtime friends.

"Ian Cresswell didn't take the scull out on a regular basis," Lynley told her. "But Valerie Fairclough takes her boat out several times a week. While the scull was indeed tied at the spot where the stones were loose on the dock, it wasn't a set position for it. People on the estate seem to tie up the watercraft wherever there's an opening."

"But someone seeing the scull in place could have loosened the stones while he was out on the lake that night, yes?" Deborah said.

"That would make it someone on the estate at that moment," her husband said. "Was Nicholas Fairclough there that night?"

"If he was, no one saw him." Lynley turned to Deborah. "What sort of reading did you get off Fairclough?"

"He seems perfectly lovely. And his wife's quite beautiful, Tommy. I can't exactly gauge the effect she has on men, but I'd guess she could make a Trappist monk give up his vows without much effort on her part."

"Something between her and Cresswell, then?" St. James offered. "With Nicholas taking issue over it?"

"Hardly, as the man's homosexual," said Lynley.

"Or bisexual, Tommy."

"And there's something else," Deborah went on. "Two things, actually. They might not be important at all, but if you want me to look for things intriguing . . ."

"I do," Lynley said.

"Then there's this: Alatea Fairclough has a copy of *Conception* magazine. It's got pages torn out of the back, and we might want to put our hands on a copy and have a look at what they are. Nicholas told me they've been trying to conceive."

St. James stirred. His expression said that the magazine meant nothing and would have meant nothing to anyone else save Deborah, whose own concerns about conceiving would probably cloud her judgement.

Lynley saw that Deborah read her husband as well as he himself had done because she said, "This isn't *about* me, Simon. Tommy's looking for anything unusual and what I was thinking . . . What if his drug use has made Nicholas sterile but Alatea doesn't want him to know that? A doctor may have told her but not him. Or she might have convinced a doctor to lie to him, for his ego, to keep him on the straight and narrow. So what if, knowing he can't give her children, she asked Ian to lend a hand in the matter, if you know what I mean?"

"Keeping it in the family?" Lynley asked. "Anything's possible."

"And there's something else," Deborah said. "A reporter from *The Source*—"

"Jesus God."

"—has been there four times, ostensibly doing a story on Nicholas. Four times but nothing's come of it, Tommy. One of the blokes at the Middlebarrow Pele Project told me."

"If it's *The Source*, there's dirt on someone's shoe soles," St. James pointed out.

Lynley thought about whose shoe soles those might be. He said, "Cresswell's lover has evidently been on the estate—on the grounds of Ireleth Hall—for some time now, working on a project for Valerie. He's called Kaveh Mehran."

"PC Schlicht mentioned him," St. James said. "Has he got motive?"

"There's the will and insurance to be looked into."

"Anyone else?"

"With motive?" Lynley told them about his meeting with Mignon Fairclough: her insinuations about her parents' marriage followed by her denial of those insinuations. He also told them about the holes in the background of Nicholas Fairclough that she'd been only too happy to fill in. He ended with, "She's rather a piece of work and I have the impression she's got a hold over her parents for some reason. So Fairclough himself might bear looking into."

"Blackmail? With Cresswell somehow in the know?"

"Emotional or otherwise, I daresay. She lives on the property but not in the house. I suspect Bernard Fairclough built her digs for her and I wouldn't be surprised if one reason was to get her out of his hair. There's another sister as well. I've yet to meet her."

He went on to tell them that Bernard Fairclough had put a videotape into his hands. He'd suggested Lynley watch it because if there was indeed someone behind Ian's death, then he needed to "see something rather telling."

This turned out to be a video of the funeral, made for the purpose of sending to Ian's father in Kenya, too frail to make the trip to say farewell to his son. Fairclough had watched it at Lynley's side, and as things turned out, it was what he *didn't* see that he wanted to point out. Niamh Cresswell, Ian's wife of seventeen years and the mother of his two children, had not attended. Fairclough pointed out that, at least to be of support to those grieving children, she might have turned up.

"He gave me a few details on the end of Ian Cresswell's marriage." Lynley told them what he knew, to which St. James and Deborah said simultaneously, "Motive, Tommy."

"Hell hath no fury. Yes. But it's not likely that Niamh Cresswell could prowl round the grounds of Ireleth Hall without being seen and so far no one's mentioned her being there."

"Still and all," St. James said, "she's got to be looked into. Revenge is a powerful motive."

"So is greed," Deborah said. "But then, so are all the deadly sins, aren't they? Why else be deadly?"

Lynley nodded. "So we'll have to see if she benefits in any way other than vengeance," he said.

"We're back to the will. Or an insurance policy," St. James said. "That information's not going to be easy to suss out while keeping your head down about why you're really here in Cumbria, Tommy."

"Not for me going at it directly. You're right about that," Lynley said. "But there's someone else who can do it."

LAKE WINDERMERE
CUMBRIA

By the time they'd concluded their meeting, it was too late for Lynley to place the call he needed to make. So instead he phoned Isabelle. Truth was, he was missing her. Truth was, he was also glad to be away from her. This wasn't due to any disinclination on his part for her company. This was, instead, due to his need to know how he felt about her when they were apart. Seeing her every day at work, seeing her several nights each week, made it nearly impossible for him to sort through his feelings for the woman aside from those that were clearly sexual. At least now he had a feeling to name: longing. Thus he knew he missed her body. What remained to be seen was whether he missed the rest of the package comprising Isabelle Ardery.

He waited till he'd got back to Ireleth Hall to place the call from his mobile. He stood just to the side of the Healey Elliott, and he punched in the number and waited for it to go through. He thought about how he was all at once wishing that she were with him. There had been something in the easy conversation between himself and his friends and something more in the way Simon and Deborah communicated with each other that made him want that for himself once again: that familiarity and assurance. He understood that, more specifically, what he really wanted was a return to the way he and his wife had talked to each other in the morning, over dinner at night, in bed together, even as one or the other of them bathed. For the first time as well, however, he realised that Helen herself didn't need to be that woman but that someone else—somewhere else—could. This felt, in part, like a betrayal of a most beloved wife, cut down through no fault of her own by a senseless act of violence. Yet he also understood that this feeling was part of getting on with life, and he knew Helen would have wanted that for him as much as she'd wanted their life together.

The ringing stopped on the other end, in London. He heard, "Damn," faintly, then the sound of Isabelle's mobile hitting something, and then there was nothing at all.

He said, "Isabelle? Are you there?" and he waited. Nothing. Again he said her name. When there was no response, he ended the call, the connection apparently gone.

He punched in her number again. The ringing began. It continued. Perhaps she was in the car, he thought, unavailable. Or in the shower. Or engaged in something that made it impossible—

"'Lo? Tommy? Joo jus' call?" And then a sound he didn't want to hear: something knocking against the side of her mobile, a glass, a bottle, what did it matter. "I's thinking of you an' here you are. How's tha' for mental tepe . . . tele . . . te*lep*athy?"

"Isabelle . . ." Lynley found he couldn't say more. He ended the call, put the mobile in his pocket, and returned to his room in Ireleth Hall.

5 NOVEMBER

Barbara Havers had spent the first part of her day off
visiting her mother in the private care home where
she was domiciled in Greenford. The call was long
overdue. She hadn't been there in seven weeks, and she'd
been feeling the weight of guilt grow heavier with every day
once she'd reached the three-week point. She'd admitted
the worst to herself: that she welcomed having work piled
upon her so she wouldn't have to go and witness the further
disintegration of her mother's mind. But there had come a
point when continuing to live with herself meant she had to
make the journey to that pebbledash house with its neat
front garden and spotless curtains hanging behind windows
that fairly gleamed in sun or rain, so she took the Central
Line from Tottenham Court Road, not because it was faster
but because it wasn't.

She wasn't liar enough to tell herself she was travelling
in this manner to give herself time to think. The last thing
she really wanted to do was to think about anything, and
her mother was only one of the subjects she didn't want
pressing in on her mind. Thomas Lynley was another: where
he was, what he was doing, and why she hadn't been
informed about either. Isabelle Ardery was yet another:
whether she was actually going to be named to the position

of detective superintendent permanently and what that would mean to Barbara's own future with the Met, not to mention to her working relationship with Thomas Lynley. Angelina Upman was still another: whether she—Barbara—could have a friendship with the lover of her neighbour and friend Taymullah Azhar, whose daughter had become a needed bit of sparkle in Barbara's life. No. The reason she took the train was avoidance, pure and simple. Additionally, the distractions afforded by the Tube were vast and continually shifting, and what Barbara wanted was distractions because they gave her conversation openers that she could use with her mother when she finally saw her.

Not that she and her mother had conversations any longer. At least not the sort of conversations one might deem normal between a mother and daughter. And this day had ultimately been no different to others in which Barbara spoke, hesitated, watched, and felt desperate to end the visit as soon as possible.

Her mother had fallen in love with Laurence Olivier, the younger version. She was completely swept away by Heathcliff and Max de Winter. She wasn't sure who he was exactly—the man she kept watching on the television screen—tormenting Merle Oberon when he wasn't leaving poor Joan Fontaine completely tongue-tied. She only knew that they were meant to be together, she and this handsome man. That he was, in reality, long dead and gone was no matter to her.

She didn't recognise the older version of the actor. Olivier doing the job on poor Dustin Hoffman's teeth—not to mention Olivier rolling round the floor with Gregory Peck—made no impact on her at all. Indeed, whenever an Olivier film other than *Wuthering Heights* or *Rebecca* was brought to her attention, she became quite ungovernable. Even Olivier as Mr. Darcy could not sway her from either of the other two films. So they looped endlessly through a television in her mother's bedroom, a feature that Mrs. Florence Magentry had installed in order to save the sanity of her other residents as well as her own. There were only so many times one could watch devious Larry destroy poor David Niven's tenuous claim on happiness.

Barbara had spent two hours with her mother. They were

heartsore hours, and she felt the pain of them all the way home from Greenford. So when she'd run into Angelina Upman and her daughter, Hadiyyah, on the pavement just outside the big house in Eton Villas where they all lived, she'd accepted their invitation to "look at what Mummy bought, Barbara" as a means of clearing her mind of the images of her mother cradling one breast tenderly as she watched the flickering screen display Max de Winter in torment over the death of his evil first wife.

She was with Hadiyyah and her mother now, having dutifully admired two ultramodern lithographs that Angelina had managed to "practically pinch, Barbara, they were such a bargain, *weren't* they, Mummy?" from a vendor in the Stables Market. Barbara admired them. Not to her taste, but she could indeed see how they were going to work in the sitting room of Azhar's flat.

Barbara gave thought to the fact that Angelina had apparently taken her daughter to one of the places absolutely *verboten* by the little girl's father. She wondered if Hadiyyah had mentioned this to her mother or if, perhaps, Angelina and Azhar had agreed in advance that it was time Hadiyyah began to experience more of the world. She had her answer when Hadiyyah clapped her hands over her mouth and said, "I for*got*, Mummy!" Angelina replied, "No matter, darling. Barbara will keep our secret. I hope."

"You will, Barbara, won't you?" Hadiyyah asked. "Dad'll be so cross if he knows where we went."

"Don't nag, Hadiyyah," Angelina said. And to Barbara, "Would you like a cup of tea? I'm parched and you look a bit rough round the edges. Difficult day?"

"Just a trip to Greenford." Barbara said nothing more but Hadiyyah added, "That's where Barbara's mum lives, Mummy. She's not well, is she, Barbara?"

Barbara certainly didn't want to entertain the topic of her mother, so she sought a different subject. Angelina being 100 percent female in ways Barbara could only dream of, Barbara pulled a topic out of the air that seemed the sort of subject a 100 percent female might wish to pursue.

Hair. More to the point, the fact that, upon Isabelle Ardery's strongly worded recommendation, she was going to have to do something with hers. Angelina had mentioned, Barbara recalled, that she knew of a beauty parlour . . . ?

"Salon!" Hadiyyah crowed. "Barbara, it's not a parlour. It's a salon!"

"Hadiyyah," her mother said sternly. "That's very rude. And *parlour* is fine, by the way. *Salon* is more modern, but it hardly matters. Don't be so silly." To Barbara she said, "Yes, of course, I do know, Barbara. It's where I get my own hair done."

"D'you think they could . . . ?" Barbara wasn't even sure what she was meant to ask for. A haircut? A styling? A colour job? What? She'd been cutting her own hair for years and while it generally looked exactly as one would expect a self-cut hairstyle to look—which was not like a style at all but rather like an application of scissors to head during a thunderstorm—it had long served the simple purpose of keeping it out of her face. That, however, was no longer going to suit, at least as far as Barbara's superior officer at the Met was concerned.

"They could do whatever you'd like them to do. They're very good. I can give you their number. And my stylist's name. He's called Dusty and he's a bit of a flamboyant arse I'm afraid—if you'll excuse me, Hadiyyah, don't tell your father I said *arse* in front of you—but if you can get past the fact that he's completely full of his own excruciating wonderfulness, he's actually quite good with hair. In fact, why don't I make you an appointment and come with you as well? Unless, of course, you think that too intrusive."

Barbara wasn't sure what she thought about having Azhar's lover along for the ride of her self-improvement. Hadiyyah had done this service before Angelina's return to her daughter's life, but making the switch to her mother and what was *implied* by making the switch to her mother . . . a movement towards friendship . . . She wasn't sure.

Angelina seemed to sense this hesitation because she said, "Well, let me fetch you that number and in the meantime, think about it. I'm completely happy to go with you."

"Where is it, exactly, this par . . . salon?"

"Knightsbridge."

"Knightsbridge?" God, now *that* would cost a fortune.

"It's not the moon, Barbara," Hadiyyah said.

Her mother lifted a warning finger. "Hadiyyah Khalidah—"

"S'okay," Barbara said. "She knows me too well. If you give me the number, I'll phone them right now. You want to come as well, kiddo?" she asked Hadiyyah.

"Oh yes yes yes!" Hadiyyah cried. "Mummy, I c'n go with Barbara, can't I?"

"You as well," Barbara said to Angelina. "I think I'll need all the help I can get for this enterprise."

Angelina smiled. She had, Barbara noted, a very pretty smile. Azhar had never told her how he'd met Angelina, but she reckoned it was the woman's smile that he'd first noticed about her. Since he was male, he'd probably gone right on to her body next, which was lithe and feminine and clothed in appealing and well-groomed ways Barbara could never have hoped to duplicate.

She took out her mobile phone in anticipation of making the call, but it rang before she was able to do so. She looked at the number and saw it was Lynley. She didn't like the delight that swept through her when she recognised his number.

"Time for a rain check on the hair," she said to Angelina. "I have to take this call."

CHALK FARM
LONDON

"What are you doing?" Lynley asked her. "Where are you? Can you talk?"

"My vocal cords haven't been cut, if that's what you mean," Barbara said. "If, on the other hand, you mean is it safe . . . God, that's what he kept saying to Dustin Hoffman, isn't it? I might be losing my bloody mind if I'm starting to quote—"

"Barbara, what are you talking about?"

"Laurence Olivier. *Marathon Man.* Don't ask. I'm at home, more or less. I mean I'm on the terrace outside

Azhar's flat, having been saved at the final moment from making an appointment to have my hair styled to please Acting Detective Superintendent Ardery. I was thinking Big Hair, circa 1980. Or one of those complicated World War II jelly-roll affairs, if you know what I mean. Masses of hair on either side of the forehead wound round something and looking like salami. I've always wondered what it was they used to get that style. Toilet rolls, p'rhaps?"

"Should I anticipate all future conversations with you to take this bent?" Lynley enquired. "Frankly, I've always thought your appeal lay in your complete indifference to personal grooming."

"Those days are past, sir. What c'n I do for you? I reckon this isn't a personal call, made to see if I'm keeping my legs shaved."

"I need you to do some digging for me, but it's got to be completely out of everyone's sight and hearing. It might involve legwork as well. Are you willing? More, can you manage that?"

"This's to do with whatever you're up to, I reckon. Everyone's talking, you know."

"About?"

"Where you are, why you are, who sent you, and all the trimmings. Common thought is you're investigating a monumental cock-up somewhere. Police corruption, with you on tiptoe fading into the woodwork to catch someone taking a payoff or someone else putting electrodes to a suspect's cobblers. You know what I mean."

"And you?"

"What do I think? Hillier's got you up to your eyeballs in something he himself doesn't want to touch with a ten-foot plastic one. You put a step wrong, you take the fall, he still smells like dewdrops on roses. Am I close?"

"On the Hillier part. But it's just a favour."

"And that's all you can say."

"For the moment. Are you willing?"

"What? To lend a hand?"

"No one can know. You have to fly beneath the radar. Everyone's but particularly—"

"The superintendent's."

"It could get you into trouble with her. Not in the long run, but in the short term."

"Why else do I breathe in our native land?" Barbara said. "Tell me what you need."

CHALK FARM
LONDON

As soon as Lynley said *Fairclough,* Barbara knew. This wasn't due to the fact that she had her fingers on the pulse of the life of everyone possessing a title in the UK. Far be that from the fact. Rather it was due to her being a devout albeit closet reader of *The Source.* She was addicted and had been so for years, an absolute victim to four-inch headlines and deliciously compromising photographs. Whenever she passed an advertising placard set up on the pavement and screaming a front-page story on sale inside this tobacconist or that corner shop, her feet went into the place of their own accord, she handed over her money, and she had a good wallow, generally over an afternoon cuppa and a toasted tea cake. Thus, *Fairclough* was a familiar name to her, not only as it referenced the Baron of Ireleth and his business—which had garnered many journalistic guffaws over the years—but also as it attached itself to his loose-living scion, Nicholas.

She also knew at once where Lynley was: in Cumbria, where the Faircloughs and Fairclough Industries were based. What she didn't know was how Hillier knew the Faircloughs and what he'd asked Lynley to do regarding the family. In other words, she wasn't sure if it was a case of we're-for-'em or we're-against-'em, but she reckoned that, if there was a title involved, Hillier was cosying up to the for-'em side. Hillier had a thing about titles, especially those that were above his own rank, which was all of them.

So this probably had to do with Lord Fairclough and not his wastrel son, long the subject of tabloid exposés along with other rich young things throwing their lives away. But the list of Lynley's interests suggested that he was casting a very wide net indeed since they involved a will, an insurance policy, *The Source*, Bernard Fairclough, and the most recent edition of *Conception* magazine. They also involved someone called Ian Cresswell, identified as Fairclough's nephew. And for good measure—if she had time to pursue the matter—someone called Alatea Vasquez y del Torres, hailing from somewhere in Argentina called Santa Maria di whatever, might bear looking into. But only if she had the time, Lynley stressed, because at the moment the real digging needed to be about Fairclough. Fairclough the father, not the son, he emphasised.

LAKE WINDERMERE
CUMBRIA

Freddie's next Internet date had spent the night and while Manette always tried to think of herself as a with-it sort of woman, this did seem a bit much to her. Her ex-husband was no schoolboy, to be sure, and he certainly wasn't asking for her opinion on the matter. But for the love of God, it had been their *first* date and where was the world going to—or more to the point, where was Freddie going to?—if men and women tried each other out in bed as a modern-day form of singing "Getting to Know You"? But that's exactly what had happened, according to Freddie, and it had been her idea. The woman's! According to Freddie, she'd said, "Really, there'd be no point in carrying on further if we're not sexually compatible, Freddie, don't you agree?"

Well, Freddie was a man, after all. Presented with the opportunity, what was he going to do, ask for six months of chastity to give them time to suss each other out on matters from politics to prestidigitation? Plus, it seemed reasonable enough to him. Times were changing, after all. So two glasses of wine at the local and home they came to take the plunge. Evidently, they'd found all their parts in working order and the experience pleasurable, so they'd done it two more times—again, this was according to Freddie—and she'd spent the rest of the night. There she'd been, having coffee with him in the kitchen when Manette came downstairs in the morning. She'd been wearing Freddie's shirt and nothing else, which left her showing a lot of leg and not a small part of where the leg came from. And like a cat with canary feathers hanging from her mouth, she said to Manette, "Hello. You must be Freddie's ex. I'm Holly."

Holly? Holly! What sort of name was that? Her former husband was going for a shrub? Manette looked at Freddie—who at least had the grace to turn puce—and then poured herself a hasty cup of coffee, after which she retreated to her bathroom. There, Freddie came to apologise for the uneasiness of the situation—not, Manette noted, for having had the woman stay the night—and he said in best Freddie fashion that in the future he'd spend the night at their places instead of the reverse. "It all just happened between us rather quickly," he told her. "I'd not intended it."

But Manette homed in on *their places*, and this was how she learned that times had changed and that instantaneous copulation had become the new form of shaking hands. She'd sputtered, "You mean, you intend to try out every one of them?"

"Well, it does seem to be the way things are done these days."

She'd tried to tell him that this was lunacy. She'd lectured him about STDs, unplanned pregnancies, entrapment, and everything else she could think of. What she didn't say was that they had a very good situation, she and Freddie, living as roommates, because she didn't want to hear him say that it was time they both moved on. At the end of it all, though, he'd kissed her forehead, told her not to worry about him, revealed he had another date that night, declared he might therefore not be home afterwards, and said he'd see her at work. He'd take his own car today, he told her, because this date lived in Barrow-in-Furness, and they were meeting at Scorpio nightclub so if she wanted to hook up seriously—Freddie actually *said* "hook up seriously"—they'd go to her place as it was apparently too far to drive to Great Urswick if their knickers were on fire.

Manette wailed, "But, Freddie . . . !" yet realised there

was nothing else she could say. She could hardly accuse him of being unfaithful or destroying what she and he had or acting hastily. They weren't married, they "had" next to nothing, and they'd been divorced long enough that Freddie's decision to get back into the world of dating—as bizarre as that world now apparently was—had not been made on the fly. He wasn't that sort of man, anyway. And one only had to look at him to understand why women would be happy to try him out as a mate: He was fresh and sweet and not half-bad-looking.

No, she had no rights here, and Manette knew it. But she mourned something lost all the same.

Nonetheless, there were things to be seen to that went beyond her situation with Freddie, and she found that she was grateful for them, although she wouldn't have thought so on the previous day after her confrontation with Niamh Cresswell. Something had to be done about Niamh, and while Manette herself was powerless when it came to the woman, she was not powerless when it came to Tim and Gracie. If she had to move a mountain to help those children, then that was what she intended to do.

She drove to Ireleth Hall. She thought there was a good chance that Kaveh Mehran would be there since he'd been long engaged in designing a children's garden for the estate, as well as overseeing the implementation of this design. The garden was intended for Nicholas's future children—and wasn't *that* like counting chickens, Manette thought—and considering the size of the garden that had been staked out, it looked as if Valerie was expecting dozens of them.

She was in luck, Manette saw upon her arrival. She traipsed round to the location of the future children's garden, which was north of the immense and fantastical topiary garden, and she saw not only Kaveh Mehran but her father as well. There was another man with them whom Manette did not recognise but reckoned was "the earl" that her sister had phoned her about.

"Widower," Mignon had told her. Manette could hear the tapping of her keyboard in the background, so she knew her sister was doing her usual multitasking: e-mailing one of her online lovers while simultaneously dismissing what she'd reckoned was a potential offline one. "It's rather obviously why Dad's dragged him up here from London. Hope springs eternal, et cetera. And now I've had the surgery and lost all the weight, he reckons I'm ready for a suitor. A regular Charlotte Lucas, just waiting for Mr. Collins to show up. God, how embarrassing. Well, dream on, Pater. I'm quite happy where I am, thank you very much."

Manette wouldn't have put it past her father. He'd been trying to offload Mignon for years, but she had him very much where she wanted him and she had no intention of making any changes. Why Bernard wouldn't show her the door or give her the boot or any other figurative cutting of ties with Mignon was beyond Manette, although once he'd built the folly for her sister some six years earlier, Manette had concluded her twin was holding back something damaging that would ruin their father if she let it be known. What that was Manette couldn't imagine, but it had to be something big.

Kaveh Mehran appeared to be showing the other two men the progress so far made on the children's garden. He was pointing hither and yon at stacks of timber beneath tarps and piles of quarried stone and stakes driven into the ground with string strung between them. Manette called out a hello and strode in their direction.

Mignon was out of her mind, Manette decided as the men turned towards her, if she thought "the widower" had been brought up from London as a potential suitor for her, a sort of "gentleman caller" in the best tradition of Tennessee Williams's psychodramas. He was tall, blond, exceedingly attractive, and dressed—even in the Lakes, for God's sake—with that kind of understated rumpled elegance that fairly screamed old family money. If he was a widower out looking for Wife Number Two or Wife Number Two Hundred and Twenty-two, he wasn't going to choose her sister to step into that position. The human animal's capacity for self-delusion was absolutely amazing, Manette thought.

Bernard smiled a hello at Manette and made the introductions. Tommy Lynley was the name of the earl and wherever he was earl of was not mentioned. He had a firm handshake, an interesting old scar on his upper lip, a nice smile, and very brown eyes at odds with his light hair. He was good at small talk, she found, and equally good at putting people at ease. Beautiful day in a beautiful place, he told her. He himself was from Cornwall originally, south of Penzance, an area which was—obviously—lovely as well, and he'd spent very little time in Cumbria. But from what he was seeing round Ireleth Hall, he knew he should make regular visits here.

Very nicely said, Manette thought. Very polite. Had he said it to Mignon she would doubtless have considered it rife with double meanings. Manette said, "Come in winter and it's likely you'll think otherwise," and then to Kaveh Mehran, "I'd like a word if you've time."

Her father had succeeded wildly in industry because he was a man fully capable of reading nuances. He said, "What's going on, Manette?" and when she gave a glance at Lynley, Bernard continued with, "Tommy's a close friend. He knows we've had a recent tragedy in the family. Has something more . . . ?"

"Niamh," Manette said.

"What about her?"

Manette glanced at Lynley and then said to her father, "I'm not sure you want . . ."

Lynley started to excuse himself but Bernard said, "No. It's fine. Stay." And to Manette, "As I said, he's a friend. It can't be anything—"

Fine, Manette thought. Whatever you like. And she said abruptly, "Niamh's not yet taken the children back. They're still with Kaveh. We need to do something about it."

Bernard glanced at Kaveh, his brow furrowed, and he murmured to Lynley, "My late nephew's wife."

"It's absolutely not right," Manette said. "She knows it, and she doesn't much care. I spoke to her yesterday. All dressed to the *ninety*-nines, she was, with a bucket of sex toys sitting out for all the world to see. She's got some bloke coming round to do the business with her, and Tim and Gracie are in the way."

Bernard cast another look at Kaveh. The young man said, "'Absolutely not right,' Manette?" He spoke politely enough, but his tone told Manette he'd misunderstood her meaning.

She said, "Oh for God's sake, Kaveh. You know I'm not talking about what you are. You can be as bent as a broken twig for all I care, but when it comes to children—"

"I'm not interested in children."

"Well, that's just the point, isn't it?" Manette snapped, choosing to misinterpret his remark. "It helps to have an interest in children if one is actually caring for them. Dad, Tim and Gracie belong with family and *whatever* he is, Kaveh's not family."

"Manette . . ." Her father's voice was minatory. Evidently, there were things in the "recent tragedy in the family" that he did indeed prefer Tommy Lynley not to know, despite what he'd said a moment earlier. Well, that was unfortunate, because he'd welcomed her to speak openly in front of the London man, so that was what she intended to do.

She said, "Ian was happy to have the children with him in Bryanbarrow. I understood that and I was on board with it. Anything to keep them away from Niamh, who's about as motherly as a great white shark, as you know very well. But Ian can't have intended Kaveh to keep them if something happened to him. You know that, Kaveh." And back to her father, "So you have to talk to Niamh. You have to order her. You have to do something. Tim's in a very bad way—he's worse than what he was like to get him into Margaret Fox School in the first place—and God knows Gracie needs a mother more than ever just now and she's going to be completely desperate for one in a year or two. If Niamh isn't willing to do the job, then someone else is going to have to step onto the pitch."

"I see the situation," Bernard said. "We'll carry on further another time."

"We can't, Dad. I'm sorry." And to Lynley, "Dirty laundry and more to come. If you haven't the stomach for it . . ."

To Bernard, Lynley said, "Perhaps there's a way I can be of help?" and something passed between them, some sort of message or assurance or *something* that assuaged what-

ever Manette's father had been concerned about in having
Lynley present at an escalating conversation.

Manette said, "Tim attacked me. No, no, I didn't get
hurt. I'm sore but that's not the point. He must be dealt
with—the whole bloody situation must be dealt with—and
since Kaveh's not going to be staying on that farm forever,
it's in everyone's best interests to deal with it now before
the farm is sold. Once Kaveh has to move house, what happens to the children? Are they going with him? And where?
This can't go on. They can't keep being uprooted."

"He left it to me," Kaveh said. "I'm not going anywhere."

Manette swung back to him. *"What?"*

"The farm, Manette. Ian left it to me."

"To *you*? Why?"

Kaveh said with a dignity Manette had to admire, "Because
he loved me. Because we were partners and that's what partners usually do: make arrangements to take care of each other
in the event of death."

Silence ensued. Into it, the sound of jackdaws burst into
the air. From somewhere the smell of burning leaves came
at them in a rush as if there were flames nearby, which there
were not.

"Men usually take care of their children as well,"
Manette said. "That farm should be Tim's, not yours. It
should be Gracie's. It should be theirs to sell, to provide for
their future."

Kaveh looked away. He worked his jaw as if this would
allow him to master an emotion. "I think you'll find there
was an insurance policy for that."

"How convenient. Whose idea was all this: the farm left
to you and insurance for them? How *much* insurance, by
the way? And exactly who does the money go to? Because
if it goes to Niamh in trust for the children—"

"Manette," her father cut in. "That's not on just now."
And to Kaveh, "Will you be keeping the farm or selling it,
Kaveh?"

"Keeping it. As for Tim and Gracie, they're welcome to
stay with me till Niamh's ready to have them back. And if
she's never ready, Ian would have wanted—"

"No, no, no!" Manette didn't particularly care to hear the rest. The point was that the children belonged with family, and Kaveh—partner to Ian or not—was not family. She said hotly, "Dad, you *must* . . . Ian *can't* have wanted . . . Does Niamh know all this?"

"What part?" Kaveh asked. "And do you think she actually cares one way or the other?"

"Does she know you've inherited? And *when* did Ian do this?"

Kaveh hesitated, as if evaluating the potential responses that he could make. Manette had to say his name twice to get him to respond at all. "I don't know," he told her.

A look passed between Bernard and Tommy Lynley. Manette saw this and knew that they were thinking what she herself was thinking. Kaveh was lying about something. The only question was which of her enquiries he was answering with "I don't know."

"You don't know what, exactly?" she asked him.

"I don't know a thing about Niamh, one way or the other. She has the insurance money, and there's quite a pile. Ian meant it to help her care for Tim and Gracie, of course, but that's because he believed that if anything happened to him, Niamh would come to her senses about them."

"Well, she hasn't. And it's not looking likely she's going to."

"If they must, then, they'll stay with me. They're established at the farm, and they're happy enough."

Ludicrous thought, that Tim Cresswell was happy. He hadn't been happy in ages. Manette said, "And what exactly is supposed to happen when you meet someone new in a month or two, Kaveh? When you move him to the farm and take up life with him? What then? What are the children supposed to do? What are they supposed to *think*?"

"Manette," Bernard murmured cautiously.

Kaveh had gone quite pale with her words, but he said nothing, although his jaw worked furiously and at his side, his right hand clenched into a fist.

Manette said, "Niamh will fight you in court for that farm. She'll contest the will. For the children."

"Manette, enough," her father said on a sigh. "There's been plenty of grief to go round and everyone needs to recover, yourself included."

"*Why* are you playing the peacemaker in this?" Manette demanded of her father. "He's nothing to us," she said with a jerk of her head at Kaveh. "He's nothing to the children. He's just someone Ian ruined his life for and—"

"I said enough!" Bernard snapped. And to Kaveh, "Excuse her, Kaveh. She doesn't mean—"

"Oh, she knows very well what she means," Kaveh said. "Most people do."

Manette sought a way out of the mire she'd created for herself by saying lamely, "All right. Look. If nothing else, you're too young to be the father of a fourteen-year-old boy, Kaveh. He needs someone older, someone experienced, someone—"

"Not homosexual," Kaveh finished for her.

"I *didn't* say that. And I don't mean that. I was going to say someone within his own family."

"You've made that point more than once."

"I'm sorry, Kaveh. It's not about you. It's about Tim and Gracie. They can't be asked to tolerate more devastation in their lives. It's destroying Tim. It's going to do the same to Gracie. I have to stop their world from falling apart even further. I hope you can understand that."

"Leave things as they are, Manette," her father said. "There are larger concerns at the moment."

"Like *what*?"

He said nothing. But there were those glances between her father and his London friend and she wondered for the first time what was going on here. Clearly, this bloke wasn't intended to press a case for love with her wily sister in the fashion of the eighteenth century: out for her money, perhaps, in order to support a crumbling estate in Cornwall. And the fact that her father had actually wanted him to hear every word of her conversation with Kaveh suggested that the quiet waters of Tommy Lynley's outward appearance were probably deep enough for Nessie to swim in. Well, that couldn't matter. Nothing could matter. She intended to do something about her cousin's children and if her father wouldn't join forces with her, she knew someone else who was likely to do so.

She threw up her hands. "All right," she said. And to Lynley, "Sorry you had to listen to all this."

He nodded politely. But there was an expression on his face that told he hadn't minded hearing the information at all.

BRYANBARROW EN ROUTE TO WINDERMERE
CUMBRIA

The previous day had been a washout. Two hours trying to thumb it to Windermere and Tim had finally given up. But he was determined today would be different.

The rain started not long after he began the most difficult part of his journey: the endless hike from Bryanbarrow village down to the main road through the Lyth Valley. He didn't expect to get a lift during this part of the route, as the cars were few and far between and if a farm vehicle happened to come by—a tractor, for example—it moved so slowly and went so little distance that he could actually make better time on foot.

He hadn't counted on the rain, though. This was stupid of him, considering it was the sodden month of sodding November and as far as he knew, it rained more in the Lakes than anywhere else in the bloody country. But because he'd left Bryan Beck farm in a state in which clear thinking wasn't exactly going on in his head, he had put a hoodie on over a flannel shirt, which he wore over a tee shirt and none of this was waterproof. He had trainers on his feet, too, and while these weren't soaked through, they were mud up to the ankles because the verges of the lane were swampy the way they always were at this time of year. As for his jeans, they were growing heavier and heavier as the rain got to them. Since they were several sizes too large anyway, the struggle to keep them up round his hips was infuriating.

He was on the main road through the valley when he scored his first lift, a spot of luck in a day that otherwise was sucking ostrich eggs. This was supplied by a farmer. He pulled over in a Land Rover that was up to its wings in crusted mud and he said, "Get in, son. You look like something dragged out of the pond. Where to?"

Tim said Newby Bridge—the opposite direction from Windermere—because he had a feeling about the bloke and the way the bloke looked at him, close and curious. He also didn't want to leave a trail once everything was over. If things went the way he wanted them to go, if his name and face showed up in the paper and this bloke recognised him, then Tim wanted the phone call he made to the cops to be one that said, "Oh, yeah, I 'member that kid. Said he was going to Newby Bridge."

The farmer said, "Newby Bridge, is it?" and pulled back onto the road. He said he could take him as far as Winster, and after that he did the usual thing, which was to ask why Tim wasn't at school. He said, "School day, innit? You doing a bunk?"

Tim was used to the maddening habit adults had of asking questions that were none of their business. It always made him want to dig his thumbs into their eyeballs. It wasn't as if they'd ask a question like that of another adult—like "Why aren't you at work today like the rest of the world?"—but they seemed to think it was open season on firing just about any question at a kid. He'd been prepared for this, though, so he said, "Check the time. Half day."

The farmer said, "Not for my three, it's not. Where d'you go to school?"

Jesus, Tim thought. Where he went to school was the farmer's business like it was his business asking Tim when his last shit had occurred. He said, "Not round here. Margaret Fox. Near Ulverston," reasonably sure that the man wouldn't have heard of the place and its reason for being. He added, "Independent school. It's boarding but I don't board."

"What's happened to your hands, then?" the farmer asked. "You don't want them to stay like that."

Tim gritted his teeth. He said, "Cut myself. Got to be more careful."

"Cut? Those don't look like you cut—"

"Look, pull over," Tim said. "You c'n let me out here."

"This's nowheres near Winster, boy." True enough. They'd gone barely a mile.

"Just let me out, okay?" Tim's voice was controlled. He didn't want it to go fierce with all that fierceness revealed, but he knew that if he didn't get out of the Land Rover *now*, he would do something and it wouldn't be pleasant.

The farmer shrugged. He pulled over. He looked long and hard at Tim as he braked, and Tim knew that the man was memorising his face. No doubt he'd be listening to the radio news next time it came on, waiting to hear about a local burglary or a spate of malicious mischief that he could pin on Tim. Well, that was the risk he'd have to take. Better that than riding farther with the bloke.

"You take care, son," the farmer said just before Tim slammed the door, hard.

"Whatever," Tim replied as the Land Rover moved on. He tore at the back of his hand with his teeth.

His next ride was better. A German couple took him as far as the road to Crook, where they turned off in search of some posh country house hotel. They spoke good English, but all they wanted to talk about to him was "ach, such rain you have in Cumbria," and when they spoke to each other— which was most of the time anyway—they spoke in German, rapid sentences about someone called Heidi.

Tim managed to get a final lift from a lorry driver just north of the Crook Road. This bloke was heading all the way to Keswick, so Windermere would be no problem, he said.

What *was* a problem was the driver's intention of using their limited time together to lecture Tim on the dangers of hitchhiking and to quiz him about his parents and did they know he was out on the roads taking lifts from strangers? You don't even know who I am, he announced. I could be Sutcliffe. I could be Brady. I could be some child molester. You understand that?

Tim bore all this without kicking the bloke in the face, which was what he badly wanted to do. He nodded, said, "Yeah," said, "Whatever," and when they finally reached

Windermere, said, "Drop me off over there by the library."
This the lorry driver did, although not without saying it
was lucky for Tim that he had no interest in twelve-year-old
boys. Because this was truly and absolutely too much, Tim
said that he was fourteen, not twelve. The lorry driver
hawked a laugh and said, "You aren't ever. And what're you
hiding under them baggy clothes? I reckon truth is you're
a girl, you are," in response to which Tim slammed the door.

He'd borne just about all that he could. If he'd done
exactly what he preferred to do at that precise moment, he
would have gone into the library and ripped up a shelf of
books. But that, he knew, would not get him an inch closer
to where he wanted to be. So he bit down hard, harder, and
then hardest of all on his knuckles till he tasted the blood
and that helped a bit and made him able to set off towards
the business centre.

Even at this time of year, there were tourists in Windermere. It was nothing like the summer, when one couldn't
move in the town without bashing straight into some fell-
walking enthusiast with a bulging rucksack on his back and
a hiking pole in his hand. Then no one local with any sense
came into town since endless tailbacks transformed every
street into nothing more than a car park. Now, though, moving about was easier, and the tourists on the pavements were
of the who-gives-a-shit sort, kitted out in green plastic bed-
sheets with their rucksacks underneath making them all
look like hunchbacks. Tim passed them by and followed the
route into the business centre, where there was not a single
tourist at all, tourists having no reason to go there.

Tim, however, had a very good reason and it was called
Shots! This was a photographic developing service, he'd
learned upon his only visit to the place, and its general purpose was to create super-enlargements for professional
photographers who came to the Lakes to memorialise its
grand vistas at all times of year.

In the window, samples of what Shots! was capable of
producing stood on large easels against a black background
curtain. Inside the shop itself, photo portraits were hanging
on the walls, digital cameras were on offer, and a display of
antique cameras was arranged in a glass-fronted bookcase

as well. There was a counter and, as Tim knew, a back room. From this room a man emerged. He was wearing a white lab coat with *Shots!* embroidered on the left breast and a plastic name tag above it. When his eyes met Tim's, his hand went quickly to that name tag. He removed it and shoved it into his pocket.

Tim thought once again how normal Toy4You looked. He was not at all what one would expect, with neat brown hair, roses in his cheeks, and wire-rimmed specs. He had a pleasant smile and he used it now. But what he said to Tim was, "This isn't a good time."

"I texted you," Tim said. "You didn't answer."

"I had no message from you," Toy4You replied. "Are you sure you sent it to the right number?" He looked directly at Tim, which was how Tim knew he was lying because that was what he himself had used to do until he'd understood how dead a giveaway it was to meet someone's eyes like that.

Tim said, "Why didn't you answer? We had a deal. We *have* a deal. I did my part. You didn't do yours."

The man's gaze shifted. It went from Tim to the doorway. This meant he was hoping that someone would enter the shop so that the conversation could go no further because he knew as well as Tim knew that neither of them wanted to be overheard. But there was no one out there, so he was going to have to talk or Tim was going to do something inside the shop . . . like make a move for those old cameras in that case or one of the digitals. He doubted Toy4You wanted any of them destroyed.

Tim said, "I *said*—"

"For what you're proposing, the risk is too great. I've thought about it, but that's how it is."

Tim grew so hot that he felt a fire being lit at his feet. It rose quickly and engulfed him and he breathed fast and hard because that seemed the best way to control it. He said, "We fucking *agreed*. You think I'm forgetting about that?" He clenched his fists, unclenched them, and looked around. "D'you even want to *know* what I can do to you if you don't keep your promise to me?"

Toy4You went to a drawer at the end of the counter. Tim tensed, reckoning he meant to pull out a gun or something, which was what would have happened in a film. But instead, he pulled out a packet of cigarettes. He lit one. He examined Tim for a very long moment before he spoke. He finally said, "Okay. All right. But if you want it to happen, I need more from you than you've given so far. That's the only thing that makes it worthwhile for me. A risk you take for a risk I take. Equality."

Tim parted his lips to speak but he couldn't at first. He'd already done *everything*. Every single damn thing. And now he was meant to do more? He said the only thing he could think of, "You promised me."

Toy4You made the sort of expression one might make upon the discovery of a seriously soiled nappy in the front seat of one's car. He said, "What's this 'you promised me'? Like some infant school pupils' arrangement, that's it? You give me your chocolate bikkie and I let you ride my skateboard? Only I eat the bikkie and then run off and you don't get your ride?"

Tim said, "You agreed. You *said*. This is fucking unfair."

Toy4You drew in long on the cigarette and watched Tim over its glowing tip. He said, "I changed my mind. That's what people do. I've assessed the risk and it's all on my part and none on yours. You want things done, you do them yourself."

Tim saw a curtain of red fall between himself and Toy4You. He knew what it meant: Action was called for and Toy4You wasn't about to call the cops to prevent him from taking it. But on the other hand, that would finish things between them and despite what he was feeling at the moment, Tim knew he didn't want to start this process all over again, searching for someone else. He couldn't face that: the days and weeks that it would take. So he said, "I swear to God, I'll tell. And when I'm done telling . . . No. Before that, I'll kill you and then I'll tell. I swear. I'll say I had to. I'll say you made me."

Toy4You lifted an eyebrow casually. "With the trail you've left on that computer of yours? I don't think so, mate." He glanced at a wall clock behind the shop counter and said, "And now it's time for you to leave."

"I'm staying." Tim's voice began to shake. The rage

filled him with both passion and need. "I'm telling every-one who walks in that door. You throw me out, I wait in the car park. Anyone comes near this place, I tell them. You call the cops to get me out of here, I tell them as well. You think I won't? You think I even care at this point?"

At this Toy4You took a moment without replying. It became so quiet within the shop that the movement of the second hand on the wall clock sounded like a gun being cocked, over and over again. Finally the man said, "Hell. Relax. Okay. You've got my short 'n curlies in your fist but I have yours as well, and you're not seeing that. As I've already said, you're taking no risk. I'm taking it all. So you're going to have to make things more worthwhile than you're making them at present. That's all I'm saying."

Tim said nothing. What he wanted to do—"at present," as Toy4You put it—was dive over the shop counter and beat the bastard to a pulp. But he remained where he was.

Toy4You said, "Really, kid, what's it going to take you to do that much: an hour, two, three? You want this bad enough, you go along. You don't want it bad enough, you phone the cops. But if you do, you have to give them some-thing to prove what you're telling them and you and I both know where that proof leads. You've got a mobile with mes-sages. You've got a computer with e-mail. There're cops out there who're going to take a look at all that and see what's what with you, and that's going to be easy. We're both in a dodgy position here, so why don't we help each other instead of trying to push each other in front of the train, eh?"

They engaged in a stare-down. From rage and need, what Tim felt altered to pure hopelessness. He didn't want to face the truth of the matter, that truth being that Toy4You had a point that Tim could not deny. So he finally said numbly, "What?"

Toy4You smiled briefly. "Not alone this time."

Tim felt his bowels get loose. He said, "When?"

That smile again, the kind of smile that acknowledges triumph. "Soon, my friend. I'll send you a text. You just be ready. Completely ready this time. Got that?"

"Yeah," Tim said because there was nothing else left, and he knew that.

LAKE WINDERMERE
CUMBRIA

After Manette had left them, Lynley told Bernard Fairclough that they needed to have a talk. Fairclough apparently anticipated this because he nodded, although he said, despite the rain that had begun to fall, "Let me take you through the topiary garden first."

Lynley reckoned that Fairclough made this offer in order to prepare himself for whatever talk was coming, but he let the other man have the time. They went in through an arched gate in a stone wall that was grey-speckled with lichen. Fairclough chatted about the site. He sounded casual enough, but doubtless he'd gone this route a hundred times: showing off what his wife had accomplished with her efforts to return the garden to its former glory.

Lynley listened without comment. He found the garden oddly beautiful. He generally preferred his shrubbery natural, but in this place box, holly, myrtle, and yew had been fashioned into fantastic shapes, some of them more than thirty feet tall. There were trapezoids, pyramids, and spirals. There were double spirals, mushrooms, arches, barrels, and cones. Paths of bleached limestone led among them and where there were no shrubs, there were parterres created from low box hedges. In these parterres yellow dwarf nasturtiums still bloomed, a contrast to the purple violas that surrounded them.

The garden was more than two hundred years old, and restoring it had been Valerie's dream upon inheriting Ireleth Hall, Fairclough told him. It had taken her years upon years with the assistance of four gardeners and photos from early in the twentieth century. "Magnificent, eh?" Fairclough said with pride. "She's amazing, my wife."

Lynley admired the garden. Anyone, he knew, would have done the same. But there was something not quite right in Fairclough's tone, and Lynley said to him, "Shall we talk here in the garden or somewhere else?"

Fairclough, obviously knowing that the time had come,

replied, "Come with me, then. Valerie's gone to check on Mignon. She'll be a while. We can talk in the library."

This turned out to be a misnomer, as there were no books. The room was a small and cosy chamber just off the great hall, with darkly panelled walls that were hung with portraits of Faircloughs long departed. A desk sat in the centre of the room, and two comfortable armchairs faced a fireplace. This was an impressive Grinling Gibbons affair surmounted by a display of old Willow pattern pottery, and a coal fire was laid within. Fairclough lit this, for the room bore a chill. Then he opened the heavy curtains that covered the lead-paned windows. Rain was streaking them.

Fairclough offered drinks. It was a little early for Lynley, so he demurred, but Fairclough poured sherry for himself. He indicated the chairs, and they sat. He said, "You're seeing more dirty laundry than I expected. I'm sorry about that."

"Every family has its share," Lynley noted. "My own included."

"Not like mine, I wager."

Lynley shrugged. He said, because at this point it had to be asked, "Do you want me to proceed, Bernard?"

"Why do you ask?"

Lynley steepled his fingers beneath his chin and looked at the coal fire. Lit by candle stubs beneath it, it was building nicely. The room would soon be quite warm. He said, "Aside from this business about Cresswell's farm, which bears looking into, you may already have the result you prefer. If the coroner has declared it an accident, you might well want to leave it that way."

"And let someone get away with murder?"

"At the end of the day, no one gets away with anything, I've found."

"What have you uncovered?"

"It's not a matter of what I've uncovered. So far, that's little enough as my hands are somewhat tied by the pretence of my being a visitor here. It's rather a matter of what I might uncover, which is a motive for murder. I suppose what I'm saying is that while this easily could have been an accident, you run the risk of discovering things about your son, your daughters, even your wife that you'd rather not know, no matter *how* your nephew died. That sort of thing happens in an investigation."

Fairclough seemed to give this some thought. Like Lynley, he directed his gaze to the fireplace and then to the Willow pattern pottery above it. One of the vases, Lynley saw, was cracked and had been repaired at some time. Long ago, he reckoned. The repair was inexpert, not like what could be done today to hide damage.

Lynley said, "On the other hand, this could indeed be a murder, perpetrated by someone you love. Do you want to face that?"

Fairclough looked at him then. He said nothing, but Lynley could see that the man's mind was ticking away at something.

Lynley continued. "Consider this as well. You wanted to know if Nicholas was somehow involved in what happened to his cousin. That was why you came to London. But what if someone else is involved, other than Nicholas? Some other member of your family. Or what if Ian wasn't the intended victim? Do you want to know that as well?"

Fairclough didn't hesitate. Both of them knew who the other intended victim would have been. He said, "No one has a reason to want Valerie hurt. She's the centre of this world. Both my world and theirs." He indicated the out-of-doors, by which Lynley took that he meant his children, and one of them in particular.

Lynley said, "Bernard, we can't avoid looking at Mignon. She has access to that boathouse every day."

"Absolutely not Mignon," Fairclough said. "She wouldn't have lifted a finger against Ian and certainly not against her own mother."

"Why not?"

"She's fragile, Tommy. Always has been. She had a head injury as a child and ever since . . . She's incapacitated. Her knees, her surgery . . . No matter . . . She wouldn't have been able to manage it."

Lynley pressed him. "If she somehow were able, has she a motive? Is there something I should know about her relationship with her mother? With her cousin? Were they close? Were they enemies?"

"In other words, did she have a reason to want Ian dead?"

"That's what I'm asking."

Fairclough took off his glasses and rubbed his eyes. "Ian advised me on financial matters, as you know. He was in charge of all finances. That was his job. He was good at that and I needed him."

"I understand," Lynley said.

"He'd insisted for a while—perhaps three years—that I cut Mignon off. He never understood that the girl *can't* work. She's never been able. Ian's point was that giving her money was what had crippled her and she was otherwise perfectly fine. It was a bone of contention between us. Not a big one and it only came up once or twice a year. But I had no intention of . . . I just couldn't. When your child's been badly injured . . . When you have children of your own, you'll understand, Tommy."

"Did Mignon know about Ian's wanting to cut her off?"

Fairclough nodded, reluctantly. "He spoke to her. When I wouldn't agree to stopping her allowance, he went to see her. He talked to her about 'bleeding money from her father,' as he put it. Mignon told me. She was hurt, of course. She told me I could cut her off at once. She invited me to do it, in fact."

"I daresay she knew you wouldn't."

"She's my child," Fairclough said.

"And your other children? Had Manette a reason to want Ian out of the picture?"

"Manette adored Ian. I think at one time she would have liked to marry him. Long before Kaveh, of course."

"And his feelings for her?"

Fairclough finished off his sherry and went to pour another. He motioned the decanter in Lynley's direction. Again Lynley demurred. "He was fond of Manette," Fairclough said. "But that was the extent of it."

"She's divorced, isn't she?"

"Yes. Her former husband works for me. Freddie McGhie. So does she for that matter."

"Is there any reason Freddie McGhie might have wanted Ian out of the way? You did tell me that you haven't definitely fixed on a successor at Fairclough Industries. How do things stand with Ian gone?"

Fairclough said nothing at first. It seemed to Lynley that they were getting close to something Fairclough preferred to ignore. Lynley raised an eyebrow. Fairclough said, "As I've said, I've not decided. Either Manette or Freddie could take over. They know the business. They've worked for me their entire careers. Freddie especially would be a good choice, despite being Manette's ex. He knows every department and he's worked in them all. I'd prefer a member of the family, as would Valerie, but if no one has the experience and the proper outlook, Freddie would be the logical one to take up the reins."

"Would you consider Nicholas?"

"That would be madness, with his history. But he's trying to prove himself to me."

"What did Ian think about that?"

"He reckoned Nick would fail. But as Nick had promised me that he was a changed man once and for all, I wanted to give him a chance to demonstrate it. He's working his way up from the bottom at the business. I rather admire him for that."

"Is that the deal you struck with him?"

"Not at all. It was his idea. I expect it's what Alatea advised him to do."

"So it's possible he could take over the company?"

"Anything's possible," Fairclough said. "As I said, it's not been decided."

"But you must have given thought to it at one point or another, else why have me come up here and look into Nicholas?"

Fairclough was silent. It was answer enough. Nicholas was, after all, the son. And the son, not the meek, was generally the one to inherit the earth.

Lynley went on. "Anyone else with a motive to be rid of Ian? Anyone you can think of with an ax to grind, a secret to keep, an issue to clear?"

"No one at all, as far as I know." Fairclough sipped his

sherry, but his eyes stayed on Lynley's over the rim of the glass.

Lynley knew he was lying, but he didn't know why. He also felt they hadn't got to the bottom of why he himself was there in the first place: at Ireleth Hall, investigating something that had already been resolved in a way that should have relieved the man. Lynley said, "Bernard, no one is actually in the clear on this except those who had no access to the boathouse. You've a decision to make if you want the truth, whatever it is."

"What sort of decision?"

"If you actually do want to get to the bottom of the matter, you're going to have to agree to let me be who I am."

"And that is?"

"A cop."

FLEET STREET
CITY OF LONDON

Barbara Havers chose a pub near Fleet Street, one of the watering holes that had long ago been a gathering place for journalists in the heyday of the newspaper business when nearly every tabloid and broadsheet had its headquarters in the immediate vicinity. Things had changed, with property in the Canary Wharf area luring more than one news organisation to the east end of the city. But not all had heeded that siren call of lower rents, and one in particular had stubbornly remained, determined to be close to the action. That was *The Source*, and Barbara was waiting for *her* source at *The Source* to show up. She'd phoned and asked him for a meeting. He'd been reluctant till she let him set the time and offered lunch. He'd still been reluctant till she mentioned Lynley. That got his attention. He asked, "How is he?" and Barbara could tell the reporter was hoping for something suitable to whet the readers' appetite in the Recovery from Personal Tragedy department. It wouldn't make the front page, but he could hope for page 3 plus photos, if the details were good.

She'd said, "I'm not prepared to say a word about a word over the phone. C'n you meet?"

That had done the trick. She hated to use Lynley that way—she hated to use him any way if it came down to it—but as he himself was the one who was asking her for information, she reckoned she was on the safe side of what was appropriate between friends.

Isabelle Ardery had been more difficult to deal with. When Barbara phoned to ask for the time off that she was owed, Ardery had been at once suspicious, as her questions of "Why? Where are you going?" indicated. Barbara had known the acting detective superintendent was probably going to be the difficult nail to pound into the board, so she'd had her excuse ready.

"Haircut," she said. "Or perhaps I should say hair*style*. I've found a place in Knightsbridge."

"So you just need the day," Ardery had clarified.

"So far," Barbara replied.

"What's that supposed to mean, Sergeant?" There was that suspicion again. The super needed to do something about the sharpness in her voice if she wanted to hide her paranoia, Barbara thought.

She said, "Have some mercy, guv. If I end up looking like last night's dinner, I'll have to find someone to repair the damage. I'll be in touch. I'm owed the time anyway."

This was no lie, and Ardery knew that. Besides, she herself had been the one to order—in the guise of making a recommendation—an improvement in Barbara's personal appearance. The superintendent had reluctantly agreed, although she'd added, "No more than two days," to make certain Barbara knew which one of them was in charge.

On her way to the pub, Barbara had taken care of another of Lynley's requests. She'd searched out the latest edition of *Conception* magazine, finding it at King's Cross Station, where a WH Smith in the railway terminal provided every journal imaginable. That had been convenient since Barbara's underground route from Chalk Farm took her through King's Cross Station anyway. So all it had involved was a brief stop there, not to mention putting up with an evaluative glance from the young man behind the till when she paid for the journal. She could see it in his eyes and in the ever-so-slightly-amused movement of his mouth: Conception? *You? Not bloody likely.* She'd wanted to pull him over the counter by the neck of his white shirt, but the dirty ring round its collar stopped her. No need to expose herself so closely to someone whose personal hygiene didn't extend to washing his clothes regularly, she'd decided.

She was leafing through *Conception* as she waited in the pub. She was wondering where they found all the perfect babies to photograph, along with all the mothers who looked dewy fresh and not at all like what they probably were, which was haggard with lack of sleep. She'd ordered herself a jacket potato topped with chili con carne and she was dipping into this and reading about the care of one's nipples during breast-feeding—who knew it was so painful? she wondered—when her inside guy at *The Source* showed up.

Mitchell Corsico came into the pub in his usual getup. He always wore a Stetson, jeans, and cowboy boots, but Barbara saw he'd added a fringed leather jacket. God, she thought, chaps and six-guns were probably next. He saw her, jerked his head in a nod, and approached the bar to place his order. He looked at the menu for a moment, tossed it down, and told the publican what he wanted. He paid for it as well, and this Barbara took for a positive sign till he walked to her table and said, "Twelve pounds fifty."

She said, "Bloody hell, what did you order?"

"Did I have a limit?"

She muttered and pulled out her purse. She dug for the cash and shoved it over as he reached for a chair and mounted it like a cowboy onto a horse. She said, "Where's Trigger?"

"Say what?"

"Never mind."

"That's bad for your arteries," he noted with a nod at her potato.

"And you ordered . . . ?"

"All right. Never mind. What's up?"

"Back-scratch situation."

She saw the wariness across his features. Who could

blame him? Corsico was the one who was usually coming to the cops for information and not the reverse. But hope crossed his features as well because he knew his stock was very low at the Yard. He'd been embedded with the police during the hunt for a serial killer nearly a year earlier, and he wasn't popular because of that.

Still, he was careful. He said, "I don't know. Let's see. What d'you need?"

"A name."

He remained noncommittal.

"There's a reporter from *The Source* been sent up to Cumbria. I need to know who he is and why he's there." At this, he began to reach into his jacket pocket, so she said, "Uh, we haven't started scratching yet, Mitch. Hold Trigger's rein, if you know what I mean."

"Oh. A horse."

"Yeah. Just like Silver. Hi ho, and all that. I'd expect you to know this, all things considered. So who's gone up there? And why?"

He considered. After a moment during which his meal arrived—roast beef and Yorkshire bloody pud and all the trimmings, and Barbara reckoned he didn't eat like *that* unless someone else was footing the bill—he said, "I need to know what's in it for me."

"That's going to depend on the value of your information."

"It doesn't work that way," he said.

"Not usually. But things have changed. New super looking over my shoulder. I have to be careful."

"An exclusive with DI Lynley would do."

"Ha! Not bloody likely."

He started to rise. Barbara knew it was show because there was no way in hell he was going to walk off and leave his roast beef and Yorkshire pud languishing uneaten at the table. But she played along and said, "All right. I'll do what I can. So you do what you can. Who's been sent to Cumbria?"

He spilled the beans as she reckoned he would. He gave her everything: Zedekiah Benjamin, a story on Nicholas Fairclough, a rejection by the editor, and a reporter's determination to mould the story into something suitable for *The Source* instead of what he'd turned in at first, which appeared to be a puff piece that belonged in *Hello!* He'd been up to Cumbria at least three times now—maybe four—trying to sex up the story enough for Rodney Aronson, but he was apparently slow on the uptake. He'd not been getting anywhere till Ian Cresswell drowned.

This was an interesting bit, Barbara thought. She asked for the dates of Zedekiah Benjamin's sojourns in Cumbria and she learned that two of those sojourns had occurred in advance of the Cresswell drowning. The second of these had ended just three days prior to the death, at which point Benjamin had apparently returned to London with his tail between his legs, having failed to suss out the sex that his editor required.

She said, "What happens to this bloke if he doesn't find the sex?"

Corsico did the knife-across-the-throat business and topped that by flipping his thumb over his shoulder in case Barbara was too dim to work out what he meant. She nodded and said, "Know where he's staying up there?"

Corsico said he didn't. But he added that Benjamin wouldn't exactly be difficult to spot if he was lurking in the bushes near someone's house.

"Why?" Barbara asked.

Because, Corsico said, he was six feet eight inches tall with a head of hair so red it looked like his skull was on fire.

"Now," he concluded, taking out his notebook, "my back's itching."

"I'll have to scratch it later," she replied.

ARNSIDE KNOT
CUMBRIA

The rain had begun during Alatea's walk. She was prepared for it, though, having seen the nasty bank of clouds approaching Arnside across Morecambe Bay, coming from the direction of Humphrey Head. What she hadn't anticipated was the strength of it. She'd known from the wind it would be coming on quickly. The fact that it altered from a quarter of an hour's downpour to a tempest was the surprise.

She was halfway to her destination when the pelting began. She could have turned for home, but she did not. It seemed to her a necessity that she complete the climb to the top of Arnside Knot. She told herself grimly that she might be struck by lightning there, and at the moment this sort of end to her life didn't actually seem like such a bad thing. She'd be done in an instant, over, out. It would be a form of the ultimate knowing in a situation in which not knowing was slowly eating her up.

The rain had abated when she began the final ascent among the auburn-coated Scottish steers that grazed freely on the hillside. Her feet sought safe purchase in the areas of limestone scree, and she grasped the trunks of the bent, wind-scarred conifers to aid her as she reached the top. Once there, she found she was breathing less heavily than she had done in earlier climbs. Soon, she told herself, she'd probably be able to jog to the top of Arnside Knot and arrive there no worse for the exertion.

From the top of the knot, she could see it all: two hundred and eighty degrees of panorama that comprised everything from the speck that was Piel Island Castle to the undulating mass of Morecambe Bay and the fishing villages strung along its shore. This vista offered endless sky, treacherous waters, and landscape of every variety. What it did not offer, however, was a glimpse into the future, and Alatea had come out into the uncertain weather in an attempt to run from what she knew she could not hope to escape indefinitely.

She'd told Nicholas part of what she'd discovered in her research, but she had not told him all of it. "She's a freelance photographer, not a location scout at all," she'd informed him. Her nerves were on edge, and she'd had a bit of sherry to still them. "Come, look, Nicholas. She has a Web site."

It had been a simple matter to find out what she needed to know about Deborah St. James. The Internet was a bottomless pit of information and one did not need to be a genius in order to use it. Find a search engine, type in a name. In the world as it was at present, one could run but one could not hide.

Deborah St. James wasn't even trying to hide. *What Do You Want Photographed?* was part of her Web site design, which contained various links showing the nature of her work. She was an art photographer, if that was the word for it. She took the kinds of photos sold in galleries: landscapes, portraits, still lifes, dramatic action shots, spontaneous moments of life captured in the streets. She worked largely in black and white, she'd had several gallery shows, and she'd been featured in photographic competitions. She was obviously good at what she did but what she did *not* do was scout locations for anyone, let alone for a company called Query Productions.

There was no such company. Alatea had discovered that as well. But that was what she did not tell her husband because she knew intuitively where telling Nicholas that part of the information was going to lead. A logical question had to be asked and Nicholas would ask it: So what is she doing here, then? Alatea didn't want him to ask that because they'd have to look at the answers. *What Do You Want Photographed?* said it all. The real matter before them—or before Alatea herself if the truth be told—was what Deborah St. James intended to do with the pictures.

Yet that was far too fragile a subject to entertain with her husband, so Alatea had said to Nicholas, "I'm not comfortable having her round here, Nicky. There's something about her that I don't like."

Nicholas frowned. They'd been in bed and he'd turned on his side to face her, propping his head on his hand. He didn't have his glasses on, which meant he couldn't see her properly, but he still looked as if he was studying her face and what he apparently thought he saw there made him say with a smile, "Because she's a photographer or because she's a woman? Because, darling wife, let me tell you this: If it's the woman part that you're concerned about, you're never going to have a single worry on that score." He'd scooted over to her to prove this declaration and she'd allowed this. She'd wanted it, even, for the sheer diversion from her thoughts that love with Nicholas produced. But afterwards the worry and the fear came sweeping back like the tidal bore in Morecambe Bay. There was no escape and the fast-rising tide threatened to drown her.

He'd sensed this. Nicholas was good at that. He could read her tension although he could not interpret it. He'd said, "Why're you so wound up about this? She's a freelance photographer, and freelancers get hired to take pictures and to hand them over to whoever hired them. That's what she's here to do." He moved away on the bed. "We need a break, I think." His face looked tender as he spoke. "We've been working too hard, too long. You've been up to your ears for months dealing with the house, and I've been running between the tower project and Barrow, so bloody caught up in getting back into my father's good graces that I haven't been paying enough attention to you. To how you're feeling, to the fact that this is all foreign to you, coming here, living here. To me, it's home, but I haven't seen that for you, it's a foreign country." He smiled regretfully. "Addicts are selfish wankers, Allie. I'm a prime example."

From this, she took up a single strand. She said, "Why do you need this?"

"A break? You? This, here in bed?" His smile, then, and, "I'd hope you wouldn't have to ask that last question."

"Your father," she said. "Why must you get into his good graces?"

When he answered, his voice showed his surprise. "Because I made his life hell for years. My mother's as well."

"You cannot rewrite the past, Nicky."

"But I can make amends for it. I took years off their lives, and I want to give those years back to them if I can. Wouldn't you want the same in my position?"

"Life," she said, "is meant to be lived by the individual living it, being true to himself. What you're doing is living your life in order to be true to someone else's perception of you."

He'd blinked and an expression of hurt touched his features and then dissipated as quickly as it had come upon him. He said, "We'll have to agree to disagree on this. And you'll have to wait and see how things turn out, how they change for me, for you, and for the family."

She'd said, "Your family—"

And he'd cut in with, "I don't mean my family. I mean our family. Yours and mine. The family we make. Things are going to continue to get better from this point on. You'll see."

In the morning, she'd tried again, but this time it was with a diversion and not with a frontal attack. She'd said, "Don't go to work today. Stay with me, stay here, don't go to the tower."

His reply of, "That's a very tempting proposition," had given her hope for an instant but he went on to say, "I must go in to work, though, Allie. I've taken a day off already."

"Nicky, you're the son of the owner. If you can't take a day off—"

"I'm a line operator in the shipping department. Someday I might be the son of the owner again. But I'm not there yet."

They were, thus, back to where they started. Alatea knew that this was the point of departure for them. He believed he had to prove himself in order to make amends for his past. In this manner he would pave a way to the future through illustrating over and over again that he was not who he once had been. While she understood this, it was not how she lived. Indeed, living in the way Nicholas was choosing to live was impossible for her.

And now there was the matter of Query Productions and the fact that it did not exist. This meant only one thing: that the presence of the photographer here in Cumbria had nothing at all to do with the work Nicholas was doing, nothing at all to do with what he was attempting to create with the Middlebarrow Pele Project, and nothing at all to do with any intention he had with regard to his parents and to transforming his life. That left only one explanation as far as she could see for the photographer's presence. *What Do You Want Photographed?* said it all.

Alatea's descent from the top of Arnside Knot took more time than the ascent had done. The patches of limestone scree were slick after the rain. Slipping upon the loose stones, falling, and tumbling down the slope were distinct possibilities. So was sliding upon the fallen leaves from the lime and chestnut trees that formed a copse lower down the hill. So safety was foremost in her mind as she made her way home in the fast-fading daylight. Safety, too, took her to the telephone soon after she walked into Arnside House.

She always kept the phone number with her. This had been the case since the very first time she'd made the call. She didn't want to do what she had to do, but she couldn't see any other choice available. She took out the card, managed a few deep breaths, punched in the numbers, and waited for the connection to go through. When it did, she asked the only question that mattered to her now.

"I don't mean to pressure you, but I do need to know. Have you considered my offer?"

"I have," the quiet voice replied.

"And?"

"Let's meet to talk it over."

"This means?"

"You're completely serious about the money?"

"Yes, yes. Of course I'm serious."

"Then I think I can do what you're asking."

MILNTHORPE
CUMBRIA

Lynley tracked them down having what Deborah called "a most indifferent curry, Tommy," which they'd found in a restaurant called Fresh Taste of India on Church Street in Milnthorpe. St. James added, "We're not spoiled for choices. It was this, takeaway Chinese, or pizza. I voted for pizza but was overruled."

They'd finished their meal and were each drinking a rather disturbingly large glass of *limoncello*, which was odd in both its size and the fact that an Indian restaurant was serving the Italian liqueur at all. "Simon likes me soused after nine in the evening," was how Deborah explained at least the size of the glass. "I become putty in his wily hands although I don't expect he's worked out how he's going to get me off the floor, out of the restaurant, and back to the hotel if I drink this entire thing."

"A trolley," St. James said. He indicated a nearby table with its unoccupied chairs. Lynley dragged one of them over and joined them.

"Anything?" St. James said to him.

Lynley knew he didn't mean food or drink. "There are motives, I'm finding. It's becoming a case of turn over a stone and find a motive." He ticked them off for his friends: an insurance policy with Niamh Cresswell as the beneficiary; the land and the farm going to Kaveh Mehran; the potential loss of funds to Mignon Fairclough; the potential gain of position at Fairclough Industries by Manette or Freddie McGhie or, for that matter, Nicholas Fairclough; Niamh Cresswell's need for revenge. "There's also something not quite right about Cresswell's son, Tim. Evidently he's a day pupil in a school called Margaret Fox, which turns out to be an institution for troubled children. A phone call got me that much but no one's saying anything else about him."

"So *troubled* could mean anything," St. James noted.

"It could." Lynley went on to tell them about the Cresswell children's being unceremoniously dumped first upon their father and his lover and now upon the lover alone. "The sister—Manette McGhie—was in quite a state about the situation this afternoon."

"Who wouldn't be?" Deborah noted. "That's ghastly, Tommy."

"I agree. The only people so far who don't seem to have motives are Fairclough himself and his wife. Although," Lynley added thoughtfully, "I do have the impression that Fairclough's holding something back. So I have Barbara looking at the London end of his life."

"But why ask you to look into matters if he's got something to hide?" Deborah asked.

"That's the question, isn't it?" Lynley said. "It hardly makes sense for a killer, who's got away with the murder, to head for the cops asking for a closer look."

"As to that . . ." He'd been to see the forensic pathologist,

St. James told Lynley. It seemed that all the i's had been
dotted and all the t's crossed. He'd had a look at the reports
and the X-rays and from the latter, it was perfectly obvious
that Ian Cresswell's skull had been fractured. As Lynley
well knew when a skull was fractured, it didn't bear the
imprint of that which had fractured it. The skull either
cracked like an egg with a spiderweb of breaks spreading
out from the point of impact or it suffered a lateral break
in the form of a semicircle on the surface. But in either case,
one needed to examine the potential instruments that could
have caused the fracture in order to decide how it had
occurred.

"And?" Lynley asked.

And this had been done. There was blood on one of the
stones remaining upon the dock when the others had dislodged and had fallen into the water. DNA analysis of this
blood indicated it had come from Ian Cresswell. There were
hairs, skin, and fibres as well, and when they were tested, they
proved to be from Ian Cresswell, too.

"I tracked down the coroner's officers who did the investigation prior to the inquest," St. James went on. "There
were two of them: a former detective from the constabulary
offices in Barrow-in-Furness and a paramedic who does
this sort of work on the side. They felt they were looking at
an accident, not a murder, but they checked all alibis just in
case."

Like Lynley, St. James ticked them off, consulting a
notepad that he withdrew from the breast pocket of his
jacket: Kaveh Mehran, he said, was at home, and although
the Cresswell children could have confirmed this, they were
not interviewed in order to spare them further trauma; Valerie Fairclough was at home on the estate, having entered
the house at five in the afternoon after fishing on the lake
and not leaving until the next morning when she went out
to speak to the gardeners working in her topiary garden;
Mignon Fairclough was at home as well although no one
could confirm her alibi that she was sending e-mails since
anyone with access to her computer and her password could
have been sending e-mails in her name; Niamh Cresswell

was en route to taking the children back to Bryan Beck farm and afterwards she was en route back to Grange-over-Sands, although no one could confirm this—

"Leaving both herself and Kaveh Mehran without confirmable alibis for a period of time," Lynley noted.

"Indeed." St. James went on: Manette and Freddie McGhie were both at home, where they remained for the evening; Nicholas was at home with his spouse, Alatea; Lord Fairclough was in London having dinner with a member of the board of his foundation. This was a woman called Vivienne Tully, and she confirmed, St. James concluded. "Of course, the essential difficulty resides in the way the man died."

"It does," Lynley agreed. "If the stones on the dock were tampered with, it could have been done at any time. So we're back to access, which roughly means we're back to nearly everyone."

"We're back to a closer examination of the dock as well as bringing up the missing stones. Either that or we're back to calling it an accident and calling it a day. I suggest a closer examination if Fairclough wants to be certain."

"He says he does."

"So we need to get into the boathouse with bright lights and someone needs to get into the water for the stones."

"Unless I can convince Fairclough to bring this all into the open, we may well have to do it on the sly," Lynley said.

"Any idea why he's playing his cards so close?"

Lynley shook his head. "It's to do with his son, but I don't know why, aside from what one would expect."

"Which is?"

"I can't imagine him wanting his only son to know his father harbours suspicions about him, no matter how chequered a past he has. He's supposed to have turned over a new leaf, after all. He was welcomed home with open arms, evidently."

"And, as you said, he has an alibi."

"Home with the wife. There's that," Lynley agreed.

Deborah had been listening to all this, but at this final mention of Nicholas Fairclough, she brought a sheaf of papers from her handbag. She said, "Barbara's faxed me the pages I wanted from *Conception* magazine, Tommy. She's overnighting the magazine itself, but in the meantime . . ." Deborah handed him the pages.

"Relevant?" Lynley could see they comprised advertisements, both personal and professional.

She said, "They fit in with what Nicholas told me about wanting to start a family."

Lynley exchanged a look with St. James. He knew the other man was thinking what he himself was thinking: How objective could Deborah be if it turned out she'd stumbled onto a woman suffering the very same problems as she herself was suffering?

Deborah saw the look. She said, "Really, you two. Aren't you supposed to remain expressionless in the presence of a suspect?"

Lynley smiled. "Sorry. Force of habit. Please continue."

She *hmmph*ed but did so. "Look at what we have here and consider the fact that Alatea—or someone—tore these pages from the magazine."

"The *someone* part of it might be important," St. James pointed out.

"I don't think it's likely someone else removed them, do you? Look. We have advertisements for just about anything you can think of relating to the process of reproduction. We have ads for solicitors who're specialists in private adoptions, ads for sperm banks, ads from lesbian couples looking for sperm donors, ads for adoption agencies, ads for solicitors specialising in surrogacy, ads looking for university girls willing to have their eggs harvested, ads looking for university boys willing to make regular deposits of semen for a price. It's become an industry, courtesy of modern science."

Lynley gauged the passion in Deborah's voice and considered what it might mean, especially as it applied to Nicholas Fairclough and his wife. He said, "Protecting one's wife is important to a man, Deb. Fairclough might well have seen the magazine and torn these pages out so Alatea wouldn't come across them."

"Perhaps," she said. "But that hardly means Alatea never knew they were there."

"All right. But how does this relate to Ian Cresswell's death?"

"I don't know yet. But if you're exploring every possible avenue, Tommy, then this has to be one of them."

Lynley looked again at St. James. The other man said, "I daresay she's right."

Deborah's expression registered her surprise. The fact that her husband chronically and, to Deborah, infuriatingly attempted to protect her from pain had long been an issue between them, born of the fact that he'd known her since she was seven years old, born of the fact that he was eleven years her senior. She said, "I think I need a second go with Alatea, Tommy. I can establish a bond with her. It will be easy enough if she's having my sort of trouble. Only a woman can know what that's like. Believe me."

Lynley was careful at this point not to look at St. James. He knew how Deborah would take it if he appeared to be asking her husband for permission like someone stepping out of a Victorian novel. So he said, "I agree. Another go is in order. See what else you can find out about her." He didn't add that she should have a care. He knew that St. James would make sure of that.

6 NOVEMBER

BRYANBARROW
CUMBRIA

Yaffa Shaw was turning out to be pure gold, much to Zed Benjamin's surprise and delight. Not only was she amusing to speak to on the phone each day—her performance as a woman besotted should have earned her a BAFTA, he decided—but she was also a twenty-four-carat helpmate in his efforts. He didn't know how she'd managed it, but she'd sweet-talked her way into looking at Ian Cresswell's will. Instead of attending university on the previous day, she'd taken the train to York, where a clerk in the probate office had apparently been so smitten by her charms that he'd slipped her the Cresswell document for a look-see and a look-see was all she needed. The woman had a bloody photographic memory, as things turned out. She phoned and recited the bequests, thus saving Zed a trip south and a wait for however long it took for the documents to be copied and posted to him. She was, in short, entirely wonderful.

So he said, "I adore you."

She said, "I'm blushing," and to his mother, who was, of course, hovering somewhere nearby, "Your son is actually making me *blush*, Mrs. B." She made some kissing noises into the phone.

Zed made some back, forgetting himself in his enthusiasm over her discovery. Then he remembered himself. He also remembered Micah waiting for Yaffa's return to Tel Aviv. Wasn't life full of irony? he thought.

After a suitable exchange of auditory hugs and vociferous kisses, they ended their call and Zed reflected on the information he had. Despite Rodney Aronson's direction as to what he was supposed to be doing in Cumbria, Zed decided that an attack on the opposing army's flank was in order. He wasn't going to speak to George Cowley about what he might and might not know about that farm, though. He was going to speak to the man's son.

Thus he got himself up to Bryanbarrow village early. The Willow and Well, with its windows conveniently situated to give a view of Bryan Beck farm, was not open yet, so Zed had to wait in his car, which he parked to one side of the village green. This was misery for him because of his size, but it couldn't be helped. Leg cramps and the distinct possibility of deep-vein thrombosis were a small price to pay for an interview that might gain him everything.

Of course, it was raining. It was a wonder to Zed that the entire Lake District wasn't a swamp, considering the weather. The endless precipitation along with the day's cold kept steaming up the windscreen of his car as he waited for Daniel Cowley to appear. He kept wiping it off with the back of his hand, which was doing nothing but getting his shirtsleeves wet as the condensation began to drip down his arm.

Finally, the boy appeared. Zed reckoned he went to school in Windermere. This was going to necessitate one of two things: Either his father was going to drive him there or he was going to catch a school bus. It didn't matter which because in any case, Zed was going to talk to him. He'd waylay him on his way into the school, or he'd offer him a lift as he hoofed it to the bus stop, which sure as hell wasn't going to be out here in the middle of nowhere.

The latter turned out to be the case. Daniel trudged across the green, around the corner, and out of the village, his head lowered and his trousers and shoes already beginning to pick up mud. Zed gave him ten minutes, reckoning that he was heading for the main road through the Lyth Valley. It was quite a walk.

By the time he pulled up next to Daniel, the boy was thoroughly soaked since, like most boys his age, he wasn't about to be seen dead or alive carrying an umbrella. Social suicide, that would be. As someone who had endured social suicide on a daily basis during his own school years, Zed understood this completely.

He lowered the window. "You need a lift somewhere?"

Daniel looked over. His eyebrows drew together. He glanced left and right and evaluated the question as the rain continued to pelt him. He finally said, "I remember you. You a pervert or something? Because if you lay a hand on me—"

"Relax," Zed told him. "This is your lucky day. I'm into girls. Tomorrow would be risky. Come on. Get in."

Daniel gave an eye roll at Zed's weak joke. Then he complied. He dropped into the passenger seat and began dripping all over it. He said, "Sorry," in reference to this.

"Not to worry."

Zed set off. He was determined to milk the kid for whatever he could, so he drove slowly. He kept his eyes on the road as a way of excusing the lack of speed: paranoid visitor worried about hitting either a sheep or Sasquatch.

Daniel said, "What're you doing round here again, anyway?"

Zed had already reckoned on his opening, which Daniel himself had inadvertently given him. "You seem worried about the local colour."

"What?" The boy screwed up his face.

"The pervert remark."

"Who wouldn't be?" Daniel said with a shrug. "Place's crawling with them."

"Well, the whole bloody district's thick with sheep, eh?" Zed remarked with a wink. "No one's safe, I reckon."

The boy observed him with that adolescent expression that telegraphed *you're a bloody idiot* far more effectively than words would have done.

Zed said, "Just a joke. Too early in the morning. Where can I drop you?"

"Lyth Valley. I catch the school bus there."

"Where to?"

"Windermere."

"I can drive you there if you like. No problem. I'm heading that way."

The boy backed away. Clearly, this was pervert territory. He said, "What d'you want, anyway? You didn't tell me why you're in the village again. What's going on?"

Too clever by seven-eighths, Zed thought. "Bloody hell, relax," he said. "I'll drop you off wherever you like. Want to get out now?"

Daniel looked at the rain. He said, "Just don't try anything. I'll punch you right in the Adam's apple and don't think I won't. I know how to do it. My dad showed me and believe me, it works. Better than the bollocks. A hell of a lot better."

"Wonderful skill," Zed agreed. He had to manoeuvre the kid into the conversation he wanted before they reached the Lyth Valley and he started screaming bloody murder or worse. So he said, "Sounds like he worries about you, your dad."

"Right. Well. We got perverts living next door to us, don't we. Pretend they just lodge together, but *we* know the truth. Dad says you can't be too careful round blokes like that, and now it's worse."

"Why?" Hallelujah, Zed thought.

" 'Cause one of them's dead and the other's going to be on the look for someone new."

That sounded like a remark coming directly from the horse's you-know-what. "I see," Zed said. "Could be the other'll just move on, though, wouldn't you say?"

"That's what Dad's waiting for," Daniel said. "He's buying the farm once it goes up for sale."

"What, that sheep farm you two live on?"

That was the one, Daniel told him. He brushed his sopping hair from his forehead and settled in for something of a natter. He seemed more comfortable with a subject that didn't deal with perverts—as he called them—because he adjusted the heat in the car to a tropical level and dug in his rucksack for a banana, which he proceeded to eat. He informed Zed that his dad wanted the farm mostly because he wanted something to pass on to Daniel himself. This,

Daniel said, was dead stupid because there was no way in hell that he intended to be a sheep farmer. Daniel wanted out of the Lakes entirely. He wanted to join the RAF. They buzzed the Lake District, did Zed know that? Wicked jets flying about three hundred feet off the ground—okay, maybe five hundred feet—and you'd be walking along when all of a sudden one of them would come roaring down the valley or just above Lake Windermere and it was bloody wicked, it was.

"Told my dad that about a thousand times," Daniel said. "He thinks he can keep me home, though. All he needs is that farm to do it."

He loved his dad, Daniel said, but he didn't want the kind of life his dad had lived. Look at the fact that Daniel's own mother deserted them. She hadn't wanted that kind of life either, but still his dad didn't understand.

"I keep telling him he should do what he's good at anyway. Everyone should."

Amen to that, Zed thought. But he said, "What's that, then?"

Daniel hesitated. Zed glanced at him. The boy looked distinctly uncomfortable. This could be the moment, Zed realised. The kid was about to confess that what George Cowley was good at was offing blokes who lived on the farm he wanted to buy. Silver, gold, platinum, and the rest. Zed was about to be handed the scoop of his life.

"Making dollhouse furniture," Daniel mumbled.

"Say again?"

"Dollhouse furniture. Furniture that goes into dollhouses. Don't you know what that is?"

Shit, damn, hell, Zed thought.

Daniel went on. "He's bloody good at it. Sounds daft, I know, but that's what he does. Sells it on the Internet as fast as he can make it. *I* tell him he should be making it full-time instead of walking round in the muck with the bloody sheep. He says it's a hobby and I should be able to tell the difference between a hobby and someone's life work." Daniel shook his head. "For him, it's that stupid farm or nothing."

Is it indeed? Zed wondered. And what was Cowley going

to do next when he learned the farm legally belonged to Kaveh Mehran via Ian Cresswell's will?

Daniel pointed to an enormous oak sitting just inside a drystone wall. That was where Zed could set him down, he said. And thanks for the ride, by the way.

Zed pulled over, and Daniel got out. At the same moment, Zed's mobile rang. He gave it a glance and saw it was London. Rodney Aronson ringing. It was a bit early for Rodney even to be at work, and this didn't bode well. Good news, though, was that Zed could report progress at last after this conversation with Daniel Cowley.

"Watch your back," was what Rodney said to him, however, without preamble.

"Why? What's happened?"

"Scotland Yard knows you're there. Keep your head down—"

When it was six feet eight inches in the air? Zed wondered.

"—and keep your eyes on Nick Fairclough. That's where you'll find whoever's been sent up there to dig into Ian Cresswell's death."

BARROW-IN-FURNESS
CUMBRIA

Manette didn't want to face the fact that her former husband hadn't come home on the previous night. More, she didn't want to face how she felt about that fact. But it was difficult not to do so.

They'd talked the subject of their broken marriage right into the ground over the years. They'd touched upon every aspect of what had happened to them and what might have happened and what would definitely happen if they didn't make some sort of change. They'd decided, ultimately, that the lack of romance had done them in, the getting-down-to-business aspect of every part of their lives, and particularly the utter lack of surprise. They'd become a couple who had to check their diaries and make appointments for an interlude of intercourse during which they both had been pretending for ages to feel something that they did not feel for each other. At the end of what had seemed like hundreds of hours of dialogue, they'd decided that friendship was more important than passion anyway. So they'd live as friends and enjoy each other's company because at the end of the day they'd always enjoyed being together and how many couples could actually say that more than twenty years along the line?

But now Freddie hadn't come home. And when he *was* home he'd taken to whistling in the mornings as he got ready for work. Worse, he'd taken to singing while he was in the shower—Freddie, *singing*, for God's sake—and he always chose the same damn song, which was driving her bonkers anyway. It was that bloody call to arms from *Les Misérables* and Manette knew if she had to hear "the blood of the martyrs will water the meadows of France!" one more time, she might water the meadows of the bathroom with Freddie's blood.

Only, she wouldn't. Not Freddie. She would never hurt Freddie.

She went to his office at work. He'd removed his jacket and was bent over his desk in his crisp white shirt and his red necktie with the ducklings on it, and he was reviewing a massive set of computer printouts. More investigation into the books, preparatory to stepping into Ian's job should her father offer it to him. If he had any sense, he would.

She said from the doorway, "So how was Scorpio?"

Freddie looked up. His expression told her he had no idea what she was talking about but he reckoned it was zodiac signs.

She said, "The nightclub? Where you and the latest date were meeting?"

He said, "Oh! *Scorpio.*" He laid the printout on his neat-as-a-pin desk. "We didn't go in, actually. We met at the door."

"Good Lord, Freddie. Was it directly to bed after that? You're a sly one."

He blushed. Manette wondered at what point in their marriage she'd stopped noticing how often he blushed and how the colour washed across his cheeks from his ears after making his ears go completely red at the tips. She also wondered when it was she'd stopped admiring how nicely his ears lay against his head like perfect shells.

He laughed. "No, no," he said. "But everyone going inside the place looked round nineteen years old and most of them were dressed like the cast of *Rocky Horror Picture Show*. So we went for a meal at a wine bar. Rigatoni puttanesca. It wasn't very good. Rather heavy on the putta and light on the nesca as things turned out." He smiled at his own silly joke and added in his usual appealingly honest fashion, "I didn't come up with that. Sarah did."

"That's her name? Sarah?" At least, Manette thought, it wasn't another shrub. She'd rather been expecting Ivy or June-short-for-Juniper as his second foray into Internet dating. But of course, ivy wasn't a shrub, was it? More like a vine. So . . . She shook herself mentally. *What* was going on inside her head? She said, "And?" although she didn't actually want to know. "Are there grisly details? I have no life, as you well know, so I'm taking the opportunity for vicarious excitement." She sauntered into his office and sat in the chair next to his desk.

He blushed, more deeply this time. "I don't like to kiss and tell," he said.

"But you did it, didn't you?"

"'Did it'? What kind of term is 'did it'?"

She cocked her head and sent him a meaningful look. "Freddie . . ."

"Well, yes. I mean, I explained all that to you: how things are these days. You know. When people go out together. So, well . . . yes, we did."

"More than once?" She hated herself for asking, but suddenly she had to know. And the reason she had to know was that in all the years they'd been together—even when they'd been twenty years old and hot for each other during the six months that they had actually *been* hot for each other—she and Freddie had never locked themselves into a passionate embrace more than once in a twenty-four-hour period.

Freddie's reaction was a look of gentlemanly shock. He said, "Manette, good Lord. There are some things—"

"So you did. More than once. More than with Holly? Freddie, are you taking precautions?"

"I think we've talked enough about this," he replied with dignity.

"So what about tonight? Are you seeing someone else tonight? Who is it tonight?"

"Actually, I'm seeing Sarah again."

Manette crossed one leg over the other. She wished for a cigarette. She'd smoked when she was in her twenties and although she hadn't thought about cigarettes in years, she suddenly wanted the comfort of doing something with her hands. As it was, she reached for a container of paper clips and played with it. She said, "I'm curious about this. Since you've done it already and that's been got out of the way, what comes next? Family photos? Or do you get on to surnames and communicable diseases?"

He looked at her strangely. Manette reckoned he was evaluating her remark, weighing it and matching its weight to a response that equaled but did not exceed it. Before he could say what she knew he was about to say—"You're upset about this. Why? We've been divorced for ages and we've decided on friendship but I never intended to be celibate for the rest of my life"—she went on with, "Well, will you be home tonight at all or should I expect you to be spending it with Sarah again?"

He shrugged, but still his face maintained that expression, which was something stuck between curious and confused. He said, "I don't know, actually."

"Of course. How could you? Sorry. Anyway, I hope you bring her home. I'd like to meet her. Just give me fair warning so I don't show up at the breakfast table without my knickers on."

"Will do. Of course. I mean, the other night was rather a spontaneous thing. I mean, with Holly. I didn't quite know then how these things tend to develop. Now that I do . . . well, of course, there are arrangements, aren't there? And explanations and whatnot?"

It was Manette's turn to look curious. It wasn't like Freddie to stumble round with his words. She said, "What's going on? God, Freddie, you didn't run off and do something . . . something rather mad, did you?" She didn't know what that madness would have been. But madness of any kind was out of character for Freddie. He was an arrow, straight and true.

He said, "No, no. It's just that I didn't tell her about . . . well, about you."

"What? You didn't say you're divorced?"

"She knows that, of course. But I didn't tell her that you and I . . . well, that we live in the same house."

"Holly knew, though. That didn't seem to be a problem for her. Lots of blokes have female flatmates and such."

"Yes, of course. But Sarah . . . It felt different being with Sarah. It felt like a risk that I didn't want to take." He picked up the printouts and he tapped them neatly together on the top of his desk. He said, "I've been out of action for ages, Manette, as you well know. I'm going by feel with these women."

She said tartly, "I'm sure you are."

She'd actually come to his office to talk to him about Tim and Gracie and about her conversation with her father as well. But now, that conversation didn't feel right to Manette. And as Freddie himself had just pointed out, in a new situation one was wise to go by feel. She got to her feet.

She said, "I won't expect to see you, then. Just take care, all right? I wouldn't like to see you . . . I don't know . . . hurt or anything." Before he could reply, she got herself out of his office and set off in search of her brother. She told herself that Freddie had his own life and she had hers and it was time she did something about that latter fact, just as Freddie was doing. She didn't know what that something was going to be, though. She couldn't imagine launching herself into the unknown world of Internet dating. Into bed with total strangers to see if a proper fit existed? She shuddered. To her that seemed to be a recipe for being cooked in a serial killer's oven, but perhaps she'd been watching too many detective programmes on the telly over the years.

She found Nicholas in the shipping department, a warehouse that served as a modest step up from where he'd laboured the previous six months. Then he'd been working on the tops of cisterns, the bowls of toilets, and kitchen sinks, seeing to the application of porcelain to the moulded clay and sliding them into the enormous kiln. In that part of the factory, the heat was intolerable and the noise was just as bad, but Nicholas had been successful there. In fact, he'd been successful in every job he'd been placed in during the last two years.

Manette knew he was working his way through all possible jobs in the factory. She'd developed a grudging admiration for this although the *why* of his doing it gave her a bit of concern. Surely he couldn't think that a few years of puttering round Fairclough Industries superseded the decades she and Freddie had worked there? Surely he didn't expect to be named managing director once their father stepped aside? The thought was ludicrous.

Today's employment for Nicholas involved bathroom basins, Manette saw. At the loading dock, with a clipboard in one hand and a pen in the other, he was comparing sizes and styles on shipping boxes to sizes and styles on an order. The basins had been delivered on a pallet by a forklift. Once Nicholas had checked them off, he would load them into a waiting lorry, the driver of which had reversed it to the shipping gate and was waiting round, smoking and generally being unhelpful.

Because the huge shipping doors were open to the lorry, it was cold in the warehouse. It was noisy as well because there was music blasting from speakers in the building, as if someone's proclivity for Carlos Santana oldies might raise the ambient temperature a bit.

Manette approached her brother. He looked up and gave her a nod of hello. Above the music, she shouted, asking him if she could have a word. His response of, "It's not near my break time," irritated her.

She said, "For God's sake, Nick. I think you can take five minutes without being sacked."

"We have a shipment going out. He's waiting." By *he* Nicholas meant the lorry driver, who didn't look exactly desperate to be on his way. He'd gone to the driver's side of the lorry and had opened its door, true. But he emerged with a Thermos from which he poured himself something that steamed in the air. He looked happy enough for the break in his routine.

She said, "I need to speak to you. It's important. Ask permission if you want to. Or shall I do that for you?"

Her brother's supervisor was approaching anyway. He tilted his hard hat back on his head, greeted her, and called her Mrs. McGhie, which rather stabbed at her heart although it was indeed her legal surname. She said, "C'n I have a word with Nicholas, Mr. Perkins? It's rather important. A family matter." She said this last as a way of reminding the man—as if he needed reminding—who Nicholas was.

Mr. Perkins looked towards the lorry and clocked the lounging driver before saying, "Five, Nick," and moving off.

Manette led the way to a quieter location, which turned out to be round the side of the warehouse. This was the gathering place for smokers, she saw, for although none were present at the moment, the ground was littered with evidence of their presence. She made a mental note to talk to Freddie about this. Then she crossed out the note and made a second one telling herself to handle it on her own.

She said to her brother, "It's Tim and Gracie," and she gave him the story with all its ins and outs: Niamh's intentions, Kaveh's responsibilities, their father's position in the matter, Tim's distress, Gracie's future needs. She ended with, "We need to do something about all this, Nick. And we need to do it soon. If we wait, there's no telling what Tim might get up to. He's that damaged by what's gone on."

Her brother removed the gloves he was wearing. From a pocket, he took out a tube of thick lotion. He began to apply this to his hands. She gave idle thought to the reason for this: keeping them soft for Alatea, no doubt. Alatea was a woman for whom a man would want to have soft hands, indeed. Nicholas said, "Isn't it Niamh's job to handle how the children are coping and everything else along those lines?"

"Well of course it is, in the natural course of events. Mothers are the carers and their children receive the care. But Niamh's not going the natural course, not that she ever

has since Ian left her, as you very well know." Manette
watched her brother massage the lotion into his hands. For
nearly two years, he'd been doing manual labour not only
at the factory but also out on the pele project near Arnside,
but one would never know it from looking at his fingers, his
nails, and his palms. They were like a woman's, only larger.
"Someone has to step up to the mark. Believe it or not,
Niamh has every intention of leaving those children with
Kaveh Mehran."

"He's a good bloke, Kaveh. I quite like him. Don't you?"

"It's not *about* liking him. For God's sake, Nick, he's not
even their family. Look, I'm as liberal minded as anyone
and while they were living with their father, that was fine
by me. Better with Ian in a household where there was love
enough to go round than with Niamh breathing fire, brim-
stone, and revenge all over them. But it's not working out,
and Tim's—"

"It has to have time to work out, doesn't it?" Nick said.
"It seems to me that Ian's not been gone long enough for
anyone to decide what's best for his children."

"That may be the case, but in the meantime, they
should be with family. If not with their mother then with
one of us. Nick, I know there was no love lost between you
and Ian. He was hard on you. He didn't trust you. He
discouraged Dad from trusting you as well. But one of us
must provide those children with a sense of security, of
familiarity and—"

"Why not Mum and Dad, then? God knows they have
enough space at Ireleth Hall."

"I've spoken to Dad and got nowhere." Manette felt a
growing need to bend her brother's will to her own. This
should have been a simple matter because talking Nicholas
into something had always been child's play, which was one
of the reasons his youth had been such a troubled one. Anyone could have talked him into anything. She said, "Look,
I know what you're trying to do and I admire you for it. So
does Dad. So do we all. Well, except Mignon, but you're not
to take that personally since she doesn't know anyone exists
on the planet other than herself."

He glanced her way. He gave her a smile. He knew Mignon as well as she did.

She said, "This would be another plank in the structure you're building for yourself, Nick. If you do this—if you take the children—it makes your position stronger. It shows commitment. It shows how capable you are of taking on more responsibility. Plus, you're closer to Margaret Fox School than Kaveh and you can take Tim there on your way to work."

"Speaking of that," Nicholas pointed out, "you're closer to Margaret Fox School than I am. You're practically in the neighbourhood. Why not you, then?"

"Nick . . ." Manette knew she was going to have to tell him the truth, so she made it brief. Freddie and dating and the new world of sex as soon as possible, which ended up with previously unknown women at the breakfast table. Hardly a suitable situation into which one might bring children, was it?

Nicholas had kept his eyes fastened on her face as she told him this. He said, "I'm sorry," when she was finished, and he went on lest she think he was saying he was sorry as a way of refusing her request to take on the children. "I know what Freddie really means to you, Manette, even if you don't," were his words.

She looked away, blinking hard. She said, "Be that as it may . . . You see . . ."

"I've got to get back to work." He put his arm round her and kissed the side of her head. He said, "Let me talk to Allie about this, okay? Something's bothering her at the moment. I don't know what. She hasn't said yet, but she will. We don't have secrets between us, so she'll bring me into the picture in a bit. Until then, you'll have to give me some time, okay? I'm not saying no about Tim and Gracie."

ARNSIDE
CUMBRIA

He knew nothing about fishing, but that was hardly the
point. Zed Benjamin understood that the point was not to
catch fish or even hope to catch fish but rather to look like
he was fishing. So he'd borrowed a rod from the tottering
owner of his B & B, who gave him chapter and verse on her
late husband and the wasted hours he'd spent with his fishing line in the waters of this lake, that stream, or whatever
bay. She handed over a tackle basket, as well, along with a
slicker that fit Zed's arm but nothing else and a pair of Wel-
lingtons that were altogether useless to him. She pressed a
folding stool upon him and wished him luck. Her husband,
she told him, had had virtually none. According to her, the
man had caught fifteen fish in twenty-five years. He could
see the record if he wanted to because she'd kept it, every
time the bloody man left the house and returned empty-
handed. Could be he'd been having an affair, she said,
because when one really put one's head to the matter—

Zed had thanked her hastily and had driven to Arnside,
where he found, with thanks to God, that the tide was in.
He'd established himself on the seawall path, just beneath
Nicholas Fairclough's house, and there he'd cast his line into
the water. The line was baitless. The last thing he wanted
was actually to catch a fish and have to do something with
it. Like touch it.

Now that Scotland Yard knew that he was in the vicinity,
he had to take care. Once they clocked him—whoever *they*
were—his job was going to be even more difficult. He
needed to know exactly who they were—assuming it was a
they, because didn't they work in teams like on the telly?—
because if he could suss them out before they sussed him
out, his position to strike a deal was going to be a hell of a
lot stronger. For if they were here on the sly, then the last
thing they would want was to have their mugs printed on
the front page of *The Source*, alerting Nicholas Fairclough
to their presence, not to mention to their intentions.

Zed had reckoned they'd turn up at Arnside House eventually. He was there to take note when that occurred.

The stool had been an excellent idea. After he took up his position along the seawall, he alternated between standing and taking a load off as the hours passed. But nothing of a suspicious nature or any nature at all happened across the lawn at Arnside House, and he was growing rather desperate to learn something—*anything*—useful to his story when Alatea Fairclough finally came outside.

She walked straight towards him and his thought was Bloody, bloody, double bloody hell. He was about to be discovered before he'd learned a damn thing useful, and wasn't that just how his luck was running these days? But she stopped far short of the seawall and stood looking out at the endlessly undulating mass of the bay. Her expression was sombre. Zed reckoned she was thinking about all the people who'd met an untimely end in this area, like those poor Chinese sods—more than fifty of them—caught in the darkness in the incoming tide and phoning home like E.T., desperate for rescue that did not come. Or the bloke and his son caught by the tide and a sudden fog bank and disoriented round by foghorns that seemed to come from everywhere. Considering this, Zed reckoned the edge of Morecambe Bay was a perishing depressing place to live, and Alatea Fairclough looked about as perishing depressed as one could get.

Hell, he thought, was she considering the possibilities of offing herself out there in the treacherous waters? He hoped not. He'd be meant to rescue her, and they'd both likely die if it came to that.

He was too far to hear its ringing, but Alatea's mobile phone seemed to go off, because she took it from the jacket she was wearing and flipped it open. She spoke to someone. She began to pace. Ultimately, she looked at her watch, which glittered on her wrist even at this distance. She glanced round as if worried she might be observed and Zed ducked his head.

God, she was a beautiful woman, he thought. He couldn't understand how she had ended up here, in the back of beyond, when a woman like her belonged on a catwalk or at least in a catalogue wearing skimpy knickers like those Agent Provocateur models with their sumptuous bosoms bursting out of brassieres and the brassieres always matching their knickers and the knickers themselves showing lots and lots of firm and delicious thigh so that one could so easily imagine all the delights of—

Zed brought himself up short. What the hell was going *on* with him? He was being completely unfair to womankind, thinking like this. He was particularly being unfair to Yaffa, who was back in London working on his behalf and helping out with the insanity of his mother and . . . But what was the point of thinking about Yaffa since Micah was on the back burner of her life, studying medicine in Tel Aviv like the good son of a mother, which Zed himself was not?

He bashed his forehead with the heel of his palm. He took a chance and cast a look back at Alatea Fairclough. She was heading back towards the house now, her phone call finished.

For a time, that appeared to be the highlight of Zed's day. Wonderful, he thought. Another nought to add to the noughts of his accomplishments in Cumbria. He spent another two hours pretending to fish before he began to pack it in and consider what to do next.

Things changed, however, as he was trudging back in the direction of the Promenade and his car, which he'd left in Arnside village. He'd just reached the end of the seawall that defined the boundary of Arnside House when a car approached and made the turn into the driveway.

It was driven by a woman. She looked as if she knew where she was going. She pulled up to the front of the house and got out, and Zed crept—as well as a man six feet eight inches tall can actually creep—back the way he'd come.

Like him, she was a redhead. She was casually dressed in jeans, boots, and a thick wool sweater the colour of moss. He expected her to walk directly to the front door, some friend of Alatea's come to call, he reckoned. But she did not do so. Instead, she began to prowl round the house like a third-rate burglar. Moreover, she took out a digital camera from her shoulder bag and started taking pictures.

Ultimately, she approached the front door and rang the bell. She waited, looking round her as if to see if anyone—like Zed himself—might be lurking in the shrubbery. While she waited, she took out her mobile and seemed to check it for text messages or something. Then the front door opened and without an exchange of more than ten words, Alatea Fairclough let her into the house.

But she sure as bloody hell did not look happy about having to do so, Zed realised. He also realised with a surge of pure joy that his wait had paid off. He had the scoop he needed. He had the sex in the story. He had the identity of the detective sent up from London from New Scotland Yard.

ARNSIDE
CUMBRIA

When Alatea answered the door, Deborah instantly read the alarm in her expression. It was out of all proportion to the appearance on her doorstep of anyone other than a surprise visitor intent upon harming her, so for a moment Deborah was taken aback. She scrambled for words and came up with, "I have a feeling Mr. Fairclough isn't at home, but it's not Mr. Fairclough I need anyway."

This promptly made things worse. "What do you want?" Alatea said abruptly. She looked beyond Deborah's shoulder as if expecting someone else to come charging round the corner of the building. "Nicky's at work." She glanced at her watch, an enormous gold and rhinestone affair that suited her well but would have looked ridiculous on a woman less dramatic in appearance. "He'll be on his way to the pele project by now."

"Not a problem," Deborah said cheerfully. "I was taking some shots of the exterior, to give the producer an idea of setting and where he can conduct his interviews. The lawn'll work wonderfully, especially if the tide's in when they're here. But there's always a chance it'll be pouring buckets, isn't there? So I'm hoping to get some shots of the interior of the house as well. Would that be all right? I don't want to trouble you. It shouldn't take long. It'll be very informal."

Alatea's throat worked with a swallow. She didn't move from the doorway.

"A quarter of an hour, I expect." Deborah tried to sound jolly: nothing to fear from me. "It's the drawing room I'm interested in, actually. There's good ambient light and some background interest as well."

Reluctant didn't do justice to the manner in which Alatea admitted Deborah into the house. Deborah could feel tension virtually oozing from the woman, and she was forced to wonder if Alatea had a man other than her husband inside somewhere, playing at Polonius behind a convenient arras.

They went towards the yellow drawing room, passing the main hall, whose sliding doors were closed. These revealed more impressive panelling along with windows combining translucent glass and stained glass fashioned in the shape of red tulips and green leaves. Someone, Deborah decided, could indeed have been lurking in that room, but she couldn't imagine who it might be.

She made light chat. The house was remarkable, she told Alatea. Had it been featured in any magazines? The Arts and Crafts movement was so clean and sympathetic, wasn't it? Was Alatea interested at all in a documentary about the restoration of this building? Had she been approached by any of the myriad television programmes that featured period homes? To all of this, Alatea's answers were monosyllabic. Bonding with the woman was not going to be a simple matter, Deborah concluded.

In the drawing room, she switched to another topic. How did Alatea like living in England? It had to be very different from what she was used to in Argentina, Deborah expected.

Here, Alatea looked startled. "How do you know I'm from Argentina?"

"Your husband told me." Deborah wanted to add, Why? Is there a problem with your being from Argentina? but she did not. Instead, she examined the room. The object was to get Alatea over to the bay window where the magazines were, so Deborah took a few shots of prospective areas in which interviews could occur, easing over in that direction.

When she got there, though, the first thing she saw was that *Conception* was gone from the fan of journals. This was going to make things tricky but not impossible. Deborah took a photo of the two chairs and the low table in front of the bay window, adjusting for the light outside so as to show both interior and exterior equally. She said as she did so, "You and I have something in common, Mrs. Fairclough." She looked up from her camera and offered a smile.

Alatea was standing by the door as if ready to bolt. She gave a polite smile and looked supremely doubtful. If they had something in common, it was clear she hadn't a clue what it was, aside from being women who were, at the moment, standing in the same room of her house.

Deborah said, "We're both trying for a baby. Your husband told me. He saw I'd seen the magazine. *Conception*?" She added a helpful lie, "I've been reading it for ages. Well, for five years now. That's how long Simon and I—that's my husband—have been trying."

Alatea said nothing to this, but Deborah saw her swallow as her eyes moved to the table where the magazine had lain. Deborah wondered if she'd removed it herself or if Nicholas had done so. She wondered, too, if Nicholas worried about his wife's state of mind and state of body as Simon worried about her own.

She said, as she took another photo, "We started out au naturel, Simon and I, hoping that nature would take its course. We went from there to monitoring. Everything from my monthly cycles to my daily temperature to the phases of the moon." She forced a chuckle. It wasn't pleasant to reveal this sort of thing to anyone, but Deborah saw the importance of doing so and, even, the potential for comfort that such a revelation could bring. "Then, there were the tests," she said, "which Simon less than adored, I can tell you. After that were the endless discussions about alternatives, visits to specialists, and talks about the other possibilities for parenthood." She paused in her photographing to say to Alatea with a shrug, "Turns out I'll never carry a baby to term. Something's wrong with the way I was manufactured. We're onto adoption now, or something else. I'd like surrogacy but Simon's not on board."

The Argentine woman had come into the room, closer now but still at a distance. Her colour had altered, Deborah saw, and she was clasping and unclasping her elegant hands. Her eyes were bright with unshed tears.

Deborah knew what she was looking at. She'd felt the same for years. She said quickly, "I'm terribly sorry. As I said, I saw the magazine when I was here earlier. Your husband said you and he were trying. He said you'd been married two years, and . . . Mrs. Fairclough, I'm *very* sorry. I hadn't meant to upset you. Please. Here. Sit down."

Alatea did sit, although not where Deborah would have wished it. She chose the inglenook of the fireplace, a padded seat just beneath a stained glass window that sent light streaming onto her crinkly hair. Deborah approached her but remained a safe distance, saying, "It's difficult. I know. I actually lost six before I found out the truth about my body. They might be able to do something about it someday, all things about science considered. But by then I'll probably be too old."

A tear streaked down Alatea's cheek. She adjusted her position, as if this would keep her from shedding more tears in front of a relative stranger.

Deborah said, "I find it odd that something so simple for some women is a complete impossibility for others."

Deborah kept expecting the other woman to respond in some way other than with tears, to admit to a fellow feeling somehow. But Alatea did not, and the only thing left was for Deborah to admit the *why* behind her intense desire to have a child, which had to do in part with the fact that her husband was disabled—*a cripple*, he called himself—and in part with what that disabling had done to his sense of himself as a man. But she had no intention of going to that place in conversation with Alatea Fairclough. It was difficult enough admitting it to herself.

So she settled on another course altogether. She said, "I think this room has better possibilities for a filmed interview than what I saw outside. And actually, where you're sitting is a wonderful location, because of the light. If you wouldn't mind, I'd like to take a quick photo of you there to illustrate—"

"No!" Alatea leapt to her feet.

Deborah took a step backwards. "It's for—"

"No! No! Tell me who you are!" Alatea cried. "Tell me why you're really here! Tell me, *tell* me!"

7 NOVEMBER

Tim hoped it was Toy4You when his mobile chimed because he was sick with the waiting. But it was bloody stupid Manette. She acted as if he'd done nothing to her. She said she was ringing to talk about their camping adventure. That was what she called it—an *adventure*—as if they were going to Africa or something and not where they would probably end up, which was in someone's bloody paddock, where they'd be cheek by jowl with sodding tourists from Manchester. She said cheerfully, "Let's get the date into our diaries, shall we? We'll want to go before it gets much later in the year. We can cope with the rain, but if it snows, we're done for. What d'you say?"

What he said was, "Why don't you leave me alone?"

She said, "Tim . . . ," in that patient voice adults tended to use when they thought he was barking, which was most of the time.

He said, "Look. Drop it. All this bollocks about you 'care about' me."

"I *do* care about you. We all care about you. Good grief, Tim, you're—"

"Don't give me that shit. All you ever cared about was my father and don't you think I know that? All *anyone* cared about was that filthy bastard and he's dead and I'm glad so leave me alone."

"You don't mean any of that."

"I bloody well do."

"No. You don't. You loved your father. He hurt you badly, but it wasn't really about you, dearest, what he did." She waited, as if for a reply from him, but he wouldn't give her the satisfaction of hearing *anything* in his voice. She said, "Tim, I'm sorry it happened. But he wouldn't have done it if he could have seen any other way to live with himself. You don't understand that now, but you will. Truly. You *will* someday."

"You don't know what the fuck you're talking about."

"I know this is difficult for you, Tim. How could it be otherwise? But your father adored you. We all love you. Your family—all of us—want you to be—"

"Shut up!" he screamed. "Leave me alone!"

He ended the call with his insides raging. It was her tone, that bloody soothing, motherly tone of hers. It was what she said. It was everything in his life.

He threw his mobile onto his bed. His body felt strung as tight as part of a high-wire act. He needed air. He went to the window of his bedroom and forced it open. It was cold outside but who bloody cared?

Outside across the farmyard, George Cowley and Dan came out of their cottage. They were talking, heads bent as if what they were saying to each other was of deadly importance. Then they approached George's wreck of a car: a Land Rover thoroughly crusted with mud, not to mention sheep shit, which was thick in its tyre treads.

George opened the driver's door and hauled himself inside, but Daniel didn't go round and get in as well. Instead, he squatted next to the door and fixed his attention on the pedals and his father's feet. George spoke and gestured and worked the pedals. Up, down, in, out, whatever. He climbed out of the wreck and Dan got in, in his place. Dan worked the pedals in a similar fashion while George nodded, gestured, and nodded some more.

Dan started the ignition then, as his father continued to talk to him. George closed the door and Dan rolled down the window. The vehicle was parked in such a way that he didn't need to reverse it to set it going, and George gestured round the triangular green. Dan set off. First time with the clutch, the accelerator, and the brakes, he went in fits, starts, and lurches. George ran alongside the vehicle like a third-rate carjacker, shouting and waving his arms. The Land Rover got ahead of him, lurched, and stalled.

George dashed over, said a few words into the driver's window, and reached inside. Watching this, Tim reckoned the farmer was going to give Dan a smack on the head, but what George did was ruffle his hair and laugh and Dan laughed as well. He started the Land Rover again. They went through the process a second time, this time with George remaining behind and shouting encouragement. Dan did a better job and George punched the air.

Tim turned from the window. Stupid gits, he thought. Two lame bastards. Like father like son. Dan'd end up just like his dad, walking in sheep shit somewhere. Loser, he was. Double loser. Triple. He was *such* a loser that he needed to be wiped from the face of the earth and Tim wanted to do it. Now. At once. Without a pause. Storming from the house with a gun or a knife or a club, only he had none of these and he needed them so badly, the worst, how he wanted . . .

Tim strode from his room. He heard Gracie's voice and Kaveh's answer, and he went in that direction. He found them in the picture room at the top of the stairs, an alcove that Kaveh used for his office. The bugger was sitting at a drafting table working on something and Gracie—dumb old stupid Gracie—was at his feet with that bloody stupid doll in her arms and wasn't she even *rocking* it and *crooning* to it and didn't she need to be brought to her senses and wasn't it time she just *grew* up anyway and what better way to do it—

Gracie screamed like he'd stuck her in the arse with a pole when he grabbed the doll. He said, "Fucking bloody idiot, for God's sake," and he slammed the doll against the edge of the drafting table before he pulled off her arms and her legs and threw her down. He snarled, "Grow up and get a life, you freak," and he spun and made for the stairs.

He stormed down them and out of the door and behind him he heard Gracie's cries, which should have felt good to him but didn't. And then there was Kaveh's voice calling his name and the sound of Kaveh coming after him. Kaveh of all people, Kaveh who'd created this whole pile of shit that was his life.

He thudded past George Cowley and Daniel, who were standing by the Land Rover, and while he didn't need even to go near them, he did anyway, just so he could shove that limp-wrist Daniel out of the way. George yelled, "Just you bloody—"

"Fuck you!" Tim cut in. He needed, he wanted, he *had* to find something because everything was cresting inside of him, his very blood was cresting and he knew if he didn't find something, his head would explode and the blood and the brains would surge out of him and while that didn't matter a whit he didn't want it to be this way and there was Kaveh calling his name, telling him to stop telling him to wait only that was the last thing he'd ever do: wait for Kaveh Mehran.

Around the side of the pub and through a garden and there was Bryan Beck. On the stream the village ducks floated and on the opposite bank wild mallards rooted through the heavy-topped grass for slugs or worms or whatever the hell it was that they ate and oh God how he wanted to feel one of them all of them crushed beneath his fist or his feet it didn't matter just to have something die die die.

Tim was in the water without knowing he was in the water. The ducks scattered. He flailed at them. Shouting was coming from every direction and some of it he realised was coming from him and then he was grabbed. Strong arms came round him and a voice in his ear said, "No. You mustn't. You don't mean to. It's all right."

And goddamn, it was the bumboy himself, the limp wrist, the queer. He had his arms and his hands on Tim and he was *holding* him God he was actually holding him touching him the filth the filth the filth.

"Get away!" Tim shrieked. He fought. Kaveh held on harder.

"Tim. Stop!" Kaveh cried. "You don't mean to do this. Come away. Quickly."

They wrestled in the water like two greased monkeys till Tim squirmed away and Kaveh fell back. He landed on his bum and the frigid water was up to his waist and he was struggling to get back to his feet and Tim felt such triumph because what he wanted was the stupid git struggling, he wanted to show him, he wanted to prove—

"I'm not a butt fucker," he screamed. "Keep your fucking hands off me. You hear me? Find someone else."

Kaveh watched him. He was breathing hard and so was Tim, but something came over his face and what it was not was what Tim wanted it to be, which was hurt, devastation, destruction.

Kaveh said, "Of *course* you're not, Tim. Did you think you might be?"

"Shut up!" Tim yelled in reply. He turned and ran.

He left Kaveh sitting in Bryan Beck, water to his waist, watching him run.

GREAT URSWICK
CUMBRIA

Manette had managed to get the tent raised by herself. It hadn't been easy and although she had always been excessively competent when it came to anything that required her to follow instructions, she hadn't done her usual perfect job with erecting the poles and the canvas, not to mention plunging the stakes into the ground, so she reckoned the whole thing would collapse on her. But she crawled inside anyway and sat Buddha-like in the opening, facing the pond at the bottom of the garden.

Freddie had knocked on her bathroom door and said he needed to speak with her. She'd said of course and could he give her a few minutes. She was just . . . whatever. He hurriedly said *absolutely* as if the last thing he wanted to know was what she was doing in the bathroom and who could blame him, really. There were some forms of intimacy that were far too intimate.

She hadn't been doing anything. She'd been killing time. She'd sensed something was going on with Freddie when they'd met at the coffeemaker midmorning. She'd come down from her room; he'd come in from outside and since he'd entered wearing what he'd been wearing the previous day, she knew he'd spent the night with Sarah. Wily one, that Sarah, Manette reckoned. She knew a gem when she saw it.

So when Freddie asked to speak with her, she reckoned the boom was going to fall. He'd seen in Sarah a potential to be the One or perhaps, Manette thought wryly, the Two, since she herself had been the One. At any rate, he probably wanted to bring her home this very night or move her into the house soon, and she wondered how she was going to cope with that.

Obviously, they'd have to sell the house and go their separate ways. She didn't want to do that because she loved this place. Not so much the house, which, admittedly, was rather pokey, but this particular little spot that had been her haven for years. It was, indeed, all about the place itself and having to leave it . . . this disquiet she was feeling. It was about the silence of Great Urswick, about the canopy of stars that hung above the village at night. It was about the pond and the resident swans that floated placidly on it and only occasionally went after an overly enthusiastic dog who stupidly tried to chase them. And it was about the old paint-flecked rowing boat tied to the dock and the fact that she could take it out onto the water and watch the sunrise or the sunset or sit in the rain if she wanted to.

She supposed it was really all about roots, having them planted somewhere and not wanting them to be torn out because transplanting often killed the plant and she didn't know what it was going to feel like when she herself had to move on.

This wasn't about Freddie, she told herself. This wasn't about Sarah or any other woman Freddie might finally choose. How could it be when she herself had been the one to bring up the spark and how they had lost it, she and Freddie? It was absolutely, utterly, and irrevocably gone and didn't he agree with her, at heart?

Manette couldn't recall the expression on Freddie's face when she had initiated this painful conversation. Had he disagreed? She couldn't remember. He was always so bloody *affable* about everything. It should have come as no surprise to her that he'd been equally affable about the idea that their marriage was as dead as roadkill. And she'd been relieved, then. Now, however, she couldn't remember why on earth she'd been so relieved. What had she been expecting of marriage, after all? High drama, sparks, and falling all over each other like randy teenagers every night? Who could sustain that? Who would want to?

"You and Freddie?" Mignon had said. "*Divorcing?* You'd better have a long look at what's out there these days before you take that step."

But this wasn't about trading Freddie in for a different model. Manette had no interest in that. It was just about being realistic, about looking squarely at the life she had and evaluating its potential for going the distance. As they'd been—best friends who occasionally made the time for a pleasant encounter between the sheets—they hadn't stood a chance of lasting. She knew it, he knew it, and they'd had to deal with it. That was what they'd done and they'd both been relieved to have it out in the open. Hadn't they?

"Here you are. What the devil are you doing out here, old girl?"

She roused herself. Freddie had come to find her, and he bore in his hands two mugs. He squatted by the tent opening and handed one over. She began to crawl out but he said, "Hang on. I've not been inside a tent in years." He crawled in to join her. He said, "That pole's going to go down, Manette," with a nod in the general direction of the troublesome part of the structure.

She said, "I could tell. One strong gust of wind, and it's over. Good place to think, though. And I wanted a trial run."

"Not at all necessary," he said. He sat next to her, Indian style, and she noted he was flexible enough to do the same as she: His knees went all the way to the ground, not like some people who couldn't manage that because they were far too stiff.

She took a sip of what he'd brought her. Chicken broth. Interesting choice, as if she were ill. She said, "Not necessary?"

"Decamping," he said, "if you'll pardon the pun. Deciding upon the out-of-doors just in case."

She frowned. "Freddie, what are you talking about?"

He cocked his head. His brown eyes seemed to twinkle at her, so she knew he was joking about something and she hated not to be in on the joke. He said, "You know. The other night? Holly? That was a one-off. Won't happen again."

She said, "You giving it up or something?"

"The dating? Good God, no." And then he blushed that Freddie blush. "I mean, I'm rather enjoying it. I'd no idea women had become so . . . so forthright in the years I was out of action. Not that I'd really been *in* action."

"Thank you very much," she said sourly.

"No, no. I didn't mean . . . What I *did* mean is that you and I, having started so young, having been together from the word go, more or less . . . You were my first, you know. My only, as a matter of fact. So to see what's going on in the real world . . . It's an eye opener, I can tell you. Well, of course you'll see for yourself soon enough."

She said, "Not sure I want to."

"Oh." He was silent. He sipped his chicken broth. She liked the fact that he'd never made any noise when he sipped. She loathed the sound of people slurping, and Freddie, for one, had *never* slurped. "Well. Anyway."

She said, "Anyway yourself. And I have no right to ask you not to bring women home, Freddie. Never fear. A heads-up would be nice, though. A phone call when she goes to the ladies or something, but even that's not compulsory."

"I know that," he said, "the thing about rights and the like. But I also know how I'd feel if I came downstairs and found some bloke dipping into a bowl of cornflakes in the morning. Bit odd, that. So mostly I'll be suggesting we meet off the beaten track, not round here. You know."

"Like Sarah."

"Like Sarah. Right."

Manette tried to read something in his voice, but she wasn't able to. She wondered if she'd ever actually succeeded in reading his voice at all. It was odd to think of it, but did one ever really know one's spouse? she wondered, and then she brought herself up short and moved away from the thought because what Freddie wasn't and hadn't been for quite a while was her spouse.

After a moment of silence broken by the sound of ducks honking from the air above them, Freddie said, "Where'd this come from, anyway?" in reference to the tent. "It's new, isn't it?"

She told him about her plans for the tent: camping with Tim, walking the fells, ending up on Scout Scar. She ended with, "Let's put it this way: He didn't enthuse when I suggested it."

"Poor kid," was Freddie's response. "What a life he's been having, eh?"

That was putting it featherlike, she thought. What in God's name was going to happen to Tim? To Gracie? To their world? She knew that if the situation in her life were different, she and Freddie would take them. She'd have made the suggestion and Freddie would have said of course, without a second thought. But she could hardly ask that of Freddie now and even if she could, she could hardly bring the children into a home where they might stumble into a strange woman walking the hallway at night in search of the loo because even if Freddie said he wouldn't be bringing Sarah or Holly or whomever else home for a trial run, there was always a chance that in the heat of the moment, he'd forget that promise. She couldn't risk it.

Out on the pond, the two resident swans came into view. Majestic and tranquil, they seemed to move without effort. Manette watched them and next to her she felt Freddie doing the same. He finally spoke again, and his tone was thoughtful.

"Manette, I've begun dealing with Ian's accounting programme."

"I did notice," she said.

"Yes. Well. I've found something there. Several things,

actually, and I'm not sure what to make of them. To be frank, I'm not sure whether they're important at all, but they need sorting out."

"What kind of things?"

Freddie moved to face her. He looked hesitant. She said his name and he went on with, "Did you know your father financed everything having to do with Arnside House?"

"He bought it as a wedding gift for Nicholas and Alatea."

"Yes, of course. But he's also paid for the entire renovation. And it's been expensive. Extremely expensive, as these things generally are, I suppose. Have you any idea why he's done that?"

She shook her head. "Is it important? Dad has gobs of money."

"True enough. But I can't imagine Ian didn't try to talk him out of tossing so much Nick's way without some sort of scheme for repayment, even if the repayment was to take a century and be made without interest. And it wouldn't have been like Ian not to have documented something like that. There's also the not-so-small matter of Nick's past. Handing so much money over to an addict . . . ?"

"I doubt Dad handed him the money, Freddie. More likely he just paid the bills. And he's a former addict, not a current addict."

"Nick himself wouldn't say *former*. That's why he takes such care about going to his meetings. But Ian wouldn't have known that and he wouldn't have thought *former*. Not with Nick's history."

"I suppose. But still . . . Nicholas stands to inherit *something* from Dad. Perhaps their arrangement was for him to enjoy his inheritance now, for Dad to see him enjoying it."

Freddie didn't look at all convinced. "D'you know he's also been paying Mignon an allowance for years?"

"What else is he supposed to do? She's had him by the short hairs ever since she fell at Launchy Gill. Honestly, you'd think Dad pushed her. He probably should have done."

"The monthly payments have increased recently."

"Cost of living?"

"What sort of cost of living does she have? And they've

increased a lot. They've doubled. And there's no way Ian would have approved of that. He had to have protested. He had to have argued not to do it at all."

Manette considered this. She knew Freddie was right. But there were matters concerning Mignon that he'd never understood. She said, "She's had that surgery, though. It wouldn't have been on the NHS. Someone would have had to pay and who else besides Dad?"

"Those payments would have been made to the surgeon, wouldn't they? These weren't."

"Perhaps they were made to Mignon so that she could pay the surgeon herself."

"Then why keep making them? Why keep paying her?"

Manette shook her head. The truth was: She didn't know. She was silent. So was Freddie. Then he sighed and she knew something more was coming. She asked what it was. He took a slow breath.

"Whatever happened to Vivienne Tully?" he said.

She looked at him but he wasn't looking back. He was instead focused on those two swans on the pond. She said, "I've absolutely no idea? Why?"

"Because for the last eight years, regular payments have gone to her as well."

"Whatever for?"

"I haven't a clue. But your father's actually been bleeding money, Manette. And as far as I can tell, Ian was the only one who knew."

CHALK FARM TO MARYLEBONE
LONDON

Barbara Havers was indulging in a snack when Angelina Upman and her daughter knocked on her door. The snack was a blueberry Pop-Tart with a side helping of cottage cheese—one needed to address at least three food groups with every meal, and this seemed to wander in the general direction of more than one food group as far as she was concerned—and Barbara crammed the rest of the pastry into her mouth before she answered the door. She could hear Hadiyyah's excited voice outside, and it was better to look virtuous with cottage cheese rather than despicable with a Pop-Tart, she reckoned.

She was also smoking. Hadiyyah took note of this. One look past Barbara and she was tapping her foot at the sight of the fag smouldering in an ashtray on the table. She shook her head but said nothing. She looked up at her mother, the virtuous nonsmoker, as if to say, You see what I'm dealing with here?

Angelina said, "We're messengers bearing both good news and bad news. May we come in, Barbara?"

God no, Barbara thought. She'd so far managed to keep Angelina out of her hovel and she'd intended to keep things that way. She'd not made the daybed, she'd not done the washing up, and she had five pairs of knickers drying on a line that she'd jerry-rigged over her kitchen sink. But really, how could she step outside into the November cold to see why Angelina and her daughter had appeared on her door-step instead of doing what Angelina herself would have done, which was open the door wide, offer coffee and tea, and be gracious to the unexpected caller?

So she stepped back and said, "Caught me just about to begin the housework," such a blatant lie that she nearly choked on it.

Hadiyyah looked doubtful but Angelina didn't know Barbara well enough to realise that, for her, housework was akin to pulling out one's eyelashes a single lash at a time.

Barbara said, "Coffee? Tea? I c'n wash a couple of the mugs," of which there were ten in the sink, along with various other bits of crockery and a pile of cutlery.

"No. No. We can't stay," Angelina said hastily. "But I did want to tell you about Dusty."

Who the hell . . . ? Barbara wondered, till she remembered that this was the name of the hairstylist in Knightsbridge who was destined to alter her appearance forevermore. "Oh, yeah," she said. She went to the table and hastily crushed out her fag.

"I've got you an appointment with him," Angelina said, "but it's not for a month, I'm afraid. He's booked. Well, he's always booked. That's the nature of success for a hairstylist. Everyone wants in to see him yesterday."

"Hair crises, yeah," Barbara said sagely, as if she knew something about this topic. "Damn. Too bad."

"Too bad?" Hadiyyah echoed. "But, Barbara, you must see him. He's the best. He'll do such a lovely job."

"Oh, I've got that point on a slice of toast, kiddo," Barbara agreed. "But I've told my guv that I'm off work getting my hair seen to, and I can't be off work for a month and I can't show up *without* my hair seen to. So . . ." And to Angelina, "Know anyone else?" because she herself certainly did not.

Angelina looked thoughtful. One perfectly manicured hand went to her cheek and she tapped upon it. She said, "You know, I think something could be managed, Barbara. It wouldn't be Dusty but it would be the same salon. He's got hangers-on there, stylists in training . . . Perhaps one of them? If I can get you in and if I went with you, I'm sure Dusty could have a wander across the salon to inspect what the stylist is doing. Would that work?"

Considering she'd spent the last ten years hacking her hair off in the shower, anything moderately more professional would be just fine. Still, Barbara thought it wise to sound somewhat uneasy about this prospect. She said, "Hmm . . . I don't know . . . What d'you think? I mean, this is important because my guv . . . She takes this stuff seriously."

"I expect it would be fine," Angelina said. "The salon's top-notch. They're not going to have just anyone in training. Shall I . . . ?"

"Oh yes, Barbara," Hadiyyah said. "Do say yes. P'rhaps we can all go to tea afterwards. We can dress up and wear hats and carry nice handbags and—"

"I don't think anyone wears hats to tea any longer," Angelina cut in. Clearly, Barbara thought, she'd read the expression of horror that had flitted across Barbara's face. She said, "What do you say, Barbara?"

Barbara really had no choice in the matter since she was going to have to turn up at the Met with a hairstyle and unless someone with some training did it, she was going to have to do it herself, which was unthinkable at this point.

She said, "Sounds good," and Angelina asked if she could use the phone. She'd make the call right from Barbara's, she said. That way they wouldn't need to engage in more backing and forthing in the matter.

Hadiyyah bounced over to where the phone was, behind the telly on a dusty shelf, and Barbara noted then that the little girl's own hair was not done in plaits as it usually was. Instead, it hung down her back in a well-brushed wavy mass, and it was neatly fastened with an ornate hair slide.

As Angelina was making her call to the salon, Barbara complimented Hadiyyah on her own locks. Hadiyyah beamed, as Barbara had reckoned she would. Mummy had done it, she said. Dad had only *ever* been able to manage plaits but this was how she'd worn it *always* before Mummy's trip to Canada.

Barbara wondered if Hadiyyah had been wearing her hair like this ever since Angelina's return, which had occurred four months earlier. God, if that was the case, what did it say about her, that she'd only noticed it just now? Barbara avoided the answer to that question, since she knew it was going to tell her that for that last four months she'd had her attention focused on Angelina herself and, worse, on Angelina and Taymullah Azhar.

"Excellent, excellent," Angelina was saying into the phone. "We shall be there. And you're certain Cedric—"

Cedric? Barbara thought.

"—will do a good job? . . . Wonderful . . . Yes, thank you. We'll see you then." Then to Barbara once she'd rung off, "We're set for three this afternoon. Dusty'll come over and give his input as well. Just remember to ignore his appalling attitude and don't take it personally. And afterwards, we'll take up Hadiyyah's idea of tea. We'll take a cab and do things properly at the Dorchester. My treat, by the way."

"Tea at the Dorchester?" Hadiyyah cried. She clasped her hands to her chest. "Oh yes, yes, yes. Do say yes, Barbara."

Barbara wanted to go to tea at the Dorchester as much as she wanted to give birth to octuplets. But Hadiyyah was looking so hopeful and, after all, Angelina had been very helpful. What else could she do?

"Tea at the Dorchester it is," she said, although she wondered what in God's name she was going to wear and how in God's name she'd survive the experience.

Once those plans were set in stone, Barbara bade her friends farewell, made herself relatively decent in appearance, and took herself over to Portland Place and Twins, Bernard Fairclough's club. She reckoned that chances were good Lord Fairclough parked himself at the club when he was in London. If that was the case, it was likely that someone who worked there would have beans to spill about the bloke if there were any beans involved.

Barbara had never been into a private club, so she wasn't sure what to expect. She was reckoning on cigar smoke and blokes walking around in Persian slippers and the sound of billiard balls clicking sonorously somewhere. She figured there would be leather wingback chairs drawn up to a fireplace and dog-eared copies of *Punch* lying about.

What she didn't expect was the ancient woman who answered the door when she rang the bell. The woman looked like someone who'd worked there since the club's inception. Her face wasn't lined; it was creviced. Her skin was tissue and her eyes were cloudy. And it seemed she'd forgotten to put in her teeth. Or she didn't have any and didn't want false ones. A possible way to diet, Barbara noted.

She might have been two thousand years old, but she was shrewd. She took one look at Barbara—head to toe—and seemed deeply unimpressed. She said, "No admittance to nonmembers without the company of a member, dear," in the voice of a woman fifty years younger. Indeed so disconcerting was it to hear her speak that Barbara had to prevent herself from looking round for a lurking ventriloquist.

Barbara said, "I was hoping to apply," to get her foot in the door. Over the woman's shoulder she could catch a glimpse of panelled walls and paintings, but that was it.

"This is a gentleman's club," she was then informed. "Women are admitted only in the company of a gentleman member, I'm afraid. Dining room only, dear. And to use the facilities, of course."

Well, that wasn't going to get her anywhere, Barbara

reckoned, so she nodded and said, "There's another matter, then," and fished out her Scotland Yard identification. "Afraid I have a few questions about one of your members, if I could come inside."

"You said you were interested in membership," the old lady pointed out. "Which is it, really? Membership or questions?"

"Both, more or less. But looks like membership isn't going to happen, so I'll settle for questions. I'd prefer not to ask them on the doorstep, though." She took a step forward.

This usually worked, but it didn't work now. The old lady held her position. She said, "Questions about what?"

"I'll need to ask them of whoever's in charge," Barbara said. "If you'll just track him down . . . ? I'll wait in the lobby. Or wherever you put the cops when they come calling."

"No one's in charge. There's a board and it's made up of members and if you wish to speak to one of them, you'll have to return on their meeting day next month."

"Sorry. That can't happen," Barbara told her. "It's a matter of a police investigation."

"And this is a matter of club rules," the lady said. "Shall I phone the club's solicitor and have him come round? Because, my dear, that's the only way you're getting in this door, aside from running straight through me."

Damn, Barbara thought. The woman gave new definition to *tough old bird*.

Barbara said, "Look, I'm going to be straight with you. I have serious questions to ask about one of your members and this could be a matter of murder."

"I see." The woman considered this, her head cocked to one side. Her hair was thick and completely white. Barbara reckoned she was wearing a wig. One didn't get this old with all the follicles still churning. "Well, my dear," the woman said, "when *could be a matter* becomes *is a matter*, we'll have something to discuss. Until then, we don't."

That said, she stepped back and closed the door. Barbara was left on the step, realising she'd lost the battle because she'd used a bloody conditional verb.

She swore and fished a packet of Players out of her bag.

She lit up and considered her next move. There had to be someone else who worked in this place, someone with information to impart: a chef, a cook, a waiter, a cleaner. Surely, the old bag didn't run the place on her own.

She descended the steps and looked back at the building. It was perfectly shut up and forbidding, a fortress for its members' secrets.

She glanced around. Perhaps, she thought, there was another way. A shop with a curious shop assistant inside, gaping out of the window at the well-heeled as they arrived and entered the club? A florist who made regular deliveries through the front door? A tobacconist selling members snuff or cigars? But there seemed to be nothing at all aside from a taxi rank on Portland Place, not far from BBC Broadcasting House.

She decided a taxi rank was possible. Drivers of cabs probably had their favourite routes and their favourite ranks. They'd know where the pickings were best and they'd haunt that area. If that was the case, it stood to reason that a cab driver could as easily cart a member of Twins somewhere as he could cart someone ducking out of the BBC.

She walked over to have a chat. The first three drivers in the line got her nowhere. The fourth was her lucky charm. The driver sounded like an extra from *EastEnders*. Barbara reckoned he spent his Sundays shouting "Pound a bowl" in the vicinity of the Brick Lane market.

He knew Lord Fairclough. He knew "most them toffs," he said. He liked to chat to them cos it rankled 'em, it did, and he liked to see how long it'd take 'em to tell 'im to plug his mug. Fairclough was always ready for a chat, when he was alone. When someone was wif him, things was diff'rent.

The *someone was with him* piqued Barbara's interest. Anyone special with him? she asked.

Oh, aye, the cab driver told her. Al'as the same bird, it was.

His wife? Barbara asked.

The cab driver guffawed.

Remember where you took him and the bird, then? she asked.

The driver smirked. He tapped his head, the repository

of all knowledge including the Knowledge. He said that course he remembered cos it was al'as the same place. And, he added with a wink, the bird was a young'n.

Better and better, Barbara thought. Bernard Fairclough and a young woman always going by taxi to the same place after meeting at his club. She asked the driver if he could take her to that place now.

He glanced at the rank of taxis ahead of him and she knew what that meant. He couldn't move off with a passenger until it was his turn or there would be hell to pay. She said she'd wait till he was at the head of the line but could he take her to the exact place and show her where Fairclough and his companion went? She showed her ID. Police business, she told him.

He said, "You got the fare?" and when she nodded, "Climb in, then, darlin'. I'm your man."

MILNTHORPE TO LAKE WINDERMERE
CUMBRIA

"Don't you see what all of this means, Simon?"

Whenever Deborah said that to him, St. James knew to take care in their conversation. She intended to attach something to the conclusion of her remarks, and in this situation what she intended to attach could put her into a dangerous position. So he said, "I don't, actually, my love. What I see is that while you were talking to her, Alatea Fairclough became upset for reasons that aren't completely clear, but those reasons don't seem to have anything to do with Ian Cresswell's death. The best course is for you to return the call from her husband and tell him something's come up and you've got to go back to London."

"Without seeing what he *wants*?" Deborah's tone was incredulous and her expression suspicious. In the way of most husbands and wives, Deborah would know his weak spots. She would also know his weakest spot was Deborah herself. "Why on earth should I do that?"

"You yourself said she knows you're not who you said

you were. You can't think she hasn't told Nicholas that. If he rang you and said he'd like a word—which he did, yes?—he's going to want that word to be about the state his wife was in when you left her."

"That's what *you* would want to talk about. *He* might want to talk to me about a dozen things. And I'm not going to know what they are unless I ring him back and agree to see him."

They were standing in the car park of the Crow and Eagle, next to his hire car, and he was due to meet Lynley at Ireleth Hall. He wasn't at this point late, but if the conversation went on much longer he was going to be. Deborah had followed him down from their room because although he'd considered their conversation finished, she had not. She was dressed to go out and this was not a good sign. She hadn't brought her shoulder bag or camera, however, so this counted in his favour.

Deborah had given him chapter and verse on her encounter with Alatea Fairclough, and as far as he was concerned Deborah's cover was blown, and it was time for her to back away from the situation. Deborah's point was that the Argentine woman's reaction had been so extreme that she had to be hiding something. Her additional point was that if Alatea was indeed hiding something, chances were very good that her husband didn't know what it was. So the only way she was going to discover what was truly going on was to speak with the man.

St. James had pointed out that, according to Lynley, a reporter from *The Source* had been nosing round the area as well, so that—in combination with a photographer who wasn't who she'd said she was—certainly would be enough to unnerve Alatea Fairclough. What did Deborah think she was hiding, anyway, a Nazi in her past? She was, after all, from Argentina.

Fiddlesticks, Deborah said.

Fiddlesticks? St. James thought. What sort of word was *fiddlesticks* in this century and what did *fiddlesticks* have to do with anything? He was wise enough not to say that, however. Instead, he waited for more, and true to form his wife didn't disappoint him.

Deborah said, "I think all of this has to do with the magazine, Simon. Alatea was perfectly fine—well, a little nervous, but otherwise fine—until I brought up *Conception*. I was attempting to get a little closer to her, I told her just a bit about our difficulties with pregnancy, and that was it. She went a bit wild and—"

"We've been over this, Deborah," he said patiently. "You can see where it leads, can't you? Her husband arrives home, she tells him you aren't who you say you are, he rings you and wants to have a chat, and that chat is going to tell you that the cover you're using to slip into his life—"

"I *told* her I was a freelance photographer. I told her what that means. I told her I was hired by Query Productions, which is a start-up company with no films made yet. I thought of that in the heat of the moment, by the way, because her next step is going to be to learn there is no start-up company called Query Productions at all, and you and I know it. I can handle meeting with Nicholas if I was able to handle that."

"You're in a very bad position," he concluded with his hand on the door handle of the car. "You need to leave this alone." He didn't say he forbade her doing more. He didn't say he wished her to do no more. Their years of marriage had taught him that in that way lay madness, so he tried to ease her in the general direction of this conclusion. At the end of the day, it was losing her that terrified him, but he couldn't say that since her next move would be to say that he wasn't going to lose her, which would lead to *his* next move, which would be about Helen's death and the crater in Tommy's life that Helen's death had caused. And he didn't want to go anywhere near Helen's death. It was too raw a place for him ever to speak of, and he knew very well that it always would be.

She said, "I can take care of myself. What's he going to do? Push me from a cliff? Knock me on the head? Something's going on with Alatea and I'm inches from knowing what it is. If it's something big and if Ian Cresswell found out about it . . . Don't you see?"

The trouble was that he did see, only too well. But he couldn't say that because it would lead only to a conclusion that he didn't want to reach, so what he did say was, "I shouldn't be long. We'll talk more when I return, all right?"

Her face wore That Look. God in heaven, she was stubborn. But she stepped away from the car and returned to the inn. Things were not close to being settled, though. He wished he'd thought to pinch her car keys.

There was nothing for it but to set out for Ireleth Hall. The arrangements were in place. Valerie Fairclough would be in the tower folly keeping her daughter occupied and away from the windows. Lynley and Lord Fairclough would be waiting for his arrival with whatever lights they'd been able to come up with to illuminate the interior of the boathouse.

St. James made good time and found Ireleth Hall with no difficulty. The gates stood open, and he coursed along the drive. Deer grazed placidly in the distance, occasionally lifting heads as if to evaluate their environment. And this was stunning, a park defined by magnificent oaks, planes, beeches, and copses of birch trees rising above expanses of rolling lawn.

Lynley came out of the house as St. James pulled up. Bernard Fairclough accompanied him, and Lynley made the introductions. Fairclough pointed the way to the boathouse. He said they'd managed to rig up some lights by using the current from an exterior bulb. They had torches as well, just in case. They also were carrying a pile of towels.

The way led through shrubbery and poplars, making a quick descent to Lake Windermere. The lake was placid, and the surroundings were soundless except for the birds and the distant noise of a motor somewhere on the water. The boathouse was a squat stone affair, with a roofline that dipped nearly to the ground. Its single door stood open, and St. James took note of the fact that it had no lock on it. Lynley would have seen this as well, and he would have already drawn the conclusion about what the lack of a lock meant.

Inside, St. James saw that a stone dock ran round three sides of the building. Several caged electrician's lights had been set up to illuminate the area of the dock where Ian Cresswell had taken his fall, and a long flex from these lights was looped over one of the building's rafters, running from there to the exterior. The lights cast long shadows everywhere save on the immediate area of the stones in question, so Lynley and Fairclough switched on their torches to do something to mitigate the gloomy spots.

St. James saw that there was a workbench at one side, most likely the spot where fish were cleaned, if the heavy smell of them was any indication. Cleaning fish meant implements to do so, so that would have to be looked into, he reckoned. The boathouse also accommodated four craft: the scull belonging to Ian Cresswell, a rowing boat, a motorboat, and a canoe. The rowing boat was Valerie Fairclough's, he was told. The canoe and motorboat were used by everyone in the family, but not on a regular basis.

St. James stepped carefully onto the area from which the stones had been dislodged. He asked for a torch.

He could see how easily a skull could be fractured if someone had fallen here. The stones were roughly hewn in the manner of those used in so many structures in Cumbria. They were slate, with the odd piece of granite thrown in. They'd been mortared into place, as any other kind of positioning would have been foolhardy. But the mortar was worn and in some spots crumbly. It would have been no difficult matter for the stones to have been loosened from it. But such loosening could have come with age as well as with intent: Generations of people stepping from boats onto the dock would have over time caused the stones to become dangerous just as well as someone deliberately dislodging them.

He moved along the mortar, looking for marks to indicate a tool had been wedged into it to serve as a lever. He found, however, that the mortar was in such bad condition that it was going to be hard to say if this or that area of crumbling was the result of anything other than age. A shiny spot would have indicated someone had used a tool to mess about with the mortar, but there didn't seem to be one.

He finally stood, having inched his way along the entire area of missing stones. Fairclough said, "What do you think?"

"It looks like nothing."

"You're certain?" Fairclough looked relieved.

"There's no sign of anything. We could bring in some more powerful lights, as well as some higher magnification. But I can see why it was deemed an accident. So far, at least."

Fairclough glanced at Lynley. "'So far'?" he said.

Lynley said, "No marks on the mortar don't indicate there are no marks on the stones that are missing." And with a wry look at his friend, "I was hoping to avoid this, you know."

St. James smiled. "I reckoned as much. I find there are distinct benefits to being moderately disabled. This happens to be one of them."

Lynley handed his torch over and began stripping off his clothes. He got down to his underwear, grimaced, and slid into the water. He said, "Christ," when the frigid water rose to his waist. He added, "At least it's not deep."

"Not that it's going to matter," St. James said. "Don't avoid the best part, Tommy. It should be easy enough. There'll be no algae on them."

"I know," he groused.

Lynley went under. It was simple, as St. James had said it would be. The dislodged stones hadn't been in the water long enough to bear algae, so Lynley was able to find them quickly and heave them to the surface. He didn't get out of the water, however. Instead he said to Fairclough, "There's something else. Can you swing some light this way?" and he went under again.

As Fairclough swung the torchlight in his direction, St. James had a look at the stones. He was concluding that they were fine since there was no shine of strike marks against them when Lynley surfaced another time. He was holding something that he slapped against the dock. He lifted himself from the water, shivering, and grabbed the towels.

St. James looked to see what he'd brought to the surface. Fairclough, still above them on the dock, said, "What've you found?"

It was a filleting knife, St. James saw, the sort of knife used when one is cleaning fish. It had a thin blade some ten inches long. Most notable of all, its state clearly indicated it had not been in the water long.

MILNTHORPE
CUMBRIA

Deborah had no idea what on earth Simon thought was going to happen to her if she rang Nicholas Fairclough back. She'd perfectly weathered the confrontation with his wife; she was determined to do the same with Nicholas.

When she returned his phone call, he asked to meet her. He began by saying that he wondered if there was anything else she needed from him. He said he understood that film-makers liked to include all sorts of footage to run during voice-overs, and there was plenty of scope for that, so he wondered if he could take her to Barrow-in-Furness to show her some of the areas where blokes lived rough. This might be important in the overall picture of things.

Deborah agreed. It was yet another chance to delve, and Tommy had wanted her to delve. Where should they meet? Deborah asked Nicholas.

He'd fetch her from her lodgings, he said.

She saw no danger in this. She had her mobile to rely upon, after all, and both Simon and Tommy were a mere phone call away. So she left her husband a note, along with the number of Nicholas's mobile, and she went on her way.

Nicholas rumbled up in an old Hillman some twenty minutes later. Deborah was waiting for him in front of the hotel, and when he suggested that they have a coffee before setting off for Barrow-in-Furness, she didn't demur.

Coffee was easy enough to come by, considering Miln-thorpe was a market town with a good-sized square just off the main road. A church comprised part of this square, rising above the town on a modest slope of land, but two of the other three sides comprised restaurants and shops. Next to Milnthorpe Chippy—apparent purveyor of all things deep-fried—there was a small café. Nicholas led her to this, but not before calling out, "Niamh? Niamh?" in the direction of a woman who was just coming out of a Chinese takeaway three doors down from the chippy.

She turned. She was, Deborah saw, petite and slender. She was also formidably well put together, especially considering the time of day, which did not suggest stilettos and cocktail wear although that was what she had on. Her dress was short, showing well-shaped legs. It was also cut in a way to flatter breasts that were full, perky, and—it had to be said—patently artificial. Directly behind her was a man in the apron of an employee of the Chinese takeaway. There was apparently some relationship between them, Deborah saw, for Niamh turned to him and spoke while he offered her a long look that was clearly besotted.

Nicholas said, "Excuse me for a moment?" to Deborah and went over to the woman. She didn't look pleased to see him. Her expression was stony. She said something to the man with her, who looked from her to Nicholas and decamped into the takeaway.

Nicholas began to speak. Niamh listened. Deborah sidled closer to catch something of their conversation, which wasn't easy as it was market day in the square, so in addition to the vehicle noise from the main road through Milnthorpe, she had to contend with housewives chattily shopping for fruit and veg as well as individuals stocking up on everything from batteries to socks.

". . . none of your concern," Niamh was saying. "And it's certainly none of Manette's business."

"Understood." Nicholas sounded perfectly affable. "But as they're part of our family, Niamh, you can understand her concern. And mine as well."

"Part of your family?" Niamh repeated. "Oh, that's a *very* good laugh. They're your *family* now but what were they when he walked out and the rest of you let it happen? Were they your *family* then when he destroyed ours?"

Nicholas looked nonplussed. He glanced round as if searching not only for listeners but also for words. "I'm not sure what any of us could have done about what happened."

"Oh, aren't you? Well, let me help you out. Your bloody father could have put a bloody end to his bloody job unless he saw reason, and that's just for a start. Your bloody father could have said, 'You do this, and I'm finished with you,' and the lot of you could have done the same. But you didn't do that, did you, because Ian had you all under control—"

"That's not actually how things were," Nicholas cut in.

"—and not a single one of you was ever willing to stand up to him. *No* one was."

"Look, I don't want to argue about that. We see things differently, that's all. I just want to say that Tim's in a bad state—"

"Do you think I don't know that? I, who had to find him a school where he could feel that the other pupils weren't pointing him out as the bloke whose father had been taking it up the chute from some Arab on the sly? I goddamn know he's in a bad state, and I'm doing what I intend to do about it. So you and your whole miserable family need to get out of our lives. You were happy enough to do that while Ian was living, weren't you?"

She stormed in the direction of a line of cars parked on the north side of the square. Nicholas took a moment, head down and obviously pondering, before he came back in Deborah's direction.

He said, "Sorry. Family matter."

"Ah," she replied. "She's a relative, then?"

"My cousin's wife. He drowned recently. She's having trouble . . . well, coping with the loss. And there're children involved."

"I'm sorry. Should we . . . ?" She gestured towards the café to which they'd been headed, saying, "Would another time be better for you?"

"Oh no," he said. "I want to talk to you anyway. The bit about Barrow? To tell you the truth, it was something of an excuse to see you."

Deborah knew he certainly wasn't referring to a desire to be with her in order to experience her charms, so she prepared herself mentally for what was to come. Since he'd rung her and requested a meeting, she'd first assumed Alatea hadn't told him the truth about their encounter. That, perhaps, had not been the case.

She said, "Of course," and followed him to the café. She

ordered coffee and a toasted tea cake and attempted to seem completely at ease.

He didn't bring up Alatea until they'd been served. Then what he said was, "I don't know how to put this, exactly, so I'll have to say it directly. You need to stay away from my wife if this documentary thing is going to work out. The filmmakers will have to know that as well."

Deborah did her best to look startled: an innocent woman completely unprepared for this turn of events. She said, "Your wife?" and then, with an attempt at dawning recognition and regret, "I upset her yesterday, and she told you about it, didn't she? I was rather hoping she wouldn't, frankly. I'm so terribly sorry, Mr. Fairclough. It was unintentional on my part. Rather emotionally clumsy, to be frank. It was the magazine that did it, wasn't it?"

To her surprise, he said rather sharply, "What magazine?"

Odd reaction, she thought. "*Conception*," she said. What she wanted to add was, Is there another magazine I should be looking into? but of course she did not. She thought feverishly back to the other periodicals that had been on the table along with *Conception*. She couldn't remember what they were, so interested had she been in that single one.

He said, "Oh. That. *Conception*. No, no. That's not . . . Never mind."

Which she could hardly do. She opted for a direct approach and said, "Mr. Fairclough, is something wrong? Is there something you'd like to tell me? Something you'd like to ask me? Is there some kind of reassurance I can give you . . . ?"

He fingered the handle of his coffee cup. He sighed and said, "There are things Alatea doesn't want to talk about, and her past is one of them. I know you're not here to delve into her background or anything but that's what she's afraid of: that you *might* start delving."

"I see," Deborah said. "Well, this isn't an investigative documentary, other than as it relates to the pele project. Certain issues about you yourself might come up . . . Are you certain she's not just worried about how the film might affect you? Your reputation? Your standing in the community?"

He laughed self-derisively. "I did enough damage to myself when I was using. No film could damage me further. No, it's to do with what Alatea did to get by before she and I met. It's stupid, frankly, for her to be so upset about it. It's nothing. I mean, it's not like she made porn films or something."

Deborah nodded gravely. She kept her face sympathetic but said nothing. Surely, she thought, he was on the verge . . . the cusp . . . the cliff's edge . . . Just the tiniest nudge might push him over.

She finally said thoughtfully, "You two met in Utah, didn't you? I went to college for a while in America. In Santa Barbara. Do you know the town? It's expensive there and I . . . Well, funds were low and there are always easy ways to make money . . ." She let him fill in the blanks for himself, with whatever his imagination might provide. The truth was she'd done nothing but go to photography school, but there was no way on earth he would know that.

He pursed his lips, perhaps considering an admission of some sort. He took a sip of coffee, set his cup back down, and said, "Well, it's underwear, actually."

"Underwear?"

"Alatea was an underwear model. She did catalogue pictures. Advertisements in magazines as well."

Deborah smiled. "And that's what she doesn't want me to know? That's hardly disgraceful, Mr. Fairclough. And let's be honest. She has the body for it. She's attractive as well. One can easily see—"

"Naughty underwear," he said. He let that sit there for a moment so that Deborah could, perhaps, absorb the information and its implications. "Catalogues for certain *types* of people, you understand. Adverts in certain *types* of magazines. It wasn't . . . they weren't . . . I mean, the underwear wasn't exactly high-class stuff. She's dead embarrassed about it all now and she's worried that someone will uncover this about her and humiliate her in some way."

"I see. Well, you can reassure her on that score. I'm not interested in her underwear past." She glanced out of the window of the café, which looked onto the market square. It was busy out there, and a queue had formed at a takeaway food stall operating from a dark green caravan with *Sue's Hot Food Bar* scrolled in white across the front of it. People sat at a few picnic tables in front of the caravan, tucking into whatever the eponymous owner was shoveling, steaming, onto paper plates.

Deborah said, "I did think it was that magazine— *Conception*—but I suppose that's more to do with me than with her. I shouldn't have brought the subject up. Do let her know I apologise."

"It wasn't that," Nicholas said. "She wants to get pregnant, certainly, but truth is I want it more than she does just now and that's making her touchy. But the real problem is this damn modeling part of her life and those pictures, which she keeps expecting to pop up in some tabloid."

As he made these final remarks, his gaze—like Deborah's—went out-of-doors. But instead of the same casual glance Deborah had given the food stall and its accompanying picnic tables, his fixed on something and his expression altered. His pleasant face hardened. He said, "Excuse me for a moment," and before Deborah could reply, he strode outside.

There he walked up to one of the individuals enjoying a Sue's Hot Food Bar meal. It was a man, who ducked his head as Nicholas approached, in an obvious effort to go unnoticed. This didn't work, and when Nicholas clutched the man's shoulder, he rose.

He was enormous, Deborah saw. He looked nearly seven feet tall. Rising quickly as he did, he knocked his cap against the furled umbrella in the centre of the table, and the cap dislodged, revealing fiery red hair.

She reached into her bag as the man stepped away from the table and listened to whatever Nicholas was saying, which appeared to be as hot as the food the man was eating. The man shrugged. Further words were exchanged.

Deborah took out her camera and began to photograph the man and his encounter with Nicholas Fairclough.

KENSINGTON
LONDON

Barbara Havers considered herself one lucky bird when the cab drove only from Portland Place to Rutland Gate, south of Hyde Park. It just as easily could have been Wapping or regions beyond and while she knew Lynley would have been good for the cab fare ultimately, she'd not brought sufficient funds to cover a lengthy journey and she doubted the driver would have been willing to take a quarter of an hour's snog in exchange for the ride. She hadn't thought of this when she hopped blithely into the vehicle, but she breathed a sigh of relief when the bloke headed west instead of east and finally turned left a short distance beyond the brick expanse of Hyde Park Barracks.

He pointed out the building in question, an imposing white structure with a panel of doorbells indicating that it was a conversion. Barbara got out, paid for the ride, and considered her options as the cab rumbled away. But not before the driver told Barbara with a wink that this was where the couple debarked, they always went inside the place together, and both of them had keys since one or the other of them would do the unlocking when they reached the door.

Conversions meant flats, Barbara knew, which in turn meant occupants, which in turn meant winkling out the identity of the occupant in question. She fished for a cigarette and paced while she smoked it. The nicotine, she reckoned, would sharpen her wits. The sharpening didn't take long.

She went to the door and saw the line of bells. Flats were marked but there were no names, as was typical in London. There was, however, one bell marked *Porter*, and this turned out to be a piece of good luck. Not every residential building in London had a porter. It upped the value of the flats within but it also cost the residents a bundle.

A disembodied voice asked her business. She said she'd come to make an enquiry about one of the flats that she'd learned would soon be coming on the market and could she possibly speak to him about the building?

The porter didn't embrace this idea with wild enthusiasm, but he did decide to cooperate. He buzzed her in and told her to come along the corridor to the back, where she'd find his office.

It was perfectly quiet inside, aside from the well-muted sound of traffic on Kensington Road, just beyond Rutland Gate. She passed along a marble floor, treading silently on a faded Turkey carpet. The doors to two ground-floor flats faced each other here, and a table upon which sat cubbies for the day's post was positioned beneath a heavy gilt mirror. She gave a quick glance to the cubbies, but like the bells outside next to the door, they offered flat numbers only and not names.

Just beyond the stairway and a lift, she found a door marked *Porter*. The porter in question opened it to her knock. He looked like a pensioner and he wore a uniform too tight in the collar and too loose in the stomach. He gave Barbara the once-over and his expression said that if she was intending to make a purchase of a flat in the building, she had better prepare herself for an accepting-offers-beginning-at situation that was going to knock her out of her high-top trainers.

He said, "Don't know about any flat on offer, do I," without any introduction.

She said, "This is a bit of a preemptive strike, if you know what I mean. C'n I . . . ?" She indicated his office and smiled pleasantly. "I'll just take a minute of your time," she added.

He stepped back and tilted his head towards a desk situated in a corner of the room. He had a nice little setup here, Barbara thought, with part of the place made into a snug sitting room complete with television currently tuned in to an ancient film in which Sandra Dee and Troy Donahue were locked in a timeless, adolescent, agonizing embrace as music swelled with a familiar theme. She thought for a moment before she came up with the title. *A Summer Place*, that was it. All about young, tormented love. Nothing quite like it, she thought. Shoot me first.

The porter saw the direction of her gaze and, perhaps determining his choice of film was some sort of revelation about him, went to the television and hastily switched it off.

That done, he moved to his desk and sat behind it. This left Barbara standing, but that apparently was his intention.

Barbara expressed what she felt was a suitable amount of gratitude for the porter's willingness to talk to her. She asked some questions about the building, the sorts of queries she expected a potential buyer might have before plunking down hard-earned cash on a piece of outrageously priced Kensington property. Age, condition, problems with heating and plumbing and ventilation, difficulties encountered with other residents, presence of undesirables, the neighbourhood, noise, pubs, restaurants, markets, corner shops, and on and on. When she'd run the gamut of everything she could possibly think of—jotting his answers in her small spiral notebook—she said, laying out her bait and hoping he'd go for it, "Brilliant. Can't thank you enough. Most of this matches up with what Bernard told me about the place."

He bit. "Bernard? That your estate agent? 'Cause like I said, I don't know of a place that's going up for sale."

"No, no. Bernard Fairclough. He told me an associate of his lives here and she apparently told him about a flat. I can't remember her name . . ."

"Oh. That'd be Vivienne Tully, that would," he said. "Don't think it's her place going up for sale, though. Situation's too convenient for that."

"Oh, right," Barbara said. "It's not Vivienne's. I thought it might be and got a bit excited about the possibility but Bernie"—she especially liked the touch of *Bernie*—"said she's quite established here."

"That'd be the case," he said. "Nice woman, as well. Remembers me at Christmas, she does, which is more than I can say for some of 'em." He shot a look at the television, then, and cleared his throat. Barbara saw that on a squat table next to a reclining chair, a plate of beans on toast was waiting. Doubtless, he wanted to get back to that as well as back to Sandra, Troy, and more of their passionate, forbidden love. Well, she couldn't exactly blame him. Passionate and forbidden love made life more interesting, didn't it?

LAKE WINDERMERE
CUMBRIA

Lynley was having a preprandial sherry with Valerie and
Bernard Fairclough when Mignon showed up. They were
in what Valerie had referred to as the small drawing room,
where a fire was doing a fine job of cutting the chill. None
of them heard Mignon enter the house—the front door
being some distance from the room in which they sat—so
she was able to make something of a surprise entrance.

The door swung open and she shoved her zimmer frame
in ahead of her. It had begun to rain again, quite heavily,
and she'd come from the folly without raingear. This
omission—which Lynley reckoned had to be deliberate—
had caused her to become wet enough to provoke a reaction
from both of her parents. Her hair was flattened, her Alice-
in-Wonderland hairband dripped water onto her forehead
and into her eyes, and her shoes and clothing were soaked.
It was not a far enough walk from the folly to the main
house to have become so wet. Lynley concluded that she'd
stood for a while in the downpour for the drama a thorough
soaking might provide. Seeing her, her mother jumped to
her feet and Lynley—who couldn't have stopped himself if
he'd tried—politely rose to his.

"Mignon!" Valerie cried. "Why've you come from the
folly without an umbrella?"

Mignon said, "I can hardly hold an umbrella while using
this, can I?" in reference to the zimmer.

"A mac and a hat might have solved that problem," her
father said guilelessly. Notably, he hadn't risen and his
expression indicated he was fully aware of her ploy.

"I forgot it," Mignon said.

Valerie said, "Here. Sit by the fire, darling. I'll fetch some
towels for your hair."

"Don't bother," Mignon said. "I'll be walking back in a
moment. You're dining soon, aren't you? As I had no invitation to join you this evening, I don't want to take up too
much of your time."

"You don't need an invitation," Valerie said. "You're

always welcome. But since you've preferred . . . because of . . ." Clearly, she didn't want to say more in front of Lynley.

Just as clearly, Mignon did. She said, "I've had a gastric band, Thomas. Big as an ox, I was. You wouldn't believe how big. Destroyed my knees heaving my fat round the planet for a good twenty years, so they'll be replaced next. The knees, I mean. Then I'll be as good as new and some bloke'll come along and take me off my parents' hands. Or so they hope."

She made her way across the room and lowered herself into the chair her mother had vacated. She said to her father, "I could do with a sherry myself," and to Lynley, "I thought at first that's why you'd come. Stupid of me, I know, but you've got to consider who my father is. Always has a scheme, my dad. I knew you were part of one as soon as I saw you. I just misjudged what the scheme actually was, thinking you'd come to have a look at me, if you know what I mean."

"Mignon, really," her mother said.

"I think I'll take those towels after all." Mignon seemed to like the idea of ordering Valerie about. She looked quite gratified when her mother went off to do her bidding. Her father in the meantime hadn't moved, so she said to him, "That sherry, Dad?"

Bernard, Lynley thought, looked like a man who was about to say something he'd regret. In any other circumstances, Lynley would have waited to see what that something was, but his natural inclination towards civility got the better of him. He set his own glass of sherry on the table next to his chair. He said, "Let me," and Bernard cut him off with, "I'll get it, Tommy."

"Make it a big one," Mignon told her father. "I've just had a successful romantic interlude with Mr. Seychelles and while normally one has a fag for afters, I'd prefer to get sloshed."

Fairclough observed his daughter. His expression was so obviously one of distaste that Mignon chuckled.

"Have I offended you?" she asked. "So sorry."

Her father poured sherry into a tumbler, a great deal of

sherry. That, Lynley thought, was certainly going to do the job if the woman tossed it back. He had a feeling she fully intended to do so.

Fairclough was handing the drink over to his daughter when Valerie returned, towels in hand. She went to Mignon and set about drying her hair, gently. Lynley expected Mignon to show a burst of irritation and to brush the ministration aside. She didn't. Instead, she allowed her hair to be seen to, along with her neck and her face.

She said, "Mother never comes for a friendly visit. Did you know that, Thomas? What I mean is that she brings me food—rather like giving alms to the poor like the lady of the manor she is—but just to drop in for a chat? That hasn't happened in years. So when it did occur today, I was all amazement. What *can* the old dear want, I thought."

Valerie dropped her hands and the towel from her daughter's hair. She looked at her husband. He said nothing. They both seemed to gird themselves for some kind of onslaught, and Lynley found himself wondering how on earth they'd got themselves into this sort of position with their own daughter.

Mignon took a healthy gulp of her sherry. She held the glass with both hands, like a priest with a chalice. "Mother and I have nothing to talk about, you see. She has no interest in hearing about my life, and believe me, I have no interest in hers. This rather limits one's conversation. After the weather, what's there to talk about? I mean, aside from her dreary topiary garden and her even drearier children's playground or whatever it is."

Her father finally said, "Mignon, are you joining us for dinner or have you another purpose for your call?"

"Do not," Mignon said, "back me into a corner. You do not want that."

"Darling," her mother began.

"Please. If there's a *darling* in the family, we both know I'm not it."

"That's not true."

"God." Mignon rolled her eyes at Lynley. "It's been Nicholas, Nicholas since the day he was born, Thomas. A son at last and all the attendant hallelujahs. But that's not what I've come here about. I want to talk about that pathetic little cripple."

For a moment, Lynley had no idea whom she actually meant. He was, of course, acutely aware that St. James was disabled since he himself had been the cause of the accident that had injured him. But to apply either *pathetic* or *little* to the man he'd known since their school days was so inapposite a description that for a moment he thought Mignon was speaking of someone else entirely. She disabused him of that notion when she went on.

"Mother didn't last as long as she was evidently supposed to last in my company. Once she left, I wondered why she'd come at all, and it wasn't difficult to suss that out. There you all were, Dad, coming up from the boathouse. You, Thomas here, and the cripple. And Thomas looked like he'd had a wetting if the towels and his hair were anything to go by. But not the cripple. He was quite dry. As you were, Dad." Another hefty gulp of sherry followed before she continued. "Now the towels suggest our Thomas went down to the boathouse prepared. He didn't just slip and fall into the water and since his clothes weren't wet, I think we've got corroboration for that assumption. Which means he went into the water intentionally. This not being the season for taking a dip in the lake, he had to have had another reason. I'm thinking that reason has to do with Ian. How am I doing?"

Lynley felt Fairclough glance his way. Valerie looked nervously from her daughter to her husband. Lynley said nothing. It was, he reckoned, up to Fairclough to confirm or deny what was going on. As far as he was concerned, being open with his reasons for his visit to Ireleth Hall was wiser than attempting to maintain a pretence for his presence.

Fairclough, however, said nothing to his daughter. She took this for assent, it seemed. She said, "So that means you believe Ian's death was no accident, Dad. At least that's what I reckoned when I saw the three of you coming up from the lake. A few seconds on the Net was actually all it took to learn who our visitor here really is, by the way. Had you wanted to keep the information from me, you needed to come up with a pseudonym."

"No one was keeping anything from you, Mignon," her father informed her. "Tommy's here at my invitation. The fact that he's also a policeman has no bearing—"

"A detective," Mignon corrected. "A Scotland Yard detective, Dad, and I assume you know that. And since he's here at your invitation and he's prowling round the boathouse in the company of *whoever* that other bloke was, I think I can connect the dots well enough." She turned in her chair so that her focus was on Lynley and not her father. Her mother had stepped away from her, towels in her hands. Mignon said to Lynley, "So you're conducting a little investigation on the sly. Engineered by . . . ? Well, it can't be Dad, can it?"

"Mignon," her father said.

She went on. "Because *that* suggests that Dad himself is innocent, which, frankly, isn't very likely."

"Mignon!" Valerie cried. "That's a terrible thing to say."

"Do you think so? But Dad's got a reason for offing our Ian. Haven't you, Dad?"

Fairclough made no reply to his daughter. His look at Mignon betrayed nothing. Either he was used to this sort of conversation with her or he knew she would go no further with what she was claiming. A tense moment passed as they all waited for more. Outside, a gust of wind sent something against the windows of the small drawing room. Valerie was the one to flinch.

Mignon said, "But then, so do I. Isn't that correct, Dad?" She leaned back in her chair, enjoying herself. Looking at her father, she nonetheless directed her next words to Lynley. "Dad doesn't know that I know Ian wanted to cut me off, Thomas. He was always poring over the books, our Ian, looking for ways to save Dad money. Well, I'm certainly one of them. There's the folly itself, which cost a bundle to build, and then there's its maintenance, as well as my own. And as you no doubt used your detective skills to suss out when you paid your call upon me, I do like to spend a bit of money here and there. Considering the piles Dad's made for the firm over the years, what I need isn't a lot, of course. But to Ian it was far more than I deserved. To his credit, Dad never agreed with him. But we both know—Dad and I—that there was always a chance that he'd change his mind and go along with Ian's suggestion to throw me out on my ear. Isn't that correct?"

Fairclough's face was stony. Her mother's face was watchful. This offered more information than either of them might have given Lynley otherwise.

"Valerie," Bernard finally said, his gaze on his daughter, "I think it's time for dinner, don't you? Mignon will be leaving presently."

Mignon smiled. She gulped down the rest of her sherry. She said pointedly, "I believe I'll need some help to get back to the folly, Dad."

"I expect you'll do fine on your own," he replied.

8 NOVEMBER

Barbara Havers shrieked when she saw herself in the bathroom mirror, having stumbled towards the loo upon rising in the early morning and having forgotten that her appearance was decidedly altered. Her heart leapt in her chest, and she swung round ready to confront the woman she saw in an oblique angle of the mirror. It was a matter of seconds only, but she felt every which way the fool as she came to her senses and all of yesterday came sweeping back in the form of a hot wave of what was not quite shame but not quite anything else, either.

She'd rung Angelina Upman on her mobile after she'd visited the building in which Bernard Fairclough's associate Vivienne Tully lived. She'd said she was in Kensington and it looked like she was going to have to cancel "the hair thing," as she called it, being so far from Chalk Farm at the moment. But Angelina enthused on the matter: Heavens, Kensington was just a hop from Knightsbridge. They'd meet there instead of going in each other's company. Hadiyyah had weighed in, hearing her mother's end of the conversation. She'd got onto the mobile and said, "You *can't*, Barbara. And anyways, you're under *orders*, you know. *And* it's not going to hurt." She'd lowered her voice and gone on to say, "And it's the Dorchester, Barbara. Tea at the *Dorches-*

ter afterwards. Mummy says they've got someone who plays the piano while you have your tea and she says someone's always walking round with silver trays *heaped* with sandwiches and she says someone brings fresh scones that're hot and then there are cakes. Lots of cakes, Barbara."

Barbara reluctantly agreed. She would meet them in Knightsbridge. Anything to be served tea sandwiches from a silver platter.

The big event at the hair salon had been what Barbara knew a pop psychologist would have called a growth experience. Dusty—Angelina's stylist—had fully lived up to her description of him. When Barbara was ensconced in the chair of one of his underlings, he'd come over from his own station, taken one look at her, and said, "God. And what century is it that you're representing?" He was thin, handsome, spiky haired, and so tan for the month of November that only hours in a tanning bed could have possibly effected such a dubious glow of precancerous health. He hadn't waited for Barbara to come up with a witty reply to this. Instead, he'd turned to the underling and said, "Bob it, foil it with one-eighty-two and sixty-four. *And* I'm going to want to check your work." He then said to Barbara, "Really, you've gone this long. You could have waited another six weeks and I'd have seen to you myself. What on earth do you use for shampoo?"

"Fairy Liquid. I use it for everything."

"You're joking of course. But it's something from the shampoo aisle in the supermarket, isn't it?"

"Where else am I supposed to buy shampoo?"

He rolled his eyes in horror. "God." And then to Angelina, "You're looking gorgeous as always," after which he air-kissed her and left Barbara in the hands of the underling. Hadiyyah he ignored altogether.

At the end of what had seemed like a period in Hades to Barbara, she had emerged from the ministrations of Dusty's underling with sleekly bobbed hair that was highlighted with streaks of shimmering blond and with subtle strands of auburn. The underling—who turned out not to be Cedric after all but rather a young woman from Essex, nice despite her four lip rings and her chest tattooes—gave

her instructions about the care and maintenance of her
locks, which did not involve the use of Fairy Liquid or anything else save a supremely costly bottle of elixir that apparently was going to "preserve the colour, improve the body,
repair the follicles," and, one assumed, alter one's social
life.

Barbara paid for it all with a shudder. She wondered if
women truly poured this much lolly into something that
could as easily be seen to in the shower every now and
again.

Nonetheless, when she showered that morning, she protected the costly hairstyle from the water by wrapping it in
cling film first. She was shrouded in an overlarge pair of
flannel drawstring trousers and a hoody and toasting herself
a strawberry Pop-Tart when she heard the excited chatter
of Hadiyyah at her door, followed by the little girl's knock
upon it.

"Are you there? Are you there?" Hadiyyah cried. "I've
brought Dad to see your new hair, Barbara."

"No, no, no," Barbara whispered. She wasn't actually
ready for anyone to see her yet, least of all Taymullah
Azhar, whose voice she could hear but whose words she
could not distinguish. She waited in silence, hoping that
Hadiyyah would assume she was already off for the day, but
really, how could she? It wasn't eight in the morning and
Hadiyyah knew Barbara's habits, and even if she hadn't
known, Barbara's Mini was in full view of Azhar's flat.
There was nothing for it but to open the door.

"See?" Hadiyyah cried, grabbing her father's hand. "*See*,
Dad? Mummy and I took Barbara to Mummy's own hairdresser yesterday. Doesn't Barbara look nice? *Everyone* at
the Dorchester noticed her."

Azhar said, "Ah. Yes. I do see," which Barbara felt was
akin to being damned with very faint praise indeed.

She said, "Bit different, eh? Scared the dickens out of
myself when I looked in the mirror this morning."

"It's not at all frightening," Azhar told her gravely.

"Right. Well. I meant that I didn't recognise myself."

"*I* think Barbara looks lovely," Hadiyyah told her father.
"So does Mummy. Mummy said the hair makes Barbara

look like light's coming from her face and it makes her eyes show nicely. Mummy says Barbara's got beautiful eyes and she must show them off. Dusty told Barbara she's to let her fringe grow out so that there's no fringe any longer as well but instead she'll have—"

"*Khushi*," Azhar cut in, not unkindly, "you and your mother have done very well. And now, as Barbara is eating her breakfast, you and I must be off." He offered a long and sombre look at Barbara. "It does suit you well," he said before he gently put his hand on his daughter's head and directed her to turn so that they could go.

Barbara watched them walk back in the direction of their flat, Hadiyyah taking a skip and a hop and chattering all the while. Azhar had always been a sober sort of bloke in the time she had known him, but she had the feeling there was something here that comprised more than his usual gravitas. She wasn't sure what it was, although since Angelina wasn't currently employed, his concerns might have had to do with the fact that he and not his partner was going to be footing the bill for their costly teatime excursion at the Dorchester. Angelina had pulled out the stops on that one, beginning with champagne with which she had toasted Barbara's burgeoning beauty, as she'd called it.

Barbara shut the door thoughtfully. If she'd put Azhar into a difficult position, she needed to do something about it and she wasn't quite sure what that was going to be other than slipping him a few quid on the side, which he was unlikely to take from her.

When she was ready for her day, she began the mental preparation for what lay ahead. Although she was still officially taking her few days off work, part of what comprised her agenda had to be a visit to New Scotland Yard. This was going to put her on the receiving end of some good-natured jibes from her colleagues once they got a look at her hair.

In another situation she might have been able to prolong the inevitable since she was still on holiday. But Lynley needed information that was going to be more easily gleaned at the Yard than anywhere else, so there was nothing for it but to head to Victoria Street and to try to avoid being noticed wherever she could.

She had a name—Vivienne Tully—but not much else. She'd tried to get more as she'd left the building in Rutland Gate and a quick survey of the cubbies for the post had given her a bit. Vivienne Tully resided in flat 6, so her small stack of letters told Barbara, and a quick dash up the stairs allowed her to find this flat on the third floor of the building. It was, indeed, the sole flat on the floor, but when Barbara knocked, she learned only that Vivienne Tully had a house cleaner who also answered the door if someone showed up while she was hoovering and dusting. One polite question about Ms. Tully's whereabouts revealed that the house cleaner spoke limited English. Something Baltic seemed to be her native tongue, but the woman recognised Vivienne Tully's name well enough and through pantomime, a magazine grabbed up from a cocktail table, and much gesturing at a longcase clock, Barbara was able to ascertain that Vivienne Tully either danced for the Royal Ballet or she'd gone to see the Royal Ballet with someone called Bianca or she and her friend Bianca had gone to a ballet dance class. In any case, it all amounted to the same thing: Vivienne Tully wasn't at home and was not likely to be home for at least two hours. Barbara's appointment to be beautified precluded her hanging about to accost the woman, so she had scarpered to Knightsbridge with Vivienne Tully a blank page upon which something needed to be written.

Her visit to the Yard was supposed to take care of this, at the same time as it allowed her to see what there was to see about Ian Cresswell, Bernard Fairclough, and the woman from Argentina whom Lynley had also mentioned: Alatea Vasquez y del Torres. So she fired up her Mini and set off towards Westminster, holding to her heart the hope that she'd see as few of her colleagues as possible as she skulked round the corridors of New Scotland Yard.

She had fairly good luck in this department, at least at the start. The only people she saw were Winston Nkata and the departmental secretary Dorothea Harriman. Dorothea, long the picture of sartorial perfection and possessing an unmatchable degree of excellence in the area of all things related to personal grooming, took one look at Barbara, stopped dead in the tracks of her crippling five-inch stilettos, and said, "Brilliant, Detective Sergeant. Abso*lutely* brilliant. Who did it?" She touched Barbara's hair with her slender and speculative fingers. Without waiting for an answer, she went on. "And just look at the sheen. Gorgeous, gorgeous. Acting Detective Superintendent Ardery is going to be delighted. You wait and see."

Waiting and seeing were the last things Barbara wanted to do. She said, "Ta, Dee. Bit different, eh?"

"*Different* does not do justice," Dorothea said. "I want the name of the stylist. Will you share it with me?"

" 'Course," Barbara said. "Why wouldn't I share it?"

"Oh, some women won't, you know. Battle of females on the prowl. That sort of thing." She took a step away and sighed, her gaze fixed on Barbara's hair. "I'm green with envy."

The idea that Dorothea Harriman might be envious of her hairstyle made Barbara want to hoot with laughter, as did the notion that she herself was intent upon capturing a man with this makeover she'd been forced to endure. But she restrained herself and gave the other woman Dusty's name as well as the name of the Knightsbridge salon. This would be right up Dee's alley, Barbara reckoned, as she had little doubt that Dorothea spent vast amounts of time and most of her wages in Knightsbridge.

Winston Nkata's reaction was less extreme, and Barbara thanked her stars for this. He said, "Looks good, Barb. Guv see you yet?" and that was it.

Barbara said, "I was hoping to avoid her. If you see her, I'm not here, okay? I mean I'm here but not here. I just need access to the PNC and some other stuff."

"DI Lynley?"

"Mum's the word."

Nkata said he'd cover for Barbara as best he could but there was no telling when Acting Superintendent Isabelle Ardery was going to appear in their midst. "Best be prepared with some sort of story," he advised. "She's not happy 'bout the inspector going off without letting her know where he'll be."

Barbara gave Nkata a closer look when he said this. She wondered what he knew about Lynley and Isabelle Ardery.

But Nkata's expression betrayed nothing and while this was habitual for him, Barbara decided it was safe to conclude that he was merely remarking upon the obvious: Lynley was a member of Ardery's team; the assistant commissioner had pulled him off to see to some matter unrelated to Ardery's concerns; she was cheesed off about this.

Barbara found an inconspicuous spot where she could access the Yard's computer with its myriad sources of information. She started first with Vivienne Tully and she began, with very little difficulty, to amass the pertinent details about her. They ranged from her birth in Wellington, New Zealand, to her education from primary school there to university in Auckland to an impressive, advanced degree at the London School of Economics. She was the managing director of a firm called Precision Gardening, which manufactured gardening tools—hardly a high-glamour job, Barbara thought—and she was also an executive director of the Fairclough Foundation. A bit of delving turned up a further connection with Bernard Fairclough, Barbara found. In her early twenties she'd been the executive assistant to Bernard Fairclough at Fairclough Industries in Barrow-in-Furness. Between her time at Fairclough Industries and Precision Gardening, she'd been an independent business consultant, which Barbara reckoned in the way of the modern world could indicate either an attempt at developing her own business or a period of unemployment that had lasted four years. As of now, she was thirty-three years old, and a photo of her showed a woman with spiky hair, quite a boyish dress sense, and a rather frighteningly intelligent face. Her eyes communicated the fact that Vivienne Tully didn't suffer fools. In conjunction with her background and her general appearance, they also suggested ferocity of independence.

As far as Lord Fairclough was concerned, Barbara found nothing curious. There was plenty curious about his wayward son, though, as Nicholas Fairclough hadn't exactly trod the straight and narrow in his teens and twenties and records showed car crashes, arrests for drink driving, bungled burglaries, shoplifting, and sale of stolen goods. He seemed a straight enough arrow now, though. He'd paid all of his debts to society and from the day of his marriage, not a hair of his head had even been ruffled.

That brought Barbara to Alatea Vasquez y del Torres, her of the mouthful name. Aside from that name, Barbara had in her crumpled notes the town from which she'd sprung, communicated to her as Santa Maria di something-or-other, which wasn't exactly helpful as she quickly found out. Santa Maria di et cetera turned out to be to the towns and villages in a Latin American country what Jones and Smith were to surnames in her own. This, she reckoned, was not going to be like pinching candy from a five-year-old.

She was considering her approach when the acting super-intendent found her. Dorothea Harriman had, alas, waxed eloquent on the subject of Barbara's hair, failing to append to her waxing a convenient lie about having seen Barbara at a location that was not New Scotland Yard. Isabelle Ard-ery thus accosted her on the twelfth floor, where Barbara had hidden herself in the Met's library, a convenient loca-tion from which she could access the Met's databases in peace and in secrecy.

"Here you are, then." The acting superintendent had come upon Barbara with the stealth of a hunting cat, and her satisfaction was feline as well. She looked like a cat, decapitated mouse in jaws.

Barbara said, "Guv," with a nod. She added, "Still on holiday," on the very slight chance that Isabelle Ardery was there to requisition her for work.

Ardery didn't go in that direction, nor did she acknowl-edge Barbara's status as being off rota for the moment. She said, "I'll see the hair first, Sergeant."

Barbara hardly wanted to know what second was going to be, considering the superintendent's tone. She stood to give Ardery a better look.

Ardery nodded. "Now that," she said, "is actually a hair-cut. We could go as far as to call it a style."

Considering what she'd paid for it, Barbara thought, they ought to be calling it a night at the Ritz. She waited for more.

Ardery walked round her. She nodded. She said, "Hair

and teeth. Very good. I'm quite pleased to know you can take direction when your feet are to the fire, Sergeant."

"I live to please," Barbara said.

"As to the clothing—"

Barbara said to remind her, "On holiday, guv?" which she believed adequately explained her ensemble of tracksuit trousers, tee shirt emblazoned with *Finish Your Beer . . . Children in China Are Sober,* red high-top trainers, and donkey jacket.

"Even on holiday," Ardery said, "Barbara, you're a representative of the Met. When you walk in the door—" Abruptly, she brushed aside whatever she'd intended to say as her gaze came to rest on Barbara's tattered notebook. She said, "What are you doing here?"

"Just needed to get some information."

"Needing to get it here suggests a police matter." Isabelle put herself in a position to see the screen of the computer's monitor. She said, "Argentina?"

"Holidays," Barbara said airily.

Isabelle looked further. She scrolled back to the previous screen and the one before that. She said, reading the list of *Santa Maria di* towns, "Developing a fondness for the Virgin Mary? Holidays suggest resorts. Skiing. Seaside visits. Jungle excursions. Adventures. Eco-journeys. Which are you interested in?"

"Oh, just playing with ideas at the moment," Barbara told her.

Isabelle turned to her. "I'm not a fool, Sergeant. If you wanted to look for holiday possibilities, you wouldn't be doing it here. That being the case and since you've asked for time off, I think it's safe to conclude you're doing some work for Inspector Lynley. Am I correct?"

Barbara sighed. "You are."

"I see." Isabelle's eyes narrowed as she thought this one through. It seemed to lead her to a single conclusion. "You've been in contact with him, then."

"Well . . . more or less. Right."

"Regularly?"

"Not sure what you mean," Barbara said. She also wondered where the hell this was going. It was not as if she had a thing with DI Lynley. If Ardery thought that, she was clearly off her nut.

"Where is he, Sergeant?" the superintendent asked directly. "You know, don't you?"

Barbara considered her answer. Truth was, she did know. Truth also was, Lynley hadn't told her. His mentioning of Bernard Fairclough had done that. So she said, "He hasn't told me, guv."

But Ardery took another meaning from the moments in which Barbara had been considering her options. She said, "I see," in a way that told Barbara she saw something other than the truth of the matter. "Thank you, Sergeant," the superintendent added. "Thank you very much indeed."

Ardery left her then. Barbara knew she could call her back before she got to the door of the library. She knew she could clarify. But she did not do so. Nor did she ask herself why she was allowing the superintendent to believe something that was patently untrue.

Instead, she turned back to her work with Santa Maria di whatever. Alatea Vasquez y del Torres, she thought. Whoever she was, and not Isabelle Ardery, was the crux of the matter in hand.

MILNTHORPE
CUMBRIA

The end product St. James had to deal with was that his wife was simply afraid. Afraid, she was projecting them into a future for which she'd come up with half a dozen alternative scenarios, none of which did anything to assuage her fears. What was to St. James a potential solution to their long-thwarted desire for a family was no solution at all to her. There were too many variables that they couldn't control, she'd argued, and reluctantly he had to admit that there was a great deal of truth in what she said. An open adoption could indeed invite into their lives not only an infant in need of a loving family but also a birth mother, birth father, birth grandparents on both sides, and

God only knew who else. It wasn't a simple matter of scooping up an infant from the arms of a social worker and—it had to be said—hoping that the child and young adult growing out of that infant would not be one who felt the need to develop a second life with a birth family he or she scouted out when of an age to do so. Deborah was completely right in this, but so was he: There would be no guarantees in any route to parenthood, he'd told her.

His brother was pressing him for an answer. This girl in Southampton couldn't wait forever, David had said. There were other interested couples. "Come along, Simon. It's either yes or no, and it's not like you not to make a decision."

So St. James had spoken to Deborah again. Again, she'd been adamant. They'd gone back and forth for a quarter of an hour, at the end of which he'd set out for a walk. They hadn't actually parted badly, but they needed a little space for the heat of their discussion to dissipate.

He'd left the Crow and Eagle and walked in the direction of Arnside, along the road that skirted the River Bela and ultimately the mudflats of Milnthorpe Sands. As he walked, he tried not to think but rather merely to breathe in the rain-washed, damp day. He needed to clear his mind of this whole adoption business once and for all. If he didn't—and if Deborah didn't—it was going to poison their marriage.

The damn magazine hadn't helped matters. Deborah had it in hand at this point, and she'd read the bloody thing from cover to cover. From a story in *Conception* she had concluded decisively that she wanted to go the surrogacy route: her egg, his sperm, a petri dish, and a host mother. She'd read a story of a six-time surrogate and the altruism she extended towards other women. "It would be our child," was the point she kept making. "Ours and no one else's." Well, it would be and it wouldn't, to his way of thinking. There were dangers here as well as dangers in the other routes of adoption.

The day was a fine one although the night had seen buckets of rain pouring down on Cumbria. But now the air felt clean and crisp, and the sky displayed an ashen wealth of cumulus clouds. Out on the mudflats, the stragglers from various flocks of birds heading to Africa and the Mediterranean still hunted for ragworms, lugworms, and tellins. He recognised the plovers and the dunlans among them but as to the rest, he could not have said. He watched them for a while and admired the simplicity of their life. Then he turned and walked back into Milnthorpe.

In the car park of the inn, he found Lynley just arriving. He walked over to join him as his friend got out of the Healey Elliott. They had a moment of mutual admiration for the saloon's sleek lines and handsome paint job before St. James said, "But you didn't come by to prompt further vehicular envy on my part, I expect."

"Any chance to lord it over you in the transportation area is a chance I must grab on to. But in this case, you're right. I wanted to talk to you."

"A mobile would have done. This was a bit of a drive."

"Hmm, yes. But part of the gaff is blown. I reckoned a few hours away from the Faircloughs wouldn't go amiss." Lynley told him of his evening encounter with Valerie, Bernard, and Mignon Fairclough. "Now that she knows Scotland Yard's involved, she'll make short work of letting everyone else know as well."

"That could be good."

"It's actually as I'd have preferred it."

"But you're uneasy?"

"I am."

"Why?"

"Because of who Fairclough is. Because of who Hillier is. Because of Hillier's damnable propensity for using me to serve his own ends."

St. James waited for more. He knew the history of Lynley's relationship with the assistant commissioner. It included at least one attempted cover-up of a long-ago crime. He wouldn't have put it past Hillier to use Lynley another time in a similar capacity in which one of their own—as Hillier would no doubt think of Fairclough, Lynley, and himself—had something serious he wished to bury and Lynley was supposed to wield the shovel. Anything was possible, and both of them knew it.

Lynley said, "It may all be a smoke screen."

"Which part of it?"

"Fairclough wanting me to look into Ian Cresswell's death. That's certainly what Mignon Fairclough indicated last evening. It was a look-no-further-than-the-bloke-who-employed-you kind of remark. It's something I'd already thought of myself and dismissed, however."

"Why?"

"Because I just can't make sense of it, Simon." Lynley leaned against the side of the Healey Elliott, arms crossed at his chest. "I can see how he'd ask for the Met's involvement if a murder had occurred and he'd been accused or suspected and wanted to clear his name. Or if one or more of his children had been accused or suspected and he wanted to clear *their* names. But this was deemed an accident from the first, so why find someone to look into it if he himself is guilty of something or if he suspects one of them is?"

"That rather suggests Mignon herself is throwing up a smoke screen, doesn't it?"

"It would explain her trying to divert attention onto her father last night. Evidently, Cresswell wanted Bernard to cut her off." Lynley explained the financial arrangement Mignon apparently had with her father. "She wouldn't have wanted that. And since Cresswell kept the books and knew every move Bernard made financially, there's the additional possibility that he wanted someone else cut off as well."

"The son?"

"He's the likely choice, isn't he? With Nicholas's past, Cresswell would have argued not to trust him with a penny, and who could blame him? Nicholas Fairclough might be a recovering methamphetamine user but that's the key word: *recovering* and not *recovered*. Addicts never recover. They merely cope day-to-day."

Lynley would know about that, St. James acknowledged, because of his own brother. "And has Fairclough handed money to his son?"

"I want to look into that. The other daughter and her husband are my means to the information."

St. James looked away. Noise and odours were coming from an open door into the back of the hotel: the crashing and banging of pots along with the smell of frying bacon and burnt toast. He said to Lynley, "What about Valerie Fairclough, Tommy?"

"As killer?"

"Ian Cresswell was no blood to her. He was her husband's nephew and he had the potential to damage her children. If he wanted to cut off Mignon and he doubted Nicholas's long-term recovery, he'd steer Fairclough away from helping them financially as Fairclough tended to do. And Valerie Fairclough's behaviour that day was decidedly strange according to Constable Schlicht: dressed to the nines, perfectly calm, a phone call announcing 'a dead man floating in my boathouse.'"

"There's that," Lynley admitted. "But she could have been the intended victim as well."

"Motive?"

"Mignon declares her father is hardly ever there. He's in London repeatedly. Havers is looking into that end of things, but if something's not right with the Faircloughs' marriage, Bernard could have hopes to rid himself of his wife."

"Why not divorce her?"

"Because of Fairclough Industries. He's run it forever and of course he'd stand to walk away with a great deal of money if it was part of a settlement unless there's some sort of prenuptial agreement we're not privy to. But as of now it's still her company, and I daresay she can throw her weight into whatever decisions are made at the place if she wants to."

"Another reason for her to want Ian dead, Tommy, if he'd been recommending decisions not to her liking."

"Possibly. But wouldn't it make more sense for her to have Ian fired? Why kill him when she had the power to cut him off as easily as he wanted to cut off two of her children?"

"So where do we stand?" St. James pointed out to him that the fillet knife they'd brought up from the water looked perfectly innocent to the naked eye, not a scratch upon it. The stones they'd also brought up bore no recent scratches to indicate they'd been jemmied away from the dock. They could get Constable Schlicht out to the boathouse and the local SOCO boys involved, but they were going to need the coroner to reopen the case and they had virtually nothing to give him in order to encourage him to have another look at Ian Cresswell's death.

"The answer lies with the people," Lynley said. "They all bear a closer looking into."

"Which means, I think, that my usefulness to you has run its course," St. James said. "Although there's a final route we might go with the fillet knife. And another conversation that might be had with Mignon."

Lynley was about to reply to these suggestions when his mobile rang. He looked at the caller and said, "It's Havers. This could tell us where we need to head next." He flipped the phone open and said, "Tell me you've got something meaningful, Sergeant, because all we're running into here is one dead end after another."

ARNSIDE
CUMBRIA

Alatea had gone out early to plant bulbs because she wanted to avoid her husband. She'd slept poorly, with her mind racing hour after hour, and at the first sign of dawn, she'd slipped out of bed and faded out of the house.

Nicholas had slept badly as well. Something was very wrong.

The first evidence of this had come over dinner on the previous evening. He toyed with his food, mostly cutting the meat and moving it round the plate, mostly slicing the potatoes neatly and piling them up like poker chips. To her question of what was bothering him, he'd smiled vaguely and said, "Just a bit off my food tonight," and ultimately he'd pushed away from the table and wandered off into the drawing room, where he'd sat in the fireplace inglenook briefly and then paced the room as if it were a cage and he the imprisoned animal on display.

When they'd gone to bed, things had been worse. With a rising feeling of dread, she'd approached him. A hand on his chest, she'd said, "Nicky, something's wrong. Tell me," although the truth was that she feared hearing his answer more than she feared her own restless mind and where it took her when she allowed it free rein. He'd said, "Nothing. Really, darling. Just tired or something. Just a bit on edge," and when she'd not been able to prevent a look of alarm washing over her features, he'd gone on to say, "You're not to *worry*, Allie," and she knew he was reassuring her that whatever was going on inside him, it bore no relationship to his past with drugs. She hadn't thought it had, however, but she played along, saying, "You might want to talk to someone, Nicky. You know how it is," and he nodded. But he looked at her with so much love in his face that she realised whatever was on his mind most likely had to do with her.

They hadn't made love. This, too, was unlike her husband because she had approached him and not the opposite, and he'd long loved to be approached by her because he was not a fool and he knew very well how disparate was everything about them, at least everything visible to a world that judged people's equality by external matters. So the fact that *she* would want *him* at least as often as he wanted her had always thrilled Nicholas, who had always responded. This, too, was a sign.

So when Alatea left the house and made her way to the garden, it was in part because she needed to do something to take her mind off the terrifying possibilities that had been assailing her throughout the night. But it was also in part to avoid seeing Nicholas because eventually what was bothering him was going to come out into the open and she didn't think she'd be able to face it.

There were several thousand bulbs to be planted. She planned the lawn to be filled with early glories of the snow so that a bank of blue upon green would fall from the house down to the seawall, and this was going to take considerable work, for which she was glad. She would not, of course, be able to complete it in this one morning. But she could make a very good start. She set upon it with shovel and spade and the hours passed quickly. When she was sure her husband would have left Arnside House to make the drive to

Barrow-in-Furness for his half day at Fairclough Industries prior to his work at the pele project, she finished up what she was doing and stretched and rubbed the sore spots on her back.

It was only when she headed to the house that she saw his car and understood that Nicholas hadn't gone to work at all. Her gaze then went from the car to the house, and the dread she felt crept up her spine.

He was in the kitchen. He was sitting at the broad oak table, and he appeared to be brooding. There was a cup of coffee in front of him, with a cafetiere and a bowl of sugar nearby. But the cup of coffee appeared undrunk and a ring of sediment round the inside of the cafetiere suggested its contents had long gone cold.

He hadn't dressed for the day. He wore the trousers of his pyjamas and the dressing gown she'd given him for his birthday. His feet were bare although he didn't seem to be bothered by the fact that the tiles on the floor would be cold against them. There was much about his appearance that wasn't right. But least right was the fact that Nicholas never missed work.

Alatea wasn't sure what to say. She went with the lead he had given her during dinner the night before. She said, "Nicky, I didn't think you were still at home. Are you ill?"

"Just needed to think." He looked at her then and she saw his eyes were bloodshot. A tingling went up her arms and felt as if it would encircle her heart. He said, "This seemed like the best place to do it."

She didn't want to ask the obvious, but not to do so would have been more obvious still, so she said, "Think about what? What's wrong?"

He said nothing at first. She watched him. He moved his gaze from her, and it seemed he was thinking about her question and all the different answers he might give. At first he said, "Manette came to see me. In the shipping department."

"Are there problems there?"

"It's Tim and Gracie. She wanted us to take them."

"Take them? What do you mean?"

He explained. She heard but didn't hear because all the

time she was busy trying to evaluate his tone. He spoke of his cousin Ian; of Ian's wife, Niamh; and of Ian's two children. Alatea, of course, knew all of them, but she had not known of Niamh's intentions towards her own flesh and blood. It was inconceivable to her that Niamh would use her children in this way, as chess pieces in a game that by all rights should have been over. She wanted to weep for Tim and Gracie and she felt the imperative of doing something for them as much as Nicholas obviously felt it. But for this to have disturbed his sleep, to have made him ill . . . ? He wasn't telling her everything.

"Manette and Freddie are the best ones to take them," he concluded. "I'm no match for Tim's problems, but Manette and Freddie are. She'd get through to Tim. She'd be good at that. She doesn't give up on anyone."

"So it seems there's a solution, yes?" Alatea said hopefully.

"Except that Manette and Freddie have split up so that throws a spanner," Nicholas said. "Their situation's odd. It's also unstable." He was silent again for a moment, and he used the moment to top up his cold coffee with more cold coffee, into which he stirred a heaped teaspoonful of sugar. "And that's too bad," he went on, "because they belong together, those two. I can't think why they split up in the first place. Except they never had kids and I think perhaps that wrecked them after a time."

Oh God, this was the crux, Alatea thought. This was where it all headed in the end. She had known it would, if not with Nicholas then with someone else.

She said, "Perhaps they didn't want children. Some people don't."

"Some people, but not Manette." He glanced at her. His face was drawn. From this, Alatea knew he wasn't telling her the truth. Tim and Gracie might indeed be in need of a stable place to live, but that was not what was bothering her husband.

She said, "There's more, though." She drew out a chair from the table and sat. "I think, Nicky, that you had better tell me."

It had long been a strong part of their relationship that

from the first Nicholas had told her everything. He'd insisted upon it because of how he'd lived in his past, which had been in a world of lies, experiencing a life defined by hiding his drug use in any way he could. If he didn't tell her everything now—despite what that "everything" might comprise—his withholding of information would be more damaging to their marriage than whatever the information itself was. Both of them knew it.

He finally said, "I believe my father thinks I killed Ian."

This was so far from what Alatea had been expecting that she was rendered speechless. There *were* words somewhere inside her, but she couldn't find them, at least not in English.

Nicholas said, "Scotland Yard's up here looking into Ian's death. Considering it was ruled an accident, there's only one reason that Scotland Yard's turned up. Dad can pull strings when he wants to. I reckon that's what he did."

"That's impossible." Alatea's mouth felt dry. She wanted to reach for Nicholas's coffee and drink it down, but she stopped herself from even moving, so unsure was she of her ability to keep the sudden trembling of her body under her control. "How do you know this, Nicky?"

"That journalist."

"What . . . ? Are you talking about that man? That same man? The one who came here . . . ? The story that never was a story at all?"

Nicholas nodded. "He's back. He told me. Scotland Yard's here. The rest is clear enough: I'm the person they're interested in."

"He said that? The journalist said that?"

"Not in so many words. But from everything that's gone on, it's obvious."

There was something more here that he wasn't telling her. Alatea could read it in his face. She said, "I don't believe it. You? Why on earth would you have hurt Ian? And why would your father think you could?"

He shrugged. She saw that he was struggling with a conflict that he couldn't bear to reveal and she herself struggled to understand what it was and what it could mean to both of them. He was deeply depressed or deeply grieved or deeply—very deeply—something else.

She said, "I think you should speak to your father. You must do this straightaway. This reporter, Nicky, he doesn't mean you well. And now this woman who says she's from the film company that doesn't exist . . . You must talk to your father at once. You must hear the truth of the matter. It's the only answer, Nicky."

He raised his head. His eyes were liquid. Her heart constricted with her love for this man, troubled soul to her own troubled soul. He said, "Well, I've definitely decided against being part of that documentary film that she was here about. I've told her that, by the way, so there's one less thing for either of us to deal with." His lips curved but it was a poor effort at a smile. It was meant to encourage her, to tell her all would be well soon enough.

Both of them knew this was a lie, however. But like everything else, neither one of them would be willing to admit that.

MILNTHORPE
CUMBRIA

"I wouldn't want to have to write it on an envelope, but they probably have some Spanish abbreviation if you're sending a letter there," Havers said. She was referring to the town in Argentina that she'd managed to come up with as being the likeliest origin of Alatea Vasquez y del Torres. "Santa Maria de la Cruz, de los Angeles, y de los Santos," she had just announced to Lynley over his mobile phone. "We're talking about a burg that's touching all the spiritual bases. It must be in an earthquake zone and hoping for divine intervention in case of the worst."

Lynley could hear her smoking on the other end. No surprise. Havers was always smoking. She wouldn't be at the Met, then. Or if she was, she was phoning from a stair-well where, he knew, she occasionally skulked for an illegal hit of the weed. He said to her, "Why this town, Barbara?" and to St. James, who had joined him to lean against the Healey Elliott, "She's onto Alatea Fairclough."

"Who're you talking to?" Havers enquired irritably. "I bloody well hate three-way conversations."

"St. James is here. I'll switch it to the speaker if I can work out how to do that."

"Oh, that'll happen on a snowy day in hell," she said. "Give it to Simon, sir. He can do it for you."

"Havers, I'm not entirely—"

"Sir." It was her patient-as-a-saint voice. There was nothing for it. He handed the mobile over to St. James. One or two buttons and both of them were listening to Havers in the car park of the Crow and Eagle.

"It's the mayor," Havers said. "I know this is spitting in the dark, sir, but the mayor's a bloke called Esteban Vega y de Vasquez and his wife's called Dominga Padilla y del Torres de Vasquez. I reckoned it could be a put-it-all-together-and-what've-you-got situation. Some of the surnames are the same as Alatea's."

"That's a stretch, Barbara."

"This came from the Internet?" St. James asked.

"Bloody hours on it. And since everything's in sodding Spanish, I'm only guessing he's the mayor. He could be the dog catcher but there was a picture of him and I can't think why the dog catcher'd be handing over the keys to the city to anyone in some picture. Well, except maybe to Barbara Woodhouse."

"She's dead," Lynley said.

"Whatever. So there's a picture of him and he's in his mayor kit and there's his wife and they're posing with someone and I can't—of course—read the caption since it's in Spanish, in which language I can actually say *una cerveza por favor* but, believe me, nothing else. But the names are in the caption. Esteban and Dominga and all the rest. So far, that's our best bet, I reckon, because I haven't been able to find anything else even close."

"We'll need someone to translate," Lynley noted.

"What about you, Simon? Spanish among your many talents?"

"Only French," St. James said. "Well, there's Latin as well, but I'm not sure how much use that would be."

"Well, we got to find someone. And we need someone else to tell us how these people come up with their surnames because I bloody don't know and can't work it out."

"It has to do with forebears," Lynley said.

"Got that much, I think. But what is it? Do they just keep lining them up back through history? Wouldn't want to have to write that on my passport application if you know what I mean."

Lynley was thinking about the language and who would serve their purposes as a translator. There would, of course, be someone in the Met, but he wasn't sure how many more people he could afford to bring in on this before Isabelle traced the lot of them back to him.

He said, "What about Alatea Fairclough herself? What've you come up with on that score when you work her into this town of Santa Maria et cetera? You're assuming she's the mayor's daughter, I take it?"

Havers said, "Can't go that way at all, sir. They seem to have five sons." She inhaled on the other end of the line and blew smoke noisily into the mobile phone. Lynley heard the rustling of paper and knew she was leafing through her notebook as well. She went on to say, "Carlos, Miguel, Angel, Santiago, and Diego. At least I reckon there are five sons. Considering the way these people string together their names, it could be one bloke, I s'pose."

"So where does Alatea fit in?"

"Way I see it, she could be the wife of one of them."

"A wife on the run?"

"Sounds very good to me."

"What about a relative?" St. James asked. "A niece, a cousin."

"I reckon that's possible as well."

"Are you working that angle?" Lynley asked her.

"Haven't been. Can do. But no way can I delve because like I said this stuff's in Spanish," she reminded him. "'Course, the Yard'll have a program to translate. You know. Something buried on the computers somewhere, away from the prying eyes of the likes of us who might actually need to use it sometime. I c'n talk to Winston. He'll know how to do it. Should I ask him?"

Lynley thought about this. He was back to what he'd considered earlier: the impact on Isabelle Ardery if she discovered he'd bled another member of her team away for his own purposes. The results of that manoeuvre wouldn't be pretty. There had to be another way to get round the problem of the Spanish language. Where he didn't want to go in his own thoughts at the moment was why it mattered to him how Isabelle would react. It wouldn't have mattered to him how a superior officer might have reacted before this. The fact that he was worried now put him on the edge of a dangerous escarpment that he didn't want to be on at this juncture in his life.

He said, "There has to be another way, Barbara. I can't get Winston into this as well. I'm not authorised."

Havers didn't point out to him that he hadn't been authorised to get her help either. She just said, "Let me . . . Well, I could ask Azhar."

"Your neighbor? He speaks Spanish?"

"He does practically everything else," she said ironically. "But I reckon if he doesn't speak Spanish, he can get me someone from the university who does. A professor, probably. A graduate student. Worse comes to worst, I c'n walk over to Camden Lock Market and listen to the tourists—if there are any at this time of year—and put my fingers on someone speaking Spanish and drag 'em to the nearest Internet café for a look at the information on the Net. I mean, there are ways, sir. I s'pose we don't need Winston."

"Ask Azhar," Lynley said, and he added, "if that doesn't put you in a difficult position."

"Why would that put me in a difficult position, sir?" Barbara's tone was suspicious and with good reason.

Lynley didn't reply. There were things between them that they didn't discuss. Her relationship with Taymullah Azhar was one of them. "Anything else?" he asked her.

"Bernard Fairclough. He's got a set of keys to the flat of a woman called Vivienne Tully. I've been there but so far no luck in seeing her. Picture of her that I tracked down makes her youngish, trendy clothes, good skin, good figure, edgy hairstyle. Another woman's basic nightmare, essentially. All I know about her is that she once worked for him, she now works in London, and she likes ballet because that's where she was yesterday. Either at a dance class or watching a performance. Her housekeeper didn't speak English, so we did it with sign language. Lots of moving body parts if you know what I mean. Bloody hell, sir, have you noticed how few people actually *do* speak English in London these days? Have *you* noticed, Simon? I feel like I'm living in the bloody lobby of the bloody United Nations."

"Fairclough has a key to her flat?"

"Sounds cosy, eh? I've another trip to Kensington on the agenda. I reckon she bears a little arm twisting. I haven't got onto the Cresswell will yet—"

No matter, Lynley told her. She could verify details, but they had that information in hand. They'd learned there was insurance that the ex-wife had come into. And according to the partner, the farm had been left to him in Cresswell's will. What she *could* do, though, was confirm these details. The date of the will might be helpful, too. Could she see to that?

Could and would, she told him. "What about the kids?"

"Apparently, Cresswell assumed the insurance money would also benefit them. That doesn't appear to be the case, however."

Havers whistled. "Always good to follow the money."

"Isn't it just."

"Which reminds me," she said, "that bloke from *The Source*? Have you run into him yet?"

"Not yet," Lynley said. "Why?"

"Because there's more to him than meets the eye as well. Turns out he was up there for three days directly *before* Ian Cresswell drowned. With him needing to beef up his story for the paper, seems like murder's a good way to do it."

"We'll take that on board," Lynley told her, "but he'd have had to get onto the Fairclough property, get down to the boathouse, fiddle with the dock, and get off the property, all unseen. You mentioned he was a big bloke, didn't you?"

"Nearly seven feet tall. A nonstarter, then?"

"It's doubtful, but at this point, anything's possible." Lynley thought about the likelihood of a seven-foot-tall redheaded reporter managing to escape the notice of Mignon Fairclough. Only in the dead of a very dark night could this have happened, he reckoned.

He said, "We've our work cut out, one way or the other." It signaled an end to their conversation and he knew the sergeant would take it that way. But before she could do so, he had to know, even if he didn't want to understand why he had to know. He said, "Are you carrying this off without the superintendent's knowledge? She still thinks you're on holiday? You've not run into her at the Met, have you?"

There was a silence. In it, he knew what the answer was. He avoided St. James's glance as he said, "Damn. That's going to make things difficult. For you, I mean. I'm sorry, Barbara."

She said airily, "Truth to tell, the guv's a bit tense, Inspector. But you know me. I'm used to tense."

MILNTHORPE
CUMBRIA

Deborah hated being at odds with her husband. This was due in part to the disparity in their ages and due in part to his disability and all the baggage attendant upon that. But most of all, it was due to the differences in their characters, which defined how each of them looked at life. Simon went at things logically and with remarkable disinterest, making it nearly impossible to argue with him because she looked at things through a cloud of emotion. In a battle where the warring armies marched onto the field from either the heart or the head, those battalions from the head won each skirmish. She was often left with that most useless of declarations to put a full stop to any heated conversation between herself and her husband: *You don't understand.*

When Simon left her in their room at the inn, she did what she knew had to be done. She phoned his brother, David, and gave him what she called *their* decision. "I so much appreciate how you've thought of us, David," she told him, and she meant every word. "But I can't get my mind round sharing a baby with its birth parents. So we're saying no."

She could tell that David was disappointed, and she had little doubt that the rest of Simon's family would be disappointed as well. But Simon's family were not being asked to open their lives and their hearts to the virtual unknown. David said, "You know, it's all a lottery, Deb, any way you go at parenthood," to which she'd said, "I do know that. But the answer's the same. The complications involved . . . I wouldn't be able to cope."

So it was over. In a day or two, the pregnant girl in question would move on her way towards another couple eager for a child. Deborah was glad she'd made the decision, but she felt disconsolate all the same. Simon wouldn't be pleased, but she couldn't see any answer other than the one she'd given. They simply had to move on.

She could tell her husband was more than ill-at-ease with going down the surrogacy route. She'd actually thought it would appeal to him since he was a scientist. But for him the miracles of modern medicine were turning out to be "dehumanising, Deborah." Locking himself up in a doctor's loo and seeing to the appropriate deposit made into the equally appropriate sterile container . . . And then there was the matter of harvesting her eggs and what that involved and the additional matter of the surrogate and monitoring the surrogate throughout the pregnancy and even finding the surrogate in the first place.

Who is this person? he reasonably asked. And how do you make sure of all the things you need to make sure of?

This person is just a womb we're hiring, was how Deborah explained it to him.

If that's what you think the extent of her involvement would be, Simon replied, then you've got your head in the clouds. We're not hiring a vacant room in her house to store furniture, Deborah. This is a life that's growing inside her body. You seem to think she'll ignore that.

There'll be a contract, for heaven's sake. Look here, in the magazine, there's a story about—

That magazine, he said, needs to go into the rubbish.

Deborah, however, didn't toss it away when he left the room. Instead, she phoned David and when she'd done so, she'd sat and looked at the copy of *Conception* that Barbara Havers had overnighted to her. She gazed at the photos of the six-time surrogate, posing with the happy families she'd helped. She reread the article. Finally, she turned to the back where the advertisements were.

Everything related to reproduction had some sort of listing, she saw, but despite the hopeful article in the magazine itself, nothing referred to surrogacy. Phoning a legal service listed on the page told her why this was the case. Advertising oneself as a surrogate mother was illegal, she learned. The hopeful mother had to find her own surrogate. A relative is best, she was told. Have you a sister, madam? A cousin? Even mothers have carried their own grandchildren for their daughters. How old is your own mother?

God, nothing was easy, Deborah thought. She had no sister, her mother was dead, she was an only child of only children. Simon's sister was a possibility but she couldn't imagine the madcap Sidney—currently in the throes of love with a mercenary soldier, for heaven's sake—allowing her million-pound model's body to be the launching pad for her brother's child. There were definite limits to sororial love, and Deborah reckoned she knew what they were.

The law was not her friend in this matter. Advertising everything else related to reproduction appeared to be entirely legal—from clinics offering money to women willing to have their eggs harvested to lesbian couples looking for sperm. There were even adverts for groups who wanted to talk donors out of donating in the first place, along with counseling services for donors, recipients, and everyone in between. There were help lines listed and assistance offered from nurses, doctors, clinics, and midwives. There were so many options heading in so many different directions that Deborah wondered someone didn't simply advertise in *Conception* with the single word *HELP!*

This thought finally took her to the matter of the magazine itself and how it had come to her attention: through Alatea Fairclough, who had torn out these very same pages that were now eating at Deborah's peace of mind. With herself in turmoil over the matter, Deborah began to see more clearly how Alatea could be viewing her own situation. What if Alatea knew she couldn't carry a baby to term? Deborah asked herself. What if she hadn't yet shared that information with her husband? What if she—just as Deborah herself was proposing to do—was searching for a surrogate mother? Here she was in England, away from her native land, away from friends and relatives who might have volunteered for the job . . . Was there someone she could turn to in their stead? Was there someone she could ask to carry her petri dish child made with Nicholas Fairclough?

Deborah thought about this. She compared Alatea to herself. She had Sidney St. James, unlikely candidate though she was. Whom did Alatea have?

There was a possibility, she realised, one that fitted in with what had happened in the boathouse at Ireleth Hall. She needed to tell Simon about it. She needed to talk to Tommy as well.

She left the room. Simon had been a good while gone on his walk, and she punched in his mobile number as she descended the stairs. Speaking with Tommy in the car park, he told her they were just about to—

She told him to wait. She was coming to meet them both.

Nicholas Fairclough was what stopped her, however. He was the last person she expected to see in the tiny lobby of the Crow and Eagle, but there he was. And he was waiting for her. He rose when he saw her and he said, "I reckoned this is where you'd be." He spoke as if she'd been making an effort to hide herself from him, and she pointed this out.

His reply of, "No, I get that much. The best place to hide anything is always in plain sight."

She frowned. He was completely altered. He was very drawn and his cherubic face had gone unshaven. He didn't seem to have had much sleep, for there were circles under his eyes. There was also nothing friendly or affable about him.

He made no preamble to his remarks. He said, "Look. I know who you really are. And here's what *you* need to know: I didn't touch Ian. I wouldn't have touched Ian. The fact that my father thinks I might have done something tells you the state our family is in, but it sure as hell doesn't tell you anything else. You"—and here he jabbed a finger at her although he didn't touch her—"need to get the hell back to London. There's sod-all to learn from hanging about. Your bloody investigation is over. And leave my wife alone, all right?"

"Are you—"

"Stay away." He backed off and when he was far enough, he turned on his heel and left her.

Deborah remained. She felt her heart pounding hard in her chest and the blood started singing in her ears. There was, she knew, only one explanation when every single statement he'd made was considered. For whatever inconceivable reason, Nicholas Fairclough actually believed that she was the Scotland Yard detective come to Cumbria to look into his cousin's death.

There was only one way he could have reached that conclusion, and her digital camera had captured that way.

MILNTHORPE
CUMBRIA

Zed Benjamin had faded out of the picture on the previous day after his brief encounter with Nicholas Fairclough in the Milnthorpe market square. Luckily, there were enough stalls in the square that he'd been able to get out of view of the café in which Fairclough had been meeting with the Scotland Yard woman, so after Fairclough had a few final words with her, all it took was a few more minutes of waiting before she emerged from the café as well. And then it was nothing to see where she was going since where she was going turned out to be the Crow and Eagle at the junction of the main road through Milnthorpe and the route to Arnside. So on this day Zed had parked himself there in the early a.m., in the vicinity of a NatWest, and he'd been skulking round the cashpoint for hours, eyes on the inn, waiting for the woman to emerge. This garnered him many a look of suspicion from people going in and out of the bank, and a few pointed words from other people using the cashpoint. He was even prodded once in the chest by an old bag telling him to "move away, laddie, or I'll have the coppers on you . . . I know your kind, I do," so he began to hope that something would happen soon on the Scotland Yard end of things or he was going to get hauled into the nick for loitering with intent.

He'd had his morning phone call with Yaffa, and this was on his mind. She hadn't returned his kissy noises, the reason turning out to be that his mother wasn't in the room and a show of affection hadn't been necessary to keep Susanna Benjamin happy. Plus, it also turned out that there were problems developing with Micah out in Tel Aviv, apparently getting a bit weary with playing Yaffa's brother Ari. In conversation with Micah, she had said *attractive* in reference to Zed. It was no big thing for goodness sake, she'd told Micah, but he hadn't been pleased. And while Zed had been dwelling on the fact that Yaffa had used the word *attractive* to refer to him, she'd gone on to say that there was, sadly enough, a very good chance that she was going to have to move on soon to other lodgings. *Quite beside himself* was how she put it in reference to Micah. She was afraid his worry over her commitment to him was going to put him off his studies. For a man in medical school, this was out of the question. But you know how it is when a man becomes uneasy about his woman, Zed.

Actually, Zed had no idea how it was when a man became uneasy about his woman since he'd so far spent his adult years avoiding women altogether.

Yaffa said that she thought she could appease her fiancé for a while longer, but only for a while. Then she would either have to move on or she would have to return to Tel Aviv.

Zed hadn't known what to say. He was hardly in a position to beg her to stay. He wasn't even sure why begging her to stay crossed his mind in the first place. Yet that entreaty was what was on the tip of his tongue at the end of their conversation. What was not on the tip of his tongue was *have a nice trip home, then*, which was something of a surprise to him.

She'd rung off before he could say anything at all. He wanted to ring her back and tell her that he'd miss her terribly, he hadn't intended her to think from his silence that he wouldn't, he'd enjoyed their every conversation, in fact she was just the sort of woman . . . But he couldn't go that far. Alas and alack, he thought. They'd have to be Keats and Fanny writing tortured letters to each other and there was an end to the matter.

Zed was so consumed with his thoughts about Yaffa and Micah and the great irony of stumbling across a woman who was—let's face it—perfect for him, only to find her engaged to another man, that when Nick Fairclough turned up at the Crow and Eagle and went inside, the importance of this didn't register at first. He merely thought, Ah, there's old Nick Fairclough, and he'd pulled his cap more firmly down on his head and slouched to reduce his size so as to make himself less noticeable. It was only after Fairclough's visit to the inn was so brief and only after he strode out with a stony expression on his face that Zed realised what one and one amounted to, which was Fairclough plus the detective equals Something Worthy of Note Happening.

Then the detective herself came out. She was on her mobile. A detective on her mobile meant that Developments were about to develop. Fairclough had left and the detective was following. Zed needed to be following as well.

His car wasn't far away. He'd parked on the pavement just a short distance down the Arnside Road, so he dashed for this as the red-haired woman went round the corner of the inn, where, no doubt, her own car was parked. He fired his car up and waited for her to emerge. No way was she going anywhere at this point without him on her tail.

He counted the seconds. They turned into minutes. What was it? he wondered. Car trouble? Flat tyre? Where the hell was she . . . ?

Finally, a car did emerge from the car park round back of the Crow and Eagle, but this was no hire car and she wasn't driving it. It was, instead, a sleek copper-coloured antique thing of the sort costing God only knew what, and it was driven by a bloke who looked perfectly at ease in it, not to mention well-heeled, because how else could he have afforded the thing? Another guest at the inn, Zed concluded. The bloke took off towards the north.

About three minutes later, another car emerged and Zed put his vehicle in gear. But *this* one was driven by a bloke as well, a serious-looking gent with too much dark hair, and he was looking grim and rubbing his head as if he needed to get rid of a migraine.

Then, at last, he saw the woman. But she was on foot. She wasn't on her mobile this time, but her face was serious and determined. Zed reckoned at first she was on her way to some location nearby and the logical place was the market square, where the cafés made good meeting spots, as did the restaurants and the Chinese takeaways, if it came down to it. But instead of heading there, she went back into the Crow and Eagle.

Zed made his decision in an instant. He switched off the car's engine and dashed after her. He could, he reckoned, follow her forever. Or he could take the bull by the horns and do some fancy dancing with it.

He pushed through the door of the inn.

MILNTHORPE
CUMBRIA

Deborah was so angry with Simon that she was far beyond seeing red. She was seeing whatever the next colour in the outrage spectrum was supposed to be.

Camera in hand, she'd found her husband with Tommy in the car park. It was, she believed, excellent luck that Tommy was with him. For Tommy was going to be on her side and she knew she was going to need an ally.

She'd given them the information in brief: Nicholas Fairclough waylaying her in the inn, Nicholas Fairclough knowing Scotland Yard was looking into the death of Ian Cresswell, Nicholas Fairclough believing that she—of all people—was the Scotland Yard detective prowling round his life. She said, "There's only one way he'd've reached that conclusion," at which point she showed them the photo she'd snapped on the previous day. This was of the red-headed man speaking to Fairclough in the market square.

She said, "Right afterwards, Nicholas wanted nothing more to do with me. We were meant to go to Barrow, but that didn't happen. And then this morning, he was in such a state . . . You see what this means, don't you?"

Tommy looked at the picture. Simon did not. Tommy said, "It's the reporter from *The Source*, Simon. Barbara described him to me. Huge, red-haired. There can't be two blokes wandering round Cumbria fitting that description and interested in Fairclough."

Better and better, Deborah had thought. She'd said, "Tommy, we can use him. Something's obviously going on with this entire lot of people and he's onto it or he wouldn't be up here. Let me make contact with him. He'll think he's got an in with the police. We can—"

"Deborah," Simon had said. It was that tone, that maddening tone of she-must-be-appeased.

Tommy had added to this, "I don't know, Deb," and he looked away for a moment. She couldn't tell if he was thinking about what she said or thinking about getting out of the car park before she and Simon had the argument he would be anticipating. For Tommy knew Simon better than anyone. He knew what *Deborah* meant when Simon said it that way. There were reasons for Simon's concern in some situations—all right, she could admit that—but there was no reason for his concern just now.

She'd said, "This is being handed to us on a platter, Tommy."

To which Tommy had said, "Barbara told me he was up here three days in advance of Cresswell's death, Deb. His intent has been to add some interest to a story on Nicholas Fairclough."

"So?"

"Deborah, it's obvious enough," Simon put in. "There's a chance that this bloke—"

"Oh, you *can't* be thinking his idea of adding interest to a story was to arrange the suspicious death of a member of his subject's own family. That's completely absurd." And as both of the men started to speak at once, she said, "No.

Wait. Listen to me. I've had a think about this and there're things you don't know. They have to do with Nicholas's wife."

It was to her advantage that neither of the men had met Alatea. Neither had met Nicholas Fairclough either, so that was an additional advantage. Tommy said, "Barbara's looking into Alatea Fairclough, Deb."

But Deborah said, "She may be doing, but she doesn't know everything," and she proceeded to tell them about those things that Alatea Fairclough had to hide. "There're photographs somewhere, according to Nicholas. She was a model, but the kind of work she did is the kind she'd prefer to keep hidden. She told Nicholas about it, but no one in his family knows. He called it 'naughty underwear' and I think we all know what you can read for that."

"What, exactly?" Simon was watching her with that *look* of his, grave and understanding and worried.

Stuff and bloody bother, Deborah thought. She said, "We can read for that everything from catalogue pictures of leather goodies for the sadomasochistic crowd to pornography, Simon. I think we can agree on that, can't we?"

"You're right, of course," Tommy said. "But Barbara's on this, Deb. She'll sort it out."

"But that's not all, Tommy. That's not everything." Deborah knew Simon would not be pleased with her next direction, but she intended to take it anyway because it had to be explored, because it was surely connected to Ian Cresswell. "There's surrogacy to consider."

Simon actually went pale at this. Deborah realised he thought she intended to bring up this most personal of matters with Tommy standing there as an arbitrator of their disagreement and their pain. She said to her husband, "Not that. I just think it's likely Alatea can't carry a baby to term. Or she's having difficulty with pregnancy. I think she's looking for a surrogate and I think that that surrogate might well be Ian Cresswell's wife, Niamh."

Simon and Tommy exchanged a look. But they hadn't seen Niamh Cresswell, so they didn't know. She went over it with them: Nicholas Fairclough's desire for a baby, Alatea's possession of a magazine with all of the advertisements in the back removed, Niamh Cresswell's appearance and the very clear indication that she'd been doing something surgically to improve it—"One doesn't have breast enhancement on the National Health" was how Deborah put it—and the simple logic of a woman who's lost her man and believes she has to have a replacement and wants to do something to increase her chances of finding that replacement . . . "Niamh has to finance all this. Carrying a baby for Alatea is the answer. It's illegal to profit from surrogacy, but this is a family matter, and who's going to know if money is exchanged? Nicholas and Alatea certainly aren't going to tell a soul. So Niamh has their baby, she hands it over, they hand her the money, and it's done."

Simon and Tommy greeted this with silence. Tommy looked down at his shoes. This was the moment when they were going to tell her she was off her nut—oh, how *well* she knew these two men in her life—so she went on. "Or perhaps, even better, Nicholas Fairclough doesn't even *know* about the arrangement. Alatea's going to fake the entire pregnancy. She's quite tall, and there's a very good chance she'd never show a pregnancy till very late in term. Niamh takes herself out of the picture for a few months and when she's ready to deliver, Alatea joins her. They come up with a pretence, they—"

"God, Deborah." Simon rubbed his forehead while Tommy shifted his feet on the ground.

Inanely, Deborah thought how Tommy always wore Lobb's shoes. They must have cost a fortune, she reckoned, but of course they would last forever and the pair he had on he'd probably had since he was twenty-five years old. They weren't scuffed, of course. Tommy's man Charlie Denton—valet, butler, man Friday, equerry, *whatever* in Tommy's life—would never have allowed scuff marks on Tommy's shoes. But they were worn and comfortable, rather like friends, and—

Simon was speaking and she realised she'd deliberately plugged her ears to his words. He would think that all this had to do with her, with them, with this stupid open adoption business, which, of course, he had no idea she'd put a stop to, so she decided to tell him then and there.

"I phoned David," she said. "I told him no. Definitely not. I can't cope with it, Simon."

Simon's jaw moved. That was all.

Hurriedly, Deborah said to Tommy, "So let's say Ian Cresswell found out about all of this. He protests. He says that their children—his and Niamh's—are already putting up with just about enough in their lives and they can't be asked to cope with their mother carrying a baby for his cousin's wife. There's too much confusion. He puts his foot down."

"They're divorced," Tommy pointed out gently.

"Since when did divorce mean people stop trying to control each other if they can get away with it? Let's say he goes to Nicholas. He appeals to him. Nicholas knows what's going on or he doesn't know but in either case, the appeal goes nowhere so Ian says he's going to have to talk to Nicholas's father about it. The last thing anyone wants is to have Bernard Fairclough drawn into this. He's already spent most of Nicholas's life believing he's a wastrel. And now this, this terrible division in the family—"

"Enough," Simon said. "Really. I do mean it. Enough."

The paternal tone behind his words was an electric shock, thirty thousand volts running through her body. Deborah said, "*What* did you say to me?"

Simon said, "It doesn't take a Freudian to know where this is coming from, Deborah."

The electric shock turned in an instant to fury. Deborah began to speak. Simon cut her off.

"This is a flight of fancy. It's time for both of us to get back to London. I've done what I can here"—this to Tommy—"and unless we want another go at the boathouse, I daresay what appears to be the case about Ian Cresswell's death is indeed the case."

That he would actually dismiss her like this . . . Deborah had never wanted to strike her husband, but she wanted it badly in that moment. *Temper, Deb, temper,* her father would have said, but never had her father been taken so lightly by this man who stood implacably before her. God, he was insufferable, she thought. He was pompous. He was so bloody self-righteous. He was always so sure, so certain, so 100 percent full of his sodding scientific knowledge, but some things had *nothing* to do with science, some things had to do with the heart, some things weren't about forensics, microscopes, bloodstains, computer analyses, graphs, charts, amazing machinery that would take a single thread and connect it to a manufacturer, a skein of wool, the sheep it had come from, and the farm on the Hebrides where that sheep had been born . . . She wanted to scream. She wanted to scratch out his eyes. She wanted—

"She does have a point, Simon," Tommy said.

Simon looked at him and his expression asked his old friend if he'd entirely lost his mind.

Tommy said, "I don't doubt there was bad blood between Nicholas and his cousin. Something's not right with Bernard as well."

"Granted," Simon said, "but a scenario in which Ian's former wife . . ." He waved off the entire idea.

Tommy then said, "But it's too dangerous, Deb, if what you're saying is true."

"But—"

"You've done good work up here, but Simon's right about going back to London. I'll take it from here. I can't let you put yourself in harm's way. You know that."

He meant more than one thing. All of them knew it. She shared a history with Tommy and even if she hadn't done, he would never allow her to come close to a danger that could take her from Simon as Tommy's own wife had been taken from him.

She said numbly, "There's no danger here. You *know* that, Tommy."

"If murder's involved, there's always danger."

He'd said all he would say on the topic. He left them, then, and left her with Simon there in the car park.

Simon had said to her, "I'm sorry, Deborah. I know that you want to help."

She'd said bitterly, "Oh, you know that, do you? Let's not pretend this isn't about punishing me."

"For what?" He sounded so *bloody* surprised.

"For saying no to David. For not solving our problem with one little word: yes. That's what you wanted, an instant solution. Without *once* considering how it would feel to me with an entire second family hovering out there, watching my every move, evaluating what sort of *mummy* I'd be . . ." She was close to tears. This infuriated her.

Simon said, "This has nothing to do with your phoning David. If you've made up your mind, I accept it. What else can I do? I might have other wishes, but—"

"And that's what counts. That's what always counts. Your wishes. Not mine. Because should my wishes be granted in any matter, the power shifts, doesn't it, and you don't want that."

He reached towards her, but she backed away. She said, "Just go about your business. We've said enough at this point."

He waited for a moment. He was watching her, but she couldn't look at him. She couldn't look at his eyes and see the pain and know how far back into his past it reached.

He finally said, "We'll talk later," and he went to his car. Another moment and he'd driven away, out of the car park and about his business. Whatever it was. It didn't matter to Deborah.

She left the car park herself. She went towards the front door of the inn. She'd got just inside when she heard someone say, "Hang on. You and I need to talk," and she turned to see that, of all people, the redheaded giant was coming in the entrance. Before she had a chance to say anything, he continued. "Your cover's been blown. It can be on the front page of *The Source* tomorrow or you and I can strike a deal."

"What sort of deal?" Deborah asked him.

"The kind that gets us both what we want."

GREAT URSWICK
CUMBRIA

Lynley knew that Simon was right about Deborah: She needed to stay clear of things from this point forward. They didn't know exactly what they were dealing with and anything that might put her into danger was unacceptable on so many levels that most of them didn't bear talking about.

He'd been wrong to bring them into this. It had seemed a simple enough job that he could sort through with their help in a day or so. That wasn't turning out to be the case, and he needed to finish things before Deborah did something that he, she, and Simon would regret.

When he left them in Milnthorpe, he headed north, then east. Then he took the road that coursed down the spatulate landmass at whose tip sat Barrow-in-Furness. Barrow wasn't his destination, however. He wanted to speak to Manette Fairclough privately, and that meant a trip to Great Urswick.

The route he followed took him through the hilly Victorian sea town of Grange-over-Sands, along the estuary where wintering birds formed a living landscape across the mudflats, establishing hierarchies in the search for food. It was abundant here, replenished daily by the tides from Morecambe Bay.

After Grange-over-Sands, the road opened to grey water, deceptive in its calm, along one side of the car and pastures on the other side, broken by the occasional line of cottages where seaside holidaymakers came in better weather. This was far south in Cumbria, not the land of the lakes so treasured by John Ruskin and William Wordsworth and his daffodils. Here most people got down to the serious hand-to-mouth of daily living, which comprised generations of fishermen out on the shifting sands of the bay, first with horses and carts and now with tractors and always within inches of losing their lives to the quicksand if they made a wrong decision. And then there was no saving them if the tide came in. There was only waiting for their bodies to turn up. Sometimes they did. Sometimes they did not.

At Bardsea, he turned inland. Great Urswick was landlocked, one of those villages that seemed to exist merely because it was at a crossroads and contained a pub. To get to it, one travelled through a countryside completely unlike the dramatic fells, slate-studded screes, and sudden eruptions of limestone of the upper lakes. This part of Cumbria looked more like the Broads. One climbed briefly through a village and then out onto a landscape flat and windswept, suitable for grazing.

Buildings in Great Urswick didn't look like part of Cumbria, either. They were prettily painted, but they were not done up in the vernacular of the Lakes. No neatly stacked slate fronted them for a consistency of appearance. Here, they were roughcast. Some even were clad in wood, a strange building material for this part of the world.

Lynley found Manette's home alongside a large pond, which appeared to be the centrepiece of the village. Swans floated on it, and it was thick with reeds here and there to protect them, their nests, and their young. There were two cars parked in front of the house, so he reckoned he could kill two birds by speaking to both Manette and her former husband, with whom, Bernard Fairclough had revealed, his daughter still lived. He went to the door.

A man answered. This, Lynley reckoned, would be Freddie McGhie. He was a decent-looking bloke, neat as a pin, dark hair, dark eyes. Helen would have declared *how squeaky clean he is, darling,* but she would have meant it in the best possible sense because everything about him was perfectly groomed. He wasn't dressed for work, but he still managed to look like someone who'd stepped out of an advertisement for *Country Life*.

Lynley introduced himself. McGhie said, "Ah yes. Bernard's guest from London. Manette said she'd met you." He sounded affable, but there was a sense of questioning in his tone. There was, after all, no reason that Bernard Fairclough's guest from London would come a-wandering into Great Urswick and knock on Freddie McGhie's front door.

Lynley said he was hoping to speak to Manette if she was at home.

McGhie glanced towards the street as if for answer to a question he didn't ask. Then he said as if remembering his manners, "Oh yes. Well, of course. It's just that she didn't mention . . ."

What? Lynley wondered. He waited politely for elucidation.

"No matter," McGhie said. "Do come in. I'll fetch her."

He ushered Lynley into a sitting room that overlooked the back garden and the pond beyond it. The dominant indoor feature was a treadmill. It was state of the art with a screen that featured readouts, buttons, and assorted gee-gaws. To accommodate it and a rubber mat for preliminary stretching, much of the other furniture in the room had been stacked and lined against a far wall. McGhie said, "Oh, sorry. Not thinking. The kitchen's better. It's just this way," and he walked on.

He left Lynley there in the kitchen for a moment and went off, calling Manette's name. As his footsteps sounded against rising stairs, however, the kitchen's exterior door opened, and Manette herself came inside. Lynley reflected—as he hadn't done before—that she looked nothing like her sister. She had her mother's height and her mother's rangy build but, unfortunately, she'd inherited her father's hair. This was sparse enough to see to her skull, although she kept the cut of it short and curly as if to hide its scarcity. She was dressed for running, obviously the person who used the treadmill in the district's often inclement weather. She saw Lynley at once and said, "Goodness. Well, hello," and her glance went to the door through which he'd come because she obviously heard her former husband calling her name.

She said, "Excuse me," and went in the same direction as McGhie. Lynley heard her call out, "Down here, Freddie. I was out for a run," and then his reply of, "Oh, I say, Manette," which was all Lynley heard because at that point their voices became hushed. He caught McGhie's "Should I . . . ?" and his "Happy to, you know," without knowing the what or the why of each. Still, when Manette returned, she had Freddie McGhie in tow. Her choice of words was apparently deliberate when she said to Lynley, "A nice surprise for us, this. Did Dad want you to pop in to see us for some reason?"

"I did want to speak to you both," Lynley said.

They exchanged a look. He realised it was more than time to drop the pretence, which hadn't worked with Mignon and which certainly wasn't going to work with anyone else.

He took out his police identification and handed it to

Manette. Her eyes narrowed. She pushed it to McGhie and while he was examining it, she asked the obvious question, "What's this about? I can't think it likely Scotland Yard's on the trail of replacing their lavatories and they've sent you up here to evaluate our line of loos. What's your guess, Freddie?"

McGhie was blushing faintly, and Lynley didn't think his growing colour had anything to do with lavatories. He said to her, "I'd thought . . ." He shrugged, one of those *you know* movements in which a couple's history allows them to communicate in a truncated fashion.

Manette barked a laugh. "I appreciate the vote of confidence," she said. "But I have a feeling the inspector here likes them a little less long in the tooth."

"Don't be stupid. You're only forty-two," Freddie said to her.

"Female years are like dog years, Freddie. When it comes to men, I'm closer to eighty. What can I do for you, Inspector?"

He said, "Your father's asked me to look into Ian Cresswell's death."

Manette's response was to McGhie. "I rest my case." There was a kitchen table at which she then sat. A bowl of fruit was in the centre of it, and she took a banana and began to peel it. She said, "Well, this must put a real pin in poor Mignon's balloon." She used her foot to push one of the other chairs out. "Sit," she told Lynley. She said the same to McGhie.

Lynley thought at first that the gesture indicated her full cooperation, but she disabused him of that notion straightaway. She said, "If Dad thinks I'm about to finger anyone for anything, I'd appreciate your telling him that kite won't fly. As a matter of fact, no kite's launching from this house at all. Honest to God, I can't believe he'd do this to his own family."

"It's more a matter that he wants to be sure of the local police," Lynley told her. "That happens, actually, more often than people think."

"What's that exactly?" Manette enquired. "Someone pops down to London and asks for a second investigation into a matter already settled by the coroner so Scotland Yard takes up the case? Just like that? Please, Inspector. You can't think I'm that stupid."

McGhie said to Lynley, "What's prompted this? It was a straightforward matter according to the coroner."

"Dad's throwing his weight," Manette said to him. "God only knows how, but I reckon he knows someone who knows someone who's willing to pull a few strings or make a donation to the widows and orphans. That's how these things happen. My guess is he wants to see if Nick's involved, no matter what the coroner said. God knows how Nick would have managed things, but with his history I daresay anything's possible." She looked at Lynley. "I'm right, am I not? You're here to see if I can assist in putting the screws on my brother."

"Not at all," Lynley said. "It's only a matter of getting a clear understanding of where everyone fits."

"What the hell is that supposed to mean?"

"It means that sometimes a death is placed too conveniently in time. A coroner wouldn't be looking at that. There'd be no reason to if the circumstances are straightforward enough."

"So that's why you're here? You're determining the *convenience*, as you say, of my cousin's drowning? And whom did Ian's death convenience? Because I must tell you it didn't convenience me. What about you, Freddie? Were you convenienced?"

McGhie said, "Manette, if Scotland Yard's here—"

"Oh bother," she cut in. "If Scotland Yard's here, my father probably handed over some cash. A new wing on their offices. Who the hell knows what else? You've been looking at the books, Freddie. You'll find it if you look hard enough. There'll be a payout that you can't understand. Beyond the others you can't understand."

Lynley said to McGhie, "Are there irregularities with the books, then, in your father-in-law's business?"

"I was joking," Manette said, and then to McGhie, "Wasn't I, Freddie?" in a tone whose meaning was *don't say a word*.

What Freddie did say was, "Former."

"What?"

"Former father-in-law."

"Yes. Of course."

"Current. Former. It doesn't matter," Manette said. "What matters is that Ian drowned, it was an accident, and if it *wasn't* an accident, you need to be looking at who was *convenienced* by his death, which wasn't me. That being the case, it seems to me, if I'm remembering this right, the big convenience is the one that fell into Kaveh Mehran's lap."

McGhie said to her, "What's going on there?"

She said to him, "I haven't told you. Kaveh's now sole owner of the farm."

"You're joking."

"Hardly. Ian left it to him. Or so he claims. I expect he's telling the truth as it wouldn't take a big effort to check out the paperwork."

"Everything's being looked into, Mrs. McGhie," Lynley said.

"But you don't think Kaveh killed Ian, do you?" Freddie McGhie asked.

"No one killed him at all," Manette said. "His death might have been opportune for someone, but it was an accident, Freddie. That entire boathouse ought to be pulled down before it collapses of its own accord. I'm surprised Mother wasn't the one to fall, smash her head, and drown. She's in there more often than Ian anyway."

McGhie said nothing, but his face altered, a subtle change in which his jaw lowered but his lips didn't part. Something had struck him with his former wife's words, something he was, perhaps, inclined to speak of if the prod was gentle enough.

Lynley said, "Mr. McGhie?"

McGhie's hand was on the table, and his fingers curled till they made a light fist. He was watching Manette, but he was also deciding: what it would mean, Lynley reckoned, if he told what he knew.

There was always tremendous value in silence. It acted upon people in much the same way that time alone in a police interview room acted. Tension was the great equaliser among men. Most couldn't handle it, especially when they themselves could so easily defuse the ticking bomb it comprised. Lynley waited. Manette's gaze met her former husband's eyes. She read there, apparently, what she didn't want to know because she said, "We don't know what *anything* means, Freddie."

To which he replied, "True enough, old girl. But we can easily guess, can't we?" And then without ceremony, he began to speak. She protested, but he made his position clear: If someone had set up the boathouse to hurt Ian Cresswell or, indeed, to hurt Manette's own mother, then everything currently in the shadows had to come out.

The way Freddie McGhie saw it, Bernard Fairclough had been running through money for a number of years. Payments to various clinics to turn Nicholas around, the wealth put into the Ireleth Hall gardens, the purchase of Arnside House at a high point in the property market, the renovation of that building to make it suitably habitable for Nicholas Fairclough and his bride, the folly built to house Mignon, her subsequent operations to allow her finally to shed the weight she'd been piling on since childhood, the follow-up surgery for the excess skin she then carted round . . .

"Ian might have been writing the cheques, but he also would've been telling Bernard to stop, stop, stop," was how McGhie put it. "Because some of this nonsense had been going on for years. There was no sense to it, as far as I can see. It was as if he couldn't stop himself. Or he felt he *had* to for some reason. Had to lay out money, I mean."

"For years?" Lynley clarified.

"Well, Nick's been a problem for a very long time, and then there was—"

"Freddie. That's enough." Manette's voice was sharp.

Freddie said, "He's got to know it all. I'm sorry, darling, but if Vivienne's somehow at the bottom of this she's got to be mentioned."

"Vivienne Tully?" Lynley said.

"You know about her?"

"I'm learning."

"D'you know where she is?" Manette asked. "Does Dad know?"

"Well, he has to, hasn't he?" McGhie said to her reasonably. "Unless Ian was paying her every month without your father's knowledge. But why in God's name would he do that?"

"The obvious reason: because she knew about him, what he was hiding from Niamh and from everyone else. She held his feet to the fire. Blackmail, Freddie."

"Come on, old girl, you don't believe that. There's only one good reason for payouts to Vivienne Tully, and we both know what it probably is."

They'd almost forgotten he was in the room, Lynley realised, so intent were they upon believing whatever it was each of them wished to believe: about Ian Cresswell, about Vivienne Tully, about the money Cresswell had paid out left, right, and centre, either on behalf of Bernard Fairclough or without his knowledge.

Aside from everyone else taking handouts from Bernard Fairclough's funds, Freddie McGhie told Lynley that Vivienne Tully—a long-ago employee, as Lynley already knew—had been receiving monthly sums for years, despite not having been employed by Fairclough Industries during that time period. This money wouldn't have anything to do with profit sharing or a pension scheme, Freddie added.

"So the payout could mean any number of things," he concluded. "A sexual harassment lawsuit Bernard was trying to avoid, an unlawful dismissal . . ." He glanced at his former wife as if for confirmation of this.

"Or Dad didn't know," was what she said. "You've said yourself: Ian might have been cooking the books all along."

To Lynley, all of the information indicated a death that was no accident. What it still did not clarify, however, was who the intended victim had actually been.

He thanked Manette and her former husband. He left them to what he reckoned was going to be a full discussion of the family situation. He could tell from Manette's reaction to the information McGhie had been giving that she was not going to let these dogs lie.

He was getting into the Healey Elliott, when his mobile rang. Havers, he thought. Clarity on its way. But he saw by the incoming number that it was Isabelle ringing.

He said to her, "Hullo, you. This is a pleasant diversion."

She said, "I'm afraid we need to talk, Thomas."

Even if she hadn't said *Thomas*, Isabelle's tone would have told him this wasn't the woman whose soft curves and warm body his hands knew and enjoyed. This was his guv, and she wasn't pleased. On the other hand, she was stone-cold sober, and he could tell that as well.

He said, "Of course. Where are you?"

"Where you should be. I'm at work."

"As am I, Isabelle."

"After a fashion. But that's not my point."

He waited for more. It was quick in coming.

"Why is it Barbara Havers can be entrusted with information and I can't? What d'you expect I'd have done with the knowledge? What *could* I have done? Marched into Hillier's office crowing, 'I know, I know, I bloody well know'?"

"Barbara's doing some digging for me, Isabelle. That's all it is."

"You lied to me, didn't you?"

"About what?"

"The entire need for secrecy. It can hardly be a hush-hush matter if Sergeant Havers is sledgehammering her way through it."

"Barbara knows no more than some names. There were matters I couldn't deal with at my end, but I knew she could. She's doing research."

"Oh, please. I'm hardly stupid, Tommy. I know how tight you are with Barbara. She'd gladly step into the iron maiden if you asked her. You say mum's the word on this one, Barb, and she'd cut out her tongue. This has to do with Bob, hasn't it?"

Lynley was flummoxed. Bob? For a moment, he had no idea what she was talking about. Then she added, "Bob, his wife, the twins. You're punishing me because unlike you I have entanglements and sometimes they get in our way."

"Are you talking about that night?" he asked. "When I turned up? When they were all there? Isabelle, good God. That happened and it's done with. I carry no—"

"Grudge? No, you wouldn't, would you? You're far too well bred for that."

"Really, Isabelle darling, you're upset about nothing. It's everything that I said it was. Hillier wants this unknown at the Met and I've kept it that way."

"It's about trust, you know. And I'm not just talking about this situation. I'm talking about the other as well. You could ruin me, Tommy. One word and I'm finished. Gone. It's done. If you don't trust me, how can I trust you? God in heaven, what've I done to myself?"

"What you've done is work yourself into a state over nothing. What do you expect I'd do to you?"

"I step out of line, I don't cooperate, I'm not quite the woman you think I should be . . ."

"And what? I march into Hillier's office and say I've been my guv's lover on the sly for the past four months, six months, two years, whatever? Is that what you think?"

"You could destroy me. I don't have that equal power over you. You don't need the job, you don't even bloody *want* the job. We're not equals in so many ways and this is the biggest one. Add to that the fact that there's no trust now and what have we got?"

"What do you mean that there's no trust now? That's ridiculous. It's completely absurd." And then the question, because he suddenly knew—was sure of it—that he'd been wrong at first about her condition. "Have you been drinking?"

Silence. It was the worst thing to ask. He wished he could unsay it. But he couldn't and her reply was soft.

"Thank you, Tommy," she said. She cut off the call. She left him looking out at Great Urswick's pond and a family of swans peacefully afloat upon the placid water.

After the detective left, Manette drove directly to Ireleth Hall. She parked on the drive and strode to the folly. She'd left with Freddie telling her that he'd had no choice but to speak, that if indeed Ian's death was no accident, they had to get to the bottom of the matter. Anyway, he'd said, it was becoming clear that there were other matters they needed to get to the bottom of, also. Well and good, had been Manette's reply. Getting to the bottom of things was exactly what she intended to do.

Mignon was at home. When was Mignon *not* at home? But she was not alone as she usually was, so Manette was forced to sit through the last part of her sister's thrice-weekly head-and-foot massage. This was administered by a grave Chinese man who drove out from Windermere for this purpose, which was an hour on the head and an hour on the feet. Which, of course, their father would pay for.

Mignon was in a reclining chair, eyes closed, as her feet were seen to: pressure, massage, whatever the hell else it all was. Manette didn't know and she hardly cared. But she understood her twin well enough to throw herself into a seat and wait because this was the only way she was going to be able to garner her sister's cooperation. Interrupt her pleasure and there would be hell to pay.

It all took a tedious half hour. Occasionally, Mignon murmured, "So lovely," or "Yes," or "A bit more pressure to the left, darling." The solemn Chinese man obliged as instructed. Manette wondered what he'd do if her sister asked him to suck on her toes.

At the end, the masseur gently wrapped Mignon's feet in a warm towel. She moaned and said, "So soon? It seemed like five minutes." Slowly, she opened her eyes and cast a radiant smile upon the man. "You are a miracle incarnate, Mr. Zhao," she murmured. "You know where to send the bill, of course."

Of course, Manette thought.

Mr. Zhao nodded and packed up his things. Oils and

unguents and whatevers. Then he was gone, as silent as an embarrassing thought.

Mignon stretched in her chair. Arms raised high over her head, toes pointed, all of it like a luxuriating cat. Then she unwrapped her feet, got up, and strolled to the window, where she stretched a bit more. She bent to touch her toes, and she worked her body to loosen her waist and her hips. Manette half expected her to start doing jumping jacks. Anything to rub in the obvious joke that Mignon was continuing to play on their parents.

"I don't know how the hell you live with yourself," Manette said.

"It's one eternal circle of excruciating pain," Mignon told her, casting a sly look in her direction. If one could project gleeful misery, Manette decided, that would come close to describing her sister's expression. "You cannot possibly know what I suffer." She strolled from the sitting room into the area set up to house her computer, careful to take her zimmer along should either of their parents make an unexpected call upon her. She tapped a few keys and spent a few moments reading something that was likely an e-mail message. She said, "Oh dear. This one's becoming something of a bore. We've got to the great-impossibility-of-our-love-darling stage, and when they get there, all the anguish and teeth gnashing put such a bloody damper on things." She sighed. "I did have such hopes for him. He seemed good for a year's go, at least, especially once he started with the genitalia photos. But what can I say? When they fall, they do fall so hard." She punched a few keys and murmured, "Bye-bye, darling. Alas, alack, and all the rest. Love springs eternal. Whatever."

"I want to talk to you," Manette said to her twin.

"I did conclude that, Manette, mere casual calls upon your siblings not being exactly your style. At least casual calls upon this sibling. That troubles me, you know. We used to be so close, you and I."

"Odd," Manette said, "I don't recall that part of our history."

"Well, you wouldn't, would you? Once Freddie came into the picture, it was all about him and how you intended to snare the poor man. He was second-best, of course, but he didn't know that. Unless, of course, you moaned the wrong name at an inopportune moment. Did you, by the way? Is that how it ended between you and Freddie?"

Manette refused to bite. She said, "Dad's haemorrhaging money. I know about the increased payments to you. We must talk about that."

"Ah, the economy," Mignon said piously. "Always such a fragile thing, isn't it?"

"Let's not play games. What's happening to the business and to Dad has nothing to do with a sudden and surprising decline in the need for lavatories, basins, and tubs since the beauty of that business is simple enough: There's always a need. But you might want to know that Freddie's been dealing with the books since Ian's death. These payouts to you must stop."

"Must they? Why? Worried I'll run through all the money? Till there's nothing left for you?"

"I think I've made myself clear: I know Dad's increased his payments to you, Mignon. It's right there in the books. It's ridiculous. You don't need the money. You're entirely taken care of. You've got to cut him loose."

"And are you having this same conversation with Nick, beloved apple of our father's eye for his entire wasteland of a life?"

"Oh, stop it. You weren't the son Dad wanted and neither was I. Is that always going to be at the centre of your thoughts? Your entire existence on earth defined straight into eternity by Daddy-didn't-love-me-enough? You've been jealous of Nick since the day he was born."

"While you haven't a jealous bone in your body?" Mignon returned to the sitting room, making her way past the boxes and the crates and the endless array of items she'd seen and fancied and bought online. "At least I know what to do with my 'jealousy,' as you call it."

"Referring to what?" Manette saw the trap too late.

Mignon smiled, the successful black widow awaiting her mate. "To Ian, of course. You always wanted Ian. Everyone knew it. Everyone tut-tutted behind your back for years.

You took Freddie as second-best, and everyone knew that as well, poor Freddie included. That man's a saint. Or something."

"Rubbish."

"Which part? The saint? The something? The wanting Ian or the Freddie knowing? It can't be the wanting-Ian part of things, Manette. Lord, it must have slain you in your trainers when Niamh came along. I expect you think even now that Niamh, being the piece of work she is, drove Ian to try it on with men instead."

"If you think back carefully," Manette said calmly, although she was burning, "you'll come up with a small problem in your scenario."

"Which is?"

"That I was married to Freddie when Ian chose Niamh. Now, that doesn't quite make things fit, does it?"

"Details," Mignon said. "Utterly insignificant. You didn't want to *marry* Ian, anyway. You just wanted to . . . well, you know. Some poking and thrusting on the sly."

"Don't be absurd."

"Whatever you say." She yawned. "Are we finished here? I'd like to have a lie-down. Massages take it out of one, don't they? So if there's nothing else . . ."

"Stop this nonsense with Dad. I swear to you, Mignon, if you don't—"

"Please. Don't be ridiculous. I'm taking what I'm owed. Everyone's doing that. I can't think why you aren't."

"Everyone? Like Vivienne Tully, for example?"

Mignon's face became shuttered, but only for the instant it took her to come up with a nonchalant reply. "You'll have to ask Dad about Vivver."

"What do you know about her?"

"What I know isn't important. It's what Ian knew, darling. And it's like I said: People take what they're owed at the end of the day. Ian knew this better than anyone. He probably took some of the dosh himself. I wouldn't be surprised. It would have been child's play. He held the purse strings, after all. How difficult would it have been for him to do some skimming, only to have Dad find out about it?

Get into that kind of chicanery and you're not going to be able to do it forever. Someone's going to get wise. Someone's going to stop you."

"That sounds like a cautionary tale you ought to heed yourself," Manette told her sister.

Mignon smiled. "Oh, I'm the exception to every rule there is," was her airy reply.

LAKE WINDERMERE
CUMBRIA

There was at least some truth in what Mignon had said. Manette had loved Ian once romantically, but it had been a young adolescent's love, insubstantial and unsustainable albeit as obvious as the longing looks she'd cast in his direction over family dinners and the desperate letters she'd written and pressed into his hand at the end of holidays when he left for school.

Ian, alas, had not shared her passion. He'd been fond enough of Manette but there had finally come that one dreadful and never forgotten moment when he'd taken her aside during a half-term holiday, had handed her a shoe box of every one of her letters unopened, and had said to her, "Listen. Burn these, Manette. I know what they are, but it's just not on." He'd spoken not unkindly because unkindness had never been his way. But firmness had, and he'd been firm.

Well, we all survive these things, Manette had thought eventually. But now she wondered if some women weren't constituted in a way to do so.

She went in search of her father. She found him on the west side of Ireleth Hall, far down on the lawn and quite near the lake. He was speaking to someone on his mobile phone, his head down as if with concentration. She considered coming upon him stealthily, but before she could do so, he concluded his call. He turned from the water to move towards the house, but when he saw her heading in his direction, he remained where he was and waited for her.

Manette tried to assess the look on his face. It was

strange that he'd come out of the hall to make a phone call.
He could, of course, have been having a walk and received
a call in the midst of it. But somehow she doubted this.
There was a furtiveness to the manner in which he slid the
mobile into his pocket.

"Why've you let all this go on?" she asked her father as
she came to his side. She was taller than he, just as her
mother was.

Fairclough said, "Which part of 'all this' are you referring to?"

"Freddie's got Ian's books. He's printed the spread-
sheets. He's got the programmes. You must have known
he'd be putting things in order after Ian."

"He's demonstrating his competency, is Freddie. He'd
like control of the firm."

"That's not his style, Dad. He'd take control of the firm
if that's what you asked of him, but that's the extent of it.
Freddie doesn't scheme."

"Are you certain?"

"I know Freddie."

"We always think we know our spouses. But we never
quite know them well enough."

"I hope you're not accusing Freddie of anything. That's
not on."

Bernard smiled thinly. "As it happens, I'm not. He's a
very good man."

"As it happens, he is."

"Your divorce . . . It always puzzled me. Nick and
Mignon"—Fairclough fluttered his fingers in the general
direction of the folly—"they had their demons, but you
didn't seem to. I was pleased when you and Freddie married. She's chosen well, I thought. To see it end, to have it
dissolve as it has . . . You've made very few mistakes in your
life, Manette, but letting Freddie go was one of them."

"These things happen," Manette said shortly.

"If we allow them," was her father's reply.

Now those were truly infuriating words, Manette
thought, all things considered. "Like you allowed Vivienne
Tully to happen?" she asked.

Bernard's gaze didn't leave her face. Manette knew what

was going on in his head. It was that rapid assessment of all the potential sources from which had sprung his daughter's question. It was also a wondering of what, exactly, Manette did know.

He said, "Vivienne Tully is in the past. She's been gone a very long time."

He was casting his line most delicately. Two could fish in these waters, though, so Manette cast hers. "The past is never as gone as we would like it to be. It has a way of coming back to us. Rather like Vivienne's coming back to you."

"I'm not sure what you mean."

"I mean Ian's been paying her off for years. Monthly, it seems. Years and years of monthly. You'll know that, of course."

He frowned. "Actually, I know nothing of the sort."

Manette tried to read him. His skin wore a glittering of sweat and she wanted that to mean something significant about who he was and what he might have done. She said at last, "I don't believe you. There was always something about you and Vivienne Tully."

He said, "Vivienne was part of a past that I allowed to happen."

"What's that supposed to mean?"

"That I failed myself in a human moment."

"I see," Manette said.

"Not everything," her father countered. "I wanted Vivienne, and she agreed to my wanting. But neither of us ever intended—"

"Oh, people never do, do they?" Manette heard the edge of bitterness in her words. Its presence surprised her. What, after all, was her father saying that in her heart she'd not suspected for years: a long-ago affair with a very young woman. What was this to her, his daughter? It was nothing at all, yet everything at once, and the hell in the moment was that Manette did not know why.

"People *don't* intend," Fairclough said. "They get caught up. They start to think rather stupidly that life owes them something beyond what they have, and when they go in that direction in their heads, the result is—"

"You and Vivienne Tully. I have to be honest. I don't

mean to hurt you but I can't see why Vivienne would have
wanted to sleep with you."

"She didn't."

"Sleep with you? Oh, please."

"No. That's not what I mean." Fairclough looked towards
the hall and then away. There was a path along Lake Windermere, rising towards a woodland that marked the far
north edge of the property. He said, "Walk with me. I'll try
to explain."

"I don't want an explanation."

"No. But you're troubled. I'm part of what troubles you.
Walk with me, Manette." He took her arm and Manette
felt the pressure of his fingers through the wool sweater
she was wearing. She wanted to loosen his grip and walk
away from him and make that departure a permanent one,
but she was as trapped as was her sister by the fact that
Bernard had wanted a son so badly. Unlike Mignon, who'd
spent her life punishing him for this desire, Manette had
tried to be that for him, adopting his ways, his postures,
his habits, his manner of speaking and standing and gazing
intently at someone with whom she was conversing and
even working in his business from the time she was able,
all to show him she was a worthy son. Which, of course,
she could never be. Then the son he'd had was unworthy
from the start, no matter how he'd redeemed himself
recently, and even that had not been enough to turn her
father's eyes upon her so he could see her merit. Thus, she
didn't want to walk with the bastard and she didn't want
to hear his lies about Vivienne Tully, whatever they were
going to be.

He said, "Children don't like to hear about their parents'
sexuality. It's unseemly."

"If this is going to be about Mother . . . some rejection
of you . . ."

"God no. Your mother never once . . . No matter. It's
about me. I wanted Vivienne for no reason other than I
wanted Vivienne. Her youth, her freshness."

"I don't want—"

"You brought her up, my dear. You must hear it
through. There was no seduction involved. Had you

thought there was?" He glanced at her. Manette saw his look but she kept her eyes fixed ahead, on the path, the way it followed the shore, the way it climbed a rise to the woods that seemed to keep receding no matter how she and her father pressed onward. He went on. "I'm not a base seducer, Manette. I approached her. She'd worked for me perhaps two months at that point. I was frank, as frank as I'd been with your mother the night I met her. Marriage between us wasn't possible, it wasn't even a thought. So I told Vivienne I wanted her for my lover, a discreet arrangement that no one would know of, something that would never stand in the way of her career, which I knew was important to her. She had a brilliant mind and an excellent future. I didn't expect her to waste that mind for a lifetime in Barrow-in-Furness or to give up that future because I wanted to be in her bed for however long she remained in Cumbria."

"I *don't* want to know this," Manette told her father, her throat aching so badly that she found speaking difficult.

"But you brought her up, so now you'll hear. She asked to have time to think about it, to consider all the ramifications of what I was proposing. For two weeks she thought. Then she came to me with her own proposal. She would try me as a lover, she said. She'd never thought of herself as anyone's mistress and she'd certainly never thought of herself as a woman attached in some way to a man older than her own father. This, she said frankly, was rather distasteful because she was not the sort of woman who found a man's money an aphrodisiac. She liked young men, men her own age, and she didn't know if she could manage even once putting up with me in her bed. She couldn't see me exciting her, she said. But if I pleased her as a lover, which she frankly did not expect, she'd agree to the arrangement. If I didn't please her, there would be—as she put it—no bad feeling between us."

"God. She could have taken you to court. It could have cost you hundreds of thousands. Sexual—"

"I knew that. But it's the madness of wanting that I was speaking of earlier. It can't be explained if you haven't felt it. It makes everything seem so reasonable, even propositioning one's employee and accepting her proposition in return." They walked on, their pace slow and the wind beginning to come off the lake. Manette shivered, and her father put his arm round her waist, pulling her closer, saying, "There's likely to be rain soon." And then he said, "So for a time, we played two different roles, Vivienne and I. At work we were the employer and his executive assistant with never the slightest indication that there was something more between us; at other times we were a man and his mistress with those daylight hours of fierce propriety providing the stimulus for what happened at night. Then, at last, she'd had enough. Her career called out to her, and I wasn't so much a fool as to stop her. I had to let her go, and as I'd promised to do so from the first, there was nothing for it but to wish her well."

"Where is she now?"

"I've no idea. The job she was offered was in London, but that was some time ago. I'd think she would have gone on from there."

"What about Mother? How could you—"

"Your mother never knew, Manette."

"But Mignon knows, doesn't she?"

Fairclough looked away. A moment passed during which a V of ducks flew overhead, swooped down towards the lake, rose above them again. He finally said, "She does. I don't know how she found out, but how does Mignon find out anything?"

"So that's why she's been able to—"

"Yes."

"But what about Ian? These payments he was making to Vivienne?"

Fairclough shook his head, then looked back at her. He said, "As God is my witness, I don't know, Manette. If Ian was paying Vivienne, it can only be that he was doing it to protect me from something. She had to have contacted him, threatened something . . . ? I just don't know."

"Perhaps she threatened to tell Mother. Like Mignon. And that's what she's doing, isn't it? Mignon's threatening to tell Mother if you don't continue to give her what she wants? What would Mother do if she knew?"

Fairclough turned to her then and it came to Manette that for the first time her father looked old. Indeed, he looked fragile, capable of breaking within someone's hands. "Your mother would be completely devastated, my dear," he said. "After all these years, I'd like to spare her that."

BRYANBARROW
CUMBRIA

Tim could see Gracie from the window. She was on her trampoline. She'd been out there for a good hour now, jumping and jumping, with her face a picture of concentration. Sometimes, she fell on her bum and rolled round on the matting. But she always got back up and resumed her jumping.

Earlier, Tim had seen her out in the garden, at the back of the house. She was digging, and he noted next to her on the ground a small cardboard box tied up with a red ribbon. When the hole she was digging got deep enough and wide enough, she put the box inside and buried it. She used a pail for the excess earth, which she spread around neatly throughout the garden, although at this time of year the garden was such a wreck that this nicety was entirely unnecessary. Before she did that spreading, though, she knelt and crossed her arms over her chest: right fist to left shoulder, left fist to right shoulder, her head tilted to one side. It came to Tim that she looked a bit like one of those angels one saw in old Victorian cemeteries, which clued him in to what she was doing. She was burying Bella, giving the doll a proper funeral.

Bella could have been repaired. Tim had done a fairly good job of destroying her, but her arms and legs might have been reattached and where she'd been scratched up from his attack upon her, the scratches might have been smoothed away. But Gracie would have none of that, just as she would have none of Tim once he'd returned from the soaking he'd given himself in Bryan Beck. When he'd changed his clothes, he went to Gracie and he'd offered to brush her hair and French-braid it, but she didn't want him near her. "Don't touch me and don't touch Bella, Timmy," was how she put it. She didn't sound sad, merely resigned.

After the doll's funeral, she went to the trampoline. There she'd been ever since. Tim wanted to stop her, but he didn't know how. He thought about ringing their mother, but he dismissed that notion as soon as it came into his head. He knew what she'd say: "She'll stop jumping when she gets tired. I'm not going to drive all the way to Bryanbarrow to pull your sister off that trampoline. If you're so bothered by it, ask Kaveh to get her off. He should enjoy the opportunity to be paternal." She'd say that last bit with a snarl in her voice. Then off she'd go to that wanker Wilcox to get herself seen to by a *proper* man. And that was how she'd think of it. Charlie Wilcox wanted to do her, so he was the real goods. While anyone *not* wanting to do her—like Tim's father, for example—was shite on oatmeal. Well, that was the truth anyway, wasn't it? Tim asked himself. His dad was shite and so was Kaveh and Tim was learning that everyone else was shite as well.

He'd come back to the house after going after the ducks in the beck. Kaveh had followed and tried to talk to him, but Tim wasn't having *anything* off that bloke. Bad enough that the wanker had put his greasy mitts on Tim. To have to talk to him on top of that . . . It just wasn't on.

Tim thought, though, that Kaveh might be able to get Gracie off the trampoline. He might also get Gracie to let Tim dig up the doll and take her off to Windermere to be repaired. Gracie liked Kaveh because that was Gracie. She liked everyone. So she'd listen to him, wouldn't she? Besides, Kaveh hadn't done anything to hurt her, aside from wrecking her entire family, of course.

Tim himself would have to *talk* to Kaveh, though. He'd have to go downstairs and find him and tell him that Gracie was outside jumping. But if he did *that*, Kaveh would probably just point out that there was nothing wrong with jumping on a trampoline, that's what trampolines were for, weren't they, and wasn't that why they'd got one for Gracie in the first place, because she liked to jump? Then Tim would have to explain that *when* she jumped for an hour as she'd done so far, it was because she was hurting inside. Then Kaveh would say the obvious thing: Well, we both know why she's hurting, Tim, don't we?

Tim hadn't intended. That was the problem. He hadn't intended to make Gracie cry. Gracie was the only person who actually mattered to him, and the truth was she'd just *been* there, in his way. He hadn't thought of what came after the moment when he snatched Bella up and pulled her arms and legs off. He'd only wanted to *do* something to make the boiling inside of him go away. But how could Gracie understand that when she had no boiling inside of her? She could only see the meanness within him that had snatched up Bella and dismembered her.

Gracie stopped for a moment outside. Tim saw that she was breathing hard. He also noticed something new about Gracie, which brought him up short. She was growing breasts and he could see the buds of them poking at the jersey that she was wearing.

This brought a searing sadness upon him. It clouded his vision, and when the cloud passed, Gracie had gone back to jumping again. And this time, he watched her little breasts as she jumped. Something, he knew, had to be done about her.

How useless would it be to pick up the phone and ring their mother? he asked himself a second time. Gracie growing breasts meant Gracie needing her mum to do something like take her to town and purchase her a baby brassiere or whatever it was that little girls wore when they started growing breasts. This went beyond just getting Gracie off the bloody trampoline, didn't it? Yes, it did, but wasn't the truth that Niamh would see this the same way she saw everything? Tell Kaveh about it, she would say. Kaveh can handle this little problem.

That was everything tied up with a bow: Whatever Gracie was going to face in her growing-up years, she was going to have to face without a mum to help her, because the one thing in life that was an absolute certainty was that Niamh Cresswell had plans for herself that didn't include the children she'd had with her louse of a husband. Thus Tim knew it was down to him or it was down to Kaveh to help Gracie as she grew up. Or it was down to them both.

Tim left his room. Kaveh was somewhere in the house, and Tim supposed now was as good a time as any to tell him that they needed to take Gracie into Windermere to get whatever she needed. If they didn't do it, the boys in her school would start to tease her. Ultimately the girls would tease her as well. Teasing her would turn into bullying her soon enough, and Tim wasn't about to have his sister bullied.

He heard Kaveh's voice as he descended the stairs. It seemed to be coming from the fire house. The door to the room was partially closed, but a shaft of light fell on the floor from inside and he heard the sound of a poker stirring coals in the grate.

". . . not actually in my plans," Kaveh was saying politely to someone.

"But you can't be thinking of staying on now Cresswell's dead." Tim recognised George Cowley's voice. He also recognised the subject. *Staying on* meant they were talking about Bryan Beck farm. George Cowley would be seeing the death of Tim's father as his chance to sweep in and buy the place. Obviously, Kaveh wasn't having that.

"I am," Kaveh said.

"Thinking of raising sheep, are you?" Cowley sounded amused by the entire idea. He probably pictured Kaveh mincing round the farmyard in pink Wellies and a lavender waxed jacket or something like.

"I'd actually hoped you'd continue renting the land as you've been doing," Kaveh said. "It's worked out so far. I don't see why it can't continue to do so. Besides the land's quite valuable if it ever came to a sale of it."

"And you reckon I'd never have the funds to make it mine," Cowley concluded. "Well, d'*you* have the funds to buy it up yourself, laddie? I reckon not. This whole place'll go on the block in a few months' time and I'll be there with the money."

"I'm afraid it won't be going on the block at all," Kaveh said.

"Why's that, then? You're not claiming he left it to you?"

"As it happens, he did."

George Cowley was silent, digesting this unexpected bit of news. He finally said, "You're taking the piss."

"As it happens, I'm not."

"No? So *where* d'you plan to come up with the death duties, eh? That'll take a real pile of dosh."

"Death duties aren't actually going to be a problem, Mr. Cowley," Kaveh said.

There was another silence. Tim wondered what George Cowley was making of all this. For the first time, he also wondered how Kaveh Mehran fit into the picture of his father's death. It had been an accident, plain and simple, hadn't it? *Everyone* had said so, including the coroner. But now it didn't seem so simple at all. And the next thing that came out of Kaveh's mouth made the matter complicated beyond Tim's imagining.

"My family will be joining me here as well, you see. Our combined resources will see to it that death duties—"

"Family?" Cowley scoffed. "What's the meaning of family in the light of day to your sort, eh?"

Kaveh didn't reply for a moment. When he spoke, then, his tone was deathly formal. "Family means my parents, for one. They'll be coming up from Manchester to live with me. Along with my wife."

The walls seemed to shimmer around Tim. The earth itself seemed to tilt. Everything he'd thought he'd known was suddenly thrown into a vortex where words meant something far beyond what they'd meant for all of his fourteen years and what he thought he'd actually understood was obliterated by the uttering of one declaration.

"Your wife." Cowley said it flatly.

"My wife. Yes." The sound of movement, Kaveh crossing to the window perhaps, or to the desk at one side of the room. Or even standing at the hearth of the fireplace, one arm on the mantel, looking like someone who knew he was holding all the good cards in the deck. "I'll be marrying next month."

"Oh, too right." Cowley snorted. "She know about your little 'situation' here, this next-month *wife* of yours?"

"Situation? What on earth do you mean?"

"You little pixie. You know 'xactly what I mean. You two arse bandits, you an' Cresswell. Wha's this, eh? Think the whole village didn't know the truth?"

"If you mean that the village knew Ian Cresswell and I shared this house, of course they knew. Beyond that, what else is there?"

"Why, you little bum fucker. You trying to say—"

"I'm trying to say that I'll be marrying, my wife will live here along with my parents, and then our children. If there's something not clear to you in that, I don't know what else to tell you."

"What about them kids? You think one'f them won't tell this next-month wife of yours what's up with you?"

"Are you talking about Tim and Gracie, Mr. Cowley?"

"You goddamn bloody well know I am."

"Aside from the fact that my fiancée doesn't speak English and wouldn't understand a word they said to her, there's nothing for them to tell anyone. And Tim and Gracie are going back to their mother. That's already in the works."

"That's that, then?"

"I'm afraid it is."

"You're a real deep one, then, aren't you, lad? Had this planned from the first, I expect."

What Kaveh said in answer, Tim did not catch. He'd heard all that he needed to hear. He stumbled from the passageway into the kitchen and from there out of the house.

LAKE WINDERMERE
CUMBRIA

St. James had decided there was a final possibility in this matter of Ian Cresswell's drowning. It was a tenuous one at best, but as it existed, he knew he had to set out to see about it. He required a single sporting implement to do so.

There was no angling shop in either Milnthorpe or Arnside, so he drove the distance to Grange-over-Sands and made his purchase in a concern called Lancasters. Lancasters sold everything from baby clothes to gardening tools and it was strung along the sloping high street as a series of shops that had obviously been snapped up by the eponymous and enterprising Lancaster family over the last hundred years in a remarkable and successful project of expansion, one shop now tumbling into the next. The governing philosophy behind them all seemed to be that what wasn't sold within the place didn't need to be bought. This being a part of the world given to fishing, what they did have was a fillet knife exactly like the one that Lynley had brought up from the water inside the Ireleth Hall boathouse.

St. James made his purchase of this, rang Lynley on his mobile, and told him he was heading to Ireleth Hall. He also phoned Deborah, but she wasn't answering. He wasn't surprised, as she would have seen he was the caller and she wasn't happy with him at the moment.

Nor, particularly, was he happy with her. He loved his wife deeply, but there were moments when the fact that they couldn't see eye-to-eye on something made him despair of their entire marriage. This despair was always a fleeting thing, a feeling that he generally reflected upon later and chuckled over when both his temper and Deborah's had cooled. Why were we so caught up in *that*? he would wonder. Matters so crucial one day were mere bagatelles the next. This one didn't seem so insignificant, however.

He took the most direct route to Lake Windermere although at another time he would have quite enjoyed taking a diversion and cruising up through the Lyth Valley. Instead, he sped along the northeastern route and ended up at the very tip of Lake Windermere, where the mass of end moraines at Newby Bridge spoke of glaciers, an ice age, and a time long ago when the village had stood at the southernmost point of the lake itself, which now lay some distance away. Then he sped north. Within moments, Lake Windermere came into view: a broad unwrinkled sheet of grey-blue reflecting the autumn-hued trees that formed woodlands along its shores.

Ireleth Hall was not far from this point, a few miles beyond the area where the Victorian beauties of Fell Foot Park offered walks and vistas that at this time of year were growing cold and forbidding but in spring would be a palette of nodding daffodils and colourful rhododendrons that grew to the height of buildings. He passed by this place and entered one of dozens of arboreal tunnels along the road: auburn and ochre where still there were leaves on the trees, skeletal branches where there were now none.

The gates were closed at Ireleth Hall, but there was a bell buried within the ivy that climbed the stone plinth forming part of its boundary wall. St. James clambered out of his hired car and rang it. As he did so, Lynley pulled up behind him in the Healey Elliott.

This made entry easy. A moment of disembodied conversation with someone who answered the bell, Lynley saying over St. James's shoulder, "It's Thomas Lynley," and that was that. They were inside, the gates creaking open like something from an old horror film, then creaking closed behind them.

They went directly to the boathouse. This was, St. James told his friend, the only other possibility in what went for his part of the investigation. While no one would ever be able to proclaim that all the circumstances surrounding Ian Cresswell's death had been completely straightforward, if there was anything to persuade the coroner to reopen the matter, this was how they would find it. And even this guaranteed nothing, he said.

For his part, Lynley declared he'd be more than happy to close matters up here and return to London as soon as possible. St. James shot him a querying look at this remark. Lynley said, "The guv's not happy with me."

"Hillier hoping for something different from what you're coming up with?"

"No. Isabelle. She's not happy Hillier's roped me into this situation."

"Ah. Not good."

"Decidedly not good."

They said nothing more on the matter, but St. James wondered about Lynley's relationship with Isabelle Ardery.

Together they'd come to see him on matters concerning an earlier case they'd worked on, and St. James was not so oblivious of the world around him that he could not see the spark that existed between them. But involvement with a superior officer was a dangerous proposition. Indeed, Lynley's involvement with anyone at the Met was a dangerous proposition.

As they walked to the boathouse, Lynley told St. James of his meeting with Bernard Fairclough's daughter Manette and her husband, explaining what they had revealed about the money that Ian Cresswell had been paying out. Either Bernard Fairclough had been a party to all of this or he had not, Lynley said. But whatever the case, Cresswell seemed to have known things that could have spelled danger for him. Had Fairclough not known about these payouts or at least some of these payouts, then in Fairclough lay the danger once he'd discovered them. Had Ian tried to put a stop to some of the payments he was making, then in the recipients of those payments lay the danger.

"It all seems to come down to money in the end," Lynley said.

"That's the case more often than not, isn't it?" St. James noted.

Inside the boathouse, there was no need for additional light. What St. James intended did not require it, and the ambient light reflecting off the lake from the bright day outside was sufficient. St. James was there to examine the condition of the rest of the stones comprising the dock. If more of them were loose than just the two that had become dislodged, then he was of the opinion that what had happened to Ian had been mere chance.

The scull was there, but the rowing boat was not. Valerie, it seemed, was out on the water. St. James went to the area where her boat had been tied. Sensible, he thought, to check here first.

He used his hands and his feet, working his way along. He knelt awkwardly, saying, "I can manage," to Lynley when the other man made a move to help him. Things seemed quite solid until he got to the fifth large stone along his way, which felt as loose as a seven-year-old's baby incisor. The sixth and seventh wobbled as well. Then the next four were fine while the twelfth was barely hanging on. It was on this twelfth one that St. James applied the fillet knife he'd bought in Grange-over-Sands. Using this on what remained of the grout in order to get the stone into a position from which it would easily tumble into the water upon the slightest touch was simple. The blade slid in, St. James did a bit of jemmying with it, and the job was done. One foot placed on it—here Lynley did the honours—and into the water it went. It was not difficult to see how someone getting out of a scull and placing all his weight upon a stone similarly jemmied would have produced what had happened to Ian Cresswell. The real question was whether the other loose stones—weighted by Lynley but unassisted by St. James's fillet knife—would fall into the water as well. One of them did. Three of them didn't. Lynley sighed, shook his head, and said, "At this point, I'm quite open to suggestions. I won't argue if going home to London is one of them."

"We need direct light."

"For what, at this point?"

"Nothing in here. Come with me."

They left the boathouse. St. James brought the fillet knife up between them. They both had a look at it and the conclusion required no microscopic examination in a forensic lab. From its use on the grout, it was deeply scratched and scored. But the one that Lynley had earlier brought up from the water had been completely unmarked.

Lynley said, "Ah. I do see."

"This clarifies matters, I think, Tommy. It's time Deborah and I went back to London. I'm not saying at this point that those stones couldn't have been loosened in another way. But the fact that the knife you brought up from the water was unmarked suggests the drowning was indeed an accident or something else was used to dislodge one of those stones. And unless you intend to cart everything from the property off to forensics for some kind of match-up with the stones that went into the water—"

"I'll need another route," Lynley finished for him. "Or I can close this up and head back myself."

"Unless Barbara Havers gives you something, I daresay that's the case. It's not a bad result, though, is it? It's just a result."

"It is."

They stood silently looking out at the lake. A rowing boat was approaching them with a woman skillfully at the oars. Valerie Fairclough was dressed for fishing but she'd evidently had no luck. When she neared them, she showed her empty bucket and called out cheerfully, "It's good we're not starving round here. I've become rather hopeless in the last few days."

"There are more loose stones on the dock inside," Lynley called back. "We've made several a bit worse. Have a care. We'll help you."

They went back inside. She glided in silently and docked the rowing boat in the exact spot where the stones were loose. Lynley said, "You've managed to choose the very worst spot. Was this where you set out?"

"It was," Valerie said. "I hadn't noticed. Are they bad?"

"Over time they'll give way."

"Like the others?"

"Like the others."

Her face relaxed. She didn't smile but her relief was palpable. St. James took note of this and he knew Lynley did likewise as Valerie Fairclough handed her fishing gear over to him. Lynley set this to one side, then extended his hand and helped Valerie Fairclough from the boat. He made the introductions between the woman and St. James.

St. James said, "You found Ian Cresswell's body, as I understand."

"I did, yes." Valerie removed the hat she'd been wearing, a baseball cap that covered her fine grey hair. This was youthfully styled and she ran her fingers through it.

"You phoned for the police as well," St. James said.

"That's correct."

"I'm rather wondering about that," St. James said. "Are you heading to the house? May we walk with you?"

Valerie glanced at Lynley. She didn't look wary. She had far too much control for that. But she'd be wondering why Lynley's friend the expert witness from London wanted to have a chat, and she'd know quite well the topic wasn't going to be her momentary lack of success as an angler. She said graciously, "Of course you may," but that quick movement at the corners of her blue eyes told a different story about how she actually felt.

They set off up the path. St. James said to her, "Had you been fishing that day?"

"When I found him? No."

"What took you out to the boathouse?"

"I was having a walk. I do that in the afternoons, generally. Once the weather gets bad with the winter, I'm rather more confined than I like to be, as we all are, so I try to get out as much as I can while the days are still fine."

"Around the property? Into the woods? On the fells?"

"I've lived here all my life, Mr. St. James. I walk wherever my fancy takes me."

"On that day?"

Valerie Fairclough glanced at Lynley. She said to him, "Would you like to clarify?" which was, naturally, a well-bred way of asking why she was being grilled by his friend.

St. James said, "This is my interest, rather than Tommy's. I've spoken to Constable Schlicht about the day Ian Cresswell was found. He told me two curious things about the phone call to nine-nine-nine, and I've been trying to understand them ever since. Well, actually, only one of the things he told me was about the phone call. The other was about you."

Now the wariness was plain to see. Valerie Fairclough stopped on the path. She ran her hands down the sides of her trousers, a movement that St. James could tell was meant to settle her nerves. He knew Lynley was aware of this from the look Lynley cast him, which was one that told him to go on in order to get what he could from her.

"And what did the constable tell you?" Valerie said.

"He'd had a conversation with the bloke at dispatch. This would be the person who took the nine-nine-nine call about Ian Cresswell's drowning. He learned that whoever made that call was remarkably calm, considering the circumstances."

"I see." Valerie spoke pleasantly enough, but the fact

that she'd stopped moving along the path suggested there were elements of Ian Cresswell's death that she didn't want St. James and Lynley to uncover. One of them, St. James knew, was now out of their sight line. The folly built for their daughter Mignon was no longer in view.

"'There appears to be a dead man floating in my boathouse,' is roughly what was said," St. James told Valerie.

She glanced away. A ripple on the surface of her face was not unlike a ripple on the surface of the lake behind them. Something swimming beneath the water or a gust of wind across it but in either case, the moment comprised an instant in which her placidity failed her. She raised a hand to her forehead and brushed an errant hair away. She'd not put her baseball cap back on her head. The sunlight struck her face, showing the fine lines of an ageing that she seemed intent upon keeping at bay.

She said, "No one knows exactly how they'll react in that kind of situation."

"I entirely agree. But the second odd thing about that day was how you were dressed when you met the police and the ambulance on the drive. You weren't dressed for walking, certainly not for an autumn walk and certainly not for anything other than a walk through the rooms of your house, I expect."

Realising the direction St. James had been heading, Lynley said, "So you see, there are several possibilities that want exploring." He gave her a moment to think about this before going on with, "You weren't at the boathouse at all, were you? You weren't the one to find the body and you weren't the one to call nine-nine-nine."

"I believe I gave my name when I phoned." Valerie spoke stiffly, but she wasn't stupid. She would know that at least this part of the game was over.

"Anyone can give any name," St. James said.

"Perhaps it's time you told the truth," Lynley added. "It's about your daughter, isn't it? I daresay Mignon found the body, and Mignon placed the call. From the folly, she can see the boathouse. If she goes upstairs to the top floor of the tower, I should guess she can see everything from the door of the building to the boats leaving it to go out on the lake. The real question, then, is whether she had a reason to arrange Ian Cresswell's death as well. Because she would have known he was out there on the lake that evening, wouldn't she?"

Valerie raised her eyes to the sky. St. James was reminded unaccountably of a suffering Madonna and what motherhood brought and did not bring to a woman brave enough to engage in everything that it comprised. It never ended with the child's entry into adulthood. It went on till death, either the mother's or the child's. Valerie said, "None of them . . ." She faltered. She looked at both of them, St. James and Lynley, before she spoke again. "My children are innocent in all matters."

St. James said, "We found a filleting knife in the water." He showed her the knife he'd used on the stones. "Not this one, of course, but one very similar."

"That would be the one I lost a few weeks ago," she said. "An accident, actually. I was cleaning a good-sized trout, but I dropped the knife and it slid into the water."

"Indeed?" Lynley said.

"Indeed," she replied. "Clumsy of me but there you have it."

Lynley and St. James glanced at each other. What they had, actually, was a lie, since the workbench for cleaning fish was on the other side of the boathouse from the spot where the filleting knife had fallen into the water. Unless St. James was very much mistaken about the nature of the tool, the knife would have had to swim in order to end up lying beneath Ian Cresswell's scull.

KENSINGTON
LONDON

In person Vivienne Tully looked exactly like the photographs Barbara had seen of her on the Internet. They were of an age—she and Vivienne—but they couldn't have been more dissimilar. Vivienne, Barbara reckoned, was exactly what Acting Detective Superintendent Ardery would have *her* become: svelte of body, sveltely clothed with all the suitable accessories, and ultra-sveltely put together when it came to hair and makeup. Indeed, if there were degrees of svelte—and Barbara reckoned there were—then Vivienne Tully had somehow managed to claw her way to the top level. On principle alone, Barbara hated her on sight.

She'd made the decision to turn up at Rutland Gate as who she was and not as who she had earlier pretended to be: someone in search of a piece of pricey Kensington property. She rang the bell for flat 6, and without asking who'd come calling upon her, Vivienne Tully—or whoever was inside her flat—had released the door's lock. At that, Barbara reckoned she was expecting someone. Very few people were foolish enough to allow callers into their buildings without giving them a proper grilling. People ended up burgled that way. People also ended up dead.

It turned out that the expected visitor was an estate agent. Barbara learned this within three seconds of Vivienne Tully's giving her a once-over. Head to toe and a look of this-can't-*possibly*-be, and Vivienne was saying, "*You're* from Foxtons?" Barbara might have taken offence at this, but she wasn't there for a beauty contest. She also wasn't there to seize the moment and run with it since there was no way on earth that Vivienne Tully was going to believe an estate agent hot to sell her property would show up at her door wearing high-top red trainers, orange corduroys, and a navy donkey jacket.

So she said, "DS Havers, New Scotland Yard. I need a word."

Vivienne didn't exactly fall back in shock, which Barbara found worthy of note. She said, "Come in. I don't have a great deal of time, I'm afraid. I've an appointment."

"With Foxtons. Got it. Selling up, are you?" Barbara looked round as Vivienne closed the door behind them. It was a gorgeous flat by anyone's standards: high ceilings, elaborate crown mouldings, hardwood floors covered by Persian carpets, a few tasteful antiques, a marble fireplace surround. It would have cost buckets in the first place and it would take barrels to purchase it now. The odd thing was, however, that there was nothing of a personal nature anywhere. One could call a few pieces of carefully chosen German porcelain personal, Barbara supposed, but the collection of antique books on a bookshelf didn't exactly look like something one browsed through on rainy days.

"I'm moving to New Zealand," Vivienne said. "Time to go home."

"Born there?" Barbara asked, although she already knew the answer. The other woman had no evident accent; she'd be able to lie if she wished.

She didn't. "In Wellington," she said. "My parents are there. They're getting older and they'd like me back in the area."

"Been in the UK a while, then?"

"May I ask what this call is about, Sergeant Havers? How may I help you?"

"By telling me about your relationship with Bernard Fairclough. That'd be a start."

Vivienne's expression remained preternaturally pleasant. "I don't think that's any of your business. Exactly what is this about?"

"The death of Ian Cresswell. It's being investigated. I expect you knew him since you worked for Fairclough Industries for a time and so did he."

"Then wouldn't the logical question be what my relationship with Ian Cresswell was?"

"I reckoned we'd get to that next. Right now it's the Fairclough angle of things that interests me." Barbara looked round the room with an appreciative nod. She said, "Very nice digs. Mind if I park myself somewhere?" She didn't wait for an answer. Instead she went to an armchair, dumped her shoulder bag next to it, and sank down into its comfortable depths. She ran a hand along the fine upholstery. Bloody hell, is this silk? she wondered. Obviously, Vivienne Tully didn't do her shopping at IKEA.

Vivienne said, "I think I told you I'm expecting—"

"Someone from Foxtons. Got it. I'm good that way. Memory like the proverbial elephant if you know what I mean. Or is it the metaphorical elephant? I never know which. Well, never mind. You'd probably like things better if I scarpered before Foxtons shows up, eh?"

Vivienne wasn't a fool. She knew it was going to be information in exchange for Barbara's departure. She went to a small sofa and sat. She said, "I worked for a time for Fairclough Industries, as you've noted. I was Bernard Fairclough's executive assistant. It was my first job straight after the London School of Economics. After several years, I went on to other employment."

"Your type generally move round in the employment game," Barbara acknowledged. "I get that. But in your case, it was Fairclough Industries, a spate of private consulting, and then this current gig you have with the gardening concern and there you've stayed."

"What of it? I wanted more job security than private consultancy offers, and once I went to Precision Gardening, I had it. I climbed the ladder there, the right person in the right place during a period of time when it was important to demonstrate equity in employment between men and women. I hardly started as managing director, Sergeant."

"But you didn't cut your ties with Fairclough."

"I don't burn bridges. I find it wise to maintain contacts. Bernard asked me to serve on the board of the Fairclough Foundation. I was happy to do so."

"How'd that come about?"

"What do you mean? Are you looking for something sinister? He asked me and I said yes. I believe in the cause."

"And he asked you because . . ."

"I assume he thought my work for him in Barrow was competent and reflective of a willingness to be useful in other ways as well. When I left Fairclough Industries—"

"Why?"

"Why did I leave?"

"Seems to me you could've climbed the career ladder there as well as anywhere else."

"Have you spent much time in Barrow, Sergeant Havers? No? Well, it didn't appeal. I had the opportunity to come to London and I took it. That's what people do. I had the kind of offer of employment that might have taken years to get in Barrow, even if I'd wanted to stay there, which, believe me, I did not."

"And here you are, then, in Lord Fairclough's flat."

Vivienne altered her position slightly, her posture—which had seemed perfect in the first place—managing to become even more so. "Whatever you're thinking, you're misinformed."

"Fairclough doesn't own this flat? Why's he got his own key, then? I reckoned he was showing up to check you weren't rubbishing the place. Doing the landlord bit, if you know what I mean."

"What does any of this have to do with Ian Cresswell, the ostensible reason for your call?"

"Not sure yet," Barbara said cheerfully. "Want to explain the situation with the keys? Especially since Fairclough doesn't, as I'd thought, own this place. Which's quite nice, by the way. Must've cost you a pile of dosh. You'd want to keep it all safe and secure, I'd think. So I'm wondering if you hand out keys willy-nilly or if you only give them to special sorts of people."

"I'm afraid that's none of your business."

"Where's our Bernard stay when he comes to London, Miss Tully? Or I s'pose I should say Ms. eh? I checked at Twins, but they don't have overnighters there, it seems. Also, they don't allow women past the threshold aside from the old bag on door duty—believe me, I found that out straightaway—unless they're in the company of a member. Turns out you're in and out all the time on Fairclough's arm, the way I heard it. Lunch, dinner, drinks, whatever, and off the two of you go by taxi and the taxi always brings you here. Sometimes you unlock the front door. Sometimes he does, with his own key. Then up you come to this . . . well, let me say it's a bloody gorgeous place . . . and after that . . . Where *does* Fairclough stow his ageing body when he's in London? That's the real question."

Vivienne rose. She would need to, Barbara reckoned. It was close to the point where the other woman would do the ceremonious tossing of her rotund body out of the front door. Meantime, Barbara meant to push things as far as she could. She saw that Vivienne's entire composure was heading in a southerly direction, and this gratified her enormously. There was, after all, a certain selfish thrill in discommoding someone so ostensibly perfect.

"No, it isn't the real question," Vivienne Tully said. "The real question is how long it will take you to walk to the door, where I shall open it for you, and then close it upon your timely departure. Our discussion is over."

"Thing is," Barbara said, "I *do* have to walk there, don't I? To the door, that is."

"Or you can be dragged, of course."

"Kicking, screaming, and howling for the neighbours to hear? Raising a ruckus the likes of which gets you noticed rather more than you'd probably like to be noticed?"

"I want you out of here, Sergeant. There's not a single thing illegal in any part of my life. I don't see what my having lunch, dinner, drinks, or anything else with Bernard Fairclough has to do with Ian Cresswell unless Bernard handed the receipts to Ian and Ian didn't want to pay the bills. But he'd hardly lose his life over that, would he?"

"Would that've been like Ian? Tight with the baron's money, was he?"

"I don't know. I had no contact with Ian once I left the firm, which was years ago. Is that all you want to know? Because, as I told you, I have an appointment."

"There's still the matter of the keys to be cleared up."

Vivienne smiled mirthlessly. "Let me wish you luck in that matter." She walked to the front door of the flat, then, and she opened it. She said, "If you don't mind . . . ?" and really, there was nothing for it but for Barbara to cooperate. She'd got what she could from Vivienne, and the fact that Vivienne had been unsurprised to have Scotland Yard come calling in the first place—not to mention the fact that she'd managed the nearly impossible feat of not putting a foot wrong during their entire conversation—told Barbara that this was a case in which forewarned had led effortlessly to forearmed. There was nothing for it but to try another route. Nothing, after all, was impossible.

She took the stairs down, rather than the lift. They deposited her opposite the table on which the postal cubbies stood. The porter was there. He'd gathered up the post from where it had been dropped into the mail slot at the front of the building, and he was in the process of distributing it. He heard her and turned.

"Back again, are you?" he said in greeting. "Still hoping for a flat?"

Barbara joined him at the table, the better to have a look at what he was putting into the cubbies. A signed declaration of *She's guilty of something* would have gone down a treat, shoved into Vivienne Tully's cubby or, better yet, handed over to Barbara to be sent along to Lynley. But everything seemed to be straightforward enough from what she could see from the return addresses of BT, Thames Water, Television Licensing, and the like.

She said, "Got an in at Foxtons. As things turn out in the world of property sales, flat six will be going on offer soon. I thought I'd have a quick look."

"Miss Tully's flat?" the porter said. "I heard naught about that. Odd, as people gen'rally tell me since there'll be some coming and going once it hits the market."

"Could be it's a sudden thing," Barbara said.

"S'pose. Never thought she'd sell, though. Not with the situation she's got. 'Tisn't easy to find nice digs where a good school's just round the corner, eh?"

Barbara felt a frisson of excitement shoot through her. "School?" she said carefully. "Exactly what school are we talking about?"

9 NOVEMBER

Zed Benjamin found that he was quite looking forward to his morning chat with Yaffa Shaw, and he wondered if this was what true partnership was like between a man and a woman. If so, he also wondered why, for years, he'd been avoiding it like a Romany beggar on the steps of a church.

When he rang her, she gave the verbal sign that his mother was within listening distance. She said, "Zed, my little puppy, let me tell you all the ways I've been missing you," and she constructed a quick paean to his intelligence, his wit, his affability, and added the warmth of his hugs for good measure.

Zed reckoned his mother would be over the moon at that. "Hmm, I'm missing you as well," he said in reply, without thinking about the ramifications of such a disclosure. He didn't, after all, have to respond other than with amused thanks for Yaffa's continuing to bamboozle his mother during their daily conversations. "If I were there, I'd show you warmth the likes of which you've never seen."

"From far more than hugs, I hope," Yaffa said.

"That," Zed told her, "you may rely on."

She laughed. "You're a very naughty boy." And then to his mother, "Mama Benjamin, our Zed's being rather naughty again."

"'Mama Benjamin'?"

"She insisted," Yaffa said, and before he could comment, she went on. "So tell me what you've uncovered, my dear. You've moved your story forward a leap, haven't you? I can hear it in your voice."

The reality Zed admitted to himself was that *this* was the real reason for his call. He wanted to crow to the woman who was pretending to be the love of his life, as any man putatively caught within the snares of adoration would wish. He said, "I've found the cop."

"Have you indeed? That's marvellous, Zed. I *knew* that you would. And will you phone your editor with this news? Will you"—she made her voice appropriately anxious—"will you come home?"

"Can't yet. I don't want to phone Rod, either. I want to have this story signed and sealed so I can hand it over and tell him it's ready to be run. Word for word with every detail chased down. I've spoken to the detective and I've struck a deal. We're going at it as a team."

"My God." Yaffa produced breathless admiration. "That's brilliant, Zed."

"She's going to be helping without knowing she's helping. We'll track down one story as far as she's concerned, but I'll end up with two and one of them is her."

"The detective's a woman, then?"

"Detective Sergeant Cotter, she's called. First name Deb. Got her nailed down. She's part of the story but she's not all of it. Turns out she's looking into the wife, Alatea Fairclough. She's not onto Nick Fairclough at all. Well, she was at first, but turns out there's something particularly iffy about the wife. Have to say I reckoned that from the first. It *never* made sense that someone like Nick Fairclough could have ended up with an Alatea."

"Oh?" Yaffa sounded interested. "Why is this, Zed?"

"He's an okay sort of bloke, but she ... His wife's drop-dead gorgeous, Yaf. I've never in my life seen anyone like her."

There was silence from Yaffa's end. Then a little "Goodness" comprised her entire response, and Zed wanted to slap himself sharply. What a bloody gaffe, he thought. He said, "She's not my type at all, of course. Cool and distant.

The sort of woman keeps a man running to do her bidding, if you know what I mean. Sort of a black widow and you're in the web? You know what black widows do, eh, Yaffa?"

"They attract males to mate with, as I recall," she said.

"Well, right. Of course. But point is, they're deadly. It's the old mate-and-die. Or rather, it's the old mate-and-be-murdered. Gives me the absolute willies, Yaffa. She's beautiful, but there's something strange going on with her. One can tell."

Yaffa seemed to take comfort from this although Zed wondered what it meant that she needed comfort, what with the loathed Micah in Tel Aviv studying to be a physician, a nuclear physicist, a neurosurgeon, and a financial wizard all rolled into one. She said, "You must be careful, then, Zed. This could be dangerous."

"Not a worry there," he told her. "Plus, I've got the Scotland Yard detective with me for added protection."

"Another woman." Did Yaffa sound sad?

"A redhead like me, but I like my women dark."

"Like this Alatea?"

"No," he said. "Not one bit like this Alatea. *Any*way, darling, this detective's got information by the bucketful. She's giving it to me in exchange for my sitting on the story for a few more days."

"But what will you tell your editor, Zed? How long can you hold off giving him something?"

"No problem there. I'll have Rodney where I want him once I tell him about the deal I've struck with the Met. He'll love that. It's right up his alley."

"You be careful, then."

"Will do, always."

Yaffa rang off then. Zed was left literally holding the phone. He shrugged and shoved the mobile into his pocket. It was only when he was on his way down to breakfast that he realised Yaf hadn't made her usual kissy noises at him. It was only when he'd tucked into his plate of watery scrambled eggs that he also realised he wished she'd done so.

MILNTHORPE
CUMBRIA

They'd passed a wretched night together. Deborah knew that Simon wasn't happy with her. They'd had a desultory dinner in the Crow and Eagle's restaurant, an establishment that wasn't exactly within breathing distance of being awarded a Michelin rosette. He'd said very little at the meal about the matter of open adoption, which Deborah knew was the source of his displeasure, just a quiet "I'd have preferred it had you not phoned David quite so soon," and that was it. What he meant, of course, was that he'd have preferred it had she waited until he could talk her into something that she did not want in the first place.

Deborah had not replied to this at first. Instead, she'd made conversation with him on other matters and waited until they'd returned to their room. There, she'd said, "I'm sorry you're unhappy about this adoption situation, Simon. But you did tell me the girl wanted to know," at which he'd observed her with his grey-blue eyes so assessing in that way he had. He'd said, "That's not really the point, though, is it?"

It was the sort of remark that could make her miserable or fire her anger, depending upon which part of her history with Simon she went to in order to receive it. She could hear it as the wife of a beloved husband whom she'd inadvertently hurt. Or she could hear it as the child who'd grown to adulthood in his house and under his gaze, recognising the disappointed-father tone in his voice. She *knew* the former but at the moment, she *felt* the latter. And sometimes it was such a pleasure just to let one's feelings fly.

So she'd said, "You know, I really *hate* it when you talk to me like that."

He'd looked surprised, which added fuel. He'd said, "Talk to you like what?"

"You *know* like what. You are *not* my father."

"Believe me, I'm aware of that, Deborah."

And that had set her off: that he wouldn't allow himself to be roused to anger, that anger simply wasn't part of who he was. It maddened her, and it had always done so. She couldn't imagine a time when it would not.

Things had developed from there in the way of all arguments. From the manner in which she'd put an end to this matter with David and the girl in Southampton, they'd found themselves examining the myriad ways in which she had apparently long required his benevolent intervention in her life. That took them ultimately into the manner in which he'd dismissed her in the car park during their conversation with Tommy. This was a primary example of why he was required to watch over her, he'd pointed out, since she could not see when she was pigheadedly putting herself into harm's way.

Of course, Simon hadn't used the word *pigheadedly*. That was not his style. Instead, he'd said, "There are times when you don't see things clearly, and you won't see things clearly. You have to admit that," in reference to her insistence in the car park that the route to investigate had everything to do with Alatea Fairclough's possession of a magazine called *Conception*. "You've reached a conclusion based on your own inclinations," he said. "You're letting your judgement become clouded because of what you want instead of relying upon what you know. You can't do that and be effective in an investigation. And none of that has any importance anyway because you shouldn't be involved in this matter at all."

"Tommy asked me—"

"If this is going to come down to Tommy, he also pointed out that you've served your purpose and there's danger likely if you go any further."

"Danger from whom? Danger from what? There *is* no danger. Oh, this is absurd."

"I agree completely," he replied. "So we're finished here, Deborah. We need to return to London. I'll see to it."

This positively made her erupt, as he'd known it would. He'd left the room to do whatever he felt needed to be done regarding their departure, and when he'd returned her anger was so icy that she saw no point in speaking to him at all.

In the morning, then, he'd packed up his things. She

pointedly did not pack up hers. Instead she'd informed him that unless he wished to carry her over his shoulder all the way to her hire car, she was remaining in Cumbria. She said, "This isn't finished, Simon," and when he said, "Isn't it," she knew he was referring to more than matters associated with the drowning of Ian Cresswell.

She said, "I want to see this through. Can't you at least try to see this is something I need to do? I *know* there're things connected to this woman . . ."

It was definitely the wrong route to take. Any mention of Alatea Fairclough would only make Simon think more determinedly that Deborah was blinded by her own desires. He said quietly, "I'll see you in London, then. Whenever you return." He gave her a half smile that felt like an arrow to her heart. He added, "Good hunting," and that was that.

All along, Deborah knew that she could have told him about her plans with the reporter from *The Source*. But had she done that, the fact that she and Zed Benjamin were going to join forces in the investigation would have come out into the open. Then, Simon would have done something to stop this from happening, and telling Tommy would have accomplished it. In keeping the truth from Simon she was actually protecting Tommy from exposure as the Scotland Yard detective. She was, effectively, giving him more time to get to the bottom of things. If Simon couldn't see that she now had a vital place in this investigation, there was simply nothing she could do about that.

Even as she and her husband had their final words at the Milnthorpe inn, Zed Benjamin was down the road in Arnside, maintaining a position from which he could see the comings and goings at Arnside House. He would text her should Alatea Fairclough leave the property. *Move* meant she was on the move, heading somewhere in her car. *Your way* meant she was heading towards Milnthorpe.

This was the beauty of Arnside, Deborah and Zed Benjamin had concluded on the previous day. Although there were narrow lanes leading out of the village that one could take to reach the other side of Arnside Knot and the hamlets beyond Arnside Knot, if one wanted a quick route out of the place, there was but a single good road upon which to travel. That road was the road to Milnthorpe. That road passed by the Crow and Eagle.

When the text message came, Simon had been gone thirty minutes. Deborah examined her mobile with a surge of excitement. *Move* and *Your way* comprised the message.

She'd already gathered her necessary belongings. In less than one minute, Deborah was down the stairs and waiting just inside the entrance to the inn with a view to the street. Through the glass half of the door, she saw Alatea Fairclough drive by and make a right turn into the A6. Three cars behind her came Zed Benjamin. Deborah was ready for him when he pulled to the kerb.

"South," she said.

"I'm on it," he replied. "Nick took off as well, looking down in the mouth. Heading for the family business, I dare say. Doing his part to keep the country well-supplied with loos."

"What do you think? Should one of us have been following him?"

He shook his head. "No. I think you're right. This little lady is at the crux of it all."

LANCASTER
LANCASHIRE

The man was huge, Deborah thought. He filled more than his side of the car. He wasn't fat, merely enormous. His seat was pushed back as far as it would go, but still he had difficulty keeping his knees out of the way of the steering wheel. Despite his size, he wasn't an intimidating presence, however. There was an odd kind of gentleness to him, which she reckoned had to make him a fish out of water when it came to his chosen employment.

She was about to comment on this when he made a remark about what he supposed to be her line of work instead. With his eyes on Alatea's car far ahead of them, he said to Deborah, "Wouldn't have taken you for a cop. I wouldn't have known who you were at all if you hadn't been nosing round Arnside House."

"What did I do to give the game away, if you don't mind my asking?"

"I just have a sixth sense about this kind of thing." He tapped the side of his nose. "Can sniff 'em out pretty easily, if you know what I mean. Goes with the territory. Has to, doesn't it."

"What territory are we talking about?"

"Journalism. Thing is," he said expansively, "you have to be able to see more than what's just on the surface in my line of work. Investigative reporting is about more than sitting at one's desk and waiting for some bloke's lifelong enemies to ring up with details of a story that'll bring down the government. You have to be adept at digging. You have to get into the hunt."

Deborah found this nonsense impossible to resist. "Investigative reporting," she said contemplatively. "Is that what you call working for *The Source*, then? They don't seem to publish investigative stories about the government very often, do they? If at all."

"Just using that as an example," he said.

"Ah."

"Hey, it's a living," he declared, doubtless picking up on her ironic tone. "Anyway, I'm a poet otherwise. And no one supports himself on poetry these days."

"No, indeed," Deborah said.

"Look, I know it's a rag, Sergeant Cotter. But I like to eat and have a roof over my head and this is how I do it. Your line of work isn't much better, I reckon, looking under stones to dig out society's scum, eh?"

Mixed metaphor, Deborah thought. Odd for a poet but there you had it. "I suppose that's one way of looking at it," she said.

"There's more than one way to look at everything."

Up ahead of them, Alatea drove onward. It became apparent soon enough that she was heading for Lancaster. Once in the environs of the city, they had to take care not to be seen by her, so they dropped back with five cars between them.

They wound through the streets. There was no question that Alatea knew exactly where she was going. She ended up in the city centre, in the small car park of a stout brick structure, which Deborah and Zed Benjamin passed by. Thirty yards from this place, Zed pulled to the kerb. Deborah swivelled in her seat to look back at the building. In some forty-five seconds, Alatea came round the corner of it from the direction of the car park and went inside.

"We need to find out what that place is," Deborah said. Considering Zed's size, he wasn't the one to accomplish this task unseen. Deborah got out, said, "Wait here," and dashed to the other side of the street, where she could keep herself somewhat hidden by using the cars parked there.

She went as far as she needed to go to be able to read the lettering above the building's entrance. *Kent-Howath Foundation for Disabled Veterans* it said. A home for soldiers wounded in war.

Deborah considered Alatea's place of birth, which she knew was Argentina. This took her ineluctably to the Falklands War. She wondered about the likelihood of an Argentine soldier ending up here for some reason, someone whom Alatea was visiting.

She was thinking about other possible wars—the Gulf Wars being the most recent ones—when Alatea emerged. She wasn't alone, but she wasn't with anyone who looked remotely like a disabled veteran. She was instead with another woman, tall like Alatea but stocky. Her appearance and ease of movement suggested she was someone who regularly favoured the type of clothing she was wearing at the moment: a colourful long skirt, loose pullover, and boots. Her long hair was unstyled, dark in colour but peppered with grey, and she wore it pulled back from her face and held with a hair slide.

They walked in the direction of the foundation's car park, talking earnestly. Considering what this meant, Deborah dashed back to where Zed had parked. She got into the car saying, "She's going to be on the move. She's got someone with her."

In response, he fired up the engine and readied himself to follow once more. He said, "What was that place?"

"Disabled soldiers' home."

"That who's with her?"

"No. She's got a woman with her. I s'pose she could be a soldier, but she's not disabled as far as I could tell. Here they come. Quickly." Deborah lunged at Zed. She threw her arms round him and drew him into what she hoped appeared to a passerby as a lovers' passionate embrace. When over Zed's shoulder she saw the car pass, she released him and saw that his face was flaming. "Sorry," she said. "It seemed best."

He stammered, "Yes. Right. 'Course," and he pulled out of the parking space and got back onto Alatea Fairclough's tail.

They headed out of the city centre. Traffic was heavy, but they managed to keep Alatea's vehicle within view. Zed Benjamin was the one who twigged first where Alatea was headed. Clear of the centre of Lancaster, it wasn't long before a hillside topped with a variety of modern-era buildings came into view.

"She's going to the university," he said. "This could take us nowhere in our information."

Deborah didn't think so. If Alatea was heading towards Lancaster University with a companion, there was going to be a reason why. She had a feeling of what that reason would be, and she reckoned it had nothing to do with a desire to pursue higher education.

Parking in this area while remaining out of sight of their quarry was something of an iffy situation. Vehicles heading to the university were made to use a peripheral road, and once they found themselves upon it, Deborah and her companion discovered that parking was restricted as well. There were cul-de-sacs for it, but very little scope for hiding within them. Obviously, Deborah thought, the university had not been designed with the thought of individuals skulking along on the tail of someone else.

When Alatea turned into one of the cul-de-sacs, Deborah told Zed to let her out of the car. When he started to protest—they were, after all, supposed to be doing this tailing of Alatea Fairclough together and he wasn't exactly sure of Scotland Yard's cooperation, he pointed out—she said, "Look. We can't go in there after them, Zed. Drop me off, and drive on. Park somewhere else. Ring me on my mobile and I'll tell you where I am. It's the only thing that's going to work."

He didn't look happy. He didn't look trustful. That couldn't be helped. She wasn't there to earn his personal faith in her character. She was there to get to the bottom of Alatea Fairclough. He'd braked the car, and that was good enough for Deborah. She hopped out, saying, "Ring my mobile," and she dashed into the cul-de-sac before he could protest.

He wasn't stupid. He knew he couldn't be seen by Alatea Fairclough or the gaff would be blown in a very large way. Deborah couldn't be seen either, but it was going to be far easier for her to hide herself from the Argentine woman and her companion than for Zed to do so.

Following them proved simpler than she had thought it would be. Providence helped. It began to rain. The downpour was sudden and it was heavy, requiring umbrellas. What better way to conceal one's identity? Deborah fished hers out of her shoulder bag and thus was able to obscure her face and, more important, cover her coppery hair.

She kept a good distance between herself and the other women. They made for the university buildings. There were plenty of students on the purpose-built campus at this time of day, which was a blessing. It was also a blessing that the university—unlike the older institutions in the country—existed largely in a single location, on the top of that hill outside of the city proper.

The two women continued to talk as they walked, heads bent together, sharing an umbrella. Alatea had her arm through the other woman's. She slipped once, and her companion steadied her. They seemed to be friends.

They didn't stop in their progress through the campus. They consulted no map. They didn't ask directions. Deborah felt a flicker of excitement at this.

Her mobile rang. She said into it, hurriedly, "We're on a central path, a sort of walkway. It goes straight across the campus."

"Deb?"

Tommy's voice. Deborah winced and called herself a fool for not having looked at the incoming caller's identity. She said, "Oh. Tommy. I thought it was someone else."

"Obviously. Where are you?"

"Why d'you want to know?"

"Because I know you. I saw that expression on your face in the car park yesterday, and I know exactly what it means. You're doing something we've asked you not to do, I take it?"

"Simon's *not* my father, Tommy. Is he with you?"

"He's asked to meet for a coffee in Newby Bridge. Deb, what're you doing? Where are you? Whose call are you waiting for?"

Deborah considered not only whether to lie to him but also whether she could carry off a lie. She sighed and said, "Lancaster University."

"Lancaster University? What's going on?"

"I'm following Alatea Fairclough. She's come here in the company of a woman from a disabled soldiers' home. I want to see where they're going." She didn't give him time to consider what this might mean, instead continuing with, "This entire situation has got to do with Alatea Fairclough. Something's not right, Tommy. I know you can sense it."

"I'm not sure I sense anything other than the distinct possibility that you're walking into trouble, Alatea Fairclough or not."

"There can hardly be trouble in my following them. They don't know I'm behind them. And even if they work that out . . ." She hesitated. To tell him more would risk his telling Simon.

He was shrewd as a fox. He said, "You didn't answer my other question, Deb. Whose call are you waiting for?"

"The journalist."

"That bloke from *The Source*? Deb, this is a mad sort of business to be engaging in. Anything can happen."

"I see nothing worse happening than my photo appearing on the front page of *The Source* with a caption misidentifying me as Detective Sergeant Cotter. And I see that as hilarious, Tommy. It's hardly dangerous."

He was silent for a moment. Ahead, Deborah saw that the women had come to their destination, which was a modern upended box of a building constructed of brick and concrete in the unattractive fashion of the 1960s.

Deborah gave them a minute to enter and to get themselves out of the lobby and into a lift. In the meantime, Tommy said, "Deb, have you any idea what it would do to Simon if something happened to you? Because believe me, I have."

She paused at the building's front door. She said gently, "Dearest Tommy." He made no reply. She knew what the question had cost him. She said, "You're not to worry. I'm quite safe."

She heard him sigh. "Take care," he said.

"Of course," she replied. "And please. Not a word to Simon."

"If he asks me—"

"He won't." And she rang off.

Immediately her mobile chimed again. Zed Benjamin demanded, "Who the hell were you talking to? I was trying to ring you. Where the hell are you?"

Deborah told him the truth. She was talking to a DI from the Met. She was standing in front of . . . Well, the building was called George Childress Centre and she was about to go inside and see what was housed here. He could join her, but she wouldn't recommend it since, as before, he was rather more difficult to camouflage than she was.

He seemed to see the sense in this. He said, "Ring me when you know anything, then. And this better not be a double cross of some kind or you're in the paper tomorrow morning and the gaff is blown."

"Absolutely understood."

She flipped the phone closed and went inside the building. There were four lifts in the lobby as well as a security guard. She knew she couldn't bluff her way past the guard for love or money, so she looked round and saw that to one side of the lobby and between two languishing bamboo plants, a glassed-in notice board was hung on the wall. She went to this and studied its information.

It identified offices, surgeries, and what appeared to be laboratories, and above all of these was something that made Deborah whisper, "Yes!" For the building itself fell under the aegis of the Faculty of Science and Technology. When she saw this, Deborah searched the list feverishly and found what she knew at heart would be there. One of the laboratories was dedicated to the study of reproductive science. Her intuition had been correct all along. She was on the right path. Simon had been wrong.

NEWBY BRIDGE
CUMBRIA

When Lynley rang off, he looked at his friend. St. James had watched him the entire time he'd been speaking to Deborah, and there were few people Lynley knew who were more adept at reading between the lines than St. James, although there actually wasn't much reading between the lines that St. James would have had to do. Lynley had framed the conversation with Deborah in such a way that her husband would understand where she was and with whom without Lynley overtly betraying her.

St. James said, "She can be the most maddening woman."

Lynley raised and lowered his fingers in a gesture that indicated his acceptance of this idea. "Isn't that the nature of women in general?"

St. James sighed. "I should have put my foot down in some fashion."

"Good Lord, Simon. She's an adult. You can hardly drag her kicking and howling back to London."

"Her point exactly." St. James rubbed his forehead. He looked as if he hadn't slept during the previous night. He continued. "It's unfortunate we needed two hire cars. I'd have been able to give her a clear choice otherwise: Come with me to Manchester airport or find your own way home."

"I doubt that would have gone down very well. And you know what her reply would have been."

"Oh yes. That's the hell of it. I do know my wife."

"Thank you for coming up here, Simon, for lending a hand."

"I would have liked to give you a more definitive answer. But it all stacks up the same way, no matter how I look at the facts: an unfortunate accident."

"Despite the plethora of motives? Everyone seems to have one. Mignon, Freddie McGhie, Nick Fairclough, Kaveh Mehran. God knows who else."

"Despite," St. James said.

"And not the perfect crime?"

St. James glanced out of the window at a copper beech hedge aflame with autumn as he considered this. They had met in a rather crumbling Victorian hotel not far from Newby Bridge, where in its lounge they were able to order morning coffee. It was the sort of place about which Helen would have happily declared *Lord, how deliciously atmospheric it is, Tommy* in order to excuse the hideous carpets, the layer of dust on the wall-mounted deer heads, and the tattered condition of the sofas and armchairs. For a moment, Lynley missed his wife with a crushing force. He breathed through it as he'd learned to do. Everything passes, he thought. This also would.

St. James stirred in his armchair and said, "There *were* perfect crimes at one time; of course. But today, it's so difficult that virtually no one can carry one off. Forensic science is too advanced, Tommy. There are ways to pick up trace evidence now that were unheard of even five years ago. Today a perfect crime would have to be one in which no one thinks there was a crime at all."

"But isn't that the case here?"

"Not with a coroner's investigation having been completed. Not with Bernard Fairclough coming to London and getting you involved. A perfect crime now is one in which there's no suspicion that there could have *been* a crime. An investigation is neither ordered nor needed, the coroner signs off on the death on the spot, the victim is conveniently cremated within forty-eight hours, and there you have it. But with the situation you've got here, all the bases were covered and there was ultimately nothing to suggest Ian Cresswell's death was anything other than what the coroner decided: an accident."

"And if Valerie and not Ian was the intended victim?"

"Exactly the same problem, as you know." St. James took up his coffee. "If this was intentional, Tommy, and if Valerie and not Ian had been the intended victim, you've got to agree there are far better ways to be rid of her. Everyone knew Ian used the boathouse as well as Valerie. Why risk killing him if she was supposed to die? And what's the motive anyway? And even if there *is* a motive for her death, trying to go at this problem through forensic data isn't going to get you anywhere."

"Because there is no forensic data."

"None that suggests this wasn't what it appears to be: an accident."

"Something other than that filleting knife could have been used to dislodge the stones, Simon."

"Of course. But the stones themselves would have borne the marks of a tool being used on them. And they had no marks. You saw that. Beyond that, look how many others were loose. That boathouse has doubtless been an accident waiting to happen for years."

"No case to present, then."

"That's my conclusion." St. James smiled regretfully. "So I'd have to say to you what I've said—quite unsuccessfully—to Deborah. It's time to go back to London."

"What about a crime of intent?"

"Meaning?"

"Meaning one *wishes* another dead. One hopes for it. One even *plans* it. But before the plan can be put into action, an accident supervenes. The intended victim dies anyway. Could we have that here?"

"We could, of course. But even if we do, the point is in this case no guilt can be established, and no one's behaviour is suggesting guilt."

Lynley nodded thoughtfully. "Still and all . . ."

"What?"

"I have the nagging feeling—" Lynley's mobile rang. He glanced at the number then said to St. James, "Havers."

"Could be something new, then."

"I can only hope." Lynley answered the call with, "Tell me something, Sergeant. At this point, anything will do."

CHALK FARM
LONDON

Barbara had placed the call to Lynley from her home. She'd
been into the Met long before the crack of dawn to engage
in some further investigating using the vast resources there.
Afterwards, not wishing to be anywhere near the place
when Acting Detective Superintendent Ardery showed her
face, she'd scarpered home. Twelve cups of coffee had seen
her through the early morning, and at this point she was so
lit up by caffeine that she doubted she'd be able to sleep for
days. She was also smoking like a steam engine going full
throttle. Her head felt as if her brain were about to begin
sending out torpedoes.

The first thing she told Lynley was, "There's a kid,
Inspector. This may be important. This may be nothing.
But turns out Vivienne Tully's got an eight-year-old daughter called Bianca. I think she also knew I was going to show
my mug on her doorstep. Her flat was swept clean of everything personal, and she didn't exactly swoon with shock
when I told her I was from the Met. I only found out about
the kid because I'm bonding with the building's porter in a
very big way. Expect an announcement soon in that quarter."

"You got inside, then."

"My talents, sir, know not a single bound. I live to
impress you." Barbara went on to tell Lynley what she'd
learned from Vivienne. She gave him everything from the
woman's education to her employment to her intention to
return to New Zealand, land of her birth. "Didn't deny a
thing about Fairclough: knowing him, acting as a board
member of his foundation, seeing him regularly for meals
and such at Twins. But she threw up a roadblock when it
came to why he has a key to her digs."

"This child, Bianca. Could she be Fairclough's?"

"Possibly. But she could also be his son's, Ian Cresswell's,
the prime minister's, or the Prince of Wales's for that matter. She could be a wild night on the town, a little whoops,
if you know what I mean. Anyway, this Vivienne hasn't

worked for Fairclough for years. She hasn't worked for him since before she even had the kid. It'd be hard to believe she's maintained a long-distance romance with him, wouldn't you say, a long-distance romance enduring enough to have had his kid?"

"Perhaps it's not a romance that's been maintained for years, Barbara. Perhaps Bianca's the result of a chance encounter that brought Vivienne back into Fairclough's life at some point."

"What? Like they find themselves in a lift somewhere, lock eyes on each other, and the rest is Bianca? I s'pose that's possible."

"He established a foundation," Lynley pointed out. "He needed board members, and she's one of them."

"Can't be that. Foundation's been around long before Bianca was a gleam in anyone's eye. Anyway, accepting a position on the foundation board's one thing. Getting involved with Fairclough and *staying* involved with him is another. Why would she want to do that? He's decades older. I've seen his picture as well and believe me, they're not close to being a physical match. Wouldn't she have preferred a bloke nearer to her own age and also available? Getting enmeshed with a married bloke is generally boarding a train to nowhere and she seems far too clever for that."

"In a sensible world she would have understood your point and made a different sort of decision. But if she didn't, you'll have to agree that there're always things making people far less than sensible, Sergeant."

Barbara heard the murmur of someone's voice in the background. Lynley identified the voice with, "Simon's saying that vast amounts of money make people less than sensible all the time."

"Okay. Right. But if the kid's Fairclough's, and if he's been doing the horizontal rumba with Vivienne Tully for God only knows how long, then why bring in a Scotland Yard investigation into his nephew's death, which has already been called an accident? He'd have to have known that everyone would be looked into, including himself. What the hell sort of risk is he taking?"

"If it's unrelated to Cresswell's death, he may be reckoning on my keeping a lid on this particular aspect of his private life."

"*If* it's unrelated," Barbara said. "But if it *is* related, that bloody well explains why Hillier picked you for this particular job, doesn't it? The earl covering up for the baron. He'd like that touch, Hillier would."

"I can't disagree. He's done it before. Anything else?" Lynley enquired.

"Yeah. I've been busy. Kaveh Mehran's not lying about ownership of that farm. Cresswell left it to him. Interesting bit is when he did it. Prepare for a drum roll: He signed the will one week before he drowned."

"That's telling," Lynley agreed. "Although one would have to wonder at a murderer so dimwitted as to kill someone one week after a will was signed in his favour."

"There is that," Havers admitted.

"Anything more?"

"Oh, I'm the early bird, all right. Getting up at ungodly hours of the morning also allows one to make international phone calls whose recipients are easy to reach because they're still in bed."

"Argentina?" Lynley guessed.

"In a pie tin. I managed to get through to the home of the mayor of Santa Maria di all the et ceteras. I tried his office first but that turned out to be a case of someone at one end saying *quien* and *que* and me on this end shouting, 'Let me talk to the bloody mayor for God's sake,' before I finally worked out the time difference and twigged I was talking to the cleaner. I had to give up that idea, but I did get to the house. And let me tell you, that was not an easy task."

"I'm all admiration, Barbara. What did you uncover?"

"The fact that no one speaks English in Argentina. Or that everyone pretends not to speak English. Have it either way. I did manage to corner someone I *think* was Dominga Padilla y del Torres de Vasquez, though. I kept repeating the name and she kept saying *si* when she wasn't saying *quien*. I went with Alatea's name, then, and this Dominga started babbling. There was a lot of *Dios mio*s and *dondes* and *gracias*es. So I wager this bird knows who Alatea is. What I need just now is someone who can talk to her."

"Are you onto that, then?"

"Like I said before, Azhar's got to know someone at the university."

"There'll be someone at the Yard as well, Barbara."

"With some fishing. But I go that route, and the guv will be all over me like groupies on a rock star. She's already asked me—"

"I've spoken to her. She knows I have you doing some work for me. Barbara, I've got to ask this. Did you tell her?"

Barbara felt deeply affronted. They had years of history, she and the inspector. That he would think she'd betray those years made her back go up. "I bloody well did not." For that was the God's truth of the matter. The fact that she'd allowed Isabelle Ardery to work it out for herself without sidetracking her with some sort of red herring was not Barbara's problem.

Lynley was silent. Barbara had a sudden anguished feeling that they were heading towards a her-or-me moment. This was the very last thing she wanted since if it came down to the superintendent or herself, she knew how unlikely it was that Lynley would make the choice that would put him at odds with his own lover. He was, after all, and she had to face it, a bloke.

So she went back to where they'd gone off track, saying, "Anyway, I'd planned to speak to Azhar. If he can come up with someone adept at Spanish, we've solved that problem and we've got the key to Alatea Fairclough."

"As to that, there's something else." Lynley told her a tale about Alatea Fairclough's modeling career in her pre–Nicholas Fairclough days. He ended with, "He told Deborah it was 'naughty underwear' and said she's embarrassed and afraid she'll be found out. Naughty underwear hardly being a crushing issue to anyone but a nun or someone marrying into the royal family, we're thinking it might be pornography instead."

"I'll see what I can do with that as well," Barbara told him.

They exchanged a few more words during which Barbara

tried to read him through his tone. Did he believe what she'd said about Isabelle Ardery and his presence in Cumbria? Did he not? And was it important, in any case, what he believed? When he ended the call, she had no answers. But she had no love for her questions, either.

CHALK FARM
LONDON

Barbara heard the sound of raised voices as she approached the ground-floor flat at the front of the property. She was already crossing the patch of lawn to the terrace in front of the flat's front doors when the unmistakable voice of Taymullah Azhar shouted furiously, "I *will* take steps, Angelina. I promise you that." Barbara froze at once. Angelina Upman cried, "Are you actually *threat*ening me?" and Azhar returned at top volume, "You can *ask* me that? This matter is settled."

Barbara spun on her heel to beat a quick retreat, but she was too late. Out of the door Azhar strode, his face as black as she'd ever seen it. He clocked her, for there was no place for either of them to hide. He turned away and hurried off the property, setting off down Eton Villas in the direction of Steeles Road.

It was a damn-and-blast moment that got worse immediately. For Angelina Upman came dashing out of the flat as well, as if going after her partner, and she clasped a fist at her mouth when she saw Barbara. They locked eyes. Angelina spun and retreated.

That painted things badly for Barbara. She was caught. Angelina had shown her friendship. Barbara could hardly slink off without asking if she could be of help. This was actually the last option she wanted to choose from the list of alternatives that she rapidly considered. She chose it anyway, however.

Angelina answered immediately when Barbara knocked on the French windows. Barbara said to her, "Sorry. I was coming to ask Azhar . . ." She ran a hand through her hair and was all at once aware of how different it felt since the previous choppiness of it was gone. This fact seemed to define what she had to do next. She said, "Bloody hell, I'm dead sorry I overheard the row. But I didn't hear much, just the last bit. I was coming to ask Azhar for a favour."

Angelina's shoulders slumped a bit. "I'm terribly sorry, Barbara. We should have kept our voices down but we're too hot tempered. I brought something up better left unsaid. There are topics Hari won't discuss."

"Triggers for a row?"

"Just that, yes." She blew out a regretful breath. "Anyway. This'll blow over. It always does."

"C'n I do anything?"

"If you don't mind a mess, you might come inside and have a cup of tea with me." Angelina then grinned and added, "Or a glass of gin, which I could bloody do with, let me tell you."

"I'll go for the tea," Barbara said. "Save the gin for next time."

Inside the flat, Barbara saw what Angelina had meant by a mess. It looked as if Azhar and his partner had resorted to hurling a few objects at each other in the midst of their row. This seemed so utterly unlike Azhar that Barbara looked from the sitting room to Angelina and wondered if she'd done all the hurling herself. There were scattered magazines, a broken figurine, an upended lamp, a shattered vase, and flowers lying on the floor in a pool of water.

Barbara said, "I c'n help you put this in order as well."

"Tea first," Angelina said.

The kitchen was untouched. Angelina made the tea and took it to a small table that sat beneath a high window through which a patch of sunlight gleamed. She said, "Thank God Hadiyyah's in school. She would have been frightened. I doubt she's ever seen Hari like that."

Barbara took the inference. Angelina herself had "seen Hari like that." She said to her, "Like I said, I was on my way to ask his help."

"Hari's? How?"

Barbara explained. Angelina lifted her teacup as she listened. She had lovely hands like the rest of her, and their tapered fingers bore shapely nails of a uniform length. She said, "He'll know someone. He'll want to help you. He likes you enormously, Barbara. You mustn't think that this"—she tilted her head in the direction of the sitting room—"is an indication of anything but two similar temperaments crashing into each other. We'll both get over it. We usually do."

"That's good to know."

Angelina took a sip of tea. "It's stupid how arguments between partners grow from nothing. One makes a suggestion that the other doesn't care for and before you know it, tempers flare. Things get said. It's ridiculous."

To this Barbara didn't know what to say. She didn't have a partner, had never had one, and had no possibility of some chance encounter leading her to having one. So arguing with one? Hurling objects at one? There was small likelihood that she'd find herself having that experience any time soon. Still, she made a mumbling, "'S hell, that, eh?" and hoped that would suffice.

"You know about Hari's wife, don't you?" Angelina asked. "I expect he's told you: how he left her but there's never been a divorce."

Barbara felt a bit prickly with this direction of conversation. "Well. Right. Yeah. I mean, more or less."

"He left her for me. I was a student. Not his, of course. I've no brain for science. But we met at lunch one day. It was crowded, and he asked to share my table. I liked his . . . well, I quite liked his gravity, his thoughtfulness. I liked his confidence, the way he didn't feel he had to answer quickly or amusingly in a conversation. He was very real. That appealed to me."

"I c'n see how it would." For it appealed to Barbara as well, and long had done. Taymullah Azhar had appeared from the first to be exactly who he seemed to be.

"I didn't want him to leave her. I loved him—I *love* him—but to break up a man's home . . . I never saw myself as such a woman. But then there was Hadiyyah. When Hari knew I was pregnant, he'd hear of nothing else but our being together. I could have ended the pregnancy, of course. But this was *ours*, you see, and I couldn't face not having her."

She leaned forward and briefly touched Barbara's hand. "Can you imagine a world without Hadiyyah in it?"

It was a simple question with an equally simple answer. "Can't," Barbara said.

"Anyway, I've wanted her to meet her siblings, Hari's other children. But he won't hear of it."

"That was the row?"

"We've gone through it before. It's the only thing we ever argue about. The answer's always the same. 'That *will* not happen,' as if he determines the course everyone's life is supposed to take. When he says that sort of thing, I don't react well. Nor do I react well when he declares that he and I will *not* be giving her a sibling either. 'I have three children,' he says. 'I will have no more.'"

"He might change his mind."

"He hasn't in years and I can't think of a single reason why he would."

"Behind his back, then? Without him knowing?"

"Take Hadiyyah to meet her siblings, you mean?" Angelina shook her head. "I've no idea where they are. I've no idea what their names are or who their mother is. She might have returned to Pakistan, for all he's told me about her."

"There's always an accidental pregnancy, I suppose. But it's a bit low, that, eh?"

"He'd never forgive it. And I've already asked him to forgive a great deal."

Barbara thought Angelina might go on at that point, revealing her reasons for having left Azhar and Hadiyyah for her "trip to Canada" as it had long been called. But she didn't do so. Instead she said, "I love Hari so much, you know. But sometimes I hate him in just the same way." She smiled at the irony of her own statement. Then she seemed to shrug it off. She said, "Wait an hour then ring him on his mobile. Hari will do whatever he can to grant your favour."

LAKE WINDERMERE
CUMBRIA

Manette had reckoned on the previous day that her father hadn't been telling the truth about Vivienne Tully. She had also reckoned that emotional cowardice was what was preventing her from pushing the subject further. It was stupid, really, but the fact of the matter was that she hadn't wanted to show any sign of weakness in her father's presence. She was *still* infuriatingly that little girl who believed she could morph herself into the son Bernard Fairclough so wanted if she tried hard enough. Big boys didn't cry, so neither would she. Thus anything that threatened a wellspring of emotion from her while her father stood there observing, evaluating, and dismissing her was something that had to be avoided.

But the subject wasn't closed. How could it be? If Ian had been making monthly payments to Vivienne Tully for years, there was more than one reason that Manette had to get to the story behind that: There was also her mother to consider. Her mother, after all, owned Fairclough Industries. It had been her inheritance. Her father might have run it for decades with great success, but it was a private company with a small but powerful board of directors. Her mother and not her father was its chairman. For Valerie's own father had been no fool. Just because Bernie Dexter had become Bernard Fairclough, this did not mean he had Fairclough blood running through his veins. So there was no way on earth that Valerie's father would have risked Fairclough Industries falling into the hands of someone who was not a Fairclough born.

She'd talked everything over with Freddie. Thankfully, he'd not had a date with Sarah on the previous night, although he'd had a lengthy conversation with the woman, his hushed voice sounding amused and affectionate. Manette had gritted her teeth through this, and when her jaw had begun to ache and the conversation did not end, she'd gone into the sitting room and used the treadmill till the sweat ran down her chest and soaked her jersey. Finally, Freddie had wandered in, his face slightly flushed and the tips of his ears quite pink. She would have concluded they'd had telephone sex, but Manette didn't see that as Freddie's style.

She ran for another five minutes to make her workout look legitimate. Freddie mouthed *wow* in ostensible admiration for her endurance and took himself into the kitchen. There she found him bent over a book of crossword puzzles, looking thoughtful and tapping the nonbusiness end of a Biro against his lip.

She said to him, "Not going out tonight?"

He said, "Giving it a bit of a rest."

"The old prong tired, is he?"

Freddie blushed. "Oh no. He's very up for the job."

"Freddie McGhie!"

Freddie's eyes got wide and then he caught the innuendo. "Lord. Didn't mean it that way," he laughed. "We decided—"

"You and the lady or you and the prong?"

"*Sarah* and I decided to slow things just a bit. Seems that a relationship should have more to it than tearing off one's clothes within ten minutes of hello."

"I'm glad to hear that," Manette said without thinking.

"Are you? Why?"

"Oh, well . . . I . . ." She thought for a moment and came up with, "I don't want you to make a mistake. To be hurt. You know."

He gazed at her. She felt the heat climb her chest and ease its way up her neck. A change of subject was needed and Manette's conversation with Bernard was just the ticket.

Freddie had listened in that Freddie way: giving her his complete attention. When she was finished, he said, "I think we both must talk to him at this point, Manette."

Manette was surprised by the strength of her gratitude. Still, she knew that they had only one option when it came to getting information from her father. It was likely that Mignon had managed to learn whatever it was she'd learned via either her impressive skills with the Internet or her dexterous turning of the screws of their father's guilt. Mignon had never been wrong about their father's preference for Nicholas. She'd merely dealt with that preference in a fashion that served her own ends from the first, becoming more expert at this the older she grew. But neither Manette nor Freddie possessed that sort of manipulative expertise. The way Manette saw it, only Valerie's presence and Valerie's learning about the money drain would move Bernard now. There was simply too much on the line—the ruin of an entire firm, just for starters—to let matters lie. If Manette's father wasn't willing to look into the money situation, to sort it out, and to stop it, she knew her mother certainly would be.

They set off for Ireleth Hall in midmorning. Soon enough the rain began to fall. Late autumn and it poured buckets in Cumbria. In another month, it would begin to snow. They'd get a bit where they lived in Great Urswick. Farther north, the steep, narrow passes over the fells would close until next spring.

When Freddie parked the car near the vast front door of Ireleth Hall, Manette turned to him. "Thanks for this, Freddie," she said.

He said, "Eh?" and looked genuinely perplexed.

"For coming along with me. I do appreciate it."

"Tosh. We're in this together, old girl." And before she could reply, Freddie was out of the car and coming round to open her own door. "Let's beard the lion before we lose our nerve. If things get bad we can always ring your sister and request an interesting diversion."

Manette chuckled. Freddie did know her family, didn't he. Well, of course he did. He'd been a member of it for nearly half his life. She said without thinking of the implications, "Why on earth did we ever divorce, Freddie?"

"Continual failure on someone's part to recap the toothpaste as I recall," he replied lightly.

They didn't knock upon the door, merely entering the long, rectangular hall where the autumn chill suggested a fire needed to be lit in the enormous fireplace. Manette shouted out a hello that seemed to echo off the walls. Freddie did likewise, calling out Bernard's and Valerie's names.

Valerie was the one who replied. They heard her walking along the corridor upstairs. In a moment, she came down. She smiled and said, "What a nice surprise to see you. Together as well." She said the last as if expecting from them a happy announcement of the reconciliation type. Not very likely, Manette thought. Her mother didn't know about Freddie and his wildly successful foray into the world of Internet dating.

Manette saw that Valerie's assumption could be extremely useful in this moment, though. She reached for her former husband's hand and said coyly, "We were hoping to have a word with you and Dad. Is he around?"

Valerie looked even more pleased. She said, "Goodness. He must be. Let me see if I can find him. Freddie dear, will you light that fire? Shall we meet in here or would you prefer—"

"Here's just fine," Manette said. She held on to Freddie's hand and looked at him, "Isn't it, Freddie?"

Freddie was, as always, blushing, which Manette considered a perfect touch. As her mother left the room he said, "I say, old girl," to which Manette replied, "Thanks for playing along," before she lifted his hand and gave it a swift and affectionate kiss. "You're a brick. Let's see to the fire. Mind the flue's open."

By the time Valerie returned with Bernard, the fire was roaring and Manette and Freddie were standing in front of it, toasting their backsides. To Manette, it was fairly clear from the expression on her parents' faces that they'd had a brief conversation about the nature of what Freddie and she had come to talk about. Her father wore a look of anticipation that equaled her mother's. No surprise there, really. They'd both adored Freddie from the day Manette had brought him home for an introduction.

Her father offered coffee. Her mother offered toasted tea cakes, chocolate gateau, biscotti from a bakery in Windermere. Both Manette and Freddie demurred politely. Manette said, "Let's sit, though," and led Freddie to one of the sofas perpendicular to the fireplace. Her parents took the other. Both of them, interestingly, sat on the edge as if ready to spring up and run at the least provocation. It was either that or being ready to dash off for a bottle of the bubbly. Hope did always spring eternal, Manette thought, when it came to what people believed was possible.

She said, "Freddie?" as an indication to him to take the bull by the horns.

He said, looking from her father to her mother, "Bernard, Valerie, it's about Ian and the books."

Alarm swept across Bernard's features. He looked at his wife as if drawing the conclusion that he'd been bushwhacked by her in a scheme with their daughter, while Valerie looked mystified although she said nothing, merely waiting for more information. Manette didn't know if Freddie noticed this. It didn't matter much, because he went on directly, saying, "I know this isn't going to go down well in some quarters, but we have to sort out a way to deal with Mignon's monthly payments. Or, preferably, to stop them altogether. And we have to get to the bottom of this matter of Vivienne Tully. What with the money that's gone into Arnside House and the money to Mignon *and* the money to Vivienne . . . I'd love you to think Fairclough Industries is awash with cash, but the truth is that along with the expense of the children's garden here at the hall, we're going to have to cut back somewhere. And sooner rather than later."

It was all so vintage Freddie, Manette thought. He was earnest and truthful, guileless to a fault. There was no possible way her father could argue that this outlay of money was not Freddie's concern. Freddie was not accusing him of anything. In addition, no one was more appropriate than Freddie to be looking through the books to see where the business stood after Ian's death anyway.

She waited for her father's response. So did Freddie. So did Valerie. The fire crackled and popped and a log rolled off the grate. Bernard took this opportunity to temporise. He took up the tongs and the hearth brush and dealt with the problem while the three of them watched him.

Valerie said, when he turned back to them, "Tell me

about the money going out to Vivienne Tully, Freddie,"
although when she said it, her eyes were fixed on her husband.

Freddie said affably, "Well, it's a bit peculiar. It's evidently been going on for years, increasing incrementally.
I've more documentation from Ian's computer accounts to
sort through, but from what I've gathered so far, it *seems*
like a large pile of money went out to her—via a bank
transfer—some years ago, then a gap of a few years with
nothing going out to her, and then a monthly allowance of
some sort appears to have begun."

"When would this have been?" Valerie asked steadily.

"Round eight and a half years ago. Now, I know she sits
on the board of the foundation, Bernard—"

"I beg your pardon?" Valerie turned to her husband and
said his name as Freddie continued with, "But that position,
as with all charitable boards, would be unpaid save for
expenses, of course. Only, what she's being paid far exceeds
any expenses unless"—and here he chuckled and Manette
wanted to kiss him for the sheer innocence of that chuckle—
"she's dining out every night with potential donors and
sending their children to public schools to boot. That not
being the case—"

"I'm getting the picture," Valerie said. "Aren't you, Bernard? Or is the truth of the matter that there's no picture
for you to get?"

Bernard was looking at Manette. Of course he would
want to know what she had told Freddie and what sort of
game they were playing with him now. He would feel
betrayed as well. What he'd told her on the previous day,
he'd told her in confidence. Well, had he told her everything, Manette thought, she might have kept the truth to
herself. But he hadn't done, had he? He'd told her just
enough to appease her in that moment, or so he had
believed.

Bernard tried to present his earlier excuse, saying, "I've
no idea why there were payments to Vivienne. It's possible
that Ian felt he had to . . ." He stumbled here, looking for a
reason. "Perhaps this was a means of protecting me."

"From what, exactly?" Valerie asked. "As I recall, Vivienne accepted employment in a more senior position with a firm in London. She wasn't dismissed. Or was she? Is there something I don't know?" And then to Freddie, "Exactly how much money are we talking about?"

Freddie named the sum. Freddie named the bank. Valerie's lips parted. Manette could see the whites of her teeth, gritted together. Her gaze fixed on Bernard. He looked away.

Valerie said to him, "How would you prefer me to interpret this, Bernard?"

Bernard said nothing.

She said, "Shall I believe she's been blackmailing Ian for some reason? Perhaps he was cooking the books and she knew it so he cooked them some more, benefitting her? Or perhaps she promised to take herself out of the picture and say nothing to Niamh of his sexual proclivities as long as he paid her . . . although that wouldn't explain why he continued to pay her once he left Niamh for Kaveh, would it, darling? So let's go with the first idea. Freddie, is there any indication Ian was cooking the books?"

"Well, only in that the payments to Mignon have increased as well. But as to any money going his own way, there's nothing—"

"Mignon?"

"Right. Her allowance has taken a rather large jump," Freddie said. "Problem with that, the way I see it, is that the jump doesn't actually match necessary expenses, if you know what I mean. Of course there was the surgery, but that would have been one payment, wouldn't it? And considering she lives right here on the property, what has she got in the way of actual expenses? I know she does tend to spend a bit on her Internet shopping, but really, how much can that cost? Well, of course, I suppose it could cost a fortune, couldn't it, if one became addicted to shopping on the Internet or something, but . . ."

Freddie babbled on a bit. Manette knew he could feel the tension between her parents and she knew his babbling was a reaction to this. He had to have known that they'd be walking into a minefield, talking to her parents together about the money going out to Vivienne and to Mignon, but in his Freddie innocence, he hadn't considered exactly how many mines lay within that field, waiting to explode.

There was silence at the end of Freddie's remarks. Valerie had her gaze concreted on Bernard. Bernard ran his hand back over his head. He opted for an attempt at redirection, saying to Manette, "I wouldn't have thought this was possible of you."

"What?" Manette said.

"You know very well. I thought our relationship was rather different to what it apparently is. My error, I see."

To which Freddie said quickly, "I say, Bernard, this has nothing to do with Manette," and with such firmness that Manette looked at her former husband. Freddie put his hand on hers and squeezed it, going on to say, "Her concerns are completely legitimate, in the circumstances. And she only knows about the payments because I told her. This is a family business—"

"And you're not family," Bernard snapped. "You were once, but you took yourself out of that position and if you think—"

"Do *not*," Manette cut in, "talk to Freddie that way. You're lucky to have him. We're *all* lucky to have him. He appears to be the only honest person working in a position of responsibility at the company."

"Does that include you, then?" her father asked.

"I'm not sure that matters," Manette told him, "because it certainly includes you." Perhaps, she thought, she would have said nothing at the end of the day, not wishing to be the one to devastate her own mother. But her father's remarks to Freddie took things too far in Manette's eyes, although she didn't pause to consider why this was the case since the only thing her father had actually said was the absolute truth: Freddie wasn't a member of the family any longer. She'd seen to that. She said to her mother, "I think Dad has something he'd like to say, something he'd like to explain about himself and Vivienne Tully."

"I'm taking that point very well, Manette," Valerie said. And to Freddie, "Stop the payments to Vivienne at once. Contact her through the bank to which the payments have gone. Tell them to inform her it's my decision."

Bernard said, "That's not—"

"I don't care what it is and it isn't," Valerie said. "Nor should you. Or have you a reason to be paying her that you'd care to explain?"

Bernard's expression was agonised. Had things been different, Manette thought she might actually have felt sorry for him. She gave passing consideration to what shits men were, and she waited for her father to attempt to lie his way out of this situation as he was surely going to do, in the hope that she would say nothing about their conversation and what he'd admitted to her about his affair with Vivienne Tully.

But Bernard Fairclough had always been the luckiest bastard on the planet, and that proved to be the case in that moment. For the door burst open as they sat there waiting for Bernard to answer, and the wind swept in. As Manette turned, thinking she and Freddie had left it off the latch, her brother, Nicholas, strode into the room.

LANCASTER
LANCASHIRE

Deborah knew the only course open to her was to speak to the woman with Alatea Fairclough. If indeed she was correct in her surmise that what was going on with Alatea had to do with conceiving a child, then she seriously doubted that Alatea was going to be willing to talk about it, especially to someone who'd already been found out as misrepresenting her true purpose in Cumbria. Nor was she likely to unburden herself to a tabloid journalist. Thus, the other woman seemed like the only possibility to get to the bottom of Alatea's odd behaviour and to learn whether it had anything to do with the death of Ian Cresswell.

She rang Zed on his mobile. He barked, "You took your bloody sweet time. Where the hell are you? What's going on? We had a deal and if you're reneging—"

She said, "They've gone into a science building."

"Well, *that's* got us nowhere in a basket. Could be she's

just taking a course. Mature student, right? The other could be doing the same thing."

"I must talk to her, Zed."

"I thought you already went that route with no result."

"I don't mean Alatea. Obviously, she's not going to talk to me any more than she's going to talk to you. I mean the other, the woman she fetched from the disabled soldiers' home. She's the one I need to talk to."

"Why?"

And here was where things got tricky. "They seem to have a relationship of some sort. They were talking quite companionably all the way from the car park to the science building. They seemed like friends, and friendships mean confidences shared."

"They also mean keeping those confidences to oneself."

"Of course. But I find that, outside of London, the Met have a certain cachet with people. Say 'Scotland Yard CID' and show your identification and suddenly what was sworn to secrecy gets offered for police consumption."

"Same thing with a reporter's work," Zed noted.

Was he joking? Deborah wondered. Probably not. She said, "I take your point, of course."

"Then—"

"I think I might be a less threatening presence."

"How so?"

"It seems obvious. First, it would be two against one: two complete strangers confronting a woman about her friendship with another woman. Second . . . Well, there's your size, Zed, which you have to admit could be rather threatening."

"I'm a lamb. She'll see that."

"Perhaps she would. But then there's the entire matter of who we are. She'll want to see our identification. Picture the result. I show her mine, you show her yours, and what's she going to think—let alone do—when she sees the Met in bed with *The Source*? It wouldn't work. The only route we have is for me to talk to this woman privately, see where that takes us, and share the information with you."

"And how'm I s'posed to know you'll do that? I see this as a bloody good route to a double cross."

"With your ability to break the story of Scotland Yard's

presence up here on the front page of *The Source* at any moment? Believe me, Zed, I'm hardly going to play games with you."

He was silent. Deborah had retreated a safe distance from the George Childress Centre. She had it in sight, but she didn't want to risk being seen by Alatea Fairclough should she and the other woman emerge. The way she reckoned, the safest route to take at this point was to return to the disabled soldiers' home and to wait there for Alatea and her companion to turn up. It could take hours, obviously, but there didn't seem to be any other choice but a long wait in Zed's car.

Which was what she told him. She also said that if he had any other ideas she would be happy to entertain them.

Luckily, he hadn't. He wasn't stupid. He did see that a direct confrontation of the two women together, right on the campus of the University of Lancaster, bore the distinct possibility of getting them nowhere. Superficially at least, the women were engaged in nothing that even looked suspicious. "Aha! What're you two doing together?" was a very likely route to "None of your business."

Zed saw that, although he made it clear to Deborah that he also didn't like it. It wasn't his style, he told her, to sit and wait. Journalists didn't do that. Journalists dug and confronted and got the story. That was at the very core of what a journalist was. That was part of the rich tradition of the profession.

Deborah wanted to scoff at that one, but she made various murmurs of assent. Too right, yes indeed, I understand. But at the moment they didn't even know the name of the woman with whom Alatea had come to the university, and without this at the very least, neither one of them could dig for anything.

She brought Zed round to her way of thinking, albeit reluctantly. He finally said he would meet her at the same spot where she'd hopped out of the car earlier. They'd head back to the disabled soldiers' home and there they would wait for the return of Alatea Fairclough and her companion. They'd lay their plans during their wait, he said. And there would *be* a plan, Sergeant Cotter. No way was he going to miss out on this story because of some double dealing at her end.

"There'll be no double dealing," Deborah said. "I recognise that you've got me in a tricky spot if I don't work with you, Zed."

He chuckled. "That's what good reporters do."

"Yes, I'm definitely learning that," she told him.

They rang off. Deborah waited a few more minutes to see if Alatea and her companion might emerge. They did not. From Deborah's recollection of the notice board inside the building's lobby, there were no lecture halls within. It was given over to offices and laboratories. This meant that Alatea and the other woman were probably not there as mature students, as Zed had suggested. And since reproductive science was one of the disciplines studied there, Deborah was certain she was on the track of what Alatea Fairclough had to hide.

VICTORIA
LONDON

Barbara Havers had to return to the Yard. She needed Winston Nkata's expertise, and other than a return to Victoria Street, the only way she reckoned she could get it was to convince him to disappear for a few hours and to meet her somewhere with access to the Web. She didn't have that at her bungalow. She didn't even own a laptop, having long considered them a drain on the time of the individuals who possessed them. The whole world of the information superhighway was too bloody much for her. She'd liked things better when everything had been controlled simply by on and off switches and when the push-button telephone and telly remotes were as far as technology had gone. Make a few calls and put the burden of information searching on someone else. That was the ticket.

Now, however, things were different. It was the investigator's mental shoe leather that got worn down, not the real thing. But while she was finally, albeit reluctantly, developing her capabilities in the area of digging through the ether of the World Wide Web, she was nowhere close to Winston's level. How *did* one locate naughty underwear ads featuring a specific model? That was the question. He would have the answer.

She reckoned she could phone him, but that wouldn't be the same. She needed to see what was on the screen as a result of his relentless Googling, clicking, and double-clicking.

So she took herself back to New Scotland Yard. She rang him from the lobby. Meet me in the library, she told him. They had a cloak-and-dagger state of affairs going on. The guv needed to be kept in the dark.

"Barb . . . ," he replied.

Barbara knew exactly what it meant when Winston used that tone. But she also knew how to quell his concerns.

"The inspector needs some information," she said. Winnie, she knew, would do anything for Lynley. "You c'n break away, can't you? It won't take long."

"What're you doing?"

"Looking up dirty pictures."

"On a Met computer? You gone dead mad?"

"Hillier's orders," she said. "Really, Winnie, d'you think I actually *want* to do this? The inspector's following up on something. It'll probably turn out to be a fat old cow modelling bras and knickers."

He said he'd meet her in the library. But he also said—and this was Winston through and through—that if he ran into the guv and she wanted to know where he was heading, he would tell her the truth.

"But you *will* try to avoid her, won't you?" Barbara clarified. "The inspector's already in trouble with her for bringing me into this. I bring you into it as well and she's going to go for his jugular."

That did it, as she hoped it would. He would avoid Isabelle Ardery as best he could.

He was, apparently, successful in this. When Barbara reached the Met's library on the twelfth floor, Nkata was waiting. He confessed that he'd run into Dorothea Harriman, however, and this wasn't good news. The departmental secretary had methods of discovery so advanced that she'd probably read Winston's intentions about the library by looking at his shoelaces. Well, it couldn't be helped.

They set to work. Winston's capable fingers flew across the keys. Once he had the spelling of Alatea Fairclough's lengthy birth name, he was unstoppable. Screen after screen flashed by. Barbara didn't attempt to keep up. Winston didn't explain what he was doing or where they were heading on the Web. He just glanced at things, made a decision of some sort, hit a few more keys, and off they went. He would have done fine in forensic computer work, Barbara reckoned. She was about to tell him this, when a furious "*Sergeants* Havers and Nkata," told her that Dorothea Harriman had let something drop and Isabelle Ardery had managed to unearth them.

Nkata swung round from the computer. If a black man could have been said to go pale, that was what happened. Barbara herself went empty. What *was* it with the bloody superintendent? she wondered. Was this about Lynley and where he was and why he wasn't performing nightly between her legs? Or was it about holding the rest of them beneath her thumbnail, like insects about to be pinned to a board?

Winston stood slowly. He looked at Barbara. She said, "I borrowed Winston for a few minutes, guv. Something I needed to look up and he's clever with this stuff. I can do it, but it takes me forever and I'm generally hopeless when it comes to figuring where to go next."

Isabelle looked her over. Her gaze rested most meaningfully on Barbara's tee shirt, which was perfectly readable since she'd flung her donkey jacket on a nearby chair. *Christ died for our sins . . . Let's not disappoint him* clearly did not amuse.

Ardery said, "Holiday's over, Sergeant Havers. I want you back at work and wearing something appropriate within an hour."

Barbara said, "Due respect, guv—"

"Don't push this, Barbara," Isabelle told her. "You may have six days, six weeks, or six months of holiday time due, but it seems rather obvious that you're not on holiday. That being the case, get back to work."

"I was only going to say—"

"Sergeant Havers!" Isabelle barked this time. "Do it now."

Barbara said it in a rush. "Guv, I can't get home and change my clothes and be back in an hour. It's impossible. Plus I need to get over to University College. If you'll let me have a day—this day, this one day more, I swear—I'm out of here in thirty seconds and I'm back tomorrow dressed like . . ." She couldn't come up with a name. "Like whoever." She wanted to add "Picture me gorgeous" but she reckoned the superintendent would respond with "I'd rather picture you dead," so she let that one go. She did add, "I twisted Winston's arm, guv. Please don't take things out on him."

"Things?" the superintendent snapped. "What *things* would those be, Sergeant Havers?"

Next to her, Barbara heard Winston moan, just a small sound that the superintendent didn't take note of, thank God. She said, "I don't know. Just . . . whatever . . . things. Stress of the job. Life."

"Referring to *what*?" Isabelle was furious now. Barbara wondered how much further she could dig herself.

"Guv, I don't know," she said, although *being without Lynley to bonk* was fairly high on her list. "I didn't mean anything by that, anyway. Just something to say."

"Yes? Well, don't play round with 'just something to say,' all right? Finish what you're doing here, then get out of this building. I'll see you here tomorrow morning and if I do not, you'll be a traffic warden in Uzbekistan by tomorrow afternoon. Is that clear?"

"Don't know how it could be clearer," Barbara said.

"And you," Isabelle said to Winston, "are coming with me."

"No sign of knickers," was what Nkata said in response, although he said it quickly and he said it to Barbara, adding, "Check out Raul Montenegro," before he left her.

Barbara waited till the superintendent and Nkata had left the Met library. She cursed her bad luck when it came to Ardery. She was going to have to start walking the perfectly straight and the excruciatingly narrow with the superintendent. Failing that, she had little doubt that Isabelle would be only too happy to drop-kick her bum into another time zone.

She replaced Winston at the computer terminal. She gazed at the screen. She read what was there—damn if it wasn't in bloody Spanish *again*—but she found the name Winston had mentioned before being carted off. *Raul Montenegro* popped out from a jumble of other words. Okay, Barbara thought, let's follow that lead.

LAKE WINDERMERE
CUMBRIA

Throughout the years, Manette had seen her younger brother in many different states, from stone-cold sober to barely conscious. She'd seen him regretful. She'd seen him earnest. She'd seen him manipulative, mournful, agitated, anxious, pleasantly high, and unpleasantly paranoid. But she'd never seen him as angry as he was when he burst through the door to Ireleth Hall, letting it crash back behind him.

As entrances went, it was damn effective. It left all of them gaping. Most conveniently, it left Bernard Fairclough in the welcome state of not having to answer any further questions about Vivienne Tully and the payments made into her bank account.

"Nicky, what's wrong?" Valerie demanded.

"Are you all right?" Bernard said. "Where's Alatea? Has something happened to her?"

"Nothing's happened to Alatea." Nicholas's voice was brusque. "Let's talk about Scotland Yard, all right? You won't mind that, will you? Will you, Manette? What about you, Freddie? I s'pose I can assume the whole collection of you are in on this."

Manette looked at her father. She wasn't about to take this on. She closed her fingers over Freddie's hand to indicate to him he wasn't to say anything either. She felt him look at her, but he said nothing. Instead, his hand turned and he wove his fingers with hers.

Bernard said, "What are you talking about, Nick? Sit down. You look awful. Are you not sleeping?"

"Don't start the bloody false concern with me," he cried. "There's someone up here from London to investigate me, and if you're about to suggest you know nothing about it, that's just not on." He strode to the fireplace. He towered over his father. "What the *hell* did you think? That I wouldn't notice? That I wouldn't work it out? That I'm so bloody addle-brained from drugs and done up with booze that I wouldn't wonder why . . . Christ in heaven, I ought to kill you and have done with it. It'd be easy enough, wouldn't it? I've apparently got such talents in the area of homicide that one more dead body in the boathouse would hardly count."

"Nicholas!" Valerie rose from the sofa. "Stop this at once."

"Oh, you're part of it, are you?" He sneered at her. "I would've thought you—"

"Not part of it. All of it," Valerie said. "Are you listening to me? I'm *all* of it."

That brought him to silence. Manette felt the shock of her mother's words, like a ball of ice forming within her stomach. But confusion replaced shock soon enough. It was easier to be confused by the declaration than it was to follow it to its logical conclusion.

"Valerie," her husband said quietly. "This isn't necessary."

"I'm afraid it is at this point." She said to Nicholas, "The police are here because of me. Your father fetched them at my request. It was not his idea. Do you understand? He went to London. He did the legwork because he knows someone at New Scotland Yard. But it was no more his idea than"—she gestured to Manette and Freddie, still holding each other's hand on the sofa—"than it was your sister's. Or Mignon's. Or anyone else's. *I* wanted this, Nicholas. No one else."

Nicholas looked like a man who'd taken a mortal blow. He finally said, "My own bloody mother. Did you actually think . . . You thought . . . ?"

"It's not quite what you're concluding," she said.

"That I might . . . that I could have . . ." Then he hit his fist on the mantelpiece. Manette winced at the force he used. "I'd kill Ian? That's what you think? That I was capable of murder? What's the matter with you?"

"Nick. Enough." Bernard had spoken. "If nothing else, you've a history of—"

"I goddamn know my history. I lived it. You bloody well don't need to recite it for me. But unless I spent a decade or two of my history in some sort of fugue, I don't recall ever lifting a hand against anyone."

"No one," Valerie said, "lifted a hand against Ian, either. That's not how he died."

"Then what the hell—"

"Valerie," Bernard said. "This will make things worse."

"They can't get worse," Nicholas said. "Unless there's another reason Mother wanted Scotland Yard up here. Want me to think that, do you? Are they investigating Manette? What about Mignon? What about Fred? Or has he just continued running to do Manette's bidding as usual?"

Manette said, "Don't you dare take this out on Freddie. And *yes* the detective has been to see us. And the first we knew there *was* a detective was when we had a Scotland Yard ID shoved under our noses."

"Well at least you got that much," he said. And to his mother, "Have you any idea—any bloody idea at all—"

"I'm sorry," she said. "I've hurt you, and I'm sorry. But there are things beyond your hurt—"

"Like what?" he shouted. And then the pieces seemed to fall into place. "Is this about the family business? Who gets what. Who runs what. Who has the power. And when and how."

"Nicholas, please. There are other things—"

"D'you think I care about any of that? D'you think I want it? D'you think that's why I'm here, back at home? I don't give a toss who runs the business. Give it to Manette. Give it to Freddie. Give it to someone off the street. Do you have any idea what this has done to Alatea, having someone actually come into our home, someone prowling round pretending to be . . . This . . . this investigator of yours has lied to us from the first, Mother. Do you understand that? She's come to the house, she's told a stupid tale about why she's here, she's frightened Allie, who now, apparently, thinks . . . Oh God, I don't know *what* she thinks, but she's in a state and if she thinks I'm using . . . Don't you see what you've done? My own wife . . . If she walks out on me . . ."

"She?" Bernard spoke. "'She's come to the house'? Nick, what are you talking about?"

"What the hell do you think I'm talking about? Your sodding Scotland Yard investigator."

"It's a man," Valerie said. "Nicholas, it's a man, not a woman. It's a man . . . We know nothing about—"

"Oh too right, Mum."

"She's telling the truth," Manette told her brother.

"He has someone with him," Bernard added. "But it's another man, Nick. A forensic specialist. Another man. If a woman's been to Arnside House to talk to you and Alatea, it's to do with something else entirely."

Nicholas blanched then. He was making connections rapidly. Manette could see that much as the thoughts passed quickly across his face.

Unaccountably he said, *"Montenegro."*

"Who?" Bernard asked.

But as swiftly as Nicholas had entered Ireleth Hall, just as swiftly he left it.

LANCASTER
LANCASHIRE

Deborah's two hours in a parked car with Zed Benjamin were broken only by a single call on her mobile. She thought it might be Simon, and she glanced to see, rapidly assessing whether she should answer or let it go to her voice mail rather than risk something less than an "official" conversation in the presence of the journalist. It was Tommy, though. She reckoned she could work with that.

She said to Zed, "My guv," and when she answered she said, "Inspector Lynley. Hullo."

"That's a formal touch."

"All due respect," Deborah told him cheerfully. She felt Zed's eyes on her. She kept her own fixed on the disabled soldiers' home.

"If only I received that at work," Tommy said. Then, "I've met up with Simon."

"I thought you might have done."

"He's unhappy with both of us. With me for getting you into this. With you for not getting out of it. Where are you now?"

"Still in Lancaster."

"How did you get there?"

"What d'you mean?"

"Deborah, Simon's rung me from your hotel."

"You said you *saw* him."

"This was afterwards. He went back to the hotel, you were gone, but your hire car's there. He's obviously concerned."

"Not enough to ring me."

"Oh, for God's sake, Deb. Have some pity on the man. He knows you're in a temper. He knows you won't answer the phone if you see he's the caller. *How* did you get to Lancaster?"

She had no choice, but she did need to be careful with her phrasing. "Mr. Benjamin from *The Source* is working with me at the moment, sir."

She heard his mild curse so she quickly went on. "I'm waiting to speak to the woman who was with Alatea. They paid a call upon someone at the Faculty of Science and Technology and we need to know why."

"Deb." She could hear in his voice that he wasn't sure what approach to take with her just now. What would work? he was wondering. An appeal to her wiser nature? A veiled reference to their own past as lovers? It was an interesting position for him to be in, she reckoned.

He said, "You know Simon wants you back in London. He's worried."

"I don't think London's wise at the moment. I'm very close to something here."

"That's exactly what he's worried about. You've been too close to a murderer once before."

Guernsey, she thought. Like Bogart and Bergman when it came to Paris, she and Simon would always have Guernsey. All right, she'd been hurt. But she hadn't died. She hadn't even been close to dying. And this was different since she had no intention of ending up inside an earthen chamber with someone in possession of an antique hand grenade. She said, "This is important somehow. A loose end needing to be tied."

"It's hard to disagree with the science behind someone's death, Deb. Simon's conclusions are sound."

"Perhaps. But there's more here than his conclusions," she said.

"I don't disagree. You're obviously finding Alatea Fairclough one of them. I have Havers on her in London, by the way."

"So you see—"

"As I said, I don't disagree. It's Simon I'm concerned about, frankly."

"So you do think he could be wrong?"

"He's far too preoccupied with you. That sometimes blinds someone to what's right in front of them. Still and all, I can't allow you—"

"No one's *allowing* anything."

"Dreadful choice of words. I can see we're going to go round and round. If nothing else, I do know you. All right, have a care. Will you do that much?"

"I will. What about you?"

"There are a few loose ends on my end as well. I'll be doing some tying. You *will* ring me if there's any reason at all, won't you?"

"Definitely, Inspector." She rang off at that. She glanced at Zed Benjamin to see if she'd carried off the conversation without raising his suspicions. But he was in the process of sinking down into his seat as best as he could. He nodded in the direction of the soldiers' home. Alatea Fairclough and her companion were just making the turn into the car park.

Deborah and Zed remained where they were, and in less than a minute, the other woman came round the side of the building and went inside. Shortly thereafter, Alatea drove out of the car park, heading off in a direction that suggested she was going to retrace her route to Arnside. This was well and good, Deborah thought. It was time to see what she could get from this other woman.

She said to Zed, "I'm off."

He said, "Quarter of an hour and I'm ringing you on your mobile."

She said, "You can do that, of course. But do consider you're my ride back to Milnthorpe so I'm hardly likely to jeopardise that."

Zed grumbled a bit. He said at the least he was getting out of the bloody car and having a stretch because two hours of waiting in, virtually, a doubled-up position had taken their toll. Deborah said this was fine with her; it was a good idea; she'd be in contact with him should he wander far while she was inside the soldiers' home.

"Oh, don't," Zed said, "worry your head on that score. I'll be close by."

Deborah had little doubt about that. He'd lurk in the bushes if he could do so, one ear pressed to a convenient window. But she knew this was as close as she was going to get to a compromise with the man, so she said she'd be as quick as she could, and she crossed the street.

Inside the Kent-Howath Foundation for Disabled Veterans, she decided on a direct approach, having very little other choice in the matter as she didn't possess police identification. She approached a reception desk and worked upon her most pleasant smile. She said to the receptionist—an antique soldier himself, by the look of him—that she'd just seen a woman come into the building: "rather tall, brown hair tied back, long skirt, boots . . . ?" She was certain this woman was a schoolmate of her own elder sister, and she would very much like to have a moment to speak with her. She knew this was a silly request. After all, the woman might turn out to be a total stranger. On the other hand, if she *was* who Deborah thought she was . . .

"You mean Lucy, I expect," the elderly man said. He was wearing a military uniform. It hung upon him like a bride to her husband on her wedding night. His neck rose from its collar, corrugated with flesh. "She's our social lady.

Games and exercises and groups and the like. Going to the pageant at Christmas. That sort of thing."

"Lucy, yes. That was her name indeed," Deborah said. "Is there *any* chance . . . " She cast a hopeful look at him.

"Always a chance for a pretty gel," he said. "Where'd you get all that lovely hair, eh?"

"Grandmother on my father's side," Deborah told him.

"Lucky you. Always had an eye for the ginger, me." He reached for a phone and punched in a number. He said, "Gorgeous woman out here asking for you, darling," and then he listened for a moment and added, "No. Someone new this is. How'd you get so popular, eh?" He chuckled at something she apparently said, rang off, and told Deborah that she'd be right out.

Deborah said confidentially, "This is terrible of me, but I can't exactly recall her surname."

"Keverne," he said. "Lucy Keverne. That'd be what she was then and what she is now as she's not married. Doesn't even have a boyfriend. I keep trying, but she says I'm too young for her, she does."

Deborah pooh-poohed this idea as was expected of her and went to wait on a wooden bench across from the receptionist's desk. She gave scattered thoughts to what on earth she was going to say to Lucy Keverne, but she had little time to consider her approach. It wasn't a minute later that the woman she'd seen with Alatea Fairclough came out into reception. She looked, understandably, a little puzzled, as she no doubt would be. Deborah reckoned that entertaining sudden visitors at her place of employment wasn't a regular feature of her job.

Up close to her, Deborah could see that she was younger than she'd previously thought when viewing her from a distance. Her hair had grey strands wound through it, but these were premature, for her face was of a woman in her twenties. She wore fashionable glasses that complemented her pleasant features.

She cocked her head at Deborah and said, "How may I help you?" as she extended her hand. "Lucy Keverne."

"Is there a place we can talk?" Deborah asked. "It's rather a private matter."

Lucy Keverne frowned. "A private matter? If you're here to discuss the placement of a relative, I'm not the person you should speak to."

"No, it's not that. This rather relates to Lancaster University," Deborah said. It was a stab in the semidarkness, the George Childress Centre into which she and Alatea had gone providing the only bit of light.

It turned out to be a good stab. "Who are you?" Lucy sounded a bit alarmed. "Who sent you?"

"Is there somewhere we can go?" Deborah said. "Have you an office?"

Lucy Keverne glanced at the receptionist as she considered the various options. She finally said to Deborah, "Come with me, then," and she took her towards the rear of the building where a sunroom looked out into a garden, which was unexpectedly large. They didn't take seats in the sunroom, however. It was already occupied. Several elderly gents were nodding over newspapers and two others were playing cribbage in a corner.

Lucy took her through the glass doors and out into the garden. She said, "Who gave you my name?"

"Is that important?" Deborah asked her. "I'm looking for some help. I thought you might be it."

"You're going to need to be more specific."

"Of course," Deborah said. "Reproduction would be what I'm talking about. I've been trying to conceive a baby for years now. It turns out I have a condition that prevents gestation."

"I'm sorry. That must be very difficult for you. But why would you think I could help you?"

"Because you went into the George Childress Centre with another woman, and I was there. I followed you here once you left the campus, hoping to speak to you."

Lucy's eyes narrowed as she evaluated this. She would have to consider the potential for danger. They were speaking in a form of code, all of which was perfectly legal at the moment. A few steps in the wrong direction, however, and they could be walking on the other side of the law of the land.

"There were two of us," Lucy said, not unwisely. "Why follow me? Why not follow her?"

"I took a chance."

"And? Did I look more fertile to you?"

"More at ease. Far less desperate. After a few years one gets to know the look. There's a hunger. It transmits from one woman to another, like a form of biological code. I don't know how else to explain it. If you haven't experienced it, you wouldn't recognise it. I have, so I do."

"All right. I can see that's possible, but I don't know what you want from me."

The truth was what she wanted. But Deborah wasn't quite sure how to get at it. She opted again for a form of her own truth. "I'm looking for a surrogate," she said. "I think you can help me find one."

"What sort of surrogate?"

"Are there different sorts?"

Lucy considered Deborah. They'd been walking on one of the garden paths, heading towards a large urn that marked one end of the garden, but now Lucy faced Deborah and crossed her arms beneath her breasts. She said, "You've not done much homework in this area, have you?"

"Clearly not."

"Well, I suggest you do so. There are egg donors, sperm donors, surrogacy involving the gestational mother's egg and donor sperm, surrogacy involving gestational mother's egg and the natural father's sperm, surrogacy with the biological mother's egg and donor sperm, surrogacy with the biological mother's egg and the natural father's sperm. If you're going to go down this route in one form or another, you have to begin with an understanding of how it all works. And," she added, "all of the legalities relating to it."

Deborah nodded, hoping she looked thoughtful. "Are you . . . Do you . . . I mean, I'm not sure how to ask this, but which route do you generally take?"

"I'm an egg donor," she said. "Usually, I'm harvested."

Deborah shuddered at the term, so impersonal, so clinical, so . . . so agricultural. But *usually* suggested that Lucy Keverne was open to other possibilities as well. She said to her, "And when it comes to surrogacy?"

"I've never been a surrogate before."

"Before? So with this woman you accompanied to the university . . . ?"

Lucy didn't reply at once. She looked at Deborah as if trying to read her. She said, "I'm not prepared to talk about her. This is a confidential matter. I'm sure you understand."

"Of course. I see." Deborah thought a bit of hand wringing would do at this point, plus an expression of desperation, which wasn't at all difficult for her to manufacture. She said, "I've spoken to clinics, of course. What they've told me is that I'm on my own when it comes to surrogacy. I mean when it comes to finding a surrogate."

"Yes," Lucy said. "That's how it is."

"They've said a friend, a sister, a cousin, even one's own mother. But how does someone like me approach all this? What do I do? Begin every conversation from now on with 'Hullo, would you consider carrying my baby for me?'" And then quite surprisingly, Deborah did feel the desperation of her position, exactly what she wished to project to Lucy Keverne. She blinked hard, feeling tears rise to her eyes. She said, "I'm sorry. Forgive me."

And this, apparently, moved Lucy Keverne, for she put her hand on Deborah's arm and drew her in the direction of a bench near a pond on which a skin of autumn leaves was floating. She said, "It's a stupid law. It's supposed to prevent women from carrying babies for profit. It's supposed to protect women altogether. Of course, it's a law made by men. I always find that rather ironic, to tell you the truth: men making laws for women. As if they know the first thing about protecting us from anything when most of the time they're the source of our problems in the first place."

"May I ask . . ." Deborah fished in her bag for a tissue. "You said that you're an egg donor . . . But if you knew someone . . . Someone close to you . . . Someone in need . . . If someone asked you . . . Would you . . ." Hesitant woman in pursuit of help, she thought. No one else would be likely to ask this question directly of a total stranger.

Lucy Keverne didn't look wary, but she hesitated. Clearly, Deborah thought, they were getting close to whatever relationship she had with Alatea Fairclough. It seemed to Deborah that Lucy herself had already named the possibilities: Alatea either needed her for her eggs or she needed her to be a surrogate. If there was another possibility, Deborah couldn't see it. Surely they hadn't been together to pay a social call upon someone in the George Childress Centre at Lancaster University.

Lucy said, "As I said, I'm an egg donor. Anything else is more than I'd take on."

"You'd never be a surrogate, then?" Hopeful, hopeful, presenting an earnest expression, Deborah thought.

"I'm sorry. No. It's just . . . too close to the heart, if you understand what I mean. I don't think I could do it."

"Would you know anyone? Anyone I could speak to? Anyone who might consider . . . ?"

Lucy looked at the ground, at her boots. They were attractive boots, Deborah thought, Italian by the look of them. Not inexpensive. Lucy finally said, "You might want to look in *Conception* magazine."

"You mean surrogates advertise in it?"

"God no. That's illegal. But sometimes someone . . . You might possibly track down a donor that way. If a woman is willing to donate eggs, she might be willing to do more. Or she could well know someone who'd help you."

"By carrying a baby."

"Yes."

"It must be . . . well, extraordinarily expensive."

"No more than having your own child aside from the in vitro part of it. The surrogate herself can only ask you for reasonable expenses. Anything more than that is, of course, against the law."

"So one has to find a woman of extraordinary compassion, I daresay," Deborah said, "for her to be willing to put herself through that in the first place. And then to hand the baby over. It would take someone special."

"It would, yes. That's what it amounts to." Lucy Keverne stood then and offered Deborah her hand to shake. She said, "I hope I've been some help to you."

She had, in some ways, Deborah thought. But in other ways there were miles still to go. Nonetheless she stood and expressed her gratitude. She knew more now than she'd

known before. How it related to the death of Ian Cresswell—
even if it related—was still unclear.

VICTORIA
LONDON

The name Raul Montenegro took Barbara Havers a few
steps forward. She got onto a photograph of the bloke, along
with an article written, alas, in Spanish. She followed a few
links by means of this article and finally found herself looking at Alatea Vasquez y del Torres. She was quite a creation,
looking like a South American film star. It was difficult to
understand what she was doing in the photo on the arm of
a bloke who resembled a toad, warts and all.

This was Raul Montenegro. He was a good eight inches
shorter than Alatea, and an even better thirty years older. He
wore a frightening Elvis Presley rug and he had a growth on
his nose the approximate size of Portugal. But he was grinning
like a cat with the cream, the canary, and sixteen mice, and
Barbara had a feeling his expression was all about possessing
the woman on his arm. Of course, Barbara couldn't be sure
of that, and there was only one way to know for certain.

She printed the page in question and she dug her mobile
out of her shoulder bag. She rang Azhar at University College London.

He would help her, of course, he told her when she had
him on his mobile. Latching on to a Spanish speaker would
not be a problem at all.

Barbara asked should she come to Bloomsbury. Azhar
said he would let her know. It would take him some time to
locate the person he had in mind who could do the translation she needed. Where was Barbara?

In the bowels of the beast, she told him.

Ah, he said. You're at work, then? Is it best if we come
to you?

Just the opposite, Barbara told him. My life is safer if I
do a runner.

Then he would ring her as soon as possible, knowing that their meeting would have to take place elsewhere, Azhar told her. And then he said carefully, "I must apologise, as well."

"Why?" Barbara asked. And then she remembered: his morning altercation with Angelina. She said, "Oh. You mean the row. Well, it happens, doesn't it? I mean, two people living together . . . One always wants to think love conquers all. Books and films and happily-ever-after with the love of one's life. I don't know much in that department, but what I do know tells me the ever-after's a road with potholes no matter who you are. Seems to me the way of the wise is to hold on to what's there, even though it's not always easy, eh? I mean, what else is there at the end of the day but what we have with our fellows?"

He was silent. In the background Barbara could hear the noise of crockery and raised conversation. He must have taken her call in a cafeteria or a restaurant. This made her think of food and the fact that she hadn't had any for hours.

He finally said, "I shall ring you back presently."

"Sounds good to me," she told him. "And, Azhar . . . ?"

"Hmm?"

"Thanks for helping me out."

"That," he told her, "will always be my pleasure."

They rang off and Barbara considered the likelihood of another run-in with the superintendent if she went in search of food. This would take her to the canteen if she had something relatively nutritious in mind. Otherwise, there were vending machines. Or there was leaving the Yard altogether and waiting somewhere for Azhar's return call. There was also having a smoke, which sounded bloody good to her at that point. This meant slinking off surreptitiously and hoping not to get caught in the stairwell. Or it meant going outside. Decisions, decisions, Barbara thought. She decided to buck up and stay and see if there was anything more that she could dig up by plugging away at Raul Montenegro.

BRYANBARROW
CUMBRIA

Tim decided to go to school without protest because Kaveh was going to have to drive him. It was the only way he was going to get Kaveh alone. And alone was where he wanted the bloke because there was no way the two of them were going to have the little talk they needed to have if Gracie was there. Gracie was already upset enough. She didn't need to hear that Kaveh had future plans with a wife, with parents, and with Bryan Beck farm that involved the elimination of irritating impediments with the surname Cresswell.

So he surprised Kaveh by getting out of bed on time and getting himself organised to go to Margaret Fox School for Terminal Nutcases such as himself. He helped Gracie get ready by setting out all her breakfast choices and making her a tuna and sweet corn sandwich, which he packed into a lunch bag along with an apple, a packet of crisps, and a banana. She thanked him with a dignity that told him she was still grieving for Bella, so one of the things he did instead of eating his own breakfast was to go to the garden and dig the doll's coffin out of the soil so that he could stuff her into his rucksack and ultimately get her repaired in Windermere. He replaced the coffin and the soil and made it look the way Gracie had left it after Bella's funeral. Then he returned to the house in time to bolt down a piece of Marmite toast before they had to leave.

He didn't say anything to Kaveh while Gracie was in the car. Instead, he waited till they'd dropped her off at her C of E school in Crosthwaite and were well on their way up the Lyth Valley. At that point, he leaned against the passenger door and studied the bloke. What came into his head was the mental picture of Kaveh taking it from his father and both of them sweating so that the dim light in the room shone slick on their skin. Only it wasn't a mental picture at all but really a memory because he'd seen it all through a sliver of open doorway and he'd been a witness to that moment of ecstasy and collapse, with his dad calling out hoarsely oh God, yes. The whole sight had been sickening to Tim, filling him with loathing and hate and horror. But it had touched something else as well, had stirred in him something unexpected, and the truth of the matter was that just for a moment the blood in him had rushed and heated. So afterwards, he'd used a pocket knife to cut himself and he'd poured vinegar on the wound to cleanse his hot and sinful blood.

But he could see how it had all come about and in the car he noted that Kaveh was young and handsome. A bent man like his dad would have fallen hard for that. Even, as things were apparently turning out, if Kaveh wasn't so bent himself.

Kaveh glanced at Tim as they headed towards Winster. Loathing, after all, was something one could feel in the air. Kaveh said rather uneasily, "It's good you're going to school this morning, Tim. Your dad would be pleased."

"My dad," Tim said, "is dead."

Kaveh said nothing. He shot another look at Tim, but the road was narrow and curved and he couldn't afford more than just that look, which Tim knew was an attempt to assess how he was feeling and what he was likely to do.

"Which makes things real good for you," Tim added.

"What?" Kaveh said.

"Dad being dead. That makes things *exceptionally* good."

Kaveh surprised him then. They were coming up to a lay-by, and he pulled into it and crushed the brake with his foot. The morning traffic was heavy. Someone honked and gave Kaveh two fingers, but he either didn't notice or he didn't care.

"What," Kaveh asked him, "are you talking about?"

"Dad, dead, and good for you, you mean?"

"Yes. That's exactly what I mean. What are you talking about?"

Tim looked out of the window. There was little enough to see. Next to the car was a drystone wall, and the wall grew ferns like the plumes on ladies' hats. There were probably sheep somewhere behind that wall, but he couldn't see them. He could only see the rise of one of the fells in the distance and a wispy crown of cloud encircling its summit.

"I asked you a question," Kaveh said. "Answer it, please."

"I don't have to answer questions," Tim said. "Not from you and not from anyone."

"You do when you make an accusation," Kaveh told him. "And that's what you've done. You can try to pretend you haven't, but that's not going to work. So why don't you tell me what you mean."

"Why don't *you* keep driving?"

"Because, like you, I don't have to."

Tim had desired this confrontation, but now he wasn't sure he really did want it after all. There he was in an enclosed car with the man for whom his father had destroyed their entire family and wasn't there a sense of menace here? Wasn't the case that if Kaveh Mehran had been capable of walking into Tim's birthday party and laying down the bald facts like a hand of cards, he was capable of pretty much anything?

No. Tim told himself he would not be afraid because if anyone was going to be afraid, it was Kaveh Mehran. Liar, cheat, rotter, and everything else.

He said, "So when's the wedding, Kaveh? And what're you planning to tell the bride? 'S she going to be brought into the picture of what you've been up to in this part of the world? Or is that why you're getting rid of me and Gracie? I don't s'pose we'll be invited to the *wedding*. Guess that'd be a bit much. Gracie'd like to be a bridesmaid, though."

Kaveh said nothing. Tim had to credit him for thinking a bit instead of blurting out something like his plans being none of Tim's business. He was probably madly going through responses since the one thing he didn't know was how Tim had managed to winkle out the truth.

Tim added, "Did you give Mum the news? Let me tell you, that's not exactly going to make her day."

What surprised Tim was what he was feeling as he spoke. He didn't know what to call it. It was filling him up inside and making him want to do something to make it go away, but he couldn't name what the feeling was, and he didn't want to. He hated it when he felt something as a result of what other people did. He *hated* that he reacted to things. He wanted to be like a sheet of glass with everything rolling off him like rain and the fact that he wasn't, that he hadn't managed it yet, that there was no indication that he'd *ever* manage it . . . This knowledge was just as bad as feeling something in the first place. It spoke of a kind of condemnation: an eternal hell of being at the mercy of everyone else and no one being at the mercy of him.

"You and Gracie belong with your mother," Kaveh said, choosing what was the easiest route for their conversation. "I've been happy to have you with me. I'd continue to be happy to have you with me, but—"

"But the wife might not be so happy about that," Tim sneered. "And with the parents as well, I guess the place would start getting a little crowded, wouldn't it? Man, this worked out perfect for you, didn't it? Like you even had it planned."

Kaveh went perfectly still. Only his lips moved. They formed words and the words were, "What exactly are you talking about?"

There was something behind those words that was unexpected, that sounded like anger but more than anger. Tim thought in that instant that danger was anger with a *d* in front of it and maybe that's where danger came from, born out of anger and what people did when anger came upon them, people like Kaveh. But he didn't care. Let the bloke do anything and what difference did it make? He'd already done his worst.

"I'm talking," Tim said, "about the fact that you're getting married, having decided—I s'pose—that taking it up the shoot from a bloke got you what you'd wanted from the first and now that you have it, you're ready to move on. You reckoned the farm is a good enough payment for what you had to do to get it, so you can bring on the wife and the kiddies now. Only, of course, there's the problem of me and what I might say in front of the wife and in front of the parents, like 'What about you and blokes, Kaveh? What about you and my dad? Why'd you change over to ladies, then? Arsehole getting stretched out of shape or some- thing?'"

"You don't know what you're talking about," Kaveh said. He glanced over his shoulder at the coming traffic. He sig- naled his intention to rejoin the stream of cars.

"I'm talking about you taking it from my dad," Tim said. "Up the arse, night after night. You think some woman's going to want to marry you if she knows what you've been up to, Kaveh?"

"'Night after night,'" Kaveh said, his brow furrowing. "'Taking it' from your dad. *What* are you talking about, Tim?" He began to move the car to the edge of the lay-by.

Tim reached over and killed the engine with a twist of the key. "You and my dad fucking each other," Tim said. "That's what I'm talking about."

Kaveh's jaw actually dropped. "Fucking . . . What's wrong with your head? What've you been thinking? That your *father* and I . . . ?" Kaveh made an adjustment to his seat, as if with the intention of settling in for a proper natter with Tim. He went on. "Your father was dear to me, Tim, a close and dear friend. I held him in the highest esteem, and we loved each other as close friends do. But that there might have been more than that . . . That he and I were . . . Are you thinking we were homosexual lovers? How could you have come to think that? I had a room in his house, only as his lodger. You know that."

Tim stared at the man. His face was perfectly serious. He was lying with such skill and such grace that for a moment Tim could actually almost quite nearly be poised on the edge of *believing* that everyone including himself had been completely wrong about Kaveh and about Tim's father and most of all about what they'd been to each other. Except Tim had been there the night his father had declared his love for Kaveh Mehran in front of his wife and his chil- dren. And Tim had seen his father with Kaveh. So he knew the truth.

"I watched you," he said. "Through the door. Didn't know that, did you? Makes your situation a bit different, doesn't it? You up on your hands and knees and Dad giving it to you in the arse and both of you liking it *just* fine. I watched you. Okay? I *watched* you."

Kaveh looked away from him for a moment. Then he sighed. Tim thought he was going to say something along the lines of being caught out and Tim needing to keep mum on the subject round Kaveh's family please. But Kaveh, it seemed, was full of surprises. He brought out another for Tim's entertainment. He said, "I used to have the same sort of dreams when I was your age. They're very real, aren't they? They're called waking dreams. They generally happen at the moment your body is making the transition from waking to sleeping and they seem so real that one actually thinks what's happening in them is life itself. People believe all sorts of things because of waking dreams: they've been abducted by aliens, they've seen someone in the bedroom with them, they've had a sexual experience with a parent or a teacher or even a mate, and on and on. But all the time they're merely asleep. As you were, of course, when you saw what you think you saw between your father and myself."

Tim's eyes widened. He wet his lips to respond but Kaveh went first.

"The fact that what you dreamed you saw between us was sexual in nature comes from the age you are, Tim. At fourteen a boy is all hormones and desire. And this is due to how his body's changing. He has dreams of sex, often. Often he ejaculates during them. And this could be—and probably is—an embarrassment to him if no one has explained it's perfectly normal. Your dad did explain this, didn't he? He ought to have done. Or perhaps your mum?"

Tim's next breath felt like a stab, not only in the lungs but in the brain and right to the centre of who he *knew* he was and not to the centre of whoever Kaveh was making him out to be. He said, "You fucking liar," and to his horror, he felt tears rising and God how he *knew* that Kaveh would use them. He could even see the endgame now, how it would all play out no matter which way he turned or what he threatened or what, indeed, he said to anyone, but especially what he said or might say to Kaveh's parents and his intended bride.

And there was no one else to tell those people the truth

about Kaveh. No one would be motivated to do it, and even if that were not the case, Kaveh's relations would themselves not be the least motivated to believe what strangers reported to them without a shred of proof. Plus, Kaveh was the consummate liar, wasn't he. He was the consummate con man and the consummate player in the chess game of life. Tim could speak the truth; he could rant; he could rail. Kaveh would know how to twist his words.

You must excuse young Tim, Kaveh would declare solemnly. You must not worry what he says and does. He goes to a special school, you know, for children who are disturbed in one way or another. There are times when he makes claims, when he does things . . . He ripped his little sister's favourite doll to pieces, for example, and just the other day or week or month or whatever I found him trying to kill the ducks in the village stream.

And people would believe him, of course. First, because people always believed what they wanted and needed to believe. Second, because every bloody word he said would be the truth. It was as if Kaveh had planned his whole game from the first, the very moment he locked eyes on Tim's dad.

Tim reached for the handle of the door. He grabbed up his rucksack and jerked the door open.

"What are you doing?" Kaveh demanded. "Stay in the car. You're going to school."

"And you're going to hell," Tim said. He leapt out and slammed the car door behind him.

VICTORIA
LONDON

Raul Montenegro certainly wasn't a dead end, Barbara Havers concluded. An hour or more of following various links connected to his name could easily have gleaned her half a ream of paper eaten up with printing stories about the bloke, so she tried to be selective. It was all in Spanish, but there were enough words similar to English for Barbara to be able to make out that Montenegro was a very big nob in industry and the industry in which he operated had something to do with natural gas in Mexico. From this she concluded that somehow Alatea Fairclough, neé Alatea Vasquez y del Torres, had got herself from Argentina to Mexico for reasons that remained unclear. She had moved herself either from a town still unknown to Barbara or, what was more likely considering the reaction of the woman to whom Barbara had attempted to speak in Argentina, she'd disappeared from Santa Maria de la Cruz, de los Angeles, y de los Santos. There, perhaps, she had lived as a member of the mayor's extended family as a niece or a cousin or, equally perhaps and probably more likely, she had been married to one of his five sons. At least that would explain all the excited *quien*s and *donde*s Barbara had heard on the other end of the line when she'd managed to get someone within the mayor's house to speak to her. Had Alatea done a runner from her marriage to one of the sons of the mayor, that son of the mayor might well like to know where she'd ended up. Especially, Barbara thought, if he and Alatea were still legally married.

All this was supposition, of course. She needed Azhar to get back to her with someone who could translate Spanish, and so far she'd heard not a word from him. So she kept struggling and following leads and vowing to take a tutorial from Winston Nkata on the use and abuse of the World Wide Web.

She also learned that Raul Montenegro was rolling in barrels of lolly. She got this from an online edition of *Hola!*, that journalistic mother ship from which *Hello!* had been launched. The two magazines were identical in their dedication to glossy photographs of celebrities of all ilks, all of whom possessed the kind of white teeth one needed to don sunglasses to gaze upon, all of whom dressed in designer gear and posed either at their own palatial estates or—if they lived too modestly for the magazine's readers— at expensive period hotels. The only difference was in the subjects of the stories, since with the exception of film actors or members of various and sometimes obscure European royal families, *Hola!* generally appeared to feature

individuals from Spanish-speaking countries, Spain itself
being the most frequently used. But Mexico had been
included more than once, and there was Raul Montenegro
with his frightening nose showing off his estate, which
appeared to be somewhere along the coast of Mexico
where there were many palm trees, lots of other colourful
vegetation, and a host of nubile girls and boys willing to
lounge at his poolside. There was also a shiny photo of
Montenegro at the helm of his yacht, with various members
of his youthful male crew striking crewlike poses around
him in their very tight white trousers and equally tight blue
tee shirts. What Barbara gathered from all this was that
Raul Montenegro liked to be surrounded by youth and
beauty since both at his home and on his yacht, there was
no one who wasn't occupying a place somewhere on the
scale between beautiful and lightning-struck gorgeous.
Where, she wondered as she looked at the pictures, did
these amazing-looking people come from? She reckoned
one never saw so many tan, lithe, supple, and scrumptious
human beings in one place outside of a casting call. Which,
of course, made her wonder if all these individuals were
indeed auditioning for something. If they were, she also
reckoned she knew what that something was. Money always
had a way of singing a siren song, didn't it? And if nothing
else, Raul Montenegro appeared to be swimming in money.

What was interesting, though, was that Alatea Fairclough neé all the rest of her names did not appear in any
of the *Hola!* pictures. Barbara compared the dates on the
magazine with the date on the article she'd found with the
photo of Alatea hanging on to Montenegro's arm. The *Hola!*
photos predated the other, and Barbara wondered if Montenegro had changed his stripes once he had Alatea on his
arm. Alatea had the kind of looks that allowed a woman to
lay down the law: You want me? Get rid of the others. Otherwise, believe me, I can easily move on.

Which brought Barbara back to the situation in Santa
Maria de la Cruz, de los Angeles, y de los Santos, whatever
that situation might be. She had to find out, so she printed
out the *Hola!* article and went back to Mayor Esteban Vega

y de Vasquez of Santa Maria di and all the rest of it. Tell me your tales, señor, she thought. At this point, pretty much anything would do.

LAKE WINDERMERE
CUMBRIA

"I've pulled Barbara Havers from your . . . Am I to call this 'your case' or what, Thomas?"

Lynley had veered to the side of the road to take the call on his mobile. He was on his way back to Ireleth Hall to go over St. James's conclusions with Bernard Fairclough. He said, "Isabelle," on a sigh. "You're angry with me. With very good reason. I'm terribly sorry."

"Yes. Well. Aren't we both. Barbara's brought Winston into things, by the way. Is that down to you as well? I put a stop to it, but I wasn't happy to find them cheek-to-cheek over a computer terminal on the twelfth floor."

Lynley lowered his head, looked at his hand on the steering wheel of the Healey Elliott. He was still wearing his wedding ring and had not been able in the months since Helen's death even to think about removing it. It was a plain gold band, engraved inside: her initials and his and the date of their marriage.

More than anything on earth, he wanted her back. That desire would continue to govern every decision he made until he was able finally and forever to let her go by embracing the fact of her death instead of struggling with its grim reality day after day. Even when he was with Isabelle, Helen was there: both the spirit of her and the delightful essence of who she had been. This was no one's fault, least of all Isabelle's. It was simply, ineluctably, how things were.

He said, "No. I didn't ask Winston's help. But please, Isabelle, don't blame Barbara for this. She's only been trying to track down some information for me."

"On this matter in Cumbria."

"On this matter in Cumbria. I'd thought, as she had time off coming—"

"Yes. I do see what you thought, Tommy."

He knew Isabelle was both wounded and hating the fact that she was wounded. When people felt like that, they needed to wound in turn, and he recognised that as well as understood it. But all of this was unnecessary at the moment, and he wanted, perhaps futilely, to make her see that. He said, "None of this was meant as a betrayal."

"And what makes you think I'm seeing it that way?"

"Because in your position, I'd see it that way myself. You're the guv. I'm not. I have no right to make requests of members of your team. Had there been any other way that I could have got the information quickly, believe me, I would have used it."

"But there was another way, and that's what concerns me. That you didn't see that other way and that you apparently still don't see it."

"You mean that I could have come to you. But I couldn't, Isabelle. I had no choice in the matter once Hillier gave the order. I was on the case and no one was to know about it."

"No one."

"You're thinking of Barbara. But I didn't tell her. She worked it out because it came down to Bernard Fairclough and things I needed to know about him, things in London and not in Cumbria. As soon as she looked into him for me, she put it together. Tell me. What would you have done in my position?"

"I'd like to think I would have trusted you."

"Because we're lovers?"

"Essentially. I suppose that's it."

"But it can't be," he said. "Isabelle, think about things."

"I've done little else. And that's a real problem, as you can imagine."

"I can. I do." He knew what she meant, but he wanted to forestall her although he could not have said exactly why. He thought it had something to do with the vast emptiness of his life without Helen and how, ultimately, as social creatures mankind did not do well in isolation. But he knew this might be the crassest form of self-delusion, dangerous both to himself and to Isabelle. Still, he said, "There has to be a separation, doesn't there? There must be a surgical cut—if you will—between what we do for the Met and who we are when we're alone together. If you go forward in this job as superintendent, there are going to be moments when you're put in a position of knowledge—by Hillier or by someone else—that you can't share with me."

"I'd share them anyway."

"You wouldn't, Isabelle. You won't."

"Did you?"

"Did I . . . ? What d'you mean?"

"I mean Helen, Tommy. Did you share information with Helen?"

How could he possibly explain it? he wondered. He hadn't had to share information with Helen because Helen had always known. She'd come to him in the bath and pour a bit of oil on her hands and work on his shoulders and murmur, "Ah, David Hillier again, hmm? Really, Tommy. I tend to think that never has knighthood caused such inflation in a man's self-esteem." He might then talk or he might not but the point was it didn't matter to Helen. What he said was a matter of indifference to her. Who he was was everything.

He hated missing her most of all. He could bear the fact that he'd been the one to decide upon when her life—such as it had been at that point, maintained by hospital machinery—would end. He could bear that she'd carried their child with her into the grave. He was coming to terms with the horror of her death's being a senseless street murder that had come from nothing and resulted in nothing. But the hole that losing her had created within him . . . He hated it so much that there were moments when its presence brought him perilously close to hating her.

Isabelle said, "What am I to make of your silence?"

He said, "Nothing. Nothing at all. Just thinking."

"And the answer?"

He'd honestly forgotten the question. "To?"

"Helen," she said.

"I wish there were one," he replied. "God knows I'd give it if I knew where to find it."

She altered then, on the edge of a coin, in that way of hers that somehow kept him unbalanced with her but still bound to her. She said quietly, "God. Forgive me, Tommy. I'm devastating you. You don't need that. I'm ringing you when I'm meant to be doing other things anyway. This isn't the time for this conversation. I was upset about Winston and that's not down to you. We'll speak later."

"Yes," he said.

"Have you any idea when you'll be back?"

That was, he thought wryly, the question in a nutshell. He looked out of the window. He was on the A592 in a heavily wooded area where the trees seemed to grow thickly right down to the shore of Lake Windermere. A few last leaves still stubbornly clung to the maples and the birches here, but another good storm would finish them off. He said, "Soon, I expect. Tomorrow, perhaps. The day after. I've had Simon with me and he's finished his part with the forensics. Deborah's still onto something, though. I'll need to be here to see that part through. I'm not sure it relates, but she's being stubborn and I can't let her stay here alone in case things go badly in some way."

She was quiet for a moment and he waited for her to make one of two choices dictated by his mention of Simon and Deborah. When she made it, he wanted to think it had been effortless for her, but he knew how unlikely this was. She said, "It's good they've been able to help you, Tommy."

"It is," he said.

"We'll speak when you return."

"We will."

They rang off then, and he spent a moment in the lay-by looking at nothing. There were facts and feelings that had to be sorted out, and he knew he would have to get to them. But for the moment, there was Cumbria, along with what needed to be sorted out here.

He drove the rest of the distance to Ireleth Hall and found the gates standing open. When he reached the hall, he saw that a car was parked in front of it. He recognised this as one of the two vehicles he'd seen in Great Urswick. Fairclough's daughter Manette would be here, then.

She'd not come alone, he discovered. She had her former husband with her, and Lynley found them with Manette's parents in the great hall, in the aftermath of what apparently had been a visit from Nicholas. When Lynley and Fairclough exchanged a look, Valerie was the one to speak.

"I'm afraid we haven't been entirely truthful with you, Inspector," she said. "And it's looking more and more like this is the moment for truth."

Lynley looked at Fairclough again. Fairclough looked away. Lynley knew he'd been used for some reason unspoken at the moment, and at this he felt the inner burning that comes from the most useless sort of anger. He said, "If you'd care to explain," to Valerie.

"Of course. I'm the reason you've been brought up to Cumbria, Inspector. No one knew this except Bernard. And now Manette, Freddie, and Nicholas know it."

For an utterly mad moment Lynley thought the woman was actually confessing to murdering her husband's nephew. The setting, after all, was perfect for it, in the best tradition of more than one hundred years of tea-in-the-vicarage and murder-in-the-library paperback novels sold in railway stations. He couldn't imagine why she might be confessing, but he'd also never been able to understand why the characters in those novels sat quietly in the drawing room or the sitting room or the library while a detective laid out all the clues leading to the guilt of one of them. No one ever demanded a solicitor in the midst of the detective's maundering. He'd never been able to sort that one out.

Valerie clarified quickly, probably in answer to the confusion on his face. It was simple enough: She and not her husband had been the one who wanted to have the death of Ian Cresswell more closely looked into.

That, Lynley thought, explained a great deal, particularly when he considered what they'd uncovered about Fairclough's private life. But it did not go the entire distance. *Why* still hung out there waiting for an answer. *Why Valerie and not Bernard?* was foremost. *Why at all?* was next since a conclusion of murder most likely would have meant that a member of her own family was culpable.

Lynley said, "I see. I'm not sure it matters entirely." He went on to explain the results of his examination of everything connected to the death in the boathouse. Everything he had looked at and everything looked at by Simon St.

James was in agreement with the coroner's conclusion. A tragic accident had taken Ian Cresswell's life. It could have happened to anyone using the boathouse. The dock's stones were ancient; some were loose. Those that had been dislodged had not been tampered with. Had Cresswell been getting out of a different sort of boat, he might have merely stumbled. But getting out of a scull was trickier. The combination of its delicate balance and the dock's loose stones had done him in. He'd pitched forward, hit his head, gone into the water, and drowned. No foul play had been involved.

In these circumstances, Lynley thought, one would expect a general sigh of relief to go around the room. One would expect something along the lines of "thank goodness" from Valerie Fairclough. But what came next was a long, tense silence in which he finally realised that something more than Ian Cresswell's death had been the real reason for the investigation. And into this silence the front door opened, and Mignon Fairclough came into the hall.

She pushed her zimmer frame in front of her. She said, "Freddie, can you manage the door, darling? It's a bit awkward for me," and as Freddie McGhie rose to do so, Valerie cut in with a sharp, "I expect you can cope quite well on your own, Mignon."

Mignon tilted her head and managed an arch look at her mother. She said, "Very well, then," and made something of a minor production out of turning herself and her zimmer and dealing with the door. She said, "There, then," when it was closed and she'd turned back to them. "Such an excitement of comings and goings today, my darlings. Manette and Freddie à deux. My heart flutters with all the possibilities attendant on that. Then Nick roars up. Then Nick roars away. And now our handsome Scotland Yard detective is back among us, pitter-pattering our collective hearts. Forgive the idle curiosity, Mother and Dad, but I couldn't bear to be outside looking in another moment with everything that's going on round here."

"It's just as well," Valerie said to her. "We're discussing the future."

"Whose, may I ask?"

"Everyone's. Including yours. I've just learned today that

for quite some time you've had something of pay rise in your monthly stipend. That's at an end. As is the entire allowance."

Mignon looked startled. Clearly, this was a turn of events she hadn't anticipated. "Mother, darling, well obviously . . . I'm disabled. I can hardly go out like this and expect to become gainfully employed. So you can't—"

"But that's where you're wrong, Mignon. I can. And I do."

Mignon looked round, apparently for the source of this sudden alteration to her circumstances. She settled her gaze on Manette. Her eyes narrowed and she said, "You little bitch. I wouldn't have thought you had it in you."

"I say, Mignon," Freddie declared.

"I expect you do," Mignon replied to him. "What else will you *say* when we begin to talk about her and Ian, Freddie?"

"There is no me and Ian and you know it," Manette cut in.

"There's a shoe box crammed with letters, darling, some of them burned but the rest in *very* good condition. I can easily fetch them. Believe me, I've been waiting years to do so."

"I had an adolescent infatuation with Ian. Make more of it if you like. It won't get you far."

"Not even the bits about 'wanting you more than I'll ever want anyone' and 'darling Ian please be my first'?"

"Oh please," Manette said in disgust.

"I could go on, you know. I've endless bits memorised."

"And none of us want to hear them," Valerie snapped. "Enough has been said. We're finished here."

"Not nearly as finished as you think." Mignon made her way to the sofa on which her sister and Freddie McGhie were sitting. She said, "If you don't mind, darling Freddie . . . ," and began to lower herself. He had no choice but to have her in his lap or to move. He opted for the second and joined his former father-in-law at the fireplace.

Lynley could see everyone regrouping mentally. All of them seemed to know something was coming, although he reckoned that no one knew what it was. Mignon had obviously been gathering information for years on the members of her family. She'd not had to use it in the past, but now she seemed to be preparing to do so. She cast one look at her sister and another at her father. She kept her eyes on him and, with a smile, said, "You know, I don't think things are going to change *quite* so much, Mother. And neither does Dad, I daresay."

Valerie took this on board easily enough. She said, "Vivienne Tully's payments are being stopped as well, if that's what you're getting at. And it *is* what you're getting at, isn't it, Mignon? You've been holding Vivienne Tully over your father's head for years, I expect. No wonder so much money's gone out to you."

"And this is turn-the-other-cheek time?" Mignon asked her mother. "Is that where we are? Where *you* are? With him?"

"Where I am, as you put it, with your father is none of your business. No one's marriage is your business."

"So let me make sure I understand," Mignon said. "He carries on with Vivienne Tully in London, he buys her a flat, he has a bloody second *life* there with her . . . and *I'm* to pay because I had the common decency not to tell you about it?"

"Please don't paint yourself as the noble character in this situation," Valerie said.

"Here, here," murmured Freddie.

Valerie continued. "You know very well why you didn't tell me about it. The information was useful and you're a common blackmailer. You ought to get down on your very capable knees and thank God I'm not asking the inspector to arrest you. Beyond that, everything about Vivienne Tully is a matter between your father and me. It doesn't concern you. She doesn't concern you. The only thing that ought to concern you is what you intend to do with your life because it's beginning tomorrow morning and I expect it to look very different from how it looks just now."

Mignon then turned to her father. She was in that moment every inch the woman holding all the valuable cards in the deck. She said to Fairclough, "Is that how you want it to be, then?"

"Mignon," he murmured.

"You've got to say. Now's the moment, Dad."

"Don't take this further," Bernard said to her. "It's not necessary, Mignon."

"I'm afraid it is."

"Valerie." Bernard appealed to his wife. He was, Lynley thought, a man who was watching his life as he'd known it come tumbling down. "I think all points have been touched upon. If we can agree upon—"

"Upon what?" Valerie broke in sharply.

"Upon showing a modicum of mercy here. That terrible fall all those years ago. Launchy Gill. She's not been well. She's never been the same. You know she's not capable of supporting herself."

"She's as capable as I am," Manette put in. "She's as capable as anyone in this room. Honestly, Dad, Mum's right, for God's sake. It's time to put an end to this nonsense. That has to be the most expensive fractured skull in history, considering how Mignon's played it."

Valerie, however, was watching her husband. Lynley could see that sweat had appeared on Fairclough's forehead. His wife apparently saw this as well because she turned to Mignon and said quietly, "Let's have the rest, then."

"Dad?" Mignon said.

"For God's sake, Valerie. Give her what she wants."

"I will not," she said. "I absolutely will not."

"Then it's time we had a chat about Bianca," Mignon declared. Her father shut his eyes.

"Who's Bianca?" Manette demanded.

"Our baby sister, as it happens," Mignon replied. She turned to her father. "Care to talk about this, Dad?"

ARNSIDE
CUMBRIA

When Lucy Keverne phoned her, Alatea Fairclough was alarmed. Their arrangement was that Lucy would never phone, either Alatea's mobile or the landline at Arnside House. Lucy had the numbers of course, because giving her the numbers had been one of the ways in which Alatea had made a stab at legitimatising that which could never be legitimate between them. But she'd impressed upon her from the first that ringing the number could bring an end to everything, and neither of them wanted that.

"What shall I do in case of an emergency?" Lucy had asked, not unreasonably.

"Then, of course, you must phone. But you'll understand, I hope, if at the moment I can't speak to you."

"We'll need some sort of code for that."

"For what?"

"For your not being able to speak at the moment. You can't just say 'I'm not able to speak to you now,' if your husband's in the room. That would be rather obvious, wouldn't it?"

"Of course. Yes." Alatea had thought about it. "I shall say, 'No, I'm sorry. I've sent for no package.' And then I'll ring you back as soon as I'm able. But it might not be at once. It might not be until the next day."

They'd agreed to this arrangement, and as things developed between them, Lucy had had no reason to phone. Because of this, all the uneasiness Alatea naturally felt in embarking upon a confidential journey with this woman had faded over time. So when Lucy rang not terribly long after their rendezvous in Lancaster, Alatea knew that something had gone wrong.

How badly wrong became clear within moments. They'd been seen at the university together, Lucy told her. They'd been seen inside the George Childress Centre. It was probably nothing, but a woman had followed them from the university back to the disabled soldiers' home. She wanted to talk about surrogacy. She was looking for a surrogate mother to carry her child. Again, it could be nothing. But the fact that this woman had settled on Lucy to talk to instead of Alatea . . .

"She claimed you have the 'look,'" Lucy said. "She claimed it was a 'look' she recognised well because she knows she has it herself. And because of this she reckoned I was the one to talk to about the possibility of surrogacy and not you, Alatea."

Alatea had taken the call in the inglenook of the main hall. It was a sheltered place, topped by a whimsical minstrel's gallery, and she liked it because it gave her a choice between the L-shaped window seat at one end of the inglenook, looking out on the lawn, or the confines of a pewlike shelter at the other side of the fireplace, one that hid her from anyone who might come into the hall.

She was alone. She'd been leafing through a design book relevant to the restoration of Arnside House, but she'd been thinking not of the house but rather of the progress she and Lucy were making. She'd been considering how each step of the process was going to be successfully managed. Very soon now, she'd decided, Miss Lucy Keverne, a struggling playwright from Lancaster who made ends meet by working as a social director in the Kent-Howath Foundation for Disabled Veterans, would come into her life as a newfound friend. From that point forward, things would be easier. They would never be perfect, but that was of no account. One had to learn how to live with imperfection.

When Lucy mentioned the woman who'd followed them, Alatea knew at once who this woman had to be. She thus put the pieces together very quickly, and she arrived at the only possible conclusion: She herself had been followed from Arnside and the red-haired woman called Deborah St. James—she of the faux documentary film—had done the following.

Alatea's earlier fears had revolved around the newspaper reporter. She'd seen *The Source,* and she knew its appetite for scandal was insatiable. The man's first visit to Cumbria had been an ordeal for her, his second a torment. But the worst his presence had ever suggested was a photograph that *might* lead to discovery. With the red-haired woman, discovery was here, just a knock-on-the-door away.

"What did you tell her?" Alatea asked, as calmly as she could manage.

"The truth about surrogacy, but she already knew most of it."

"Which truth are we talking about?"

"The various ways and means, the legalities, that sort of

thing. I'd thought at first there was nothing in it. It rather made sense in a bizarre sort of way. I mean, when women are desperate . . ." Lucy hesitated.

Alatea said quietly, "Go on. When they're desperate . . . ?"

"Well, they will go to extremes, won't they? So, considering everything, how extreme was it, really, that a woman who's gone to the George Childress Centre for a consultation would see us at some point in one corridor or another, perhaps as she's coming out of someone's office . . ."

"And what?"

"And think there was a chance. I mean, essentially that's how you and I met."

"No. We met via an advertisement."

"Yes. Of course. But the feeling is what I'm talking about. That sense of desperation. Which was what she described. So I believed her at first."

"At first. Then what?"

"Well, that's why I've rung you. When she left, I walked with her to the front of the building. The way one does, you know. She headed up the street and I thought nothing of it, but I walked to a window along the corridor and happened to see—quite by chance—that she'd reversed directions. I thought she intended to come back for another word, but she passed altogether and got into a car some way down the street."

"Perhaps she'd forgotten where she'd parked," Alatea said, although she reckoned there was more to come, something that had further intrigued Lucy. And so there was.

"That's what I thought at first. But when she got to the proper car, it turned out that she hadn't come alone. I couldn't see who was with her, but when she reached the car, the door swung open as if someone had pushed it from inside. So I continued to watch till the car drove by. She wasn't driving. It was a man. That made it all suspicious, you see. I mean, if she had her husband with her, why not come to talk to me together? Why not mention him? Indeed, why not say he was waiting in the car? Why not say he was in agreement with her in the matter? Or he was against her in the matter? Or he was anything at all? But she said nothing. So on top of her story of having stumbled upon us, the fact that there was a man—"

"What did he look like, Lucy?"

"I didn't get a good look, merely a quick glimpse. But I thought it best to ring you because . . . Well, you know. We're on very thin ice as things stand and—"

"I can pay more."

"That's not why I'm ringing. Good heavens. That's all been agreed to. I'm not about to squeeze more money out of you. Of course, money's always nice, isn't it, but we've agreed on a sum and I'm not the sort to go back on my word. Still, I wanted you to know—"

"We must get on with it, then. And soon. We must."

"Well, that's just the thing, you see. I'm suggesting we slow things down a bit. I think we need to make sure this woman—whoever she is—is completely out of the picture. Perhaps then in a month or two—"

"No! We've made our arrangements. We *can't.*"

"I think we should, Alatea. I think we must. Look at it this way: Once we know it was just a one-off—this woman turning up—a strange coincidence meaning nothing, then we'll move forward. I'm at bigger risk than you, after all."

Alatea felt numb, someone straitened on all sides with those sides pressing in till she reached the point when she'd no longer be able even to breathe unconstricted. She said, "I'm in your power, of course."

"Alatea. My dear. This *isn't* about power. This is about safety. Yours and mine. This is about dancing round the law. I daresay this is also about a number of other things as well, but we've no need to touch on those."

"What sort of things?" Alatea demanded.

"Nothing. Nothing. It's just a turn of phrase. Listen, I must get back to work. We'll speak in a few days. Till then, you're not to worry, all right? I'm still on board. Just not at this precise moment. Not till we know for certain that this woman's appearance in my life meant nothing."

"How will we know that?"

"As I said. We'll know it if I don't see her again."

Lucy Keverne rang off then, amid urgings and murmurings that Alatea was not to worry, was to remain calm, was to have a care. She—Lucy—would be in touch. *They* would be in touch. *Everything* would go according to plan.

Alatea sat in the inglenook for several minutes, trying to understand what her options were or whether, at this point, she had any options left. She'd known from the first that the red-haired woman had spelled danger, no matter what Nicholas had said about her. Now that Lucy had seen her in the presence of a man, Alatea finally saw what the danger was. Certain people had no right to live as they wished to live, and she'd had the misfortune of having been born as one of those wretched people. She had great beauty, but it meant nothing. It was, indeed, what had doomed her from the first.

At the far end of the house, she heard a door slam. She frowned, rose quickly, and looked at her watch. Nicky should have gone to work. From there he should have gone to the pele project. But when he called her name and sounded panicked in the calling of it, she knew he'd gone elsewhere.

She hurried to find him. She called out, "Here, Nicky. I'm here."

They met in the long oaken corridor, where the light was dimmest. She couldn't read his face. But his voice frightened her, so intense was it. "It's down to me," he said. "I've ruined everything, Allie."

Alatea thought of the previous day: Nicholas's distress and the fact that Scotland Yard was in Cumbria looking into the circumstances of Ian Cresswell's death. For a terrible moment, her conclusion was that her husband was confessing to his cousin's murder, and she felt light-headed as she was struck with the knowledge of where this terrible admission could take them should they not be able to hide the truth. If terror had a presence, it was there in the darkened corridor with them.

She took her husband's arm and said, "Nicky, please. You must tell me very clearly what's wrong. Then we can decide what to do."

"I don't think I can."

"Why? What's happened? What can be so terrible?"

He leaned against the wall. She held on to his arm, and she said to him, "Is it this Scotland Yard matter? Have you been to speak to your father? Does he actually think . . . ?"

"None of that matters," Nicholas said. "We're surrounded by liars, you and I. My mother, my father, probably my sisters, that damn reporter from *The Source*, that filmmaking woman. Only I didn't see it because I was so intent on *proving* myself." He spat the penultimate word. "Ego, ego, ego," he said, and with each repetition, he hit his forehead with his fist. "All I cared about was proving to everyone—but especially to them—that I'm not the person they used to know. The drugs are gone, the alcohol is gone, and they're gone forever. And *they* were meant to see that. Not only my family but the whole bloody world. So I took every opportunity to show myself off and because of *that* and nothing else, we're where we are just now."

His mention of the filmmaking woman sent fear coursing down Alatea's spine. More and more, everything was coming down to that woman whom they had blindly admitted into their home with her camera, her questions, and her apocryphal concern. From the first, Alatea had known there was something very wrong about her presence. And now she'd been to Lancaster to see Lucy Keverne. So quick she was to follow the clues. Alatea wouldn't have thought it was possible. She said, "Where are we, then, 'just now,' Nicky?"

He told her and she tried to follow. He spoke of the reporter from *The Source* and of that man's belief that the red-haired woman had come from New Scotland Yard. He spoke of his parents and a confrontation he'd had with them that day over this very matter in the presence of his sister Manette and Freddie McGhie. He spoke of his mother and her admission to having brought Scotland Yard into the mix. And he spoke of the surprise of all of them when he railed about the detective who'd been sent into his house, the woman who'd upset Alatea so very much . . . And that was where he stopped.

Alatea said carefully, "What then, Nicky? Did they say something? Did something more occur?"

His words sounded hollow. "She's not the Scotland Yard

detective at all. I don't know who she is. But because she's been hired to come up to Cumbria . . . to take those photographs . . . Oh, she *claimed* she needed none of you, that you weren't going to be part of that bloody film, but someone *had* to hire her because there *is* no filmmaker and she's *not* Scotland Yard and do you see why it's down to me, now, Allie? What's going to happen is down to me. I thought it was bad enough that my parents wanted a detective to investigate Ian's death because of me. But then to know that *nothing* that's happened here in this house, with that woman, has anything to do with Ian's death but rather has happened because I agreed, because of my ego . . . because a stupid story in a stupid magazine gave someone a licence, a clue, a way in . . ."

She knew, then, where this was heading. She supposed she'd known where it had been heading all along. She murmured the name: "Montenegro. You think she was hired by Raul?"

"Who the hell else could it possibly be? And I did this to you, Allie. How am I supposed to live with that?"

He pushed past her. He made his way along the corridor and into the drawing room. There, she could see him more clearly in what remained of the daylight. He looked ghastly, and for a completely mad moment she felt herself responsible for this although he and not she had been the one to allow the putative documentary scout into their lives. But she couldn't help herself. It was the role he played in their relationship, just as his role was to need her so desperately that from the first he had questioned nothing about her as long as he'd been assured of her love. Which was what she herself had been looking for: a place of permanence where she could abide, where no one would ask the kind of dangerous questions that grew from a moment's wonder.

Outside, Alatea could see that the afternoon was bringing on midautumn's dusk. The sky and the bay beneath were identical in colour, with grey clouds encroaching on apricot streaks cast across both water and air by the setting sun.

Nicholas went to the bay window. He sank into one of the two seats there, and he dropped his head into his hands. "I've failed you," he said. "I've failed myself."

Alatea wanted to shake her husband. She wanted to tell him that this was *not* the time for him to feel himself the sun round which all the brewing troubles revolved. She wanted to shout that he could not possibly begin to understand how bad things were about to become for both of them. But to do any of that was to waste what little ability she had left to come up with a way to forestall an inevitable conclusion of which he was still entirely ignorant.

Nicholas thought that Raul Montenegro's reintroduction into her life meant the end of things. He could not possibly have known the truth of the matter: Raul Montenegro was only the beginning.

BLOOMSBURY
LONDON

Barbara took herself to Bloomsbury in order to be in his vicinity when she finally heard from Taymullah Azhar. Faced with her need to get more information on the topic of Raul Montenegro—not to mention sorting out everything that there was to sort out about Santa Maria de la Cruz, de los Angeles, y de los Santos—she reckoned an Internet café was in order. She'd kill two birds while she waited for Azhar to produce a Spanish translator for her.

Before Nkata had left the Met's library, he'd said softly, "Look for key words and follow the trail. It's not brain surgery, Barb. You'll get better as you go on." From this, Barbara reckoned that she was to do searches on the names she came across in the articles she had, regardless of what language the articles were in. When she found an Internet café not far from the British Museum, then, that was what she did.

It was not the most pleasant environment in which to conduct her Web search. She had stopped to purchase an English/Spanish dictionary on the way to the spot, and now she was sandwiched between an overweight asthmatic in a mohair sweater and a gum-popping Goth with a septum ring and a score of eyebrow studs who kept receiving calls on her mobile phone from someone who, apparently, did not believe she was sitting at a computer because each time he rang, she barked, "Well then, come to the bloody place if you don't believe me, Clive . . . Don't be so bloody *stoop*id. I'm not fucking e-mailing anyone. I can't, can I, since you keep bloody ringing me every thirty seconds."

In this atmosphere, Barbara tried to concentrate. She also tried to ignore the fact that the mouse looked like it hadn't been disinfected since the day it had come out of its box. As best she could, she attempted to type without actually touching the keys, hitting them only with her fingernails, although these were mostly too short to make a proper job of it. But she reckoned the keyboard was crawling with everything from the bubonic plague to genital warts, and she didn't intend to leave the place with her future writ large in the clutches of some disease.

After a few false trails, she was able to find an article on the mayor of Santa Maria et cetera that included a picture. It looked like an anniversary photograph—perhaps a graduation picture?—but in any case, it was something having to do with the nuclear family because they were all spread out on the steps of an unidentifiable building: the mayor, his wife, and their five sons. Barbara examined this picture.

One fact was obvious immediately, with or without a translation: In the roll of the genetic dice, the five sons of Esteban and Dominga had hit the jackpot. Barbara read their names: Carlos, Miguel, Angel, Santiago, and Diego. They were a handsome lot, ranging in the photo from nineteen years old down to seven years old. But a scrutiny of the article told Barbara that the picture had been taken twenty years earlier, so any of them could easily have been married at this point, perhaps one of them to Alatea. The next step, according to Nkata's explanation of how these things worked, would be to check on the five sons. Carlos would be first. All Barbara had to do was cross her fingers.

No luck, though, as far as any marriage went. She found Carlos far more easily than she would have thought possible, but he appeared to be a Catholic priest. There was an article that seemed to be about his ordination, and the entire family posed with him again, this time on the steps of a church. His mother was clinging to his arm, gazing up at him adoringly; his father was grinning, a cigar clutched in his hand; his brothers were looking vaguely embarrassed at all the attendant religious hoopla. So much for Carlos, Barbara thought.

She went on to Miguel. Again, it didn't take long. Indeed, it was so easy that Barbara wondered why she hadn't been checking up on her neighbours for years. In the case of Miguel, she found his engagement picture. The wife-to-be looked vaguely like an Afghan hound, all hair and thin face with a suspicious lack of forehead suggesting a paucity of marbles in the prefrontal lobe. Miguel himself was a dentist, Barbara decided. Either that or he was in need of dental work. Her Spanish dictionary was a little iffy on the topic. But at any rate, it didn't seem to matter. It took her no step closer to discovering anything about Alatea Fairclough.

She was about to go on to Angel when her mobile chimed out the first two lines of "Peggy Sue." She flipped it open, said, "Havers," and heard Azhar—at long last—telling her that he had found someone who could translate Spanish for her. "Where are you at present?" he asked.

"Internet caff," she told him. "I'm down the street from the BM. I c'n come to you. Easier than anything. Cafeteria near your office or something?"

He was silent for a moment, perhaps thinking about this. At last he said there was a wine bar in Torrington Place, near Chenies Mews and Gower Street. They would meet her there in a quarter of an hour.

"Right," she said. "I'll find it." She printed the documents she'd so far found and went to the till, where the shop assistant named an exorbitant price for them and said, "Colour printer, luv," when Barbara protested.

"Colour robbery more like it," Barbara said. She took her copies in a paper bag and made it over to Torrington Place, where the wine bar was easy to spot and Azhar was waiting inside with a leggy girl in a cashmere jacket upon whose shoulders spilled a luxury of dark curls.

Her name was Engracia, no last name provided, and she was a graduate student from Barcelona. The girl smiled at Azhar as he passed this information to Barbara. "I will do what I can to help you," she said, although Barbara reckoned it was Azhar to whom she wished to be useful, and who could blame her? They made a nice-looking couple. But then, so did Azhar and Angelina Upman. So would Azhar and pretty much anyone.

She said, "Ta," to the girl. "In my next life I plan to be multilingual."

"I shall leave you to it, then," Azhar said.

"Heading back?" Barbara asked him.

"Heading home," he replied. "Engracia, my thanks."

"De nada," she murmured.

At one of the tables inside the wine bar, Barbara handed over the documents, beginning with the article that accompanied the photograph of the mayor and his family. She said, "I got a Spanish/English dictionary, but it wasn't much help. I mean, it *was* . . . a bit. But looking up every word . . ."

"Of course." Engracia read for a moment, holding the article in one hand while she played with a gold hoop earring with the other. After a moment, she said, "This is connected to an election."

"For mayor?"

"*Si.* The man—Esteban—he runs for mayor of the town and this article introduces him to people. It's an article without import . . . how do you call this?"

"A puff piece?"

She smiled. She had very nice teeth and very smooth skin. She wore lipstick but it was barely noticeable, so perfectly had it been chosen. "Yes. A puff piece," she replied. "It says in the town there is such a large family of the mayor that if his family members all vote, he will win the election. But that, I believe, is a joke because it also says the town's population is seventy-five thousand people." Engracia read a bit further and said, "There is information about his wife, Dominga, and about her family. Both families have lived in Santa Maria de la Cruz, de los Angeles, y de los Santos for many years, many generations."

"What about the boys?"

"The boys . . . Ah. Carlos is a seminarian. Miguel wishes to be a dentist. Angel"—she pronounced it Ahn*hail*—"plans to study architecture and the other two boys are too young to know, although Santiago says he wants to be an actor and Diego . . ." She read further and chuckled. "It says he wishes to be an astronaut in the unlikely event that Argentina develops a space programme. That is a little joke, I think. The reporter was humouring him."

There wasn't a lot of grist in all that, Barbara reckoned. She brought out the next pieces, both of them about Raul Montenegro. She handed them over with, "What about these?" And she asked Engracia if she wanted a glass of wine or something since they were taking up space in the wine bar, which wasn't going to turn out to be a popular move if they didn't place an order.

Engracia said mineral water would be nice, and Barbara fetched it for her along with a glass of the house plonk for herself. When she returned with the drinks, she saw that Engracia was concentrating on the article whose accompanying photo had Alatea hanging on Montenegro's arm. This, she said, was an article about a very important fundraiser in Mexico City, having to do with the construction of a symphony music hall. The man was the biggest contributor to this project and consequently would have the honour of naming the music hall.

"And?" Barbara said, expecting the hall to be named for Alatea since she was looking so pleased as she hung on his arm.

"Magdalena Montenegro Centre for Music," Engracia said. "Named for his mama. Latin men are close to their mothers, as a rule."

"What about the woman with him in the picture?"

"It says only that she is his companion."

"Not his wife? Lover? Partner?"

"Only his companion, I'm afraid."

"Could be a euphemism for lover or partner?"

Engracia studied the photo a moment. "This is difficult to say. But I do not think so."

"So she could have been merely his evening's companion? Even an escort he hired for the night?"

"It is possible," Engracia said. "She could even be someone who stepped into the picture with him at the moment, I suppose."

"Damn, damn, damn," Barbara muttered. And when Engracia looked remorseful, as if she'd somehow failed, Barbara said, "Oh, sorry. Not you. Just life."

"I see this is important to you. Can I help in some other way?" Engracia asked.

Barbara thought about this. There *was* something else. She calculated the time difference and said, "Let me make a phone call," and she took out her mobile. "They don't speak English at the other end, so if you c'n talk to whoever answers . . ."

She explained to Engracia that they were phoning the mayor's home in Santa Maria et cetera. The four-hour time difference made it early afternoon there. Her job was to see if there was information to be had about one Alatea Vasquez y del Torres should someone answer the phone.

"The woman in the picture," Engracia said with a nod at the article about Raul Montenegro.

"That would be the case," Barbara told her.

When the call went through and the phone began ringing, she handed the mobile over to the Spanish girl. What happened next was rapid-fire Spanish during which Barbara caught only Alatea's name. Coming from Argentina, though, she could hear the sound of a woman's voice. It was high and excited, and she could see from Engracia's intent expression that something was developing from this call to Santa Maria de la Cruz, de los Angeles, y de los Santos.

There was a pause in the dialogue and Engracia glanced at Barbara. She said, "That was a cousin, Elena Maria."

"Do we have the wrong number, then?"

"No, no. She's at the house visiting. Dominga—the mayor's wife?—this is her aunt. She's gone to fetch her. She's most excited to hear Alatea's name."

"Pay dirt," Barbara murmured.

"This is . . . ?"

"Sorry. Just an expression. We might be getting somewhere."

She smiled. "Ah. 'Pay dirt.' I like this very much." Then her expression altered as a distant voice bridged the thousands of miles between London and Argentina. The rapid-fire Spanish began again. There were many *comprendos* and many more *si*s. A few *sabe*s? and several *no sabo*s and then *gracias* over and over again.

When the call was completed, Barbara said, "Well? Yes? What've we got?"

"A message for Alatea," Engracia said. "This woman Dominga says to tell Alatea she must come home. She says to tell her that her father understands. She says the boys also understand. Carlos, she says, has made all of the family pray and what they pray for is for her safe return."

"Did she happen to mention who the hell she is?"

"A member of the family, it seems."

"A sister who didn't get in that old picture? A sister born after the picture was taken? A wife of one of the boys? A cousin? A niece? What?"

"She did not say, at least not clearly. But she told me the girl ran from her home when she was fifteen. They thought she went to Buenos Aires and they search for her there for many years. Particularly Elena Maria searches. Dominga said Elena Maria's heart was broken and Alatea must be told that as well."

"How many years are we talking about that she's been gone, then?"

"Alatea? Thirteen," Engracia said.

"And she ended up in Cumbria," Barbara murmured. "By what route and how the hell . . . ?"

She'd been speaking to herself but Engracia replied, reaching for one of the copied articles she'd already looked at. Barbara saw it was the piece on Raul Montenegro. Engracia said, "Perhaps this man helped her? If he has enough money to pay for a symphony music hall, he has more than enough to purchase a ticket to London for a beautiful woman, no? Or a ticket to any place else. Indeed, to any place she might like to go."

LAKE WINDERMERE
CUMBRIA

They were like a tableau for thirty seconds or so, although the thirty seconds seemed much longer. During this period, Mignon directed her gaze from one person to another and her face blazed with a triumph that she'd obviously been waiting years to feel. Manette felt like a character in the midst of a stage play. This was the climax of the drama, and everything afterwards was going to provide them with the catharsis guaranteed in all Greek tragedies.

Valerie was the first person to move. She stood and said in that well-bred fashion of hers that Manette knew so well, "Please excuse me," and she began to leave the great hall.

Mignon said in a burble of laughter, "Don't you want to know more, Mum? You can't leave now. Wouldn't you like to have it all?"

Valerie hesitated, then turned and looked at Mignon. "You make a very good case for strangling one's children at birth," she said, and she left them.

The inspector followed her. Obviously, new light was being shed upon everything and there was now a very good chance, Manette thought, that he was reconsidering whatever conclusions he'd drawn about Ian's death. She was doing the same herself because if Ian had known about this child of her father's . . . if he'd made some kind of threat regarding this child and what he knew about her . . . if, indeed, it had come down to a choice between the truth being revealed or a lie continuing to be lived . . . Manette saw how her cousin's life had been in danger, and she reckoned the detective saw it as well.

She didn't want to believe what Mignon had revealed about this child Bianca, but she could see by the expression on her father's face that Mignon's revelation was the truth. She didn't know how she felt about this, and she didn't know when she might even be able to sort through her feelings in the matter. But she saw how Mignon felt about it: just another reason to blame their father for whatever she believed had been lacking in her life.

Mignon said to him happily, "Oh my, Dad. Well, at least you and I are going down in this ship together, aren't we? I do expect there's some consolation in that for you. To be doomed but to see your favourite child—that *would* be me, wouldn't it?—doomed alongside you? Rather like King Lear and Cordelia. Only . . . Who's playing the Fool?"

Bernard's lips were as thin as a bowl of workhouse gruel.

He said, "I think you're rather mistaken, Mignon, although you've got the serpent's-tooth part of it bang on the money."

She wasn't the least taken aback. "D'you think marital forgiveness actually runs that far?"

He said, "I don't think you know the first thing about marriage or forgiveness."

At this Manette glanced at Freddie. He was watching her, his dark eyes concerned. She understood he was worried for her, anxious about how she was taking in being a witness to her family's destruction. Before her eyes, the world as she'd known it was undergoing a cataclysmic change. She wanted to tell him she could cope with that, but she knew she didn't want to cope alone.

Mignon said to their father, "Did you really think you could keep Bianca a secret forever? My God, what an enormous ego you have. Tell me, Dad, what was poor little Bianca to make of everything when she learned about her father and his other family? His *legitimate* family. But you hadn't got that far along in your consideration of the future, had you? As long as Vivver was willing to play the game your way, you probably didn't think one moment beyond what kind of fuck she was and how often you could manage it."

"Vivienne," her father replied, "is going home to New Zealand. And this conversation is quite finished."

"I'll say when it's finished," Mignon told him. "Not you. Never you. She's younger than *we* are, this Vivienne of yours. She's younger than Nick."

Bernard walked to the front door then, passing Mignon to do so. She tried to grab his arm, but he shook her off. Manette expected her sister to use that gesture as an opportunity to topple from the sofa to the floor and proclaim herself the victim of abuse, but instead, she merely carried on talking. She said, "I'll speak to Mother. I'll tell her the rest. How long you've been having an affair with Vivienne Tully: Is it ten years, Dad? Longer than that? How old she was when it all began: She was twenty-four, wasn't she? Or was she younger? How Bianca came about: She wanted her, didn't she? She wanted a baby and *you* did as well, didn't you, Dad? Because when Bianca was born, Nick was still out there doing his Nick thing and you were still hoping that someone, somewhere, some bloody time was going to give you a decent male child, weren't you, Dad? And won't Mother just love hearing that?"

Bernard said, "Do your worst, Mignon. It is, I think, what you've always wanted."

"I hate you," she said.

"As always," he replied.

"Did you hear me? I *hate* you."

"For my sins," Bernard said, "believe me, I know. And perhaps I deserve it. Now leave my house."

There was a moment of impasse during which Manette thought her sister might refuse. Mignon stared at her father as if waiting for something that Manette knew very well was never going to appear. Finally, she shoved her zimmer to one side. She smiled, rose, and strolled easily out of her father's life.

When the door was closed upon her, Bernard took a linen handkerchief from his pocket. He wiped his glasses with it, then he used it against his face. Manette could see that his hands were shaking. Everything was on the line for him, not the least a marriage of more than forty years.

He finally looked from Manette to Freddie and back to Manette. He said, "I'm so sorry, my dear. There are so many things . . ."

"I'm not sure they matter any longer." How odd, Manette thought. She'd waited most of her life for this moment: with herself in a superior position and Bernard made vulnerable, with Bernard looking at her and actually seeing her, not as a daughter, not as a substitute for the kind of son he'd wished for, but as a person in her own right, fully capable of anything he himself could do. She no longer knew why all of that had been so important to her. She only knew that she didn't feel what she'd expected to feel with his recognition of her washing over her at last.

Bernard nodded. He said, "Freddie . . ."

Freddie said, "If I'd been told, I would have probably stopped it all from happening. But then, I don't know, do I? I'm not sure."

"You're a good, honest man, Fred. Stay that way." Bernard excused himself and went to the stairs. He climbed them heavily and Manette and Freddie listened to his footfalls. Eventually, they faded. A door closed quietly somewhere above them.

"We should probably leave, old girl," Freddie said to Manette. "If you're able, that is."

He came to her and she allowed him to help her to her feet, not because she needed it but because it felt good to feel someone solid at her side. They left the great hall and went outdoors. It wasn't until they were in the car and heading along the drive in the direction of the gate that she began to weep. She tried to do this silently, but Freddie glanced in her direction. He pulled the car over at once and stopped. Gently, he took her into his arms.

He said, "It's a tough one. Seeing one's parents like that. Knowing how one has demolished the other. I expect your mother knew something wasn't quite right, but perhaps it was easier just to ignore it. That's the way these things are sometimes."

She cried against his shoulder but she shook her head.

He said, "What? Well, of course, your sister's mad as a rabid dog, but there's nothing much new in that, is there? I do wonder, though, how you managed to emerge so . . . well, so normal, Manette. It's rather miraculous when you think about it."

At this, she wept harder. It was all too late: what she now knew, what she should have seen, and what she finally understood.

LAKE WINDERMERE
CUMBRIA

Lynley found Valerie Fairclough walking along one of the paths already laid out in the unfinished children's garden. When he joined her, she began to speak as if they had been interrupted in the midst of a conversation about this very spot. She pointed out where work on the wrecked ship had already begun and told him about the ropes, swings, and sand that would be a feature of it. She indicated the spot designated for monkey bars and a roundabout. She took him past the smaller children's section, where horses, kangaroos, and large frogs already stood on their heavy spring bases, waiting for riders who would laugh and crow with the simple fun of bouncing upon them. There would be a fort as well, she said, because boys loved forts to play soldiers in, didn't they? And for the girls there would be a playhouse stocked with everything in miniature that one would find in a real house because wasn't the truth of the matter— and all sexism aside—that girls liked to play inside houses and make up games in which they were married with children and a husband who came home at night and presided over dinner?

She laughed mirthlessly when she said that last bit. Then she went on to say that the children's area would be, in short, every child's dream place to play.

Lynley thought it all quite odd. What she was building was more suitable for a public park than a private home. He wondered what her expectation of its use really was, whether she had a larger picture in mind, one that meant opening Ireleth Hall to the public in the manner of so many great houses across the country. It was quite as if she'd known an enormous change was coming and was preparing for it.

He said to her, "Why did you arrange for me to come to Cumbria?"

Valerie looked at him. At sixty-seven years old, she was a striking woman. In her youth she would have possessed great beauty. Beauty and money: a powerful combination. She could have chosen from a score of men of similar background to her own, but she had not done so.

"Because I've suspected for quite some time."

"What?"

"Bernard. What he was up to. I didn't know for certain that he was 'up to' Vivienne Tully, of course, but I probably should have realised that as well. When he didn't mention her after the second time she and I met, those trips to London of his that became more frequent, so many things associated with his foundation that needed his attention . . . There are always signs, Inspector. There are always clues, red flags, whatever you wish to call them. But it's generally easier to ignore them than to face the unknown that's going to arise out of the wreckage of a forty-two-year marriage." She picked up a discarded plastic coffee cup, something left by one of the workers. She frowned at this and crushed it into her pocket. She shaded her eyes and looked out at the lake, at storm clouds that were brewing on the hills to the west. "I am surrounded by liars and knaves. I wanted to smoke them out of their hiding places. You"—and here she cast him a small smile— "you were my fire, Inspector."

"What of Ian?"

"Poor Ian."

"Mignon could have killed him. She had motive, a very strong motive if it comes to that. By your own admission, she was in the boathouse. She could have gone in there earlier and loosened the stones somehow, in an undetectable way. She could even have been in there when he returned. She could have pulled him from the scull, pushed him from it . . ."

"Inspector, that sort of revenge is far beyond Mignon's ability to plan. Besides, she would have seen no immediate monetary gain in that. And the only thing Mignon has ever been able to see clearly is the monetary gain of the moment." She turned from the lake then and looked at Lynley. She said, "I knew the stones were loose. I'd told Ian as much, more than once. He and I were the only ones who used the boathouse regularly, so I told no one else. There was no need. I warned him to take care getting in and out of his scull. He said not to worry, that he would take care and when he had a moment, he'd fix the dock. But I think that night he had other things on his mind. He must have done. It was quite out of the ordinary that he came to row that late anyway. I think he wasn't paying close enough attention. It was always an accident, Inspector. I knew that from the first."

Lynley considered this. "And that filleting knife I found in the water with the stones?"

"I threw it there. Just to keep you here, in case you decided too soon it was an accident."

"I see," he said.

"Are you terribly angry?"

"I ought to be." They turned and headed back towards the house. Above the walls of the topiary garden, the towering mass of shaped shrubbery loomed and behind it Ireleth Hall itself, sand coloured and teeming with history. He said, "Didn't Bernard think it unusual?"

"What?"

"Your asking for an investigation into his nephew's death."

"Perhaps he did, but what could he say? 'I don't want that'? I would have asked why. He would have tried to explain. Perhaps he would have said it was unfair to Nicholas, to Manette, to Mignon to suspect them, but I would have argued it's better to know the truth about one's children than to live a lie and that, Inspector, would have taken us far too close to the truth Bernard himself didn't want me to know. He had to run the risk you wouldn't unearth Vivienne. He really had no choice in the matter."

"For what it's worth, she's returning to New Zealand."

She made no response to this. She took his arm as they worked their way along the path. She said, "What's odd is this: After more than forty years of marriage, a man often becomes a habit. I must consider whether Bernard is a habit I would prefer to break."

"Might you?"

"I might. But first I want the time to think." She squeezed his arm and looked up at him. "You're a very handsome man, Inspector. I'm sorry you lost your wife. But I hope you don't intend to remain alone. Do you?"

"I haven't thought about it much," he admitted.

"Well, do think about it. We all have to choose eventually."

WINDERMERE
CUMBRIA

Tim spent hours in the business centre waiting for the time to be right. It hadn't taken him that long to reach the town once he'd left Kaveh that morning. He'd leapt over a dry-stone wall and jogged across a lumpy paddock in the direction of dense woods comprising fir trees and birches. He'd remained there—in a shelter of autumn-hued bracken backed by the trunk of a fallen spruce—until he was certain Kaveh had driven off, and then he'd worked his way over to the road to Windermere, where two lifts took him to the middle of town, at which point he began his search.

He'd had no luck in finding a restorer of broken toys. At long last, he'd had to settle upon an establishment called J. Bobak & Son, a shop dedicated to the repair of all things electrical. Inside this place three aisles crammed with broken kitchen appliances led to the back, where J. Bobak turned out to be a woman with grey plaits, a lined face, and bright pink lipstick that ran up the cracks above her lips while Son turned out to be a kid in his twenties with Down's syndrome. She was tinkering with something that looked like a miniature waffle iron. He was working on an old-time wireless that was nearly the size of a Mini. All round both Son and his mother stood various appliances in various stages of repair: television sets, microwaves, mixers, toasters, and coffeemakers, some of which looked as if they'd been waiting for expert electrical ministrations for a decade or more.

When Tim presented J. Bobak with Bella, she'd shaken her head. This poor lump of arms and legs and body couldn't be repaired at all, he was told, even if J. Bobak & Son repaired toys, which they did not. At least, she couldn't be repaired in a way that would be pleasing to her owner. He'd be better off saving his money to buy a new doll. There was a toy shop—

It had to be *this* doll, he told J. Bobak. He knew it was rude to interrupt and the expression on J. Bobak's face indicated she was about to tell him so. He went on to explain the doll belonged to his little sister and their dad had given it to her and their dad was dead. This got to J. Bobak. She laid the doll's pieces out on the shop counter and pursed her bright pink lips thoughtfully. Her son came to join her. He said, "Hi," to Tim, and "I don't go to school any longer but *you're* supposed to be in school, eh? Betcher doing a bunk today." His mum said, "Trev, you see to your own job, luv. There's a good boy," and patted him on his shoulder as he snuffled noisily against his arm and went back to the enormous radio.

She said to Tim, "Sure you don't want to buy a new doll, luv?"

As could be, Tim told her. Could she repair it? There was no other shop. He'd tried all over town.

She said reluctantly that she'd see what she could do, and Tim told her he would give her the address where the doll had to be sent when it was completed. He took out a crumpled wad of bank notes and some coins, all of which he'd cadged over time from his mother's bag, his father's wallet, and a tin in the kitchen where Kaveh kept pound coins to use when he ran out of money and hadn't thought to stop at the cash point in Windermere on his way home from work.

J. Bobak said, "What? You not coming back for it yourself?"

He said no. He wouldn't be here in Cumbria by the time the doll was repaired. He told her to take as much money as she liked. She could send any change back with the doll. Then he gave her Gracie's name and the address, which was simple enough. Bryan Beck farm, Bryanbarrow, near Crosthwaite. Gracie might well be gone by then, but even if she'd returned to their mother, certainly Kaveh would send the doll on. He'd do that much, no matter what sort of lie he was living with his pathetic little wife at that point. And she'd be pleased to see it, would Gracie. Perhaps she'd even forgive Tim for having wrecked the poor doll in the first place.

That done, he'd found his way to the business centre and there he stayed. On his way, with what remained of his money he bought a packet of jam mallows, a Kit Kat bar, an apple, and a nachos kit of chips and salsa and refried beans, and, squatting between a filthy white Ford Transit and a wheelie bin overloaded with soaking Styrofoam, he ate it all.

When the car park began to empty as people left the various businesses for the day, he ducked behind the wheelie bin and kept out of sight. He fixed his eyes upon the photo shop and just before the hour when it was to close, he went across to it and opened the door.

Toy4You was taking the cash drawer out of the till. His hands full, he didn't have the chance to remove his name tag. Tim saw part of it, *William Con—*, before the man flicked away. He ducked into the back and when he returned, he was without the cash drawer and without the name tag. He was also without good humour.

He said, "I told you I'd text. What're you doing here?"

Tim said, "It happens tonight."

Toy4You said, "Get this straight: I'm not playing power games with some fourteen-year-old. I told you I'd let you know when I had it set up."

"Set it up now. You said not alone this time and that means you know someone. Get him over here. We're doing it now." Tim pushed past the man. He saw Toy4You's face darken. It didn't matter to Tim if it came to blows. Blows were just fine. One way or another, things were going to be concluded.

He went into the back room. He'd been here before, so nothing about it surprised Tim. It wasn't a large space, but it was divided into two distinct sections. The first was for digital printing, supplies, and articles relating to the photographic business. The second, at the far end of the room, was a studio in which subjects posed for their pictures in front of various backgrounds.

At the moment, the studio took the form of a photographic parlour from another century, the sort of place where people used to pose stiffly, sitting or standing or both. It contained a chaise longue, two plinths upon which sat artificial ferns, several overstuffed chairs, thick faux curtains drawn back with fancy tasselled cords, and a backdrop. The backdrop made it look as if anyone posing had dragged their furniture outside to the top of a cliff: It comprised a painted landmass ending in a deep sky filled with cumulus clouds.

Tim had learned that this setup was all about contrast. And contrast, he'd also learned, was all about two things being in direct opposition to each other. When this had been explained to him on his first visit, he'd thought immediately of the contrast between what he'd once counted upon as his life—a mum, a dad, a sister, and a house in Grange-over-Sands—and what his life had been reduced to, which was nothing. Entering the space now, he thought about the contrast between how Kaveh Mehran had lived with his dad at Bryan Beck farm and how Kaveh Mehran intended to live in what was going to go for the next phase of his miserable excuse for a life. When this thought came upon him, Tim forced himself to think instead of the real contrast that lay ahead, which was the contrast between the mock innocence of this setting for photos and what the photos themselves consisted of.

Toy4You had explained all this to him the first time he had posed for the pictures as he had been instructed to pose. Certain kinds of people, he'd been told, liked to look at or purchase photos of nude young boys. They liked the boys posing in certain ways. They liked to see certain body parts. Sometimes it was just the suggestion of a body part, and sometimes it was the real thing. Sometimes they wanted a face included in the picture. Sometimes they didn't. A pout was good. So was something Toy4You referred to as a you-can-have-it look. Make a stiffie for the camera, and it was even better. Certain people would pay a good sum of money for a picture of a boy, a pout, desire in the eyes, and a decent stiffie as well.

Tim had gone along. He, after all, had been the one to start this ball rolling towards its destination. But money wasn't what he'd wanted. He'd wanted action and so far that action had been denied him. That was going to change.

Toy4You had followed him into the back room. He said to Tim, "You need to leave. I can't have you here."

Tim said, "I already told you. Call your friend or whoever it is. Tell him I'm ready. Tell him to get down here. We're doing the pictures now."

"He's not about to do that. No fourteen-year-old tells him how to run his affairs. He tells us when the time is right. We don't tell him. What is it about this that you don't understand?"

"I don't *have* the time," Tim protested. "The time is *now*. I'm not waiting any longer. If you want me doing it with some bloke, then this is your chance because you're not getting another."

"That's the way it is, then," Toy4You said with a shrug. "Now get out."

"*What?* You think you'll find someone else to do it? You think it'll be that easy?"

"There are always kids looking for money," he said.

"For a picture, maybe. They'll take your money for a picture. They'll stand there naked and maybe they'll even do it hard. But the rest? You think someone'll do the rest? Someone besides me?"

"And *you* think you're the only one who's found me online? You think this is a bit of work I've just taken up recently for my health or something? You think you're the first? The one and only? There're dozens of you out there and they're willing to do it the way I want it done because they want the money. They don't make the rules, they follow the rules. And one of the rules is that they don't show up—this is twice now, you little bugger—and make demands."

Toy4You had been standing among the supplies, but he came forward as he spoke. He wasn't big and Tim had always reckoned he could take him down if that was going to be necessary, but when the man grabbed him by the arm, Tim felt a strength emanating from him that he hadn't suspected was there.

"I don't play games," Toy4You told him. "I don't get manipulated by little bits of boy-ass like you."

"We had a deal and—"

"Bugger your deal. It's over. It's off."

"You promised. You *said*."

"I don't need this shit."

Toy4You jerked him, hard. Tim saw that he meant to eject him from the premises. That couldn't happen. He'd worked too hard and he'd done too much. He pulled away.

He cried, "No! I want it to happen, and I want it now," and he began to tear at his clothes. He pulled off his anorak, his heavy sweater. Buttons flew from his shirt as he ripped it off. He began to shout. "You promised. If you don't do it, I'll go to the cops. I swear. I will. I'll tell them. What I did. What you want. The pictures. Your friends. How to find you. It's all on my computer and they'll know and—"

"Shut up! Shut *up*!" Toy4You looked back over his shoulder, in the direction of the shop. He strode to the doorway that had brought them both into the back room and he slammed it shut. He returned to Tim. He said, "Christ, calm down. All *right*. But it can't happen now. Can't you get that?"

"I want . . . I swear . . . The cops'll come."

"All right. The cops. I get it. I believe you. Just calm the fuck down. Look. I'm going to make the call. Now. In front of you. I'll set it up for tomorrow. We'll do the pictures then." He appeared to think for a moment; then he looked Tim over. He said, "It'll be film, though. Live action. And all the way this time. You understand?"

"But you said—"

"I'm taking a risk here!" Toy4You roared. "You'll make it worth my while. Do you want it or not?"

Tim flinched, cowed. But he knew fear only for a moment before he said, "I want it."

"Good. Two blokes as well. Do . . . you . . . get . . . it? You and two blokes and the real thing, live on film. Do you know what that means? Because no way in hell are we starting this and finding out midway that you've changed your mind. You and two blokes. Say you understand."

Tim licked his lips. "Me and two blokes. I understand."

Toy4You looked him over, as if expecting something to ooze from his pores that would indicate the future. Tim stood his ground. Toy4You nodded sharply and punched in some numbers on the phone.

Tim said, "And after . . . when it's over . . . you promise . . ."

"I promise. When it's over, you die. Just like you want it. However you want it. You get to make the rules for that."

10 NOVEMBER

When Lynley phoned her early in the morning, he was clever enough to ring the inn and not her mobile. Because of this, Deborah answered. Simon or Tommy, she'd reckoned, would ring the mobile. She'd see the caller's number and decide whether to answer or not. Even the reporter from *The Source* rang her mobile. A call on the phone inside her hotel room meant Reception was probably enquiring about the length of her stay.

Thus, Deborah winced as Lynley's pleasant baritone came over the line. When he said, "Simon's not happy with either of us," she could hardly pretend he'd phoned the wrong number.

It was quite early, and she was still in bed. Clever Tommy to have thought of that as well: Catch her before she left the inn, and there was little she could do to avoid him.

She sat up, pulled the blankets closer against the chill, and said as she rearranged the pillows, "Well, I'm not happy with Simon, either."

"Right. I know. But as it happens, he was correct, Deb. From the start."

"Oh, isn't he always?" she said tartly. "What are we talking about anyway?"

"Ian Cresswell's death. He could have prevented it if he'd

been paying closer attention to where he was tying up his scull that night."

"And we've reached this conclusion because . . . ?" Deborah waited to hear him say he'd reached his conclusion because of Simon's insufferably logical presentation of the facts, but he didn't go in that direction. Instead he told her about a family imbroglio he'd witnessed among the Faircloughs and a conversation he'd had with Valerie Fairclough afterwards.

He concluded it all with, "So it seems I've been brought up here as a means of Valerie's delving into her husband's doings. It was a fool's errand with me as the fool. Hillier as well. I daresay he's not going to be happy when I tell him how we've both been used."

Deborah shoved off the blankets, swung her legs over the side of the bed, and looked at the clock. She said, "And you believe her?" as she read the time. A phone call from Tommy at six thirty in the morning could mean only one thing and she was fairly certain she knew what that was.

He said, "In the ordinary course of things, I might not. But with the coroner's conclusion and with Simon's assessment, along with what Valerie told me—"

"She could be lying. There are motives, Tommy."

"Without anything more than motives, there's no case to present, Deb. That's how it works. Frankly, people often have motives to do away with other people. They often have the wish to do away with other people. And still they never lift a finger against them. That's what apparently happened here. It's time to return to London."

"Even without putting the matter of Alatea Fairclough to rest?"

"Deb—"

"Just listen to me for a moment: Everything about Alatea suggests secrecy. People with secrets have motive to do all sorts of things to protect those secrets."

"That may be, but whatever she might have done or might be doing to protect her secrets—assuming she has them—what she didn't do was murder Ian Cresswell. That's why we came up here. We now know the truth. As I said, it's time to go home."

Deborah got out of the bed. The room was cold. She shivered and moved to the electric fire. It had clicked off in the night, and she turned it on. There was moisture climbing the window, against which she brushed her hand to look out at the day. It was still quite dark outside, she saw, the road and the pavement wet. The glitter of the streetlamps and the traffic lights on the corner winked brightly against it.

She said, "Tommy, those missing pages from *Conception* magazine have said from the first that something's going on with Alatea."

"I don't disagree," was his perfectly reasonable reply. "And we have a good idea of what that something is. Conception. But you already knew that. Didn't Nicholas Fairclough tell you that when you first met?"

"Yes. But—"

"It's reasonable that she wouldn't want to talk about this with a stranger, Deborah. Do you like to talk about it with anyone?"

That was an unfair blow, and he had to know it. But Deborah wasn't about to let her reaction to the question get the better of her ability to reason. She said, "None of this makes much sense, talking about conception or not. This woman, Lucy Keverne, told me she has her eggs harvested. All right. Perhaps she does. Then what was she doing at Lancaster University in the company of Alatea Fairclough? Why was she in the George Childress Centre with her?"

"Perhaps donating an egg to Alatea," Lynley said.

"The egg needs to be fertilised. Wouldn't Nicholas need to be there?"

"Perhaps Alatea had his sperm with her."

"In a turkey baster, you mean?" Deborah asked pointedly. "So why would Lucy be there as well?"

"To donate eggs on the spot?"

"Really? Fine. All right. Then why wouldn't Nicholas be there to donate sperm as fresh as possible, real little swimmers, that sort of thing?"

Lynley sighed. Deborah wondered where he was. On a landline somewhere since his sigh had come to her so clearly. This suggested he was still at Ireleth Hall. He said,

"Deb, I don't know. I don't know how it's done. I don't know how it all works."

"I know you don't. But I do, believe me. And one thing I know is that even if they do the business with one egg or two dozen from Lucy and sperm from Nicholas, they're not implanting them in Alatea on the spot. So *if* Lucy's a donor as she claims to be and *if* she's giving Alatea eggs for some reason and *if* sperm from Nicholas are being used—"

"None of it matters," Lynley cut in firmly. "Because it has nothing to do with Ian Cresswell's death and we need to get back to London."

"You need to. I do not."

"Deborah." His voice was losing that patient tone. Deborah heard Simon in it. How alike they were at the end of the day, he and Tommy. The differences between them were only superficial.

"What?" she asked sharply.

"I'm heading back to London this morning. You know that's why I've phoned. What I'd like to do is stop in Milnthorpe, follow you to the car hire so you can return your car, then take you back to London with me."

"Because you don't trust me to get there on my own?" she demanded.

"I rather wanted the company," he replied. "It's a long drive."

"She *said* she'd never be a surrogate, Tommy. If all she's going to do is donate eggs for Alatea to use, why not just say that? Why tell me she wouldn't discuss it?"

"I have no idea. And it's not important. It doesn't matter. Ian Cresswell's death was no one's fault but his own. He knew about the loose stones in the boathouse. He didn't take care. That's where things lie, Deb, and nothing about this woman in Lancaster is going to change that. So the question is: Why can't you let it go? And I think we both know the answer to that."

His words were quiet enough, but they were unlike Tommy. They spoke of the degree to which Simon had persuaded him to take his side. But then, why wouldn't he? Deborah asked herself. They had years of history, Tommy and Simon. They had decades of history. They shared one terrible automobile accident and the love for a murdered woman as well. These things bound them to each other in ways she would never be able to surmount. That being the case, there was only one alternative.

She said, "Very well. You win, Tommy."

"What does that mean?"

"It means that I'll go back to London with you."

"Deborah . . ."

"No." She gave a hearty sigh, one she knew he'd be able to hear. "I do mean it, Tommy. I give up. What time shall we leave?"

"Are you being quite serious?"

"Of course I am. I'm stubborn, but I'm not a fool. If there's no point carrying on with this business, then there's no point, is there."

"You do see—"

"I do. One can't argue with forensics. That's how it is." She waited a moment for this to sink in. Then she repeated, "When do we leave? You woke me up, by the way, so I'll need time to pack. To shower. Do my hair. Whatever. I'd like breakfast as well."

"Ten o'clock?" he said. "Thank you, Deb."

"I do see it's better this way," she lied.

WINDERMERE
CUMBRIA

Zed Benjamin had barely slept. His story was crumbling. What had started out too hot to be handled without oven gloves was fast becoming cold fish on a platter. He hadn't the slightest clue what to do with the information he had because he had no information that amounted to a blockbuster of a story. In his daydreams it had been an exposé, front page material in which was revealed that a secret investigation launched by New Scotland Yard was digging up dirt about Nicholas Fairclough and about what *truly* went for his recovery from years of drug abuse, which was the murder of a cousin standing in the way of his success.

It was the tale of a bloke who had managed to pull the wool over the eyes of his parents, his family, and his fellows by posing as a do-gooder while all the time engaged in vile machinations to eliminate someone blocking his access to the family fortune. The story was accompanied by photos—DS Cotter, Fairclough, his wife, the pele project, and Fairclough Industries among others—and its length and quality begged for a leap onto page 3 and from there to 4 and 5 as well. All of it rested beneath the byline *Zedekiah Benjamin*. His name in journalistic lights.

For that to happen, however, the story had to be about Nicholas Fairclough. But, if nothing else, his day with DS Cotter had proved that Nick Fairclough was of no interest to the Met. The day had also proved that Fairclough's wife was a monumental dead end.

"Nothing, I'm afraid," was how the red-haired detective had reported upon her interview with the woman they'd followed from the Kent-Howath Foundation for Disabled Veterans to Lancaster University and back again, all in the company of Alatea Fairclough.

"What d'you mean 'nothing'?" had been Zed's demand.

She'd said the woman—Lucy Keverne was her name—and Alatea had gone to see a specialist at the university about "female troubles." They were Lucy's "female troubles," evidently, and Alatea had accompanied her as a friend.

"Shit," he'd muttered. "That's bloody nowhere, isn't it?"

"It does put us back to square one," she replied.

No, he thought. It put *her* back to square one. It put him in danger of losing his job.

He found that he wanted to talk to Yaffa. She was wise, and if anyone was going to be able to suggest how he could get himself out of this mess and onto a story that Rodney Aronson would find a suitable return for the money invested by *The Source*, it was going to be Yaffa.

So he rang her. When he heard her voice, he felt nearly overcome with relief. He said, "Morning, darling."

She said, "Zed, hel*lo*," and, "Mama Benjamin, it's our lovely man ringing," to tell him Susanna was somewhere nearby. "I miss you, dearest." And she laughed at something Susanna said in the distance. She said, "Mama Benjamin tells me to stop trying to ensnare her son. He is an uncatchable bachelor, she tells me. Is that true?"

"Not if you're trying to do the catching," he replied. "I've never had bait I wanted to bite so badly."

"You wicked boy!" And to the side, "No, no, Mama Benjamin. I will absolutely *not* tell you what your son is saying. I will say that he's making me a bit faint, though." And to Zed, "You are, you know. I'm quite light-headed."

"Well, good thing it's not your head I'm interested in."

She laughed. Then she said in a completely altered voice, "Ah. She's gone into the loo. We're safe. How are you, Zed?"

He found he wasn't ready for the shift from Yaffa the Putative Lover to Yaffa the Co-conspirator. He said, "Missing you, Yaf. I wish you were with me."

"Let me help you from a distance. I'm happy to do that."

For an insane moment, Zed thought she was actually suggesting phone sex, and in his present state, that would have been a welcome diversion. But then she said, "Are you close to the information you need? You must be worried about the story."

That brought him round, cold water on his ardour. He said with a groan, "That bloody story." He told her where he was with it. He told her everything, as he'd been doing all along. And as she'd been doing all along, she listened. He concluded with, "So there's sod-all to report on. I could massage the facts and write that Scotland Yard's up here investigating Nick Fairclough due to the untimely and suspicious death of his cousin, who happened to hold the purse strings of Fairclough Industries, and we all know what that means, don't we, gentle readers? But the truth of the matter happens to be that Scotland Yard look like they're investigating Alatea Fairclough and getting about as far with her as I've got with her husband. We're in the same position, the Met and I. The only difference is this detective can toddle back to London and give the high-ups the all-clear, but if I return without a story, I'm done for." He heard his tone as he concluded and he said hastily, "Sorry. I'm whingeing a bit."

"Zed, you can whinge all you need to."

"Ta, Yaf. You're . . . well, you're just how you are."

He could hear the smile in her voice when she said, "Thank you, I think. Now let us put our heads together. When one door closes, another opens."

"Meaning?"

"Meaning perhaps it's time you did what you were intended to do. You're a poet, Zed, not a tabloid journalist. Remaining one is going to bleed your soul of its creative power. It's time for you to write your poetry."

"No one supports himself on his poetry." Zed laughed self-derisively. "Look at me. I'm twenty-five years old and I'm living with my mum. I can't even support myself as a reporter, for the love of God."

"Ah, Zed. Don't talk this way. You need only someone to believe in you. *I* believe in you."

"Bloody lot of good that does me. You're going back to Tel Aviv."

There was a silence at the other end. Into it came the indication of another phone call to Zed's mobile. He said, "Yaffa? You still there?"

"Oh yes. I'm here," she said.

The other call was insistent. Rodney, probably. It was close to the time he had to face the music. He said, "Yaffa, I've got another call. I probably should—"

"I don't have to," she said quickly. "I don't even need to. You think about that, Zed." Then she rang off.

For a moment he stared at nothing at all. Then he took the other call.

It was the Scotland Yard detective. She said, "I'm going to speak to this woman in Lancaster again. There's more here than meets the eye. It's time you and I worked together to twist her arm."

BARROW-IN-FURNESS AND GRANGE-OVER-SANDS
CUMBRIA

One of the last people Manette expected to see turn up on the premises of Fairclough Industries was Kaveh Mehran. As far as she could recall, he'd never been there before. Ian had certainly never taken him round for formal introductions, and Kaveh hadn't come on his own expecting to be introduced. Nearly everyone knew, of course, that Ian had walked out on his marriage because of a young man. But that was the extent of it. So when Kaveh was shown into her office, she blinked in confusion before she realised he'd probably come to collect Ian's personal belongings. It needed to be done and no one had yet thought about doing it.

His reason for showing up at the firm, however, turned out to be somewhat different. Tim was missing. He'd jumped out of Kaveh's car on the previous morning on the way to school, and he'd not returned home last night.

Manette said, "Did something happen? Why did he jump out of your car? Did he go to school? Did you phone the school?"

The school, Kaveh said, had phoned the house yesterday. Tim was absent, and when one of the day pupils didn't turn up, the school rang the home because . . . well, because of the sort of school it was, if Manette knew what he meant.

Well, of course she bloody knew what he meant. The whole family knew what Margaret Fox School was all about. It was hardly a secret.

Kaveh then said that he'd driven the route from Bryanbarrow to Margaret Fox School that morning to see if Tim was, perhaps, hitchhiking there. On the way, he'd stopped in Great Urswick on the chance that Tim had gone to Manette's home to spend the night or was holed up somewhere on her property without her knowledge. He'd stopped at the school next. And now he was here. Could Tim be here?

"Here?" Manette asked. "D'you mean in the factory? Of course he's not here. What would he be doing here?"

"Have you seen him at all? Has he phoned? For obvious reasons, I haven't checked with Niamh." Kaveh had the grace to look uncomfortable, but Manette knew there was something rather large and important that he wasn't saying.

"I've not heard from him. And he's not been in Great Urswick. Why'd he jump out of your car?"

Kaveh looked over his shoulder, as if he wanted to close the door to her office. This alone made Manette gird herself for something she wasn't going to want to hear.

He said, "I think he overheard a conversation I was having with George Cowley."

"The farmer? What on earth . . . ?"

"It was about the future, the farm. I expect you know Cowley's wanted the farm for himself."

"Ian told me, yes. And what of the farm and Mr. Cowley?" And why would Tim care a fig about either? she wondered.

"I mentioned to Mr. Cowley my intentions regarding Bryan Beck farm," he said. "I suspect Tim overheard."

"And what are your intentions? Are you thinking of raising sheep yourself?" Manette sounded tart and couldn't help it. The farm, after all, should have gone to Tim and Gracie. It should not now be the sole property of this man who'd done his best to ruin their lives.

"To keep it, of course. But also . . . I did tell him that Tim and Gracie would be returning to their mother. Tim may have overheard that."

Manette drew her eyebrows together. She knew, of course, that this was the logical progression of events. Farm or no farm, Tim and Gracie could hardly continue to live with their father's lover now that their father was dead. It wouldn't be easy moving to their mother's home—Niamh being Niamh—but there wasn't an alternative as long as they were underage. Tim would understand this. He would doubtless have been expecting it, and he doubtless would also have been preferring it. So would have Gracie. Thus, to have this piece of information set him off to the extent that he would jump out of Kaveh's car and run off . . . ? This didn't make sense.

She said, "I don't mean to be offensive, Kaveh, but I can't imagine the children would want to live with you now that their dad's dead. So is there something else . . . ? Is there something you're not telling me?"

Kaveh looked at her squarely. "If there is, I can't tell you what. Will you help, Manette? I don't know what else—"

"I'll handle it," she said.

When he'd departed, she phoned the school. For ease of information, she claimed to be Niamh. She learned at once that Tim wasn't there for a second day. The school was worried, as it would be. Losing one of their pupils could mean all sorts of things and not a single one of them was good.

Manettte phoned Niamh next. The answer machine took the call in Niamh's irritating purr, doubtless designed as a siren's song for potential suitors. Manette left a message, but then switched to, "Tim? Are you there, listening to this? If you are, pick up, love. This is your cousin Manette."

Nothing, but of course, that didn't mean much. If he was in hiding, he was hardly going to reveal it to someone searching for him. And he would know Manette was looking for him. He would know everyone was looking for him.

There was nothing to do but set out on a search. Manette didn't want to do it alone, however. She went to Freddie's office. Not there. She went to Ian's office, and there Freddie was, beavering away at Ian's computer, trying to make sense of the money trails. She watched him for a moment before she spoke. She thought, Dear Freddie, and her heart hurt briefly, as if making her aware of its presence for the first time in years.

She said, "Have you a moment, Fred?"

He looked up, smiled. "What's up?" And then, "What's happened?" because he read her as well now as he'd read her when they were married.

She told him the gist: Tim was missing, and she needed to make the drive to Niamh's, which seemed to be the only place left where he could be in hiding. But she didn't want to make the drive alone. Or better said, she didn't want to confront Tim alone. Things were iffy with the boy. She felt a little . . . well, a little in need of backup if it was going to come down to another confrontation with him.

Of course, Freddie agreed. When had Freddie not agreed? He said, "In a tick. Meet you at the car," and he set about doing whatever he needed to do to close up shop for a while.

He was as good as his word. In less than ten minutes, he was climbing into the passenger seat of her car, saying, "Don't want me to drive?"

She said, "One of us might have to jump out and tackle him, and I'd rather it was you, if you don't mind."

They made good time to Grange-over-Sands, taking the

coastal route along the empty bay. When they pulled up in front of Niamh's white house, it was to see her on the doorstep bidding a fond farewell to the same bloke Manette had encountered the last time she'd been in Grange-over-Sands. Charlie Wilcox of Milnthorpe Chinese takeaway fame, she thought. She murmured his name to Freddie, but she didn't need to say anything more about the man's relationship with Tim and Gracie's mother. Niamh herself was making that clear enough.

She was wearing a dressing gown with enough leg showing through its opening at the moment to indicate she had nothing on beneath it. Charlie was wearing last night's clothing, an out-on-the-town getup with a jacket and trousers, white shirt, and tie rakishly unknotted round his neck. Niamh cast a quick look in the direction of Manette's car and then gave herself to a serious good-bye kiss, locking her leg around poor Charlie's leg and doing a bit of bump and grind against him. Her mouth was so wide upon his she might have been excavating for his wisdom teeth with her tongue.

Manette sighed. She glanced at Freddie. He was blushing. He shot her a look. She shrugged.

They got out of the car as the kiss ended. Charlie was walking dazedly to his Saab still parked in the drive, and he nodded a hello that was utterly unembarrassed. Seemed like he was getting quite comfortable coming and going and doing what Niamh needed to have done, Manette thought. Just like a plumber seeing to the pipes. She snorted at the thought and approached the front door.

Niamh hadn't closed it. She'd gone inside, however, most likely thinking that Manette and Freddie would do likewise. They did, shutting the door behind them.

Niamh called, "I'll be with you in a moment. I'm putting on something decent."

Manette didn't comment on this. She and Freddie went to the sitting room, which displayed the remains of a tryst: wine bottle, two glasses, a plate bearing crumbs and bits of cheese and chocolate, sofa cushions shoved onto the floor, and a pile of Niamh's clothing lying nearby. Niamh was, Manette thought, certainly having the time of her life.

"Sorry. Haven't got to this yet."

Manette and Freddie turned at the sound of Niamh's voice. Her "something decent" turned out to be a black leotard, which hugged every curve of her body and did everything possible to emphasise her breasts. These stood to attention like infantrymen in the presence of their commanding general. Their nipples strained against the thin cloth.

Manette glanced at Freddie. He was looking out of the sitting room window, at the fine view of the bay that it provided. With the tide out, plovers and knots by the thousands were in. Freddie wasn't a bird man, but he was giving them considerable attention. The tips of his ears were absolutely magenta.

Niamh smiled slyly at Manette. She said, "Now. What can I do for you two?" and she bustled round as well as one could be said to bustle in a leotard. She put the cushions back onto the sofa and plumped them nicely, then picked up the wine bottle and glasses and took them into the kitchen. There the remains of a Chinese takeaway dinner were on the worktops and the table. It seemed that Charlie Wilcox was providing all sorts of sustenance, Manette thought. Stupid sod.

Manette said to her, "I phoned. Did you not hear it, Niamh?"

She fluttered her fingers in a pooh-pooh gesture. "I never answer the phone when Charlie's here," she said. "Would you? In my position?"

"I'm not sure. Which one *is* your position? Oh, never mind. I don't care to know. Yes, I'd answer the phone if I heard the message and the message was about my son."

Niamh was at the worktop, picking up the takeaway cartons, inspecting them for remains that were salvageable. "What about Tim?" she asked.

Manette felt Freddie come into the kitchen behind her. She moved to one side to give him room. She glanced at him. He stood with his arms crossed inspecting the mess. Freddie wasn't big on the pickings of daily life being left round to clutter up a place.

Manette gave Niamh the story in brief. One missing son,

two days truant from school. "Has he been here?" she finished, fairly sure of the answer.

"Not that I know of," Niamh said. "I haven't been home every moment. I suppose he could have come and gone."

"We'd like to check," Freddie said.

"Why? D'you think he's under a bed? Do you think I'm hiding him from you?"

"We think he might be hiding from *you*," Manette put in. "And who could blame him? Let's be honest, Niamh. There's a limit to what life can ask one boy to endure, and I expect he's reached his."

"What, exactly, are you saying?"

"I think you know very well. And with what you've been up to—"

Freddie touched her arm briefly to halt her words. He said reasonably, "Tim might have slipped into the house while you were sleeping. He could be in the garage as well. D'you mind awfully if we have a look? It'll just take a moment and then we'll be out of your hair."

Niamh's expression said she'd have liked to carry the conversation further, but Manette knew that doing so would lead them in the single direction Niamh would want to go. Ian's sins against her and against the family constituted the broken record of her life, and she had no wish to repair it. No matter Charlie Wilcox and his Chinese takeaway. Niamh would never get beyond Ian's betrayal because she had no wish to do so.

She said, "Do as you like, Freddie," and turned her back to begin putting the kitchen in order.

Searching the house was the business of less than five minutes. It was small, and upstairs there were three bedrooms and a bathroom. Tim would hardly have hidden himself in his mother's room, since doing so would have risked having to listen to Niamh's lovemaking, likely to be an acoustically enthusiastic affair. That left his room and Gracie's room. Manette took these on as Freddie did the honours with Niamh's garage.

They met back in the sitting room. They shook their heads. Time to move to another location. But Manette felt that she couldn't do so without a final word with Tim's mother. Niamh emerged from the kitchen with a cup of coffee. She made no offer of the like to her unwanted visitors. All to the good, Manette thought, as she didn't want to remain any longer than it would take to say what needed to be said.

This was, "It's time for the children to come home. You've made your point, Niamh, and there's really no reason to take it further."

Niamh said, "Oh dear," and went to a chair, beneath which something had been shoved. She brought it out and shot them a coy smile. "Charlie will have his games," she said.

Manette saw it was a sex toy, a vibrator by the looks of it, complete with various attachments in various shapes that lay on the floor as well. Niamh scooped these up and placed them along with the vibrator on the coffee table. She said, "What point are you talking about, Manette?"

"You know very well what point I'm talking about. It's the same point that sent you on your way to the plastic surgeon, and it's the same point that has that poor stupid bloke sniffing round you every night."

"Manette," Freddie murmured.

"No," Manette said. "It's time someone took her to task for this nonsense. You have two children and a duty to those children and *that* has nothing to do with Ian, with his rejection of you, with his love for Kaveh, with—"

"Stop it!" Niamh hissed. "I will not have that name spoken inside this house."

"Which one? Ian, the father of your children, or Kaveh, the man he left you for? You were hurt. Fine. All right. Everyone knows it. You had a right to be and, believe me, everyone knows that as well. But Ian's dead and the children need you and if you can't see that, if you're so self-absorbed, if you're so bloody needy, if you have to continue to prove to yourself over and over that some man—any man, for the love of God—wants you . . . What on earth is the matter with you? Were you ever a mother to Gracie and Tim?"

"Manette," Freddie murmured. "Really."

"How *dare* you." Niamh's voice was fury. "How bloody

dare you. To stand there . . . to tell me . . . you who threw *away* a man for—"

"This isn't about me."

"Oh, it never is, is it? You're perfect, aren't you, while the rest of us are beneath your contempt. What do you know of what I went through? What do you know of discovering that the man you love has been meeting with other men for *years*? Public lavatories, city parks, nightclubs where they grope each other and stick their cocks into strangers' arseholes? Do you know how it feels to have that knowledge descend on you? To realise your marriage has been a sham and, worse, that you've been exposed to every possible variety of filthy disease because the man you've given your life to has been living a lie for years? Don't you tell me how to live my life now. Don't you bloody tell me I'm all about myself, I'm needy, I'm pathetic, I'm whatever else is on your goddamn mind . . ."

She'd begun to weep as she spoke, and she dashed the tears away from her face. She said, "Get out of here and don't come back. If you do, Manette, I swear to God I'll phone the police. I want you out of here and I want you to leave me alone."

"And Tim? And Gracie? What of them?"

"I can't have them here."

It was Freddie who spoke. "What d'you mean?"

"They remind me. Always. I can't bear it. Them."

Manette's lips parted. She took in the meaning behind Niamh's words. She finally said, "Why on earth did he choose you? Why did he not see?"

"What?" Niamh demanded. "What? *What?*"

"From the very first, you were totally about yourself. Even now, Niamh. That's how it is."

"I don't know what you're talking about," Niamh said.

"Don't worry about that," Manette said. "I finally do."

LANCASTER
LANCASHIRE

Deborah felt a twinge of guilt about Lynley, but a twinge
was all she allowed herself to feel. He would arrive at the
Crow and Eagle, and she wouldn't be there, but he wouldn't
know she'd gone to Lancaster since her hire car would still
be sitting in the car park. She reckoned he'd think at first
she'd gone for a final walk round Milnthorpe, perhaps over
to the town's market square or beyond it to the church to
have a look at the graveyard. Or perhaps, he'd think, she'd
gone along the route to Arnside for a stroll to watch the
marsh birds. For the tide was out, and the mudflats were
thickly populated at the moment with flocks of every sort
of bird one could think of, wintering in Britain from harsher
climes. There was the bank, as well, just across the road
from the hotel. He might think she'd be there. Or perhaps
still at breakfast. But in any case, it didn't matter. What
mattered is that she wouldn't be there for him to cart home
to Simon. She could have left him a note, of course. But she
knew Tommy. One indication that she was on her way to
Lancaster for another go with Lucy Keverne on the subject
of Alatea Fairclough and he'd be after her like a hound
chasing down a hare.

After her phone call to him, Zed Benjamin arrived in
record time. She was waiting for him just inside the doorway
of the inn—having booked herself in for at least one more
night—so she stepped outside and into his car as soon as
he'd made the three-point turn that would put them in the
direction of Lancaster.

She didn't tell him she'd lied to him earlier about why
Lucy Keverne and Alatea Fairclough had been together at
Lancaster University. The way she reckoned it, she didn't
owe *any* tabloid reporter a thing, be it the truth, a pack of
lies, or even a spurious apology.

She made the situation simple for Zed: She reckoned
that Lucy Keverne had lied to her on the previous day. Her
tale about some kind of female problem needing to be
looked into by someone at the university didn't make

sense the more Deborah had thought about it. After all, Lucy had gone to a reproductive centre and why would she need the support of a friend for that? She might want the support of a husband or a partner if she had reproduction on the mind, but a friend . . . ? No, it seemed more likely that there was something more going on between Lucy Keverne and Alatea Fairclough and she—Deborah— needed Zed's presence in order to find out.

Being orientated towards *The Source*, Zed immediately jumped to a secret lesbian liaison between Lucy Keverne and Alatea Fairclough. Looking for a connection with the death of Ian Cresswell, he went from there to the dead man knowing about the secret lesbian liaison and threatening to tell Nicholas Fairclough about it. Zed offered several variations on this theme, most of which included Lucy Keverne and Alatea Fairclough managing to do away with Ian Cresswell together, which was fine with Deborah as it kept Zed occupied and away from questioning why on earth a putative detective from New Scotland Yard would welcome *The Source* into the midst of an ongoing investigation.

What she did tell him was that she reckoned it was going to come down to money. What she didn't tell him was that if Lucy Keverne had been advertising herself as an egg donor, as she claimed, then she hadn't been doing it out of the goodness of her heart but rather for the cash. Zed was going to hand over tabloid money for her story, whatever her actual story was. He didn't know that yet, but he would soon.

The one subject Deborah didn't think about was why this part of the Cresswell case was important to her. The local coroner had been convinced that the death of Ian Cresswell had been an accident. Simon was absolutely certain of that fact, and it was his job to be certain of such things. Tommy had agreed. It seemed as if the entire reason for Tommy to be in Cumbria had relatively little to do with Ian Cresswell's death in the first place, so for her to be tenaciously maintaining that there was more here than met the eye was a matter calling for close introspection. Deborah knew that at heart but she didn't want to go there in mind. The chain of thought created by such self-examination was not going to be pleasant.

At the Kent-Howath Foundation for Disabled Veterans, she said, "Here's how it has to be," to which Zed replied, "Wait a bloody minute," doubtless at the thought that once again he would be playing chauffeur while she gathered information that she might or might not share with him. Well, who could blame him for being miffed? she asked herself. The last time they'd gone this route, he'd ended up with little more than a half-empty tank of petrol.

"I'll ring you once I have her alone," she said. "If she sees us both at once, I guarantee, she'll not say another word about Alatea Fairclough. And why should she? If she's up to something illegal, she's hardly going to confess it, is she?"

He didn't ask why the hell they were there at all, then, which was just as well. Deborah knew she was going to have to do some considerable fancy dancing with Lucy Keverne, and she needed most of her wits to do that, not to create fictive reasons for why Zed had to play the part she was going to orchestrate for him. She didn't really know if she'd get that far with Lucy Keverne anyway. She was flying without radar on this one.

The same old gentleman who'd welcomed her on the previous day did so today. He remembered her because of her hair, which was one of the few benefits, she reckoned, of being a redhead. He asked if she wanted to speak with Miss Lucy Keverne again. He held up a sheaf of papers and said, "Reading 'er play, I am, and lemme tell you if it's not a West End winner, then I'm the Queen of Sheba."

So she was a playwright, Deborah thought, perhaps supporting herself by working here at the disabled soldiers' home and topping up her funds with the occasional donation of eggs? That was the grimmest sort of news to be had, since perhaps the *only* action she'd been taking in the company of Alatea Fairclough was in the nature of research. Well, one way or another they had to know, Deborah thought. Meanwhile, she had no intention of letting on that she'd been told about the playwriting. No need to give the woman in advance a direction in which to spin her story.

Lucy's face registered surprise when she walked into the lobby and saw who was waiting to speak to her. Then her face altered at once to suspicion.

Deborah didn't give her a chance to speak first. She quickly strode to her and placed a hand on her arm. She said to her quietly, "Here's what you need to know, Ms. Keverne. New Scotland Yard is here in Cumbria and so is a reporter from *The Source*. One way or another you're going to end up telling your story—the true one this time—and it's up to you how and when you want to tell it."

Lucy said, "I can't—"

"You've no choice any longer. I deceived you yesterday. I apologise for that, but I'd hoped to get to the root of the matter without bringing in anyone who might make you uncomfortable. Obviously, Alatea Fairclough's being investigated. The trail has led directly to you."

"I've done nothing illegal."

"So you say," Deborah said. "And if that's the case—"

"It *is*."

"—then you can decide which route has more to offer you."

Lucy's eyes narrowed. The word *offer* had done the trick. "What are you talking about?"

Deborah looked round furtively and said with great meaning, "We can't speak here in the lobby."

"Come with me, then."

Even better, Deborah thought.

This time, they didn't go to the garden but rather to an office, which seemed to be her own. There were two desks in it, but the other wasn't occupied. Lucy closed the door behind them and stood in front of it. She said, "Who's offering what?"

"Tabloids pay for their stories. You must know that."

"Is that who you are?"

"A tabloid journalist? No. But I've got one with me, and if you'll consent to talk to him, I'm here to make sure you get paid for what you have to say. My part is to assess the value of the story. You tell me, I negotiate with him."

"That can't possibly be how it works," Lucy said shrewdly. "What are you, then? An agent for *The Source*? Some kind of . . . what? News scout or something?"

"I'm not sure it matters who I am," Deborah said. "I think it matters more what I have to offer. I can ring the DI from New Scotland Yard who's here in Cumbria on a matter of murder or I can ring a journalist who'll walk in, listen to your story, and pay you for it."

"*Murder?* What's going on?"

"That's not important at the moment. This situation between you and Alatea Fairclough is. You must decide. What's it to be? A visit from New Scotland Yard or a journalist happy to hear what you have to say?"

Lucy Keverne thought this over while outside the office, some sort of trolley trundled down the corridor. She finally said, "How much, then?" and Deborah breathed more easily now that Lucy was swimming closer to the bait.

She said, "I suppose that depends on how sensational your story is."

Lucy looked towards a window that faced the garden in which she and Deborah had spoken on the previous day. A gust of wind shuddered the slim branches of a Japanese maple outside, dislodging the rest of the leaves still clinging to it stubbornly. Deborah waited with *please please please* running through her mind. This was, she knew, the only option left to get at the truth. If Lucy Keverne didn't go for it, there was nothing more to do but return to London as bidden.

Lucy finally said, "There is no story. At least, there is no story that could possibly interest *The Source*. All there is is an arrangement between two women. I'd make more of it if I could, believe me, because I could use the money. I'd prefer not to work here. I'd prefer to sit at home and write my plays and send them off to London and see them produced. But that's not happening any time soon, so I work here in the mornings and I write in the afternoons and occasionally I top up my income by donating eggs, which was why I placed the advertisement in *Conception* magazine. I told you this."

"You also told me you would never consider being a surrogate."

"All right. That part wasn't true."

"So why did you lie about this yesterday?"

"Obviously, it was a private matter. It's still a private matter."

"And the money?"

"What about it?"

"As I understand how everything works," Deborah pointed out, "you're paid for allowing your eggs to be harvested. But if you're a surrogate for someone, you receive nothing. Just your expenses. Eggs equal profit while surrogacy comes from the goodness of your heart. Isn't that how it works?"

Lucy was silent. Into her silence, Deborah's mobile rang. She jerked it impatiently from her shoulder bag and saw the incoming number.

"Are you playing me for a bloody idiot?" Zed demanded when she answered. "What the hell's going on?"

"I'm going to have to ring you back," she said.

"No sodding way. I'm coming in."

"That's not a good idea."

"No? Well, it's the best I've come up with. And when I get there, there'd better be a story waiting for me and it'd better have to do with Cresswell's murder."

"I can't promise—" But he ended the call before she could finish. She said to Lucy, "*The Source* reporter is on his way in. This is out of my hands unless you wish to tell me more, something I can spin to keep him away from you. It's to do with money, I expect. You've agreed to be a surrogate for Alatea, and Alatea is willing to pay you more than just your expenses, isn't she? That would put you on the wrong side of the law. It explains why you misdirected me yesterday."

Lucy said with some passion, "Look at me. Look at this job. All I need is time to finish my play, to have it workshopped, to be able to revise it, and I *don't* have time and I *don't* have money and the surrogacy agreement between us was going to give me both. So you can make a story out of that if you'd like, but I hardly think it'll sell any papers. Do you?"

She was, of course, dead right. *Scion of Fairclough Fortune in Illegal Surrogacy Deal* might sell some newspapers, but the story would have legs only if there existed a bouncing baby whose winsome picture could be run along with the tabloid's disclosure, along with a typical tabloid caption, something like *Purchased Baby Fairclough, Sold by Surrogate Mum for £50,000.* The story of an illegal deal going unfulfilled couldn't even be sold to *any* tabloid since there would be nothing to prove it save Lucy's claim, which would be denied by Alatea Fairclough. The story of a deal in which an infant could be produced as proof would be hot and lively, but since there was no baby to speak of, there was also no story.

On the other hand, Deborah now knew why Alatea Fairclough was in a panic about her. The only question was whether Ian Cresswell had discovered this situation in some manner and had threatened Alatea in the one way she could be threatened by him: through money. If Lucy was to be paid for the surrogacy, then the money would have had to come through Ian Cresswell. He had been the man in control of the Fairclough fortune. Unless she had funds of her own, Alatea would have had to strike some kind of deal with Ian.

This of course brought up Nicholas Fairclough's role in the surrogacy arrangement. He would have had to know and to agree, which meant he would have had to be part of digging up the funds to pay for everything.

She said to Lucy, "What about Nicholas, Alatea's husband?"

Lucy said, "He only—" but that was as far as she got.

The maddening Zed Benjamin burst into the room. He said to Deborah, "Enough of these Scotland Yard double crosses. We're doing this together or not at all."

Lucy cried, "Scotland Yard double crosses? Scotland *Yard*?"

Zed said to her, jerking his thumb at Deborah, "Who the hell d'you think you've been talking to here? Lady Godiva?"

ARNSIDE
CUMBRIA.

Alatea had managed to send Nicholas off to work. He hadn't wanted to go and chances were very good, she knew, that he wouldn't stay there. But the only thing she had to cling to at this point was a semblance of normalcy, and what constituted normal was Nicky heading to Barrow and after that to the pele project.

He'd been unable to sleep again. He was filled with remorse, seeing himself as the person who was bringing Raul Montenegro down upon her.

Nicky knew they'd been lovers, she and Raul. She'd never lied about that. He'd also known she was on the run from Montenegro. In a world in which fixated stalking had become just one more thing a woman had to worry about, Nicky had had no trouble believing that she needed to be protected from this multimillionaire from Mexico City, a powerful man determined to have what she'd promised him, a man in whose home she'd lived for five years.

But Nicky had never known everything about her, about Raul, and about what they'd been to each other. The only one who knew the story from start to finish was Montenegro himself. He'd changed his life to be with her; he'd altered hers to bring her into a world she'd had no chance to make her own before she'd met him. But there had been elements of Raul that he'd never made quite clear to her, just as there had been elements of herself that she'd never made quite clear to him. The result had been a nightmare from which the only chance of awakening was to run.

She was pacing and considering her final options when Lucy Keverne rang. She made her announcement tersely: The woman from the previous day had returned, and she hadn't come alone. "I had to tell her the truth, Alatea. Or at least a version of it. She left me no choice."

"What do you mean? What did you tell her?"

"I kept it simple. I told her that you've had trouble becoming pregnant. She does think your husband knows, however. I had to make her think that."

"You didn't tell her about the money, did you? How much I'm paying . . . Or the rest . . . She doesn't know the rest?"

"She knows about the money. She worked that out easily enough because I'd told her about the egg harvesting yesterday and she knew money was connected to that, so she reckoned there had to be money connected to the surrogacy, and I could hardly deny it."

"But did you tell her—"

"That's all she knows. I needed money. End of story."

"Not about—"

"I didn't tell her how, if that's what you're worried about. She doesn't know—and no one will *ever* know, I swear it—about faking the pregnancy. That part is yours and mine to hold: the 'friendship' between us, the holiday together too close to the due date, the delivery of the baby . . . She knows nothing of that and I didn't tell her."

"But *why* did you—"

"Alatea, she gave me no choice. It was either tell her or face arrest, and that would hardly put me into the position of helping you later, when all this dies down. *If* it dies down . . ."

"But if she knows and then there's a baby later on . . ." Alatea went to the bay window and sat. She was in the yellow drawing room, its cheerful colour doing little to mitigate the dull grey day outside the house.

"There's more, Alatea," Lucy said. "I'm afraid there's more."

Alatea's lips felt stiff as she said, "What? What more?"

"She had a reporter with her. The choice she gave me was to talk to him or to have Scotland Yard—"

"Oh my God." Alatea slumped in the chair, her head lowered, her hand holding her brow.

"But why is Scotland Yard interested in you? And why is *The Source* trying to write about you? I *have* to ask because the one thing you promised—you guaranteed this, Alatea—was that no one could possibly root out the deception. Now between Scotland Yard and a tabloid, we both stand in very good stead to be—"

"It's not you. It's not me," Alatea told her. "It's Nicky. It's the fact that his cousin drowned."

"What cousin? When? What's this got to do with you?"

"Nothing. It's got nothing to do with me and nothing to do with Nicky. It's just what brought Scotland Yard up here in the first place. The journalist was here to do a story on Nicky and the pele project, but that was weeks ago and I don't know why he's come again."

"This is a mess," Lucy said. "You do know that, don't you? Look. I do think I've managed to keep the reporter from getting a story out of all this. What's there to report? You and I talking about a surrogacy arrangement? There's no story in that. But as to the woman . . . She claimed that she could produce the detective from Scotland Yard with a wave of her hand and he said that she *was* the detective, which she denied. But she wouldn't say more and by that time things were falling apart and . . . For the love of God, who *was* this woman, Alatea? What does she want with me? What does she want with you?"

"She's gathering her information," Alatea said. "She's making sure she knows who I am."

"What do you mean, who you are?"

The instrument of another, she thought, eternally never who I wish to be.

VICTORIA
LONDON

Barbara Havers spent the morning keeping her nose to Isabelle Ardery's assigned grindstone, which had a great deal to do with meeting a clerk from the CPS on the invigorating subject of comparing all the statements taken from everyone connected to the summer death of a young woman in a north London cemetery. She hated this kind of work, but she did everything save salute when Ardery gave it to her. Better to prove herself in ways beyond her manner of dress, she reckoned, which was today letter perfect, as a matter of fact. She'd donned her A-line skirt, navy tights, and perfectly polished court shoes—well, there was one little scuff but some spit had taken care of that—and she'd topped this with a new wool sweater that was finely knitted and *not*, mind you, of her usual heavy-gauge fisherman's variety. Over that she'd shrugged into a subtle plaid jacket and she'd even put on the single piece of jewellery she owned, which was a filigree necklace purchased the previous summer at Accessorize in Oxford Street.

Hadiyyah had heartily approved of her ensemble that very morning, which told Barbara she was developing more skill in the putting-oneself-together-professionally department. She'd come to Barbara's bungalow as Barbara was indulging in the last bit of her Pop-Tart, and heroically she'd ignored the fag smouldering in the ashtray in favour of complimenting Barbara on her growing talents in fashion.

Barbara noted that Hadiyyah was not wearing her school uniform, and she asked about this. "Holiday today?"

Hadiyyah bounced from foot to foot, hands on the back of one of the two chairs at Barbara's kitchen table, which was little larger than a chopping board and generally did duty as that as well. The little girl said, "Mummy and I . . . It's *special*, Barbara. It's for Dad and I must take the day off school. Mummy phoned and said I was ill today but it was only the *littlest* lie because of what we have planned. It's a surprise for Dad." She hugged herself in glee. "Oh, just wait, wait, *wait*," she cried.

"Me? Why? Am I part of the surprise?"

"*I* want you to be. So Mummy says you can know but you mustn't say a word to Dad. D'you promise? See, Mummy says she and Dad had a row—well, adults do row sometimes, don't they—and she wants to give him a cheer-you-up surprise. So that's what we're doing today."

"Taking him somewhere? Surprising him at work?"

"Oh no. The surprise'll be when he gets home."

"Special dinner, I'll bet."

"Much, *much* better than that."

To Barbara's way of thinking, there wasn't anything better than a special dinner, especially if she wasn't the one who had to cook it. She said, "What, then? Tell me. I'm sworn to secrecy."

"D'you promise and double promise?" Hadiyyah asked.

"Triple promise if that will do it."

Hadiyyah's eyes danced along with her feet. She pushed away from the table and spun so that her hair flew round her shoulders like a cape. She said, "My brother and sister! My brother and sister! Barbara, did you know I have a brother and a sister?"

Barbara felt the smile melt from her face. She forced it back on. "A brother and sister? Really? You have a brother and a sister?"

"I do, I do," Hadiyyah cried. "See, Dad was married once before and he didn't like to tell me 'cause I s'pose he thought I was too young. But Mummy told me and she said it's not such a *bad* thing to be married once before, is it, and I said no, of course it isn't 'cause lots of kids have parents who aren't married any longer and I know them from school. So Mummy said well that's what happened with Dad only his family got so cross with him that they didn't want him to see his children anymore. And that's not nice, is it?"

"Well, I suppose not," Barbara said, but she was developing a very bad feeling about where this was heading and what the possible outcome would be. And how the hell had Angelina Upman tracked these people down? she wondered.

"*So* . . . " Hadiyyah allowed a dramatic pause.

"Yes?" Barbara prompted.

"So Mummy and I are going to fetch them!" she cried. "Won't that be a wonderful surprise! I get to meet them, and I'm ever so excited to have a brother and a sister I never knew. And Dad gets to see them next and *he'll* be ever so excited as well 'cause Mummy says he's not seen them in years and *she* doesn't know how old they are, even, except she thinks that one of them is twelve and the other is fourteen. Imagine, Barbara, I got an *older* brother and sister. D'you think they'll like me? I hope so 'cause I know I'll like them."

Barbara's mouth had gone so dry that she could hardly move her jaw, so tightly were her cheeks adhering to her teeth. She gulped a mouthful of tepid coffee and said, "Well, well, well," which was just about the only thing she could manage while her brain was racing with thoughts of the bloody-hell-what-should-I-do variety. Friendship demanded that she warn Azhar of the impending disaster about to befall him: Angelina Upman presenting him with a fait accompli that he would have had neither time nor opportunity to prevent. But did friendship extend that far? she asked herself. And if she told him, what would he do and what effect would whatever he did have on Hadiyyah, who was, as far as Barbara could see, the most important person involved?

Ultimately, Barbara had done nothing because she couldn't come up with a plan that didn't culminate in utter havoc being wrought upon too many lives. Talking to Angelina felt like a betrayal of Azhar. Talking to Azhar felt like a betrayal of Angelina. It seemed the better course to stay out of it altogether and let nature—or whatever it was—take its course. She'd have to be there to sweep up the pieces but perhaps there would be no pieces to sweep up. Hadiyyah, after all, deserved to know her brother and sister. Perhaps everything would come out of the wash of affairs smelling sweet as roses in June. Perhaps.

Thus Barbara had taken herself to work as usual. She'd made certain Superintendent Ardery got the complete eyeful of her day's ensemble, although she'd presented herself to Dorothea Harriman for a thumbs-up first. Harriman had been copious in her praise—"Detective Sergeant Havers, your hair . . . your makeup . . . stunning . . ." —although when she'd gone on to talk about a new mineral-based foundation that Barbara *had* to try and did the detective sergeant want to pop out at lunchtime and see if they could find it locally, Barbara drew the line. She'd said thanks, made her bow to Superintendent Ardery, who'd handed her the demands from the CPS while she spoke to someone on the phone about, "What sort of cock-up is this, anyway? Are you people ever on top of things over there?" which Barbara assumed had to do with SO7 and matters pertaining to forensics. She herself got down to work with the CPS clerk and it was some time later when she was finally able to resume the work she'd been doing for Lynley.

This was easier than before since Ardery had to leave to

attend to the cock-up apparently and if it *was* a forensics cock-up, she'd be across the river for God only knew how long. The moment Barbara learned she was out of the building—it always paid to be on friendly terms with the blokes who manned the Yard's underground car park access—she was out of there like a cannonball and on her way to the Met's library, excuses made to the CPS bloke, who was happy enough to take a very long lunch hour.

Barbara took her English/Spanish dictionary with her. Having gathered enough information on the first two sons of Esteban Vega y de Vasquez and Dominga Padilla y del Torres de Vasquez—the first two sons being the priest Carlos and the dentist Miguel—and having seen a good enough photo of Miguel's wife to know that no amount of plastic surgery in the world could have turned her into Alatea Fairclough, Barbara was ready to move on to Angel, Santiago, and Diego to see what she could unearth. If none of them had a connection with Alatea, then she was going to have to look at the rest of the extended family, and from what the Spanish student had told her on the previous day, there could be hundreds of them.

As it turned out, there was very little on Angel, who, despite his name, appeared to be the black sheep of the family. Using her dictionary and moving at a pace so tedious that she thought her outrageously expensive Knightsbridge haircut might grow out before she discovered anything useful, she ultimately was able to put together the fact that he'd caused a car crash that had crippled his passenger for life. The passenger had been a fifteen-year-old girl.

Barbara followed this lead—the fifteen-year-old girl being at least the first female she'd come across aside from Miguel's unfortunate wife—but she came up with nothing but a dead end. No photo was available of her and while there was one of Angel, he appeared to be round nineteen years old and it didn't matter anyway because after the accident, he dropped directly off the media map. If he was North American and preferably from the United States, at that point he would either have gone into a rehab programme or discovered Jesus, but this was South America and whatever happened to him after that accident, the available media didn't talk about it. Too small a fish, probably. They'd quickly moved on to other things.

So did she. Santiago. She found a story about the boy's first communion. At least she reckoned it was his first communion because he was standing in a neat arrangement of children in suits (the boys) and bride getups (the girls) and either the Moonies had decided to begin marrying them off when they were round eight years old or this was a group of children who, as Catholics in Argentina, had just been elevated to worthy recipients of the Sacrament. It was rather odd that there would be a story about a group first communion, so Barbara struggled through a bit of it. She got the gist: that the church had burned down and they'd been forced to have their first communion in a city park. Or so it seemed to Barbara's extremely limited skill with Spanish. Truth was, the church could have been destroyed by a flood. Or even an earthquake. Or perhaps they'd tented the place for termites because God, God, *God* this was tedious work having to translate everything a single word at a time.

She squinted at the photo of the children and looked at it one girl at a time. She brought out the Internet picture she had of Alatea Fairclough and she began to compare it to each of the girls. Their names were listed and there were only fifteen of them and certainly she could do an Internet search on each of them but that would take hours and she didn't have hours because once Superintendent Ardery returned, if she wasn't beavering away at the witness statements she'd been ordered to deal with at the side of the CPS clerk, there would be hell to pay.

She considered choosing the most likely suspect among the girls and having an age progression done upon her. But she hardly had the time and she certainly *didn't* have the authority. So she went back to the Santiago trail because if he had nothing more to offer her, there was nothing else to do other than to move on to Diego.

She found an older picture of Santiago playing Othello sans black pancake in the eponymous play as an adolescent. There was a final picture of him with the school football team and an enormous trophy, but then there was nothing. Just like Angel of the car crash, he fell off the radar. It was as if once the boys reached mid-adolescence, if they hadn't accomplished something important—preparing for the priesthood or for dentistry being cases in point—then the local news media lost interest in them. Either that or they became useless to their father politically. Because, after all, he *was* a politician, with a politician's bent for trotting out his family in election years to demonstrate their essential wholesomeness for the voters.

Barbara thought about this: family, politics, the voting public. She thought about Angel. She thought about Santiago. She stared at every photo she'd come up with and she ended with the children in the park at their first communion. Finally, she picked up the photograph of Alatea Fairclough again.

"What *is* it?" she whispered. "Tell me your secrets, luv."

But there was nothing. A string of noughts stretched out to infinity.

She muttered a curse and reached for the mouse to log off the Internet and get back to Diego—the final brother—later. But then she looked a last time at the football photo, then at Othello. From them she went to Alatea Fairclough. Then Alatea on Montenegro's arm. Then she went back to the first communion. Then she riffled through the photos of Alatea Fairclough's modelling years. She went back and back and back through those photos, back through time, back to the first one she could find. She studied it. She finally saw.

Eyes on the terminal's screen, she reached for her mobile. She punched in Lynley's number.

BRYANBARROW
CUMBRIA

"Can she be forced?" Manette asked Freddie. They were coursing through the Lyth Valley at a good speed, with Freddie behind the wheel. They'd just made the turn into the southwest end of it, where the emerald fields spread out behind crusty drystone walls on either side of the road and the fells rose above them with peaks that wore the grey shawls of cloud on their shoulders. It would be misty up there, and soon it would be misty on the valley floor as well. A good fog was probably going to develop as the day wore on.

Manette had been consumed by their conversation with Niamh Cresswell. How, she wondered, could she have known Niamh for so many years without really knowing her at all?

Freddie, it seemed, had been thinking thoughts unrelated to Niamh and their call upon her because he glanced Manette's way and said, "Who?"

"Niamh, Freddie. Who else? Can she be forced to take the children back?"

Freddie looked doubtful. "I don't know the law when it comes to parents and children. But, really, old girl, what sort of plan would that be, to get the law involved?"

"Oh Lord, I don't know. But we should at least find out what the options are. Because the very idea that she'd just leave Tim and Gracie to their fate . . . especially little Gracie . . . Good God, Freddie, does she expect them to go into care? Can she *give* them into care, for that matter? *Can't* someone force her . . . ?"

"Solicitors, judges, and social services?" Freddie asked. "How d'you see that sort of thing affecting the children? Tim's in a bad enough way already, what with Margaret Fox School and all that. I daresay knowing his mum has been forced by a court to take him back would send the poor lad right over the edge."

"Perhaps my mum and dad, then . . . ?" Manette suggested. "With that enormous play area she's building . . . ? Mum and Dad could take them. They've got the space, and the kids would love to be near the lake and to use the play area, certainly."

Freddie slowed the car. Up ahead, a flock of sheep were being moved from one paddock into another in a manner typical to Cumbria: They were in the middle of the road with a border collie directing them and the farmer strolling along behind. The pace was, as always, glacial.

Freddie changed gears and said to Manette, "Tim's a bit

old for play areas, wouldn't you say, Manette? And anyway, what with this business with Vivienne Tully just coming to light, having the kids move into Ireleth Hall might be even worse for them than . . . well, than whatever other arrangement can be made."

"Of course, you're right." Manette sighed. She thought about everything she'd learned in the last twenty-four hours about her parents, but especially about her father. She said, "What d'you think she's going to do?"

"Your mother?" He shook his head. "No idea."

"I've never understood what attracted her to Dad in the first place," Manette said. "And believe me, I haven't a *clue* what Vivienne saw in him. Or continues to see in him, because it's looking like she's been seeing him for years. Why on earth would she ever have found Dad attractive? It can't be money. The money's mother's, not his, so if they'd divorced he'd do fine but he wouldn't have been exactly rolling in the dosh. I mean, of course he's always had access to it and perhaps Vivienne never knew it wasn't actually his . . . ?"

"It's unlikely that she even thought of money when it came to your dad," Freddie replied. "I expect it was his self-assurance. Women like that in a man, and your father's always had self-assurance in spades. I wager it's what attracted your mother to him."

Manette glanced his way. He was still watching the sheep on the road, but the tips of his ears were giving him away. There was more here than met the eye, so she said, "And . . . ?"

"Hmm?"

"The self-assurance bit."

"Right. Well. I've always admired that about your father. Honestly? Wished I had just a bit of what he's got." The ears got redder.

"You? Not self-assured? How can you say that? And look at all the women who've been crawling on their knees across broken glass to get at you lately."

"That sort of thing is easy, Manette. It's the biological imperative. Women want a man without knowing why they want him. All he has to do is perform. And if a man can't perform when a woman's pulling his trousers down to have a ride on the pogo stick—"

"Freddie McGhie!" Manette laughed, in spite of herself.

"It's true, old girl. The whole species dies out if the bloke can't do it when a woman's getting him ready for it, so that's all it is. Biology. The performance is rote. Technique isn't, of course, but any bloke can learn a decent technique." The sheep ahead of them reached the next field, where the gate stood open between the drystone walls. The border collie expertly got them through, and Freddie put the car back into gear. He said, "So we can say your dad developed a good technique, but he had to have something to attract women in the first place, and that's his confidence. He has the sort of confidence that makes a man believe he can do anything. And not only does he believe he can do anything, but he proves it to people."

Manette could see how this was the case, certainly when it came to her parents' relationship. Their initial meeting was part of family lore, that fifteen-year-old boy strutting up to eighteen-year-old Valerie Fairclough and announcing his intentions towards her. She'd been intrigued by his cockiness in a world where his kind generally knew where to find their forelocks. That feeling of intrigue was all Bernie Dexter had required. The rest was history.

She said, "But, Freddie, you can do anything, as well. Have you never believed that about yourself?"

He shot her a diffident smile. "Couldn't hang on to you, could I? And what Mignon said yesterday . . . ? I always knew you preferred Ian. P'rhaps that was the crux of our problems."

"That isn't true," Manette protested. "The seventeen-year-old girl I was might have preferred Ian. The woman I became preferred no one but you."

"Ah," he said. But he said nothing more.

Nor did she, although she could feel an uneasiness come between them, a tension that hadn't been there before. She kept quiet as they made the turn that would take them up to Bryanbarrow village and, ultimately, to Bryan Beck farm.

When they arrived, it was to see a removals van in front of the cottage where George Cowley and his son, Daniel, lived. When they parked and began to approach the old manor house, Cowley came out of the cottage and, apparently seeing them, strolled over to have a word. It was brief enough to begin with: "Got what he wanted all along, I dare say." He spat unappealingly on the stone path that led past Gracie's trampoline to the front door. "See how he likes to have a farm not bringing in a bloody penny and he'll be changing his tune."

"I beg your pardon?" Freddie was the one to speak. He didn't know George Cowley and while Manette knew him by sight, she'd never actually spoken to the man.

"He's got Big Plans, he has," Cowley said, using upper-case by means of his intonation. "We're finished here, me an' Dan. We take our sheep with us, and let him see how he likes it. *And* let him see his way to finding another farmer willing to rent the land and live in that hovel over there and pay through the nose for the pleasure. Him and his wife and family."

Manette wondered if the cottage was actually large enough for a man, his wife, and a family as well, but she didn't say anything. Just, "Is Tim here, Mr. Cowley? We're looking for him."

"Don't know, do I?" George Cowley said. "Something wrong with that kid anyways. And the other's an odd one, 's well. Jumping on that trampoline for hours. Bloody glad, I am, to be gone from this place. You see that bollock licker, you tell him I said so. You tell him I don't believe his nonsense for a bloody minute, no matter what he's got up his sleeve."

"Certainly. Will do," Freddie said. He took Manette's arm and steered her to the front door. Under his breath he said, "Best give him a very wide berth, hmm?"

Manette agreed. Clearly, the man was a bit off his nut. What on earth had he been talking about?

No one was at home in the old manor house, but Manette knew where a spare key was kept, beneath a lichen-covered concrete mushroom half-buried in the garden at the base of an old wisteria, leafless now with its massive trunk climbing towards the roof. Key in their possession, they entered. The door took them through a passage and into the kitchen, where everything was pin-neat and the old woodwork of the sagging cabinets had been polished to a glow. The place looked better than it had looked prior to Ian's death. Clearly, Kaveh or someone else had been at work upon it.

This gave Manette a feeling of disquiet. She was of a mind that devastating grief should produce in someone an equal devastation of spirit, of the sort that precluded doing one's house up as if in the expectation of visitors. But nothing was out of place in this room, not a single cobweb clung to the heavy oak ceiling beams, and even in the hidden area high above the old fireplace where meat had once hung to be smoked and preserved during long winters, it appeared that someone had used a mop and a cleaning agent on the smoky walls.

Freddie said, "Well, no one can claim he's letting the place go to ruin, eh?" as he looked round.

Manette called out, "Tim? Are you here?"

This was mostly for effect, since she knew very well that even if Tim was present, he was hardly going to come leaping down the stairs or in from the fire house, open-armed in greeting. Nonetheless, they checked the place systematically as they went: The hallan was empty, the fire house was as well. Like the kitchen, every room into which they popped their heads was neat and clean. It all looked as it had when Ian had been alive, only better kept up, as if a photographer might be arriving at any moment to shoot pictures for a magazine article on Elizabethan buildings.

They went up the stairs. A building of this age would have hidey-holes aplenty, and they did their best to search them out. Freddie voiced his opinion that Tim was long gone and who could really blame him after what he'd been going through. But Manette wanted to make absolutely sure. She looked under beds and poked into wardrobes and even pressed on some of the ancient panelled walls to see if there were hidden chambers. She knew she was being ridiculous but she couldn't help herself. There was something essentially wrong with the entire picture of Bryan Beck Farm, and she was intent upon understanding what it was because for all they knew the real truth was that Kaveh had done something to Tim to drive him off and then had made a show of looking for him afterwards.

Tim's bedroom was the last place they looked, and here, too, all was in order. The fact that it was the bedroom of a fourteen-year-old boy was nowhere in evidence, although his clothing still hung in the wardrobe, and his tee shirts and jerseys were folded within the chest of drawers.

"Ah," Freddie said, approaching a table that did service as a desk beneath a window. On this sat Tim's laptop computer, its top open as if it had been recently used. "This might give us something," he told Manette. He sat down, stretched his fingers, and said, "Let's see what we can see."

Manette went to his side and said, "We don't have his password. What do we know about delving into other people's computers without passwords?"

Freddie looked at her and smiled. "Ah, you of little faith," he said. He began to whittle away at the problem, which didn't turn out to be much of a problem at all. Tim's computer was set to remember his password. They needed only his user name, which Manette knew since she had done her best to e-mail Tim regularly. The rest, as Freddie said, was bingo.

He chuckled at the ease of it all and said to Manette, "I do wish your back had been turned, old girl. You might actually have thought I was some sort of genius."

She squeezed his shoulder. "You're genius enough for me, my dear."

As Freddie set about examining e-mails and trails to various websites, Manette looked at what was on the desk along with the computer. School books, an iPod with its docking station and speakers, a notebook filled with disturbing pencil drawings of grotesque alien beings consuming various body parts of humans, a book on bird watching—where had *that* come from? she wondered—a pocketknife that she unfolded to see a chilling brown crust of blood on its largest blade, and a map printed from the Internet. She took this last and said, "Freddie, could this be—?"

Car doors slammed outside the house. Manette leaned over the table to look out of the window. She thought it likely that Kaveh had returned, that, perhaps, he'd found Tim himself and had brought him home, in which case she and Freddie would need to be off the boy's computer post-haste. But the arrivals weren't Kaveh, as things turned out. They were, instead, an older Asian couple, possibly Iranian like Kaveh. With them was a teenage girl, who looked up at the manor house with a long-fingered hand pressed against her lips. She shot a glance at the older couple. The woman took her arm and together all three of them approached the front door.

They had to belong to Kaveh in some fashion, Manette thought. There were few enough Asians in this part of Cumbria, and hardly any at all in the countryside. They'd come on a surprise visit, perhaps. They'd come to call on their way from Point A to Point Z. Who knew *why* they'd come? It didn't matter because they'd knock on the door and no one would answer and then they'd skedaddle so that she and Freddie could get on with things.

But that didn't happen. Apparently with a key in their possession, they let themselves inside. Manette murmured, "What on earth . . . ?" And then, "Freddie, someone's arrived. It's an older couple and a girl. I think they belong to Kaveh. Shall I . . . ?"

Freddie said, "Damn. I'm getting somewhere here. Can you . . . I don't know . . . Can you handle them in some way?"

Manette left the room quietly, closing the door behind her. She made a suitable amount of noise as she descended the stairs. She called out, "Hullo? Hullo? C'n I help you?" and she came face-to-face with everyone in the passage between the kitchen and the fire house.

The best course was bluffing, Manette decided. She smiled as if there was nothing unusual in her being inside the manor house. She said, "I'm Manette McGhie. I'm Ian's cousin. You must be friends of Kaveh? He's not here at the moment."

They were more than friends of Kaveh, as it happened. They were his parents come up from Manchester. They'd brought his fiancée, newly come from Tehran, to see what was going to be her home in a few short weeks. She and Kaveh had not yet met. It was not the usual done thing for her future in-laws to bring the bride to call, but Kaveh had been anxious—well, what bridegroom wouldn't be?—and so here they were. Just a little premarital surprise.

The girl's name was Iman and she'd dropped her gaze in an appealingly diffident fashion while all this was being said. Her hair—copious, lustrous, and black—fell forward to hide her face. But the glimpse Manette had caught of it had been enough to see she was very pretty.

"Kaveh's fiancée?" Manette's smile froze as she took this on board. At least there was an explanation now for the pristine state of the house. But as to everything else, these waters were deep and this poor girl was probably going to drown in them. Manette said, "I had no idea Kaveh was engaged. Ian never told me about that."

Whereupon the waters became deeper still.

"Who is Ian?" Kaveh's father asked.

EN ROUTE TO LONDON

When his mobile rang, Lynley was nearly seventy miles from Milnthorpe, fast approaching the junction for the M56, and more than a little disturbed. He'd been played for a fool by Deborah St. James, and he was far from happy about it. He'd turned up at the Crow and Eagle as agreed at half past ten, expecting to find her with her bags packed and ready for the drive back to London. He'd not been concerned at first when she was not waiting for him in the lobby since he'd seen her hire car in the car park, so he knew she was somewhere about the place.

"If you'd ring her room, please," he'd said to the receptionist, a girl in a crisp white blouse and black wool skirt who'd done so obligingly with a "Who shall I tell her . . . ?"

"Tommy," he said, and he saw the flash of a knowing look strike her features. The Crow and Eagle was, perhaps, a hotbed of hot beds—as Sergeant Havers would have put it—a central location for daily assignations among the landed gentry. He added, "Fetching her for the drive back to London," and then was immediately irritated with him-

self for doing so. He walked away and studied the ubiquitous rack of brochures featuring tourist highlights in
Cumbria.

The receptionist cleared her throat after a moment and
said, "No answer, sir. Could be she's in the dining room?"

But she wasn't. Nor was she in the bar, although what
Deborah would have been doing in the bar at half past ten
in the morning was a mystery to him. Since her car was
there, right next to where he'd parked the Healey Elliott,
he sat down to wait. There was a bank across the street from
the hotel, a market square in the town, an old church with
an appealing graveyard . . . He reckoned she could be having a final look round the place before the long drive.

It didn't occur to him for some ten minutes that if the
receptionist had been ringing Deborah's room, she clearly
hadn't yet checked out of the hotel. When it *did* occur to
him, he moved fairly rapidly from there to a conclusion of
"Bloody maddening woman."

He rang her mobile at once. Of course, it went immediately to her voice mail. He said, "You must know I'm rather
unhappy with you at the moment. We had an arrangement,
you and I. Where the hell are you?" but there was nothing
more to add. He knew Deborah. There was no point in trying to move her from the obdurate stand she had taken with
regard to matters in Cumbria.

Still he had a look round the town for her before he left,
telling himself he owed Simon that much. This ate up more
of his day and accomplished nothing save an extended study
of Milnthorpe, which, for some reason, appeared to have a
plethora of Chinese takeaways round the market square.
He finally returned to the inn, wrote her a note, left it with
the receptionist, and went on his way.

When his phone rang on the approach to the M56, then,
he thought at first it was Deborah, ready to be profuse with
her apologies. He answered without glancing at the incoming number, barking, "What?" only to hear Sergeant
Havers's voice instead.

She said, "Right. Well. Hullo back at you. Which one is
it, then? Did you have a personality transplant or a toss-
and-turn night?"

He said, "Sorry. I'm on the motorway."

"Heading . . . ?"

"Home, where else?"

"Not a good idea, sir."

"Why? What's going on?"

"Just ring me when you can talk. Find a services area. I don't want you crashing that expensive motor of yours. I've already got the Bentley on my conscience."

The next services area was a Welcome Break, and he had to travel some way to find it. It was a quarter of an hour before he got there, but the car park wasn't crowded and there was virtually no one inside the unappealing sprawl of sticky-floored cafeteria, shops, newsagents, and children's play area. He bought himself a coffee and took it to a table. He rang Havers's mobile.

"Hope you're sitting down," were her words when she answered.

"I was sitting down the first time we spoke," he reminded her.

"Okay, okay." She brought him up to the minute on what she'd been doing, which appeared mostly to be keeping out of Isabelle Ardery's sight in order to do research on the Internet, for which she seemed to be developing a distinct liking. She talked about a Spanish graduate student; her neighbour Taymullah Azhar, with whom Lynley was acquainted; the town of Santa Maria de la Cruz, de los Angeles, y de los Santos; and finally the five sons of the mayor of that town. She ended with the purpose of her call, always someone who liked to build to dramatic moments:

"And here's the situation in a nutshell. There is no Alatea Vasquez y del Torres. Or perhaps better put: There is and there isn't an Alatea Vasquez y del Torres."

"Hadn't you already established that Alatea's probably from another part of the family?"

"To borrow unblushingly from rock 'n' roll history, sir: That was yesterday and yesterday's gone."

"Meaning?"

"Meaning Alatea's from this part of the family. She's just not Alatea."

"Who is she, then?"

"She's Santiago."

Lynley tried to take this in. Around him, a cleaner was industriously mopping the floor, casting meaningful glances in his direction as if with the hope he'd vacate the premises, giving access to the floor beneath his chair. He said, "Barbara, what on earth do you mean?"

"I mean exactly what I say, sir. Alatea is Santiago. Santiago is Alatea. Either that or they are identical twins, and if I remember my biology correctly, there is no such thing as identical twins of the male-female sort. A biological impossibility."

"So we're talking about . . . What, exactly, are we talking about?"

"Cross-dressing, sir. Impeccable female impersonation. A tasty secret one would hope to keep from the family, wouldn't you say?"

"I would say, yes. In certain circumstances. But in these circumstances—"

Havers cut in. "Sir, here's how it is: The trail on Santiago goes dead when he's about fifteen years old. That's when, I daresay, he started passing himself off as someone called Alatea. He ran away from home round then as well. I got that, among other details, from a phone call to the family."

She began to tell him what she'd learned from her earlier meeting with the graduate student Engracia after that call the young woman had placed to Argentina: the family wanted Alatea to come home; her father and her brothers now understood; Carlos—"He's the priest," Havers reminded Lynley—*made* them understand; everyone was praying for Alatea's return; they'd been searching for years; she must not continue to run; Elena Maria's heart was broken—

"Who's Elena Maria?" Lynley felt as if his head were filling with wet cotton wool.

"Cousin," Havers said. "Way I figure it, Santiago did a runner because he liked to cross-dress, which—let's face it—probably didn't go down a treat with his brothers and his dad. Latin types, you know? Macho and all that, if you'll pardon the stereotyping. Anyway, somewhere along the line he met up with Raul Montenegro—"

"Who the dickens—"

"Rich bloke in Mexico City. Rolling in enough lolly to build a concert hall and name it for his mum. Anyway, Santiago meets him, and Raul likes him, as in Raul *likes* him, because Raul likes to bat for the same side, if you know what I mean. *And* he prefers his partners young and nubile. From what I've seen in photos, he prefers them well oiled as well, but that's neither here nor there, eh? Anyway, we've got heaven in a basket for these two blokes. On the one hand we have Santiago, who likes dressing up and making himself up like a woman, which, over time, he's learned to do bloody well. On the other hand, we have Raul, who meets Santiago and has no problem whatsoever with Santiago's dressing habits since he—Raul—is bent like a twig but would rather not have anyone actually know that. So he takes up with Santiago, who, when he's fixed himself up, looks like a gorgeous dolly bird, and Raul can even take him out in public. They keep company, so to speak, until something better comes along."

"That something better being . . . ?"

"Nicholas Fairclough, I expect."

Lynley shook his head. It was all so wildly improbable. He said, "Havers, tell me: Are you surmising all this, or do you actually have any real facts?"

She was unoffended. "Sir, it all fits. Santiago's mum knew exactly who we were talking about when Engracia asked her about Alatea. She didn't know who Engracia was other than someone looking for Alatea, so she also wouldn't have known that we'd already turned up the fact that there were only sons in the family. Since we knew there were only sons, Engracia and I both thought Alatea was someone else in the extended family—just like you did—but when I followed the trail on Santiago and then went back in time with Alatea's modelling pictures to find the youngest ones of her . . . Believe me, sir, she's Santiago. He ran off to take up life as a woman with no one the wiser because of how he looks, and once he met Raul Montenegro, he was set. Things probably just went swimmingly between them— Alatea and Raul—till Nicholas Fairclough came along."

Lynley had to admit there were possibilities in this. For

Nicholas Fairclough, former drug addict and drunk, was probably not going to want his parents to know that he was now living with a man posing as his wife, with a false marriage certificate the only documentation that would give this person the right to remain in the country anyway.

"Could Ian Cresswell somehow have discovered all this?" Lynley said, more to himself than to Havers.

"Give that barker a bone" was how Havers put her agreement to this consideration. "'Cause all things considered, sir, when he first saw her, who'd have known what he was looking at better than Ian Cresswell?"

MILNTHORPE
CUMBRIA

Deborah was feeling rotten even before the receptionist at the Crow and Eagle handed her Tommy's message. For everything that she'd been trying to do was falling apart at the seams.

She'd tried to draw the horrible reporter from *The Source* along the primrose path of there being no story to be got from what they learned from Lucy Keverne in Lancaster. Since Zed Benjamin still thought of Deborah as the Scotland Yard detective he'd assumed her to be from the first, she had hoped that when she said, "Well, my work here is finished," he'd go along and conclude his own work was finished in Cumbria as well. After all, if the putative detective had decided there was no case to answer, it stood to reason there was also no story.

But that was not how Zed Benjamin looked at matters, as things turned out. He said the story was just beginning.

This had filled Deborah with horror at what she might be exposing Alatea and Nicholas Fairclough to, so she had asked Zed Benjamin what sort of story he thought he had. "Two people want to pay a woman more than they're supposed to pay her to be a surrogate mother for their child," she pointed out. "How many people like that are there in the country? How many people don't have a friend or a relative who's willing to be a surrogate for free, just for compassion's sake? It's a ridiculous law and there's no story to write."

But again, that wasn't how Zed Benjamin saw it. The law itself *was* the story, he declared. It produced desperate women looking for desperate remedies using desperate means to attain them.

Deborah said, "Pardon me for saying so, Mr. Benjamin, but I hardly think *The Source* is going to issue a clarion call for women's reproductive issues upon your recommendation."

"We'll see," he'd promised.

They'd parted ways at the door to her lodgings, and she'd trudged inside, only to be given a sealed envelope with her name written on the outside in a cursive she recognised from years of receiving letters from Tommy while she studied photography in California.

The message was brief: *Deb, What can I say? Tommy.* And it was true enough. What *could* he say? She'd lied to him, she'd ignored his phone call on her mobile, and now he was as upset with her as Simon was. What a mess she'd made of things.

She went to her room and began to pack up her belongings. As she did so, she considered the various ways in which she'd utterly bollocksed up everything. First, there was the matter of Simon's brother, David, whom she'd strung along by refusing to make up her mind about the open adoption he was trying to arrange purely out of a desire to help them. Then there was Simon, whom she'd alienated in any number of ways but particularly by being so bloody minded about remaining in Cumbria when it was clear that their real business in the county—which had been to assist Tommy with his enquiry into Ian Cresswell's death—was completed. Finally, there was Alatea Fairclough, whose hopes for a surrogacy were now probably dashed by Deborah's bashing into her private affairs when all she wanted was what Deborah herself wanted: the chance to bring a child into the world.

Deborah stopped packing for a moment and lowered herself to the bed. She thought about how much of her life had been dominated over the last few years by something completely out of her control. It was beyond her power to grant her own wish. She could do nothing to make herself a mother simply because she wanted to be one. Alatea Fairclough had probably gone through exactly what she herself was going through.

Deborah could see at last why the South American woman had been so fearful of her presence and so reluctant to talk to her. She and her husband were set to *pay* someone to carry a baby for them and for all she knew, Deborah had been sent there to Cumbria by Lancaster University's reproduction scientists to sniff out the truth behind her arrangement with Lucy Keverne before they went forward with all the procedures required for a surrogate pregnancy. And there'd be a handful of them, no doubt about it. None of which would begin until the scientists and the doctors were certain about Alatea Fairclough and the surrogate.

So Deborah had been dogging the poor woman since the moment she herself had set foot in Cumbria when all along, she and Alatea Fairclough had in common the most agonising of desires, something granted so easily to other women, something often even deemed a "mistake" in the lives of other women as well.

Deborah realised she owed apologies everywhere for how she'd conducted herself over the past few days. She had to begin those apologies with one to Alatea Fairclough. Before leaving Cumbria for the south, she resolved, that was what she was going to do.

MILNTHORPE
CUMBRIA

So much of what Zed had said to the Scotland Yard detective was bluster, and he knew it. After he dropped her off at her hotel, he didn't return to Windermere. Instead, he went across the main road through Milnthorpe and made his way to the street that ran east to west along the market square. There was a Spar shop at a junction where another street led off to a grim-looking housing estate of unremittingly grey roughcast, and he parked nearby and went inside. It was cluttered and hot and it suited both his mood and his thoughts.

He browsed aimlessly for a few minutes before caving in and buying a copy of *The Source.* This he carried the short distance to Milnthorpe Chippy, which stood not far from an impressive butcher shop in whose front window an array of venison pies was displayed.

Inside the chippy, Zed bought a double order of haddock and chips and a Fanta Orange. Once he had his food arranged on the table in front of him, he unfolded *The Source,* and he girded himself to look at the day's lead story and, worse, at its byline.

That louse Mitchell Corsico had both. It was a nothing story, a real piece of rubbish: A very minor member of the royal family had been outed with a bastard child who was mixed-race, photos included. She was a girl. She was five years old. She was also pretty in that way that mixed-race people often are, having received the best of every chromosome from her progenitors. Her royal father could not accede to the throne unless the present monarch and family and extended family were all partying on a ship in the Atlantic the moment that it hit an iceberg, and that detail robbed the story not only of legs but also toes. However, this fact clearly was of no matter to Mitchell Corsico or, obviously, to Rodney Aronson, who would have made the decision to give the tale the front page, no matter *how* minor the minor member of the royal family was.

The front page suggested this could well be the explosive revelation of the year, the decade, or even the century, and *The Source* was squeezing it like the udders of a dying cow. Rodney had given it the full treatment: three-inch headline, photos grainy and otherwise, the byline for Mitch, and a jump to page 8—now *that* said volumes about what Rodney really thought he was offering for public consumption, didn't it?—where the story went into the uninspiring background of the child's mother and the even less inspiring background of the minor royal, who, unlike a lot of the monarchical family, at least had been born with a chin.

Of course, the tabloid had to take care, political correctness being all the rage. But really, it was a who-bloody-gives-a-toss piece to offer to the public anyway. Zed's conclusion was that it had to have been a very slow day in the sewers for this to be what Rodney had come up with.

Zed reckoned this might actually put him in a good position to snag the front page when he lined up his Cumbria facts and worked them into a story. So he pushed *The Source* to one side, doused his haddock and chips with malt vinegar, popped open his Fanta Orange, and began to sort through what he'd gathered on Nick Fairclough and the delectable Alatea.

Big was not a word that could be used to describe the story he had. The Scotland Yard detective had been right in that. Nick Fairclough and his wife were going to pay a woman more than just her expenses to have a baby for them, and while this wasn't legal, it also wasn't a story. The question was how to make it into one, a sensational one, or at least a member-of-the-royal-family-has-a-bastard-child one.

Zed considered his options, which were all those details he had to work with. Essentially, he had eggs, sperm, man, woman, another woman, and money. Whose eggs, whose sperm, which man, which woman, and whose money? were the various topics to be massaged into an epic piece of journalism.

Here, too, there were possibilities. Perhaps poor Alatea's eggs were not good enough (was there such a thing? he wondered) to do what they needed to do, such as to drop (did they drop?) into her wherever to meet up with Nick's you-know-what. Since they weren't good enough, someone else's eggs had to be used. But Nick and Alatea didn't want the family wise to this for reasons of . . . what? Inheritance? What were the laws on inheritance these days? Was there an inheritance involved, anyway, beyond a firm manufacturing toilets and other unappealing products, the mention of which could turn the story into a real boffola with Zed the butt of every joke in Fleet Street? Or perhaps Nick's swimmers weren't up to the job? Years of drug use had rendered them too weak to make the journey or to do much poking when they reached the destination? So someone else's swimmers were being used with the resulting baby being passed off as a bona fide Fairclough? That would be nice.

Or perhaps it was all about the money that was going to be paid to Lucy Keverne? With Nick's history, wasn't it possible that he was selling a little something on the side—other than toilets—to collect enough money to pay the woman? Could the doctors be on the take as well? That was another possibility.

By the time Zed had finished his double order of haddock and chips, he'd reached the conclusion that the best angle from which to write the tawdry tale of buying a baby-making machine—which was how he was going to sell it to Rodney—was to begin with Nick Fairclough. His reasoning behind this was simple enough. He knew human nature, perhaps not perfectly but well enough. And what he knew about human nature told him that the moment he and the Scotland Yard detective had left Lucy Keverne, she'd picked up the phone to ring Alatea Fairclough and to let her know the worst.

That left him with Nick and putting a little pressure on him for the real tale behind the deal with the woman in Lancaster.

He gathered up his copy of *The Source* and returned to his car. He glanced at his watch and saw from the time of day that Nicholas Fairclough would probably be at the Middlebarrow Pele Project. So to the pele project Zed would go.

His route took him past the Crow and Eagle and onto the route that led to Arnside. He zipped alongside Milnthorpe Sands, which were indeed sands at the moment—albeit soupy ones—because the tide was gone as if it had never been, leaving the River Kent a narrow gleam of water at the edge of which curlews, plovers, and redshanks high-stepped in their endless search for food. Beyond, from the direction of Humphrey Head, the fog was beginning to creep towards the shore. The mist was heavy, and the air was laden. Moisture clung to cottage windows and dripped from trees. The road was wet and slick.

At the pele project, Zed parked not far from the tower itself. He saw no one working at present. But when he got out of the car into the damp air, he heard at once a burst of raucous male laughter, and he followed this to its source, which turned out to be the dining tent. Within, all of the men were gathered. They sat at the tables, but they were not eating. Their attention was fixed on an older bloke who stood before them in a posture of ease, with one foot up on a chair and his elbow resting on his knee. He appeared to be telling the others some sort of tale. The others appeared to be enjoying it mightily. They were also enjoying cups of coffee and tea, and their cigarette smoke made the atmosphere eye stinging.

Zed clocked Nick Fairclough at the same instant that Nick Fairclough clocked him. He'd been sitting at the far side of the tent, his chair tipped back and his feet on the tabletop, but he dropped the chair legs to the ground as his eyes met Zed's. He came rapidly over to the tent's entrance.

He took Zed by the arm and directed him outside. He said, "It's not an open meeting," and he didn't sound particularly friendly about it. At this Zed concluded that he'd witnessed a bit of what kept the men on the straight and narrow: Alcoholics Anonymous, Jonesing Johnnies United, Hogs for Hope, or whatever it was. He also concluded that he wasn't going to be welcomed back into Nicholas Fairclough's life with open arms. Well, that couldn't be helped.

"I'd like a word," Zed said to him.

Fairclough tilted his head towards the tent, replying, "I've a meeting, as you saw. It'll have to wait."

"Don't think that's possible, actually." Zed took out his notebook to underscore the declaration.

Fairclough's eyes narrowed. "What's this about?"

"Lucy Keverne."

"Who?"

"Lucy Keverne. Or perhaps you know her by another name? She's the surrogate you and your wife are employing."

Fairclough stared at him and Zed recognised immediately what the look on the other man's face was telling him. The expression itself said, *Are you mad?* The reason for the question, however, had nothing whatsoever to do with madness.

"Surrogate?" Fairclough said. "Surrogate for what?"

"What do you think?" Zed said. "A surrogate mother.

I'd like to talk to you about the deal you and your wife have struck with Lucy Keverne to carry your child."

"Deal?" Nicholas Fairclough said. "There is no deal. What the hell are you talking about?"

Zed felt the pleasure of the moment wash through him at the same time as *bingo* chimed in his mind. He had his story.

"Let's take a little walk," he said.

BRYANBARROW
CUMBRIA

Manette was still trying to take in the information as she climbed the stairs, having settled Kaveh's parents and his fiancée in the fire house and having assembled for them tea and biscuits, which she'd delivered on a tray she'd rustled out of a kitchen cupboard. God alone could explain why she'd done the bit with the tea, she thought, but at the end of the day she reckoned good manners, in conjunction with habit, would always out.

They'd cleared up the confusion about who, exactly, Ian Cresswell had been in Kaveh's life, at least as far as his parents had known. A few moments' discussion of this matter had produced the revelation that, in his parents' minds, Kaveh merely lodged chastely with the owner of a farm and the Christian name of said owner had never yet been mentioned in any phone calls, notes, cards, or letters from their son. Miracle of miracles, the farm owner had supposedly left the farm to Kaveh in his will when he himself had—as they say in the vernacular—unexpectedly bought the farm. More miracle of miracles, this at last freed Kaveh to marry, since he now had a home into which he could welcome his wife. Of course, he'd not *needed* a home, as Mum and Dad had tried to point out to him time and again, year after year, since he and his wife could live with his parents in a manner traditional to their people in Iran, where extended families dwelt together for generations. But Kaveh had been a modern young man with the ideas of a modern *British* young

man, and British young men did not bring wives home to
live with their parents. It was not the done thing. Although,
truth to tell, the opposite was going to happen: Kaveh was
insisting that his parents join him and his soon-to-be-wife
on the farm. It was, they said, a successful conclusion to a
decade of badgering him to give them grandkids.

The amount that these good people did not know about
their son was staggering, and Manette made the quick decision not to be the person to burst their bubble. She felt a
tug of guilt about poor Iman and the future that lay before
her marrying a man who would most likely set out to lead
a double life not unlike the one Ian himself had led. But
what could she do about it? And if she did something—such
as saying, "Excuse me, don't you know Kaveh's been having
it off with blokes for years?"—where would that take them
aside from into an imbroglio that was not her concern?
Kaveh could do what he liked, she decided. His family
would discover the truth eventually. Or they would remain
blissfully or purposefully ignorant of the matter. Her job at
the moment was to find Tim Cresswell. But at least she
knew why Tim had run off. Doubtless, Kaveh had filled him
in on his upcoming nuptials. That would have pushed the
poor lad over the edge.

But into *what*? was the question. She returned to Tim's
bedroom to see if Freddie was making any headway into
answering it.

He was, apparently. He was still at Tim's laptop, but he'd
turned it away from the door, so someone entering the room
couldn't see its screen. That someone being her, Manette
reckoned. His face was grave.

She said, "What is it?"

"Pornography. It goes back quite a way in time."

"What sort are we talking about?" She made a move to
go round his chair, which he'd also shifted so that he could
see when she came into the room. He held up his hand.
"You don't want to see this, darling."

"Freddie, what *is* it?"

"It starts out mild, not much more than what you'd see
if a boy managed to get his hands on one of those magazines
they keep encased in black wrappers. You know what I

mean. Naked women showing off their privates in rather more detail than is actually attractive photographically. Boys do this kind of thing all the time."

"Did you?"

"Well . . . Yes and no. I was more of a breast man, frankly. Their artful presentation and all that. But times do change, eh?"

"And then?"

"Well, I met my first girlfriend when I was young enough for this to be—"

"Freddie, dear, I'm talking about the computer. Is there something more? You said it starts out mild."

"Oh. Yes. But then it goes on to men and women engaged . . . Well, you know."

"Still normal curiosity, perhaps?"

"I'd say. But then it changes to men with men."

"Because of Ian and Kaveh? Perhaps because of his own doubts?"

"Always a possibility. A likelihood, even. Tim would have wanted to understand. Himself, them, whatever." But Freddie sounded so sombre when he said all this that Manette knew there was more.

She said, "And then what, Freddie?"

"Well, then it switches from photographs to film. Live action. And the actors—or whoever they are—change as well." He rubbed at his chin and she could hear the *scritch* of his palm against the whiskers on his flesh and it came to her how comforting a sound that was, although she couldn't have told him why.

She said, "Do I want to know how the actors change?"

"Men and boys," he said. "Young boys, Manette. They look round ten to twelve years old. And the films themselves . . ." Freddie hesitated before he looked at her squarely, his dark eyes reflecting the depth of his concern. "Young boys 'performing' on older men, sometimes alone but more often in groups. I mean, it's always just one young boy but sometimes there's more than one man. There's even . . . well, it's a mockery of the Last Supper except it isn't feet-washing that 'Jesus' is engaged in and 'Jesus' looks round nine years old."

"Dear God." Manette tried to put it together: why Tim's interest would have gone from naked women displaying their genitals to male/female sex to male/male sex and then eventually to man/young boy sex. She didn't know enough about young adolescent males to understand if this was natural curiosity or something more sinister. She feared the latter. Who wouldn't? she thought. She said, "What d'you think we should . . . ?" but had no way to frame the rest of the question because she didn't know what the next step was beyond handing it all over to the police and a child psychologist and hoping for the best from there. She said, "I mean, for him to be searching this stuff out . . . We'll have to tell Niamh, at the very least. But of course, what good will that do?"

Freddie shook his head. "He's not been searching, Manette."

"I don't understand. You just said—"

"Aside from the pictures of women and men and the male/male sex, which we might be able to attribute to his confusion about his father and Kaveh, he's not been searching at all."

"Then . . . ?" She twigged. "He's been *sent* this stuff?"

"There's a trail of e-mails from someone calling himself Toy4You. They lead all the way back to a chat room for photography. I should guess that various routes through that chat room lead on to types of photography or photographic models or quirky photography or nude photography or any number of potential subjects from which users can then go into more-private chat rooms for more-private chats. The Web is called *the Web* for a reason. Threads lead everywhere. You just have to follow them."

"What does this Toy4You have to say?"

"What you'd expect of a slow seduction. 'Bit of harmless fun,' 'shows affection,' 'between consenting adults, of course,' 'must be of age,' and then the switch to 'Have a look at this and tell me what you think,' 'would *you* ever consider,' et cetera."

"Freddie, what's Tim saying in reply?"

Freddie tapped his fingers on the desk. He appeared to be trying to formulate an answer. Either that or he was attempting to put together the pieces. Manette prompted him by saying his name again. He finally said, "Tim actually appears to be striking a bargain with this person."

"With Toy4You?"

"Hmm. Yes. The bloke—I assume it's a bloke—says in the last one, 'You do something like this and I'll do whatever you want.'"

"What's 'this'?" Manette asked, although she wasn't sure she wanted to know.

"He's referring to another video attached."

"Do I want to know?"

"Garden of Gethsemane," Freddie said. "But the Roman soldiers don't make any arrest."

Manette said, "My God." And then with her eyes widening and her hand lifted to cover her mouth, "'I'll do anything you want'? Freddie, oh my God, do you think Tim arranged for this person to kill Ian?"

Freddie rose quickly, the chair scraping the floor. He came to her and said, "No, *no*," and touched her cheek briefly. "That last one . . . It postdates Ian's drowning. Whatever Tim wants, it's something besides his father's death. And it looks to me like he's going to receive it in exchange for being part of a pornographic film."

"But *what* could he want? And where *is* he? Freddie, we have to find him."

"We do indeed."

"But how . . . ?" Then she recalled the map she'd seen and she rustled for it again among the items that had been on Tim's desk. She said, "Wait, wait," and then she found it. But a glance told her the map was going to be of little use. For it was an enlarged section of some unnamed town and unless Freddie knew where Lake, Oldfield, Alexandra, Woodland, and Holly Roads were, they were going to have to waste time trying to rustle up a street atlas, sort out how to use this information on the Internet, or perform some magical feat to discover what town in Cumbria contained these places.

She said, "It's nothing, *nothing*. It's just streets, Freddie," and she shoved the map at him. She said, "What next? We must find him. We must."

He gave the map a glance and folded it quickly. He unplugged the laptop and said, "Let's be off."

"Where?" she asked. "Where on earth . . . Do you *know*?" God, she thought, why had she *ever* divorced this man?

"No idea," he said. "But I've a notion who will."

ARNSIDE
CUMBRIA

Lynley made excellent time. The Healey Elliott had been designed originally as a racing car, and despite its age it did not disappoint. He had no flashing lights to use, but the time of day and year did not make them necessary. He was coursing off the motorway in an hour's time, at which point the slickness of the streets and the heaviness of the mist encouraged him to have care with regard to his speed.

The difficult bit was getting from the motorway over to Milnthorpe and from Milnthorpe to Arnside. Off the motorway, the roads were narrow, not one of them was straight, there were few lay-bys into which slow drivers could pull to allow him to pass, and every farmer in Cumbria appeared to have chosen this day to move his tractor like a lumbering pachyderm from one spot to another.

Lynley felt a sense of rising urgency. It had to do with Deborah. God only knew what she would stumble into at this point, but she was obstinate enough to do something mad that would put her straight into the path of danger. How, he wondered, did Simon manage not to wring her neck?

Along the route from Milnthorpe to Arnside, at last, he saw the fog. Unlike the little cats' feet of the poem, this bank of grey was moving across the empty plain of Morecambe Bay's ebbed tide with startling swiftness, as if pulled along by unseen horses dragging a mantle of coal smoke behind them.

He slowed at Arnside village. He'd not been to Arnside House, but he knew where it was from Deborah's description. He passed a pier jutting into the wide and waterless channel of the estuarial River Kent and he braked to allow a woman with a pushchair to cross the street, a child hanging on to her trousers with a mittened hand and otherwise bundled against the chill. As they crossed—taking their bloody time about it, he thought, and why *was* it that when one was in a hurry, all occasions conspired against one?—he read the sign warning all the dangers of this place. *Fast Rising Tides!* it shouted, *Quicksands! Hidden Channels! Danger! Beware!* Why on earth, he wondered futilely, would someone want to bring up children here when one wrong move at one wrong time of day would snatch them towards a watery end?

The woman and child crossed safely to the pavement on the other side of the road. He went on. Through the village, down the Promenade with its display of Victorian mansions lined up on a rise of land overlooking the water, and then he was on the drive into Arnside House, where the Promenade ended. The building was set at an angle that made the most of its view, across an expanse of lawn from the water. That view was obscured today as the fog became more and more like wet cotton wool, once singed by fire.

Arnside House itself looked deserted, with no lights burning in the windows despite the gloom of the day. He couldn't decide if this was bad or good. No car meant, at least, there was a very good chance that Deborah had not bulldogged her way into a bad situation. The best scenario of all would be no one at home, but he couldn't rely on that.

He braked the Healey Elliott at the top of the driveway, where the gravel shaped into a winnow for parking. When he got out of the car, he found that the air had altered in the few hours he'd been gone. It felt nearly tubercular in his lungs. He moved through it like someone separating curtains, along the path to the heavy front door.

He heard the bell ring somewhere inside the place. He expected no answer, but this was not the case. He heard footsteps against a stone entry, and the door swung open. Then he faced the most beautiful woman he'd ever seen.

He was unprepared for the shock of Alatea Fairclough: the tawny skin, the wealth of wild, curly hair captured in tortoiseshell slides, the large dark eyes and sensuous mouth, the shape of a woman who was entirely woman. Only her hands betrayed her, and even then it was only by their size.

He had no trouble at all seeing how Alatea and Nicholas Fairclough had duped everyone around them. Had Barbara Havers not sworn this woman was, in fact, Santiago Vasquez y del Torres, Lynley would not have believed it. Truth to tell, he still couldn't. So he was careful with his words.

"Mrs. Fairclough?" he said. When she nodded, he took out his identification. He said, "DI Thomas Lynley, New Scotland Yard. I've come to talk to you about Santiago Vasquez y del Torres."

She went white so quickly that Lynley thought she would faint. She took a step away from the door.

He repeated the name. "Santiago Vasquez y del Torres. It seems the name's familiar to you."

She felt behind her for the oak bench that ran the length of one of the panelled walls of the entrance. She lowered herself onto it.

Lynley shut the door behind him. There was little light. What there was came from four small windows in the entrance, all of them stained glass in a stylised pattern of red tulips surrounded by greenery, which cast a subtle glow against the skin of the woman—or, he thought, whatever she was—who sat slumped on the bench.

He still wasn't certain of his facts, but he chose to take a stab at being direct and waiting for the consequences. So he said, "We must speak. I've reason to believe you're Santiago Vasquez y del Torres from Santa Maria de la Cruz, de los Angeles, y de los Santos in Argentina."

"Please don't call me that."

"Is that your true name?"

"Not since Mexico City."

"Raul Montenegro?"

She reared up at that, her back against the wall. "Has he sent you? Is he here?"

"I've not been sent by anyone."

"I don't believe you." She rose then. She hurried past him, nearly losing her footing on the step that gave access through a doorway into a dark corridor panelled, like the entrance, in oak.

He followed her. A short distance along the corridor, she slid open two pocket doors with stained glass panes of lilies surrounded by drooping fronds, and she passed through them and into a hall. It was half restored and half in tatters, an odd mixture of medieval revival and Arts and Crafts, and there she made for an inglenook fireplace, where she sat in the most sheltered corner, drawing her knees up to her face.

"Please leave me," she said, although she seemed to be speaking more to herself than to him. "Please leave."

"I'm afraid that's not possible."

"You must leave. Don't you see? No one here knows. You must leave at once."

Lynley thought it unlikely that no one knew. Indeed, he thought it wildly improbable. He said, "I daresay Ian Cresswell knew."

At that she raised her head. Her eyes were luminous, but her expression was shifting from distraught to confused. "Ian?" she said. "There's no possible way. How could he ever have known?"

"As a homosexual man, still in the closet, his was a double life. He would have come into contact with people like you. It would have been easier for him than for other people to recognise—"

"Is that what you think I am?" she asked. "A homosexual man? A transvestite? A cross-dresser?" A dawning knowledge came over her face. She added, "You're thinking that I killed Ian, aren't you? Because he . . . what? He discovered something? Because then he threatened to betray me if I didn't . . . what? Pay him money that I didn't have? Oh my God, had that only been the case."

Lynley found himself quite down the rabbit hole. The nature of her initial response to the name Santiago Vasquez y del Torres had indicated she was indeed the long-ago adolescent boy who'd run off from the town of his birth and somehow ended up on the arm of one Raul Montenegro. But her reaction to the suggestion that Ian Cresswell had come to know who and what she was was beginning to alter Lynley's thoughts on the subject.

She said, "Ian didn't know. No one here knew. Not a single person."

"Are you telling me that Nicholas doesn't know?" Lynley stared at her. He tried to take her in. Making sense of what she was telling him demanded he take a leap into an area that was completely unknown to him. He was like a blind man trying to get himself to a hidden doorway in a room cluttered with furniture whose misshapen nature only confused him. He said, "If that's the case, I don't quite understand. *How* could Nicholas not have known?"

"Because," she said, "I never told him."

"But I daresay his own eyes . . ." And then Lynley began to understand what she was actually revealing about herself. If she'd never told Nicholas Fairclough about Santiago Vasquez y del Torres, and if Nicholas Fairclough's own eyes hadn't told him, there was only one reason for this.

"Yes," she said, apparently reading the dawning knowledge on his features. "Only my immediate family in Argentina know, along with one cousin, Elena Maria. And Elena Maria, she always knew. Right from the first, even when we were children." Alatea pushed her hair from her face, a distinctly feminine gesture that was discommoding to Lynley, putting him off balance, as perhaps she intended. "She shared with me: her dolls when we were children, her clothes and her makeup when we grew older." Alatea looked away for a moment, then back at him directly, her expression earnest as she said, "Can you understand this? It was a way for me just to be. It was the *only* way for me just to be, and this Elena Maria understood. I don't know how or why, but she simply did. Before anyone, she knew who and what I was."

"A woman." Lynley finally put it into words. "Trapped in a man's body. But still a woman."

"Yes," Alatea agreed.

Lynley took this in. He could see that she was waiting for his reaction, perhaps steeling herself to whatever it would be: revulsion, confusion, curiosity, disgust, pity, abhorrence, interest, acceptance. She'd been one of five brothers in a world where being male equated with being accorded privileges that women had had to fight for and were still fighting for. She would know that most men would never comprehend why any man from that world would wish to change the gender into which he'd been born. Yet this, apparently, was what she had done, as she went on to clarify, saying:

"Even when I was Santiago, I was a woman. I had the body of a male. But I was not male. To live like that . . . belonging nowhere . . . having a body that is not your own body . . . so that you look upon it with loathing and would do anything to alter it in order to be who you are . . ."

"So you became a woman," Lynley said.

"I transitioned," she said. "This is what it's called. I left Santa Maria because I wished to live as a woman and could not do it there. Because of my father, his position, our family. Many things. And then came Raul. He had the money I needed to become a woman and he had his own needs. So we made a deal, he and I. No one else was involved and no one else knew." She looked at him then. Over the years, he'd seen the various expressions that flitted across the faces of desperate, crafty, or sly people when they attempted to play with the truth. They always thought they could hide who they were, but only the sociopath ever succeeded. Because the reality was that eyes were indeed windows into the soul, and only the sociopath was soulless.

There was a bench seat opposite Alatea's position in the inglenook. Lynley went to it and sat. He said, "The death of Ian Cresswell—"

"I had nothing to do with that. If I were to kill anyone, it would be Raul Montenegro, but I don't want to kill him. I never wanted to kill him. I just wanted to flee him, and even then it wasn't because Raul's intention was to betray who I am. He wouldn't have done that because he needed to have a woman on his arm. Not a real woman, you see, but a man who could pass as a woman, to safeguard his reputation in his world. What he didn't understand and what I didn't tell him was that I didn't want to pass as a woman because I already was one. I only needed surgery to make it so."

"He paid for it?"

"In exchange, he thought, for the perfect relationship between two men, one of whom looks to all of the world like a woman."

"A homosexual relationship."

"A form of one. Which really cannot exist when one of the partners is not of the same sex, you see. Our problem—mine and Raul's—was that we did not clearly understand each other before we began this . . . this venture. Or perhaps I deliberately misunderstood what he wanted from me because I was desperate and he was my only way out."

"Why do you think he's pursuing you now?"

She said without irony or self-congratulation, "Wouldn't you, Thomas Lynley? He spent a great deal of money to make me, and he's had little enough return on his investment."

"What does Nicholas know?"

"Nothing."

"How can that be?"

"I had the final surgery many years ago in Mexico City. When I knew I could not be what Raul wanted me to be, I left him. And Mexico. I was here and there, never remaining any place long. Finally, I was in Utah. And so was Nicky."

"But you would have had to tell him—"

"Why do you think that?"

"Because . . ." Well, it was obvious. There were certain things her body was never going to be able to do.

She said, "I thought I could go forever as a woman without Nicky knowing. But then he wished to come home to England, and he wished even more to make his father proud. He saw a single way to do it, a certain guarantee of his father's happiness. We would do what neither of his sisters had managed to do. We would have a child and give Bernard a grandchild and this would heal forever the damage Nicky had done to his relationship with his father—and his mother—during all his years of addiction."

"So now you must tell him."

She shook her head. "How can I tell him of such betrayal? Could you?"

"I don't know."

"I could love him. I could be a lover to him. I could make a home for him and do everything a woman might do for a man. Except this one thing. And to submit to a doctor's examination as to why I haven't yet become pregnant . . . ? I've lied to Nicky from the first because I was used to lying, because that's what we do, because that's what we have to do to get on in the world. It's called *stealth* and it's how we live. The only difference between me and the rest of the people who have transitioned from male to female is that I hid it from the man I love because I thought if he knew he would not wish to marry me and take me to a place where Raul Montenegro would never find me. That was my sin."

"You *know* you must tell him."

"I must indeed do something," she said.

ARNSIDE
CUMBRIA

He was drawing his car keys from his pocket when Deborah drove her hire car up to Arnside House. He remained where he was, and their eyes locked on each other. She pulled up next to the Healey Elliott, got out, and stood there looking at him for a moment. At least, he thought, she had the grace and decency to look regretful.

She said, "I'm so sorry, Tommy."

"Ah," he said. "Well."

"Have you waited all this time?"

"No. I was on my way back to London, about an hour from here. Barbara rang my mobile. There were a few loose ends. I thought it best to tie them."

"What sort of loose ends?"

"None that actually have anything to do with Ian Cresswell's death as things turn out. Where have you been? Lancaster again?"

"You know me too well."

"Yes. There'll always be that between us, won't there?" He looked past her to see that during his time inside Arnside House, the fog had reached the seawall. It was beginning to billow up and over it, reaching long cold fingers onto the lawn. He needed to leave at once in order to reach the motorway before the mist became impenetrable. But with it fast making all of Cumbria dangerous, he didn't see how he could in conscience depart unless Deborah was with him.

Deborah said, "I needed to speak to her one more time—Lucy Keverne—but I knew you'd not allow it."

Lynley raised an eyebrow. "I don't 'allow' or not allow anything. You're a free agent, Deborah. I told you on the phone I merely wanted your company on the drive back to town."

She dropped her head. That red hair of hers—always her most becoming feature—swung down from her shoulders and he saw how quickly it was being affected by the mist. Curls of it were separating, forming other curls. Medusa, he thought. Well, she'd always had that effect on him, hadn't she?

"As it turns out, I was right," she said. "I mean, there was more to the story than Lucy Keverne told me. I'm just not sure it would go far as a motive for anyone to murder Ian Cresswell."

"What is it, then?"

"That Alatea was indeed going to pay her to carry a baby, more than her expenses, that is. So . . . Well, I suppose the story's not as sensational as I thought it might be. I can't really imagine anyone committing murder over it."

This told Lynley that Lucy Keverne—whoever she was—either didn't know the full truth about Alatea Fairclough or she'd not told the full truth to Deborah. For the actual story was sensational in spades. Driven by those three prongs that dominated human behaviour—sex, power, and money—the story gave anyone in possession of it reason to ride it as far as it would go. But to murder as well? Deborah was probably correct in this. The one part of the story Ian Cresswell might have been murdered over was the part of the story Lucy Keverne had not known, if Alatea Fairclough was to be believed. And he thought she was.

"And now?" he said to Deborah.

"Actually, I've come to apologise to Alatea. I've made her life a misery for these past days, and I think I've put paid to her plans with Lucy as well. I didn't intend to, but that infernal reporter from *The Source* burst into our conversation and announced that I was the Scotland Yard detective in Cumbria to investigate Ian Cresswell's death and—" She sighed. She shook her hair off her shoulders and fingered it back in a gesture exactly like Alatea's. She said, "If I've made Lucy afraid to carry this baby for Alatea, Tommy, I've done her a serious wrong. She'll have to go back to square one and find another surrogate. I thought . . . Well, we have something in common, she and I, don't we? This business about babies. I wanted to tell her that much at least. Along with an apology. And the truth about who I am."

She meant well, Lynley thought, but he couldn't help wondering if she would make things worse for Alatea. He didn't see how. Deborah didn't know the full truth and he wasn't about to tell her. There was no need at this point. His business was finished here, Ian Cresswell was gone, and who Alatea Fairclough was and what she would reveal to her husband were matters for a divinity, which he certainly was not.

Deborah said, "Will you wait for me? I'll not be long. Perhaps at the hotel?"

He thought about it. It seemed the best solution. Still he said, "If you change your mind, ring me this time, all right?"

"I promise," she said. "And I won't change my mind."

MILNTHORPE
CUMBRIA

Zed didn't go back to his B & B in Windermere. All things considered, it was too far to drive with what he had simmering on the back burner of his brain. And what he had was a stop-the-presses story, one that he had to get written in order to stop those presses as soon as possible. He felt more alive than he had in months.

Nick Fairclough had tried to hide everything from him, but he succeeded just about as well as a fat man trying to remain unseen by hiding behind a sapling. From start to finish, the poor dumb bloke had been completely in the dark about what his wife had been cooking up with Lucy Keverne. The way Zed reckoned it, the two women had planned to go the turkey baster route and spring the situation on poor Nick when Lucy was too far up the duff for Nick to cry foul and demand they do something about it. Zed didn't quite have all the finer points of the tale since so far Nick had been as mute as a lump of coal on the topic of his semen and what Alatea had been doing with it or whether, even, she'd got her hands on it, but the way he saw it, that was a minor detail. The crux of the story was a husband being duped by two women for a delicious reason that was bound to emerge once the first part of the tale appeared on the front page of *The Source*. Within twenty-four hours of that occurring, the usual suspects would crawl out from beneath their rocks to spill whatever beans they were holding in their pots on the topic of Nick, Lucy, and Alatea. Not to mix too many metaphors, Zed thought, but the truth behind his kind of journalism was that one story always led to another like day to night to day again. First, though, he had to get the story he had thus far onto the front page of the paper. And oh what a story it was: Scotland Yard in Cumbria to investigate a murder only to stumble upon a nefarious plot in which a duplicitous wife meets a scheming young playwright willing to sell off her womb like a room to let. There were shades of prostitution here as well, Zed reckoned. For if Lucy Keverne was selling one part of her body, didn't it stand to reason that at one time or another she'd been selling other parts of her body as well?

Since Zed's route took him by the Crow and Eagle, he pulled into its car park. They'd have an Internet connection here, wireless or otherwise, because how likely was it that a hotel hoping to stay in business in this day and age existed sans a connection to the Web? No hotel at all. He put his money on that.

He had no laptop with him, but that wasn't going to matter. He intended to hand over a wad of cash for the use of the hotel's computer. At this time of year there weren't going to be hordes of potential tourists sending enquiries to the place via e-mails needing instantaneous answers. Twenty minutes online was all he required. He'd fine-tune the piece once Rod read it. And Rod *would* read it. For as soon as Zed was finished with the piece, he'd fire it off to his editor and ring him as well.

Zed zipped into the car park and gathered up his notes. These he always carried with him. They were his stock in trade, his jewels, his little precious. Where he went, they went, for the simple reason that one never knew where a story would appear.

Inside the place, he approached the reception desk with his wallet out and his money ready. He counted out one hundred pounds. He'd put it on his expense account later. Right now, though, there was a story waiting.

He leaned over her desk and put the money onto the keyboard of the young woman's computer. Its screen was on, but she hadn't been using it. Instead, she'd been yammering on the phone to someone apparently requiring information about the exact dimensions of every bedroom in the place. She looked at Zed, then at the money, then at Zed. She said, "Moment, please," into the phone and held the earpiece against her bony shoulder as she waited for Zed's explanation.

He gave it quickly enough. And she was quick enough to decide. She rang off on whoever had been at the other end of her phone conversation, scooped up the money, and said, "Let voice mail take the calls if any come in. You won't say . . . ?" and she gestured round to complete her question.

"You've gone to see about a room for me," he assured her. "I've just booked in and you're letting me use this thing to check for crucial messages. Twenty minutes?"

She nodded. She pocketed the ten- and twenty-pound notes and headed for the stairs to play her part. He waited till she'd mounted them and made the turn round the landing before he began to write.

The story led in every direction. Its parts were like tributaries pouring into the Amazon, and all he had to do was paddle up them. He began to do so.

He went first with the Scotland Yard angle and the irony attached to it: A detective sent up to Cumbria to investigate the drowning of Ian Cresswell ends up stumbling upon an illegal surrogacy deal that could—bet on it—lead to an entire illegal surrogacy ring that fed on the desperation of couples struggling to conceive. Then he touched on the artistic angle: The struggling playwright so desperate to support herself that she was willing to sell her body in pursuit of the higher calling of her art. He moved directly from there to the deception angle and was pounding away at the tale of Nick Fairclough's ignorance in the matter of his wife's deal with Lucy Keverne when his cell phone rang.

Yaffa! he thought. He needed to tell her that all was well. She would be worrying about him. She would want to encourage him. She would have words of wisdom and he wanted to hear them and more than that he wanted to interrupt her with the news of his impending triumph.

"Got it," he said. "Darling, it's hot."

"I didn't know you and I were that close," Rodney Aronson said. "Where the bloody hell are you? Why aren't you back in London by now?"

Zed stopped typing. "I'm not in London," he said, "because I've got the story. All of it. From bloody alpha to sodding omega. Hold the front page because you're going to want this plastered across it."

"What is it?" Rodney didn't sound like a man experiencing a come-to-Jesus moment.

Zed rattled it all off: the surrogacy deal, the starving artist, the husband in ignorance. He saved the very best for last: the humble reporter—that would be me, he pointed out—working hand-in-glove with the detective from New Scotland Yard.

"She and I cornered the woman in Lancaster," Zed announced. "And once we had her—"

"Hang on," Rodney said. "'She and I'?"

"Right. The Scotland Yard detective and I. She's called DS Cotter. Detective sergeant. She's the one investigating the Cresswell death. Only she got sidetracked onto Nick Fairclough and his wife and as it turned out, that was a dynamite direction. Not for her, of course, but for me."

Rodney said nothing at his end. Zed waited for the kudos to flow. He waited in vain. For a moment he thought they'd been cut off. He said, "Rod? You there?"

Rodney finally said, "You are one fucking loser, Zedekiah. You know that, don't you? One fucking class-A loser."

"Sorry?"

"There *is* no Detective Cotter, you idiot."

"But—"

"Detective Inspector *Lynley* is up there, the bloke whose wife took a bullet from a twelve-year-old kid last winter. Sound familiar? It was front-page news for two weeks." He didn't wait for Zed to make a reply. Instead he went on with, "Jesus, you are pathetic, you know? Get back to town. Collect your wages. You and *The Source* are through."

ARNSIDE
CUMBRIA

Alatea saw them in the driveway. Their body language told her everything. This was not a conversation between strangers who happen to come upon each other in passing at the same destination. This was an exchange between colleagues, friends, or associates. The exchange was one of information shared. She could tell this much when the woman tilted her head towards Arnside House in the manner of someone speaking about it. Or, more likely, speaking about a person within it. Or, most likely, speaking about her. About Alatea, once Santiago. About her past and what would now be her future.

Alatea didn't wait to see anything more pass between the woman and the man from Scotland Yard. Her world was collapsing so quickly around her that the only idea she had in her mind was flight. She would have run like a lioness in pursuit of food if she had a single place she could go, but her routes were limited so she was forced to calm herself long enough to think, just to *think*.

The woman needed confirmation of Alatea's identity.

The detective, obviously, would give it, courtesy of Alatea herself, who could have denied, who *should* have denied, but who had not thought quickly enough to deny. That much was established, for what else could they have to discuss with each other? The only questions that possibly remained were those that Alatea herself could ask. Had the woman outside with the Scotland Yard detective sent photos of Alatea to Raul Montenegro already? If she had not, was she open to bribery, a payment for maintaining silence, for reporting to Raul that Santiago Vasquez y del Torres, who had become Alatea Vasquez y del Torres, who had married Nicholas Fairclough to escape a past that tied her to a man she had learned to hate, was not in Cumbria, was not in England, was nowhere in the UK to be found? If she was open to bribery, Alatea was safe. Only for now, of course. But now was all she had.

She ran to the stairway. She flew to the bedroom she shared with Nicholas and from beneath the bed, she brought out a locked box. A key from her dressing table gained her access, and within the box she had money. Not a lot, not a fortune, not what Raul was paying to find her, surely. But along with her jewellery, perhaps there was enough to tempt this woman who was closing in now, who was hearing the truth from the detective even as Alatea gathered what she could to keep that truth from spilling out of the hidden corners of her life.

She was back downstairs when the expected knock sounded against the front door. The woman would not know Alatea had seen her in conversation with Inspector Lynley. For a moment this gave Alatea the upper hand, and she intended to use it.

She pressed her slick hands against her trouser legs. She closed her eyes briefly and said, *"Dios mio por favor,"* and then she opened the door with as much assurance as she could muster.

The red-haired woman spoke first, saying, "Mrs. Fairclough, I've not been truthful with you. May I come in and explain?"

"What do you want from me?" For her part, Alatea was

stiff and formal. There was *nothing* to shame her, she told herself. She had already paid the price of Raul's help in altering her body. She would not pay more.

"I've been following you and watching you," the woman said. "You must know that—"

"What is he paying you?" Alatea asked.

"There's no money involved."

"There's always money involved. I can't afford to pay what he's paying, but I ask you . . . No, I beg you . . ." Alatea turned from the woman to where she'd placed the strongbox and her jewellery. "I have this," she said as she scooped up these things. "I can give you this."

The woman took a step backwards. She said, "I don't want these things. I'm here only to—"

"You must take them. And then you must leave. You don't know him. You cannot know what people like him are capable of."

The woman thought, her brows drawn together and her eyes on Alatea as she weighed the words she'd heard. Alatea thrust the money and the jewellery at her once again, but the woman nodded and she said, "Ah. I do see. I'm afraid it might be too late, Mrs. Fairclough. Some things are unstoppable and I think he could be one of them. There's a desperation to him . . . He doesn't say exactly but I get the impression there's a lot on the line for him just now."

"He'd make you believe that. That's how he is. It was clever of him to use a woman. For reassurance, he thinks. To calm my fears. While all the while his intention is to destroy me. He has the power to do this and he intends to use it."

"There's no story, though. No real story. Not a story that a paper like *The Source* would care about."

"And this is supposed to reassure me?" Alatea demanded. "What does a story in *The Source* have to do with anything? What does it have to do with what he's asking of you? You've photographed me, haven't you? You've followed me and you've photographed me and that's the proof he wants."

"You don't understand," the other woman said. "He doesn't need proof. These types never do. Proof is nothing to them. They start their business just this side of the law and if they slip over onto the other side, they have a score of solicitors to take care of the problem."

"Then let me buy your photos," Alatea said. "If he sees them, if he sees me in them . . ." She took off her wedding rings, the diamond and the band. She took off a large emerald that Valerie Fairclough had given her as a wedding gift. She said, "Here. Please. Take these as well. In exchange for your photos."

"But photos are nothing. They're meaningless without words. It's the words that count. It's what's written that counts. And anyway, I don't want your money and I don't want your jewellery. I just want to apologise for . . . well, for everything but especially for how I might have ruined things for you. We're much the same, you and I. With different cause, I daresay, but otherwise the same."

Alatea clung to what an apology from this woman might mean. She said, "So you won't tell him?"

The woman looked regretful. "I'm afraid he knows. That's the point. That's why I've come. I want you to be ready for what might come next and to know it's my fault and to know how terribly sorry I am. I tried to keep things from him, but these people have ways of finding things out and once he came to Cumbria . . . I'm so sorry, Mrs. Fairclough."

Alatea took this in fully and realised what it meant, not only to her but to Nicky and to their life together. She said, "He's *here*, in Cumbria?"

"He's been here for days. I thought you would have known. Didn't he—"

"*Where* is he now? Tell me."

"Windermere, I think. Other than that, I don't know."

Nothing else remained to be said, but many things remained to be done. Alatea said good-bye to the woman and like someone in a dream, she gathered everything she'd brought down from the bedroom in the hope of bribing her. It was just as well, she thought, that the woman had refused her offerings. She would need them now herself in the coming days, for she'd run out of options.

She went back up the stairs to the bedroom and threw

the jewellery and money onto the bed. From the box room at the end of the corridor, she brought out a small valise. There was little enough time to gather the things she would need.

Back in the bedroom, she went to the chest of drawers. It stood between two windows and the sound of a car door slamming outside drew her attention to the front of the house again. She saw that, on the worst possible day, Nicky had come home from the pele project early. He was now in conversation with the red-haired woman. He was violent faced. His voice grew loud although through the glass of the window, Alatea could not understand his words.

But understanding the words didn't matter. Only the fact that they were speaking to each other mattered. That in conjunction with Nicky's expression gave testimony to the topic between them. Seeing this, Alatea saw also that even when it came to escape, she was out of options. She could not leave in her car, for Nicky and the woman stood on the fan of gravel across which she would need to drive. She could not go by foot to the railway station at the far end of Arnside village, for the only route there went directly between her husband and the woman where they stood talking. So she prayed for some kind of answer to come to her and she paced the room until she saw it. It was through the window, just as the vision of Nicky and the red-haired woman had been. But it was the window on a wall perpendicular to that which overlooked the driveway. This window offered a view of the lawn and beyond it the seawall sketched a stony line of demarcation between the lawn and the sea walk along the bay, beyond which was the bay itself.

Today was one of the days during which the tide had ebbed for miles. This meant the remaining sands were hers. She could cross them and make for Grange-over-Sands a few miles away. Another railway station awaited her there. All she needed to do was to reach it.

Just a few miles, then. That was all she needed, and she would be free.

WINDERMERE
CUMBRIA

Tim had spent the night beneath a caravan at Fallbarrow Park, at the edge of the lake. On his way there from Shots!, he'd pinched a blanket from the Windermere fire station, where a smoke-scented stack of them just inside an open door seemed like a message telling him that here were his means of passing the time until Toy4You was ready for him. He himself was ready for Toy4You. He felt the need for escape like a weight on his chest. Soon, he told himself, he'd have the only answer he'd wanted to the question that his life had become since Kaveh Mehran had sauntered into it.

The caravan provided him shelter from the night's rain, and against a tyre and huddled into his stolen blanket, he escaped the worst of the cold. Thus he'd slept rough and when he returned to the business centre towards the end of an afternoon the day of which he'd spent sulking round the town, he looked as bad as he felt, most of his bones aching and every inch of him reeking.

Toy4You directed one glance at him and had one whiff of him and said, in brief, "No way in hell." He pointed him in the direction of the loo, told him to do what he could to make himself less malodorous, and when Tim emerged he handed him three twenty-pound notes. "Go into town and get something decent to wear," he told him. "If you think you're going to meet your fellow actors looking like that, think again. They won't want anything to do with you."

Tim said, "What's the problem? It's not like we'll have our clothes on, is it?"

Toy4You made a thin line of his lips. "Get something to eat, as well. I don't want you complaining in the middle of things that you've missed your dinner."

"I'm not going to complain."

"That's where they all begin."

"Fuck," Tim said as he took the money. "Whatever."

"Exactly right," Toy4You said sardonically. "That's the spirit, mate. Fuck whatever."

When he left Shots!, Tim headed back for the shops. He found, oddly enough, that he was hungry. He'd thought it unlikely he'd ever be eating again, but a hunger came on him as he passed the fire station again and the scent of bacon on the grill formed a cloud through which he passed. The smell made his mouth water unexpectedly. It put him in mind of breakfasts in his childhood: hot bacon rolls and scrambled eggs. His stomach rumbled accordingly. Okay, he thought, so he would find something to eat. He'd get the clothing first, though. He knew where an Oxfam was in the centre of town, and that would do when it came to trousers and some kind of jersey. No way in hell was he about to purchase something new from one of the other shops. Waste of money, that. He wouldn't need new clothes after today.

At Oxfam he found a pair of old corduroy trousers, worn in the arse, but they were in his size and that was good enough for Tim. To this he added a polo-neck sweater and as he already had shoes, socks, and an anorak, he needed nothing else. The purchase left him with plenty of money to buy a meal, but he reckoned he'd just get a sandwich from the grocery, perhaps a bag of Kettle Chips and a drink as well. The rest he'd post to Gracie inside a card. He'd write a message about taking care of herself first and worrying about the rest of the world later because *no one*, he would tell her, was about to take care of her no matter how nice she tried to be to them. Then he'd apologise about Bella. He still felt dead awful that he'd damaged Bella. He hoped the woman at the electronics repair shop could fix her properly.

It was funny, though, Tim thought as he left Oxfam with his purchases and made for the grocery. He was actually feeling a bit lighter. He'd made a decision and relief came with it. It was odd to consider that for so very long he'd felt so terribly wretched when all he ever had had to do was simply decide.

WINDERMERE
CUMBRIA

They had to wait nearly a half hour at the police station in Windermere, which was where Freddie drove them. They had Tim's laptop with them as well as the map the boy had printed out. Both of them had thought that simply walking into the police station and announcing they had information about a child pornography ring was going to light a serious conflagration under someone's office chair, but that had not been the case. Like a doctor's surgery, they had to wait their turn and as each moment passed, Manette's anxiety climbed roofward.

"It's all right, old girl," Freddie had murmured more than once. He'd taken to holding her hand as well, and he made gentle finger circles upon it, just as he'd done in the early days of their marriage. "We'll manage it all in time."

"Whatever *it* is," Manette said. "Freddie, you and I both know it could already have happened. It could be going on while we're waiting here. He could be . . . they could be . . . I blame Niamh for this."

"No point in blaming," Freddie said quietly. "That's not going to get us the boy."

When at last they were ushered into an office, Freddie quickly logged on to Tim's e-mail and brought up the exchanges the boy had had with Toy4You as well as the photos and videos that had been sent to him. Once again and ever the gentleman, Freddie made sure that Manette couldn't see what the films were, but she could tell from the expression on the constable's face that they were indeed as bad as Freddie had indicated.

The constable picked up a phone and punched in three numbers. He said to whoever answered, "Connie, you're going to want to look at a laptop I've got my paws on . . . Will do." He rang off and said to Freddie and Manette, "Five minutes."

"Who's Connie?" Manette asked.

"Superintendent Connie Calva," he said. "Head of Vice. Have anything else?"

Manette remembered the map. She fished it out of her bag and handed it over. She said, "Tim had this amongst the things on his desk. Freddie thought it best to bring it. I don't know how useful . . . I mean, we don't know the streets involved. They could be anywhere."

Freddie said, "I reckoned you'd have someone who could go back and find the map Tim began with. This is an enlargement he printed. The full map should be easy enough to find for someone better versed than I am in Internet maps."

The constable took it from Freddie, reaching into his desk simultaneously and bringing out a magnifying glass. It was the oddest thing for him to have, Manette thought, harking back to Sherlock Holmes. But he made a reasonable use of it, applying it to the map in order to read the names of the streets more clearly. He was saying as he did all this, "This sort of thing's usually done in Barrow, at the constabulary. We've a forensic computer specialist there and . . . Ah. Hang on. This is easy enough."

He looked up at them as a woman in jeans, knee-high leather boots, and a tartan plaid waistcoat stepped into the room, presumably Superintendent Calva. She said, "What've we got, Ewan?" and nodded to Manette and Freddie.

Ewan handed over the laptop and waved the map at her as well. "Enough of the bad nasty on that to make you fear lightning strikes from God," he said in reference to the computer. "And this is a printout map of the area round the business centre."

"You know where these streets are?" Manette asked. It seemed too much to hope for.

"Oh, aye," Ewan said. "They're right here in town. Not ten minutes away."

Manette grabbed Freddie's arm but spoke to the constable. "We must go there at once. They intend to film him. They'll be doing it there. We must stop them."

The constable held up his hand. "Bit of trouble with that route," he said.

Connie Calva had gone to a desk nearby and had begun to study the laptop as she removed a piece of gum from its silver wrapper and folded it into her mouth. She wore the weary expression of a woman who'd already seen it all, but that expression altered as she moved from image to image. Manette could tell when she'd reached the videos. She stopped chewing. Her face altered to a careful blank.

"What sort of trouble?" Freddie was asking in the meantime.

"These streets are lined with private homes and B & B's. There's a fire station there and, like I said, a business centre as well. We can't go barging in left and right without something to go on. The laptop's filled with it, aye, but how d'you make the connection between the laptop and this map aside from the user having found the map online? D'you see what I mean? Now you've brought us some excellent information, and Superintendent Calva will get onto it directly. And when we know more—"

"But the boy is missing," Manette cried. "He's been gone for over twenty-four hours. And with this on his computer and a blatant invitation to be part of a film in which God only knows what is about to happen . . . He's fourteen years old."

The constable said, "Got that. But we've the rule of law—"

"Bugger the law!" Manette cried. "*Do* something."

She felt Freddie then. His arm went round her waist. "Ah yes," he said. "We see."

She cried, "Are you mad?"

"They've got to follow their procedure."

"But, Freddie—"

"Manette . . ." His gaze shifted to the door, and his eyebrows rose. "Let's let them get on with it, eh?"

She knew that he was asking for her trust, but in that moment she trusted no one. Still, she couldn't take her eyes off Freddie, who was on her side in all things. She haltingly said, "Yes, yes, all right," and once they'd given every possible piece of information they could to the constable and to Superintendent Calva, they went out to the street.

"What?" Manette said to Freddie in anguish. *"What?"*

"We need a map of the town," Freddie told her, "which we should be able to find in a bookshop easily enough."

"And then?" she asked him.

"Then we need a plan," he said. "Either that or one monumental, excellent piece of luck."

WINDERMERE
CUMBRIA

They had the latter. The police station was on the outskirts of town, straddling Bowness-on-Windermere and Windermere itself. When they left the station, Freddie drove farther into Windermere, and they were travelling up Lake Road just coming upon New Road when Manette spotted Tim. He was leaving a small grocery, a striped blue and white plastic bag in his hands. He was inspecting its contents, and he fished inside to bring out a bag of crisps, which he proceeded to tear open with his teeth.

Manette cried, "There he is! Pull over, Freddie."

"Hang on, old girl." Freddie drove on.

She cried, "But what are you—" and she squirmed in her seat. "We'll lose him!"

A short distance along, Freddie pulled to the kerb, once Tim was safely behind them and walking in the opposite direction. He said to Manette, "You've got your mobile?"

"Of course. But, Freddie—"

"Listen, darling. There's more involved here than just scooping up Tim."

"But he's in danger."

"As are a lot of other children. You have your mobile. Set it to vibrate and follow him. I'll park and ring you. All right? He should lead us to wherever they're going to film, if that's what he's here for."

She saw logic in this, cool and clear-headed Freddie logic. She said, "Yes, yes, of course. You're right," and grabbed her bag and made certain of her mobile. She started to get out of the car but then she stopped and turned to him.

"What?" he said.

"You're the most wonderful man, Freddie McGhie," she told him. "Nothing that's happened before this moment matters as much."

"As much as what?"

"As my loving you." She shut the car door smartly before he replied.

ARNSIDE
CUMBRIA

Nicholas Fairclough made very short order of letting Deborah feel his wrath. He jerked his car to a halt in the driveway and leapt out onto the gravel. He strode towards her saying, "Who the hell *are* you, then? What are you doing here?" For a man whose previous meetings with her had been conducted in such a mild-mannered fashion, Fairclough was completely transformed. If eyes could be said to blaze, his were doing just that. "Where is he? How much time do we have?"

Deborah felt pinned by the ferocity of the questions and only able to express herself inarticulately. She stammered, "I don't know . . . How long do these things take? I'm not sure. Mr. Fairclough, I tried . . . You see, I did tell him there was no story to be had because that's the truth of the matter. There is no story."

Fairclough drew himself up at that, as if Deborah had placed her hand on his chest to stop him. He said, "Story? What? Who the hell *are* you? Christ, d'you work for *The Source* as well? Montenegro didn't send you?"

Deborah frowned. "*The Source*? No. That's something entirely . . . Who on earth's Montenegro?"

Nicholas looked from her to Arnside House and back to her. "Who the hell *are* you?" he demanded.

"Deborah St. James, as I always was. As I said I was."

"But there's no film. There's no documentary. We've worked that out. There's bloody *nothing* you've told us that's true. So what do you want? What do you know? You've been to Lancaster with that bloke from *The Source*. He's told me as much. Or can I not believe him, either?"

Deborah licked her lips. It was cold and damp and miserable out of doors and the fog was becoming thicker as they spoke. She wanted a coal fire and something hot to drink if only to hold the cup in her hands, but she couldn't leave with Fairclough blocking her way, and her only option left was the truth.

She was there to help the Scotland Yard detective, she informed Nicholas Fairclough. She'd come with her husband, a forensic specialist who evaluated evidence during investigations. The newsman from *The Source* had, for some reason, concluded that she was the detective from the Met and she'd let him think that in order to give the real detective and her husband time to do the work they'd come to do regarding the death of Ian Cresswell undisturbed by a tabloid.

"I don't know anyone called Montenegro," she concluded. "I've never heard of him. If it is a him, and I daresay it is? Who is he?"

"Raul Montenegro. Someone trying to find my wife."

"So that's what she meant," Deborah murmured.

"You've talked to her?"

"At cross purposes, I expect," Deborah said. "She must have thought we were speaking of this Raul Montenegro while I thought we were speaking of the reporter from *The Source*. I'm afraid I told her he's in Windermere, but I meant the reporter."

"Oh my God." Fairclough headed towards the house, saying over his shoulder. "Where is she now?"

"Inside," and as he began to jog towards the door, "Mr. Fairclough? One thing more?"

He stopped, turned. She said, "I tried to tell her this. I tried to apologise. What I mean is . . . The surrogacy situation? You've absolutely nothing to fear. I told Mr. Benjamin there was no story in it and there isn't. And besides, I completely and utterly understand. We're rather . . . Your wife and I . . . We're rather sisters in this matter."

He stared at her. He was pasty faced anyway, but Deborah saw that now all colour had left his lips as well, rendering him ghostlike in appearance, aided by the fog that curled at his feet. "Sisters," he said.

"Yes indeed. I, too, so much want a baby and I haven't been able to—"

But he was gone before she was able to conclude.

WINDERMERE
CUMBRIA

When Tim returned to Shots!, Toy4You was behind the counter chatting with an Anglican priest. They both turned as Tim entered the shop, and the priest gave him the kind of once-over that spoke of an evaluation being made. Tim concluded he was there as a fellow actor for Toy4You's film, and he registered this with a lurch of his gut that rapidly formed itself into a hot ball of anger. A fucking vicar, he thought. Just another bleeding hypocrite like the rest of the world. This pathetic excuse for a human being stood up in front of a congregation every Sunday and did his bit with the Word of God and handed out communion wafers and then on the side when no one was the wiser off he went to do his filthy business with—

"Daddy! Daddy!" Into the shop burst two children—a boy and a girl—in neat school uniforms and behind them a woman looking rather harried and studying her watch and saying, "Darling, I am *so* terribly sorry. Are we too late?" She went to the priest and kissed his cheek and linked her arm through his.

The priest said, "Mags, ninety minutes. Really," and sighed. "Well, William and I have examined Abraham and Isaac, Esau and Jacob, Ruth and Naomi and the alien corn, and the brothers of Joseph from every angle, and it's been most illuminating and—I think that William will agree—entertaining as well. But, alas, you *are* too late now. We'll have to rearrange. William's got something on, and I've an appointment as well."

Murmurs of apology, profuse, from the wife. Children hanging upon the priest's either hand. A rescheduling of the family's annual Christmas picture to be sent to all the relatives and off they went.

Tim was hanging back, lurking in a corner of the shop with the pretence of examining the digital cameras all locked to their display shelves and rather in need of dusting. When the priest and his family made their noisy, happy exit, Tim came forward. *William Concord* was on Toy4You's name tag. Tim wondered what it meant that the bloke kept it on as he approached. He reckoned it had nothing to do with having forgotten to remove it. Toy4You wasn't a forgetful kind of man.

He came round the counter and locked the door of the shop. He reversed the *Open* sign to *Closed.* He turned off the overhead lights and jerked his head to indicate that Tim was to follow him into the back.

Tim saw that the back of the shop had been altered, and it was little wonder that Toy4You wasn't able to accommodate the priest and his family for their yearly photo. A man and a woman were in the process of setting up an entirely different design from what had been in the studio, and now a rough replica of a Victorian children's nursery stood in place of the dramatic columns and background sky. As Tim watched them at work, they brought in three narrow beds, one of them occupied by a child-sized department store mannequin wearing Shrek pyjamas and, oddly, a schoolboy cap. The other two were empty and at the foot of one the woman laid an enormous stuffed dog, a St. Bernard by the look of it. The man rolled into position a faux background window that opened onto a starry night sky, and in the distance, a crude representation of Big Ben shone with the hour midnight.

Tim didn't know what to make of all this until another individual materialised from the storage area. Like Tim, he was a young adolescent. Unlike Tim, he was very sure of himself and moved with purpose onto the set, where he leaned against the mock window and lit a cigarette. He was outfitted head to foot in green, with slippers that curled up at the toes and a cocked hat set at a jaunty angle on his head. He jerked his chin in a hello to Toy4You as the other two individuals faded through the storage area, from which Tim could hear the murmur of conversation and the sound of shoes and clothes dropping to the floor. As Toy4You did some business with a rolling tripod and a rather impressive video camera, the man and the woman returned to the set. She was now in a white nightdress with a high ruffled neck. He was outfitted as a pirate captain. Unlike the other two, he was the only one wearing a mask, although the hook that emerged from his right sleeve was enough of a clue to the permanently clueless as to the bloke's supposed identity. Of course, the permanently clueless would never wonder what he was meant to be doing in Victorian London instead of where he should have been which was, naturally, on a sailing ship in Never Never Land.

Tim looked from these characters to Toy4You. He felt momentarily queasy as he wondered what his part was supposed to entail. Then he spied a nightshirt lying at the foot of one of the beds with a pair of round-framed spectacles folded on top, and from this he understood that he was the older of the two brothers and at some point meant to put on the costume provided.

It all seemed the height of stupid to Tim, but there was a modicum of relief in the setup. When he'd seen the Last Supper film and the Jesus-in-the-garden piece, he'd reckoned they'd be engaged in something equally blasphemous here, although he hadn't liked to think what it would be. And while he truly didn't much care at this point whether the subject of their film was going to be blasphemous or not, he'd rather worried over the possibility that his upbringing *would* out at the very last moment, and he'd find himself unable to perform according to whatever directions would be recited to him from the other side of the camera.

He needn't have worried as things turned out. As Wendy moved onto the nursery set and Captain Hook took up a position off-camera, Toy4You approached Tim with a small glass of water, which he handed over. From his pocket, he took a vial and from the vial, he shook out two different pills. He gave them to Tim with a nod that indicated he was meant to swallow them.

"What're . . . ?"

"Something to help with authentic close-ups," Toy4You said. "Among other things."

"What d'they do?"

A smile flicked at the corners of his mouth. Whiskers grew there. He hadn't shaved well that day. "They aid with the performance we require of you. Go ahead. Take them. You'll see soon enough how they work, and I expect you'll enjoy their effect."

"But—"

Toy4You's voice altered. He whispered fiercely, "Take them, goddamn it. This is what you wanted so bloody *do* it. We've not got all night."

Tim swallowed them. He felt nothing and wondered if they were something to make him relax or to make him unconscious. Were they the date-rape drug? Was that a pill? He wasn't sure. He said, "Do I put on that nightshirt? I'm John Darling, aren't I?"

"You're only half-stupid then," Toy4You said. "Just stand by the camera till you get the call."

"What call?"

"Christ. Shut up and see." And to Peter Pan and Wendy, he said, "You two ready?" And without waiting for an answer, he moved behind the camera and the other young boy and the nightgowned woman took up position: the boy on the edge of the windowsill and the woman kneeling upright on the bed.

Tim saw from the lighting that her nightgown was so sheer that all of her was visible through it. He swallowed and wanted to look away, but he found he couldn't for she was lifting the nightgown slowly and sensually over her head as Peter Pan advanced upon her. She presented her breasts to him and Toy4You said, "Now," to Tim.

"But what'm I s'posed to *do*?" he asked desperately, even as he felt the stirring within him as all of his organs began doing what they were meant by nature to do.

"Getting to bed a bit late, you are," Toy4You murmured as he filmed the action on Wendy's bed, where she was lowering Peter's tights and Peter was presenting himself to the camera. She began to minister to him. "Up to the wee hours reading in the library, you were. Into the nursery you go, only to find your sister and Peter Pan in the midst of tut tut tut. But you fancy Peter yourself once you see what he's got on him, you do."

"So I . . . ? What do I do?"

"Fuck it, just go onto the set. Follow your inclinations, for God's sake. I know you have them. We both know you have them."

And the worst was he did. He *did*. Because even as they were holding their whispered conversation, Tim couldn't tear his eyes away from what was being filmed. And he didn't know what it meant that Peter unveiled himself engorged with blood and Tim kept watching and his body kept reacting and he *wanted* to watch and he wanted something else only he didn't know what it was.

"Go. Bloody go," Toy4You said. "Peter and Wendy will show you what to do." He looked away from the camera for a moment, directing his gaze to Tim's crotch. He smiled. "Ah. The miracles of modern medicine. Don't worry about a thing."

"What about him?" Tim asked as Toy4You turned back to the camera.

"Who?"

"The . . . Captain . . . You know . . ."

"Don't worry about him either. He fancies Peter. Always has done. Fancies all the Lost Boys. Fancies you as well. He'll show up and sort you out for consorting with Peter once Wendy exits stage right. Okay? You got it? Now get bloody in there because we're wasting time."

"How's he going to sort me?"

Toy4You shot him a look. "Exactly the way you've wanted to be sorted from the first. All right? Got it?"

"But you said you would—"

"Fuck it, you idiot. What did you really expect? Death on a biscuit? Now go. *Go*."

MILNTHORPE
CUMBRIA

Deborah drove back to the Crow and Eagle in Milnthorpe as the fog began to billow across the road in a great grey mass like the effluent of a thousand smokestacks somewhere out in the bay. The railway viaduct that took trains into the Arnside station was only a shadowy form that she passed beneath on her way out of the village, and Milnthorpe Sands was entirely lost to view with only the wading birds closest to shore punctuating the grey with a darkness that huddled and shifted in a solid mass as if the ground itself were sighing.

The headlamps of cars did little to pierce the gloom, merely reflecting the light back onto the driver. When, occasionally, a pedestrian was present—foolhardy enough to be walking along the verge in such weather—he emerged without warning as if popping out of the ground like a Halloween ghoul. It was an unnerving experience to be on the road. Deborah was grateful when she reached the car park of the inn without incident.

Tommy was waiting for her as he'd promised. He was in the bar with a coffee service in front of him and his mobile pressed to his ear. His head was bent and he didn't see her, but she caught the remainder of his conversation.

"Quite late," he was saying. "Shall I come to you anyway? I've no idea of the time and perhaps you'd rather . . . Yes. All right . . . Quite anxious as well. Isabelle, I'm terribly sorry how this has . . . Indeed. Very well. Later, then. Right . . ." He listened for a moment and evidently felt Deborah's presence for he turned in his chair and saw her approaching. He said, "She's just arrived so I daresay we'll be off in a few moments," with a raised eyebrow in Deborah's direction, to which she nodded. "Very good," he said. "Yes. I have the key with me."

He rang off. Deborah wasn't sure what to say. Two months earlier, she'd concluded that Tommy was sleeping with his superior officer. What she hadn't worked out was how she felt about the fact. It was a given that Tommy had to move on with his life, but the *how* of his moving on was something that made her unsure of her footing with him.

She settled for, "Could I have a coffee before we leave, Tommy? I promise to swill it like a priest going after the altar wine."

"Swilling won't be necessary," he replied. "I'll have another. I'd prefer both of us wide awake for the drive. It's going to be a long one."

She sat as he went to place the order. He'd been doodling

on a paper napkin, she saw, as he'd spoken to Isabelle Ardery in London. He'd sketched a rough cottage in a wide meadow somewhere, with two smaller buildings and a stream nearby and hillsides rising on either side. Not bad by the look of it, she thought. She'd never considered Tommy as an artist.

"A second calling," she said to him, indicating the sketch when he turned to the table.

"One of a thousand similar places in Cornwall."

"Thinking of going home?"

"Not quite yet." He sat, smiled at her fondly, and said, "Someday, I suppose." He reached for the napkin, folded it, and put it into the breast pocket of his jacket. "I've rung Simon," he told her. "He knows we'll be coming home."

"And?"

"Well, of course, he finds you the most maddening sort of woman. But, then, don't we all?"

She sighed, saying, "Yes. Well. I think I've made things worse, Tommy."

"Between you and Simon?"

"No, no. I'll put that right. It does help to be married to the most tolerant man on the planet. But I'm talking about Nicholas Fairclough and his wife. I've had an awkward conversation with her, followed by an awkward conversation with her husband."

She told him about both conversations, sketching in all the details as she remembered them, including the reactions of both Alatea and her husband. She explained Alatea's offer of jewellery and money and she included the revelation about the man Montenegro. Tommy listened as he always had done, his brown eyes fixed on hers. Their coffee service came as she was talking. He poured them both a cup as she was concluding.

Her final words were, "So all along, Alatea apparently thought I was talking about this Raul Montenegro while I thought we were talking about the reporter from *The Source*. I suppose it wouldn't have mattered much, except for the fact that I told her he was in Windermere—at least I think that's where he went when he dropped me here after Lancaster—

and when I told her that, she simply panicked, obviously thinking I meant Montenegro. Nicholas panicked as well."

Lynley added a packet of sugar to his coffee. He stirred it, looking thoughtful all the while. Indeed, he looked so thoughtful that Deborah understood something she should have recognised earlier.

She said to him, "You know what's actually going on with these people, don't you, Tommy? I expect you've known from the first. Whatever it is, I wish you'd told me. At least I could have refrained from blundering in and doing whatever it is I've now managed to do to them."

Lynley shook his head. "Actually, no. I think I've known less than you since I'd not met Alatea before today."

"She's beautiful, isn't she?"

"She's quite . . ." He seemed to search for a better word, perhaps a more accurate one. He lifted his fingers as if to say that any choice he made would not do her justice. He settled on, "Rather amazing, actually. Had I not known about her before going to see her, I would never have believed she began life as a man."

Deborah felt her jaw loosen with the surprise that swept through her. She said, "What?"

"Santiago Vasquez y del Torres. That's who she was."

"What do you mean *was*? Is she impersonating . . . ?"

"No. She had surgery, financed by this bloke Montenegro. His intention, apparently, was to have her play his female lover in public to maintain his reputation and social position but, in private, to make love to her as a male to a male."

Deborah swallowed. "Dear God." She thought about Lancaster, about Lucy Keverne, about what she and Alatea Fairclough could have and must have actually planned between them. She said, "But Nicholas . . . Surely he knows?"

"She hasn't told him."

"Oh, surely, Tommy, he'd be able to tell. I mean . . . Good heavens . . . There'd be signs, wouldn't there? There'd be marks of incisions, scars, whatever."

"In the hands of a world-class surgeon? With all the tools

at hand? With lasers to deal with potential scarring? Deborah, everything would be altered. Even the Adam's apple can go. If the man's appearance was feminine to begin with—because of an extra X chromosome perhaps—then the shift to female would be even simpler."

"But not to tell Nicholas? Why wouldn't she have told him?"

"Desperation? Worry? Fear of his reaction? Fear of rejection? With Montenegro looking for her and apparently having the funds to go on looking indefinitely, she would need a safe place. To achieve it, she allowed Nicholas to believe what he wanted to believe about her. She married, giving her the right to remain in England once she came here."

Deborah saw how this fitted in with what Tommy and Simon had come to Cumbria to do. She said, "Ian Cresswell? Did she murder him? Did he know?"

Lynley shook his head. "Consider her, Deborah. She's something of a masterpiece. No one would know unless there was a reason to delve back into her past, and there was no reason. For all intents and purposes, she's Nicholas Fairclough's wife. If anyone bore looking into with regard to Ian's death, it would have been Nicholas. As things happened, we didn't need to go that far because Simon was right from the first and so was the coroner. There's not a single sign of Ian Cresswell's death being anything other than an accident. Someone may have wanted him to die. His death might have been a convenience to more than one person. But no one orchestrated it."

Deborah said, "And now that terrible reporter's going to write his story about this surrogacy situation and Alatea's photo will be in the paper and I'm *responsible*. What can I do?"

"Appeal to his better angels?"

"He works for *The Source*, Tommy."

"There is that," he admitted.

Her mobile rang. Deborah hoped it was Zed Benjamin, reporting on a change of heart. Or perhaps Simon, telling her he understood the passions that had driven her to make such a mess of things at Arnside House. But it turned out to be Nicholas Fairclough, and he was in a panic. "What've you *done* to her?"

Deborah's first horrified thought was that Alatea Fairclough had harmed herself. She said, "What's happened, Mr. Fairclough?" and she looked at Tommy.

"She's gone. I've searched the house and the grounds. Her car is still here and she couldn't have passed us in the driveway without being seen. I've walked the length of the seawall as well. She's gone."

"She'll be back. She won't have gone far. How could she have done, with the weather so bad?"

"She's gone onto the sands."

"Surely not."

"I tell you, she's gone onto the sands. She has to have done. It's the only place."

"She's taken a walk, then. To have a think. She'll be back soon and when she comes back, you can tell her I was talking about the reporter from *The Source*, not Raul Montenegro."

"You don't understand," he cried. "God in heaven, you don't understand! She's not coming back. She can't come back."

"Whyever not?"

"Because of the fog. Because of the quicksands."

"But we can—"

"We can't! Don't you see what you've done?"

"Please, Mr. Fairclough. We can find her. We can phone . . . There's going to be someone—"

"There's no one. Not for this, *not* for this."

"This? What's this?"

"The tidal bore, you stupid woman. The floodwaters are coming. The siren's just gone off. Today's a tidal bore."

WINDERMERE
CUMBRIA

When her mobile phone finally vibrated, Manette was in a welter of nerves. She was lurking in the car park of the business centre, close to a wheelie bin. Tim had gone inside a business called Shots!—a photographic studio by the look of the front window, which displayed enormous enlargements of the village of Ambleside in autumn—and he'd been followed some minutes later by a harried-looking woman with two children in tow. That woman had left moments later on the arm of an Anglican priest, and they'd all climbed into a Saab estate car and vanished, upon which time someone within Shots! had switched the *Open* sign to *Closed* and Manette had given up on Freddie and phoned the police.

Her conversation with Superintendent Connie Calva was as unproductive as it was brief, and Manette ended it by wanting to hurl her mobile onto the tarmac of the car park. She told the head of Vice about the business centre and what was going on and how the *Open* sign had been turned to *Closed* and they both knew what that meant, didn't they, because Tim Cresswell, aged fourteen, was here to film one of those horrible, soul-destroying pieces of filth and the police had to come and they had to come *now*.

But Connie Calva said they had to get Tim's laptop to Barrow, where the forensic computer specialist would go through it and discover the exact location from which Toy4You had been sending his e-mails, whereupon they would apply for a search warrant and—

"Bugger that for a lark!" Manette whispered fiercely. "I'm telling you exactly where he is, exactly where this Toy4You monster is, exactly where they're going to film, and you bloody goddamn better get someone over here to deal with this. *Now*."

To this Superintendent Calva had replied in the nicest possible voice, which indicated she was used to speaking with people on the edge, which was something they probably taught in training college. It was a case of Mrs. McGhie,

I know you're upset and worried but the only way to bring down something like this so that the entire thing doesn't get thrown out of court on its ear is to do it within the confines of the law. I know you don't like this and I certainly don't like it. But we have no choice.

Manette said, "Bugger the confines of the bloody law!" and she ended the call.

Then she rang Freddie because God only knew where he was. He answered at once, saying, "Damn it, Manette. I rang you. You were supposed to—"

"Talking to the police," she cut in. "I had to. Freddie, he's in a photo studio. Where *are* you?"

"Walking back from the railway station. Where are you?"

"The business centre." She told him the route, surprising herself with her own memory.

He repeated it back to her and she said, "Hurry. Please do hurry. Freddie, the police won't come. When I rang them, they said they need a search warrant, they need to take that computer to Barrow, they need to . . . God, I don't know what. And he's *in* there and they're going to film him. I just know it, but I couldn't make her see."

"Darling, I'm on my way," he said.

"I'll try to get inside the shop," she told him. "I'll bang on the door. They'll stop what they're doing, won't they? Surely?"

"Manette, do nothing. Do you understand me? These are dangerous people. I'm on my way. Wait."

Manette didn't know how she could. But she rang off after promising him that until he arrived . . . There was no way she could do that, although she tried. Three minutes of waiting did her in.

She ran to the front door. It was locked, as she knew it would be, but that was of no account. She banged upon it. She rattled it. It was mostly glass, but the glass was thick and the door was unmoving, even in its jamb. And as for the noise possibly disturbing the action inside Shots!— whatever that action was—she could see how unlikely the case was that she was achieving that. For a door behind the shop counter was also closed, and if they were filming within the building, noise would also be associated with that.

She bit her nails. She looked around. She thought of the possibilities and came up with the back of the business centre. For the shops in the centre would have more than one door, surely? In case of fire, only one means of egress from a place of business had to be illegal, didn't it?

She dashed round the back, only to encounter a line of doors and all of them unmarked. She hadn't thought to count up the shops in front in order to do the same in the rear, so she went back round the front at a run to do so, just as Freddie came tearing into the car park.

She flung herself towards him. He was breathing like a mountaineer without oxygen. He gulped out, "Treadmill. Starting tomorrow," and then, "Which one? Where?" as she clung to his arm.

She told him that the door was locked, that there was an inner door, that there were also doors round the back. She said that she could bang on the back door and Freddie could wait at the front door for all of them to come pounding out of the place to make a run for it. When they did that—

"Absolutely not," he said. "We're not about to set these people off. They've a lot vested in not getting caught. We need the police."

"But they won't come!" she wailed. "I told you that. They won't come unless they get a bloody warrant."

Freddie looked round the car park. He spied the heavy wheelie bin. He said to Manette, "Oh, I think we can give them a reason to come."

He trotted over to the wheelie bin and put his shoulder to it. She saw what he intended and joined him in the effort. They began to roll the bin towards the shops, picking up speed on a slope of the car park. As they approached the front of Shots!, Freddie murmured, "Give it your best now, darling. And hope he set the burglar alarm."

He had done. So they discovered when the wheelie bin crashed through the front door of the photo shop and the alarm began to howl.

Freddie winked at Manette and rested his hands on his thighs to catch his breath. "Voilà," he said.

"Bob's your uncle," she replied.

MORECAMBE BAY
CUMBRIA

Alatea was motionless, a statue more than two miles from where she'd leapt off the seawall and into the empty channel of the River Kent. When she'd set off from Arnside, she'd seen the fog but at that point she could still make out in the distance the peninsula that was Holme Island, and she knew that round the tip of it lay Grange-over-Sands and escape.

She'd thought to put on her hiking boots, deciding she had just time for that and an anorak as Nicky and the red-haired woman had their conversation out on the driveway. She'd grabbed her bag, faded out of the house via the drawing room doors, and made for the seawall. She'd swung herself over it and out onto the sands, where she'd begun to run as best she could.

The channel and the bay it fed into both were virtually waterless. The River Kent was a mere leapable creek at that point. The water of the bay was nonexistent. She had sufficient time to make the crossing, she reckoned, as long as she took care. She knew how to do that. She had a walking stick to help her and even if she hit a patch of the quicksand for which the bay and its surrounds were notorious, she knew what to do should she become caught in it.

What she hadn't counted on was the fog. While she'd seen it far to the northwest of Arnside, and while she knew the likelihood of its advancing towards shore, what she hadn't understood was how quickly it was going to roll in. And roll it did, like a diaphanous barrel of immense proportions that silently rumbled forward, inexorably, swallowing everything in its path. When it reached her, Alatea knew in an instant that this was more a pestilential miasma than was it mere fog because she understood that this substance brought with it a deadly danger. What began as a vapour—nothing more than a hoary veil that was cold and damp but still not impossible to navigate—within moments became a grey drapery so thick that it felt to Alatea as though her eyes were playing tricks upon her for the simple reason that she could not see and this seemed impossible because it *was* daylight, but other than the fact that the sun was out somewhere rendering visible the colours of her boots, her anorak, and the fog itself, she could see nothing at all. There was no depth to her vision. No width. No height. There was only fog.

She'd had no choice but to turn back for Arnside, which was closer than Grange-over-Sands. But in less than five minutes she'd stopped moving forward because she no longer knew if it was forward that she was moving.

There were sounds that should have helped her negotiate the route back to her home, but she couldn't tell where they were coming from. The first she heard was the train crossing the railway viaduct, which spanned the Kent Channel from Arnside and ultimately carried passengers onward to Grange-over-Sands. But she couldn't make out whether the train was going to or coming from Grange-over-Sands, and further, she couldn't even tell in what direction the railway track lay. According to her reckoning, it should have been to her left if she was on the route back to Arnside, but it sounded as if it was coming from behind her, which would mean she was heading out to sea.

She turned to correct her course, then, and began to walk again. She hit a puddle, sank up to her calf, and quickly pulled back. Someone shouted in the distance somewhere. She couldn't tell where the shout was coming from, but it sounded close, and this was good. She turned towards it and resumed her progress.

A tractor roared. At least it sounded like a tractor. But it was directly behind her—or so it seemed—so *that* would be the best route to shore. She turned towards it. She called out—"Hello? Hello? I'm here. Over here," but she heard nothing in reply, only the tractor's engine, and it seemed to groan and strain, as if the machine was pulling an inconceivably heavy load.

And then a horn honked. Yes, she thought, *that* way was the road. Only, the road seemed to be where the sea was supposed to be and if she went in that direction, she'd be lost, surely. She would wander among the little hillocks of sand, through the puddles, and ultimately she'd stumble into a scour, where the waters of the bay did exactly that: scoured out the sand to form a trough upon which sand resettled in a new form that was too much liquid to bear the weight of anything other than the smallest bird. And then she would sink.

She stopped again. She turned. She listened. She called out. In reply came the cry of a gull. A moment later the air seemed to part for an instant with the sound of a gunshot or the backfire from a car. Then silence, utter and complete.

That was the moment Alatea knew there was no escape. That there never had been any real escape. From this instant out in the far east part of Morecambe Bay there *might* be some form of either flight or rescue. But from her life and the lies she'd constructed so that she might dwell safely within it, there was not. It was time she faced up to that, she decided. For every occasion of her life had led her to a moment of revelation she'd foolishly thought she could avoid forever. But there simply was no avoiding it any longer. That was the only truth that remained.

All right. So be it. She would take what was coming to her because she surely deserved it. She opened her bag. It was only when she found her purse, her chequebook, her makeup case, and not her mobile phone inside that she saw in her mind's eye where she had left the device, sitting on the kitchen worktop plugged into a socket, recharging itself. She stared mutely into her bag then and understood that speaking the truth to Nicholas was not the final challenge remaining for her.

Hers would be to take the leap into accepting the icy embrace of what was inevitable. How could she have thought it would ever have been otherwise? she wondered. For hadn't each step she'd taken since she'd run away from her family brought her to this single spot on earth in this one perilous moment of time?

There had never really been an escape—only a

postponement—and she finally understood this. While science and surgery had provided her a way to shed the terrible carapace that had been her prison, rendering her the strangest of strangers in a very strange land, there was no taking flight from what had gone into her making and this was the stuff of her memories, which could not be shed no matter how she tried.

The worst part, she thought, had been the boxing lessons that followed the declaration that her brothers couldn't be expected to fight the battles of Santiago Vasquez y del Torres forever. It was time Santiago learned to defend himself against bullies, his father insisted. But the fear was bright like a silver coin in his eyes as he spoke, and he frowned with more than concern and displeasure when Santiago didn't want horseplay with his brothers, when Santiago wasn't interested in building fortresses or playing soldiers, in wrestling, in trying to direct his pee as far as Carlos could. And the fear was bright in his mother's eyes when she came upon her Santiago playing dressing-up, cradling a doll, or planning a tea party with cousin Elena Maria.

The faces of Santiago's parents said the same thing without speaking: What have we borne into this world? His father's worry was an obvious one for a man of his culture, his age, his religion, and his upbringing. He worried he had foisted upon the world another depraved homosexual. His mother's worry was more subtle and more in keeping with her nurturing disposition in general. How would her Santiago cope in a world ill equipped to understand him?

Escape at the time meant Elena Maria. To her Santiago had told it all. She'd heard his explanation of being a soul inside a body that he did not even recognise as his own. He looked out of this body, he told her, and looked down upon it and *saw* it was male and *knew* it as male, but it did not function as the body of a male and he did not wish it to function so. He couldn't even stand to touch it, he said. It was like touching someone else.

I don't know what it is, he told her, I don't know what it means, I just don't want it, I can't live with it, I have to be rid of it, and if I can't be rid of it then I will die I swear I will die.

With Elena Maria, then, there was relief. For those few

hours, for a day trip to one of the larger towns, for a weekend once in which they were adolescent girls on their own at a beach . . . This allowed the young Santiago to see what he truly wanted, what he had to be. But this could not happen in a world in which his father believed that toughening him up was the only answer. In order to live as he had been born to live, Santiago had run, and he'd continued running until he'd run into the arms of Raul Montenegro.

So was the worst really those boxing lessons? Alatea asked herself now. Or was the worst the promise that Raul Montenegro had held out to her and the reality of how she'd been intended to keep up her end of the bargain they'd struck with each other? She wasn't sure. But what she did know was that Raul Montenegro was a driven man. Just as he'd been unwavering in his promise to fulfill the feminine dreams of his young lover Santiago Vasquez y del Torres, so was he equally unwavering in his decision to find Alatea Vasquez y del Torres so that she could repay him in coin he'd long ago determined.

And now here she was, as lost as ever, with no choice left but to move or to die. So she moved in the direction she hoped against hope was Arnside, although she no longer knew. Within ten yards she hit the quicksand, a scour she had feared she'd stumble upon. In an instant she was up to her thighs. And cold, cold. So horribly cold.

No panic was necessary, she told herself. She knew what to do. Nicholas had told her. A long-ago walk across the expanse of the empty bay and she remembered his words. It's completely counterintuitive, darling, but you've got to do it, he had said.

She knew that. She prepared herself.

That was when the siren began to blare.

ARNSIDE
CUMBRIA

"Are you certain, sir?" the voice asked Lynley. The man at
the Coast Guard station on Walney Island spoke with the
kind of calm authority meant to soothe whoever was phoning
in an emergency of the sort that Lynley was reporting. He
spoke with cool-headed reason, which could lead to a decision, because he and he alone had the authority to put the
wheels in motion. "I don't want to launch a boat out into the
bay unless we know for a fact that the woman's out there.
Conditions are deadly. Has she rung on her mobile? Was
there a note?"

"Neither. But we're certain." Lynley described for the
officer the position of the house, the lack of an escape route,
and what they'd done to attempt to find Alatea Vasquez y
del Torres. The only possibility besides the bay had been
the walk along the seawall: a public footpath that branched
into half a dozen other public footpaths leading to Arnside
Knot, to the village of Silverdale, and ultimately onto the
Lancaster Coastal Way. But Alatea didn't know those footpaths other than the footpath to Arnside Knot and she had
no reason to climb to the knot in the fog while she had every
reason to try to make a run for it across the bay.

"What reason would this be, sir?" the officer had asked,
not unreasonably.

Lynley told him he was in the midst of an enquiry into a
drowning, which could have been a murder, and all the et
ceteras. He was not only stretching the truth of the matter.
He was actually lying to the man. But there seemed no
choice available other than setting out themselves for Arnside Knot to search for her there, which he'd managed to
persuade Nicholas Fairclough to do, hopeless task though
it was.

Fairclough had agreed to do this, although he'd built a
bonfire first on the seawall path. This Deborah was keeping
at a roar, feeding into it armfuls of whatever was flammable:
logs, branches, newspapers, magazines, old pieces of furniture. The fire had attracted the attention of the fire brigade

as well as the good citizens of Arnside, who joined in the effort to make from these combustibles a beacon that might glow through the fog and signal to Alatea the route she needed to take in order to return.

It was more something to do than was it useful, and Lynley knew this. For if Alatea was indeed out there in Morecambe Bay and if the tide was coming in, it was hardly likely that she'd be able to outrun it. Hence his call to the Coast Guard.

The officer on Walney Island said to him, "Sir, I can put out a boat, but let's not deal in fantasy here. Visibility just now is less than twenty yards. The bay is over one hundred square miles. With the combination of fog and the tidal bore . . . I'm not putting a crew out there on a whim."

"I assure you, this is not a whim," Lynley told him. "Surely if you set a course for Arnside—"

"We'll chance it, all right," the officer cut in. "But she's a dead woman, sir, and we both know that. Meanwhile, ring the lifeboat service to see what they can do to assist. You might want to phone the Guide to the Sands for his opinion as well."

The Guide to the Sands was established across the water to the south of Grange-over-Sands, near a little enclave called Berry Bank. He sounded a kindhearted soul when Lynley rang him. But in more than fifty years of walking curious day-trippers across Morecambe Bay and after a lifetime spent between cockling from the fishing village of Flookburgh to trawling for shrimp in the River Leven, he bloody well knew how to read the sands, sir, and if a lady was out there in the fog for any reason on God's good earth—and he didn't much care to know the reason—she was well on her way to being a corpse and "that's the unfortunate truth of the matter, I'm sorry to tell you."

Was there nothing to be done? Lynley asked. For the Coast Guard was setting out from Walney Island and he was about to ring the RNLI for a lifeboat as well.

Depends on how many corpses you want to look for when the fog lifts, was how the Guide to the Sands put it. But he made one thing clear: After all his years of reading the sands and knowing the safe routes from those fraught with danger, he wasn't about to join the foolhardy who went out now in search of anyone.

Nor, it turned out, was the RNLI. They were volunteers, after all. They were trained to help and they wanted to help. But they needed water to launch their boats, sir, and the bay was at present empty. While it was true that it wasn't going to be empty for long, when the water rushed in, it was going to take that woman quickly because if she didn't drown, hypothermia would get her. They'd set off with the tide as soon as they were able, but it was useless. We're so sorry, sir.

So the fire roared and someone thought to bring a loud-hailer from which Alatea's name was shouted continuously. In the meantime, out in the distance somewhere, the phenomenon that was the tidal bore was coming. Awesome to witness, Lynley heard someone murmur. But deadlier to encounter.

WINDERMERE
CUMBRIA

The burglar alarm was loud enough to raise skeletons from tombs. They had to shout to each other to be heard above it. They used all their force to wedge the wheelie bin into the shop in order to give themselves a means of access, and once inside, Freddie turned to Manette and yelled, "You wait here," which, naturally, she was not about to do.

He went for the inner door and rattled its handle. It was locked, and although he yelled, "Open this! Police!" and then "Tim! Tim Cresswell!" it was clear to them both that whoever was within the other room wasn't about to cooperate.

"I'll have to break it."

Manette read his lips rather than heard him. She said, "How?" because of all the things Freddie was, he was hardly a man in possession of the brute force that was needed to break in a door. And this door wasn't like a telly door or a film door, substantial in appearance but in reality flimsy enough to be kicked in with a single thrust of a manly foot powered by an even manlier thigh. This was a door with intentions, and those intentions were to keep out trespassers.

Nonetheless, Freddie went at it. First with his foot. Then with his shoulder. Then they took turns and all the time the burglar alarm kept howling. It was a good five minutes— perhaps more—when they finally broke the lock through the doorjamb. Freddie stumbled inside the inner room, shouting over his shoulder, "Manette, you must wait."

Again, she ignored him. If he was walking into danger, she wasn't about to let him walk into danger alone.

They were in a digital printing room that gave onto a storeroom. Two aisles comprised this, at the end of which strong lights were shining, although the rest of the place was in darkness. The alarm's noise continued unabated, so they watched for movement from the shadows. But a cold breeze wafting towards them spoke of an escape having been effected out of the back door. They could only hope someone had been left behind. They could only hope that someone was Tim.

At the far end where the light was brightest, they saw the crude film set. Manette took it all in in an instant—beds, window, Big Ben in the distance, dog at the foot of a bed— before she saw him. He was a figure lying on his side in what looked like a nightshirt. But the nightshirt was pulled above his head, green tights were tied round the top of it like a sack, and the boy himself lay on his side with his hands bound in front of him and his genitals on display. He was fully erect. An X on the floor not far from the bed on which he lay indicated where the camera had been positioned and what its primary focus had been.

Manette said, "Oh God."

Freddie turned to her. She read his lips because there was no way to hear him, not while the alarm kept shrieking like a banshee come to claim a soul. *You stay here. You stay here.*

Because she was frightened at that point, she remained where she was. If Tim was dead, the truth of the matter was that she simply did not want to see.

Freddie went to the bed. Manette saw his lips form *he's bleeding* and then *Tim old man I say old man* as he reached for the tights that bound the nightshirt closed above Tim's head.

Tim's body jerked. Freddie's lips said *Easy there. It's Freddie my man let me get you out you're all right old man* and then he had the nightshirt released from its binding and he was lowering it gently to cover Tim's body and Manette saw from the boy's eyes and his face that he was drugged which in that moment she thanked God for because if he was drugged there was a small chance that he would not remember what had happened to him here.

Phone the police, Freddie said.

But she knew there was no need for that. Even as she approached Ian's son where he lay on the bed, even as she reached to untie his hands, the alarm ceased howling and she heard the voices.

"Bloody damn mess," someone called out from the shop itself.

How true, she thought.

MORECAMBE BAY
CUMBRIA

Everything you do in quicksand is counterintuitive, Nicky had told her. When you hit it, your inclination is to freeze in place. It seems that struggling will make you sink faster. Any movement at all will presage more danger and an inconceivable end. But you must remember several things, darling. The first is that you have no idea how deep the sand really is. You're only in a scour and while it *might* be deep enough to swallow a horse or a tractor or an entire tour coach, it's more likely that you're in one of the shallower scours, which will suck you in only to your knees or, at worst, your thighs, leaving you otherwise free until rescue comes. *But* you don't want to discover that—especially if you're going to go in up to your chest—because if you sink that far there's no getting out because of the suction involved. At that point only more water can get you out, water from a fire hose blasting into the sand to free you or water from the incoming tide driving sand from the scour again. So you must move quickly once you're in the sand. If you're very lucky, it's not deep and before it can suck upon your boots and entrap them, you can move across it or back away from it. If you can't do that, then you must lie on the surface of the quicksand. Lie down upon it as soon as you're able. You'll see that you'll sink no deeper and you'll be able to roll away from it.

But no matter the words of her husband, who had lived his life in this strange part of the world, to Alatea the thought was madness. She was in the sand up to her thighs, so no quick movement out of the scour was possible. This meant lying on the top of the sand. And she could not bring herself to do it. She told herself to. She said aloud, "You must, you *must*," but all she could think of as she settled more slowly downward was the insidious movement of the sand inching up her supine body, crawling into her ears, touching her cheeks, slithering like menace incarnate towards her nose.

She wanted to pray but her mind would not produce the appropriate words that could effect a miracle. Instead, what it produced were images, and central to them was Santiago Vasquez y del Torres, thirteen years old, a runaway only as far as the closest city to Santa Maria de la Cruz, de los Angeles, y de los Santos. There in a church he had stowed himself for refuge, dressed in Elena Maria's clothing, face painted with Elena Maria's cosmetics, a shoulder bag containing some little money and a change of clothing and three tubes of lipstick, and a scarf covering hair that was too long for a boy and too short for a girl.

When the priest found her, he called her *my child* and *daughter of our Heavenly Father* and he asked her if she was there to confess. And confession seemed like the path she should take—"Go, Santiago. Go where God points," Elena Maria had whispered—so Santiago Vasquez y del Torres had confessed. Not to sin but to his need for help because if he could not be what he needed to be, he knew he would end his life.

The priest listened. He spoke gently of the grave sin of despair. He said that God did not create mistakes. Then he said, "Come with me, child," and together they walked to the rectory, where Santiago was given absolution for whatever sin he had committed in running from his home and a meal of beef and boiled potatoes, which he ate slowly as he looked round the simple kitchen, where the priest's housekeeper eyed him with thick black eyebrows drawn together and a furrowed brow. When he was finished with his meal, he was led to a parlour to rest, my dear child, for your journey has been a long and difficult one, has it not? And yes it had, oh it had. So he lay on a sofa covered in corduroy and he fell asleep.

His father awakened him. Face like a stone mask, he'd said, "Thank you, Padre," and he'd taken his wayward son by the arm. "Thank you for everything," and he'd made a hefty donation to the church or perhaps to the betraying priest himself, and home they had gone.

A beating would change him, his father decided. So would being locked into a room until he saw clearly the crime he had committed not only against God's law but also against his family and their good name. And nothing would change about his situation—"Do you understand me, Santiago?"—until he agreed to stop this mad behaviour.

So Santiago had tried on manhood, for all the ill-fitting suit of clothes it was. But pictures of naked ladies shared in secret with his brothers only made him want to be like the ladies, not to have them, and when his brothers touched themselves in guilty pleasure at the sight of these women, the thought of touching himself in a similar way made him both nauseous and faint.

He did not develop as a boy: hairy of arm and leg and chest, bearded and needing to shave. It was so clear that something was wrong with him, but the only answer seemed to be toughening him up with contact sports, with hunting, with rock climbing, with daredevil skiing, with anything, in short, that his father could think of to make him into the man he was intended by God to be.

For two long years Santiago made the attempt. For two long years Santiago saved every bit of money he could. At fifteen, then, he ran for the final time, and he made it by train to Buenos Aires, where no one knew he was not a female unless he wished to make the fact known to them.

Alatea recalled the train ride: the sound of the engine and the scenery passing. She recalled her head against the cool glass of the window. She recalled her feet upon her suitcase. She remembered her ticket being punched and the man saying, *Gracias, señorita*, and being *señorita* from that time forward as the train carried her away from her home.

She could almost hear the train at this moment, so vivid was the memory of that time and that place. It rumbled and roared. It gushed and it thundered. It took her relentlessly into her future and even now she was on it, escaping her past.

When the first of the water hit her, she understood that what she'd been hearing was the tide. She realised then what that siren had meant. This was the tidal bore coming, coming as fast as a horse could gallop. And while the water meant that she would soon be free of the scour that held her fast, she understood that there were things from which she would never be free.

She thought of how thankful she was that she would not suffocate in the sand, as she had feared she might. As the first of the water crashed against her body, she understood also that she would not drown. For one did not drown in water such as this. One merely lay back and fell asleep.

11 NOVEMBER

There had been nothing, really, that could be done. All of them had known it. All of them had pretended otherwise. The Coast Guard went out into the fog, taking the route from Walney Island into Lancaster Sound. But it was miles from there into Morecambe Bay and miles farther into the channel of the River Kent. She could have been anywhere, and this was something that everyone had known as well. If it had been the tidal bore alone, there might have been a chance—slight though it was—that she could be found. But with the tidal bore conjoining the fog, the situation had been without hope from the very first. They did not find her.

The RNLI had attempted to help as well, once there was enough water for them to set out. But they hadn't got far before they knew that it was a body they would be looking for. With this the case, for them to remain out in the fog ran the risk of there being more bodies to find at the end of the day, and to compound the tragedy was foolish. Only the Guide to the Sands could assist, they reported to Lynley upon their return to land, for the Guide's job in a situation such as this was to speculate on the probable places that a body would wash up. His job was to help them find the body as quickly as possible because if they did not find it when the fog lifted, there was a very good chance they would not find it at all. The water would wash it away, and the sand would bury it. Some things out in Morecambe Bay were never found and some things lay buried for one hundred years. It was the nature of the place, the Guide to the Sands told them.

Lynley and Deborah had gone into Arnside House at last, after hours upon hours of stoking the bonfire, even after the point when the tidal bore had surged into and then filled the channel and all of them knew there was not a single hope left. But Nicholas wouldn't leave the fire, so they continued to feed it with him, even as they cast worried looks upon his devastated face. He wasn't ready to stop until evening, when exhaustion had combined with knowledge and the dawning of grief to rob him of the desire to continue. Then he'd stumbled towards the house, and Lynley and Deborah had followed him as the people of Arnside village parted to let them pass and their words of sympathy had matched the looks of sorrow on their faces.

Inside the house, Lynley had phoned Bernard Fairclough. He reported only the barest of facts: that his son's wife was missing and probably drowned out in Morecambe Bay. Apparently out for a walk, Lynley told them, and caught up in the tidal bore.

"We'll be there at once," Bernard Fairclough had said. "Tell Nicholas we're on our way."

"They'll want to know if I'm going to use now," Nicholas said numbly when Lynley relayed his father's message. "Well, who wouldn't worry that I might, with my history, eh?" He went on to say that he would not see them. Or anyone else, if it came to that.

So Lynley had waited and when Nicholas's parents arrived, he gave them the information. And he himself decided that his part in all this was not to betray Alatea. He would hold her secrets in his heart. He would take her secrets to his grave. He knew that Deborah would do the same.

It was too late by then to begin the journey back to London, so he and Deborah had returned to the Crow and Eagle, booked two rooms, had a largely silent dinner, and had gone to bed. In the morning, when he could bear to talk, he phoned New Scotland Yard. There were, he saw, seven messages on his mobile phone. He didn't listen to any of them. He rang Barbara Havers instead.

He told her briefly what had happened. She was silent except for the occasional, "Oh damn" and "Oh hell, sir." He told her that they would need to get word to Alatea's family in Argentina. Could Barbara find the graduate student once again and make the necessary phone call? Yes, she could, she told him. She was that bloody sorry about the way things had worked out, as well.

Havers said, "How are you, sir? You don't sound good. Anything else I c'n do at this end?"

"Tell the superintendent that I was detained in Cumbria," he said. "I'll be on my way in an hour or two."

"Anything else I should tell her?" Havers asked. "Want me to let her know what's happened?"

Lynley considered this only briefly before he made his decision. "Best to let things lie as they are," he said.

She said, "Right," and rang off.

Lynley knew he could trust her to do as he'd asked, and it occurred to him, then, that he'd not thought at all about ringing Isabelle. Either on the previous night or this morning upon waking from a very bad sleep, he'd not considered her.

Deborah was waiting for him when he descended the stairs into reception at the Crow and Eagle. She was very ill looking. Her eyes grew bright with tears when she saw him, and she cleared her throat roughly to keep them from falling.

She was sitting on a wooden bench opposite the reception desk. He sat next to her and put his arm round her shoulders. She sagged into him, and he kissed the side of her head. She reached for his other hand and held it, and he felt the change in both of their bodies as they began to breathe as one.

He said, "Don't think what you're thinking."

"How can I not?"

"I'm not sure. But I know that you mustn't."

"Tommy, she would never have gone out into the bay if

I hadn't been pursuing this whole mad surrogate mother business. And that had nothing to do with Ian Cresswell's death, which you and Simon knew all along. I'm at fault."

"Deb darling, secrets and silence caused all of this. Lies caused this. Not you."

"You're being very kind."

"I'm being truthful. It was what Alatea couldn't bear to tell him about herself that took her onto the sands. It was that information that took her to Lancaster in the first place. You can't make her secrets and her death your fault because they're not, and that's how it is."

Deborah said nothing for a moment. Her head was bent and she seemed to be studying the toes of her black leather boots. She finally murmured, "But there're things one *must* be silent about, aren't there?"

He thought about this, about everything that remained and would remain forever unspoken between them. He replied with, "And who knows that better than we two?" and when he loosened his arm from her shoulders, she looked at him. He smiled at her fondly. "London?" he said.

"London," she replied.

ARNSIDE
CUMBRIA

No matter Nicholas's desire for solitude, Valerie had insisted to her husband that they would remain in Arnside House the rest of that night. She'd phoned Manette to give her the news, telling her to stay away. She'd phoned Mignon as well but with little worry that Mignon would bring herself all the way to Arnside since she'd been holed up in her tower from the moment she'd understood that her parents had no intention of continuing to be at her monetary, emotional, and physical beck and call. Mignon hardly mattered to Valerie at this point, anyway. Her concern was Nicholas. Her worry was what he might do in the wake of this disaster.

His message to them via the detective from New Scotland Yard had been terse but forthright. He wanted to see no one. That had been all.

Valerie had said to Lynley, "She'll have people in Argentina. We'll need to let them know. There will be arrangements . . ."

Lynley had told her that the Met would handle informing Alatea's people since he had an officer who had tracked them down. As for arrangements, perhaps they all ought to wait to see if a body could be found.

She hadn't thought of that: that there might not be a body. There had been a death so there *would* be a body, she wanted to insist. After all, a body was a form of finality. Without one, how would grief ever be navigated?

When Lynley had left with the woman he'd introduced as Deborah St. James—unknown to Valerie and, frankly, unimportant at this point save the knowledge that she'd been present during the time of Alatea's disappearance— Valerie climbed the stairs and made her way to Nicholas's room. She'd said to the panels of his door, "We're here, darling. Your father and I. We'll be downstairs," and she'd left him alone.

Throughout the long night, she and Bernard had sat in the drawing room, a fire burning in the grate. Near three in the morning, she'd thought she heard movement above them on the first floor of the house, but it turned out to be only the wind. The wind blew away the fog and brought with it the rain. The rain beat against the windows in steady waves and Valerie thought aimlessly about heaviness enduring for a night but joy coming in the morning. Something that came from the Book of Common Prayer, she recalled. But the words did not apply in this terrible case.

She and Bernard did not speak. He attempted to draw her into conversation four times, but she shook her head and held up her hand to make him stop. When he finally said, "For the love of God, Valerie, you must talk to me sometime," she understood that in spite of everything that had passed in the last twelve or more hours, Bernard actually wanted to talk about *them*. What was wrong with the man? she asked herself wearily. But then, hadn't she always known the answer to that?

It was just after dawn when Nicholas came into the drawing room. He'd moved so quietly, she hadn't heard him and he was standing in front of her before she realised it was not Bernard who'd entered the room. For Bernard had never left the room, although that, too, was something she hadn't taken note of.

She started to get to her feet. Nicholas said, "Don't."

She said, "Darling," but she stopped when he shook his head. He had one eye closed as if the lights in the room were painful to him, and he cocked his head as if this would help bring her into focus.

He said, "Just this. It's not my intention."

Bernard said, "What? Nick, I say . . ."

"It's not my intention to use again," he said.

"That's not why we're here," Valerie said.

"So you stayed because . . . ?" His lips were so dry they seemed to stick together. There were hollows beneath his eyes. His cherub hair was flat and matted. His spectacles were smudged.

"We stayed because we're your parents," Bernard said. "For the love of God, Nick—"

"It's my fault," Valerie said. "If I hadn't brought the Scotland Yard people up here to investigate, upsetting you, upsetting her—"

"If it's anyone's fault, it's mine," Bernard said. "Your mother is blameless. If I hadn't given her cause to want an investigation, no matter the bloody reason—"

"Stop." Nicholas raised his hand and dropped it in an exhausted movement. He said, "Yes. It's your fault. Both of you. But that doesn't really make a difference now."

He turned and left them in the drawing room. They heard him shuffle along the corridor. In a moment they heard him trudging up the stairs.

They went home in silence. As if knowing they were coming down the long drive from the road—perhaps she'd been watching for them from the roof of the tower, where, Valerie now knew, she'd doubtless been skipping up the stairs to spy upon everyone for years—Mignon stood waiting for them. She'd wisely discarded the zimmer frame, no doubt understanding that her jig was decidedly up, and she was wrapped up in a wool coat against the cold. The morning was fine as it sometimes is after a good rain, and the sun was as bright as an undashed hope, casting gold autumn light on the lawns and the deer grazing upon them in the distance.

Mignon advanced on the car as Valerie got out. She said, "Mother, what happened? Why did you not come home last night? I was sick with worry. I couldn't sleep. I nearly phoned the police."

Valerie said, "Alatea . . ."

"Well, of course Alatea," Mignon declared. "But why on earth did you and Dad not come *home*?"

Valerie gazed at her daughter, but she couldn't quite seem to make her out. Yet hadn't that always been the case? Mignon was a stranger and the workings of her mind were the foreign country in which she dwelt.

"I'm far too tired to speak to you now," Valerie told her, and headed for the door.

"Mother!"

"Mignon, that's enough," her father said.

Valerie heard Bernard following. She heard Mignon's wail of protest. She paused for a moment then turned back to her. "You heard your father," she said. "Enough."

She went into the house. She was monumentally exhausted. Bernard said her name as she made for the stairs. He sounded tentative, unsure in ways that Bernard Fairclough had never been unsure.

She said, "I'm going to bed, Bernard," and she climbed the stairs to do so.

She was acutely aware of the need for a decision of some sort. Life as she'd known it was something of a shambles now, and she was going to have to work out how to repair it: which pieces to keep, which pieces to replace, which pieces to send to the rubbish tip. She was also aware of how much the burden of responsibility fell upon her shoulders. For she had known all along about Bernard and his life in London, and that knowledge and what she'd done with that knowledge were the sins that would weigh on her conscience till the end of her days.

Ian had told her, of course. Although it was his own

uncle whose use of the firm's money he was reporting upon, Ian had always recognised where the true power in Fair-clough Industries lay. Oh, Bernard ran the day-to-day business and, indeed, made many of the decisions. Bernard, Manette, Freddie, and Ian had together kept the concern moving forward, modernising it in a way that Valerie would never have considered. But when the board met two times a year, it was Valerie who took the position at the head of the table, and not one of them ever questioned this because that was how it had always been. You could climb the ranks, but there was a ceiling and breaking through it was a matter of blood, not strength.

"Something curious and rather unsettling," was how Ian had reported it to her. "Frankly, Aunt Val, I'd thought not to tell you at all because . . . Well, you've been good to me and so has Uncle Bernie, of course, and for a while I thought I might be able to move funds around and cover the expenditures, but it's got to the point where I can't quite see how to do it."

A nice boy Ian Cresswell had been when he'd come to live with them to attend school after his mother's death in Kenya. A nice man Ian Cresswell had become. It was unfortunate that he'd hurt his wife and children so badly when he'd decided to live the life he'd been intended to live from birth, but sometimes these things happened to people and when they did, you had to muddle on. So Valerie had seen his concern, she'd respected the battle of loyalties he was fighting, and she was grateful that he'd come to her with the printouts that showed where the money was going.

She'd felt ghastly when he'd died. Accident though it was, she couldn't help thinking that she hadn't stressed enough the perilous condition of that dock in the boathouse. But his death had given her the opening she'd been looking for. The only suitable manner in which Bernard could be dealt with, she'd decided, was humiliation in front of his entire family. His children needed to know exactly what sort of man their father was. They'd abandon him, then, to his London mistress and his bastard child, and they'd circle the wagons of their devotion around their mother, and that would be how Bernard would pay for his sins. For the children were Faircloughs by blood, the three of them, and they would not brook the obscenity of their father's double life for an instant. Then, after a suitable amount of time had passed, she would forgive him. Indeed, after nearly forty-three years, what else was Valerie Fairclough to do?

She went to her bedroom window. It looked out upon Lake Windermere. Thankfully, she thought, it did not look out on the children's garden that now probably would not be. Instead, what she gazed upon was the great wide platter of the lake itself, still as a mirror flung onto the earth, reflecting—as a mirror would do—the fir trees along the shore, the fell rising opposite the land of Ireleth Hall, and the great cumulous clouds, which were the usual aftermath of a stormy night. It was a perfect autumn day, appearing clean and polished. Valerie looked upon it and knew she didn't belong in it. She was old and used up. Her spirit was dirty.

She heard Bernard come into the room. She didn't turn. She heard his approach and she saw from the corner of her eye that he'd brought a tray with him and was placing it on the demi-lune table between the room's two lakeside windows. Above this table, a large mirror hung, and reflected in it Valerie saw the tray held an offering of tea, toast, and boiled eggs. She also saw reflected her husband's face.

He was the one to speak first. "I did it because I could. My life's been like that. I've done what I've done because I could do it. I suppose it was a challenge to myself, much like winning you. Much like making more of the firm than your father and grandfather had been able to do. I don't even know what it means that I've done what I've done, and that's the worst of it because that tells me I might well do it all again."

"Isn't that a comforting thought," she said dryly.

"I'm trying to be honest with you."

"Another highly comforting thought."

"Listen to me. The devil of it is that I can't say it meant nothing to me because it did mean something. I just don't quite know what."

"Sex," she said. "Virility, Bernard. Not being such a little man, after all."

"That hurts," he said.

"As it's intended." She looked back at the view. There were things to know before she decided and she might as well know them, she told herself. "Have you always?"

He did her the courtesy of not misunderstanding. "Yes," he said. "Not all the time. Only occasionally. All right, frequently. Usually when business took me elsewhere. Manchester, perhaps. Birmingham. Edinburgh. London. But never with an employee until Vivienne. And even with her, it was like the rest, at first. It was because I *could*. But then things went further between us and I thought I saw a way to have two lives."

"Clever you," she said.

"Clever me," he replied.

She glanced at him then. Such a little man, actually. He was shorter than she by nearly five inches. Small, a little delicate, mischievous looking, cocky, grinning . . . My God, she thought, all he needed was a hunchback, a doublet, and tights. She'd been as easily seduced as the Lady Anne. She said to him, "Why, Bernard?" and when his eyes narrowed, she added, "Why two lives? One is usually more than enough."

"I know that," he said. "It's the curse I live with. One life was never enough for me. One life didn't . . . I don't *know*."

But she knew and perhaps she'd known all along. "One life couldn't prove to you that you were more than Bernie Dexter from Blake Street in Barrow-in-Furness. One life could never do that."

He was silent. Outside the honking of ducks drew Valerie's attention back to the window, and she saw a V of them flying in the direction of Fell Foot Park, and she thought of how ducks taking flight or landing made such a silly, awkward spectacle but ducks in flight were as graceful as any bird and the equal of any bird doing what birds do. It was only the getting there that was strange and different.

Bernard said, "Yes. I suppose that's it. Blake Street was the pit I climbed out of but its sides were slippery. Any wrong move, and I'd slide back down. I knew that."

She moved away from the window then. She went to the tray and saw he'd brought only enough for her. One cup and saucer, two boiled eggs but only one egg cup, cutlery for one, a single white napkin. He wasn't so certain of himself after all. There was a small mercy in this.

"Who are you now?" she asked him. "Who do you want to be?"

He sighed. "Valerie, I want to be your husband. I can't promise that this—the two of us, you and I and what we've built—won't all end up going down the Fairloo in another six months. But that's what I want. To be your husband."

"And that's all you have to offer me? After nearly forty-three years?"

"That's all I have to offer," he said.

"Why on earth would I accept that? You as my husband with no promise of anything else, such as fidelity, such as honesty, such as . . ." She shrugged. "I don't even know any longer, Bernard."

"What?"

"What I want from you. I no longer know." She poured herself a cup of tea. He'd brought lemon and sugar, no milk, which was how she'd always taken it. He'd brought toast without butter, which was how she'd always eaten it. He'd brought pepper but no salt, which was how she'd always seasoned her boiled egg.

He said, "Valerie, we have history together. I've done you—and our children—a terrible wrong and I know why I've done it and so do you. Because I'm Bernie Dexter from Blake Street and that's all I've had to offer you from the first."

"The things I've done for you," she said quietly. "To you, for you. In order to please you . . . to satisfy you."

"And you have," he said.

"What it took from me . . . You can't know that, Bernard. You'll never know that. There's an accounting that needs to be made. Do you understand that? *Can* you understand that?"

"I do," he said. "Valerie, I can."

She was holding her cup of tea to her lips, but he took the cup from her. He placed it carefully back onto its saucer.

"Please let me begin to make it," he said.

GREAT URSWICK
CUMBRIA

The police had taken Tim directly to hospital in Keswick. Indeed, they'd radioed for an ambulance to do so. Manette had insisted that she ride inside the vehicle with the boy because if she knew nothing else about Tim's condition and the prospects for his healing, she knew that he needed to be close to what was standing in place of his immediate birth family from this time forward. That was Manette.

The alarm had still been howling like a warning of the apocalypse's imminent arrival when the police burst onto the scene. Manette had been sitting on the makeshift bed with Tim's head in her lap and his body shrouded by the nightshirt, and Freddie had been crashing about looking for the guilty parties—long since flown—as well as for evidence of what had been going on in this place. The camera was gone, as was any sign of a computer, but in their haste the other members of the cast and crew of the spectacle being filmed had overlooked such items as a jacket containing a man's wallet and credit cards, a woman's bag containing a passport, and a rather heavy safe. Who knew what would be inside? Manette thought. The police would find out soon enough.

Tim had said nothing other than two numbly spoken sentences. The first was "He promised" and the second "Please don't tell." He wouldn't clarify who promised what to whom. As to what he meant with "Please don't tell," that was fairly clear. Manette rested her hand on his head—his hair too long, too greasy, too unnoticed by anyone for far too long—and she repeated, "No worries, Tim. No worries."

The police had comprised uniformed constables on the beat, but when they saw what they had walked into, they'd used their shoulder radios and made a request for detectives and officers from Vice. Thus Manette and Freddie had found themselves face-to-face with Superintendent Connie Calva once again. When she stepped into the room and swept her gaze over the Victorian bedroom, the open window, Big Ben in the distance, the dog at the foot of the bed, the discarded costumes, and Tim lying with his head in Manette's lap, she had said, "Did you ring for an ambulance?" to the constables, who nodded. Then to Manette, she said, "I'm sorry. My hands were tied. It's the law," and Manette had turned away. Freddie had said, "Don't tell us about the goddamn law," and he'd spoken so fiercely that Manette felt such a wave of tenderness sweep over her that she wanted to weep for how stupid she'd been not to see Freddie McGhie clearly before this moment.

Superintendent Calva took no offence. She fixed her eyes on Manette and said, "You stumbled upon this, I take it? Heard the burglar alarm, saw the mess outside, and reckoned what was going on? That's what happened?"

Manette looked down at Tim—he'd begun to shiver— and she made her decision. She cleared her throat and said no, they hadn't just stumbled upon the scene, although thank you, Superintendent, for assuming they might have done. She and her husband—she forgot to refer to Freddie as *former* or *erstwhile* or anything other than what he'd once been to her when she'd had common sense—had broken into the place. They had taken the law into their own hands and would have to embrace the consequences. They hadn't arrived soon enough to stop some piece of filth from raping a fourteen-year-old boy and filming it for the delectation of perverts around the globe, but she and Freddie would leave that part of it in the hands of the police, as well as what the police wished to do about the fact that they—she and her husband, as she referred to him again—had broken and entered, or whatever the police wished to call it.

"An accident, I think," Superintendent Calva had said. "Perhaps malicious mischief by persons unknown? In either case, these wheelie bins need to have better braking devices on them, ones that lock, I daresay, so they can't get out of hand and roll into the front doors of shops." She'd looked round the place and directed her officers to begin the process of collecting evidence. She'd concluded with, "We'll need a statement from the boy."

"But not now," Manette told her.

They'd taken him then. Tim had been handled tenderly by the emergency staff at the hospital in Keswick and ultimately released to his cousin Manette. She and Freddie had taken him home, provided him with a warm bath, heated soup for him, buttered soldiers to go along with it, sat with him as he ate it, and put him to bed. Then they had retired to their separate bedrooms. In hers Manette had spent a sleepless night.

In the early morning, with darkness still pressing against the windows, she made coffee. She sat at the kitchen table and gazed unseeing at her reflection in the glass, backed by night outside and the pond somewhere in that night and somewhere on the pond the swans tucked into the reeds together.

She considered what they had to do next, which was to phone Niamh. She'd already phoned Kaveh to tell him only that Tim was safe and inside her own home at this point and would he please let Gracie know so that she wouldn't worry about her brother?

Now she had to do something about Niamh. As Tim's mother, Niamh had a right to know what had occurred, but Manette wondered about Niamh's *need* to know. If she were informed and Tim learned she had been informed and she did nothing after *being* informed, the boy would be further devastated, wouldn't he? And wasn't that one pill of pain he didn't need to swallow? On the other hand, Niamh had to be told something at some point since she knew her son had gone missing.

Manette sat there at the kitchen table going back and forth and in and out, trying to make a decision. Betraying Tim seemed unthinkable to her. On the other hand, he was going to need help. Margaret Fox School could give it to him if he cooperated with them. But when had Tim been known to cooperate? And did what happened to him mean he might cooperate now? Why should he, for God's sake? Whom could he trust?

God, it was such a mess, Manette thought. She didn't know where to begin to help the boy.

She was still sitting at the table in the kitchen when Freddie came into the room. She realised she must have dozed in her chair, because it was fully light outside by then and Freddie was dressed and pouring himself a cup of coffee when she snapped to.

"Ah, she lives." Freddie came to the table with his mug of coffee, took hers, and dumped its cold contents into the sink. He gave her a fresh cup and rested his hand on her shoulder briefly. "Buck up, old girl," he said to her affably. "You'll feel better after having a good run on that blasted treadmill of yours, I daresay."

When he sat opposite her, Manette noted that he was dressed in his best suit, which was not something he ever put on when he went to work. He had on what he called his weddings-baptisms-and-funerals togs, which he wore with a crisp white shirt with French cuffs and a linen handkerchief folded into the breast pocket of his jacket. He was 100 percent Freddie McGhie, at ease with himself and sparkling from his head to the tips of his polished shoes, quite as if the previous day had not been a nightmare beginning to end.

He nodded at the handset of the phone, which Manette had left sitting in front of her on the table while she dozed. He said, "Hmm?" in reference to this, and Manette told him she'd phoned Kaveh. He said, "What about Niamh?" to which her reply was, "That's the question, isn't it?" She told him that Tim had begged her not to tell his mother. He'd amplified on "Please don't tell" when she'd gone into the bedroom to make sure he had everything he needed for the night.

"I suppose I should ring her, though," Manette concluded, "just to let her know he's with us, but I'm reluctant even to do that much."

"Why?"

"The obvious," she said. "The same reason Tim doesn't want me to tell her anything from yesterday: Sometimes it's just easier to speculate what might happen rather than to know the truth about people. Tim can think—or *I* can think, let's admit it—that she won't care or she won't do anything or she'll just feel bothered by the news and that's it. But he—and I—won't know for sure, will we? So he—and I—can also think, Perhaps if she knew, though, she'd jump into action, she'd shed this skin of indifference that she's been wearing, she'd . . . I don't know, Freddie. But if I phone her, I can't avoid finding out the complete truth of Niamh Cresswell. I'm not sure I want to know it just now, and Tim certainly doesn't."

Freddie listened to all this in his usual fashion. He finally said, "Ah. I see. Well, that can't be helped, can it," and he reached for the phone. He gave a glance to his watch, punched in a number, and said, "Bit early, but with good news early is always welcome." And then after a moment, "Sorry, Niamh. It's Fred. Have I awakened you? ... Ah. Bit of a restless night here ... Really? So glad of it ... I say, Niamh, we've got Tim over here ... Oh, bit cold from exposure. He was sleeping rough, the imp ... Ran into him in Windermere, quite by chance. Manette's looking after him ... Yes, yes, that's just it. Could you phone the school and let them know ... Oh. Well, of course. Certainly ... You've put Manette on his card as well, eh? Very good of you, Niamh. And I say, Manette and I would very much like to have Tim and Gracie stay here with us for a while. How d'you feel about that? ... Hmm, yes. Oh grand, Niamh ... Manette will be thrilled. She's quite fond of both of them."

That was it. Freddie ended the call, put the handset back on the table, and took up his coffee once again.

Manette gaped at him. "What on earth are you doing?"

"Making the necessary arrangements."

"I see that. But have you gone mad? We can't have the children here."

"Whyever not?"

"Freddie, our lives are a terrible muddle. What Tim and Gracie don't need is another uncertain situation in which to live."

"Oh yes. A muddle. I do know that."

"Tim thought that man was going to kill him, Freddie. He needs help."

"Well, that's understandable, isn't it? The killing part. He must have been terrified. He was in the midst of something he didn't understand and—"

"No. *You* don't understand. He thought that man meant to kill him because that was the deal they'd struck. He told me last night. He said he'd agree to the film if this Toy4You person would kill him afterwards. Because, he said, he lacked the bottle to kill himself. He wanted to, but he couldn't. And above everything he didn't want Gracie to think he'd been a suicide."

Freddie listened to this gravely, chin on his thumb and index finger pressed against his lips. He said, "I see."

"Good. Because that boy's in such a state of confusion and emotion and passion and hurt and . . . God, I don't know what else. So to bring him here, into this situation, perhaps permanently . . . How could we do that to him?"

"First of all," Freddie replied after a moment of thought, "he's in a very good school where he can sort himself out if he's a mind to it. Our part is to give him that mind. He's wanting a mum and a dad to stand behind him and believe in him and in the possibility that one can actually pick up the pieces of one's life and go on."

"Oh, very well and good, but how long can we give him that if we take him now?"

"What do you mean?"

"Come along, Freddie," Manette said patiently, "don't be obtuse. You're quite a wonderful catch and one of these women you're dating is going to reel you in. Then Tim and Gracie will face another broken situation and how can we ask either one of those children to go through that?"

Freddie looked at her steadily and said, "Ah. Well. Have I been wrong, then?"

"Wrong about what?"

"About us. Because if I have, I'll dash back upstairs and get myself out of my wedding togs."

She looked at him till she could no longer see him for her blurring of vision. She said, "Freddie . . . Oh, Freddie . . . No. You're not wrong."

"Excellent. I was feeling . . . well, a bit more certain than perhaps I should have done, so I spoke to the registrar, who's perfectly willing to make an exception in our case and allow us a wedding. Today. I'll need a best man and you'll want a bridesmaid. Shall I rouse Tim for the job?"

"Do," Manette said. "I'll phone Gracie."

ST. JOHN'S WOOD
LONDON

Zed Benjamin sat in the car park outside his mother's flat, and he stared at the route he needed to walk to get inside. He knew what awaited him there, and he wasn't anxious to confront it. It wasn't going to take long for his mother to work out the fact that he'd lost his job, and that was going to be a real teeth grinder to deal with. In addition to that, there was Yaffa to be faced, and what he really didn't want to see was her expression when she listened to the tale of how he'd failed in every possible way pursuing his story of the century in Cumbria.

Worse, he felt like hell. He'd awakened that morning in a budget hotel along the motorway. He'd left Cumbria at once on the previous day, directly after speaking to Rodney Aronson and collecting his things in Windermere. He'd driven as far as he could towards London before he'd had to stop for the rest of the night. That night had been spent in a grubby room reminiscent of those Japanese sleeping boxes he'd once read about. He felt as if he'd attempted slumber inside a coffin. Make that a coffin with a loo, he thought.

He'd risen that morning as rested as a man could be after having a fight break out in his hotel corridor at three a.m., necessitating an appearance by the local police. He'd got back to sleep at half past four, but at five the various workers for the day shift in the various shops and takeaway food stalls of the services area had begun to arrive, and they did their arriving with the accompaniment of the slamming of car doors and the shouts of greeting to each other, so round half past the hour, Zed had given up on sleep altogether and crammed himself into the upright packing crate that went for a shower in the bathroom.

He'd gone through the rest of his morning rituals by rote: shaving, cleaning his teeth, dressing. He hadn't felt like eating, but he wanted a cup of coffee and he was in the cafeteria of the services building when the daily newspapers arrived.

Zed couldn't help himself. It was force of habit. He'd picked up a copy of *The Source* and had taken it back to his table to see that the tabloid was running a follow-up to the earth-shattering Corsico piece about the mixed-race child of the minor royal. The paper was giving it Major Breaking Story treatment, this time with the banner headline *He Declares His Love* accompanied by suitable photographs. It seemed that the minor royal in question—who appeared to be getting more minor by the moment—intended to marry the mother of his bastard child since the revelation of his relationship to the woman had just obliterated her career as a third-rate Bollywood star. Turn to page 3 to see who the mother of the bastard child might be . . . ? Zed did so. He found himself looking at a sensuous woman with more than her share of mammaries, posing with her royal suitor cum fiancé with their child abounce on the royal's knee. He was grinning toothily, on his face a self-satisfied expression declaring to the men of his country, "Look what I managed to get for myself, you wankers." And it was true. The idiot had a title to recommend himself. Whether he had brains to go with the title was another matter entirely.

Zed had tossed the paper to one side. What a load of tosh it all was, he thought. He knew what would be going on at *The Source* as a result of this piece and the one that had preceded it, though. It would be celebration of Mitchell Corsico's unerring ability to sniff out a story, shape the public debate, and manipulate a member of the Royal Family—no matter how obscure—to take an action predetermined by the tabloid. He—Zedekiah Benjamin, struggling poet—was better off shot of the place.

He shoved his way out of his car. He could no longer avoid the inevitable, he thought, but he could damn well paint it as a positive alteration in his life if the proper words would come to him.

He had nearly reached the door when Yaffa came out of the building. She was wrestling with her rucksack, so he reckoned she was on her way to the university. She didn't see him, and he considered ducking into the shrubbery in an attempt to hide from her, but she looked up and clocked him. She halted.

She stammered, "Zed. What a . . . well, what a . . . a lovely surprise. You didn't say you were returning to London today."

"It won't be so lovely when I give you the news why I'm here."

"What's wrong?" She sounded so concerned. She took a step towards him and put her hand on his arm. "What's happened, Zed?"

"The sack."

Her lips parted. How soft they looked, he thought. She said, "Zed, you've lost your job? But you were doing so well! What about your story? The people in Cumbria? All of the mystery surrounding them and what they were hiding? What *were* they hiding?"

"The how and why and who-knows-what-and-when about having babies," he told her. "There's nothing else."

She frowned. "And Scotland Yard? Zed, they cannot have been investigating having babies."

"Well, that's just the worst of it, Yaff," he admitted. "If there was anyone from Scotland Yard up there, I never saw him."

"But who was the woman, then? The Scotland Yard woman?"

"She wasn't Scotland Yard. Haven't the foggiest who she *was* and it doesn't much matter now I'm through, eh?" He was carrying his laptop, and he shifted it from one hand to the other before going on. "Fact is," he said, "I was rather enjoying our little charade, Yaff. The phone calls and all that."

She smiled. "Me, too."

He shifted the laptop again. He didn't seem to know what to do with his hands and his feet all of a sudden. He said, "Right. Well. So when d'you want to schedule our breakup? Better be sooner rather than later, you ask me. If we don't engineer it in the next couple of days, Mum'll be talking to the rabbi and baking the challah."

Yaffa laughed. She said in a way that sounded like teasing, "And is that such a very bad thing, Zedekiah Benjamin?"

"Which part?" he asked. "The rabbi or the challah?"

"Either. Both. Is that so bad?"

The front door opened. An elderly woman toddled out, a miniature poodle in the lead. Zed stepped aside to let her pass. She looked from him to Yaffa to him. She leered. He shook his head. Jewish mums. They didn't even have to be one's mum to be one's mum, he thought with resignation. He said to Yaffa, "I don't think Micah would much like it, do you?"

"Ah, Micah." Yaffa watched the old lady and her poodle. The poodle lifted its tufted leg and did some business against a shrub. "Zed. I fear there is no Micah."

He peered at her earnestly. "What? Damn. You broke up with the bloke?"

"He never was the bloke," she said. "He was ... Actually, Zed, he never was at all."

It took Zed a moment. Then the moment felt like the dawn although it was morning and broad daylight in front of his mother's flat in St. John's Wood. He said, "Are you telling me—"

She broke in with, "Yes. I'm telling you."

He began to smile. "What a very clever girl you are, Yaffa Shaw," he said.

"I am," she agreed. "But then I always have been. And yes, by the way."

"Yes to what?"

"To wanting to be your wife. If you will have me despite the fact that I set out to ensnare you with your own mother's help."

"But why would you want me now?" he asked. "I have no job. I have no money. I live with my mum and—"

"Such are the mysteries of love," she declared.

BRYANBARROW
CUMBRIA

Gracie came dashing outside the moment the car stopped at the front gate. She flung herself at Tim and clung to his waist and Tim could barely take in her words, so rapidly did they come at him. He was having a bit of trouble taking in the rest of things as well. Cousin Manette had phoned Margaret Fox School to bring them up to date on his whereabouts; she'd requested permission for Tim to miss just one more day; she'd promised she'd have him back there tomorrow; she'd dressed herself in a peacock silk skirt and a milky-coloured cashmere pullover and a grey tweed jacket with a scarf that made all the colours good together; and she'd said they all had a wedding to attend at which Tim was going to have to be best man. That is, if Tim was willing to do so.

Tim saw from her face that the wedding was her own. He saw from Freddie's face that he was going to be the bridegroom. He said, "I guess," but he looked away quickly from the happiness that was blazing between his cousin and her soon-to-be-once-again husband and he thought how he didn't belong in that blaze, how to enter it even for a moment promised the bleak reality of leaving it as well. And he was tired of the constant leaving that had been colouring his life. He added, "What'm I s'posed to wear?" because clearly he had nothing suitable in Great Urswick.

"We shall find something perfect," Manette had replied, her arm through Freddie's. "But first, Gracie. Kaveh's kept her home from school because, of course, I shall need a bridesmaid."

Which was the topmost subject on Gracie's mind as she hung on Tim's waist. "A wedding, a wedding, a wedding!" she sang. "We're going to a wedding, Timmy! C'n I get a new dress, Cousin Manette? Should I wear white tights? Will there be flowers? Oh, there must be flowers!"

Gracie needed no answer to any of this, for she went on to other matters, all of them having to do with Tim and Bella. "You must never run off again," she told him. "I was

that worried and scared, Tim. I know I was cross with you
but it was 'cause you hurt Bella, but Bella's only a doll and
I do know that. It's just that, see, Dad gave her to me and
he let me pick her out myself and she was special 'cause of
that, but I'm *so* glad you're back, and what're you going to
wear?" And then to Manette and Freddie, "Will there be
guests? Will there be cake? Cousin Manette, *where* will you
get flowers? Are your mum and dad coming as well? What
about your sister? Oh, I expect the walk would be too much
for her."

Tim had to smile, and it was odd because he hadn't felt
like smiling in more than a year. Gracie was like a newly
bloomed flower, and he wanted to keep her that way.

All of them went into the house so that Tim could find
something to wear to a wedding. He climbed the stairs to
his room while Gracie remained chatting to Manette and
Freddie below but once inside, the place looked different
to him. He saw things and knew them for his belongings,
but somehow they weren't really his. He resided there, but
he didn't reside there. He wasn't sure what this meant or
how to feel about it.

He had nothing nice to wear to a wedding. All he had
was his school uniform and he certainly didn't intend to
wear that.

He thought for a moment about what it would mean if
he took the next necessary step. It seemed an enormous
one, something that might engulf and drag him under in
ways he could neither anticipate nor recover from. But there
was a wedding, and it was Manette and Freddie's wedding,
and there seemed nothing else to do but to go into his
father's bedroom and to search round and ultimately pull
from beneath the bed the black garbage bags of his father's
clothing that Kaveh had shoved there, preparatory to cart-
ing them all off to Oxfam in advance of bringing his bride
to the farm.

Ian's trousers were large on Tim, but a belt did the trick
and in another year they would probably fit him anyway.
He sifted through the rest of the clothing: more trousers
and shirts, ties and waistcoats, tee shirts and sweaters, and
he thought of how well his dad had dressed and of what this

meant about who his dad had been. Just a bloke, Tim thought, just an ordinary bloke . . .

Hurriedly, he grabbed up a shirt, a tie, and a jacket. He went back to the others, who were waiting for him in the old kitchen of the manor house, where Gracie was taping a note to Kaveh onto the cupboard in which he kept his tea. *Gracie and Timmy have gone to a wedding!* was written on the note. *What fun!*

After this, the lot of them set off to Windermere. On the way out to the car, though, they saw George Cowley removing the last of his belongings from the tenant's cottage. Daniel was there, hanging back a bit, and Tim wondered that Dan wasn't in school. Their eyes met, then slid away from each other. Gracie called out, "Bye, Dan. Bye, Dan. We're off to a wedding and we don't know if we'll *ever* be back!"

It wasn't until they'd wended their way from Bryan-barrow village to the main road through the Lyth Valley that Manette turned in her seat and spoke to them. She said, "What *if* you never came back at all, Gracie? What if you and Tim came to Great Urswick and lived with Freddie and me?"

Gracie looked at Tim. She looked back at Manette. Her eyes were round with expectation, but she turned her gaze to the window and the passing scenery it offered her. She said, "Could I bring my trampoline?"

Manette said, "Oh, I think we have room for that."

Gracie sighed. She moved on the seat to be closer to Tim. She rested her cheek on his arm. "Lovely," she said.

So the drive to Windermere was spent in a tangle of plans being laid. Tim closed his eyes and let the sounds of their conversation wash round him. Freddie slowed the car as they came to the town and Manette said something about the register office, which was when Tim opened his eyes again.

He said, "C'n I do something first? I mean, before the wedding?"

Manette turned to him and said of course he could, so he directed Freddie to the appliance repair shop where he'd left Bella. The doll had been seen to. Her arms and legs were reconnected. She'd been cleaned up. She wasn't what she'd been before Tim had pounced upon her, but she was still unmistakably Bella.

"Thought you wanted it posted," the woman behind the counter said to him.

"Things changed," Tim said as he accepted the doll.

"Don't they always," the woman said.

In the car, he handed Bella to his sister. She clutched the doll to her budding little bosom and said, "You mended her, you *mended* her," and cooed to the thing as if it were a live baby and not a realistic depiction of one.

He said, "I'm sorry. She's not as good as new."

"Ah," Freddie said as he moved the car away from the kerb, "but which one of us is?"

12 NOVEMBER

CHELSEA
LONDON

When Lynley and Deborah arrived back in London, it was after midnight. They'd made the drive mostly in silence although Lynley had asked her if she wanted to talk. She knew he understood that she was carrying the heavier of both of their burdens because of her part in Alatea's flight and her death, and he wanted to relieve her of at least part of the weight. But she couldn't allow it. "May we just be quiet with each other?" she'd asked him. And so they had been, although from time to time he'd reached over and covered her hand with his own.

They hit traffic near the junction for Liverpool and Manchester. They came upon roadworks near Birmingham and a tailback from an accident at the junction for the A45 to Northampton. At this last, they got off the motorway for a meal and spent ninety minutes hoping the route would be less congested at the meal's conclusion. They didn't reach the Cricklewood roundabout until midnight and Chelsea at half past the hour.

Deborah knew that her husband was still up, despite the time. She knew he would be waiting for her in his study on the ground floor of the house because before she climbed the front steps to the door, she saw that the light was on.

She found him reading. He had the fire on, and Peach

was snoozing in front of it on a cushion that Simon had placed there for her. The dachshund removed herself from this only slowly as Deborah entered, and she stretched her front legs and then her back legs before toddling over for a late-night greeting.

Simon set his book to one side. Deborah saw it was a novel, which was unusual for him. Simon was strictly a non-fiction reader, favouring biographies and the recounting of superhuman acts of survival in the wild. Shackleton was his foremost hero.

He got to his feet, always an awkward business for him. He said, "I wasn't sure what time."

She said, "Traffic was bad in places." And then, "Tommy told you?"

He nodded, his grey eyes taking in her face and gauging—as he always would—her expression and what it said about her state of mind. He read upon her the heaviness she felt and he said, "He rang me when you stopped for petrol. I'm terribly sorry, my love."

She stooped to pick up the dachshund, who squirmed in her arms and tried to climb to her face. "You were right about everything," Deborah said to her husband as she rubbed her cheek against the dog's silky head. "But then, you usually are."

"It gives me no pleasure."

"Which part? Being right always or being right just now?"

"Neither one gives me pleasure. And I'm not always right. In matters of science I feel fairly certain that the ground I'm walking on is solid. But in matters of the heart, in matters affecting you and me . . . Believe me, I have no idea, Deborah. I'm a wanderer in the dark."

"It was *Conception*. It became some sort of obsession for me. I saw a sisterhood forming between us because of that magazine and I let that thought—the thought that someone was as determined as I was, as . . . as *empty* as I was—dominate everything else. So I'm responsible for her death. If I hadn't made her feel so vulnerable. If I hadn't frightened her. If I hadn't pursued her. I thought she was talking about that mad journalist from *The Source* when all along *she* thought I'd come from the man who'd been searching for her."

"The man she *thought* had been searching for her," Simon corrected her gently. "When you hold your truths as close as she did, those truths can undermine your life. The world becomes a suspicious place. You were there at Tommy's request, Deborah. The rest came from her."

"But we both know that's not quite the truth," Deborah said. "I made more of what I saw in Arnside House because I wanted to. And both of us, Simon, know exactly why I did that." She went to one of the armchairs and sat. Peach settled into her lap. Deborah caressed the dog and then said to her husband, "Why's she not sleeping with Dad?"

"I required her presence. I didn't want to wait for you alone."

Deborah took this in. "How strange," she finally said. "I wouldn't have thought alone would bother you. You've always been so self-contained, so sure."

"That's how I've seemed to you?"

"Always. How else could you seem? So cool, so rational, so confident. Sometimes I just want you to explode, Simon, but you never do. And now even with this . . . There you stand. You're waiting for something from me—I can feel that—but I simply don't know what it is—"

"Do you not?"

"—or how to give it to you."

Simon sat then, not in the chair where he'd been sitting when she'd entered the room, but rather on the arm of hers. She couldn't see his face, and he couldn't see hers. She said, "I simply must get past this. I do understand that. But I don't know how to do it. Why can I not get past this, Simon? How can I *not* be obsessed with something I want so much?"

"Perhaps to want it less," he said.

"How do I manage that?"

"Through resignation."

"But that means I've given up, that *we've* given up. So where does that leave me?"

"Wandering," he said.

"Hungry," she said. "That's what it's like. Inside of me, always. This . . . this hunger that nothing is able to assuage.

It's horrible. It's why I always feel . . . well, empty. I know I can't keep living this way, but I don't know how to make the hunger stop."

"Perhaps you're not meant to," he said. "Perhaps you're meant to cope with it. Either that or to come to realise that the hunger and the appeasement of the hunger are two entirely different things. They're unrelated. One will never quell the other."

Deborah thought about this. She considered how much of herself—and the way in which she'd lived so long—had been tied up with a single unfulfilled desire. She finally said, "This is not who I want to be, my love."

"Then be someone else."

"Where on earth do I begin with *that* project?"

He touched her hair. "With a good night's sleep," he said.

WANDSWORTH
LONDON

Lynley had thought about going directly home from Chelsea. His town house in Belgravia was less than five minutes by car from the St. Jameses' home. But as if of its own volition, the Healey Elliott had taken him to Isabelle's, and he was putting his key in the lock and letting himself inside before he truly thought about why he was doing so.

The flat was dark, as it would be at this time of night. He went to the kitchen and turned on the dim light above the sink. He examined the contents of the fridge and after this, hating himself for doing so but doing it anyway, he looked through the rubbish in its bin, opened and closed the cupboards quietly, and glanced into the oven to make sure it was empty.

He was doing this last when Isabelle came into the room. He didn't hear her. She'd flipped on the overhead lights before he was aware of her presence, so he had no idea how long she'd watched him prowling through her kitchen on his search.

She said nothing. Nor did he. She merely looked from

him to the open oven door before she turned and went back to her bedroom.

He followed her, but in the bedroom it was more of the same and he couldn't help himself. His glance went to the bedside table, to the floor next to the bed, to the top of the chest of drawers. It was as if an illness had come over him.

She watched him. That he'd awakened her from sleep was obvious. But what *sort* of sleep, how it had been induced, *if* it had been induced . . . These were suddenly troubling matters that he had to sort out. Or so he'd thought until he saw her expression: Acceptance, along with its clansman resignation, was in her eyes.

He said, "In a thousand different ways, I'm sorry."

"As am I," she replied.

He went to her. She wore only a thin nightgown and this she lifted over her head. He put his hand on the back of her neck—warm with sleep, it was—and he kissed her. She tasted of sleep interrupted and of nothing else. He broke from her, looked at her, then kissed her again. She began to undress him and he joined her in the bed, pulling the covers away, off, to the floor, so that nothing could come between them.

But it was there nonetheless. Even as their bodies joined, even as she rose above him and his hands sketched curves from her breasts, to her waist, to her hips, even as they moved together, even as he kissed her. It was all still there. No avoiding, he thought, no running, no escape. The pleasure of their connection was a celebration. It was also, however, a pyre that bore the touch of a torch and then did what pyres always do.

Afterwards, their bodies slick and satisfied, he said, "That was the last time, wasn't it?"

She said, "Yes. But we both knew that." And after a moment, "It couldn't have worked, Tommy. But I have to say how I wanted it to."

He sought her hand, which lay palm-down on the mattress. He covered it, and her fingers spread. His curved into hers. "This isn't about Helen," he told her. "You must know that."

"I do." She turned her head and her hair fell against her

cheek for a moment. It had become mussed during their lovemaking, and he smoothed it for her, brushing it back and behind her ear. "Tommy, I want you to find someone," she said. "Not to replace her, for who could replace her? But someone to continue your life with. Because that's all life is, isn't it? Just continuing, going on."

"I want that as well," he said. "I wasn't sure at first and it's likely there'll be days when I step backwards another time and tell myself there's no real life without Helen in it. But that will be a moment's thought only. I'll come through it and out of it. I'll move on."

She reached up and used the back of her fingers against his cheek. Her expression was fond. She said, "I can't say that I love you. Not with my demons. And not with yours."

"Understood," he said.

"But I wish you well. Please know that. No matter what happens. I do wish you well."

BELGRAVIA
LONDON

It was half past three in the morning when Lynley finally returned to his home in Eaton Terrace. He let himself inside the silent house, felt for the light switch to the right of the heavy oak door, and flipped it on. His eyes lit on a pair of women's gloves that had been resting in place against the newel post at the bottom of the stairway for the last nine months. He studied them for a moment before he crossed the entry, took them in hand, and held them briefly to his nose for a final scent of her, faint but there, the smell of citrus. He felt the gloves' softness against his cheek before he placed them in a small drawer of the coat tree near the door.

It came to him that he was very hungry. The feeling was odd. It had been many months since he'd experienced real, honest hunger in the pit of his stomach. Mostly, he'd been going through the motions of eating just to keep his body alive.

He went to the kitchen. There, he opened the refrigerator

and saw that it was well stocked as always. God knew he was pathetic as a cook, but he reckoned he could manage scrambled eggs and toast without burning the house to the ground.

He removed what he would need for his makeshift meal, and he began to search for the proper utensils with which to cook it. He had not got far before Charlie Denton stumbled into the room in his dressing gown and slippers, wiping his spectacles on his belt.

Denton said, "What're you doing in my kitchen, m' lord," to which Lynley replied as he always had done with a patient "Denton . . ."

"Sorry," Denton said. "Half-asleep. What the bloody hell are you doing, *sir*?"

"Obviously, I'm making something to eat," Lynley told him.

Denton came to the worktop and examined what Lynley had laid out: eggs, olive oil, marmite, jam, sugar. "What, exactly, would that be?" he enquired.

"Scrambled eggs and toast. Where do you keep the frying pan, for God's sake? And where's the bread? That shouldn't require a search party, should it?"

Denton sighed. "Here. Let me. You'll only make a bloody mess of everything and I'll be cleaning it up. What were you intending with the olive oil?"

"Doesn't one need something . . . So the eggs don't stick?"

"Sit, sit." Denton waved at the kitchen table. "Look at yesterday's paper. Go through the post. I've not put it on your desk yet. Or do something useful like setting the table."

"Where's the cutlery?"

"Oh for God's sake. Just sit."

Lynley did so. He began to go through the post. There were bills, as always. There was also a letter from his mother and another from his aunt Augusta, both of whom refused to have anything to do with e-mail. Indeed, his aunt had only recently begun resorting to a mobile to make her pronouncements from on high.

Lynley set both letters to one side and unfurled a handbill from the elastic band that had kept it rolled. He said, "What this?" and Denton glanced his way.

"Don't know. Something on the doorknob," he replied. "They were up and down the street yesterday. I hadn't looked at it yet."

Lynley did the looking. He saw that it was an advertisement for an event at Earl's Court in two days' time. Not the normal sort of event, he found, but rather an exhibition of a sport. The sport was flat track roller derby, and he saw that Boadicea's Broads from Bristol—love the alliteration, he thought—were going to meet London's Electric Magic in an exhibition match-up that was described with large print that read *The Spills! The Chills! The Thrills! Come to witness the spectacular artistry and skate-to-kill drama of the women who live for the jam!*

Below this were the names of the sportswomen, and Lynley couldn't stop himself from reading through the list, from looking for one name in particular, a name he had certainly never thought he'd see again. And there it was: Kickarse Electra, the nom de guerre of a large-animal veterinarian from the zoo in Bristol: one Daidre Trahair, a woman who took the occasional country weekend in Cornwall, where he had met her.

Lynley smiled at this. Then he chuckled. Denton looked up from the scrambling of eggs and said, "What?"

"What do you know about flat track roller derby?"

"What in hell is that, if one might ask?" Denton enquired.

"I think we ought to find out, you and I. Shall I purchase tickets for us, Charlie?"

"Tickets?" Denton looked at Lynley as if he'd gone half-mad. But then he fell back against the stove, and he struck a pose, one arm lifted to his forehead. He said, "My God. Has it actually come to *this*? Are you—dare I say—asking me out on a date?"

Lynley laughed in spite of himself. "I appear to be doing so."

"What *have* we come to?" Denton sighed.

"I've absolutely no idea," Lynley answered.

15 NOVEMBER

CHALK FARM
LONDON

The day hadn't been an easy one for Barbara Havers. It had largely depended upon the use of two skills that she possessed, alas, in minuscule proportion. The first was an ability to ignore the obvious. The second was the production of compassion for persons unknown.

Ignoring the obvious meant saying nothing to DI Lynley about whatever it was that had happened between him and Superintendent Ardery. From what Barbara could tell, their personal relationship was finished. There was a sadness in both of them that they each attempted to mask with courtesy and kindness, and from this Barbara took the fact that their breakup was a mutual decision, which was, at least, all to the good. It would have been a real nightmare in the workplace had one of them wished to end their affair while the other continued to cling like a starfish to a piling. At least this way, they both could forge onward without blameful glances and meaningful remarks being flung about by the aggrieved party for the next six months. But they were feeling the end of things. There was so much melancholy in the air round them that Barbara decided that avoidance was the better part of valour in this situation.

Her lack of skill in the compassion department didn't relate to Lynley and Superintendent Ardery, though. Neither of them was about to unburden a heavy heart onto her shoulders, so she was relieved about that. She was less relieved when she met Engracia in the wine bar near Gower Street a second time and asked the Spanish student to place another phone call to Argentina.

While Engracia spoke to Carlos, the brother of Alatea Vasquez y del Torres, Barbara fed her the information. He happened to be there at his parents' home, making a call upon his mother, and in his company was his cousin Elena Maria, with whom Engracia also spoke. She went between what Barbara was telling her and what the Argentines were saying in reply, and in this manner they navigated the waters of a family's sorrow.

Please tell them Alatea has drowned . . . please let them know that as of yet there is no body . . . because of the conditions in Morecambe Bay where she was lost . . . the sands shift due to the tide . . . it has to do with various elements . . . rivers running into it, something that's called the tidal bore, mudflats, quicksand . . . we do believe the body will turn up and we've been given a good idea where . . . will be buried by her husband . . . yes, she was married . . . yes, she was very happy . . . she'd merely gone for a walk . . . so terribly sorry . . . I'll see about photos, yes . . . so understandable that you'd want to know . . . definitely an accident . . . definitely an accident . . . absolutely no doubt that it was a terrible and tragic accident.

Whether it was or wasn't an accident didn't matter, Barbara thought. In the final analysis, dead was dead.

She and Engracia parted outside the wine bar, both of them feeling the regret of having to pass along the news of Alatea's death. Engracia had wept as she'd spoken to Carlos and then to Elena Maria, and Barbara had marvelled at this: at the idea of weeping over the death of someone she had never met, in fellow feeling with individuals thousands of miles away whom she would also never meet. What was it that prompted such a rush of compassion within one? she wondered. What was wrong with her that she didn't feel it? Or was this separation of self from event merely part and parcel of the career she'd chosen?

She didn't want to think about any of it: Lynley's gloom,

Isabelle Ardery's melancholy, an Argentine family's grief. So on the way home that evening, she thought instead of something more pleasant, which was her upcoming dinner. This would comprise steak and kidney suet-topped pie thrown into the microwave, a can of red wine popped open, toffee cheesecake, and a cup of reheated morning coffee afterwards. Then an evening propped up on the daybed with *Passion's Sweet Promise* open on her lap and an hour or two to discover if Grey Mannington would finally embrace his love for Ebony Sinclair in typical romance novel fashion having much to do with heaving bosoms, muscular thighs, probing tongues, and searing pleasures. She'd turn the electric fire on within the mousehole fireplace as well, she thought. For it had been bitterly cold all day, and the promise of a deadly winter was being made each morning, written in the frost on her windowpanes. It was going to be a bad one and a long one, she thought. Best get out the woolies and prepare to sleep nightly between brushed-cotton sheets.

At home, she saw that Azhar's car was in the driveway, but the lights were not on in the family's flat. They were probably out to dinner, she reckoned, having walked the short distance to Chalk Farm Road or Haverstock Hill. Perhaps everything had worked out after all, she thought. Perhaps Azhar's other children and his never-divorced wife were at this moment dining en famille at the local Chinese with Azhar, Hadiyyah, and Angelina. Perhaps they'd all come to terms with a brilliant way to share in each other's lives, the wife forgiving the husband for having walked out on her for a university student whom he'd impregnated, the husband abjuring guilt for having done so, the former university student proving her worth as mother and quasi-stepmother to all of the children, everyone living in one of the odd family situations becoming so prevalent in their society . . . It could have happened, Barbara thought. Of course, all the pigs in England could have taken to the air today as well.

Meantime, it was as cold as the heart of a serial killer and she hurried down the path alongside the Edwardian house. It was very dimly lit as two of the five garden lights had burnt out and no one had replaced them yet, and it was darker still at the front of her bungalow since she'd not thought to turn the porch light on when she'd left that morning.

There was enough illumination, however, to see that someone was sitting on the single step in front of her door. This was a hunched figure, forehead on knees, fists raised to temples. The figure rocked slightly and when he raised his head at her approach, Barbara saw that it was Taymullah Azhar.

She said his name as a question, but he didn't speak. She saw then as she approached that he was wearing only one of his workday suits, no overcoat or hat or gloves, and as a result he was shivering so badly that his teeth made a death rattle inside his skull.

Barbara cried, "Azhar! What's happened?"

He shook his head, a compulsive movement. When she dashed to him and helped him to his feet, he managed only two words, "They've gone."

Barbara knew at once. She said, "Come inside," and with one arm round his waist, she unlocked the door. She guided him to a chair and helped him sit. He was icy cold. Even his clothing felt stiff, as if it were in the process of freezing to his skin. She raced to the daybed and pulled off the counterpane. She wrapped this round him, put on the kettle, and went back to the table to warm his hands with hers. She said his name because it was the only thing she could think of to say. To ask "What's happened?" once again meant she was going to find out, and she didn't think she wanted to know.

He was looking at her, but she could tell he wasn't seeing her. His were the eyes of a man gazing into the void. The kettle snapped off, and Barbara went to it, flung a bag of PG Tips into a mug, and sloshed the boiling water in after it. She carried the tea to the table with a spoon and sugar and a carton of milk. She slopped some of both into the mug and told him to drink. She told him he had to get warm.

He couldn't hold the mug, so she did this for him, raising it to his lips, one hand on his shoulder to keep him steady. He took a gulp, coughed, and took another. He said, "She's taken Hadiyyah."

Barbara thought he had to be mistaken. Surely, Angelina and Hadiyyah had only gone for Azhar's other children. Surely, despite the foolhardy nature of what Angelina Upman had planned, it would only be a matter of an hour or so before Angelina and Hadiyyah tripped up the path with those children in tow and the Big Surprise about to unfold. But Barbara knew—she *knew*—she was lying to herself. Just as Angelina had lied.

Over Azhar's shoulder, Barbara saw that her answering machine was blinking with messages. Perhaps, she thought, perhaps, perhaps . . .

She curved Azhar's hand round the tea and went to the machine. Two messages were indicated, and the first voice she heard was Angelina's. "Hari will be quite upset tonight, Barbara," the woman's pleasant voice said. "Will you check on him at some point? I'd be ever so grateful." There was a pause before Angelina went on with, "Make him understand this isn't personal, Barbara . . . Well, it is and it isn't. Will you tell him that?" And then following that brief and inconclusive message, the second was Azhar's voice breaking on, "Barbara . . . Barbara . . . Their passports . . . her birth certificate . . . ," and his terrible sobbing before the line went dead.

She turned back to him. He was bent over the table. She went to him. She said, "Oh my God, Azhar. What has she *done*?" Except the worst of it was that she knew what Angelina Upman had done, and she realised that had she only spoken, had she told him about the "surprise" that Hadiyyah had revealed to her, he might well have twigged what was about to happen and he might well have been able to do something to stop it.

Barbara sat. She wanted to touch him but she was afraid that a gesture of concern from her might shatter him like glass. She said, "Azhar, Hadiyyah told me about a surprise. She said she and her mum were planning to fetch your other children, the children . . . the children from your marriage, Azhar. Azhar, I didn't know what to tell you. I didn't want to betray her confidence . . . and . . . Bloody hell, what is *wrong* with me? I should have said something. I should have done something. I didn't think . . ."

He said numbly, "She doesn't know where they are."

"She must have found out."

"How? She doesn't know their names. Not the children's. Not my wife's. She couldn't have . . . But Hadiyyah would have thought . . . Even now she must think . . ." He said nothing more.

"We must phone the local police," Barbara said, even though she knew that it was useless. For Hadiyyah wasn't with a stranger. She was with her own mother, and no divorce existed with complicated custody arrangements attached to it, for there had been no marriage in the first place. There had only been a man, a woman, and their daughter who had lived, for a short time, in relative peace. But then the mother had run off and although she'd returned, it now was clear to Barbara that Angelina Upman's intention had always been to come for her child and to leave again: first to soothe Azhar into a false sense of all being well and then to take Hadiyyah away from her father and to fade with her into obscurity.

How they had all been duped and used, Barbara thought. And what, what, *what* was Hadiyyah going to think and feel when she began to understand that she had been ripped away from the father she adored and the only life she had ever known? To be taken . . . ? Where, Barbara thought, *where*?

No one vanished without a trace. Barbara was a cop, and she knew very well that no one ever managed to flee without a single clue being left behind. She said to Azhar, "Take me to the flat."

"I cannot go in there again."

"You must. Azhar, it's the route to Hadiyyah."

Slowly, he got to his feet. Barbara took his arm and guided him along the path to the front of the house. At the flagstone area before the door, he stopped but she urged him forward. She was the one to open the door, though. She found the lights and she switched them on.

Illumination revealed the sitting room, altered by Angelina Upman's impeccable good taste. Barbara saw the alteration now for what it was and for what it had been, which was just another way to seduce. Not only Azhar but

Hadiyyah and Barbara herself if it came down to it. *What fun we shall have doing it, darling Hadiyyah, and how we shall surprise your father!*

Azhar stood there between the sitting room and the kitchen, immobile and ashen. Barbara thought there was every chance the man might simply pass out, so she took him into the kitchen—the room least altered by Angelina—and she sat him at the small table there. She said, "Wait." And then, "Azhar, it's going to be all right. We're going to find her. We'll find them both." He didn't reply.

In his bedroom, Barbara saw that all of Angelina's belongings were gone. She couldn't have packed everything and taken it off in suitcases, so she must have shipped things on ahead with no one the wiser. This meant she'd known where she was going and, possibly, to whom. An important detail.

On the bed, a strongbox lay, its lid open and its contents dumped out. Barbara looked through all this, noting insurance papers, Azhar's passport, a copy of his birth certificate, and a sealed envelope with *Will* written on the front in his neat cursive. As he had said, everything relating to Hadiyyah was missing, and this state of affairs was underscored by the little girl's bedroom.

Her clothing was gone with the exception of her school uniform, which lay on the bed, spread out as if in mockery of tomorrow morning when Hadiyyah would not be there to don it. Also still there was her school rucksack, and inside her schoolwork was neatly placed within a three-ring binder. On her little desk, tucked beneath a window, her laptop was in position and sitting on top of it was a small stuffed giraffe that, Barbara knew, had been given to Hadiyyah by a good-hearted girl in Essex the previous year, in Balford-le-Nez on the pleasure pier. Hadiyyah, Barbara thought, would want that giraffe. She would want her laptop. She would want her school things. She would want—above everything else—her father.

She returned to the kitchen where Azhar sat, staring at nothing. She said to him, "Azhar, you're her father. You have a claim upon her. She's lived with you since she was born. You've a building full of people right here who're going to testify to that. The police will ask them and they'll say you're the parent of record. Hadiyyah's school will say that as well. Everyone—"

"My name is not on her birth certificate, Barbara. It never was. Angelina would not put it on. It was the price I paid for not divorcing my wife."

Barbara swallowed. She took a moment. She forged ahead. "All right. We'll work with that. It doesn't matter. There are DNA tests. She's half you, Azhar, and we'll be able to prove it."

"In what manner without her here? And what does it matter when she is with her mother? Angelina defies no law. She defies no court order. She does not fly in the face of what a judge has told her must be the way in which Hadiyyah is shared. She's gone. She's taken my daughter with her, and they are not returning."

He looked at Barbara and his eyes were so pained that Barbara couldn't hold his gaze. She said uselessly, "No, no. That's not how it is."

But he put his forehead against his upraised fists and he hit himself. Once, twice, and Barbara grabbed his arm. She said, "*Don't*. We'll find her. I swear we'll find her. I'm going to phone now. I'm ringing some people. There are ways. There are means. She's not lost to you and you must believe that. *Will* you believe it? Will you hang on?"

"I've nothing to hang on to," he told her, "and I've less to hang on for."

CHALK FARM
LONDON

Who could she blame? Barbara asked herself. Who on God's bloody earth could she possibly blame? She had to blame someone because if she could not find a person to wear the mantle of guilt, she was going to have to blame herself. For being seduced, for being awed, for being stupid, for being—

It all came down to Isabelle Ardery, she decided. If the

bloody superintendent hadn't ordered, insisted, recommended strongly that Barbara alter her appearance, none of this would have happened because Barbara wouldn't have come to know Angelina Upman in the first place so she would have maintained a distance from her that might have allowed her to see and to understand . . . But what, really, did that matter because Angelina had intended to take her daughter away from the very first, hadn't she, and *that* had been the argument Barbara had heard that day between Angelina and Azhar. It had been her threat and his reaction to her threat. Azhar had lost his temper, as any father might, in the face of her declaration that she would take away his child. But when Angelina had explained the cause of the argument to Barbara, Barbara had stood there in her little shop of deceit, and she'd bought up her lies, every one of them.

She didn't want to leave Azhar alone, but she had no choice once she decided to make her phone call. She didn't want to do it in his presence because she wasn't sure of the outcome despite her words of assurance to the man. She said, "I want you to lie down, Azhar. I want you to try to rest. I'll be back. I promise you. You wait here. I'll be gone a little while because I have some phone calls to make and when I return, I'll have a plan. But in the meantime I have to phone . . . Azhar, are you listening? *Can* you hear me?" She wanted to ring someone to come to him and to comfort him in some way, but she knew there was no one other than herself. All she could do was get him into his bedroom, cover him with a blanket, and promise she would return as soon as she could.

She hurried to her bungalow to place the call. There was only one person she could think of who might be of help, who would be able to think clearly in this situation, and she rang his mobile.

Lynley said, "Yes? Barbara? Is that you?" over a tremendous roaring of noise and music in the background. Barbara felt a surge of gratitude and she said, "Sir, sir, yes. I need—"

He said, "Barbara, I can't actually hear you. I'm going to have to—"

His voice was overwhelmed by the cheers of a crowd.

Where in God's name *was* he? she wondered. At a football game?

He said as if in answer, "I'm at the exhibition centre. Earl's Court . . ." More cheers and roaring and Lynley saying to someone, "Charlie, has she gone out of bounds? My God, the woman's aggressive. Can you tell what's happened?" Someone said something in reply and this was followed by Lynley's laughter. Lynley laughing, Barbara realised, as she'd not heard him laugh since before last February, when it had seemed his laughter had died forever. He said into his mobile, "Roller derby, Barbara," and she could barely hear him over the background noise although she managed to catch ". . . that woman from Cornwall" and she thought, Is he on a date? With a woman from Cornwall? What woman from Cornwall? And what is roller derby? And who is Charlie? Someone otherwise called Charlotte? He *couldn't* mean Charlie Denton, could he? What on earth would Lynley be doing out and about with Charlie Denton?

She said, "Sir, sir . . . ," but it was hopeless.

Another roar from the crowd and he said to someone, "Is that a point?" and then to her, "Barbara, may I ring you back? I can't hear a thing."

She said, "Yes," and she thought about texting him instead. But there he was in a moment of happiness and pleasure and how on earth could she tear him from it when the truth of the matter—as she bloody well knew despite her words to Azhar—was that there was nothing he could do? There was nothing anyone could do officially. Whatever happened next was going to have to happen in an extremely unofficial manner.

She ended the call. She stared at the phone. She thought of Hadiyyah. It had been only two years since Barbara had met her, but it did seem as if she'd known her the length of her very short life: a little dancing girl with flying plaits. It came to Barbara that Hadiyyah's hair had been different the last few times she'd seen her and she wondered how much different it was going to become in the ensuing days.

How will she make you look? Barbara wondered. What will she tell you about your disguise? More, what will she tell you about where you're going once it becomes clear there are no half siblings for you to meet at the end of your journey? And where will that journey take you? Into whose arms is your mother fleeing?

For this was the truth of the matter, and what could be done to stop it when Angelina Upman was only a mother who'd come to claim her child, a mother who'd returned from "Canada" or wherever she'd been with whomever she'd been with, who was, of course, the very same person to whom she was running, some bloke who'd been seduced by her, just like Azhar, just like all of them, seduced into waiting instead of believing . . . *What* had Angelina done and where had she gone?

She had to get back to Azhar, but Barbara began to pace. Every black cab in London, she thought. Every mini cab, and there were thousands. Every bus and after that the CCTV films from the Chalk Farm Tube station. Then the railway stations. The Eurostar. After that the airports. Luton, Stansted, Gatwick, Heathrow. Every hotel. Every B & B. Every flat and every hidey-hole there was from the centre of London working out to the edges and then beyond. The Channel Islands. The Isle of Man. The inner and outer Hebrides. Europe itself. France, Spain, Italy, Portugal . . .

How long would it take to find a beautiful light-haired woman and her dark-haired little girl, a little girl who was going to want her father soon, who was going to manage — God in heaven, she *would* manage, wouldn't she? — to get to a phone and to ring her father so that she could say, "Daddy, Daddy, Mummy doesn't know I'm ringing and I want to come *home . . .* "

So do we wait for the call? Barbara asked herself. Do we set out to find her? Do we simply pray? Do we convince ourselves with any amount of lies that no harm is meant and no harm will be done because this is, after all, a mother who loves her child and who *knows* above all that Hadiyyah belongs with her father, because he's given up everything to stand at her side and has, as a result, absolutely nothing without her?

God, how she wanted Lynley to be there. He would know what to do. He would know what to say. He would listen to the entire anguished tale and he would have the right words of hope to give to Azhar, the words she herself couldn't muster because she hadn't the skill. She hadn't the heart. But still she had to do something, say something, find something, because if she didn't, what sort of friend was she to a man in agony? And if she couldn't find the words or develop a plan, was she in truth a friend at all?

It was nearly ten o'clock when Barbara finally went to her bungalow's small bathroom. Lynley had not yet rung her back, but she knew he would. He would not fail her because DI Lynley did not fail people. That was not who he was. So he would ring as soon as he was able, and Barbara believed this—she clung to this—because she had to believe something and there was nothing else left to believe and she certainly didn't believe in herself.

In the bathroom she turned on the shower and waited for the water to heat. She was shivering, not from the cold, for the electric fire had finally warmed the bungalow, but rather from something else far more insidious and more deeply felt than frigid temperature against one's skin. She looked at herself in the mirror as the steam began to seep from the shower. She studied the person she had become at the behest of others. She thought of the steps that had to be taken to find Hadiyyah and to return the little girl to her father. The steps were many, but Barbara knew the first one.

She went to the kitchen for a pair of scissors, a nice sharp pair that sheared easily through the bones of chickens although she'd never used them for that or, as it happened, for anything else. But they were perfect for the need she had now.

She returned to the bathroom, where she shed her clothes.

She adjusted the temperature of the water.

She stepped into the shower.

There, she began to hack off her hair.

SEPTEMBER 6, 2010
WHIDBEY ISLAND, WASHINGTON

ACKNOWLEDGEMENTS

As an American writing a series set in the UK, I am continually in the debt of people in England who willingly help me in the early stages of my research. For this novel, I'm extremely grateful to the staff and owners of Gilpin Lodge in Cumbria who provided me a lovely safe haven from which to launch my exploration into the countryside that became the backdrop for this novel. The Queen's Guide to the Sands—Cedric Robinson—was a generous and invaluable source of information on Morecambe Bay, having spent all of his life living on the bay and most of his life guiding people across its perilous expanse at low tide. Mr. Robinson's wife, Olive, graciously welcomed me into their eight-hundred-year-old cottage and allowed me to pick her brains as well as those of her husband during my time in Cumbria. The ever resourceful Swati Gamble of Hodder and Stoughton once again proved that, armed with the Internet and a telephone, nothing is impossible for her.

In the United States, Bill Solberg and Stan Harris helped me in matters pertaining to lakeside life, and a chance encounter with Joanne Herman in the San Francisco greenroom of a Sunday morning talk show put me in possession of her book *Transgender Explained for Those Who Are Not*. Caroline Cossey's book *My Story* elucidated better than anything the pain and confusion of gender dysphoria and the prejudice one faces having made the decision to do something about it.

I'm grateful for the support of my husband, Thomas McCabe; for the always cheerful presence of my personal assistant, Charlene Coe; and for the readings of early drafts of this novel done by my longtime cold reader, Susan Berner, and by Debbie Cavanaugh. My professional life is made smoother through the efforts of my literary agent, Robert Gottlieb of Trident Media Group, as well as my British publishing team of Sue Fletcher, Martin Nield, and Karen Geary at Hodder and Stoughton. With this novel, I join a new American publishing team at Dutton, and I'm grateful for the confidence in my work expressed by my editor and publisher, Brian Tart.

Finally, to my readers who are interested in Cumbria and its crowning jewel—the Lake District—all of the places in this novel are real, as is the case in all my books. I have merely picked them up and moved them when necessary. Ireleth Hall stands in for Levens Hall, the home of Hal and Susan Bagot; the Faircloughs' boathouse can actually be found in Fell Foot Park; Arnside House stands in for Blackwell, the Arts and Crafts beauty on the shore of Lake Windermere; Bryan Beck farm grew from an Elizabethan manor house called Townend; and Bassenthwaite village became Bryanbarrow village, complete with ducks. Playing God with locations such as these is part of the pleasure of writing fiction.

Elizabeth George
Whidbey Island, Washington

Read on for a sneak peak
at another Lynley novel by Elizabeth George

JUST ONE EVIL ACT

Available now.

ynley was still sitting there in front of the hotel in his car when his mobile rang. He was still feeling the pressure of Daidre's lips against his cheek and the sudden warmth of her hand on his arm. So deep was he into his thoughts that the mobile's ringing startled him. He realised at its sound that he'd not phoned Barbara Havers back as he'd said he would. He glanced at his watch.

It was one a.m. Couldn't be Havers, he thought. And in the way that the mind will go spontaneously from one thought to another, in the time it took to fish the mobile from his pocket, he thought of his mother, he thought of his brother, he thought of his sister, he thought of emergencies and how they generally did occur in the middle of the night because no one made a friendly call at this hour.

By the time he had the mobile out, he'd decided it had to be a disaster in Cornwall, where his family home was, a heretofore-unknown Mrs. Danvers in their employ having set the place alight. But then he saw it was Havers ringing again. He said into the phone hastily, "Barbara, I am so sorry."

"Bloody hell," she cried. "Why didn't you ring back? I've been sitting here. And he's alone over there. And I don't know what to do or what to tell him because the worst of it is that there's sod all *anyone* can do to help and I know it and I lied to him and said we'd do something and I need your *help*. Because there has to be something—"

"Barbara." She sounded completely undone. It was so unlike her to babble like this that Lynley knew something was badly wrong. "*Barbara*. Slow down. What's happened?"

The story she told came out in disjointed pieces. Lynley was able to pick up very few details because she was speaking so fast. Her voice was odd. She'd either been weeping—which hardly seemed likely—or she'd been drinking. The latter made little sense, however, considering the urgency of the story she had to tell. Lynley put together what he could, just the salient details:

The daughter of her neighbour and friend Taymullah Azhar was missing. Azhar, a science professor at University College London, had come home from work to find the family flat stripped of nearly all possessions belonging to his nine-year-old daughter as well as to her mother. Only the child's school uniform remained, along with a stuffed animal and her laptop, all of this lying on her bed.

"Everything else is gone," Havers said. "I found Azhar sitting on my front step when I got home. She'd rung me, too—Angelina had done—sometime during the day. There was a message on my phone. Could I look in on him this evening? she'd asked me. 'Hari's going to be upset,' she said. Oh yes, too right. Except he's not upset. He's destroyed. He's wrecked. I don't know what to do or to say, and Angelina even made Hadiyyah leave that giraffe behind and we *both* know why because it meant a time when he'd taken her to the seaside and he'd won it for her and when someone took it off her on the pleasure pier—"

"Barbara." Lynley spoke firmly. "*Barbara*."

She breathed in raggedly. "Sir?"

"I'm on my way."

CHALK FARM
LONDON

Barbara Havers lived in north London, not far from Camden Lock Market. At one in the morning, getting there was merely a matter of knowing the route, as there was virtually no traffic. She lived in Eton Villas, where parking one's car depended upon very good luck. There was none of that at an hour when the residents of the area were all tucked up into their beds, though, so Lynley made do with blocking the driveway.

Barbara's digs sat behind a conversion, a yellow Edwardian villa done into flats at some point during the late twentieth century. She herself occupied a structure behind it, a wood-framed building that had once done duty as God only knew what. It had a tiny fireplace, which suggested it had always been used as some sort of living space, but its size suggested that only a single occupant had ever lived there, and one needing very little room.

Lynley cast a glance at the ground-floor flat inside the conversion as he made his way along the paved path towards the back of the villa. This was, he knew, the home occupied by Barbara's friend Taymullah Azhar, and the lights within it were still blazing out onto the terrace in front of the flat's French windows. He assumed from his conversation with Barbara that she'd been inside her own digs when he'd spoken to her, though, and when he got behind the villa, he saw the lights were on inside her bungalow as well.

He knocked quietly. He heard a chair scraping against the floor. The door swung open.

He was unprepared for the sight of her. He said, "God in heaven. What have you done?"

He thought in terms of ancient rites of mourning in which women chopped off their hair and poured ashes upon the stubble that remained. She'd done the first, but she'd skipped the second. There were, however, ashes aplenty on the small table in what went for the kitchen. She'd sat there for hours, it seemed to Lynley, and in a glass dish that had served as her ashtray, the remains of at least twenty cigarettes lay crushed, spilling burnt offerings everywhere.

Barbara looked ravaged by emotion. She smelled like the inside of a fireplace. She was wearing an ancient chenille dressing gown in a hideous shade of mushy-peas green, and her sockless feet were tucked into her red high-top trainers.

She said, "I left him over there. I said I'd be back but I haven't been able to. I didn't know what to tell him. I thought if you came . . . Why didn't you ring me? Couldn't you tell . . . Bloody hell, sir, where the hell . . . Why didn't you . . . ?"

"I'm so sorry," he said. "I couldn't hear you on my mobile. I was . . . It doesn't matter. Tell me what happened."

Lynley took her arm and guided her to the table. He took away the glass dish of cigarette dog ends as well as an unopened packet of Players and a box of kitchen matches. He put all of this on the worktop of her kitchen area, where he also set the kettle to boil. He rustled in a cupboard and came up with two bags of PG Tips as well as some artificial sweetener, and he excavated through a sink filled with unwashed crockery till he discovered two mugs. He washed them, dried them, and went to the small refrigerator. Its contents were as appalling as he'd expected they would be, heavily given to takeaway food cartons and to-be-heated ready-made meals, but among all of this he found a pint of milk. He brought it out as the kettle clicked off.

Throughout everything, Havers was silent. This was completely uncharacteristic of her. In all the time he'd known the detective sergeant, she'd never been without a comment to toss in his direction, particularly in a situation like this one in which he was not only making tea but actually giving some thought to toast as well. It rather unnerved him, this silence of hers.

He brought the tea to the table. He placed a mug in front of her. There was another sitting near to where the cigarettes had been, and he removed this. It was cold, a skin of someone's indifference to it floating on its surface.

Havers said, "That was his. I did the same thing. What is it about tea and our bloody society?"

"It's something to do," Lynley told her.

"When in doubt, make tea," she said. "I could do with a whiskey. Or gin. Gin would be nice."

"Have you any?"

" 'Course not. I don't want to be one of those old ladies who sip gin from five o'clock in the afternoon till they're comatose."

"You're not an old lady."

"Believe me, it's out there."

Lynley smiled. Her remark was a slight improvement. He pulled the other chair out from the table and joined her. "Tell me."

Havers spoke of a woman called Angelina Upman, the apparent mother of Taymullah Azhar's daughter. Lynley himself had met both Azhar and the girl Hadiyyah, and he'd known that the mother of this child had been out of the picture for some time prior to Barbara's purchase of the leasehold on her bungalow. But he'd not been told that Angelina Upman had waltzed back into the lives of Azhar and Hadiyyah the previous July, and he'd never learned that not only were Azhar and the mother of his child not married but also that Azhar's name was not on the birth certificate of the girl.

Other details came pouring forth, and Lynley tried to keep up with them. It hadn't been due to the fashion of the times that Azhar and Angelina Upman had remained unmarried. Rather, there had been no marriage possible between them because Azhar had left his legal wife for Angelina, and this was a woman he'd refused to divorce. With her, he had two other children. Where they all lived was something Barbara didn't know.

What she did know was that Angelina had seduced Azhar and Hadiyyah into believing she'd returned to take her rightful place in their lives. She needed to obtain their trust, Barbara said, so that she could lay her plans and execute them.

"That's why she came back," Barbara told him. "To get everyone's trust. Mine included. I've been a bloody idiot most of my life. But this one . . . I've sodding outdone myself."

"Why did you never tell me any of this?" Lynley asked.

"Which part?" Havers asked. "Because the bloody-idiot part I would've expected you already knew."

"The part about Angelina," he said. "The part about Azhar's wife, the other children, the divorce or lack thereof. All of that. Any of that. Why didn't you tell me? Because you certainly must have felt . . ." He could say no more. Havers had never spoken of her feelings either for Azhar or for his young daughter, and Lynley had never asked. It had seemed more respectful to say nothing when the truth, he admitted, was that saying nothing had just been the easier thing to do.

"I'm sorry," he said.

"Yeah. Well, you were occupied anyway. You know."

He knew she was talking about his affair with their superior officer at the Met. He'd been discreet. So had Isabelle. But Havers was no fool. She hadn't been born recently, and she was nothing if not acutely percipient when it came to him.

He said, "Yes. Well. That's over, Barbara."

"I know."

"Ah. Right. I expect you do."

Havers turned her tea mug in her hands. Lynley saw it bore a caricature of the Duchess of Cornwall, helmet-haired and square-smiled. Unconsciously, she covered this caricature with her hand as if in apology to the unfortunate woman. She said, "I didn't know what to tell him, sir. I came home from work and I found him sitting on my front step. He'd been there hours, I think. I took him back to his flat once he'd told me what happened—that she'd taken off and that Hadiyyah was with her—and I had a look round and I swear to God, when I saw she'd taken everything with her, I didn't know what to do."

Lynley considered the situation. It was more than difficult and Havers knew this, which was why she'd been immobilised. He said, "Take me to his flat, Barbara. Put on some clothes and take me to his flat."

She nodded. She went to the wardrobe and rooted around for some clothes, which she clutched to her chest. She started to head towards the bathroom, but she stopped. She said to him, "Ta for not mentioning the hair, sir."

Lynley looked at her shorn and ruined head. "Ah, yes," he said. "Get dressed, Sergeant."

CHALK FARM
LONDON

Barbara Havers felt appreciably better now that Lynley had arrived. She knew she should have been able to do something to take hold of the reins of the situation, but Azhar's grief had undone her. He was a self-contained man and had always been so in the nearly two years that she had known him. As such, he'd played his cards so close that most of the time she could have sworn he had no cards at all. To see him broken by what his lover had done and to know that she herself should have recognised from their first meeting that something was up with Angelina Upman and with all of Angelina Upman's overtures of friendship towards her . . . This was enough to break Barbara as well.

Like most people, she'd seen only what she wanted to see in Angelina Upman, and she'd ignored everything from red flags to speed bumps. Meantime, Angelina had seduced Azhar back to her bed. She'd seduced her daughter into abject devotion. She'd seduced Barbara into unwitting conspiracy through garnering her cooperative silence about everything having to do with Angelina herself. And this—her disappearance with her daughter in tow—was the result.

Barbara got dressed in the bathroom. In the mirror she saw how terrible she looked, especially her hair. Her head bore great bald patches in spots, and in other spots the remains of what had been an expensive Knightsbridge hairstyle sprang out of her scalp like so many weeds waiting to be pulled from a garden. The only answer to what she'd done to herself was going to be to shave her head completely, but she didn't have time to do that just then. She came out of the bathroom and rooted for a ski cap in her chest of drawers. She put this on and together she and Lynley returned to the front of the house.

Everything was as she'd left it in Azhar's flat. The only difference was that instead of sitting staring at nothing, Azhar was walking aimlessly through the rooms. When, hollow-eyed, he looked in their direction, Barbara said to him, "Azhar, I've brought DI Lynley from the Met."

He'd just emerged from Hadiyyah's bedroom. He was

clutching the little girl's stuffed giraffe to his chest. He said to Lynley, "She's taken her."

"Barbara's told me."

"There's nothing to be done."

Barbara said, "There's always something to be done. We're going to find her, Azhar."

She felt Lynley shoot her a look. It told her that she was making promises that neither he nor she could keep. But that was not how Barbara saw the situation. If they couldn't help this man, she thought, then what was the point of being cops?

Lynley said, "May we sit?"

Azhar said yes, yes, of course, and they went into the sitting room. It was still fresh from Angelina's redecoration of it. Barbara saw it now as she should have seen it when Angelina unveiled it to her: like something from a magazine, perfectly put together but otherwise devoid of anyone's personality.

Azhar said as they sat, "I telephoned her parents once you left."

"Where are they?" she asked.

"Dulwich. They wished not to speak to me, of course. I am the ruination of one of their two children. So they will not contaminate themselves through any effort to be of assistance."

"Lovely couple," Barbara noted.

"They know nothing," Azhar said.

"Can you be sure of that?" Lynley asked.

"From what they said and who they are, yes. They know nothing about Angelina and, what's more, they do not want to know. They said she made her bed a decade ago, and if she doesn't like the smell of the sheets, it's not down to them to do anything about that."

"There's another child, though?" Lynley said, and when Azhar looked confused and Barbara asked, "What?" he clarified with, "You said you were the ruination of one of their two children. Who is the other and might Angelina be with this person?"

"Bathsheba," Azhar said. "Angelina's sister. I know only her name but have never met her."

"Might Angelina and Hadiyyah be with her?"

"They have no love for each other as I gather these things," Azhar said. "So I doubt it."

"No love for each other according to Angelina?" Barbara asked sharply. The implication was clear to both Lynley and Azhar.

"When people are desperate," Lynley said to the man, "when they plan something like this—because it *would* have taken some planning, Azhar—old grudges are often put to rest. Did you ring the sister? Do you have the number?"

"I know only her name. Bathsheba Ward. I know nothing else. I'm sorry."

"Not a problem," Barbara said. "Bathsheba Ward gives us something to start with. It gives us a place to—"

"Barbara, you are being kind," Azhar said. "As are you"—this to Lynley—"to come here in the dead of night. But I know the reality of my situation."

Barbara said hotly, "I told you we'll find her, Azhar. We *will*."

Azhar observed her with his calm, dark eyes. He looked at Lynley. His expression acted as acknowledgement of something Barbara didn't want to admit and certainly didn't want him to have to face.

Lynley said, "Barbara's told me there's no divorce involved between you and Angelina."

"As we were not married, there is no divorce. And because there was no divorce between me and my wife—my legal wife—Angelina did not identify me as Hadiyyah's father. Which was, of course, her right. I accepted this as one of the outcomes of not divorcing Nafeeza."

"Where is Nafeeza?" he asked.

"Ilford. Nafeeza and the children live with my parents."

"Could Angelina have gone to them?"

"She has no idea where they live, what their names are, anything about them."

"Could they have come here, then? Could they have tracked her down, perhaps? Could they have wooed her out there?"

"For what purpose?"

"Perhaps to harm her?"

Barbara could see how this was entirely possible. She

said, "Azhar, that could be it. She could have been taken. This could look like something it isn't at all. They could have come for her and taken Hadiyyah as well. They could have packed everything. They could have forced her to make that call to me."

"Did she sound like someone under duress in the phone message, Barbara?" Lynley asked her.

Of course, she had not. She'd sounded just as she'd always sounded, which was perfectly pleasant and completely open to friendship. "She could have been acting," Barbara said, although even she could hear how desperate she sounded. "She fooled me for months. She fooled Azhar. She fooled her own daughter. But maybe she wasn't fooling at all. Maybe she never intended to leave. Maybe they came for her out of the blue and they've taken her somewhere and she had to leave that message and they forced her to sound—"

"You can't have it both ways," Lynley said, although his voice was kind.

"He is right," Azhar said. "If she was forced to make a phone call, if she was taken from here—she and Hadiyyah—against her will, she would have said something in that phone call to you. She would have left a sign. There would be some indication, but there is not. There is nothing. And what she did leave—Hadiyyah's school uniform, her laptop, that little giraffe—this was to tell me that they are not returning." His eyes grew red-rimmed.

Barbara swung to Lynley. He was, she had long known, the most compassionate cop on the force and quite possibly the most compassionate man she'd ever met. But she could see upon his face that what he felt—beyond sympathy for Azhar—was knowledge of the truth in front of them. She said to him, "Sir. *Sir.*"

He said, "Aside from checking with the families, Barbara . . . She's the mother. She's broken no law. There's no divorce with a judge's decree and a custody ruling that she's defying."

"A private enquiry, then," Barbara said. "If we can do nothing, then a private detective can."

"Where am I to find such a person?" Azhar asked her.

"I can be that person," Barbara told him.